Mental Illness, Medicine and Law

The International Library of Medicine, Ethics and Law

Series Editor: Michael D. Freeman

Mental Illness, Medicine and Law

Edited by

Martin Lyon Levine

University of Southern California, Los Angeles, USA

Routledge
Taylor & Francis Group

LONDON AND NEW YORK

First published 2009 by Ashgate Publishing

Published 2016 by Routledge
2 Park Square, Milton Park, Abingdon, Oxon OX14 4RN
711 Third Avenue, New York, NY 10017, USA

Routledge is an imprint of the Taylor & Francis Group, an informa business

British Library Cataloguing in Publication Data
Mental illness, medicine and law. – (The international
    library of medicine, ethics and law)
    1. Mental health laws 2. Medical ethics
    I. Levine, Martin
    344'0419

Library of Congress Control Number: 2008931962

ISBN 9780754621218 (hbk)

Contents

This book is dedicated with love to Martha

Acknowledgements

The editor and publishers wish to thank the following for permission to use copyright material.

AAAS for the essays: Amos Tversky and Daniel Kahneman (1974), 'Judgment under Uncertainty: Heuristics and Biases', *Science*, **185**, pp. 1124–31. Copyright © 1974 AAAS; George L. Engel (1977), 'The Need for a New Medical Model: A Challenge for Biomedicine', *Science*, **196**, pp. 129–36. Copyright © 1977 AAAS.

American Medical Association for the essay: Arthur J. Barsky and Jonathan F. Borus (1995), 'Somatization and Medicalization in the Era of Managed Care', *Journal of the American Medical Association*, **274**, pp. 1931–34. Copyright © 1995 American Medical Association.

American Psychiatric Publishing, Inc. for the essays: Lars Kjellin, Kristina Andersson, Inga-Lill Candefjord, Tom Palmstierna and Tuula Wallstein (1997), 'Ethical Benefits and Costs of Coercion in Short-Term Inpatient Psychiatric Care', *Psychiatric Services*, **48**, pp. 1567–70. Copyright © 1997 American Psychiatric Publishing; Paul S. Appelbaum (2002), 'Privacy in Psychiatric Treatment: Threats and Responses', *American Journal of Psychiatry*, **159**, pp. 1809–18. Copyright © 2002 American Psychiatric Publishing; Martin L. Levine and Martha Lyon-Levine (1984), 'Ethical Conflicts at the Interface of Advocacy and Psychiatry', *Hospital and Community Psychiatry*, **35**, pp. 665–66. Copyright © 1984 American Psychiatric Publishing; Alexander Gralnick (1985), 'Build a Better State Hospital: Deinstitutionalization Has Failed', *Hospital and Community Psychiatry*, **36**, pp. 738–41. Copyright © 1985 American Psychiatric Publishing; Richard Lamb (1984), 'Keeping the Mentally Ill Out of Jail', *Hospital and Community Psychiatry*, **35**, p. 529. Copyright © 1984 American Psychiatric Publishing; Paul S. Appelbaum (1994), 'Mental Health Law and Ethics in Transition: A Report from Japan', *Hospital and Community Psychiatry*, **45**, pp. 635–36 and 644. Copyright © 1994 American Psychiatric Publishing; Kenneth S. Kendler (1999), 'Setting Boundaries for Psychiatric Disorders', *American Journal of Psychiatry*, **156**, pp. 1845–48. Copyright © 1999 American Psychiatric Publishing; Donna M. Norris, Thomas G. Gutheil and Larry H. Strasburger (2003), 'This Couldn't Happen to Me: Boundary Problems and Sexual Misconduct in the Psychotherapy Relationship', *Psychiatric Services*, **54**, pp. 517–22. Copyright © 2003 American Psychiatric Publishing; Paul S. Appelbaum and Linda Jorgenson (1991), 'Psychotherapist-Patient Sexual Contact After Termination of Treatment: An Analysis and a Proposal', *American Journal of Psychiatry*, **148**, pp. 1466–72. Copyright © 1997 American Psychiatric Publishing; Paul S. Appelbaum (2001), 'Abuses of Law and Psychiatry in China', *Psychiatric Services*, **52**, pp. 1297–98. Copyright © 2001 American Psychiatric Publishing; Renée L. Binder (2002), 'Liability for the Psychiatrist Expert Witness', *American Journal of Psychiatry*, **159**, pp. 1819–25. Copyright © 2002 American Psychiatric Publishing; Stephen A. Green and Sidney Bloch (2001), 'Working in a Flawed Mental Health Care System: An Ethical Challenge', *American Journal of Psychiatry*, **158**, pp. 1378–83. Copyright © 2001

Yozmot Heiliger for the essays: Ron L.P. Berghmans and Guy A.M. Widdershoven (2003), 'Ethical Perspectives on Decision-Making Capacity and Consent for Treatment and Research', *Medicine and Law*, **22**, pp. 391–400. Copyright © 2003 YOZMOT; T. Mozes, S. Tyano, I. Manor and R. Mester (2002), 'Informed Consent: Myth or Reality', *Medicine and Law*, **21**, pp. 473–83. Copyright © 2002 YOZMOT.

Series Preface

Few academic disciplines have developed with such pace in recent years as bioethics. And because the subject crosses so many disciplines, important writing is to be found in a range of books and journals, access to the whole of which is likely to elude all but the most committed of scholars. The International Library of Medicine, Ethics and Law is designed to assist the scholarly endeavour by providing in accessible volumes a compendium of basic materials drawn from the most significant periodical literature. Each volume contains essays of central theoretical importance in its subject area, and each throws light on important bioethical questions in the world today. The series as a whole makes available an extensive range of valuable material (the standard 'classics' and the not-so-standard) and should prove of inestimable value to those involved in the research, teaching and study of medicine, ethics and law. The fifteen volumes together – each with introductions and bibliographies – are a library in themselves – an indispensable resource in a world in which even the best-stocked library is unlikely to cover the range of materials contained within these volumes.

It remains for me to thank the editors who have pursued their task with commitment, insight and enthusiasm, to thank also the hard-working staff at Ashgate – theirs is a mammoth enterprise – and to thank my secretary, Anita Garfoot, for the enormous assistance she has given me in bringing the series from idea to reality.

MICHAEL FREEMAN
Series Editor
Faculty of Laws
University College London

Introduction

Legal and Ethical Frontiers in Mental Illness

The essays in this volume survey current legal and ethical issues in mental illness. Part I deals with the seriously ill – those whom laypeople may call 'crazy' or 'mad'. The 'normal person' is discussed in Part II – and later in this Introduction I will address the rationale for including that topic in a volume on mental illness. Part III deals with issues of the therapist, including the psychiatrist and other professionals, and the overall treatment system.

The essays were selected from a survey of the literature in medicine, mental health and law. Key issues where those domains overlap were identified – including such standard legal questions as patients' rights and the doctor's powers and responsibilities – and the most interesting essays were chosen.

In some instances, essays were chosen for their focus on cutting-edge issues, rather than on more familiar topics. Under the rules governing the series to which this volume belongs only full essays could be used – not excerpts from articles or books. To permit broader coverage shorter essays were favoured, making it necessary to exclude the very long essays so beloved of American law journals. Several of the essays chosen for this collection present cross-national information, to the extent practicable within the English-language literature.

A Non-Lawyer's View of the Law

There is a culture conflict between medicine and law on how to deal with the mentally ill, a conflict which provides the context for the essays in this volume. Lawyers for patients work for their rights. That can include a right to obtain treatment and rights within treatment, but sometimes what lawyers seek to vindicate is a right to the *least intrusive alternative* treatment or even a right to refuse treatment altogether. Doctors, on the other hand, work for the patient's interests as they understand them, not for their rights – an instance of a well-known distinction between interests and rights. Doctors may regard lawyers as preventing them from doing what is best for their patients and sometimes joke wryly about leaving patients to 'die with their rights on', in the often-quoted phrase of psychiatrist Darold Treffert (1973). This volume deals with the relationship of the legal and medical perspectives on mental illness.

Doctors, like other non-lawyers, may think that law consists of rules and that for each legal question there is an answer. They may find some of those legal answers to be repugnant to their idea of what is best medically or ethically. Then doctors, as non-lawyers often do, may conceive of their alternatives as whether to decide to submit and comply with the law, to ignore or consciously violate it, or to seek to evade the legal rule through some technicality.

In comparison, the same doctors, applying their medical knowledge, have memorized acronyms suggesting the medical steps for each situation (see, for example, Welsh, 2003). However, they also know that medical science includes contradictory research, gaps in knowledge and changes in best practice. They understand that medicine is an art as well as a science.

Doctors should realize that the law is similarly complex. In important medical-legal cases, legal arguments can be made on both sides, and a choice of action sometimes requires a willingness to take a certain amount of legal risk in the pursuit of medical goals.

Principle-Based and Process-Based Approaches

As to ethical issues, there, too, doctors are sometimes taught a set of generative principles, if not specific rules. The so-called 'Georgetown Mantra' of bioethics, taught to generations of medical students, is based on the principles of beneficence, non-maleficence, autonomy and justice (Beauchamp and Childress, 2009). But important real-life questions of ethics, like those of medicine and law, are too complex for any mantra to solve.

I propose a four-step process for doctors approaching ethical dilemmas; it can be generalized to other professionals. The first step is for the doctor to try assiduously to recognize when an action he or she is contemplating raises ethical issues, not just medical ones. That recognition requires the doctor to take a step back from questions of diagnosis and treatment and use an ethical sensitivity to signal that more thought is needed.

The second step is to realize there is typically not just a single applicable ethical value or principle, but conflicting principles – a war of values that potentially govern the choice of action.

The third step I recommend is that the doctor does not make an individual decision among the rival values, but instead seek advice from those who can appropriately give it. In a hospital setting, sources of ethical counsel might be an organized ethics committee or the chief of service. In private practice, it might be a senior colleague or a medical society official. A traditional source of advice for a physician is a lawyer suggested by the doctor's malpractice insurance company, but that perspective is likely to be risk-averse and narrowly legal rather than more broadly ethical.

The fourth step is to define more precisely the role the doctor is playing at that moment and to clarify just how the ethical values and principles apply. For example, a doctor may realize that his or her role at that time is that of offering the patient (or the patient's representative) information on the costs and benefits of alternative medical options. Or a doctor may realize that following what the patient says may not actually honour the patient's autonomy. Sometimes, clarifying the doctor's role and the relevant values makes it easier for the doctor to define the ethical course of action.

Law, Medicine and Ethics: A Case Illustration

An example of a controversy involving medicine, ethics, law and a mentally incompetent patient is the *Georgetown College* case.[1] A patient entered Georgetown University Hospital for emergency care, having lost two-thirds of her body's blood supply from a ruptured ulcer. Her

---

[1]   Application of President & Directors of Georgetown College, Inc., 118 US App. DC 80; 331 F.2d 1000; 1964 US App. LEXIS 6510; 9 ALR.3d 1367, application for rehearsing en banc denied, 118 US App. DC 90; 331 F.2d 1010; 1964 US App. LEXIS 6509; 9 ALR.3d 1381 (DC Circuit, 1964).

condition worsened to the point that she was *in extremis*. Her physician, Dr Edwin Westura, the chief medical resident, concluded that blood transfusions were immediately necessary to save her life. Mrs Jessie Jones's condition rendered her *non compos mentis*, not of sound mind, and it made no legal difference that the cause was not ongoing 'lunacy', but a temporary state caused by her physical condition. The patient's husband refused to give his consent to transfusions, citing the family's religious beliefs.

The doctor identified an ethical conflict and understood the conflicting values at play: his medical training and his personal sense of morality counselled him to give transfusions and save the patient's life, but he was prevented from doing so by the maxim of medical ethics dictating respect for the patient's autonomy.[2] And he potentially faced legal liability whether he disobeyed the family's directions or followed them and let his patient die.

The doctor took what was, in my view, the proper course and, rather than decide himself, brought others into the situation, turning to his superiors at the hospital. A series of steps quickly involved, in turn, the president of Georgetown University, Father Bunn; the university attorney, Edward Bennett Williams, one of the nation's best-known lawyers; and a court from which an immediate decision was sought.

Judge J. Skelly Wright of the US Court of Appeals for the District of Columbia Circuit held an emergency hearing at the bedside. I was present as his law clerk, was asked to offer my recommendation to the judge, and assisted in drafting the ultimate opinion. With an urgent decision necessitated by the medical situation there was no time for legal research until afterwards. After considering the complex situation, Judge Wright decided 'to act on the side of life'. While still at the hospital he authorized the transfusions.

The patient's family and church did not seek to overturn the judge's decision while she was receiving the transfusions. But, after she had recovered, they contested the decision, in order to avoid a precedent being set that their religious views could be overridden.

The full Court of Appeals declined to take up the case, but nevertheless produced a set of clashing published opinions by some of the judges. Judge Warren Burger, later to become Chief Justice of the United States, wrote that whatever the moral dilemma faced by a doctor if a patient refuses medical treatment, courts have no right to hear the case. Judge Wright's view was different: when patient and doctor disagree on a life-or-death treatment decision, a court has jurisdiction to decide whether or not to authorize treatment.

On the merits of the decision, Judge Wright's understanding was that the patient and her family did not want her to die, but that, because of their religious beliefs, they did not want to be the ones to give consent for transfusions. Complex abstract arguments could be made both ways but, with a quick decision necessary, he was unwilling to let the patient die.

The *Georgetown College* case is a dramatic illustration of how domains of medicine, ethics and law can overlap in the treatment of a patient unable to function with normal mental competence.

---

[2]   Georgetown University is also the source of the famous ethical mantra, of beneficence, non-maleficence, respect for autonomy, and justice (Beauchamp and Childress, 2009).

The Seriously Ill

I now turn to a discussion of the essays in this volume. Part I deals with the seriously mentally ill and tackles seven subjects in a series of chapters.

Involuntary Treatment

Traditional legal questions involving the mentally ill have included the criteria and processes for involuntary treatment. A well-known method of authorizing involuntary psychiatric treatment has been a court proceeding leading to a *civil commitment* to a mental health institution. An alternative legal process has been a court appointment of a relative, friend or impartial person to be *guardian* of the mentally ill individual. The guardian is then legally recognized as the decision-maker for the individual, with a power extensive enough to consent to the individual's inpatient treatment, even over his or her protest. In some jurisdictions the term 'conservator' is used instead of guardian. A well-known distinction is between a guardian or conservator *of the person*, who makes decisions involving his or her life, and a guardian or conservator *of the estate* or property, who manages the person's assets.

Modern legal reform efforts have argued that *limited guardianship* is often more appropriate, allowing the mentally ill individual to make many decisions of ordinary life, while the guardian makes a limited range of decisions, such as those involving treatment.

These traditional proceedings deal with long-term treatment. A less traditional question is whether the law should provide a method to order involuntary mental health treatment on a short-term basis. As to this question, Chapter 1 by Lars Kjellin *et al.* considers inpatient care, and my USC colleague Elyn Saks (Chapter 2) considers outpatient treatment.

Treatment Rights

For those in treatment, there are arguments to recognize a broad set of legal rights, as discussed by Douglas Marty and Rosemary Chapin (Chapter 3). Paul Appelbaum's essay (Chapter 4) deals with a specific important claim: the right to privacy.

The range of legal treatment rights recognized for consumers of mental health services may strike physicians as surprisingly wide. No jurisdiction recognizes them all, and the list of rights recognized varies greatly from place to place. Many rights were suggested a quarter-century ago by the President's Commission on Mental Health (1978), and a patients bill of rights was recommended to the states by Congress (but not made legally enforceable) in the Mental Health Systems Act of 1980. Martha Lyon-Levine and I, with psychiatrist Jack Zusman (1982, 1985), surveyed the statutes of the fifty US states, and found that there were statutes enacted in one or more jurisdictions that recognized a patient's right to:

- *Basic Rights*: treatment and least restriction of liberty, freedom from restraint or seclusion, other civil rights, no reprisals for assertion of rights
- *Rights Concerning Treatment*: appropriate treatment and services, individual treatment plan, treatment based on plan, periodic review, aftercare plan, humane treatment environment, privacy for personal needs, safety, discharge referrals

- *Consent and Communication Rights*: ongoing participation, refuse treatment, nonparticipation in experimentation, converse privately, telephone and mail, visitors
- *Information and Record Rights*: explanation re treatment, explanation re experimentation, confidentiality of records, access to records, information re rights, confidentiality of records and access after discharge, posted notice of rights
- *Grievance and Access Rights*: assert grievances, fair grievance procedure, access to advocate, access by legal representative
- *Other Rights*: sales, contracts, vote, storage of goods, compensation for work, education (for children), fingerprinting and photos prohibited, physical exercise and outdoor recreation, spiritual treatment, choice of physician, nourishing diet, conjugal visits or contact with opposite sex

Patient Autonomy

In Chapter 5 Bruce Winick employs the perspective he calls 'therapeutic jurisprudence', familiarly known as TJ, to discuss the right of a mentally ill person to refuse treatment. TJ is an intellectual movement of legal scholars aiming to achieve wide changes in the law: its bold goal, that may strike outsiders as counterintuitive, is that legal interventions should be structured so that they are likely to have a psychologically positive therapeutic effect.

The right to refuse treatment can be analysed as grounded in the individual's ethical claim for respect of his or her autonomy. There are, however, inherent contradictions in respecting patient autonomy while the individual is seriously mentally ill: can a mentally ill person be regarded as exercising autonomy? Can forcing the person to undergo treatment be justified as promoting long-term autonomy? Janet Ritchie, Ron Sklar and Warren Steiner (Chapter 6) approach the topic by considering whether psychiatry can borrow from the field of end-of-life care the concept of advance directives.

Advocacy

A patient's legal and ethical claims, like those just mentioned, may be recognized in principle or on paper, but, to make them real, an advocate can be essential. The right to an advocate can be thought of as the master right that makes the realization of all other rights possible. In Chapter 7 D.P. Olson discusses protection and advocacy services, and in Chapter 8 Martha Lyon-Levine and I discuss the ethical conflicts at the interface of advocacy and psychiatry, drawing on a USC programme she directed that trained patient advocates in mental health. Some psychiatrists welcomed such advocates as part of the treatment team, but others resented their intrusion into traditional medical decision-making prerogatives.

The Social Construction of Madness

In conflict with the traditional medical perspective, some psychiatric patients and their advocates refuse the 'patient' designation and prefer to be regarded as 'consumers of mental health services'. Even some US government agencies use that vocabulary and go further, referring to 'consumers/survivors' of mental health treatment (Cf. Bassman, 1999). The Church of Scientology is well known for its opposition to all psychiatry; it has founded the Citizens Commission on Human Rights to fight psychiatry and operates Psychiatry: An Industry of Death, a museum in Hollywood.

Discussions of mental illness, by both doctors and the public, generally regard its existence as an objective fact, but there are those who view it as being socially constructed. Being a mental patient is, after all, a social role, played in the context of others who recognize that role. Some argue that it is the attitudes and actions of others, not objective medical reality, that creates the role of mental patient.

Thomas Szasz, himself a psychiatrist, is a scholarly opponent of much of psychiatry. His short essay in this volume (Chapter 9) represents his many publications, best known for the claim that mental illness is 'a myth' (Szasz, 1960). That claim relates to a variety of overlapping views held by several authors: that there is not a biological basis for mental symptoms; that bizarre behaviour is not a matter of impaired brain functioning; that symptomatic behaviour is chosen; that a patient's beliefs and actions are equally entitled to respect as those of people regarded as healthy; or that – as a matter of definition – the word 'illness' should be reserved for physical maladies.

I have debated Szasz, admiring his passion for defending the interests of mentally ill people, but critiquing his analysis. For example, in opposition to the claims of Szasz and similar writers, modern research is finding that psychiatric illness can be demonstrated to have a basis in the physical world. Increasingly, the brain correlates of mental processes can be imaged. In addition, brain plasticity has also been demonstrated, showing that the physical brain, the biological substrate of the mind, can itself be changed by mental functioning. The interrelationship between brain functioning and mental disease or health is sufficient to show that mental illness is no myth, no fantasy, although scientists and philosophers still seek to fathom the mysteries of consciousness and its vicissitudes.

In another approach related to the topic of social construction of mental illness, J.R. McMillan (Chapter 10) considers issues of dangerousness and responsibility. The prolific work of my former student Michael Perlin is represented in this volume by his essay, written with Deborah Dorfman, discussing the novel concept of sanism, conceptualized by analogy with racism and sexism (see Chapter 11). Attitudes about the mentally ill are often harmful and inaccurate stereotypes, underscored by conscious or unconscious feelings of repugnance – in a word, discrimination. That the mentally ill are, as a whole, more dangerous than others seems doubtful.

Legal Concepts of Insanity Many ethicists place the mentally ill outside the realm of those who can be held morally accountable and subjected to punishment. Long-standing legal rules purport to do the same, and the precise wording of the definition of insanity, which prevents a finding of criminal guilt, has been the subject of intense debate by scholars, judges and legislators. The legal concept of insanity refers to a mental state at the time of the alleged crime, which prohibits the accused from being found guilty. 'Knowledge of right and wrong' is one among many definitions of this legal concept of sanity. Despite the innumerable books, articles, cases and statutes dealing with the definition of legal insanity, relatively few cases lead to a judgement of 'not guilty by reason of insanity'.

Such a verdict leads to a long period in a locked facility, generally for as long as, or far longer than, the imprisonment that would have followed a guilty verdict. Before a defence lawyer chooses to offer an insanity defence in a non-capital case, it would be prudent to discover the relative conditions of the locked psychiatric hospital and the criminal prison that are alternative destinations for the client.

The legal concept of competence to stand trial, as differentiated from insanity, refers to the time of the court proceeding, not the time of the alleged crime, and is often phrased as the capacity to understand the charges and the situation and to cooperate with counsel for the defence. The mentally ill person swept up in the criminal justice system is far more likely to be found incompetent to stand trial than to be found not guilty by reason of insanity. But the incompetency finding will also lead to a long period in a locked psychiatric facility.

Influenced by the persistence of discriminatory attitudes and unjustified fears, the criminal justice system is often used to place mentally ill persons in locked facilities where they are out of sight of the general public.

Deinstitutionalization

Deinstitutionalization is the modern movement to end the practice of using either commitment or guardianship to require seriously mentally ill people to be long-term inpatients, held involuntarily in locked facilities. In the United States those facilities were generally state hospitals, where the patients supposedly received psychiatric treatment, but may in fact have been warehoused – that is, held without likelihood of cure for many years or for their whole lives.

The deinstitutionalization movement had two facets: the closure of the state hospitals was paired with plans to extend mental health treatment in the local community as a replacement. Generally, as events unfolded, the closure of state hospitals did occur, with great savings to government budgets, but the community treatment centres were not funded. With no other alternative treatment available, large numbers of mentally ill people were then left with nowhere to go but the streets, homeless and without work or social support. The essay by Aileen Rothbard and Eri Kuno (Chapter 12) argues that the deinstitutionalization movement was a success; Alexander Gralnick (Chapter 13) argues that it failed.

In jurisdictions where the policy of deinstitutionalization has been adopted into law, it has become more difficult to obtain a civil commitment order to place a mentally ill person in a state institution. Nevertheless, the mentally ill may still be subjected to involuntary treatment in locked facilities: the process is now likely to be part of the criminal law, rather than civil. It is triggered if a mentally ill person becomes involved in the criminal justice system – convicted of a crime, found not guilty by reason of insanity, or even just held for trial. In Chapter 14 my USC colleague Richard Lamb discusses keeping the mentally ill out of jail.

Cross-Cultural Psychiatry

The final section in Part I deals with cross-cultural psychiatry and is introduced by Arthur Kleinman, who argues, in Chapter 15, that 'illness' should be defined as the personal, interpersonal, and cultural reaction to a biological or psychological 'disease', and reports that culture shapes depressive illness among Chinese in Taiwan and elsewhere, who are likely to experience depression somatically. The next essay by Paul Appelbaum (Chapter 16) reports from Japan on mental health legal and ethical issues. In Chapter 17 Roland Littlewood considers racial bias in psychiatric diagnosis, and Jacqueline Wallen (Chapter 18) considers culturally appropriate treatment. If both biology and culture influence mental functioning, we will expect to see both similarities and differences across societies and ethnic groups, both in mental illness and in how others see it and respond to it.

The Ordinary Mind

In Part II, I turn from the seriously ill to the ordinary mind, – that is, what is sometimes called the 'normal neurotic' or the 'worried well'.

Many people assume that ordinary thinking is rational, and draw a sharp distinction between 'sane' and 'crazy' people. Economists have long used models assuming that people function through cold-blooded rationality, seeking to maximize utility, and philosophers have used the term *akrasia*, 'weakness of will', to label the failure to do what careful thought concludes to be the right or rational thing to do.

However, psychoanalysts suggest that, for all of us, much of our mental functioning: involves emotions as well as thought; is not easily accessible to consciousness; reflects internal compromises, ambivalence and defences; seeks symbolic as well as real-world goals; and transfers on to current adult situations and individuals the perceptions and feelings that the individual first experienced in childhood – or invented at that time in an attempt to understand the world as a child.

Beyond psychoanalysis, the discipline of cognitive psychology has found new methods, employing ordinary scientific tools, to study consciousness and less-than-conscious mentation. In addition, contemporary brain-imaging science has begun to detect many of the mental functions whose existence psychoanalysts derived from listening to patients. And a new field, behavioural economics, explores through experiments the irrationalities that pervade the everyday functioning of people regarded as wholly normal.

The Psychological Underpinnings of Law

The opening chapter of Part II deals with a different area, the psychological underpinnings of law. Both psychological causes and psychological effects are important: psychological reasons that help explain why legal institutions arise and are accepted, and explorations of the psychological effect of what legal actors do. Two essays by Tom Tyler represent his research: one on civil commitment proceedings in particular (Chapter 19), and the other on the broader theme of social justice (Chapter 20). In Chapter 21 Dennis Fox discusses the psychological implications of the very legitimacy of the law.

The Law's Assumption of Rationality

The vision of the ordinary not-so-rational mind is expressed in the work of Amos Tversky and Daniel Kahneman. Kahneman was awarded the Nobel Prize in Economics for his research on human judgement and decision-making under uncertainty. Their work is represented by an essay on the law's assumption of rationality (Chapter 24).

The common cognitive errors their research elucidates are similar to the phenomena psychoanalysis explores, but there are differences. Freudian slips, for example, are affect-laden and, though unconscious, appear to have a meaning or purpose. And psychoanalysts regularly find unconscious transference: adults tend to choose to engage with people who are like significant people from their childhood, or who can be induced to behave similarly, or who are misperceived to be similar. In other instances of transference, adults take on the role of a significant person from their childhood and seek, induce or perceive others in current life to be like they themselves were as children. Psychoanalysts find that feelings and actions influenced by transference to be well nigh ubiquitous, contrary to the assumption that most people are 'rational'.

One example of not-very-rational functioning is the so-called 'false memory syndrome', discussed in an essay by Fiona Raitt and Suzanne Zeedyk (Chapter 23), as well as in an essay representing the body of work by Elizabeth Loftus (Chapter 22). Some therapists have elicited from adults or children what seem to be detailed, previously repressed, memories of abuse they suffered. Research by others indicates that these apparent memories are iatrogenic phenomena, produced by the suggestive methods employed by the therapists.

Controversies over false memories of abuse are important: they involve legal cases where defendants may receive long sentences and suffer intense moral criticism. The topic is also significant for understanding memory and the patient–therapist relationship. False memory syndrome is an example *par excellence* of ethical and legal issues in the domain of mental illness and health.

Overdiagnosis and Overmedication

The psychiatric approach to mental problems may overreach: mentally ill patients may be overdiagnosed and overmedicated with psychotropic medication. This section of Part II is introduced by George Engel's essay on the need for a new medical model (Chapter 25). In Chapter 26 Arthur Barsky and Jonathan Borus discuss the issues of overmedicalization in the context of managed care, and in Chapter 27 Kenneth Kendler argues for setting boundaries for psychiatric disorders. The next pair of essays deal with issues of overmedication of young people, Daniel Safer (Chapter 28) discusses stimulants and Thomas Newman (Chapter 29) writes about treating children with antidepressants.

Enhancement

The final pair of essays in Part II, by Holger Breithaupt and Katrin Weigmann and by Paul Root Wolpe (Chapters 30 and 31 respectively), deal with an ethical issue looming on the horizon: the possibility of enhancing mental functioning. This topic involves improvement rather than impairment, yet our ethical sensitivity is alerted when contemplating departures from the assumed normal.

The Therapist

Part III turns to the therapist, rather than the patient or people in general. An aside on terminology may be useful for some lay readers of this volume, although the terms are familiar to professionals. In this Introduction I may refer to 'therapists' or 'doctors' to refer to all mental health professionals, but distinctions do exist.

Psychiatrists are medical doctors with hospital-based specialist training, who see their practice as part of medicine. In the contemporary understanding of psychiatric best practice they may largely use psychotropic medication, often with little time in their busy schedules available for listening to patients.

Psychologists are usually PhDs with graduate school training, emphasizing research and statistical methods, and those specializing in clinical psychology have post-doctoral training in psychotherapy. They are trained in the effects of medication, but not in its dispensation.

A *psychotherapist* (or therapist), whose technique emphasizes listening and verbal interventions, may be a psychiatrist, but in the current world is more likely to be a clinical psychologist, or a social worker with an MSW degree (perhaps one who has achieved the designation LCSW, licensed clinical social worker). In some countries master's level psychologists can do therapy, and some jurisdictions recognize new professions, with degrees like MFT, a master's degree in marriage and family therapy.

Psychoanalysts are mental health clinicians with advanced training in the form of treatment first inaugurated by Freud, which attempts to understand the influence of a person's past and unconscious determinants. Traditionally, psychoanalysts had prior qualifications as psychiatrists before studying in psychoanalytic institutes, but nowadays there are other routes to psychoanalytic training, such as education as a clinical psychologist or my own background as a university teacher of psychoanalysis and law. Less intensive treatment using a psychoanalytic approach is often called *psychodynamic psychotherapy*.

Informed Consent

The first three essays in Part III are on informed consent. Current law embodies the ethical norm that the doctor can only recommend treatment, while it is up to the patient, if competent, to decide whether or not to accept it. A corollary of this norm is that the patient's consent must be an informed one, given after the doctor has explained not only the risks and benefits of the treatment, but also its alternatives.

An essay by my teacher, Jay Katz (Chapter 32), and another by T. Mozes and colleagues (Chapter 34), considers whether the idea of informed consent is a mere fairytale or myth. All too often, the patient does not receive the information necessary to decide, or does not comprehend it if received.

Moreover, the doctor–patient relationship frequently beclouds autonomous patient decision-making. Psychoanalysts have long studied similar matters under the heading of transference that I mentioned earlier. Freud's original comments on transference dealt with a doctor–patient relationship: he concluded that the patient tends to unconsciously confuse the doctor with some significant person from his childhood and so transfers on to the doctor feelings that had been appropriate to the earlier figure. If unduly influenced by a positive transference, a patient may accept whatever he or she believes the doctor wants, without making an independent judgement.

The legal idea of informed consent is tied up with the concept of decision-making capacity, which Ron Berghmans and Guy Widdershoven (Chapter 33) consider as an ethical issue. The legal status of competence, with its authority to make certain decisions, is supposed to rest on the factual existence of certain psychological capacities. As I argued above while mentioning guardianship, people may be competent to make some decisions, such as those pertaining to daily life, but not others, such as those concerning the disposition of their estate or important treatment choices.

Trust and Confidentiality

To a large extent psychotherapy rests on a foundation of the patient's trust in the doctor, whether that trust is founded in fact or based on a positive transference. An aspect of this trust is the belief that what is said will be kept confidential. It is an ethical maxim dating back to Hippocrates that the doctor will keep private what the patient discloses. The classical version of the Hippocratic duty was 'What I may see or hear in the course of the treatment or even outside of the treatment in regard to the life of men, which on no account one must spread abroad, I will keep to myself, holding such things shameful to be spoken about'. In Chapter 36 David Lowenthal presents case studies illustrating the duties of the modern therapist; in Chapter 35 Ansar Haroun and Grant Morris say that psychiatrists sometimes deceive; in Chapter 37 Stephen Green analyses the ethical limits of confidentiality.

Boundary Violations and Dual Relationships

The law itself imposes limits on confidentiality. The therapist is often under legal obligations to report child abuse and to warn a potential victim of likely violence by the patient (*Tarasoff* v. *Regents*, 1976). The doctor may be privileged to disclose information necessary to secure an emergency involuntary hospitalization of the patient, if suicide is feared or there is sufficient danger to others, and sometimes on the basis of the patient's inability to care for him- or herself.

Trust is but one aspect of a larger doctor–patient model in which the doctor owes loyalty to the patient. Two chapters deal with challenges to that model. It sometimes happens that doctor and patient have an additional relationship alongside that of healing: famously, Freud analysed his own daughter, Anna; a patient may offer to pay in services rather than money; doctor and patient may have a pre-existing acquaintanceship within a small community; or, most dramatically, doctor and patient may develop a sexual relationship.

The concept of multiple or dual relationships is used in the separate essays by Jeffrey Younggren and Michael Gottlieb (Chapter 38) and by Vincent Rinella and Alvin Gerstein (Chapter 39). In Chapter 40 Donna Norris, Thomas Gutheil and Larry Strasburger use a different concept, that of boundary violation where the doctor has crossed the line. Both scholars and the law may differentiate dual relationships that exist during treatment from those that develop after the treatment is ended. In Chapter 41 Paul Appelbaum, in his third appearance in this volume, considers, with his co-author Linda Jorgenson, psychotherapist–patient sexual contact after termination of treatment.

Divided Loyalties

The dual relationship concept concerns role conflicts when both relationships are with the patient; in other common situations, the therapist has a relationship with a third party that may create divided loyalties. The doctor may be paid by someone other than the patient – for example, by the patient's employer, by the parent of a child being treated, or, most commonly, by an insurance company. In Chapter 43 Martha Lyon-Levine and I discuss the ethical issues of divided loyalties, and in Chapter 44 James Dwyer offers philosophical reflections on loyalty conflicts. Paul Appelbaum (Chapter 42) considers the Chinese experience with abuses that can be created by divided loyalties.

The Psychiatrist as Expert

A special role which the doctor may be called on to play is that of expert witness. 'Expert' in this context means those who are recognized as such by a court in a specific judicial proceeding, based on their training, knowledge and experience. Once acknowledged to be experts, they are allowed to testify even though they are not percipient witnesses to the events in controversy, and they are permitted to testify as to their opinions. Psychiatrists or other experts can offer an opinion based on either their own observations of, say, a criminal defendant, or on the basis of medical records, or even on the basis of assumed or hypothetical facts.

Two essays by Paul Appelbaum (Chapter 45) and by Alan Stone (Chapter 46) consider the ethical issues through a parable of the forensic psychiatrist. A second essay by Stone (Chapter 48) asks whether capital punishment creates a special ethical problem for the forensic psychiatrist. In addition, Renée Binder (Chapter 47) considers the possible liability of the psychiatrist expert witness.

Practising in a Flawed System

Turning from the individual level to that of the system, ethical challenges are created by the flaws in the mental health system and, in particular, by the managed care system. These issues are discussed in a pair of essays by Stephen Green and by Green and Sidney Bloch (Chapters 49 and 50). Systemic pressures can have significance, overwhelming issues of the individual doctor–patient dyad.

The Ethical Psychiatrist

The final section in this volume presents essays spanning the issues involved in being an ethical psychiatrist. In Chapter 52 Laura Roberts, Cynthia Geppert and Robert Bailey highlight the issues of essential ethics skills, informed consent, the therapeutic relationship and confidentiality.

Robert Reece (Chapter 51) calls for a new medical ethics for mental health administration, and the final essay, by Sameer Sarker and Gwen Adshead (Chapter 53), writing in the British context, calls for a code of ethics in psychiatry, under a ringing call for 'protecting altruism'.

Acknowledgements

My survey of the medical, legal and mental health literature on these topics draws on the research librarians of the University of Southern California Law School, whose support for scholarship approaches the ideal.

As a university, the USC is committed to interdisciplinary research, a commitment symbolized by the joint appointments I enjoy in the USC Gould School of Law, the Leonard Davis School of Gerontology and the Keck School of Medicine.

The UPS Foundation, the charitable arm of the United Parcel Service, supports my work as part of its concern for people and their problems, and endowed the chair of which I am honoured to be the inaugural holder.

I thank Dr Martha Lyon-Levine and Dr Ralph S. Levine and owe debts of gratitude to my research assistants Alicia Bartley and, especially, Debbie Lusardi. Thanks also to my son, Ben Levine, a keen student of psychoanalytic issues.

References

Bassman, R. (1999), 'The Psycology of Mental Illness: The Consumers/Survivors/Ex-mental Patients' Perspective', *Psychology Bulletin*, **34**(1), pp. 14–16.

Beauchamp, T.L. and Childress, J.F. (2009), *Principles of Biomedical Ethics* (6th edn), New York and Oxford: Oxford University Press.

Lyon, M.A., Levine, M.L. and Zusman, J. (1982), 'Patients' Bills of Rights: A Survey of State Statutes', *Mental Disability Law Reporter*, **6**, pp. 178-201.

Lyon-Levine, M., Levine, M.L. and Zusman, J. (1985), 'Developments in Patients' Bills of Right Since the Mental Health Systems Act', *Mental and Physical Disability Law Reporter*, **9**, pp. 146-52

President's Commission on Mental Health (1978), *Report to the President*, vols. I, IV, Washington: US Government Printing Office.

Szasz, T.S. (1960), 'The Myth of Mental Illness', *American Psychologist*, **15**, pp. 113-18.

Tarasoff v. *Regents of the University of California* (1976), 17 Cal. 3d 425, 551 P. 2d 334, 131 Cal. Rptr. 14, Supreme Court of California.

Treffert, D.A. (1973), 'Dying with their Rights On', *Prism*, **2**, pp. 49-52.

Welsh, C.J. (2003), '"TRAPPED": A Mnemonic for Taking a Substance Use History', *Academic Psychiatry*, **27**, p. 289.

Part I
The Seriously Ill

Involuntary Short-Term Treatment

[1]

Ethical Benefits and Costs of Coercion in Short-Term Inpatient Psychiatric Care

Lars Kjellin, Dr.Med.Sc.
Kristina Andersson
Inga-Lill Candefjord, B.S.
Tom Palmstierna, M.D., Ph.D.
Tuula Wallsten, M.D.

Objective: The study examined the outcome of psychiatric inpatient care in terms of patients' reports of ethical benefits, which were defined as fulfillment of the ethical principles of beneficence and autonomy, and ethical costs, which were defined as any violation of those principles. _Methods:_ A consecutive sample of 84 committed patients and a random sample of 84 voluntarily admitted patients in psychiatric care in two Swedish counties were studied. The patients were assessed twice by a psychiatrist, at admission and at discharge or after three weeks of care. They were also interviewed by a clinical psychologist at discharge or after three weeks. Four aspects of the ethical benefits or costs of their care were examined—whether they reported improvement in mental health, being treated with respect, not being violated as a person, and not being exposed to measures against their will (aside from commitment). _Results:_ The great majority of all patients reported improvement as a result of the psychiatric care. A third of the committed patients and more than half of the voluntarily admitted patients experienced ethical benefits only, without ethical costs. Twenty-three percent of the committed patients and 13 percent of the voluntary patients experienced ethical costs only, without ethical benefits. Some of the patients who experienced ethical costs only were also rated by a psychiatrist as not improved. _Conclusions:_ Few patients had no measurable benefits of care. For committed as well as voluntary patients, an association was found between perceived respect for autonomy and self-reported improvement in mental health. (_Psychiatric Services_ 48:1567–1570, 1997)

Coercion in psychiatric care may be considered necessary to ensure that a mentally ill person receives care and to secure the person's safety as well as the safety of others. In conflict with the ethical obligation to respect the individual's autonomy, an ethical obligation to use compulsory care may exist. Thus an essential question is whether involuntarily hospitalized patients will improve under psychiatric care or be prevented from doing harm to themselves or other persons. Another question that needs to be empirically investigated involves the extent to which ethical principles are violated to achieve these outcomes.

The aim of this study was to examine the outcome of psychiatric inpatient care in terms of ethical benefits, or the fulfilment of ethical principles,

versus ethical costs, or the violation of ethical principles. These issues were explored using data from an ongoing study of the quality of mental health care in two Swedish counties (1). For the study reported here, committed and voluntarily admitted patients were compared.

Outcome was studied in terms of the fulfilment of two basic principles of medical ethics (2). The principle of beneficence sets forth the obligation to benefit others, and the principle of autonomy establishes the obligation to respect the right of the individual to self-determination. The study focused on several questions. To what extent was the patient's mental health and level of functioning improved at discharge or after a period of care? To what extent was the patient's right of autonomy violated? Was respect for the patient's autonomy related to improvement in mental health? Did some patients experience only ethical benefits, and did some experience only ethical costs?

Methods

Legal prerequisites

According to the Swedish Compulsory Mental Care Act (4), which was in force at the time of the study, a combination of two prerequisites is required for care "independent of [one's] own will." The first is having a serious mental illness or mental disorder requiring inpatient care. The second has three aspects—being a danger to one's health or life or to others, having a grossly disruptive way of life, or having an absolute

Dr. Kjellin, Ms. Andersson, and **Ms. Candefjord** _are affiliated with the department of psychiatric research at Västerås Hospital, S-721 89 Västerås, Sweden._ **Dr. Kjellin** _is also affiliated with the department of social medicine at Uppsala University in Uppsala, Sweden._ **Dr. Palmstierna** _is with the St. Göran clinic of dependence disorders at the Karolinska Institute in Stockholm._ **Dr. Wallsten** _is with the department of psychiatry at Uppsala University._

Table 1

Mean scores at admission and change in scores after hospitalization on the Global Assessment of Functioning scale (GAF) for committed and voluntarily admitted patients, by whether they did or did not report improvement from hospitalization[1]

| Score or change | Committed | | | | Voluntarily admitted | | | |
| | Improved | | Not improved | | Improved | | Not improved | |
	Mean	SD	Mean	SD	Mean	SD	Mean	SD
GAF at admission	33.7	12.1	28.7	10.4	43.2	14.7	39.6	9.3
GAF change[2]	19.5	16.3	17.1	22.0	12.2	15.5	2.5	11.4

[1] Admission GAF ratings were available for 82 committed patients (62 improved and 20 not improved) and 83 voluntary patients (63 improved and 20 not improved); data on changes in GAF ratings were available for 71 committed patients (52 improved and 19 not improved) and 66 voluntarily admitted patients (48 improved and 18 not improved).

[2] Wilcoxon rank-sum test, $z=-2.25$, $p<.05$ for the difference between improved and not improved voluntary patients

need for inpatient care to improve one's condition.

Sample and design

The study was conducted in 1991 in two Swedish counties with a total of about 500,000 inhabitants. The settings were the psychiatric departments at a university hospital in one county and at a central hospital in the other. A consecutive sample of patients committed to inpatient psychiatric care and a random sample of voluntarily admitted patients were included. Patients under age 18 and over age 69 were excluded, as were those with alcohol and drug use disorders, mentally retarded people, offenders with mental disorders, people with severe dementia, and patients discharged within three days of admission.

The patients were assessed twice by a psychiatrist—at admission and at discharge, or after three weeks of care, whichever occurred earlier. They were diagnosed at discharge or three weeks according to *DSM-III-R* criteria, and psychiatric status was assessed at both time points by the Global Assessment of Functioning scale (GAF) (3). At discharge or three weeks, the patients were also interviewed by a clinical psychologist.

Short-term outcome at discharge or three weeks was examined using several measures. First, self-reported change in mental health was assessed by asking patients, Considering your mental problems, how do you feel now compared with the time of admission? Answers were cat-

egorized as improved or not improved. Second, patient satisfaction with care was assessed by the question What is your opinion of the psychiatric care you have received? The answers were categorized as satisfied or not satisfied. Third, change in level of functioning was assessed based on psychiatrists' ratings of patients on the GAF. An increase of 10 points or more in the GAF rating was considered to indicate an improvement.

Fourth, respect for the patient's autonomy was assessed by asking the patient several questions: Have you been respected on the ward as a person? Have you at any time during your stay on the ward felt violated as a person? Have you been exposed to measures against your own will?

A total of 84 committed patients and 84 voluntarily admitted patients participated. Forty of the committed patients (48 percent) and 53 of the voluntarily admitted patients (63 percent) were women. The median age of the committed patients was 39 years and of the voluntarily admitted patients 39.5 years. Among the committed patients, 54 (64 percent) had a diagnosis of psychosis (schizophrenia, delusional disorder, schizoaffective and schizophreniform disorders, or atypical psychosis), 26 patients (31 percent) had a mood disorder, and four patients (5 percent) had other diagnoses. Among the voluntarily admitted patients, 29 (35 percent) had a diagnosis of psychosis, 37 (44 percent) had a mood disorder, and 18 (21 percent) had other diagnoses.

Interrater reliability and data analysis

The interrater reliability of the interviews carried out by the psychologists was assessed in 20 interviews. During these interviews, one or two persons were present to rate the answers. The mean reliability calculated with generalized kappa for polychotomous data and two or more raters (5) was .96. The interrater reliability of the GAF ratings, by means of two independent raters, was calculated with a linear correlation to be .96 (6).

Differences between groups were analyzed by the chi square test, Fischer's exact probability test, or the t test when appropriate. Differences in GAF ratings were analyzed using the Wilcoxon rank-sum test (7). The significance level was set at .05.

Results

Improvement

Improvement at discharge or at three weeks was reported by 62 patients in the group of committed patients (76 percent) and 63 patients in the voluntarily admitted group (76 percent); 20 patients (24 percent) from both groups reported they were not improved. Thirty-eight of the committed patients (46 percent) and 45 of the voluntary patients (54 percent) reported at discharge or three weeks that they were satisfied with the care they had received. (Two of the committed patients and one of the voluntarily admitted patients did not answer the question.) However, among the 20 patients from each group who reported no improvement, two committed patients (10 percent) and six voluntary patients (30 percent) reported being satisfied with their care. None of these differences was significant.

Among both the committed patients and the voluntary patients no significant differences were found in gender, age, or diagnosis between patients who reported improvement and those who did not.

Data on change in GAF ratings were available for 73 committed patients and 66 voluntarily admitted patients. A total of 47 patients in the committed group (64 percent) and 31 in the voluntary group (47 percent) were rated as improved, a nonsignif-

Table 2

Self-reports of violations of autonomy by committed and voluntarily admitted patients, by whether they did or did not report improvement from hospitalization

| | Committed | | | | | | Voluntarily admitted | | | | | |
| | Improved (N=62) | | Not improved (N=20) | | | | Improved (N=63) | | Not improved (N=20) | | | |
Violation	N	%	N	%	χ^2†	p<	N	%	N	%	Test statistic[1]	p<
Not respected as a person	13	21	9	45	4.17	.05	3	5	8	40	—	.001
Felt violated as a person	23	37	14	70	6.69	.01	9	14	7	37	—	.05
Exposed to measures against one's will	30	48	17	85	9.12	.01	12	19	6	30	—	ns
At least one of the above	35	56	19	95	12.43	.001	19	30	11	58	4.70	.05

† df=1 for all comparisons
[1] Except for the final item, all comparisons were evaluated by Fischer's exact test. The final item was evaluated by a chi square test (df=1).

icant difference. Table 1 shows the relationship between self-reported and clinician-rated improvement. Among the committed patients, those who experienced improvement were more improved as measured by the GAF than those who did not experience improvement, but the difference was not statistically significant. Among the voluntary patients, the patients who reported improvement were rated as having significantly greater improvement on the GAF than those who reported no improvement.

Violation of autonomy
Twenty-two of the committed patients (26 percent) reported they had not been respected as a person, compared with 11 of the voluntarily admitted patients (13 percent). Thirty-eight of the committed patients (45 percent) reported they had felt violated as a person, compared with 16 of the voluntary patients (19 percent). Forty-eight of the committed

patients (57 percent) reported they had been exposed to measures against their will, compared with 18 of the voluntary patients (21 percent). Thus 55 of the committed patients (65 percent) and 30 of the voluntary patients (36 percent) responded affirmatively to at least one of the three measures of violation or autonomy during hospitalization.

Improvement and autonomy
As shown in Table 2, among the committed patients, a significantly larger proportion of the group that reported no improvement also reported a violation of autonomy. Similar results were found among the voluntarily admitted patients.

Among the 47 committed patients who were rated as improved on the GAF, 28 patients (60 percent) reported a violation of autonomy. Twenty (80 percent) of those rated on the GAF as not improved reported such a violation. Among the 31 voluntary patients who were rated as improved,

nine (29 percent) reported a violation of autonomy. Fourteen (40 percent) of those rated as not improved reported a violation. None of these differences was statistically significant.

Self-reported ethical benefits
Patients were considered to have experienced only ethical benefits if they reported improvement and did not report an autonomy violation. Those who experienced only ethical costs reported no improvement and reported at least one autonomy violation. Some patients experienced benefits as well as costs. For purposes of this analysis, patients who were rated as improved but did not report improvement were regarded as not improved.

Table 3 shows the proportions of patients reporting ethical benefits without costs, ethical benefits as well as costs, and ethical costs without benefits. Of the 19 patients in the committed group who experienced only costs, six (7 percent of the entire sample) were rated as not improved on the GAF. Of the 11 patients in the voluntary group who experienced only costs, seven (8 percent of the entire sample) were rated as not improved on the GAF.

Discussion and conclusions
The main focus in this study was on determining the balance between ethical benefits and ethical costs among committed and voluntarily admitted patients. The majority of both patient groups reported experiencing improvement after being given psychiatric care. Similar results

Table 3

Self-reported ethical benefits and costs among among committed and voluntarily admitted patients

| | Committed (N=82) | | Voluntarily admitted (N=83) | |
Patient group	N	%	N	%
Patients with only ethical benefits[1]	27	33	44	53
Patients with ethical benefits and costs	36	44	28	34
Patients with only ethical costs[2]	19	23	11	13

[1] Self-reported improvement and no self-reported autonomy violations
[2] No self-reported improvement and at least one self-reported autonomy violation

have been found in other studies (8). In this study, one-third of the committed patients reported ethical benefits only—that is, they reported improvement and did not report violations of their autonomy. This finding indicates that once patients are involuntarily hospitalized, they may improve without further violations of autonomy during care.

More than half of the voluntarily admitted patients reported ethical benefits only. A nonnegligible proportion of the patients, 23 percent of the committed patients and 13 percent of the voluntary patients, reported ethical costs only, but few of them were rated as not improved according to the GAF.

Even if no improvement was reported or rated, a positive outcome of care may have been achieved in terms of calming the patient down or preventing the patient from doing harm to self or others. Thus the involuntary admission may have been justified.

Self-reports about improvement were associated with fulfillment of the principle of autonomy. Compared with patients who reported improvement, those in both the committed and the voluntary groups who reported no improvement more frequently reported a violation of autonomy. It may be that patients get better if they are treated more respectfully, or that patients who get better more often perceive they have been treated with respect. Other studies have reported that patients who believed that they were involuntarily admitted were less satisfied with care (9), that patients who reported their stay and treatment to be helpful had been active participants in their treatment program (10), and that commitment can be at least partly accepted by patients if they feel that they have been treated with respect, concern, and fairness (11).

Among both committed and voluntary patients, improvement was more often self-reported than rated on the GAF. Similar results have been found in other studies (10). A stronger association was found between reported and rated outcome among the voluntarily admitted patients than among the committed patients. This finding could reflect the fact that it is easier to reach a treatment alliance with a voluntarily admitted patient.

When interpreting the results of the study, the relatively small and selective samples and the fact that the data were self-reported should be kept in mind. Considering the explorative nature of the study, however, the samples were of suitable size, although differences that were not found to be statistically significant might have been significant in a larger sample. The high interrater reliability for the interviews makes it reasonable to assume that the self-reports reflected the experiences of the patients. Scales for measuring perceived coercion at admission have now been developed (10–12). Methods for assessing the fulfillment of the principle of autonomy during the care process as a whole must be developed and applied in a variety of settings.

The aim of both involuntary and voluntary psychiatric care must be to achieve as many benefits as possible at the lowest possible cost. This study presents a model of how to empirically examine some aspects of the balance between ethical benefits and costs. Few patients in the study experienced no benefit from care. Showing respect to both committed patients and voluntarily admitted patients and avoiding integrity violations and coercive measures seem to be important conditions for a positive outcome of care. ◆

Acknowledgments

The study was supported by grants from the Swedish Council for Social Research and by the Uppsala and Västmanland County Councils.

References

1. Kjellin L, Westrin CG, Eriksson K, et al: Coercion in psychiatric care: problems of medical ethics in a comprehensive empirical study. Behavioral Sciences and the Law 11:323–334, 1993

2. Beauchamp TL, Childress JF: Principles of Biomedical Ethics, 2nd ed. New York, Oxford University Press, 1983

3. Diagnostic and Statistical Manual of Mental Disorders, 3rd ed, rev. Washington, DC, American Psychiatric Association, 1987

4. Lag om ändring i lagen (1966:293) om beredande av sluten psykiatrisk vård i vissa fall [Compulsory Mental Care (certain cases) Act]. Svensk Författningssamling 782: 1–10, 1982

5. Bartko JJ, Carpenter WT: On the methods and theory of reliability. Journal of Nervous and Mental Disease 163:307–317, 1976

6. Lindström E, Palmstierna T, Wallsten T, et al: Key symptoms in patients with a psychotic syndrome in need of compulsory care. European Journal of Psychiatry 8:5– 14, 1994

7. JMP: Statistics and Graphics Guide: Statistical Software for the Macintosh. Research Triangle, NC, SAS Institute, 1994

8. Monahan J, Hoge SK, Lidz CW, et al: Coercion and commitment: understanding involuntary mental hospital admission. International Journal of Law and Psychiatry 18:249–263, 1995

9. Svensson B, Hansson L: Patient satisfaction with inpatient psychiatric care. Acta Psychiatrica Scandinavica 90:379–384, 1994

10. Nicholson RA, Ekenstam C, Norwood S: Coercion and the outcome of psychiatric hospitalization. International Journal of Law and Psychiatry 19:201–217, 1996

11. Lidz CW, Hoge SK, Gardner W, et al: Perceived coercion in mental hospital admission. Archives of General Psychiatry 52:1034–1039, 1995

12. Gardner W, Hoge S, Bennett N, et al: Two scales for measuring patients' perceptions of coercion during mental hospital admission. Behavioral Sciences and the Law 11:307–321, 1993

[2]

INVOLUNTARY OUTPATIENT COMMITMENT

Elyn R. Saks
University of Southern California Law School

This article offers a novel approach to outpatient commitment (OPC). After distinguishing 4 varieties of OPC, the article shows how 3 are easy to justify, whereas "preventive outpatient commitment" (POC) requires more careful scrutiny. The article argues that, as a general matter, POC is not justified, except for on a "one free shot" basis. The hope is that patients will come to appreciate the benefits of treatment in the community and will become voluntarily compliant; after one free shot, they are in a much better position to decide. The consequences of noncompliance are also explored.

Involuntary outpatient commitment (OPC)[1] has been hailed as a godsend in an age in which the extremes of widespread forcible hospitalization and widespread release from hospitalization have been recognized as utter failures.[2] OPC

Correspondence concerning this article should be addressed to Elyn R. Saks, University of Southern California, The Law School, Los Angeles, California 90089-0071. E-mail: esaks@law.usc.edu

---

[1] In this article, I refer to involuntary outpatient commitment as *OPC* or *outpatient commitment*, and I refer to involuntary inpatient commitment as *involuntary commitment, civil commitment, involuntary hospitalization*, or *forcible hospitalization*.

[2] By now, there is a considerable body of literature on OPC. Perhaps the most thoughtful and comprehensive account is that of Ken Kress (2000). For theoretical studies, see, e.g., Scheid-Cook (1991); Stein and Diamond (2000); Swanson et al. (1997); and Tavolaro (1992). For accounts that discuss the costs and benefits of OPC, see, e.g., Bloom (1986); Fulop (1995); Geller (1986); Gutterman (2000); Hoge and Gottole (2000); Leong (1987); Mulveny, Geller, and Roth (1987); Smith (1995); Swanson et al. (2000); and Wilk (1988a, 1988b). For accounts of the three different varieties of OPC, see below; see also, e.g., McCafferty and Dooley (1990); Slobogin (1994); and Wilk (1988a). For accounts of whom OPC should be applied to, see, e.g., Appelbaum (1986); Brooks (1997); Mental and Physical Disability Law Reporter (1986); Mulveny, Geller, and Roth (1987); and Wilk (1988a). Some commentators would apply it only to the incompetent, see, e.g., Hoge and Gottole (2000); and Munetz, Geller, and Frese (2000); and other require that the patient accede voluntarily to the OPC, see, e.g., Brooks (1987). Why patients do comply is an open question; some think it may have to do with a general respect for the law, see, e.g., Lefkovitz et al. (1993), while others cite the case of patients who are misled about the coercive power of the state under this rubric, see, e.g., Geller (1986). (On misperceptions of patients about OPC generally, see, e.g., Borum et al. (1999).) In terms of sanctions for noncompliance, there are different views: some discuss forcing medication (see, e.g., Appelbaum (1986); Keilitz and Hall (1985); and Miller and Fiddleman (1984)); and others, return to the hospital (see, e.g., Miller (1992); Mulvey, Geller, and Roth (1987). Some explicitly discuss hospitalization on a lower showing than for civil commitment (see, e.g., Miller (1992); and others discuss the need for ample process if the patient is to be returned to the hospital (see, e.g., Slobogin (1994)). In terms of sanctions, enforcement problems with OPC are discussed frequently. See, e.g., Appelbaum (1986); Fulop (1995); Geller (1986); Miller (1988); Miller and Fiddleman (1984); and Wilk (1988b). Certain studies review the laws on OPC (see, e.g., Keilitz and Hall (1985); McCafferty and Dooley (1990); Miller (1988); and Torrey and Kaplan (1995)), while others review the empirical studies on OPC (see, e.g., Draine (1997) (discussing methodological issues too); Miller (1988); Swartz et al. (1995) (good on methodological issues, e.g., separating out aggressive case management); Swartz et al. (1997) (discussing methodological limitations of earlier studies); and Wilk (1998a)). Some commentators report on their own studies,

involves coercion and loss of liberty, but arguably less so than inpatient commitment. It widens the net of those coerced, but it also permits many to remain in the community who would otherwise be hospitalized. OPC reduces hospital recidivism and increases voluntary compliance in the future. How could anyone object to it?

Of course, people do object to it, and not wholly without reason. In this article, I propose and attempt to justify a limited use of so-called preventive outpatient commitment (POC). First I lay out the three varieties of OPC that have been identified in the literature. Next I argue that two of those varieties—together with another less explicitly identified variety—are easy cases. I then turn to POC and propose a complex standard to be applied in this case: I argue there should be "one free shot" of POC when patients are not incompetent; and patients may self-bind to POC in the future.[3] (This complex standard is consistent with my views on involuntary inpatient commitment and forcible medication, which I elaborate in *Refusing Care: Forced Treatment and the Rights of the Mentally Ill* [Saks, 2002].[4] I refer readers to that book for justification of that position there.) Finally, I discuss the sanction for noncompliance. My conclusion is that there should be a limited role for POC.

The Varieties of Outpatient Commitment and the Easy Justification of Several

Commentators divide OPC into three varieties. The first is conditional release from hospitalization, occurring after a period of hospitalization has resulted in improving the patient's condition. The second is a form of OPC in which committing courts order OPC as a less restrictive alternative to involuntary hospitalization. The third type is POC, under which an individual may be compelled to accept treatment in the community on a lesser standard than that required for involuntary hospitalization.

Another variety of OPC that is not mentioned much in the literature involves involuntary medication in the community of someone who is incompetent to decide on medication and would have wanted it if competent. This variety does

---

see, e.g., Hiday and Goodman (1982); Hiday and Scheid-Cook (1987); Miller (1992) (reviewing the experience of a state); Policy Research Associates, Inc., for New York City Department of Mental Health, Mental Retardation and Alcoholism Services (1998); Swanson et al. (2000); Swartz et al. (1999); and Van Putten, Santiago, and Berren (1988). Other commentators present individual case studies, see, e.g., Geller (1986); Lefkovitz et al. (1993); and Schneider-Braus (1986). Certain commentators take a comparative perspective, looking at other countries, see, e.g., Davies (2000); and Lefkowitz et al. (1993). The empirical studies report on a variety of outcomes. For instance, some talk about a future increase in the voluntary use of services by those formerly committed to OPC, see, e.g., Hiday and Scheid-Cook (1987); and Van Putten et al. (1988). Others talk about a decrease in future hospital admissions and lengths of stay, see, e.g., Fernandez and Nygard (1990); and Munetz et al. (1996). Other outcomes generally are discussed in the individual empirical studies, see above; see also Scheid-Cook (1991). And data on the use of OPC are discussed in Torrey and Kaplan (1995). Certain commentators talk about alternatives to OPC, such as conditional release and the use of guardians, see, e.g. Torrey and Kaplan (1995), and some prefer efforts at aggressive outpatient services that are provided voluntarily, see, e.g., Fulop (1995); and Tavolaro (1992).

[3]See *infra* note 14 for a definition of self-binding. See Saks (2002).

[4]Saks (2002).

not easily fit in the above schema. In some places such a person would be committable as an inpatient, so this would be the second variety of OPC—a less restrictive alternative. In others, the individual would not be committable as an inpatient, so this would be an instance of the third variety. However, most commentators distinguishing the three varieties are thinking of OPC when the person is dangerous or might devolve into dangerousness—not when he is incompetent. Therefore it might be plausible to construe this a fourth variety of OPC.

The first, second, and fourth varieties of OPC are easy to justify. If someone has been in a hospital and is well enough to leave under certain conditions, imposing those conditions makes sense. (In a way, this variety is an instance of the second: the person remains committable as an inpatient, but is given the opportunity of a less restrictive alternative if he will subject himself to certain conditions. To the extent this variety of OPC is an instance of the third variety, it is more problematic and is justifiable to the extent that variety is.)

The second variety of OPC also seems justifiable on its face, although there are some complexities here. If someone is committable as an inpatient, then allowing him to stay in the community subject to taking medications is a less restrictive alternative. (This is not necessarily because hospitalization per se is less restrictive, see below; but because being given a choice between hospitalization and medication is less restrictive.)

The second variety has some complexities, though. How can we allow someone truly dangerous to remain in the community? Aren't we really committing to OPC those dangerous patients who are less dangerous or for whom the evidence of dangerousness is less? If so, then even though we are using the word "dangerous," the standard for when the dangerous are committed as inpatients versus outpatients is different: the *really* dangerous are hospitalized, and the less dangerous get OPC. This then looks like the third variety of OPC.

I think there is something to this criticism, but in the end it doesn't carry the day. Two things can be said. First, if the less dangerous would have been committed as inpatients in the past, then OPC is a less restrictive alternative. Second, it may be that some for whom the danger is really patent are nevertheless given OPC because they tend to be compliant when pressure is exerted. As a result, they are as dangerous as other inpatients but their danger can be contained outside the hospital. For these reasons, I am inclined to think that the second variety of OPC is sensible and should be its own category.

What about the fourth variety of OPC, when an individual is incompetent to decide on medication and would have wanted it if competent? In general, why should incompetent patients be subject to involuntary treatment? This question returns us to an inquiry I posed in *Refusing Care;* namely, what is special about mental patients that we should treat them differently? We could arguably treat them differently, on the one extreme, because their suffering compels our action, and on the other, because they are incompetent.

Should we involuntarily treat someone to alleviate his suffering and disability? But is there not a real question as to why the patient should not decide which alternative he prefers? Why should the state have the right to choose medication, for instance—with all that entails—over suffering and disability? If the alleviation of suffering and disability were enough to justify forced treatment, there would be no reason not to force treatment on those physically ill as well; yet we let the physically ill decide whether or not they will accept treatment.

Incompetency is a more plausible standard. In effect, this standard means that, in the context of the rights of the mentally ill, psychiatric patients are treated no differently than physically ill patients, whose choices are also not honored when they are incompetent.

It makes sense not to honor the choices of the incompetent. They do not understand what is at stake in their decisions, nor can they appreciate or reason with the information. We cannot rely on the incompetent to know and protect their own interests. There is a place, then, for forcing medication on outpatients (viz., on those who are incompetent and would have wanted medication if competent), just as there is for inpatients in the same circumstances. These are patients, again, who cannot be expected to protect their interests, and we respect their autonomy by honoring what we determine to be their competent wishes.

If this is correct, then incompetence to decide on treatment is a sufficient justification for involuntarily medicating outpatients as much as inpatients. It does not respect patient autonomy to defer to the choices of those who are incompetent to decide, and it does respect patient autonomy to defer to what would be their competent choices. This is true for outpatients no less than for inpatients. When patients meet the conditions specified here, they should be subject to involuntary medication if they will not comply voluntarily. This distinguishes this fourth variety of OPC from POC, in which I argue we should give the patient a choice between medication in the community and hospitalization. The question in the next section is whether we shouldn't compel medication, either by force or by giving a hard choice, in order to prevent or shorten hospitalization—a very different rationale for forced outpatient treatment.

Medication to Shorten or Prevent Civil Commitment to a Hospital

If incompetence is a sufficient basis for forcible treatment in the community, is it a necessary condition in general? Or should we not rather allow outpatient treatment to prevent or shorten commitment, even when the patient is competent? This, I take it, is the rationale of the third variety of OPC–preventive outpatient commitment: The person is committed to outpatient treatment in order to keep him stable in the community even though he would not meet the inpatient commitment standards.

Forcible medication to avoid inpatient commitment seems an illegitimate reason to medicate an outpatient against his will. Indeed, we do not permit inpatient forcible medication to shorten commitment when the patient is competent. Although forcible medication is less costly than civil commitment, cost seems rarely, if ever, a sufficient justification to abridge so important a right. Many choices people make (e.g., to smoke) are costly to society, yet we don't force them to behave otherwise. Avoiding civil commitment might also be thought to be justified by the fact that the intrusion on liberty is greater with civil commitment than with forcible medication. But this is not clear; I shall consider this issue below, when I discuss the consequences of noncompliance in OPC.

Most important for our purposes here, why should we not let the patient himself decide what he would prefer? If he prefers confinement to forcible medication, then the latter is the greater intrusion.

POC in fact allows commitment if the patient, among other things, is not dangerous, but can reliably be predicted to deteriorate to dangerousness—and to require civil commitment—if not treated; he is given a choice between medication and commitment. But then could one not argue that with POC, properly understood, one is simply putting the person's beliefs to the test? That is, one is requiring him to decide between hospitalization and medication in the community. If he truly does prefer hospitalization, he can make that choice. This is an important point, and it does mean that we are not literally forcing medication to avoid hospitalization; we are coercing it. We are giving the person a hard choice: "If you really prefer civil commitment to medication, then we will civilly commit you."

But the question then becomes, why are we coercing a competent person to choose medication or hospitalization, when she could well believe that *no medication in the community* is the best choice for herself? As a competent patient, why does she not get to decide what is best for herself? In the same way, we do not tell competent physically ill patients that they must receive treatment in the community for, say, their lupus or we will put them in a hospital. True, we are not literally *forcing* the lupus patient to be treated, but the example makes plain that coercion is nearly as bad as force itself.

Of course, one could say that this does not make sense in the case of the lupus patient, whereas it does in the case of the psychiatric patient, because treatment in the community may well be what keeps the psychiatric patient out of the hospital, but the same is not true with the lupus patient. But we can make up a fact here: if lupus patients do not get treatment in the community they will eventually have to be hospitalized. We still, I think, would not give them a hard choice between treatment and hospitalization, but would allow them, if competent, to choose to wait and eventually be hospitalized, if that is what the outcome turned out to be.

Now one could, however, say there is an important difference here. With the psychiatric patient, unlike the lupus patient, we may eventually require hospitalization because the patient becomes dangerous. So we, the community, have an interest in making sure the patient does not devolve into needing involuntary inpatient treatment which we do not have with the lupus patient. If the psychiatric patient needs involuntary inpatient treatment it generally means that he has become a danger; and that is putting ourselves at risk.

This seems to be an important difference; however, it is no more sufficient to justify forcing/coercing treatment of a competent patient than simply preemptively committing someone who looks as if he may become dangerous (as in the prior case, if we wait, it may become too late). Because of our commitment to liberty and dignity, we tolerate a certain amount of insecurity. And of course with non-mentally ill people we tolerate a huge amount of danger—think of violent felons who are released from prison. In addition, the evidence is very clear that most mentally ill people (at least the non-substance abusing) are no more a threat than anyone else. Once again, preventing or shortening commitment—even though there is potentially something in it for us, and not just the patient—is not a sufficient basis for POC, at least as a general matter.

It must nevertheless be acknowledged that this is not an easy position to take.

For is not the evidence overwhelming that outpatient commitment helps? It reduces hospital recidivism in a significant percentage of cases if combined with aggressive treatment of 6 months or longer; and it results in a greater likelihood that the patient will voluntarily remain in treatment once the commitment period is over.

On the other hand, more studies are needed to replicate those that exist. And there are, indeed, studies going the other way. Perhaps more important, these good outcomes must be weighed against the costs of outpatient commitment (e.g. all those patients coerced to no good end). And we must study more systematically whether aggressive outpatient treatment, with, for example, outreach workers going to people's homes when they do not show up for appointments, would not be a better use of resources.

Finally, while giving a choice of medication in order to avoid hospitalization is preferable to forcing medication, it is still a coercive choice, as I argued above. It is unclear why competent people should be put to this choice. For these reasons, I would not, as a general rule, allow POC in order to avoid hospitalization.

One Free Shot

I would, however, allow one free course of outpatient commitment, under certain specified conditions. For instance, the patient would need to have a record as a revolving door patient, so we know we are coercing those who indeed reliably deteriorate into dangerousness. In addition, the patient, while not incompetent, would need to be psychotic and impaired. I would allow the commitment to last 6 months, or however long the best evidence suggests is necessary to get patients to become voluntarily compliant. Indeed, encouraging future voluntary treatment is an important outcome of a limited use of outpatient commitment.[5]

The reasons for allowing one free shot here are as follows: the patient might not appreciate the benefits of continuous medication in the community until he has been forced to experience them. And once he has experienced them he may be enormously grateful and subsequently choose voluntary compliance.

To be more explicit about the rationale for a one-free-shot regime, I note that the patient is impaired, if not incompetent, at the decision point.[6] As such, her

---

[5]What if it took two, or three, free shots to secure these benefits? First, note that we have no evidence that this is so. Absent evidence, there is good theoretical reason to prefer one free shot, namely, that is the point at which the patient will have sufficient experience to make a choice— experience of both the illness and the intervention. Second, even if it were so, there are some troubling aspects of preferring the non-impaired choice that agrees with us over the non-impaired choice that doesn't. This is a difficult question. For further thoughts about it, see *Refusing Care.*

[6]On why "impaired" choices, and not just "incompetent" choices, are sometimes not entitled to respect, see *Refusing Care.* It is important to note, however, that my proposal allows coercing a medication decision absent incompetence, while many cases say that competent patients have a right to refuse medication absent an emergency. *See, e.g., Mills v. Rogers, Rivers v. Katz, and Riese v. St. Mary's Hospital.* It is not my task here to formulate the best constitutional argument for my position. I will note that there are many cases which do not allow competent patients to refuse—and which deny that the constitution requires allowing them to. Whether we endorse these decisions or not, it is also the case that this particular rationale for allowing medication has never been addressed by the courts; it may be that, given the benefits of keeping someone in the community, as well as the fact that medication is not forced, but the patient is just given a hard choice, this proposal would pass

choice is less worthy of respect. In addition, she may be somewhat "not herself," and when she is restored to her healthy, unimpaired self, she endorses the choice we have made for her. Again, the choice made by the "different self" is less worthy of respect; "different selves" know the true self less well and are less committed to tending to its needs and wants. Moreover, even though we are somewhat preferring one self over the other when we point to the retrospective gratitude, it is unduly skeptical not to prefer the choice of the healthy self.

Finally, by enforcing one course of outpatient commitment, one is putting the person in the best position to make an intelligent choice about medication in the community in the future. Before the period of outpatient commitment, the patient will not have experienced six months of wellness in the community, but afterward, he will. We therefore bring the patient to a place of maximal competence—both because his mental state is improved and because he will have experienced a period of stability that he may like—and we allow him to make the best choice for himself.

But why isn't the one free shot of medication in the hospital sufficient basis for the patient to self-bind?[7] If he or she hasn't chosen to do that, surely we must wait until he or she becomes incompetent or dangerous before we medicate him or her. But it may be the case that some may not appreciate the benefits of treatment *in the community* without forced treatment there for 6 months. They may have failed to self-bind because they deluded themselves that they could survive in the community without medications, or they may have mistaken the unpleasantness of being hospitalized for that of being medicated. In any case, one free shot of consistently doing well in the community for six months may be what gets the patient to want to maintain his gains.[8]

It will be clear that this one free shot of outpatient commitment proposal shares features with Alan Stone's famous "thank you" theory of commitment.[9] It should be clear, however, that there are important differences too. Most prominently, my proposal allows only *one* free shot; Stone would allow commitment generally under his standards given the prospect of retrospective thanks. I also want to be clear that, while retrospective gratitude is sufficient in my view to justify our actions, it is not necessary. For me, the justification for the one-free-shot regime is that it positions the patient maximally to decide, both because he is more competent and because he has more information.

---

constitutional muster. I leave to others the hard task of putting this argument in terms the constitution cognizes.

[7]*Refusing Care* allows this.

[8]Throughout this discussion I have been assuming that compliance with medication is a good thing, and that getting people to want to comply is therefore also a good thing. I confess that in the case of serious mental illness I think that medication is generally helpful, if not essential. By the same token, I think competent patients should generally have authority to decide this question for themselves, and there may certainly be cases where not taking medication is in a patient's best interests, at least as he conceives them.

[9]See Stone (1976). There is considerable literature discussing whether patients are indeed grateful for their treatment. Findings include that many are indeed grateful—or think they have received good care or some such—but that voluntary patients tend to be grateful more often than involuntary. For an extended discussion of the evidence, see *Refusing Care*.

The Sanction for Noncompliance

If patients are noncompliant during the period of outpatient commitment, what should the consequences be? Some jurisdictions allow the person to be rehospitalized only if he or she meets inpatient commitment standards. Others allow unjustified noncompliance to suffice. Still others simply forcibly medicate patients in the community.

Let us look first at the option of allowing noncompliance to suffice for hospitalization or requiring dangerousness (i.e., meeting inpatient commitment criteria) before doing so. It may seem that the latter gives no teeth to the outpatient commitment: one must comply or one will be committable only under the circumstances under which one would have been committable anyway. In fact, however, there are some consequences: the person may be returnable to the health facility by the police where she will be evaluated and an effort made to persuade her to take her medications. At the very least one comes to the attention of the authorities much sooner.

In addition, some patients probably comply because they think they have to. If this is just a matter of respecting a court order, that seems fine to me. If the patients are under the mistaken impression that they have to take the medications, or they will be forced to take them, then that is not so fine. Some of the evidence suggests that some patients are under this misimpression, and some doctors encourage it. Patients should be aware of the real consequences of their noncompliance—greater likelihood of hospitalization, rather than forced medication, in this scenario.

Indeed, it seems to me that if patients really knew that all they risked from noncompliance was greater scrutiny of their behavior, they may not have much incentive to comply. I would therefore allow, on the one free course (or subsequent self-bound-to courses), that noncompliance itself, unless appropriately justified, should itself be a basis of inpatient commitment; again, on this one free course, patients should be given the choice of medication or hospitalization. The advantages in the way of encouraging compliance in the future by giving patients 6 months of doing well on medication—and perhaps, maybe even probably, coming to appreciate it—may justify the costs.

But why should we give the patient a choice between compliance and hospitalization, rather than just enforcing compliance: forcibly medicating the patient in the community? There are two dimensions to this question. First, is it better to give people a choice, albeit a hard choice, than to simply force what we think best? And second, if the patient will not make a choice, are we better off forcing hospitalization than medication?

As for the first question, the answer seems clear. Even a hard choice is a choice, and coercion is better than force. Even if medication is a better choice than hospitalization, this is simply an abstract principle, and individual patients may feel differently. It enlarges patients' freedom to let them decide for themselves.

As for the second question, the answer is less clear. One could say that if the patient is given a choice between compliance and hospitalization, and chooses noncompliance, he is choosing hospitalization. But he may totally disagree with this characterization. He may see himself as choosing noncompliance and non-hospitalization—it's just that nobody will let him do that.

Assuming that the patient refuses to make the choice we put to him, are we better off forcing hospitalization or forcing medication? At first blush, one might think the case for compulsion is easier to make for medication than for hospitalization. Consider that taking medication is less stigmatizing than being civilly committed; it is between the patient and his doctor. By contrast, inpatient civil commitment is a public affair, right down to the existence of a public record.[10]

Further, medication has less effect on one's liberty, at least in its grossest manifestations: it does not confine the patient to a particular place, regulate whom he can see and when, and so on. Finally, medication has much more beneficial effects on one's mental status than hospitalization. Medications are real treatments, while hospitalization is at best a safe haven—rarely does it result in the remission of mental illness. (One need only reflect on the census in mental hospitals before and after the advent of psychotropic drugs to see that this is so.)

Arguments on the other side, however, are stronger. Force, that is, is more difficult in the case of medications, and therefore it should be permissible, generally, only when the patient is incompetent. While medications are less stigmatizing than hospitalization, they are also far riskier to one's health. Death itself is a possibility, as are considerable discomfort and an irreversible, sometimes grotesque movement disorder.[11] Indeed, the latter makes medication potentially far more stigmatizing than hospitalization, because people who develop the disorder look mentally ill to all the world.[12]

And, while hospitalization involves greater restrictions on one's liberty than medication, medication in a sense involves greater intrusion into one's person. Medication changes one's mental state—one's very thought processes—and in a way that can't be resisted by any effort. Thus, it is a deep intrusion into the person's psychic integrity. People probably care more about their freedom of mentation than their locomotor freedom. Therefore, we should abridge this freedom only on a greater showing.

Finally—and to return to our first point—if patients are forcibly medicated when they do not comply, we are altogether taking choice away from them: either they take the medication or they take the medication. Again, a coerced choice may be better than no choice at all. And that some patients refuse to make a choice does not mean that we should deprive the many others who would want it of that opportunity.

If all of this is right, it is better to make hospitalization on unjustified

---

[10]The patient's outpatient commitment may have involved a public record. But if the further sanction is forcible medication, rather that involuntary inpatient commitment, the patient will not suffer the stigma of a further public record—and this time of inpatient commitment.

[11]Neuroleptic malignant syndrome, though rare, can result in death. It must be conceded, of course, that untreated mental illness can also lead to death, e.g. through suicide, and it is unclear that deaths caused are greater than deaths saved, although the death rate of those already hospitalized must be less than of those wholly untreated. Tardive dyskinesia (TD), the irreversible movement disorder, can also be quite problematic to patients. Risk increases with lifetime dose, and estimates of prevalence rates suggest that it occurs quite often. The newer medications seem to have less risk of TD.

[12]I do not think that only those who know of TD make this connection. Students have often commented that the movement disorders of the mentally ill they see on the streets are what make them think the person is mentally ill.

noncompliance the sanction than either to force medication or to force hospitalization only if ordinary civil commitment criteria are met.[13] As noted earlier, if the patient is incompetent and would have wanted medication if competent, then this is a permissible basis for forcing medication. But in the ordinary preventive outpatient commitment context, where patients are not strictly incompetent, patients should be given the hard choice of medication in the community or hospitalization.

Self-Binding

After the period of one free shot of POC, I would allow the patient to self-bind[14] not only to future treatment, but also to continuing or future POC, even though it would not otherwise be required. A patient might feel she would be more likely to comply continuously with treatment if she were under coercion for an extended period. While under self-binding principles, she could be required to be treated, she might prefer being required to make a hard choice to literally being forced. That might, in her view, not only be most consistent with he autonomy interests, but also be most effective in terms of treatment response.

One question would be whether the outpatient treatment to which the patient has self-bound should remain in force even if the patient becomes unimpaired and wishes to revoke her consent. That is, can the patient self-bind to 6 months of treatment even if she later becomes unimpaired and no longer wishes to be subject to it? I would suggest not; once the patient is unimpaired, her current wishes must be respected. Certainly on later occasions than the one free shot, my inclination would be to require the patient to remain impaired if he is to continue to be subject to a self-binding contract to outpatient commitment, because in this scenario it is the patient's unimpaired consent that justifies the coercion.

Still, it seems clear that there is a place for self-binding to outpatient commitment. The hope is eventually to encourage continuous voluntary compliance.[15]

---

[13]There may be practical problems with this suggestion, in that patients refusing medications will now take up scarce hospital beds. But these patients may be persuaded to take medications by the hospital personnel. And they will only be subject to such hospitalization one time. Finally, we can set the length of hospitalization at some reasonable amount so as not to strain resources too much.

[14]By "self-binding," I mean to indicate using "advance directives" or "living wills" or entering into a "Ulysses contract." There is a considerable literature on the use of such devices in the mental health context. See, e.g., Appelbaum, 1982, 1991; Backlar, 1995; Backlar and MacFarland, 1996; Brock, 1993; Cuca, 1993; Dixon, 1992; Dresser, 1992; Macklin, 1987; Perling, 1993; Radden, 1992; Rosenson and Kasten, 1991; and Winick, 1996. There is also an interesting issue of *Psychology, Public Policy, and Law* (Winick, 1998) devoted to this topic.

[15]Constitutional questions, of course, could arise on either the one-free-shot or the self-bound-to course of POC when the sanction of hospitalization absent dangerousness is triggered: one might then be civilly committing, without more, a nondangerous person who could survive safely in the community on her own or with the help of willing and responsible family or friends. And *O'Connor v. Donaldson* seems to preclude this. But *Donaldson* did not address the issue of the permissibility of such commitment for the sake of inducing a patient to take the medications which would allow her to remain safely in the community—and that, only during one course of outpatient commitment. As that issue was not addressed, we do not know how the Court would come down. And there are certainly arguments that this would be a permissible deprivation of liberty under the

Conclusion

My conclusion is that forced outpatient medication should be allowed if the patient is incompetent or if the patient has self-bound to it. Under limited circumstances, patients should be subject to "preventive commitment" (i.e., they should be given a choice between involuntary medication and involuntary hospitalization). However, preventative commitment should be allowed only under a one-free-shot regime, with the ultimate hope being to induce the patient voluntarily to accept treatment in the future, or at least to self-bind to future treatment or future outpatient commitment.

References

Appelbaum, P. S. (1982). Can a subject consent to a Ulysses contract? Commentary. *Hastings Center Report, 12,* 27–28.

Appelbaum, P. S. (1986). Outpatient commitment: The problems and the promise. *American Journal of Psychiatry, 143,* 1270–1272.

Appelbaum, P. S. (1991). Advance directives for psychiatric treatment. *Hospital and Community Psychiatry, 42,* 983–984.

Backlar, P. (1995). The longing for order: Oregon's medical advance directive for mental health treatment. *Community Mental Health Journal, 31,* 103–108.

Backlar, P., & MacFarland, B. H. (1996). A survey on use of advance directives for mental health treatment in Oregon. *Psychiatric Services, 47,* 1387–1389.

Bloom, J. D. (1986). The Tarasoff decision, dangerousness and mandated outpatient treatment. *International Journal of Offender Therapy and Comparative Criminology, 30,* 7–10.

Borum, R., Swartz, M., Riley, S., Swanson, J., Hiday, V. A., & Wagner, R. (1999). Consumer perceptions of involuntary outpatient commitment. *Psychiatric Services, 50,* 1489–1491.

Brock, D. W. (1993). A proposal for the use of advance directives in the treatment of incompetent mentally ill persons. *Bioethics, 7,* 247–256.

Brooks, A. D. (1997). Outpatient commitment for the chronically mentally ill: Law and policy. *New Directions for Mental Health Services, 36,* 117–128.

Cuca, R. (1993). Ulysses in Minnesota: First steps toward a self-binding psychiatric advance directive statute. *Cornell Law Review, 78,* 1152–1186.

Davies, S. (2000). Involuntary out-patient commitment and supervised discharge. *British Journal of Psychiatry, 177,* 183.

Dixon, G. (1992). The Minnesota advance psychiatric directive: Protecting patient decision-making. *Minnesota Medicine, 75,* 33–34.

Draine, J. (1997). Conceptualizing services research on outpatient commitment. *The Journal of Mental Health Administration, 24,* 306–315.

Dresser, R. (1992). *Autonomy revisited: the limits of anticipatory choices.* Baltimore: Johns Hopkins University Press.

Fernandez, G. A., & Nygard, S. (1990). Impact of involuntary outpatient commitment on the revolving-door syndrome in North Carolina. *Hospital and Community Psychiatry, 41,* 1001–1004.

---

limited conditions specified in the text—all of the arguments given for why this makes sense as a policy matter, so that liberty is not being wrongly or arbitrarily denied. Finally, I wish to say that I take my task to be proposing the most sensible regimen concerning OPC; I am not making a constitutional argument, and I leave to others more skilled in that arena to make such an argument.

INVOLUNTARY OUTPATIENT COMMITMENT   105

Fulop, N. J. (1995). Involuntary outpatient civil commitment: What can Britain learn from the U.S. experience? A civil liberties perspective. *International Journal of Law and Psychiatry, 18*, 291–303.

Geller, J. L. (1986). The quandaries of enforced community treatment and unenforceable outpatient commitment statutes. *The Journal of Psychiatry & Law, 14*, 149–158.

Gutterman, J. (2000). Waging a war on drugs: Administering a lethal dose to Kendra's Law. *Fordham Law Review, 68*, 2401–2444.

Hiday, V. A., & Goodman. R. R. (1982). The least restrictive alternative to involuntary hospitalization, outpatient commitment: its use and effectiveness. *The Journal of Psychiatry & Law, 10*, 81–96.

Hiday, V. A., & Scheid-Cook, T. L. (1987). The North Carolina experience with outpatient commitment: A critical appraisal. *International Journal of Law and Psychiatry, 10*, 215–232.

Hoge, M. A., & Grottole, E. (2000). The case against outpatient commitment. *The Journal of the Anerican Academy of Psychiatry and the Law, 28*, 165–170.

Keilitz, I., & Hall, T. (1985). State statutes governing involuntary outpatient civil commitment. *Mental & Physical Disability Law Reporter, 9*, 378–397.

Kress, K. (2000). An argument for assisted outpatient treatment for persons with serious mental illness illustrated with reference to a proposed statute for Iowa. *Iowa Law Review, 85*, 1269–1386.

Lefkovitch, Y., Weiser, M., & Levy, A. (1993). Involuntary outpatient commitment: Ethics and problems. *Medicine and Law, 12*, 213–220.

Leong, G. B., Bursten, B., & Geller, J. L. (1987). Letters to the editor: Outpatient civil commitment. *American Journal of Psychiatry, 144*, 694–695.

Macklin, A. (1987). Bound to freedom: The Ulyses contract and the psychiatric will. *University of Toronto Faculty Law Review, 45*, 37–68.

McCafferty, G., & Dooley, J. (1990). Involuntary outpatient commitment: An update. *Mental & Physical Disability Law Reporter, 14*, 277–287.

Mental and Physical Disabilities Law Reporter. (1986). Case law developments: Civil commitment. [all sections]

Miller, R. D. (1988). Outpatient civil commitment of the mentally ill: An overview and an update. *Behavioral Sciences & the Law, 6*, 99–118.

Miller, R. D. (1992). An update on involuntary civil commitment to outpatient treatment. *Hospital and Community Psychiatry, 43*, 79–81.

Miller, R. D., & Fiddleman, P. B. (1984). Outpatient commitment: Treatment in the least restrictive environment? *Hospital and Community Psychiatry, 35*, 147–151.

Mills v. Rogers, 457 U.S. 291 (U.S.S.Ct)

Mulvey, E. P., Geller, J. L., & Roth, L. H. (1987). The promise and peril of involuntary outpatient commitment. *American Psychologist, 42*, 571–584.

Munetz, M. R., Geller, J. L., & Frese, F. J. (2000). Commentary: Capacity-based involuntary outpatient treatment. *The Journal of the American Academy of Psychiatry and the Law, 28*, 145–148.

Perling, L. J. (1993). Health care advance directives: Implications for Florida mental health patients. *University of Miami Law Review, 48*, 193–228.

Policy Research Associates. (1998). *Final report on the Research Study of the New York City Involuntary Outpatient Commitment Pilot Program.* Delmar, NY: Author.

Rivers v. Katz, 495 N.E. 2d. 377 (N.Y. 1986).

Radden, J. (1992). Planning for mental disorder: Buchanan and Brock on advance directives in psychiatry. *Social Theory and Practice, 18*, 165–186.

Rogers v. Commissioner of the Department of Mental Health, 458 N.E.2d. 308 (Mass. 1983)

Riese v. St. Mary's Hospital Medical Center, 271 CalRptr 199, 203 (Cal. Ct. App. 1987).

Rosenson, M. K., & Kasten, A. M. (1991). Another view of autonomy: Arranging for consent in advance. *Schizophrenia Bulletin, 17,* 1–7.

Saks, E. R. (2002). *Refusing care: Forced treatment and the rights of the mentally ill.* Chicago: University of Chicago Press.

Scheid-Cook, T. L. (1991). Outpatient commitment as both social and least restrictive alternative. *The Sociological Quarterly, 32,* 43–60.

Schneider-Braus, K. (1986). Civil commitment to outpatient psychotherapy: A case study. *Bulletin of the American Academy of Psychiatry and Law, 14,* 273–279.

Slobogin, C. (1994). Involuntary community treatment of people who are violent and mentally ill: A legal analysis. *Hospital and Community Psychiatry, 45,* 685–689.

Smith, C. A. (1995). Use of involuntary outpatient commitment in community care of the seriously and persistently mentally ill. *Issues in Mental Health, 16,* 275–284.

Stein, L. I., & Diamond, R. J. (2000). Commentary: A "systems"-based alternative to mandatory outpatient treatment. *The Journal of the American Academy of Psychiatry and the Law, 28,* 159–164.

Stone, A. A. (1976). *Mental health and law: A system in transition.* New York: Jason Aranson.

Swanson, J. W., Swartz, M. S., George, L. K., Burns, B. J., & Hiday, V. A., Borum, R., & Wagner, H. R. (1997). Interpreting the effectiveness of involuntary outpatient commitment: A conceptual model. *Journal of the American Academy Psychiatry Law, 25,* 5–16.

Swanson, J. W., Tepper, M. C., Backlar, P., & Swartz, M. S. (2000). Psychiatric advance directives: An alternative to coercive treatment? *Psychiatry, 63,* 160–172.

Swartz, M. S., Burns, B. J., George, L. K., Swanson, J., Hiday, V. A., Borum, R., & Wagner, H. R. (1997). The ethical challenges of a randomized controlled trial of involuntary outpatient commitment. *Journal of Mental Health Administration, 24,* 35–43.

Swartz, M. S., Swanson, J. W., Wagner, H. R., Burns, B. J., Hiday, V. A., & Borum, R. (1999). Can involuntary outpatient commitment reduce hospital recidivism?: Findings from a randomized trial with severely mentally ill individuals. *American Journal of Psychiatry, 156,* 1968–1975.

Swartz, M., Burns, B. J., Hiday, V. A., George, L. K., Swanson, J., & Wagner, H. R. (1995). New directions in research on involuntary outpatient commitment. *Psychiatric Services, 46,* 381–385.

Tavolaro, K. B. (1992). Preventative outpatient civil commitment and the right to refuse treatment: Can pragmatic realities and constitutional requirements be reconciled. *Medicine and Law, 11,* 249–267.

Torrey, E. F., & Kaplan, R. J. (1995). A national survey of the use of outpatient commitment. *Psychiatric Services, 46,* 778–784.

Van Putten, R. A., Santiago, J. M., & Berren, M. R. (1988). Involuntary outpatient commitment in Arizona: A retrospective study. *Hospital and Community Psychiatry, 39,* 953–958.

Wilk, R. J. (1988a). Implications of involuntary outpatient commitment for community mental health agencies. *American Journal of Orthopsychiatry, 58,* 580–591.

Wilk, R. J. (1988b). Involuntary outpatient commitment of the mentally ill. *Social Work,* 133–137.

Winick, B. J. (1996). Advance directive instruments for those with mental illness. *University of Miami Law Review, 51,* 57–95.

Winick, B. J. (Ed.). (1998). Advance directive instruments for health and mental health care [special issue]. *Psychology, Public Policy, and Law, 4(3).*

Treatment Rights

[3]

ETHICS IN COMMUNITY MENTAL HEALTH CARE

The Legislative Tenets of Client's Right to Treatment in the Least Restrictive Environment and Freedom from Harm: Implications for Community Providers

Douglas A. Marty, M.S.W.
Rosemary Chapin, Ph.D.

ABSTRACT: For over four decades, national legislation has supported efforts to move persons with severe and persistent mental illness out of restrictive hospital settings and into community based services. Within institutional walls, numerous duties of state have been established to help ensure humane and effective treatment. However, the legal protections afforded hospitalized residents have not appeared to follow these individuals into the community. This article analyzes relevant case law and attempts to establish similarities between the state hospital's duty to protect its residents and the responsibility of community mental health centers to do the same for the persons

Doug Marty is a Ph.D. student and affiliated with the Office of Social Policy Analysis at the University of Kansas. Rosemary Chapin is Associate Professor, School of Social Welfare, University of Kansas.

Address correspondence to Doug Marty, OSPA, School of Social Welfare, Twente Hall, University of Kansas, Lawrence, Kansas 66045-2510; e-mail dougm@sw1.socwel.ukans.edu.

Ethics in Community Mental Health Care is a special section within *Community Mental Health Journal* designed to remind our readers about special problems that accompany the delivery of care to our clients.

Anyone wishing to submit a philosophical or ethical piece to this special section should write to Patricia Backlar, Department of Philosophy, Portland State University, P.O. Box 751, Portland, Oregon 97207.

they serve. The authors argue that the client's right to freedom-from-harm must receive increased attention and community based service providers will have to enhance their capacity to deliver more effective risk management services if mental health reform is to become a successful social policy.

The drive toward community based services for people with severe and persistent psychiatric disabilities which underpins mental health reform has also presented U. S. state and local policy makers with an array of difficult dilemmas. In many states, mental health reform legislation has been hailed as a "landmark" legal initiative in the state's history (Mechanic & Rochefort, 1990; Rapp & Moore, 1995). A primary effect of this effort has been to nationally divert citizens challenged with severe and persistent psychiatric disabilities from the upheaval and restrictiveness of hospital admission. Public psychiatric hospital beds have been significantly reduced across the nation. In 1955, over 558,000 severe and persistent psychiatrically disabled persons resided in state hospitals. By 1994, that number dropped to just under 72,000 (Torrey, 1997). It is not enough, however, to merely close state hospitals. Federal and state legal processes have mandated the shifting of hospital dollars to community mental health providers (CMHP). These mandates established the mechanisms for developing community based service opportunities and resources at the local level for the severe and persistent psychiatrically disabled at risk of institutionalization.

Throughout the nation, creating these community based services fell on the shoulders of the local mental health provider(s). However, nationally accepted treatment protocols like those provided for the state hospitals by the Joint Commission on Hospital Accreditation (JCHAO) are not yet in place for CMHPs. JCHAO guidelines not only reflect present "best practice" knowledge but also current legal considerations as well. In the absence of nationally recognized standards, community mental health providers need to carefully consider the developing legal and judicial actions supporting people receiving community based services so that they may implement effective and appropriate service delivery policies.

Deinstitutionalization and the development of community based services has its roots embedded in three tenets of legal debate. They are: (1) the right of the individual to receive treatment, (2) the right to treatment in the least restrictive setting, and (3) the right to freedom from harm (Rapson, 1981). Although by no means an unqualified success, the closure of hospital beds across the nation and the emerging community support services have established community treatment for previously hospitalized persons and that service has been provided in the least restrictive setting for the majority of those affected (Torrey, 1997). However, there has been much less practical and judicial attention given to the principle of assisting persons with managing potential psychological and physical risks to self and others outside of the hospital (risk management). Historically, once an individual is discharged from the inpatient unit, issues surrounding the client's right to be protected from harm has received scant attention from community service providers. In this paper we argue that freedom from harm is a critical and essential, yet often-overlooked, component germane to the success of effective community based services and mental health reform.

LEGISLATIVE AND JUDICIAL BACKGROUND

Legislative initiatives enacted following the Second World War directly influence contemporary services for persons with severe and persistent mental illness. The Mental Health Act, passed in 1946, established the National Institute for Mental Health (NIMH). NIMH has been a consistent provider of funds and research initiatives to states for the advancement of the understanding of the trauma of mental illness. Under the Kennedy administration, the Community Mental Health Construction Act of 1963 established public funding for the creation of mental health centers. In 1966, federal legislation was passed allowing states to capture Medicaid funding for mentally ill persons living in nursing facilities which provided an alternative for many hospitalized individuals (Mechanic & Rochefort, 1990). In 1980, the Mental Health Systems Act recognized the need for additional public funding for services targeted to the "chronically mentally ill." Senator Edward Kennedy introduced PL 99-660 in 1985. The bill is known as the State Comprehensive Mental Health Services Plan Act of 1986. The Act provided block grants to states for the development of comprehensive mental health services. Further, it required each state to establish an Advisory Council on Mental Health Planning as well as authorized block grants to states for demonstration projects to provide services for the homeless chronically mentally ill.

With the passage of the Americans with Disabilities Act in 1990, persons challenged by severe and persistent mental illness are more protected from discrimination than ever before (Seicshnaydre, 1992). The Act specifically prohibits forms of discrimination including: exclusion; denial of services, programs, or activities; unequal treatment; separate or different treatment when unnecessary; failure to make necessary accommodations; establishing eligibility criteria that screens out disabled persons; and the failure to provide services in the most integrated setting appropriate to the needs of the disabled individual.

The foundation upon which the judiciary standards directing the development of community based services have been established is predicated on the premise that relief for a complainant will not be upheld unless the individual has been forced to forfeit a right that is guaranteed under the Constitution (Costello & Preis, 1987). This forfeiture would constitute a threat to the person's personal liberty. For persons with severe and persistent psychiatric disabilities, liberty means "avoiding confinement in a hospital or other institution and, equally important, functioning in the community as an autonomous person to the maximum extent possible, given the limits of their disabilities" (pg. 1533).

The Right to Treatment

Judiciary action has been crucial to the advancement of rights and services for committed and institutionalized persons with psychiatric disabilities. The classic case that established the foundation for the right to treatment was Wyatt v. Stickney (1974) (Mechanic, 1999). The Fifth Circuit Court found that persons residing in a psychiatric hospital have the constitutional right to receive individual treatment that permits them a reasonable opportunity to improve their mental condition. The decision was predicated on the Due Process Clause of the Fourteenth Amendment (Rapson, 1981). The Fourteenth Amendment prohibits the limitations of individual liberties without due process of law. Even though a state may commit a person to an institution if that person exhibits dangerous behavior or is unable to provide self-care, they must be afforded treatment. Confinement within the institution restricts individual liberty. Should the state fail to provide adequate treatment that attempts to ameliorate the dangerous behavior or develop self-care skills, the state would be in a position of imposing permanent loss of individual liberty, violating its constitutional responsibility to promote the welfare of its citizenry.

In Youngberg v. Romeo (1982), the Supreme Court upheld the plaintiffs claim that the institutionalized Romeo has "constitutionally protected liberty interests under the Due Process Clause of the Fourteenth Amendment to reasonably safe conditions of confinement, freedom from unreasonable bodily restraints, and such minimally adequate training as reasonably may be required by these interests." Further, the judgment stated that in determining what is "reasonable," courts must show deference to the judgment of a qualified professional.

The Right to Treatment in the Least Restrictive Environment

The basis for treatment in the least restrictive alternative draws from the broad constitutional principle of "less drastic means" (Rapson, 1981). Basically, the state through hospital confinement cannot continue its liberty impingement if there are less restrictive alternatives that would produce similar treatment results. In Lake v. Cameron (1967), a person wandering the streets was committed to a psychiatric hospital. The plaintiff challenged the commitment, and the District Court held on statutory grounds that the hospital was required to assess other less restrictive placements prior to commitment. Unfortunately for the plaintiff, alternative treatment placements and/or programs did not exist and she remained in the hospital. Even though court decisions built a strong foundation for community based treatment, during the late sixties and seventies, the lack of community based programs inhibited the treatment of individuals within the community. Up to this point, there had been no court decision that addressed the state's responsibility in ordering the creation of services outside of the institution. In 1975, Dixon v. Weinberger provided the breakthrough in defining the state's responsibility to develop a community based continuum of care (Rapson, 1981). The court found on behalf of the committed plaintiff and ordered the government to develop a spectrum of community based programs and facilities that would allow the establishment of the least restrictive principle to come to fruition.

Following the tenets of the decision regarding courts showing deference to the judgment of a qualified professional in the Youngberg case, three other court decisions found a constitutional right to community based treatment. In Johnson v. Solomon (1979), the court reasoned that by exercising its protective power to commit an individual to hospitalization, it created a state of obligation to provide treatment which included community based services if those services were the least drastic means to achieve the reinstatement of the individual's liberty interests (Rose, 1987). In Clark v. Cohen (1986) and Thomas S v. Morrow (1987), professional judgments indicated that institutional confinement was not considered to be adequate treatment. Both persons were assessed to be able to reside in the community if they were given adequate supports (Costello & Preis, 1987). In both cases, the right to be afforded the opportunity to receive treatment in the least restrictive environment outside of the hospital was "based on a clear professional consensus that 1) institutional confinement and treatment were not consistent with good professional standards and 2) community based care was" (p. 1548).

Recently in Olmstead et al. v. L.C. (1999), the Supreme Court held that the state violated the ADA in failing to place two hospitalized persons with mental disabilities in the community. The Court opinion concluded that states are required to place persons with mental disabilities in community settings rather than in institutions when the state's treatment professionals have determined that: (1) community placement is appropriate, (2) the transfer from institutional care to a less restrictive setting is not opposed by the individual, and (3) the placement can be reasonably accommodated (pp. 11–18).

The Right to Freedom from Harm

Unlike the relatively clear judicial precedents establishing a person's right to treatment in the least restrictive environment, the right to freedom from harm has been less articulated and understood. Under the Eighth Amendment, all persons have the right to freedom from harm based on the Amendment's cruel and unusual punishment clause. In New York State Association for Retarded Children v. Rockefeller (1973), the court ruled that the hospitals poorly maintained physical environment, inadequate staffing patterns, and repressive treatment methods subjected hospitalized residents to cruel and unusual punishment (Rapson, 1981). The court suggested that "an environment in which the mental condition of a retarded individual is certain to regress violates the eighth amendment just as surely as does an environment in which a patient is likely to suffer the loss of an eye or a tooth" (p. 224).

The above case involved the state's duty to protect a person under state custody. At least three cases suggest that the state could be held liable for the safety of its citizenry beyond a formal custodial relationship. In Martinez v. California (1980), the Supreme Court found that municipalities may have an affirmative duty to protect if a "special relationship" exists between a municipality and the claimant (Weed, 1987). However, the Court offered no specific guidelines for what constituted a special relationship. In Jensen v. Conrad (1984), the court considered what factors could contribute to the establishment of a special relationship. One of those factors considered was whether the state expressly stated its desire to provide affirmative protection to persons of a particular class (Weed, 1987). In Estate of Bailey v. County of York

(1985), the court held a municipality liable for its failure to adequately investigate an abused child's home despite the absence of a legal relationship between the child or family and the county (Weed, 1987). On appeal, the ruling court stated that "government control or custody is not a prerequisite for municipal liability" (p. 300). A "special relationship" may also exist if state statute declares that individuals have a legal claim of entitlement (Alexander, 1993). In Board of Regents v. Roth (1972), the Supreme Court upheld a plaintiff's claim for an entitlement because once a state establishes its desire to provide a program or service, all eligible persons have a property interest in that program. A special relationship is thereby established between the state and persons who meet program or service guidelines. Many states have passed legislation that identifies specific target populations for service. These rulings indicate that states may have a duty to protect non-custodial citizens if a special relationship exists between that citizen and the state.

There is also a precedent charging health care providers with the responsibility to disclose potentially harmful consequences of a client's decision or treatments. In Canterbury v. Spence (1972), the Court held that " the test for determining whether a particular peril must be divulged is its materiality to the patient's decision: all risks potentially affecting the decision must be unmasked" (p. 1078). This decision clarified the responsibility of providers to disclose all but the most insignificant and highly improbable risks associated with the treatment and decisions of persons they serve (Herr, Arons, & Wallace, 1983). For providers of community based mental health services that do not disclose risk potentials to clients, they and their agency are vulnerable to plaintiff relief.

Last, the court itself has shed light on how a legal argument might be constructed to allow a plaintiff to receive relief due to the state's failure to protect its citizenry. In DeShaney v. Winnebago County Department of Social Services (1987), a mother sued the protective service agency on the grounds that they failed to protect her child from the abusive husband. The child had been in and out of state custody due to a history of abuse by the father. The child had been returned home and the father granted visitation. While with the father, the child was beaten so severely that he became comatose. Due to the extent of the injuries, the child will probably never be able to leave an institution for the profoundly retarded. The Court denied relief based on the grounds that the state played no part in causing the injuries and consequently, the due process clause of the 14th Amendment did not impose an affirmative duty of protection from the state (Bullis, 1990). However, elements of a potentially successful argument can be gleaned from careful examination of this case.

Although relief was not granted, the DeShaney decision might prove to have significant consequences for defining the state's responsibility to protect its citizenry from harm (Winchenbach, 1989; Bullis, 1990; Alexander, 1993). First of all, three justices gave dissenting opinions. The dissenting judges agreed that the case *did* represent an argument under a federally protected liberty right. This would have established the right of the plaintiff to rely on the protective service agency's actions to protect the child from harm. Second, the Court suggested that relief could have been granted if it was proven that the caseworker failed to protect the child based on an arbitrary decision not to act due to the client's race, sex, disability or other constitutionally impermissible category which would represent a discrimination action (Bullis, 1990). Further, the DeShaney argument was based on the due process clause of the 14th Amendment. Although this argument did have some support from the dissenting judges, had the plaintiffs argued as well that because state statute promised to protect abused children, the family was therefore entitled to protection, the outcome of the ruling may have been different. This argument may have given rise to relief for the plaintiff as evidenced in the aforementioned Roth decision which decreed that an eligible individual is entitled to any provision outlined by state statue (Alexander, 1993).

Although no single case has been mounted using all of the above arguments, providers need to be aware of the possibility that a new era of liability and risk management may soon be upon us. In summary, the right of persons to be afforded protection from harm could be based on the following conditions:

1. A person is under custodial care of the state;
2. A "special relationship" exists between the individual and the state;
3. A provider or service agency fails to disclose risks associated with its service or treatment;
4. A caseworker makes an arbitrary decision not to protect the client based on the persons sex, race, disability or other discriminatory category; and
5. State law defines itself as a protector of its citizenry.

DISCUSSION

The mounting judicial rulings which have explored provider duty to protect points to risk management implementation as a necessary practice component to be included in the service delivery system. Mental health reform has brought many positive changes to the lives of persons challenged with psychiatric disabilities. The establishment of community based services and the development of resources have largely brought about these changes. However, after careful examination of case law and the judicial precedents that establish the foundation for an individual's right to freedom from harm, it is clear that if providers do not concern themselves with the protection of clientele, it is ethically and legally vulnerable to damage litigation.

Despite the apparent success of mental health reform thus far, further evaluation is necessary to provide a clearer picture of the national consequences of the movement. Community based services which have replaced institutional settings have been hailed as a success in some states and a failure in others (Winchenbach, 1989; Mechanic & Rochefort, 1990; Torrey, 1997). In some states the effort to thoughtfully implement services appears to compliment the right of persons previously hospitalized to receive treatment and to receive those services in the least restrictive environment. However, the consistency of "best practice" techniques being utilized throughout the nation has yet to be established.

The development, incorporation, and monitoring of nationally accepted standards for practice would greatly aid our ability to more clearly understand the consequences of mental health reform initiatives. For example, without such monitoring one way states could appear to be successfully reducing their hospital population is by diverting people to nursing facilities without a mental health component (Stiles, Culhane, & Hadley, 1996). It does not appear possible at this time to determine the extent of this practice locally let alone nationally. This "diversion" method certainly points to issues surrounding how mental health providers may practice risk management for challenging persons without having to develop creative, effective, and responsive community support services in the least restrictive environment. In a legal challenge, persons "diverted" to nursing homes may be deemed as exposed to repressive treatment methods and thereby subject to cruel and unusual punishment. Further, this practice is not consistent with the intent of mental health legislation. This illustration of possible "risk management" practice clearly points to the need for national attention to the development of practice standards for providers of service with persons with severe and persistent mental illness. Such attention not only helps ensure consistent service for a vulnerable population, but also helps to protect providers from possible litigation involvement. By developing and implementing accepted practice guidelines that integrate risk management protocol into service delivery, providers could come together in support of state of the art practice as well as present a unified voice against any unwarranted threat of litigation.

Mental health reform is a landmark piece of legislation in U.S. history. State governments have begun to provide the necessary services and resources to a very disadvantaged population. Now, it is the authors' opinion that states must take the next step and work together to define the necessary elements involved with the delivery of services based on "best practice" principles related to standards of practice and thoughtful risk management procedures. The development of accepted guidelines of practice for persons with severe and persistent mental illness residing in the least restrictive environment should at least include in principle:

- Defined target population and service priorities;
- Services that are specific to the needs of the individual and designed to enable people to live in the least restrictive environment;
- Services that respect the rights of all citizens;
- Explicit statement of desired practice outcomes;
- Specific mechanisms to monitor the delivery of services; and
- Risk management protocol.

At a minimum, specific components of a risk management policy and procedure process should include:

- A centralized policy and procedure mandate that defines CMHP and state responsibilities to "protect" the persons they serve;
- A mandated set of procedures that addresses protective interventions that balance consumer risks with their dignity and agency liability (These procedures should at least include: the process for identifying risk potential, the obligation to disclose, time lines for documentation as well as the dissemination of information, and a process that encourages the establishment of partnerships or alliances with all invested parties);
- A centralized client grievance reporting procedure to help ensure adequate provider response to their service population as well as permitting the identification of service needs; and

- The provision of funds for statewide training and resources necessary to implement the risk management policy.

CONCLUSION

This legislative review indicates that fundamental elements of the mental health reform initiative need further definition before the success of the initiative can be realized. First, ideally nationally, but certainly state and local stakeholders (consumers, family members, providers, governing bodies) need to develop consensus around standards of service delivery for persons with severe and persistent mental illness residing in the least restrictive environment. Second, as a component of those standards, further attention to provider risk management practice is necessary. It is clear that the potential exists for damage litigation to be brought against the state or provider for its failure to protect the people mental health reform was established to empower.

The simplest solution for the state may be to change the language and/or intent of the law. For example, through legislation the state could eliminate statutes that express a desire to protect its vulnerable citizenry. Or, the state could do nothing and wait for the courts to decide its liability. The consequences of either of these actions would be devastating to consumers who have found a "quality" of life never thought possible prior to the legislation. Therefore it is hoped that states and providers become proactive in development of practice standards and effective risk management guidelines that further enhances, yet more efficaciously defines the current law. To do less casts a shadow on the potential for success of mental health reform.

REFERENCES

Alexander, R. (1993). The legal liability of social workers after DeSchaney. *Social Work, Vol. 38, Number 1, January*, 64–68.

Board of Regents v. Roth, 408 U.S. 564 (1972).

Bullis, R. K. (1990). Cold comfort from the Supreme Court: Limited liability protection for social workers. *Social Work, Vol. 35, Number 4, July*, 364–366.

Canterbury v. Spence, 409 U.S. 1064 (1972).

Clark v. Cohen, 794 F. 2d (1986).

Costello, J. C. & Preis, J. J. (1987). Beyond least restrictive alternative: A constitutional right to treatment in the community. *Loyola of Los Angeles Law Review, June*, 1527–1557.

DeShaney v. Winnebago County Department of Social Services, 812 F 2d 298 (7th Cir., 1987).

Dixon v. Weinberger, 405 F. Supp. 974 (D.D.C., 1975).

Estate of Bailey v. County of York, 768 F.2d 503 (3rd Cir. 1985).

French, L. (1987). Victimization of the mentally ill: An unintended consequence of deinstitutionalization. *Social Work, Nov–Dec, Vol 32(6)*, 502–505.

Herr, S. S., Arons, S., & Wallace, R. E. (1983). *Legal rights and mental health care.* Lexington, Mass.: Lexington Books.

Jensen v. Conrad, 747 F. 2d, 185 (4th Cir., 1984).

Johnson v. Solomon, 485 F. Supp. 278 (D. Md., 1979).

Lake v. Cameron, 267 F. Supp. 155 (D.D.C., 1967)

Martinez v. California, 444 U.S. 277, (1980).

Mechanic, D. & Rochefort, D. A. (1990). Deinstitutionalization: An appraisal of reform. *Annual Review of Sociology, 16*, 301–327.

Mechanic, D. (1999). *Mental health and social policy.* Boston: Allyn and Bacon.

New York State Association for Retarded Children v. Rockefeller 357 F. Supp. 752 (1973).

Rapp, C. A. & Moore, T. D. (1995). The first 18 months of mental health reform in Kansas. *Psychiatric Services, Vol. 46, No. 6*, 580–585.

Rapson, R. (1981). The right of the mentally ill to receive treatment in the community. *International Journal of Law and Psychiatry, Winter–Spring*, 13–34.

Rose, S. (1987). A State's duty to develop community-based mental health treatment. *The Journal of Contemporary Health Law and Policy, Spring*, 281–308.

Seicshnaydre, S. (1992). Community mental health treatment for the mentally ill—when does less restrictive treatment become a right? *Tulane Law Review, June*, 1971–2001.

Stiles, P. G., Culhane, D. P., & Hadley, T. R. (1996). Before and after deinstitutionalization: Comparing state hospitalization utilization, staffing, and costs in 1949 and 1988. *Administration and Policy in Mental Health, 23 (6)*, 513–525.

Talbott, J. A. (1979). Deinstitutionalization: Avoiding the disasters of the past. *Hospital and Community Psychiatry, 30 (9)*, 621–624.

Thomas S. v. Morrow, 781 F.2d 367 (1987).

Torrey, E. F. (1997). *Out of the shadows.* New York: John Wiley & Sons, Inc.

Weed, J. (1987). The Third Circuit Widens the Scope of Section 1983: Estate of Bailey v. County of York. *Journal of Contemporary Law, Vol. 32:285*, 297–311.

Winchenbach, L. (1989). Snake pits and slippery slopes: DeShaney Revisited. *ABA Journal, September*, 62–65.

Wyatt v. Stickney, 325 F. Supp. 373 (1974).

Youngberg v. Romeo, 457 U.S. 307, 322 (1982).

[4]

Privacy in Psychiatric Treatment: Threats and Responses

Paul S. Appelbaum, M.D.

Objective: The author provides an overview of the current status of privacy in psychiatric treatment, with particular attention to the effects of new federal regulations authorized by the Health Insurance Portability and Accountability Act (HIPAA).

Method: The author reviews the ethical and legal underpinnings for medical privacy, including the empirical data supporting its importance; discusses those portions of the new federal regulations most relevant to psychiatric practice; and suggests steps that psychiatrists can take to maintain their patients' privacy in the new environment.

Results: Medical ethics and law, in keeping with patients' preferences, traditionally have provided strong protection for the information that patients communicate while receiving medical care. In general, release of information has required patients' explicit consent. However, limitations of the consent model and technological innovations that permit the aggregation of computerized medical information have led to pressure for greater access to these data. Although the new federal regulations offer patients some additional protections (including security for psychotherapy notes), they also mark a retreat from reliance on patient consent and open up records to previously unauthorized uses, among them law enforcement investigations and marketing and fundraising by health care organizations. However, states retain the power to provide higher levels of protection.

Conclusions: The new regulatory environment is less friendly to medical privacy but still leaves a great deal of discretion in physicians' hands. A commitment to protecting privacy as an ethical norm can be advanced by psychiatrists' requesting patients' consent even when it is not required, by ensuring that patients are aware of the limits on confidentiality, and by avoiding unnecessary breaches of privacy in the course of providing psychiatric care.

(Am J Psychiatry 2002; 159:1809–1818)

A long distance truck driver with a clean driving record is fired after his health insurance company informs his employer that he sought coverage—which the insurer denied—at an alcohol treatment clinic (1).

Newspaper accounts report that a health maintenance organization (HMO) with more than a million members has made computerized medical records of patients, including notes of psychotherapy sessions, available to all clinical personnel at every site (2). After the disclosure, psychotherapy notes are withdrawn from the computerized system.

A major university medical center discloses that thousands of patient records have been posted in error on its publicly available web site. Officials believe the records were available for 2 months before the mistake was discovered (3).

P rivacy of communications between patients and physicians has long been a cornerstone of medical treatment. Since the Hippocratic Oath enjoined physicians not to tell of those things that "should not be published abroad" (4, p. 5), doctors and their patients generally have assumed that they could communicate in confidence the information necessary to conduct medical care. That has been particularly important in psychiatry, where the ability of patients to convey potentially embarrassing information is essential for accurate diagnosis and effective treatment. Although exceptions to the privacy of medical information have always existed, they were relatively circumscribed and seemed to reinforce, rather than undermine, the general rule.

In recent years, however, the assumption that medical information will remain a private matter between patients and physicians has been challenged by a series of changes in how medical records are kept and in the nature, oversight, and financing of medical practice. These changes include the formulation of a team approach to patient care (5), requirements for reporting behaviors such as child and elder abuse, aggressive government monitoring of care financed by public payers (6), demands by private insurers and managed care companies for access to patient records before authorizing payment (7), and the rapid computerization of medical record keeping, accompanied by the development of the Internet (8). Both the popular media and the professional literature evidence the resulting sense of unease about the potential loss of privacy of medical information (9, 10).

These concerns about the privacy of data generated in medical encounters, along with a growing recognition of the value of medical records for commercial, research, and governmental purposes, have combined to create a rapidly changing regulatory environment. Physicians and patients alike now face profound perturbations in the rules that have governed the disclosure of medical information. To clarify the current situation—with particular attention to psychiatric practice—this paper reviews the ethical and legal underpinnings of medical privacy and the sources of pressure for change, offers an overview of new federal regulations that are likely to alter profoundly many aspects of medical privacy, and provides suggestions to psychiatrists both for maintaining their patients' privacy in the new environment and for political and other initiatives that may mitigate the regulations' negative impact.

The Underpinnings of Medical Privacy

Privacy, as used in this discussion, is the interest that persons have in maintaining control of information about them; medical privacy refers specifically to information concerning persons' medical conditions. Confidentiality, a term that often is used interchangeably with privacy, refers more narrowly to the obligation to maintain privacy assumed by someone who enters into a relationship marked by the promise that information that is disclosed will not be revealed to others.

Ethical Underpinnings

What accounts for the long-standing tradition in medicine of protecting patients' privacy? Medical ethicists point to two deep-seated ethical rationales. The justification most commonly offered is a consequentialist or utilitarian one: if patients are to provide the information required for physicians to diagnose and treat them effectively, they must trust that their physicians will not disclose these data to third parties [11]. In the absence of some guarantee of privacy, patients will either avoid coming for care, or if they do come, will withhold information necessary for treatment. This rationale seems particularly potent in psychiatry, where the information elicited from patients includes symptoms, behaviors, thoughts, and affects that might cause embarrassment, stigma, and discrimination were they to become generally known.

Consequentialist justifications can be susceptible, at least in principle, to empirical testing. Surveys of patients and of the population at large have confirmed that most people value highly the privacy of their medical information. For example, a recent Gallup survey conducted for the Institute for Health Freedom found that 78% of respondents felt that the confidentiality of their medical records was very important [12]. As a corollary, there was strong opposition to giving nonmedical groups access to medical records. Thus, 95% of respondents opposed banks' having access to their records; 92% felt similarly about govern-

ment agencies; 84% opposed access by the police, lawyers, or employers; and 82% opposed insurance companies' seeing their records without their consent. Studies of psychiatric [13, 14] and other mental health patients [15, 16] have revealed similar attitudes.

In keeping with utilitarian theory, those advocating a consequentialist basis for privacy must show that, in its absence, medical care would not be provided as effectively, i.e., that patients would withhold information from their caregivers or decline to come for treatment. Although this argument seems self-evident to many privacy advocates, few attempts have been made to support this reasoning empirically, and the results have been mixed. A survey sponsored by the California Health Foundation revealed that 15% of a national sample reported doing something out of the ordinary to protect their medical privacy, including not seeking care and giving inaccurate or incomplete information [17]. Probably the strongest data exist for adolescents, 25% of whom in one study said they would forego care if they thought their parents might find out [18]. Another study of 2,224 high school students showed that those who perceived that their communications with physicians were confidential were more likely to have had pelvic exams and to have discussed sexual behavior and substance abuse with their doctors [19]. On the other hand, 8% of respondents in that study reported that they actually had foregone care because of a fear that their parents would learn about their treatment.

Studies of mental health treatment have yielded mixed results, but often because the methods used were less than optimal. Some studies utilizing nonclinical samples (e.g., university students) found that varying the level of assurance of confidentiality did not affect the amount of information disclosed in an interview [20, 21], although other studies reached contrary conclusions [22]. The relevance of these studies to real-life settings, however, is questionable. In the only two studies of this sort to examine patients currently receiving mental health treatment, when a variety of limitations on confidentiality were described, willingness to disclose and actual disclosure of information were reduced [23, 24]. Overall then, although there are data suggesting that patients in mental health settings are similar to those in general health settings in the extent to which their disclosures may be negatively impacted by a lack of privacy, the number of studies is small and the data are not robust. Nonetheless, belief remains strong in the field that potential adverse effects on treatment constitute the strongest rationale for protection of patients' privacy.

Some students of medical privacy, however, impelled in part by the relative paucity of data supporting consequentialist justifications—especially in psychiatric treatment—have suggested that a second ethical argument be considered. They argue that medical privacy can better be justified by using what ethicists refer to as a deontologic approach, i.e., considering privacy as a good in itself, rather than seeing its value only in the positive effect it may have

PAUL S. APPELBAUM

on patients' health (25, 26). Most often, the role of privacy in advancing individual autonomy is identified as the basis for this claim. One commentator speaks of the "insulation that privacy provides so that as self-conscious beings we can maintain our self-respect, develop our self-esteem, and increase our ability to form a coherent identity and set of values, as well as our ability to form varied and complex relationships with others" (27, p. 213).

Although a deontologic argument for medical privacy can be applied to medical care in general, it probably works best for psychotherapy per se. The ability to speak freely with another person about one's innermost thoughts, fears, and passions is clearly dependent on the belief that one's revelations will go no farther. Creating a space within which this sort of dialogue can occur is likely to facilitate the conscious exploration of alternative modes of thought and behavior on which truly autonomous functioning rests. A society like ours, built on the premise that individual autonomy ought to be encouraged, should be receptive to the claim that protecting the privacy of the psychotherapeutic relationship carries positive social value. Indeed, insofar as psychiatrists deal largely with conditions that often impair autonomous function, the same argument might be advanced for psychiatric treatment in general.

The practical import of these ethical arguments is the widespread acceptance among members of the medical profession of the principle that physicians owe patients a duty of confidentiality, unless patients release them from it by offering consent for the disclosure of information. Embodied in the American Medical Association's *Principles of Medical Ethics* is the admonition that "[a] physician...shall safeguard patient confidences within the constraints of the law" (28, p. 2). The American College of Physicians, representing the nation's internists, is still more explicit: "To protect patient confidentiality, information should only be released with the written permission of the patient or the patient's legally authorized representative" (29). Similarly, the American Psychiatric Association's *Annotations* to the AMA's *Principles* holds that "[a] psychiatrist may release confidential information only with the authorization of the patient or under proper legal compulsion" (28, p. 6). The medical profession's ethical commitment to protecting privacy seems clear. However, since the boundaries of the profession's ethical duties appear to be circumscribed by the law, the parameters of legal protection for medical information assume particular significance.

Legal Underpinnings

Legal protection of medical privacy is a much more recent and fragmentary phenomenon than many people suppose. The law's first foray in this area was aimed at preventing the courts from compelling disclosure of information that physicians obtained in their attendance on patients. Abandoning the common law rule that the courts had the right to every person's testimony, New York in 1828 passed the nation's first statute establishing a physician-patient

testimonial privilege. Under the privilege, patients had the right to prevent their physicians from testifying in regard to any information patients may have communicated in the course of treatment. In the century that followed, many states emulated New York, passing privilege statutes of their own (30). However, the courts were often hostile to medical privileges, since they were seen—not unreasonably—as complicating the adjudicatory process. Given that these privileges were usually defended on consequentialist grounds—i.e., as necessary to encourage patients to seek medical care—they were also susceptible to attack on the basis that patients with significant illnesses would pursue treatment regardless of whether a privilege existed, because patients typically did not need to communicate sensitive information to obtain medical care. By the mid-20th century, physician-patient privileges began to fall from favor, although they still exist in many jurisdictions.

As enthusiasm for physician-patient privileges declined in the second half of the 20th century, there was a concomitant rise in the number of states creating privileges designed specifically to cover mental health treatment, often denominated psychotherapist-patient privileges. Today, every jurisdiction in the United States offers some sort of privilege for treatment by mental health professionals, by no means limited to psychotherapy (31). Often riddled with exceptions (which may include, for example, testimony related to criminal offenses, child custody, and child abuse and testimony in cases in which patients have based a legal claim on some aspect of their mental state), these statutes nonetheless provide some real protection for patients. In 1996, the U.S. Supreme Court, exercising the discretion afforded it in the Federal Rules of Evidence, gave judicial recognition to a psychotherapist-patient privilege for the federal courts (31). The Court's decision in *Jaffee v. Redmond* offered strong support for privacy in psychotherapeutic treatment: "The psychotherapist privilege serves the public interest by facilitating the provision of appropriate treatment for individuals suffering the effects of a mental or emotional problem. The mental health of our citizenry, no less than its physical health, is a public good of transcendent importance" (31). Although the precise dimensions of the federal privilege will be determined by subsequent cases, it is worth emphasizing that it is likely to cover mental health treatment in general, rather than being limited to psychotherapy per se (32).

Parallel to the growth of privileges for treatment by mental health professionals has been the development of state statutes regulating the circumstances under which medical information can be disclosed to others besides the courts. These statutes create a patchwork of regulation, often focused on particular disorders, such as AIDS, or on diagnostic information, such as genetic testing (33). Forty-five states and the District of Columbia have statutes specifically addressing release of mental health information (34). Although their provisions vary greatly, many statutes address the criteria for a valid consent to release of information, specify when information can be disclosed to other health professionals and to family members who may be involved in patients' care, and enumerate the circumstances under which access to data is allowed for other purposes, including research, public health needs, and quality improvement efforts (34).

While state legislatures were limiting the circumstances in which medical information can be disclosed without patients' consent, state courts were recognizing causes of action under which patients who were harmed by unauthorized disclosures could obtain appropriate compensation. A typical case, echoing decisions in other jurisdictions (e.g., references 35–37), is *Alberts v. Devine*, a 1985 decision of the Massachusetts Supreme Judicial Court (38). Alberts, a minister who had sought psychiatric treatment from Devine, lost his pulpit when the psychiatrist acquiesced in the request of Alberts's superiors and revealed the nature of his condition to them. The court held that patients have "a valid interest in preserving the confidentiality of medical facts communicated to a physician or discovered by the physician through examination." Hence, "a violation of that duty [of confidentiality], resulting in damages, gives rise to a cause of action sounding in tort against the physician" (35). Not only was Devine liable to compensate Alberts for the harm he suffered, but Alberts's superiors, who had induced Devine to violate his duty, were held liable as well. Like the other courts that have ruled in this area, the Massachusetts court recognized exceptions to the requirement of confidentiality when a danger existed to third parties or when disclosure was otherwise required by law.

To this point, the focus has been largely on state law and regulation, since until recently the federal government left regulation of medical privacy largely to the states. One important exception is embodied in the Public Health Service Act, which establishes special protections for the records of patients who receive treatment for alcohol or drug abuse in federally supported, specialty treatment programs (39). The resulting regulations strictly limit disclosure without the patient's consent to situations in which an emergency exists, a crime has been committed at the program, information has been obtained relating to child abuse, a court—applying a set of criteria that includes balancing the benefits and harms of disclosure—orders release, and a small number of other circumstances (40).

In sum, the impact of law on medical privacy by and large has been complementary to the thrust of the medical profession's ethical codes. Although there are a number of discrete exceptions, often involving a risk of harm to third parties (e.g., child abuse) or the superordinate needs of the courts, physicians have been obliged to respect patients' medical privacy. Patient consent has been the sine qua non required for disclosure of information, and physicians can be subject to civil actions, licensure proceedings, and, sometimes, criminal penalties for violation of that rule.

Pressure for Change

From where have the pressures come to alter these traditional approaches to the protection of patients' medical privacy? In part, there has been greater recognition in recent years of the limitations of the consent-based model. With medical care increasingly being rendered by large entities, rather than restricted to the physician-patient dyad, a growing number of caregivers and support staff gained access to patients' records. In 1982, internist Mark Siegler declared confidentiality "a decrepit concept," as he documented how as many as 100 people in his university hospital might have a legitimate need to examine a patient's medical record (5). During the intervening two decades, with outpatient care increasingly rendered in HMOs or large group practices, a similar effect has been seen for ambulatory care records. Since obtaining patients' consent each time someone other than their physicians accesses their records is impractical, many health care facilities have begun obtaining blanket consent for all staff to view patient records, or simply have assumed that patients acquiesced in staff members' having access, when that was necessary for their care. In these settings, the traditional model of consent for each disclosure fell by the wayside.

The number of people with access to patients' records was further magnified with the growth of third-party payers in the mid-20th century and the development of managed care in the late 1980s and 1990s. Tighter management of authorizations for payment, with the goal of holding down medical costs, often involves requests for large amounts of patient information—including entire medical records—as part of managed care companies' utilization review procedures (7). Although patients may be asked for consent, either at the inception of treatment or at the time the information is requested, they generally feel that they have no genuine choice about releasing information, since insurance coverage for their care is dependent on their agreement (41). Once the information is in the companies' hands, these entities are not bound by the traditional duties that have attached to physicians and, by extension, the facilities in which they deliver care. Thus, insurers and managed care companies have been free to transfer medical information to insurance industry databanks (42), pharmacy benefit management companies (43), or even patients' employers (44), without limits on further redisclosure.

At the same time that these developments were calling into question the efficacy of a consent-based approach, technological advances opened up new possibilities for the use of medical data. An influential 1991 report by the Institute of Medicine endorsed the adoption of computerized medical records as likely to improve the quality of care, advance medical science, lower health care costs, and enhance medical education (45). Just 3 years later, another Institute of Medicine panel enthusiastically sup-

PAUL S. APPELBAUM

ported the development of regional health data organizations that would aggregate medical information from all encounters of every patient, a process that would be greatly facilitated by computerized record systems (46). Among the uses that were envisioned for the resulting data were identifying patterns of illness and unmet needs; documenting inappropriate, wasteful, or harmful services; locating "cost-effective care providers"; and improving the quality of care—although the committee recognized that the very existence of easily accessible data of this sort would inevitably generate additional unanticipated requests for access. The Clinton administration's unsuccessful proposal for health care reform adopted this vision, embracing a national network of databases that would track every health care encounter (33).

If fully implemented, a web of computerized record systems feeding into a network of regional data banks would create what its proponents referred to as a "health information infrastructure" (10, 33). Large employers, insurers, hardware and software makers, law enforcement agencies, and researchers—each for their own reasons—lined up in support. Although the Clinton health proposal was defeated, the first steps toward establishing this infrastructure were taken in 1996, with the passage of the Health Insurance Portability and Accountability Act (HIPAA) (Public Law 104-191). Among its provisions, the bill charged the Secretary of the Department of Health and Human Services (DHHS) with developing a "unique health identifier," a code that would allow each person's medical contacts to be aggregated from birth to death. Some such means of tracking individuals is an absolute requirement for the implementation of a system of regional or national data banks. (The Clinton administration imposed a moratorium on the development of a unique health identifier in August 1998, until medical privacy legislation was adopted; the HIPAA mandate, however, remains unchanged, and the process can be restarted at any time [44].)

Since many of the proponents of a health information infrastructure acknowledged that it would raise substantial concerns about medical privacy (33, 46), HIPAA required the Secretary of the Department of Health and Human Services (DHHS) to submit to Congress within 1 year "detailed recommendations on standards with respect to the privacy of individually identifiable health information."

The Secretary's report appeared in late 1997 (47). Recognizing that the traditional reliance on patient consent would make the goal of a databank network unattainable and pointing to the existing limitations of consent as a means of protecting patients' privacy, the Secretary recommended, "that the traditional control on use and disclosure of information, the patient's written authorization, be replaced by comprehensive statutory controls on all who get health information for health care and payment purposes" (47).

Under the DHHS proposal, patients would have lost control over release of their medical records, with the process governed instead by federal regulation. Congress, which had been trying for several years to pass privacy legislation, found itself caught between advocates of greater accessibility of medical records and privacy proponents. Recognizing that it was unlikely to break the logjam, Congress wrote into the HIPAA law a deadline of August 1999 for the passage of comprehensive medical privacy legislation. If the deadline was not met, DHHS would be empowered to draft binding regulations to accomplish what Congress could not. When Congress failed to pass a bill, DHHS issued draft regulations in late 1999 (48) and, after an extended comment period, published final regulations in December 2000, during the waning days of the Clinton administration (49). After a period of reconsideration, the regulations were formally promulgated by the Bush administration in April 2001 (50). Final changes, before implementation, appeared in August 2002 (51).

As the first effort to establish national standards for the privacy of medical information, these regulations (often referred to as the "HIPAA regulations" to denote their statutory lineage) are of immense significance. When they go into effect in April 2003, they will alter the way every physician deals with patient information and will affect the privacy rights of all persons who receive medical care. Moreover, far from codifying existing practice, the new rules will effect substantial changes in the handling of medical record information, limiting access without patient consent in a few areas, but broadening it beyond current bounds in a number of others. The regulations reflect the pressure that has been growing over the past decade to sacrifice individual control over medical data in favor of the purported social benefits of easier access to that information.

The New Federal Regulations

The privacy regulations themselves take up 31 pages of small print in the *Federal Register*; an accompanying official commentary occupies another 336 pages (49), with additional changes adding to the mass of detail (51). Rather than attempting to summarize this complex regulatory structure in its entirety, this section focuses on those elements of the regulations that are likely to be of greatest concern to psychiatrists. Broader summaries are beginning to appear (52), and interested readers are encouraged to review the regulations themselves in preparation for the changes they will bring.

Who must comply with the new rules? Under the terms of HIPAA, DHHS was authorized to write regulations that apply to health plans (e.g., insurers, HMOs, self-insurance programs), health care clearinghouses (i.e., entities that process health information), and health care providers who transmit any health information in electronic form. The latter is interpreted broadly to include submission of claims, processing of bills, and transmission of other patient-related information. Indeed, even practitioners who do not use computers themselves, but who contract with billing services that transmit information electronically would be covered by the regulations (49, p. 82476). For now, it appears that clinicians who make no use of electronic transmission of data and contract with no other entities to do so on their behalf are exempt from the provisions of the HIPAA rules. As electronic submission of claims becomes routine, this group is likely to shrink considerably. Almost all the entities affected by the regulations (with the exception of small health plans, which have an extra year) have been given until April 14, 2003, to come into compliance with their terms.

Use and Release of Information for Treatment, Payment, and Health Care Operations

The rules governing use and release of individually identifiable information under the regulations differ according to the purposes for which the information is being used or disclosed. For those functions most closely related to the delivery of health care—denoted "treatment, payment and health care operations"—holders of health information need no longer obtain consent from their patients, though they can if they choose to (51, p. 53268). Instead, they are authorized by the regulations themselves to use and disclose the information, with few exceptions. Under these provisions, other caregivers, disease management companies, pharmacy benefit managers, utilization reviewers, quality improvement consultants, and many others will receive identifiable information without patient consent or knowledge. The regulations do require that covered entities make good-faith efforts to provide notice of their information policies to patients the first time service is rendered and to obtain patients' written acknowledgment. According to DHHS, this provision is designed in large part to offer patients an opportunity to ask questions about and discuss the information practices of those to whom they will be revealing health-related information. But the entities' ability to disclose such information is not dependent on patients' agreement; indeed, the regulations authorize such disclosure even over patients' specific objections.

This approach to use of health information, which negates the traditional reliance on patient consent, was initially proposed in DHHS Secretary Shalala's report in 1997 (47) and was reflected in the draft regulations issued by the Clinton Administration in 1999 (48). But when the final version of the Clinton regulations appeared at the end of 2000, they embodied an alternative approach that asked patients to provide blanket written consent for use and release of their medical information at the time of enrollment into a health plan or the inception of treatment (49, p. 82810). The Bush Administration's decision to reject patient consent as the basis for disclosure of information was premised in part on the assertion that the Clinton consent

requirement provided little meaningful protection for patients in any event. Clearly, the Administration was also responding to objections from the health care, pharmacy, and insurance industries, among others, about the cost and inconvenience associated with reliance on written consent. Thus was lost the historic right of patients to control dissemination of their medical records. This represents the most profound change in traditional practices wrought by the HIPAA regulations.

Use and Release of Information for Other Purposes Requiring Authorization

Except for treatment, payment, health care operations, and the special categories described in the following section, all other uses of identifiable health information require something that the regulations refer to as the patient's "authorization" but that resembles consent as most physicians and facilities are familiar with the term (51, p. 53268). The authorization forms must indicate the information to be used or disclosed, the purposes to which it will be put, and the recipient of the information, and they must contain an expiration date. Thus, for example, for information to be disclosed to a patient's employer for use in a hiring or promotion decision, the patient must provide this kind of written authorization. For non-health-care uses that are not addressed specially elsewhere in the regulations, this provision offers real protection for patients' privacy.

Use and Release That Does Not Require Consent or Authorization

Twelve uses are identified specially as justifying the release of identifiable health information without patients' consent or authorization, and generally without their even being told that disclosure has occurred. Some of these uses of information are familiar to clinicians and consistent with current practice, for example, "to avert a serious threat to health or safety" (49, p. 82817) or to report child abuse or neglect (49, p. 82814). Other provisions are more problematic. Thus, during litigation, health information can be released in response to a request for discovery or a subpoena from an attorney—even one representing a party adverse to the patient—as long as the attorney provides assurance that reasonable efforts have been made to notify the patient of the request (49, p. 82814). The absence of a requirement for judicial review of these requests means that, unless patients respond quickly enough to block disclosure, attorneys will be able to obtain medical records of parties to the case and conceivably of their witnesses as well.

Law enforcement lobbied heavily during the process of drafting these regulations for greater access to medical records. In the final version, police officers can be given access to records on the basis of an administrative request, without judicial review (49, p. 82815). Disclosure of identifying information and some details of patients' treatment can occur in response to a simple inquiry from a law enforcement officer for the purposes of "identifying or locating a suspect, fugitive, material witness or missing person." If the police desired to enter a person's house to examine their possessions for any of these reasons, they would be required to obtain a search warrant from a magistrate and to demonstrate probable cause that the search will discover information related to the crime. However, under the HIPAA regulations, police can search medical records without ever having to step before a judge to demonstrate the reasonableness of their request. Separate provisions permit disclosure to national security agencies and the Secret Service that go well beyond current practices; the Secret Service, for example, has gone to great lengths to train its agents to work within the limits imposed by state law and requirements for patient consent (53), but the regulations would free them of that burden.

Fundraising also constitutes an exception to the usual requirements for consent or authorization (49, p. 82820). Holders of health information can disclose to other entities that are assisting them in raising funds the identity of their patients, demographic information, and the dates that health care was provided. This can be particularly problematic for patients treated in psychiatric or other specialized facilities, where identification of the locus of treatment indicates the nature of the patient's condition. A similar exemption exists for disclosure of information for the purpose of marketing services delivered by the facility that originally treated the patient (49, p. 82819). A set of complex rules governs marketing by health care providers and health plans, requiring authorization if information is being sold for marketing purposes, but allowing information to be used for many forms of marketing by the information holders themselves and their business associates (51, p. 53267).

Access to medical records for research purposes was a contentious issue as the regulations were being formulated. Researchers, particularly those using existing data bases, objected to the possibility of being required to obtain consent from every person whose data they wished to access (54, 55). In response, DHHS allowed the requirement for authorization for research use to be waived by an Institutional Review Board constituted according to the federal Common Rule that governs most research in this country, or by a privacy board set up specifically for the purpose (49, p. 82816; 51, p. 53270). The criteria largely reflect current practices, including a demonstration that the research presents no more than a minimal risk to subjects and could not be practicably carried out without the waiver. This represents a reasonable accommodation of the interests of both researchers and patients (56).

Use and Release of Psychotherapy Notes

Of particular interest to psychiatrists, psychotherapy notes have been given protections by these regulations that were not afforded to any other medical records (49, p. 82811). Psychotherapy notes cannot be released, with a small number of exceptions, without the explicit authorization of the patient. Moreover, neither treatment nor payment by insurers can be conditioned on release of psychotherapy notes. This provision reflects a recognition by DHHS that the information contained in psychotherapy notes is likely to be qualitatively different from that found elsewhere in the medical record. In the preamble to the regulations, DHHS specifically cites the rationale of the U.S. Supreme Court's decision in *Jaffee v. Redmond* (31) as motivating its treatment of this issue.

Although these extra safeguards for psychotherapy notes will be welcomed by most therapists, they are not quite as sweeping as they seem at first blush. In order to qualify for this protection, the notes in question must be kept separate from the patient's medical record, requiring a second chart in many cases. Excluded from protection are information about medication prescription and monitoring, start and stop times, modalities and frequencies of treatment furnished, results of clinical tests, and summaries of diagnosis, functional status, treatment plan, symptoms, prognosis, and progress to date. Thus, a great deal of sensitive information—for example, most of the information routinely collected during an intake evaluation—that would ordinarily be protected under a psychotherapist-patient privilege such as *Jaffee*'s, will not qualify for protection under this provision. A more effective means of protecting sensitive psychiatric information would have been to extend the protections now afforded to psychotherapy notes to the entire record of psychiatric treatment.

Other Provisions of the Regulations

There are several other aspects of the regulations of which clinicians should be aware. Patients are granted fairly sweeping rights to have access to and obtain a copy of their medical records, except for psychotherapy notes. Only a small number of exceptions to this general rule exist, the most significant of them being when "the access requested is reasonably likely to endanger the life or physical safety of the individual or another person" (49, p. 82823). If patients believe that the information in their record is inaccurate, they will have the right to request an amendment to the record. Denials of these requests must be justified in writing, and patients must be given the opportunity to submit a statement of disagreement, which becomes part of their medical record. Some states already have patient access provisions similar to these, but this will be new to much of the country and will create a uniform national standard of practice.

As a general rule, when releasing information from a patient's record, reasonable effort must be made "to limit protected health information to the minimum necessary to accomplish the intended purpose of the use, disclosure, or request" (49, p. 82805). The primary exception to this rule is when disclosure is being made to a health care provider for purposes related to treatment. When a request for information is made by another entity covered by the regulations, holders of medical records will be permitted to rely

PRIVACY IN PSYCHIATRIC TREATMENT

on the requester's judgment that the latter has asked for the minimum necessary amount of information (57).

Along with learning the new rules for disclosure of medical record information, clinicians will have to meet a number of administrative requirements. Each "provider"—even a single physician's office—will need to develop formal privacy policies and procedures and designate a staff person as a "privacy official" who will receive complaints from and provide information to patients (49, p. 82826). All staff members must be trained in these policies, and, as noted, new patients will need to be provided with a notice of the relevant privacy practices. Patients have the right to receive an accounting of all disclosures from their medical records in the past 6 years, except for those made for treatment, payment, and health care operations, those they themselves have authorized, and a small number of other categories. Every provider will need to create and sign contracts with all business associates who are given access to identifiable information about patients (e.g., billing and transcription services, accountants, etc.) binding them to observe the terms of the regulations—to which, under the terms of HIPAA itself, they would not otherwise be subject. Medical societies have expressed considerable concern about the costs of implementing these provisions, especially for solo practitioners and small practices. General medical and specialty groups—including the American Medical Association and the American Psychiatric Association—have begun producing detailed guides for their members that provide advice on applying the regulations to their own practices.

Given that extensive state law and regulation already exist in this area, a final important consideration is how the federal regulations relate to these rules. As a general matter, the HIPAA regulations preempt state laws that are less protective of patients' privacy, creating a uniform floor of protection throughout the country (49, p. 82801). States retain the authority, however, to enforce a higher level of privacy protection, which means that practitioners will need to be aware of both the laws in their own jurisdictions and the federal rules. Other state laws that are not preempted by the regulations include those requiring reporting of events of public health significance, such as child abuse or communicable diseases, and laws relating to controlled substances. A procedure has been established for the Secretary of DHHS to determine whether a state law is more or less protective of privacy—something that may not always be clear, for example, when the same statute is more protective in one area and less in another.

Evolution of the Regulations

Although it appears at this point that the general form of the regulations will be retained for the indefinite future, there are likely to be some changes in specifics. DHHS has indicated that it will issue a set of guidance documents clarifying some aspects of the regulations and responding to frequently asked questions; the first of those advisories

has already appeared (57). In addition, DHHS has the power to seek additional changes in the regulations, through its formal rule-making process, on a yearly basis.

More frontal assaults on the regulations have already begun. Two state medical societies have filed a lawsuit seeking to block implementation of the regulations, primarily on the grounds that Congress acted unconstitutionally in delegating power to DHHS to fashion these rules, without providing sufficient guidance (58). There are also rumblings from various congressional sources regarding legislation that would delay implementation or replace the regulations with statutory guidelines. However, since DHHS was empowered to enact these regulations only after years of failure by Congress to pass just such a bill, it seems unlikely that Congress will step back into this thicket.

Protecting Patient Privacy Under the HIPAA Regulations

What is the future of patient privacy in psychiatric treatment? The HIPAA regulations, although they take some positive steps toward greater privacy protection—limiting sale of medical information and providing greater security for psychotherapy notes, for example—fall far short of an optimal balancing of patients' interests with demands for access to patient-identifiable data. When the regulations go into effect in 2003, consent will no longer be required for disclosures related to treatment, payment, and health care operations. New avenues for access to medical information have been created (e.g., for law enforcement), while gaps in current protections have been addressed only in part (e.g., disclosures for purposes of marketing) or not at all. As an example of an area neglected by the regulations, no overt limits are set on the excessive demands of managed care companies for patient records in their utilization review process (although it is possible that the provision described earlier for the "minimum necessary" disclosure may be helpful over the long run here).

Despite the sweeping nature of these regulations, it is important to reflect on the ways in which greater privacy protections can be made available to patients. Perhaps most crucial is the fact that the HIPAA regulations do not override state laws that are more protective of medical privacy. Thus, in states that have case law, statutes, or regulations mandating, for example, patient consent before the release of medical information, those rules will take precedence over the less stringent federal regulations. States without such rules will retain the opportunity to adopt new laws restricting access to medical data. The insurance and managed care industries and representatives of large corporations can be expected to continue lobbying Congress to revoke HIPAA's nonpreemption provision, so as to impose a uniform set of federal regulations on the nation as a whole. For now, however, more protective state laws take precedence. Patients, clinicians, and professional as-

PAUL S. APPELBAUM

sociations desiring greater privacy safeguards are likely to direct their efforts toward their state houses.

Moreover, the regulations, which generally permit but do not require disclosure in the various circumstances they address, leave a great deal of discretion in the hands of health care professionals and facilities. Practitioners, clinics, and hospitals are not precluded from creating policies of their own that are more protective than the federal rules, so long as the data are stored locally. They might, for example, require informed consent before each disclosure of information, except for routine billing data. Although the regulations do not require holders of medical information to agree to limits on disclosure that are requested by patients, clinicians retain the discretion to do so. Thus, patients who are particularly concerned that their psychiatric record not be disseminated beyond their psychiatrist's office can negotiate specific limits that, once agreed to, would be binding on the psychiatrist. Even demands for information by attorneys, law enforcement, and other entities authorized under the HIPAA regulations to make such requests need not be acceded to by clinicians without patient consent, unless required by some other law.

An additional safeguard that clinicians can employ is to discuss with patients at the inception of treatment the limits on confidentiality of disclosed information. The new federal regulations, as noted, require that patients be informed in writing of a practitioner's or facility's privacy policies, but those documents may turn out to be insufficiently informative for many patients. A clear description of the foreseeable risks to privacy that might be material to a patient's decision to disclose sensitive information and a willingness to discuss ways of protecting privacy (e.g., omitting certain information from the record, or limiting it to a separate set of psychotherapy notes) could go a long way toward helping patients understand the privacy risks they face. Data from several studies suggest that information about limits to confidentiality is already the information that therapists reveal most frequently to patients at the start of treatment (59–62), although by no means do all patients receive such information (63, 64).

Nor can clinicians afford to ignore their behavior outside the realms directly governed by the HIPAA regulations and state law. Reports of discussions about patients in public elevators (65) or of psychiatric records being discarded in a dumpster when a practice is closed (66) point out how greatly patients' privacy rests in their physicians' hands. Complicated dilemmas relating to patients' privacy will only grow as the use of information technology proliferates (67) and as new medical techniques such as genetic profiling become common (68). Already clinicians must attend to protecting privacy when using web sites, e-mail, cell phones, voice mail, faxes, and other communications technology (69). In the long run, psychiatrists' dedication to the ethical principles underlying medical privacy will remain one of the most important protections that can be offered to patients.

Received Sept. 4, 2001, revision received Jan. 16, 2002, accepted Feb. 4, 2002. (Further revisions were made in August 2002, after changes in the federal regulations authorized by HIPAA were issued.) From the Department of Psychiatry, University of Massachusetts Medical School. Address correspondence to Dr. Appelbaum, Department of Psychiatry, University of Massachusetts Medical School, Worcester, MA 01655; appelbap@ummhc.org (e-mail).

References

1. Goldstein A: Long reach into patients' privacy: new uses of data illustrate potential benefits, hazards. Washington Post, Aug 23, 1999, p A1
2. Bass A: HMO puts confidential records on-line: critics say computer file-keeping breaches privacy of mental health patients. Boston Globe, March 7, 1995, p 1
3. Upton J: Michigan medical records accidentally posted on Web. Detroit Free Press, Feb 12, 1999
4. Resier SJ, Dyck AJ, Curran WJ: Ethics in Medicine: Historical Perspectives and Contemporary Concerns. Cambridge, Mass, MIT Press, 1977
5. Siegler M: Confidentiality in medicine: a decrepit concept. N Engl J Med 1982; 307:1518–1521
6. Questions raised about Medicaid investigators. Psychiatr News, Nov 17, 1989, p 17
7. Corcoran K, Winslade WJ: Eavesdropping on the 50-minute hour: managed mental health care and confidentiality. Behav Sci Law 1994; 12:351–365
8. US Congress, Office of Technology Assessment: Protecting Privacy in Computerized Medical Information, OTA-TCT-576. Washington, DC, US Government Printing Office, Sept 1993
9. Appleby J: File safe? health records may not be confidential. USA Today, March 23, 2000, p 1
10. Appelbaum PS: A "health information infrastructure" and the threat to confidentiality of health records. Psychiatr Serv 1998; 49:27–28, 33
11. Gillon R: Philosophical medical ethics: confidentiality. Br Med J 1985; 291:1634–1636
12. Public Attitudes Toward Medical Privacy. Submitted to the Institute for Health Freedom. Princeton, NJ, The Gallup Organization, Sept 2000. www.forhealthfreedom.org/Gallupsurvey/IHF-Gallup.html
13. Schmid D, Appelbaum PS, Roth LH, Lidz CW: Confidentiality in psychiatry: a study of the patient's view. Hosp Community Psychiatry 1983; 34:353–355
14. Appelbaum PS, Kapen G, Walters B, Lidz CW, Roth LH: Confidentiality: an empirical test of the utilitarian perspective. Bull Am Acad Psychiatry Law 1984; 12:109–116
15. McGuire JM, Toal P, Blau B: The adult client's conception of confidentiality in the therapeutic relationship. Prof Psychol Res Pr 1985; 16:375–384
16. VandeCreek L, Miars R, Herzog CE: Client anticipations and preferences for confidentiality of records. J Counsel Psychol 1987; 34:62–67
17. Medical Privacy and Confidentiality Survey. Oakland, Calif, California Health Foundation, Jan 28, 1999. http://admin.chcf.org/documents/chcf/survey.pdf
18. Cheng TL, Savageau JA, Sattler AL, DeWitt TG: Confidentiality in health care: a survey of knowledge, perceptions, and attitudes among high school students. JAMA 1993; 269:1404–1407
19. Thrall JS, McCloskey L, Ettner SL, Rothman E, Tighe JE, Emans SJ: Confidentiality and adolescents' use of providers for health information and for pelvic examinations. Arch Pediatr Adolesc Med 2000; 154:885–892

PRIVACY IN PSYCHIATRIC TREATMENT

20. McGuire J, Graves S, Blau B: Depth of self-disclosure as a function of assured confidentiality and videotape recording. J Couns Dev 1985; 64:259–263

21. Muehleman T, Pickens BK, Robinson F: Informing clients about the limits to confidentiality, risks and their rights: is self-disclosure inhibited? Prof Psychol Res Pr 1985; 16:385–397

22. Nowell D, Spruill J: If it's not absolutely confidential, will information be disclosed? Prof Psychol Res Pr 1993; 24:367–369

23. Kremer TG, Gesten EL: Confidentiality limits of managed care and clients' willingness to self-disclose. Prof Psychol Res Pr 1998; 29:553–558

24. Taube DO, Elwork A: Researching the effects of confidentiality law on patients' self-disclosures. Prof Psychol Res Pr 1990; 21: 72–75

25. Shuman DW, Weiner MF, Pinard G: The privilege study, part III: psychotherapist-patient communications in Canada. Int J Law Psychiatry 1986; 9:393–429

26. Imwinkelried E: The rivalry between truth and privilege: the weakness of the Supreme Court's instrumental reasoning in *Jaffee v Redmond*, 518 US 1 (1996). Hastings Law J 1998; 49: 969–990

27. DeCew JW: The priority of privacy for medical information. Soc Philosophy and Policy 2000; 17:213–234

28. American Psychiatric Association: The Principles of Medical Ethics With Annotations Especially Applicable to Psychiatry. Washington, DC, APA, 1998

29. American College of Physicians: Ethics manual. Ann Intern Med 1998; 128:576–594

30. Shuman DW: The origins of the physician-patient privilege and professional secret. Southwestern Law J 1985; 39:661–687

31. Jaffee v Redmond, 518 US 1 (1996)

32. Finley v Johnson Oil Company, 199 FRD 301, 2001 US Dist Lexis 1645 (SD Ind, Jan 18, 2001)

33. Gostin LO: Health information privacy. Cornell Law Rev 1995; 80:451–528

34. Petrila J: Legal and ethical issues in protecting the privacy of behavioral health care information (with appendix on state mental health law confidentiality provisions), in Privacy and Confidentiality in Mental Health Care. Edited by Gates JJ, Arons BS. Baltimore, Paul H Brookes, 2000, pp 91–125, 219–232

35. Horne v Patton, 291 Ala. 701 (1974)

36. MacDonald v Clinger, 84 A 2d 482 (NY 1982)

37. Hague v Williams, 37 NJ 328 (1962)

38. Alberts v Devine, 479 NE 2d 113 (Mass 1985)

39. 42 United States Code, Section 290dd-2

40. Samuels PN: Confidentiality of alcohol and other drug patient records, in Privacy and Confidentiality in Mental Health Care. Edited by Gates JJ, Arons BS. Baltimore, Paul H Brookes, 2000, pp 173–192

41. Kinzie, JD, Holmes JL, Arent J: Patients' release of medical records: involuntary, uninformed consent? Hosp Community Psychiatry 1985; 36:843–847

42. Garfinkel S: Database Nation: The Death of Privacy in the 21st Century. Sebastopol, Calif, O'Reilly & Associates, 2000

43. Lo B, Alpers A: Uses and abuses of prescription drug information in pharmacy benefit management programs. JAMA 2000; 283:801–806

44. Scarf M: The privacy threat that didn't go away: brave new world. New Republic, July 12, 1999, pp 16–18

45. Dick RS, Steen EB (eds): The Computer-Based Patient Record: An Essential Technology for Health Care. Washington, DC, National Academy Press, 1991

46. Donaldson MS, Lohr KN (eds): Health Data in the Information Age: Use, Disclosure, and Privacy. Washington, DC, National Academy Press, 1994

47. Confidentiality of Individually Identifiable Health Information: Recommendations of the Secretary of Health and Human Services, Pursuant to Section 264 of the Health Insurance Portability and Accountability Act of 1996. Washington, DC, Office of the Secretary, US Department of Health and Human Services, Sept 11, 1997. http://aspe.hhs.gov/admnsimp/pvcrec0.htm

48. Office of the Secretary, Department of Health and Human Services: Standards for privacy of individually identifiable health information. Federal Register 1999; 64:59918–60065

49. Office of the Secretary, Department of Health and Human Services: Standards for privacy of individually identifiable health information; final rule. Federal Register 2000; 65:82462–82829 (www.hhs.gov/ocr/hipaa)

50. Office of the Secretary, Department of Health and Human Services: Standards for privacy of individually identifiable health information. Federal Register 2001; 66:12434

51. Office of the Secretary, Department of Health and Human Services: Standards for privacy of individually identifiable health information. Federal Register 2002; 67:53182–53273

52. Gostin LO: National health information privacy: regulations under the Health Insurance Portability and Accountability Act. JAMA 2001; 285:3015–3021

53. Disclosure of Mental Health Information: A Secret Service Guide to Applicable State Law. Washington, DC, US Secret Service, Department of the Treasury, 1997

54. Melton LJ III: The threat to medical-records research. N Engl J Med 1997; 337:1466–1470

55. Simon GE, Unützer J, Young BE, Pincus HA: Large medical databases, population-based research, and patient confidentiality. Am J Psychiatry 2000; 157:1731–1737

56. Appelbaum PS: Protecting privacy while facilitating research (editorial). Am J Psychiatry 2000; 157:1725–1726

57. Standards for Privacy of Individually Identifiable Information. Washington, DC, Office for Civil Rights, Department of Health and Human Services, 2001. http://www.hhs.gov/ocr/hipaa/finalmaster.html

58. Landa AS: HHS sued over medical privacy rules. Am Med News, Aug 6, 2001, pp 5, 7

59. Talbert FS, Pipes RB: Informed consent for psychotherapy: content analysis of selected forms. Prof Psychol Res Pr 1988; 19: 131–132

60. Beeman DG, Scott NA: Therapists' attitudes toward psychotherapy informed consent with adolescents. Prof Psychol Res Pr 1991; 22:230–234

61. Somberg DR, Stone GL, Claiborn CD: Informed consent: therapists' beliefs and practices. Prof Psychol Res Pr 1993; 24:153–159

62. Jensen JA, McNamara JR: Parents' and clinicians' attitudes toward the risks and benefits of child psychotherapy: a study of informed-consent content. Prof Psychol Res Pr 1991; 22:161–170

63. Baird KA, Rupert PA: Clinical management of confidentiality: a survey of psychologists in seven states. Prof Psychol Res Pr 1987; 18:347–352

64. Nicolai KM, Scott NA: Provision of confidentiality information and its relation to child abuse reporting. Prof Psychol Res Pr 1994; 25:154–160

65. Ubel PA, Zell MM, Miller DJ, Fischer GS, Peters-Stefani D, Arnold RM: Elevator talk: observational study of inappropriate comments in a public space. Am J Med 1995; 99:190–194

66. Schwartz J: When public goes private: why were psychiatric files blowing down our street? Washington Post, Dec 22, 1996, p C1

67. Hodge JG, Gostin LO, Jacobson PD: Legal issues concerning electronic health information: privacy, quality, and liability. JAMA 1999; 282:1466–1471

68. Laurie GT: Challenging medical-legal norms: the role of autonomy, confidentiality, and privacy in protecting individual and familial group rights in genetic information. J Legal Med 2001; 22:1–54

69. Gutheil TG, Appelbaum PS: Clinical Handbook of Psychiatry and the Law, 3rd ed. Philadelphia, Lippincott Williams & Wilkins, 2000

Patient Autonomy

[5]

The Right to Refuse Mental Health Treatment:

A Therapeutic Jurisprudence Analysis

Bruce J. Winick*

Introduction

The controversy concerning the recognition and definition of a right to refuse mental health treatment has largely ignored the question of whether such recognition would be therapeutically beneficial or detrimental to the patient. Would such recognition lead to refusal of needed treatment so that patients will "rot with their rights on," as some have suggested?[1] Will allowing offenders the choice whether to participate in correctional rehabilitation programs increase recidivism? Will patients forced to accept mental health treatment over objection improve and come, in time, to thank their doctor, retrospectively approving beneficial treatment they never would have accepted voluntarily?[2] On the

*Professor of Law, University of Miami School of Law, Coral Gables, Florida, P.O. Box 248087, 33124-8087, U.S.A.

Preliminary versions of this article were presented at meetings of the International Academy of Law and Mental Health and the American Psychology-Law Society, and I appreciate the comments of colleagues at these meetings. I also appreciate the research assistance of Joyce Golden and Karen Kaminsky. This article, in a somewhat revised form, will appear as a chapter in my forthcoming book, THE RIGHT TO REFUSE MENTAL HEALTH TREATMENT: A CONSTITUTIONAL AND THERAPEUTIC JURISPRUDENCE ANALYSIS.

[1] See, e.g., Appelbaum & Gutheil, The Boston State Hospital Case: "Involuntary Mind Control," the Constitution, and the "Right to Rot," 137 AM. J. PSYCHIATRY 720 (1980); Gutheil, In Search of True Freedom: Drug Refusal, Involuntary Medication, and "Rotting with Your Rights On," 137 AM. J. PSYCHIATRY 327 (1980) (editorial).

[2] See, e.g., A. STONE, MENTAL HEALTH LAW: A SYSTEM IN TRANSITION 69–70 (1975) (describing this reaction as the "thank-you" theory); D. WEXLER, MENTAL HEALTH LAW 45-48 (1981) (analyzing the "thank you" theory in context of narcotics abusers); Gove & Fain, A Comparison of Voluntary and Committed Psychiatric Patients, 34 ARCH. GEN. PSYCHIATRY 669, 675 (1977); Kane, Quitkin, Rifkin, Wegner, Rosenberg & Borenstein, Attitudinal Changes of Involuntarily Committed Patients Following Treatment, 40 ARCH. GEN. PSYCHIATRY 374, 376 (1983); Schwartz, Vingiano & Beziganian-Perez, Autonomy and the Right to Refuse Treatment: Patient's Attitudes After Involuntary Medication, 39 HOSP. & COMMUNITY PSYCHIATRY 1049 (1988) (empirical study showing that medication refusers treated over objection, if rehospitalized, would assent to drug treatment); but see Beck & Golowka, A Study of Enforced Treatment in Relation to Stone's "Thank You" Theory, 6 BEHAV. SCI. & L. 559, 565 (1988) (empirical study of involuntarily hospitalized patients showing no evidence to support "thank you" theory in 62% of cases).

other hand, might recognition of a right to refuse treatment empower patients and offenders in ways that could have therapeutic value? Might it provide them with a context in which they could acquire decisionmaking skills, learn to engage in self-determining behavior, and attain functional capacities that will be useful in community adjustment? Will providing patients and offenders with treatment choice enhance the potential that such treatment will be efficacious? Will according patients (or offenders) a right to refuse treatment change the therapist–patient (or counselor–offender) relationship in ways that will enhance or diminish its therapeutic potential?

These are questions that have not been examined empirically, but which are critical to resolving the right to refuse treatment dilemma. Whether a right to refuse treatment should be recognized ultimately may be a constitutional question, but judicial and statutory definitions of its parameters and of the procedural requirements necessary to implement it can be critically affected by the answers to these empirical questions. Moreover, because constitutional adjudication itself usually involves the balancing of conflicting interests, the answers to these questions should provide data that is essential to a constitutional analysis of the right to refuse treatment. This article accordingly attempts a therapeutic jurisprudence analysis of the right to refuse treatment.[3] It examines principles of cognitive and social psychology and psychodynamic theory in order to speculate about the likely impact of recognizing that patients and offenders have a right to refuse treatment, and a corresponding opportunity to choose such treatment. It is hoped that this theoretical speculation will generate empirical investigation that, in turn, will aid in a more informed development of the law in this area.

The Psychological Value of Choice

An extensive body of psychological literature points to the positive value of allowing individuals to exercise choice concerning a wide variety of matters affecting them.[4] Patient choice in favor of treatment, for example, appears to be an important determinant of treatment success.[5] Treatment imposed over objection may not work as well. Patients, like people generally, often do not respond well when told what to do. This may be even more true of criminal

---

[3]Therapeutic jurisprudence suggests the need for an assessment of the therapeutic impact of legal rules. The law itself impacts upon therapeutic values — sometimes positively, but sometimes negatively. While other considerations may properly shape legal rules, a sensible policy analysis of law should take into account its consequences for the health and mental health of the individuals and institutions it affects. Therapeutic jurisprudence accordingly calls for theoretical speculation about and empirical investigation of the therapeutic or antitherapeutic effects of the law. *See generally* D. Wexler & B. Winick, Essays in Therapeutic Jurisprudence (1991); Wexler & Winick, *Therapeutic Jurisprudence as a New Approach to Mental Health Law Policy Analysis and Research*, 45 U. Miami L. Rev. 979 (1991). In our prior writings, David Wexler and I have suggested the need for a therapeutic jurisprudence assessment of the right to refuse treatment. *See* Wexler & Winick, *supra* at 303, 310–11; Wexler & Winick, *supra* at 990–92. This article attempts such an analysis.

[4]*See* Winick, *On Autonomy: Legal and Psychological Perspectives*, 37 Vill. L. Rev. 1705, 1755–68 (1992) (summarizing literature on the psychology of choice).

[5]Winick, *Competency to Consent to Treatment: The Distinction Between Assent and Objection*, 28 Hous. L. Rev. 15, 46–53 (1991).

offenders, who have demonstrated their unwillingness or inability to behave in accordance with society's rules. Unless people themselves see the merit in achieving a particular goal, they often will not pursue it or will do so only half-heartedly. Indeed, sometimes even when the costs of noncompliance with a goal are high, some people may resent the pressure imposed by others and refuse to comply. Sometimes they even may act perversely in ways calculated to frustrate achievement of the goal. By contrast, an individual voluntarily accepting treatment is exercising choice. The law strongly favors allowing individual choice rather than attempting to achieve public or private goals through compulsion.[6] Aside from the political values reflected in this preference, it is strongly supported by utilitarian considerations.

Cognitive and social psychology provide a theoretical explanation for why permitting individual choice may have the effect of enhancing the potential for success.[7] People directed to perform tasks do not feel personally committed to the goal or personally responsible for its fulfillment.[8] This feeling may apply even for tasks the individual is directed to perform in furtherance of his or her own best interests, such as medical treatment. When physicians do not allow patient participation in treatment decisions and do not explain treatment to them, patients often fail to comply with medical advice.[9] Choice, on the other hand, may bring a degree of commitment which mobilizes the self-evaluative and self-reinforcing mechanisms that facilitate goal achievement.[10] To the extent that a patient's agreement to accept a course of treatment recommended by a therapist constitutes an affirmative expression of choice by the patient in favor of treatment, such choice itself may be therapeutic. Compliance with a treatment plan is often indispensable to successful treatment.[11] Unless patients show up for scheduled appointments or take their prescribed medication, treatment cannot succeed. This would seem especially true for treatments like psy-

---

[6]Winick, *supra* note 4, at 1707–55.

[7]*See* S. BREHM & J. BREHM, PSYCHOLOGICAL REACTANCE: A THEORY OF FREEDOM AND CONTROL 301 (1981); Carroll, *Consent to Mental Health Treatment: A Theoretical Analysis of Coercion, Freedom, and Control,* 9 BEHAV. SCI. & L. 129, 137–38 (1991); Winick, *Harnessing the Power of the Bet: Wagering with the Government as a Means of Accomplishing Social and Individual Change,* 45 U. MIAMI L. REV. 737, 752–72 (1991) (hereinafter *Wagering with the Government*; Winick, *supra* note 5, at 46–53; Winick, *Competency to Consent to Voluntary Hospitalization: A Therapeutic Jurisprudence Analysis of Zinermon v. Burch,* 14 INT'L J. L. & PSYCHIATRY 169, 192–99 (1991) (hereinafter *Competency to Consent to Voluntary Hospitalization*).

[8]A. BANDURA, SOCIAL FOUNDATIONS OF THOUGHT AND ACTION: A SOCIAL COGNITIVE THEORY 338, 363, 368, 468–69, 470–71, 475–76, 478–79 (1986).

[9]P. APPELBAUM, C. LIDZ & A. MEISEL, INFORMED CONSENT: LEGAL THEORY AND CLINICAL PRACTICE 28 (1987); D. MEICHENBAUM & D. TURK, FACILITATING TREATMENT ADHERENCE: A PRACTITIONER'S GUIDE-BOOK 20, 76–79 (1987); B. MOYERS, HEALING AND THE MIND 50 (1993); *see* Appelbaum & Gutheil *Drug Refusal: A Study of Psychiatric Inpatients,* 137 AM. J. PSYCHIATRY 340, 341 (1980); Shultz, *From Informed Consent to Patient Choice: A New Protected Interest,* 95 YALE L. J. 219, 293 & n.323 (1985). Treatment adherence in general increases when the patient is given choice and participation in the selection of treatment alternatives and goals. *See* MEICHENBAUM & TURK, *supra* at 157, 159, 175; Kanfer & Gaelick, *Self-Management Methods, in* HELPING PEOPLE CHANGE 334–47 (F. Kanfer & A. Goldstein eds. 1986).

[10]BANDURA, *supra* note 8, at 338, 363, 368, 468, 478–70; BREHM & BREHM, *supra* note 7, at 301; MEICHENBAUM & TURK, *supra* note 9, at 156–57; Carroll, *supra* note 7, at 129, 137–38.

[11]*See generally* MEICHENBAUM & TURK, *supra* note 9.

chotherapy, correctional counseling, and other forms of verbal therapy,[12] and even for many forms of behavioral therapy.[13] These techniques all are largely dependant for their success on the conscious involvement and active cooperation of the patient. However, patient involvement and cooperation would seem essential for even organic forms of treatment.

The conscious, voluntary agreement to accept a course of treatment constitutes the setting of a goal. The setting of explicit goals is itself a significant factor in their accomplishment.[14] This "goal-setting effect" is "one of the most robust . . . findings in the psychological literature."[15] The conscious setting of a goal is virtually indispensable to its achievement.[16] A patient's voluntary agreement to a course of treatment recommended by a therapist constitutes the setting of a goal, the acceptance of a prediction by the therapist that the patient can achieve the goal and will do so, and at least an implicit undertaking by the patient that he or she will attempt the task. The therapist's prediction that the proposed therapy will succeed and the patient's acceptance of this prediction set up expectancies that help to bring about a favorable treatment outcome.[17]

A patient's expectancies concerning treatment success, as well as a number of other cognitive mechanisms, seem to be significantly related to treatment response. There is increasing recognition that the mind plays a crucial role in both the patient's susceptibility to a variety of medical conditions and his or her response to treatment.[18] In its treatment of illness, medicine traditionally has focused almost exclusively on treating the body, often neglecting the role

---

[12]*See* Council of the Am. Psychiatric Ass'n, *Position Statement on the Question of Adequacy of Treatment*, 123 AM. J. PSYCHIATRY 1458, 1459 (1967) ("[I]t may be said in general that the effectiveness of the psychotherapies is proportional to the degree of cooperation that is present . . . . "); Katz, *The Right to Treatment—An Enchanting Legal Fiction*, 36 U. CHI. L. REV. 755, 777 (1969); Michels, *Ethical Issues of Psychological and Psychotherapeutic Means of Behavior Control: Is the Moral Contract Being Observed?*, 3 HASTINGS CENTER REP. 11, 11 (1973); Stromberg & Stone, *A Model State Law on Civil Commitment of the Mentally Ill*, 20 HARV. J. LEGIS. 276, 328 (1983); Winick, *The Right to Refuse Mental Health Treatment: A First Amendment Perspective*, 44 U. MIAMI L. REV. 1, 83–84 (1989).

[13]*See* E. ERWIN, BEHAVIOR THERAPY: SCIENTIFIC, PHILOSOPHICAL AND MORAL FOUNDATIONS 180–81 (1978); MEICHENBAUM & TURK, *supra* note 7, at 150; Bandura, *Behavior Therapy and the Models of Man*, 29 AM. PSYCHOLOGIST 859, 862 (1974); Marks, *The Current Status of Behavioral Psychotherapy: Theory and Practice*, 133 AM. J. PSYCHIATRY 253, 255 (1976); Winick, *Legal Limitations on Correctional Therapy and Research*, 65 MINN. L. REV. 331, 360–61 (1981); Winick, *supra* note 12, at 80.

[14]Campbell, *The Effects of Goal-Contingent Payment on the Performance of a Complex Task*, 37 PERSONNEL PSYCHOLOGY 23, 23 (1984); Huber, *Comparison of Monetary Reinforcers and Goal Setting as Learning Incentives*, 56 PSYCHOL. REP. 223 (1985); Kirschenbaum & Flanery, *Toward a Psychology of Behavioral Contracting*, 4 CLINICAL PSYCHOL. REV. 598, 603–09 (1984); Locke, Shaw, Saari & Latham, *Goal Setting and Task Performance 1969–1980*, 90 PSYCHOL. BULL. 125, 125–31 (1981); Terborg & Miller, *Motivation, Behavior, and Performance: A Closer Examination of Goal Setting and Monetary Incentives*, 63 J. APPLIED PSYCHOL. 29, 30–31 (1978).

[15]Campbell, *supra* note 14, at 23; Locke, Shaw, Saari & Latham, *supra* note 14, at 145.

[16]BANDURA, *supra* note 8, at 469 ("Those who set no goals achieve no change . . . . ").

[17]*See id.* at 412–13, 467; Deci & Ryan, *The Empirical Exploration of Intrinsic Motivational Processes*, 13 ADVANCES IN EXPER. SOC. PSYCHOLOGY 39, 59 (1980).

[18]*See generally* N. COUSINS, HEALTH FIRST: THE BIOLOGY OF HOPE AND THE HEALING POWER OF THE HUMAN SPIRIT (1990); H. DIENSTFREY, WHERE THE MIND MEETS THE BODY: TYPE A, THE RELAXATION RESPONSE, PSYCHONEUROIMMUNOLOGY, HYPNOSIS, BIOFEEDBACK, NEUROPEPTIDES, AND THE SEARCH

of the mind. Even when fighting organic illnesses with organic treatment techniques, the role of the mind may be significant in producing positive outcomes.[19] Expectancy theory helps to explain the therapeutic power of such phenomena as the placebo effect, the Hawthorne effect, and the medicine man.[20] Although as yet imperfectly understood, these phenomena suggest the existence of a powerful relationship between a patient's expectations that he or she will improve and his or her perceived and even actual improvement. An increasing variety of medical and psychological conditions are treated with hypnosis and positive imaging techniques that ask the patient to visualize his or her body fighting illness and the ultimate restoration to health.[21] The positive attitudes and expectations thereby created are thought to allow the patient to

---

FOR IMAGERY, AND THE MIND'S EFFECT ON PHYSICAL HEALTH (1991); H. DUNBAR, EMOTIONS AND BODILY CHANGES (1954) (discussing psychosomatic medicine, a psychological approach to medicine treating the mind and body as one entity); MOYERS, *supra* note 9; Engel, *The Need for a New Medical Model: A Challenge for Biomedicine*, 196 SCIENCE 129 (1977) (proposing a psychosocial view of health, taking into account the interaction of biological, psychological, and social factors in the onset of physical disorders); Frank, *The Faith that Heals*, 137 JOHNS HOPKINS MED. J. 127 (1975) (observing that diverse modes of medical treatment owe their success or failure to the patient's state of mind and expectations, and not solely to the treatment regimen itself).

[19]*See* COUSINS, *supra* note 18, at 192 (commenting on the role of patient's outlook and attitudes on the onset and course of disease); *id.* ("[T]he wise physician makes a careful estimate of the patients' will to live and the ability to put to work all the resources of spirit that can be translated into beneficial biochemical changes."); *id.* ("[F]ew things are more important than the psychological management of the patient" in all medical contexts.); *id.* at 217–20 (discussing survey of oncologists showing their belief that positive patient attitude and participation in treatment were beneficial); MOYERS, *supra* note 9, at 130 (commenting on the role of lifestyle and attitudes on such conditions as cancer and heart disease).

[20]*See, e.g.*, J. BOURKE, THE MEDICINE MEN OF THE APACHE 2 (1971) (observing that the ability to inspire belief in patients that he has "the gift" is a prerequisite to being "a diyi" or medicine man); H. BRODY, PLACEBOS AND THE PHILOSOPHY OF MEDICINE: CLINICAL, CONCEPTUAL, AND ETHICAL ISSUES 18–20 (1980) ("[T]he patient's expectations of symptom change is held to be causally connected to the change that occurs"); M. JOSPE, THE PLACEBO EFFECT IN HEALING 93–108, 130 (1978) (analyzing the Hawthorne effect in terms of expectancy theory); O. SIMONTON, S. MATTHEWS-SIMONTON & J. CREIGHTON, GETTING WELL AGAIN 22 (1978); Beecher, *The Powerful Placebo*, 159 J.A.M.A. 1602 (1955) (documenting the power of the placebo); Evans, *Expectancy, Therapeutic Instructions, and the Placebo Response, in* PLACEBO: THEORY, RSEARCH, AND MECHANISMS 215, 222–24 (1985) (concluding that the "placebo response is mediated by expectations generated within the context of the doctor-patient relationship"); Frank, *Biofeedback and the Placebo Effect*, 7 BIOFEEDBACK & SELF-REGULATION 449 (1982) (examining placebo effect in terms of expectancy theory); Horvath, *Placebos and Common Factors in two Decades of Psychotherapy Research*, 104 PSYCHOL. BULL. 214, 215 (1988) ("Expectancy factors have been shown to influence therapeutic outcome"); Wolf, *Effects of Placebo Administration and Occurrence of Toxic Reactions*, 155 J.A.M.A. 339 (1974) (documenting beneficial effects of placebos). For an alternative analysis of the placebo effect in terms of classical conditioning, *see* DIENSTFREY, *supra* note 18, at 86–87; Ader, *The Placebo Effect as Conditioned Response, in* EXPERIMENTAL FOUNDATIONS OF BEHAVIORAL MEDICINE: CONDITIONING APPROACHES 47 (R. Ader, H. Weiner & A. Baum eds. 1988).

[21]*See, e.g.*, P. BROWN, THE HYPNOTIC BRAIN: HYPNOTHERAPY AND SOCIAL COMMUNICATION (1991); G. EPSTEIN, HEALING VISUALIZATIONS: CREATING HEALTH THROUGH IMAGERY (1989); M. ERICKSON, THE COLLECTED PAPERS OF MILTON H. ERICKSON ON HYPNOSIS (E. Ross ed. 1988); Barber, *Changing "Unchangeable" Bodily Processes by (Hypnotic) Suggestion: A New Look at Hypnosis, Cognition, Imagining, and the Mind-Body Problem, in* IMAGINATION AND HEALING (A. Sheikh ed. 1984); Orne & Dinges, *Hypnosis, in* 2 COMPREHENSIVE TEXTBOOK OF PSYCHIATRY 1501, 1511–12 (H. Kaplan & B. Sadock eds. 5th ed. 1989); Wilson & Barber, *The Fantasy-Prone Personality: Implications for Understanding Imagery, Hypnosis, and Parapsychological Phenomena, in* IMAGERY: CURRENT THEORY, RESEARCH AND APPLICATION 340 (A. Sheikh & J. Wiley eds. 1983).

mobilize his or her psychic resources in ways that may play a critical role in the therapeutic process.[22]

How do these positive attitudes and expectancies work to influence treatment success? Social cognitive theory posits that predictions and expectations concerning the achievement of goals, including treatment goals, stimulate feelings of self-efficacy in the individuals which in turn spark action and effort in furtherance of the goal.[23] The setting of treatment goals serves to enhance motivation and increase the patient's effort through self-monitoring, self-evaluation, and self-reactive processes.[24] Setting such goals helps to structure and guide the patient's behavior over the often long course of treatment.[25] It provides direction for the patient and focuses his or her interest, attention, and personal involvement in the treatment.[26] A patient's voluntary acceptance of a therapist's treatment recommendation may facilitate an internalization of the treatment goal that can produce the personal commitment and expenditure of energy needed to achieve it.[27]

Motivation to succeed is an ingredient in goal achievement. Ability to accomplish a goal, although necessary, will not produce success by itself; unless individuals are motivated to succeed, they will not commit the effort needed to bring about success. Psychologist Edward Deci's distinction between intrinsic and extrinsic motivation[28] helps to explain why choice works better than compulsion. Intrinsic motivation involves self-determining behavior and is associated with "an internal perceived locus of causality, feelings of self-determination, and a high degree of perceived competence or self-esteem."[29] With extrinsic motivation, on the other hand, the perceived locus of causality is external and feelings of competence and self-esteem are diminished.[30] When people are allowed to be self-determining, they function more effectively, with

---

[22]*See* COUSINS, *supra* note 18, at 237–39 (discussing the psychic interplay and its effects on wound healing, the course of progressive illnesses such as AIDS, and the functioning of the immune system); DIENSTFREY, *supra* note 18; MOYERS, *supra* note 9, at 48; Dubos, *Introduction, in* N. COUSINS, ANATOMY OF AN ILLNESS AS PERCEIVED BY THE PATIENT: REFLECTIONS ON HEALING AND REGENERATION 11, 18, 22–23 (1979); Shultz, *supra* note 9, at 292–93.

[23]*See* BANDURA, *supra* note 8, at 413. *See also* Rotter, *Generalized Expectancies for Internal Versus External Control of Reinforcement*, 80 PSYCHOL. MONOGRAPHS 1 (1966) (behavior varies as a function of the individual's generalized expectancies that outcomes are determined by his own actions or by external sources beyond his control); Horvath, *supra* note 20, at 218 ("The belief that the treatment works in the manner outlined in the rationale motivates the client to perform the tasks of the therapy.").

[24]*See* BANDURA, *supra* note 8, at 469–72; MEICHENBAUM & TURK, *supra* note 9, at 158–61.

[25]*See* BANDURA, *supra* note 8, at 469.

[26]*See id.* at 472.

[27]*Cf. id.* at 477–78 (observing that pledging goal commitments publicly, or to other people, enhances the amount of personal effort expended in their pursuit).

[28]*See* E. DECI, INTRINSIC MOTIVATION (1975) (hereinafter INTRINSIC MOTIVATION) (reviewing studies in intrinsic motivation and discussing development of its interplay with extrinsic rewards and controls); E. DECI, THE PSYCHOLOGY OF SELF-DETERMINATION (1980) [hereinafter THE PSYCHOLOGY OF SELF-DETERMINATION]; Deci & Ryan, *supra* note 17, at 41–43, 60–63, 67.

[29]DECI, THE PSYCHOLOGY OF SELF-DETERMINATION, *supra* note 28, at 41.

[30]*Id.*

a higher degree of commitment and greater satisfaction.[31] These feelings increase motivation to succeed, stimulate positive expectations and attitudes, and spark effort.[32]

The exercise of treatment choice also may trigger what Leon Festinger described as "cognitive dissonance"—the tendency of individuals to reinterpret information or experience that conflicts with their internally accepted or publicly stated beliefs in order to avoid the unpleasant personal state that such inconsistencies produce.[33] Cognitive dissonance affects not only perception, but behavior as well, producing effort in furtherance of the individual's stated goal in order to avoid the dissonance that failure to achieve it would create.[34] In the treatment context, cognitive dissonance can cause the patient to mobilize his or her energies and resources in order to accomplish the treatment goal. These motivating effects of cognitive dissonance will be even stronger to the extent that the patient's commitment to achievement of the goal is made to a respected therapist or counselor or publicly communicated to others whose respect the patient values.[35]

Thus, according to several strands of psychological theory, voluntary choice of treatment, particularly if recommended by a trusted and respected therapist or counselor, engages a number of important intrinsic sources of motivation and creates the positive expectancies that help to bring about treatment success.[36] These intrinsic sources of motivation and positive expectancies are more likely to be activated when the individual makes a choice that he or she regards as voluntary. To the extent that a decision is externally imposed on the individual, or the individual perceives the choice to be coerced, motivation to succeed predictably will be reduced. The positive expectancies and attitudes that appear to be so significant to treatment response would seem likely to occur only to the extent that a real contractarian relationship exists between therapist and patient. The condition of voluntary choice is satisfied in most outpatient treatment contexts, but perhaps rarely in traditional public mental hospitals, where clinicians dictate treatment that is imposed whether or not the patient con-

---

[31]*Id.* at 208–10. *See also* C. KIESLER, THE PSYCHOLOGY OF COMMITMENT: EXPERIMENTS LINKING BEHAVIOR TO BELIEF (164–67 (1971) (finding most effective method for behavior therapists to obtain desired results with patients was to give patients perception that they had freedom and control).

[32]*See* BANDURA, *supra* note 8, at 390–449; DECI, THE PSYCHOLOGY OF SELF-DETERMINATION, *supra* note 28, at 208–10; M. FRIEDMAN & G. LACKEY, JR., THE PSYCHOLOGY OF HUMAN CONTROL: A GENERAL THEORY OF PURPOSEFUL BEHAVIOR 72–74 (1991) (noting that control leads to self-confidence, which in turn leads to positive behavior); Deci & Ryan, *supra* note 17, at 41–42, 60–61.

[33]L. FESTINGER, A THEORY OF COGNITIVE DISSONANCE 2–3, 18–24, 73 (1957) [hereinafter COGNITIVE DISSONANCE]; L. Festinger, CONFLICT, DECISION, AND DISSONANCE 43 (1964). For a review of empirical studies on cognitive dissonance, *see* J. Brehm & A. Cohen, EXPLORATIONS IN COGNITIVE DISSONANCE 221–44 (1962).

[34]FESTINGER, COGNITIVE DISSONANCE, *supra* note 33, at 19.

[35]*See* BANDURA, *supra* note 8, at 477–78; MEICHENBAUM & TURK, *supra* note 9, at 170, 174; *Winick, Wagering with the Government, supra* note 7, at 763–64.

[36]*See supra* notes 7–35 and accompanying text. *See generally* BANDURA, *supra* note 8, at 467, 471–72; DECI, INTRINSIC MOTIVATION, *supra* note 28; DECI, THE PSYCHOLOGY OF SELF-DETERMINATION, *supra* note 28; Carroll, *supra* note 7, at 129, 137–38; Deci & Ryan, *supra* note 17, at 41–42, 60–63, 67.

sents,[37] or in prisons in which treatment is given involuntarily[38] or is perceived to be a condition of release. Some jurisdictions, however, recognize a right to refuse treatment that is applicable in public mental health institutions and prisons,[39] and institutionalized individuals in these jurisdictions are able, at least theoretically, to exercise treatment choice. To the extent that these jurisdictions honor a right to refuse, the goal-setting effect, cognitive dissonance, and other psychological mechanisms producing intrinsic motivation would be possible. The ability of a patient or prisoner to internalize the goal would seem to be enhanced to the extent he perceives his choice as voluntary, and undermined to the extent he perceives it to be coerced. To the extent coercion prevails in public hospitals and prisons, the therapeutic effects of choice discussed here would seem unlikely to be achieved.

This theoretical explanation of the therapeutic value of choice finds support in empirical research in a variety of areas suggesting that allowing individuals to exercise choice increases the likelihood of success. For instance, research with children has demonstrated that involving them in treatment planning and decisionmaking leads to greater compliance and increases the efficacy of treatment.[40] Similarly, allowing students to make choices about educational programs causes them to work "harder, faster, and [react] more positively to the situation than when they [are] unable to make such choices."[41] Anecdotal reports and informed clinical speculation, supported by several empirical studies, suggest that medical and mental health treatment are more effective when provided on a voluntary rather than involuntary basis.[42] An extensive review

---

[37] *See, e.g., Dautremont v. Broadlawn Hosp.*, 827 F.2d 291, 298 (8th Cir. 1987) (hospitalized civil patients may be involuntarily treated with psychotropic drugs against their will).

[38] *See, e.g., Washington v. Harper*, 494 U.S. 210 (1990) (upholding involuntary administration of antipsychotic medication to prisoner).

[39] *See, e.g.,* 2 M. PERLIN, MENTAL DISABILITY LAW: CIVIL AND CRIMINAL §§ 5.01–69 (1989); Winick, *supra* note 12; Winick, *The Right to Refuse Psychotropic Medication: Current State of the Law and Beyond, in* THE RIGHT TO REFUSE ANTIPSYCHOTIC MEDICATION 7 (D. Rapoport & J. Parry eds. 1986).

[40] *See, e.g.,* Lewis, *Decision Making Related to Health: When Could/Should Children Act Responsibly?, in* CHILDREN'S COMPETENCE TO CONSENT 75, 76–77, 78–79 (G. Melton, P. Koocher & M. Saks eds. 1983); Melton, *Children's Competence to Consent, A Problem in Law and Social Science, in* CHILDREN'S COMPETENCE TO CONSENT, *supra* at 1, 11; Melton, *Decision Making by Children: Psychological Risks and Benefits, in* CHILDREN'S COMPETENCE TO CONSENT, *supra* note 21, 30–31, 37; Melton, *Children's Participation in Treatment Planning: Psychological and Legal Issues,* 12 PROF. PSYCHOL. 246, 250–51 (1981).

[41] Bringham, *Some Effects of Choice on Academic Performance, in* CHOICE AND PERCEIVED CONTROL 131, 140 (L. Perlmutter & R. Monty eds. 1979). *See also* Amabile & Gitomer, *Children's Artistic Creativity: Effects of Choice in Task Materials,* 10 PERSONALITY & SOC. PSYCHOL. BULL. 209, 213 (1984) (restriction of choice negatively affected creativity); Deci, Nezlek & Sheinman, *Characteristics of the Rewarder and Intrinsic Motivation of the Rewardee,* 40 J. PERSONALITY & SOC. PSYCHOL. 1, 9 (1981) (students in autonomy-oriented classrooms shown to have higher intrinsic motivation and self-esteem than students in control-oriented classrooms).

[42] *See* AM. PSYCHIATRIC ASS'N TASK FORCE REPORT NO. 34: CONSENT TO VOLUNTARY HOSPITALIZATION 1 (1993) (voluntary hospitalization may lead to more favorable outcomes compared to involuntary hospitalization); *id.* at 5 ("The American Psychiatric Association strongly believes that it is preferable whenever possible for patients to be able to initiate their own psychiatric treatment."); APPELBAUM, LIDZ & MEISEL, *supra* note 7, at 28; S. BRAKEL, J. PARRY & B. WEINER, THE MENTALLY DISABLED AND THE LAW 178, 181 n.34 (3d ed. 1985); BREHM & BREHM, *supra* note 7, at 301; MEICHENBAUM & TURK, *supra* note 9, at 175; Appelebaum, Mirkin & Bateman, *Empirical Assessment of Competency to Consent to*

of the literature on psychotherapy and psychotropic medication, the two most prevalent forms of treatment for those suffering from mental illness, found no persuasive evidence that coercive application of these techniques to involuntarily committed patients was effective.[43]

While more research is needed before definitive conclusions can be reached concerning the effectiveness of treatment applied coercively,[44] the available evidence supports the conclusion that patient choice increases the likelihood of treatment success and that coercion does not work as well. Choice seems to increase positive outcomes in a variety of treatment contexts, although the question of its impact on patients with psychosis has not been adequately studied. For example, a patient in a florid state of schizophrenia, who is disoriented and hallucinating, may not possess a sufficient degree of competence to make a meaningful choice in favor of treatment.[45] How much understanding and volition are necessary to engage the psychological mechanisms discussed earlier that can contribute to a positive treatment response? Will choice by such a patient have the effect of producing the positive expectancies

---

Psychiatric Hospitalization, 183 Am. J. Psychiatry 1170, 1170 (1981); Carroll, *supra* note 7, at 129, 137–38; Culver & Gert, *The Morality of Involuntary Hospitalization, in* The Law-Medicine Relation: A Philosophical Exploration 159, 171 (S. Spicker, J. Healy & T. Engelhardt eds. 1981); Freedberg & Johnston, *Effects of various Sources of Coercion on Outcome of Treatment of Alcoholism*, 43 Psychol. Rep. 1271, 1271, 1277 (1978); Nicholson, *Correlates of Commitment Status in Psychiatric Patients*, 100 Psychol. Bull, 241, 243–44 (1986); Perlin & Sadoff, *Ethical Issues in the Representation of Individuals in the Commitment Process*, 45 Law & Contemp. Probs. 161, 190–91 (1982); Rogers & Webster, *Assessing Treatability in Mentally Disordered Offenders*, 13 Law & Hum. Behav. 19, 20–21 (1989); Stein & Test, *Alternatives to Mental Hospital Treatment*, 37 Arch. Gen. Psychiatry 392, 392–93 (1980); Stromberg & Stone, *supra* note 12, at 327, 328; Ward, *The Use of Legal Coercion in the Treatment of Alcoholism: A Methodological Review, in* Alcoholism: Introduction to Theory and Treatment 272 (D. Ward ed. 1980); Note, *Developments in the Law—Civil Commitment of the Mentally Ill*, 87 Harv. L. Rev. 1190, 1399 (1974). *See also* Washington v. Harper, 494 U.S. 210, 249 n.15 (1990) ("The efficacy of forced drugging is also marginal; involuntary patients have a poorer prognosis than cooperating patients.") (Stevens, J., dissenting); Rennie v. Klein, 462 F. Supp. 1131, 1144 (D. N.J. 1978) ("[T]he testimony . . . indicated that involuntary treatment is much less effective than the same treatment voluntarily received.").

[43]Durham & La Fond, *A Search for the Missing Premise of Involuntary Therapeutic Commitment: Effective Treatment of the Mentally Il*, 40 Rutgers L. Rev. 303, 351–56, 367–68 (1988) (hereinafter *Involuntary Therapeutic Commitment*). *See also* Durham & La Fond, *The Empirical Consequences and Policy Implications of Broadening the Statutory Criteria for Civil Commitments*, 3 Yale L. & Policy Rev. 395 (1985) (analyzing adverse effects of a statutory broadening of civil commitment standards).

[44]*See* Wexler & Winick, *supra* note 3, at 248 n.101 (noting the scarcity and inadequacy of existing studies and suggesting the need for more empirical research on the issue).

[45]*See* Zinermon v. Burch, 494 U.S. 113 (1990) (patient with schizophrenia who was delusional and hallucinating and who expressed the view that the mental hospital he was entering was "heaven" held incompetent to consent to voluntary hospitalization). This article does not analyze the concept of competency. For analysis of competency in various legal contexts, see Winick, *Competency to be Executed: A Therapeutic Jurisprudence Perspective*, 10 Behav. Sci. & L. 317 (1992) (competency to be executed); Winick, *supra* note 5 (competency to consent to treatment); Winick, *Competency to Consent to Voluntary Hospitalization*, *supra* note 7 (competency to consent to hospitalization); Winick, *Incompetency to Stand Trial: An Assessment of Costs and Benefits, and a Proposal for Reform*, 39 Rutgers L. Rev. 243 (1987) (competency to stand trial). Nor does this article examine the conditions under which an incompetent patient's choice may be overridden pursuant to the state's *parens patriae* power. *See* Winick, *supra* note 4, at 1772–77. Recognition that patients have a constitutional right to refuse treatment does not, of course, mean that a patient's right is absolute. For analysis of when state interests may outweigh the patient's asserted right to refuse treatment, see Winick, *supra* note 13 (examining state interests in correctional rehabilitation); Winick, *supra* note 39 (examining state interests in the civil context).

and intrinsic motivation that seem to be related to favorable treatment outcome? Theoretical explanations for the relationship between patient choice and treatment success are based on studies with less impaired populations. Can these findings be generalized to more impaired patients suffering from at least severe cases of major mental illness? These questions remain largely unexamined empirically.

Even if such patients do not possess competence to enable their choices to trigger these positive psychological effects, however, allowing them as great a degree of choice as circumstances permit may still be therapeutic. The aim of treatment interventions for acutely psychotic patients is to ameliorate severe symptomatology and restore the patient to as great a degree of competence as is possible. After a brief period of medication, for example, most seriously disturbed patients will be sufficiently competent that their choices about future treatment presumably will have positive therapeutic value.

An additional therapeutic value of choice, especially for disabled and disadvantaged populations like mental patients and criminal offenders, is that having and making choices is developmentally beneficial. Except for young children, and sometimes even including them, the more choice we give individuals, the more they will act as mature, self-determining adults. Indeed, a sense of competency and self-determination provides strong intrinsic gratification and may be a prerequisite for psychological health.[46] Treating individuals as competent adults able to make choices rather than as incompetent subjects of our paternalism, pity, or even contempt, predictably will have a therapeutic effect. This may be especially true for mental patients, who too often are infantilized by the treatment they receive from institutional clinicians and staff.[47] But it also may be true for prisoners, particularly those incarcerated for lengthy periods, who develop a form of institutional dependency.[48]

The denial of choice—which occurs in a legal system that rejects a right to refuse treatment—can be antitherapeutic, producing what in therapeutic jurisprudence terminology is called "law related psychological disfunction."[49] Exercising self-determination is thought to be a basic human need.[50] A variety of studies show that allowing individuals to make choices is intrinsically motivating, while denying choice "undermines [their] motivation, learning, and

---

[46]Carroll, *supra* note 7, at 129, 137–38; Deci & Ryan, *supra* note 17, at 42, 61, 72–73.

[47]*See generally* E. GOFFMAN, ASYLUMS: ESSAYS ON THE SOCIAL SITUATIONS OF MENTAL PATIENTS AND OTHER INMATES 3–74(1962) (discussing the phenomena of institutional dependence); Devillis, *Learned Helplessness in Institutions,* 15 MENTAL RETARDATION 10 (1977); Doherty, *Labeling Effects in Psychiatric Hospitalization: A Study of Diverging Patterns of Inpatient Self-labeling Process,* 32 ARCH. GEN. PSYCHIATRY 562 (1975). *See also* Johnson v. Solomon, 484 F. Supp. 278, 308 (D. Md. 1979) ("Inappropriate and excessive hospitalization fosters deterioration, institutionalization, and possible regression.") (footnotes omitted). In addition to breeding learned helplessness, *see* Devillis, *supra; infra* note 53 and accompanying text, such total institutions condition passivity and helplessness by reinforcing it and by discouraging assertiveness and autonomous behavior.

[48]*See* GOFFMAN, *supra* note 47, 16–17, 25–31, 39, 53–55, 61, 68–70.

[49]*See* WEXLER & WINICK, *supra* note 3, at 313; Wexler & Winick, *supra* note 3, at 979, 994.

[50]DECI, THE PSYCHOLOGY OF SELF-DETERMINATION, *supra* note 28, AT 208–09 (discussing "intrinsic motivation" as providing energy for various functions of will). *See also* H. HARTMANN, EGO PSYCHOLOGY AND THE PROBLEM OF ADAPTATION (1958) ("independent ego energy"); White, *Motivation Reconsidered: The Concept of Competence,* 66 PSYCHOL. REV. 297 (1959) ("effectance motivation").

general sense of organismic well-being."[51] Indeed, the stress of losing the opportunity to be self-determining may cause "severe somatic malfunctions" and even death.[52] When people feel they have no influence over matters that vitally affect them, they may also develop what Martin Seligman called "learned helplessness." Seligman's experimental work with animals and human subjects led him to posit that repetitive events outside an individual's control may produce a generalized feeling of ineffectiveness that debilitates performance and undermines motivation and perceptions of competence.[53] Institutionalized individuals coerced into accepting treatment might come to view themselves as incompetent in ways that could perpetuate and perhaps even worsen their mental health and social problems. This loss of control may produce depression[54] and decrease motivation.[55] Moreover, it may set up expectancies of failure in the individual that may undermine commitment and diminish subsequent performance.[56]

Denying people a sense of control over important areas of their lives thus can have strongly negative consequences. By contrast, when individuals exercise control and make choices, they experience increased opportunities to build skills necessary for successful living. As a result, they may gradually acquire feelings of self-efficacy, which in turn become important determinants of motivation and performance.[57] Hopefully, if given meaningful choices, these individuals will come to view themselves as in control of their lives, rather than as mere passive victims of forces they can neither understand nor control—a feeling that undoubtedly contributes to the existence and continuation of a variety of social and health problems. Treating individuals as competent adults able to make choices and to exercise a degree of control over their lives rather than as incompetent subjects of governmental paternalism and control predictably will have a beneficial effect.

Having a role in making important decisions, such as those involving treatment, can only increase patient satisfaction and confidence in the treatment process,[58] which inevitably increases patient compliance and motivation to suc-

---

[51]Deci, The Psychology of Self-Determination, *supra* note 28, at 209 (discussing studies).

[52]*Id.*

[53]M. Seligman, Helplessness: On Depression, Development, and Death (1975); Human Helplessness: Theory and Applications (J. Garber & M. Seligman eds. 1980); Maier & Seligman, *Learned Helplessness: Theory and Evidence*, 105 J. Experimental Psychol. 33 (1976); Overmier & Seligman, *Effects of Inescapable Shock Upon Subsequent Escape and Avoidance Responding*, 63 J. Comp. & Physiological Psychol. 28 (1976). Seligman, *Learned Helplessness*, 23 Ann. Rev. Med. 407 (1972). *See also* Brehm & Brehm, *supra* note 7, at 378 (1981); Lenore Walker, The Battered Woman 42–54 (1979) (applying learned helplessness to the battered woman syndrome); Peterson & Bossio, *Learned Helplessness, in* Self-Defeating Behaviors: Experimental Research, Clinical Impressions, and Practical Implications 235 (C. Peterson & Bossio eds. 1989); Thornton & Jacobs, *Learned Helplessness in Human Subjects*, 87 J. Experimental Psychol. 367 (1971).

[54]*See* Friedman & Lackey, *supra* note 32, at 73; Peterson & L. Bossio, *supra* note 53, at 26.

[55]*See* Deci, Nezlek & Sheinman, *supra* note 41; Deci & Ryan, *supra* note 17, at 59.

[56]*See* Friedman & Lackey, *supra* note 32, at 73.

[57]*See* Bandura, *supra* note 8, at 390–449; Brehm & Brehm, *supra* note 7, at 301, 376; Carroll, *supra* note 7, at 129, 137–38; Deci & Ryan, *supra* note 17, at 41–42, 60–61.

[58]Wexler, *Doctor-Patient Dialogue: A Second Opinion on Talk Therapy through Law*, 90 Yale L. J. 458, 469 (1980) (book review).

ceed. Particularly for institutionalized individuals who have developed a form of institutional dependency or learned helplessness, experiencing a measure of control over important decisions can itself be therapeutic. This conclusion is supported by research on nursing home residents, which demonstrated that providing them increased choices and responsibilities produced improvement in their conditions.[59] Exercising choice and experiencing a sense of control over important events in their lives can be a tonic for institutionalized mental patients and prisoners.

Thus, the potential for successful treatment in many contexts would appear to increase when the individual chooses treatment voluntarily rather than through coercion.[60] Individuals coerced to participate in a treatment program—for example, by court order; as a condition of diversion, probation, or parole; by correctional authorities; or by authorities in psychiatric settings—often just go through the motions, satisfying the formal requirements of the program without deriving any real benefits.[61] Indeed, such coercion may backfire, producing a negative "psychological reactance" that sets up oppositional behavior leading to failure.[62] Coercion may also trigger a form of the "overjustification effect," in which the individual may accomplish a specified goal, but because he or she attributes his or her performance to external pressure, will not experience any lasting attitudinal or behavioral change.[63] In contrast, the voluntary choice of a course of treatment involves a degree of internalized commitment to the goal often not present when the course of treatment is imposed involuntarily.[64]

Voluntary treatment therefore seems more likely to be efficacious than treatment that is coerced. These psychological perspectives on the value of choice in the therapeutic context, and on the corresponding disutility of coercion, may help to explain why treatment in the typical public mental hospital[65] and correctional rehabilitation in the typical prison[66] often have been ineffective. These psychological insights suggest that the therapist–patient (or counselor-

---

[59]Langer & Rodin, *The Effects of Choice and Enhanced Personal Responsibility for the Aged: A Field Experiment in an Institutional Setting*, 34 PERSONALITY & SOC. PSYCHOL. 191 (1976).

[60]*See* APPELBAUM, LIDZ & MEISEL, *supra* note 9, at 28; N. MORRIS, THE FUTURE OF IMPRISONMENT 24 (1974); Carroll, *supra* note 7, at 137–38; Deci & Ryan, *supra* note 17, at 59, 61; Winick, *supra* note 13, at 353, 360, 422; Winick, *supra* note 5, at 46–53; Winick, *supra* note 7, at 192–99; Winick, *Restructuring Competency to Stand Trial*, 32 UCLA L. REV. 921, 980 (1985).

[61]*See* COMMITTEE ON PSYCHIATRY AND LAW OF THE GROUP FOR THE ADVANCEMENT OF PSYCHIATRY, PSYCHIATRY AND SEX PSYCHOPATH LEGISLATION: THE 30S TO THE 80S 889 (1977); AMERICAN FRIENDS SERVICE COMM., STRUGGLE FOR JUSTICE: A REPORT ON CRIME AND PUNISHMENT IN AMERICA 97–98 (1971); Winick, *supra* note 13, at 344–46; Winick, *supra* note 12, at 83–87.

[62]*See* J. BREHM, A THEORY OF PSYCHOLOGICAL REACTANCE (1966); BREHM & BREHM, *supra* note 7, at 300–01.

[63]*See* R. PETTY & J. CACIOPPO, ATTITUDE AND PERSUASION: CLASSIC AND CONTEMPORARY APPROACHES 169–70 (1981); Carroll, *supra* note 7, at 129, 137–38; Deci, *Effects of Externally Mediated Rewards on Intrinsic Motivation*, 18 J. PERSONALITY & SOC. PSYCHOL. 105 (1971).

[64]*See supra* notes 7–10 and accompanying text; Carroll, *supra* note 7, at 129, 137–38; Deci & Ryan, *supra* note 17, at 59, 61.

[65]*See, e.g.*, Durham & LaFond, *Involuntary Therapeutic Commitment, supra* note 43.

[66]*See, e.g.*, D. LIPTON, R. MARTINSON & J. WILKS, THE EFFECTIVENESS OF CORRECTIONAL TREATMENT (1975); PANEL ON RESEARCH ON REHABILITATIVE TECHNIQUES OF THE NATIONAL RESEARCH COUNCIL,

offender) relationship in the typical institution – in which treatment (or correctional rehabilitation) is imposed coercively, or on a basis not perceived by the patient (or offender) as truly voluntary – may frustrate rather than facilitate achievement of the therapeutic goal.

Enhancing the Therapeutic Relationship

These psychological perspectives also suggest that according patients and offenders a right to refuse treatment might have the salutary effect of restructuring the therapist–patient (and counselor–offender) relationship in ways that will enhance its therapeutic potential. There is increasing recognition that in psychotherapy, the therapist–patient relationship itself plays an essential role in producing positive outcomes.[67] The effectiveness of psychotherapy is heavily dependent on the quality of the therapeutic relationship. The most effective therapeutic relationships are those in which mutual trust and acceptance are established and maintained and in which the patient perceives that the therapist cares about and is committed to pursuing his interests.[68] Patients improve as a result of therapeutic relationships that generate the perception that the therapist is interested in and dedicated to the patient's well-being.[69] To succeed, the therapist must establish his or her credibility and trustworthiness at an early time in the relationship. A relationship in which the therapist is permitted to treat the patient as an object of paternalism whose participation in the therapeutic decisionmaking process is unnecessary and undesirable will not inspire such trust and confidence, and therefore may be counterproductive. Indeed, a relationship in which the therapist ignores the patient's expressed wishes concerning treatment may produce the perception that the therapist is more concerned with the welfare of the institution than with that of the patient, and is not truly committed to the patient's best interests. A paternalistic approach that ignores the patient's wishes and concerns is likely to be perceived as offensive by the patient and an affront to his or her dignity and personhood.[70]

THE REHABILITATION OF CRIMINAL OFFENDERS: PROBLEMS AND PROSPECTS 5 (L. Sechrest, S. White & E. Brown eds. 1979).

[67]E.g., BREHM & BREHM, *supra* note 7, at 151–55, 300–01; WEXLER & WINICK, *supra* note 3, at 173; Deci & Ryan, *supra* note 17, at 70; Lambert, Shapiro & Bergin, *The Effectiveness of Psychotherapy*, *in* HANDBOOK OF PSYCHOTHERAPY AND BEHAVIOR CHANGE 157–211 (S. Garfield & A. Bergin eds., 3d ed. 1986) (hereinafter HANDBOOK).

[68]*See* authorities cited in *supra* note 67. The therapist-patient relationship, although especially significant in the context of psychotherapy, is also important in all areas of medical practice. *See, e.g.*, COUSINS, *supra* note 18, at 18 (discussing confidence by the patient in the doctor and in the patient's own healing resources); MOYERS, *supra* note 9, at 50 (discussing a "prevention partnership in which a patient is empowered to be a partner with . . . [the doctor] in the healing process."); Appelbaum & Gutheil, *supra* note 9, at 341 (noting correlation between adherence to drug treatment by psychiatric inpatients and the quality of the doctor-patient relationship).

[69]BREHM & BREHM, *supra* note 7, at 151–52, 300–02; WEXLER & WINICK, *supra* note 3, at 173; Beutler, Crago & Arizmendi, *Therapist Variables in Psychotherapy Process and Outcome*, *in* HANDBOOK, *supra* note 67, at 280–81; Orlinsky & Howard, *Process and Outcome in Psychotherapy*, *in* HANDBOOK, *supra* note 67, at 311.

[70]*See* J. FEINBERG, HARM TO SELF 4–5, 23, 27 (1986); Goldstein, *For Harold Lasswell: Some Reflections on Human Dignity, Entrapment, Informed Consent, and the Plea Bargain*, 84 YALE L.J. 683, 691 (1975);

Rather than producing trust and confidence, such an approach can inspire resentment and resistance.

Therapists, particularly those in public institutions, too often seem to misperceive the importance of the therapist–patient relationship. Not only do these therapists thereby forego therapeutic opportunities, but by their actions they may actually create a harmful division between therapist and patient. Too often there is no real connection or sense of community between therapist and patient. As a result, no real sense of trust and confidence develops on the part of the patient. Yet such trust and confidence may be a prerequisite for engaging those positive attitudes and expectancies that play an important role in producing a successful treatment response. There are therapists who could learn much from the teachings of theologian Martin Buber, whose writings explore the nature of relationships based on mutual dialogue.[71] Buber's notion of an "I–Thou" relationship characterized by mutual respect, openness, and affirmation of the other can be a useful model for restructuring the therapist–patient relationship. This model can transform the therapeutic relationship from one of paternalistic monologue to one of true dialogue, thereby increasing its therapeutic potential.

Recognition of a right to refuse treatment can reshape the therapist–patient relationship into a tool that is both more humane and more effective. It will increase the likelihood that therapists will respect the dignity and autonomy of their patients, and recognize their essential role in the therapeutic process. This reshaping of the therapist's role can increase the potential for a true therapeutic alliance in which therapists treat their patients as persons.[72] The result can be more patient trust, confidence, and participation in decisionmaking in ways that can cause patients to internalize treatment goals. A therapeutic relationship restructured in this fashion can enhance the patient's intrinsic motivation and the likelihood that the goal-setting effect, commitment, and the reinforcing effects of cognitive dissonance will occur.

A real therapist–patient (or counselor–offender) dialogue concerning treatment planning and decisionmaking can only bolster the patient's faith in the therapist and in his or her dedication to the patient's best interests. This faith and the expectations it generates may be essential to producing the Hawthorne effect or other interactive mechanisms that can increase the likelihood of therapeutic success.[73] Without trust, the therapeutic opportunities provided by the therapist–patient relationship are drastically reduced.

The need for trust, cooperation, and open communication is particularly important in the context or psychotherapy and other forms of verbal counsel-

---

Meisel & Roth, *Toward an Informed Discussion of Informed Consent: A Review and Critique of the Empirical Studies*, 25 ARIZ. L. REV. 265, 284 (1983); Winick, *supra* note 5, at 17.

[71]*See* M. BUBER, I AND THOU (1937); M. BUBER, BETWEEN MAN AND MAN (1947). For a proposal calling for the restructuring of the attorney-client relationship in the poverty law context that builds upon Buber's work, see Alfieri, *The Antinomies of Poverty Law and a Theory of Dialogical Empowerment*, 16 N.Y.U. REV. L. & SOC. CHANGE 659 (1987–88).

[72]*See* P. RAMSEY, THE PATIENT AS PERSON: EXPLORATIONS IN MEDICAL ETHICS (1970).

[73]*See* JOSPE, *supra* note 20, at 93–108, 130; text accompanying *supra* note 20.

ing, which are totally dependent on willing patient communication in the therapeutic relationship. What Freud characterized as the "fundamental rule" of
psychotherapy requires the patient to communicate openly and candidly with
the therapist.[74] Such basic techniques for probing the patient's unconcious
as free association and interpretation of dreams necessitate a patient who is
forthcoming with the therapist. Patient cooperation, necessary for these verbal
techniques to have any chance of succeeding, assume a high degree of patient
trust in the therapist and a relationship that is basically contractarian rather
than coercive in nature.

The ability of the therapist successfully to manipulate the transference phenomenon is similarly dependent upon a high degree of patient trust in the
therapist. Transference is the process by which the patient's feelings, thoughts,
and wishes concerning certain important figures in his or her life (particularly
in early life) are transferred or displaced to the therapist.[75] This process is an
essential device by which the therapist helps the patient to understand his or
her emotional problems and their origins. Transference is a key element in the
therapist–patient alliance.[76] Indeed, it has been characterized as "unequivocally
the heart of psychoanalysis."[77] Freud himself strongly stressed the role of transference as an ally of the analyst and the motivating force in treatment.[78] According to Freud, a positive transference provides the "strongest motive for
the patient's taking a share in the joint work of analysis."[79] Transference thus
is both a crucial therapeutic tool and a motivating force for committing the
patient to the therapeutic alliance. It is the "unconscious affective bond that
forms the basis for analytic work and underlies the patient's desire to remain
in treatment . . . ."[80]

For transference to play this essential role in the therapeutic relationship,
the therapist must gain the patient's trust and inspire confidence and respect.
A basic sense of trust is a prerequisite to the optimal functioning of the working alliance. Patients "often require an awareness of the person and personality
of the analyst as someone appropriately interested, caring, warm, and wishing
to be helpful at the beginning of treatment in order to establish the self-object
transferences that stabilize the treatment and make optimal therapeutic work

---

[74]S. FREUD, AN OUTLINE OF PSYCHOANALYSIS, *in* 23 STANDARD EDITION OF THE COMPLETE PSYCHO-
LOGICAL WORKS OF SIGMUND FREUD 141 (1964).

[75]*See, e.g.,* AM. PSYCHIATRIC ASS'N, A PSYCHIATRIC GLOSSARY 106 (6th ed. 1988) (hereinafter A PSYCHI-
ATRIC GLOSSARY); Adler, *Transference, Real Relationship and Alliance,* 61 INT'L J. PSYCHO-ANAL. 547,
547 (1980); Greenson, *The Working Alliance and the Transference Neurosis,* 34 PSYCHOANAL. Q. 155
(1965); Karasu, *Psychoanalysis and Psychoanalytic Psychotherapy, in* 2 COMPREHENSIVE TEXTBOOK OF
PSYCHIATRY 1442, 1446–47 (H. Kaplan & B. Sadock eds., 5th ed. 1989).

[76]*See* A PSYCHIATRIC GLOSSARY, *supra* note 75, at 106; Adler, *supra* note 75, at 548 ("[T]ransference
and alliance seem inextricably intermeshed.").

[77]Karasu, *supra* note 75, at 1446.

[78]*See* Adler, *supra* note 75, at 548; Friedman, *The Therapeutic Alliance,* 50 INT'L J. PSYCHOANAL. 139
(1969).

[79]S. FREUD, ANALYSIS TERMINABLE AND INTERMINABLE, *in* 23 THE COLLECTED WORKS OF SIGMUND
FREUD 233 (1937), *cited in* Adler, *supra* note 75, at 548.

[80]Karasu, *supra* note 75, at 1446.

possible."[81] Indeed, "[n]o analysis can proceed without the functioning of a rational, trusting therapeutic alliance."[82]

There is increasing recognition that the key to successful psychotherapy is the therapeutic alliance itself. The classical analytic concept of the psychotherapist–patient relationship envisioned the therapist as a neutral screen for the patient's transferential projections. But this concept has more recently been broadened to focus attention on the therapeutic value of the relationship itself. This broadening is often discussed as the "real relationship."[83] It represents more than a mere acknowledgement of the therapist's humanness, but also a recognition that what is transformative or curative in the therapeutic process is the actual, caring, human relationship between therapist and patient.[84] Thus, the therapeutic relationship itself is a therapeutic agent. To reach its therapeutic potential, the therapist must establish an environment of safety and trust.[85] A voluntary relationship in which the patient sees the therapist as his or her agent, assisting him or her to accomplish goals that the two of them define, rather than as a paternalistic director of the process, is more likely to create the atmosphere of trust and openness that is necessary for the therapeutic relationship to bring about healing and change.

A legal system in which the therapist needs the informed consent of the patient is thus more conducive to allowing the relationship itself to realize its potential as a therapeutic agent. An informed consent requirement, by encouraging a therapist–patient dialogue, can create a significant therapeutic opportunity. Discussion and negotiation about a patient's objections to treatment can provide an important context for probing conscious and unconscious resistance, for fostering a positive transference, and for earning the patient's trust and confidence.

A therapeutic relationship characterized by voluntariness rather than coercion is particularly important in the institutional contexts—hospital and

---

[81]Adler, *supra* note 75, at 553. *See also* Viederman, *The Real Person of the Analyst and his Role in the Process of Psychoanalytic Cure*, 39 J. AM. PSYCHOANALYTIC ASS'N 451, 457–58 (1991) (need for first phase of analysis to offer an environment of safety and trust in the therapist-patient relationship in order for the therapeutic potential of transference to be achieved). For a parallel perspective drawn from cognitive psychology, see BREHM & BREHM, *supra* note 7, at 151–53, 300–01; Deci & Ryan, *supra* note 17, at 70.

[82]Karasu, *supra* note 75, at 1449.

[83]*See, e.g.,* Adler, *supra* note 75.

[84]Personal communication from Daniel C. Silverman, M.D., Associate Psychiatrist In Chief, Beth Israel Hospital, Boston, Massachusetts, and Assistant Professor of Psychiatry, Harvard Medical School, Cambridge, Massachusetts, June 3, 1991. *See, e.g.,* Aaron, *The Patient's Experience of the Analyst's Subjectivity*, 1 PSYCHOANALYTIC DIALOGUE 29, 33 (1991) ("The relational approach that I am advocating views the patient-analyst relationship as continually established and re-established through ongoing mutual influences in which both patient and analyst systematically affect, and are affected by, each other. A communication process is established between patient and analyst in which influence flows in both directions."); *id.* at 41 (analysis viewed as co-participation); *id.* at 43 (analysis viewed as "mutual," with "both patient and analyst functioning as subject and object, as co-participants"); Adler, *supra* note 75 at 552–54; Binstock, *The Therapeutic Relationship*, 21 J. AM. PSYCHOANALYTIC ASS'N 543 (1973); Hoffman, *Discussion: Toward a Social-Constructivist View of the Psychoanalytic Situation*, 1 PSYCHOANALYTIC DIALOGUE 74, 75 (1991) (a real personal relationship and a mutual exploration of each one's perception of the analytical relationship creates the opportunity "for a special kind of affective contact with the analyst that is thought to have therapeutic potential").

[85]Karasu, *supra* note 75, at 1449; Viederman, *supra* note 81, at 548.

prison—in which the right to refuse treatment question most often arises. It is in these contexts that distrust of the therapist and concern about his conflicting allegiance to his institutional employer is at its highest. For therapy to be successful, the therapist or counselor must distance himself from the institution's security and management staff and functions. The institutional resident, accustomed to being treated as an object—as a means to the accomplishment of institutional ends—will naturally be suspicious and distrustful of therapists who treat him on a coercive basis. Providing therapy or counseling on a truly voluntary basis will provide a sharp contrast to the way the individual is treated by other institutional staff and can establish a climate that may allow the patient or offender to view his therapist as an ally. It can break down distrust and inspire confidence in and commitment to the therapeutic relationship, which can emerge as an oasis in the desert of institutional life.

These considerations favoring a therapeutic relationship based on voluntariness obviously have special force in the context of verbal psychotherapy or counseling. They also seem applicable, however, in the context of behavior therapy, many of the techniques of which, in order to succeed, require patient cooperation and involvement as well as trust and confidence in the therapist.[86] Moreover, although to a considerably lesser extent, these considerations may apply as well even in the context of the organic treatment techniques. Choosing the appropriate medication, for example, and maximizing the potential that it will be used appropriately, will often require communication with the patient and a high degree of cooperation.[87]

In all types of medical decisionmaking, allowing the patient to exercise choice inevitably enriches and improves the quality of the decisionmaking process.[88] Successful treatment planning and implementation require a thorough analysis of the patient's problems, of the social context that often perpetuates them, and of the patient's strengths and weaknesses. Patient trust, cooperation, and full and open communication are essential if the therapist is to obtain this information from the patient, who frequently is the best, if not the

---

[86] *See supra* note 13 and accompanying text.

[87] *See* Appelbaum & Gutheil, *supra* note 9, at 341. In addition, many of the organic treatment techniques, like psychotropic drugs, are not administered in isolation, but are part of an integrated treatment plan that involves verbal psychotherapy or counseling. In the case of schizophrenia or severe depression, for example, medication is needed to control symptoms that would prevent the patient from accepting other forms of therapy. Antipsychotic drugs that minimize the visual or auditory hallucinations or agitation that often characterize schizophrenia, and antidepressant drugs that control the severe withdrawal and feelings of worthlessness and profound sadness that often characterize major affective depression, are necessary to render the patient accessible to verbal, social, and occupational therapy approaches. Even if such medication would be effective in reducing severe symptomatology when administered coercively, the verbal therapy that should follow the reduction in symptoms would seem to be more effective to the extent that the individual chooses it voluntarily.

[88] *See* J. Katz, The Silent World of Doctor and Patient 102–03 (1984) (analyzing the informed consent doctrine as furthering the doctor-patient relationship); Cousins, *supra* note 22, at 55 ("[F]ull communication between the patient and physician is indispensable not just in arriving at an accurate diagnosis but in devising an effective strategy for treatment."); Altman, *Health Official Urges Focus by Doctors on Caring as well as Curing: A More Active Role for Patients is Recommended,* N.Y. Times, § 1, at 6, col. 3 (Aug. 15, 1993) ("Doctors need to consider their patients as knowledgeable allies, not as passive recipients of care, and involve them fully in the entire care process, including decision-making about treatment . . . .") (*quoting* Michael H. Merson, M.D., World Health Organization official).

only, source. Moreover, the aphorism "two heads are better than one" is especially apt in this context. Higher quality treatment decisionmaking is more likely when the therapist–patient dialogue, kept open by allowing the patient a legal right to participate in decisionmaking, produces the decision rather than the therapist making it unilaterally. Treatment decisionmaking often involves difficult value choices. How risks and benefits of alternative courses of treatment are weighed depends on the incentive preferences of the individual. The therapist will not always share the patient's values and preferences. Moreover, when the therapist is not the patient's long-term physician – as in mental institutions and prisons – he or she will be unaware of their absent dialogue. The doctor may "know best" about the clinical aspects of risks and benefits of alternative treatments.[89] However, the doctor cannot possess knowledge superior to that of the patient concerning the patient's preferences. Dialogue, although it may cost more in terms of therapist time, produces treatment decisionmaking that is more accurate and thus more likely to be efficacious. In addition, the patient is more likely to accept and comply with treatment when the decision is a product of a process in which he or she has participated.[90]

Conclusion

For all kinds of medical and psychological treatment there would seem to be strong therapeutic value in having a meaningful dialogic process between therapist and patient resulting in mutual decision-making. Such a process will enhance communication in the therapeutic relationship and increase the quality of clinical decisionmaking. It will also foster patient trust and confidence in the therapist, facilitating positive patient attitudes and expectancies that can play an important role in treatment success.

In a legal system that allows the therapist to make medical decisions unilaterally without patient participation and consent, a dialogic process would largely be unnecessary and would frequently be dispensed with. Recognizing a right to refuse treatment will foster the possibility of a meaningful dialogic process, thereby enhancing the potential that the therapist–patient relationship itself will serve as a therapeutic agent. Moreover, in a legal system that denies patients a right to refuse treatment, patients will be deprived of the opportunity to make treatment choices for themselves, and of the therapeutic advantages that seem to be associated with choice. A patient deprived of the right to choose against a particular treatment cannot exercise the kind of choice in favor of it that will engage the positive expectancies and intrinsic motivation that can be so important to a successful treatment response.

The right to refuse treatment, rather than frustrating treatment, may thus actually advance the goal of successful therapy and rehabilitation. Instead of viewing the right to refuse treatment with suspicion and patients who refuse treatment with contempt, therapists should understand the right to refuse as providing an important therapeutic opportunity. Indeed, a right to refuse treatment may be an indispensable condition to a meaningful therapeutic alliance.

---

[89]*But see* KATZ, *supra* note 88, at 166–69 (discussing the uncertainty inherent in medical science).

[90]*See* KATZ, *supra* note 88, at 103; MEICHENBAUM & TURK, *supra* note 9, at 63, 71–76, 84–85.

This theoretical analysis of the likely impact of recognizing a right to refuse treatment — and a corresponding opportunity of patients and offenders to choose it — strongly suggests that therapeutic values will be furthered by the reshaping of the therapist–patient relationship that will result from recognition of the right. Although empirical work is needed to test these assumptions and their applicability to seriously impaired patients, psychological and psychodynamic theory would seem to provide significant support for the recognition of a right to refuse treatment and for its effective implementation.

[6]

Advance Directives in Psychiatry

Resolving Issues of Autonomy and Competence

Janet Ritchie,* Ron Sklar,† and Warren Steiner†

Introduction

Advance directives have been championed and debated in the literature, es-poused by patient advocates, and incorporated or proposed in the majority of Canadian provinces and nearly every U.S. state. Advance directives allow in-dividuals to make decisions for future medical treatment while they are com-petent to do so in anticipation of future incompetence. While intuitively it would seem that advance directives are unquestionably beneficial to patients and their caregivers, and to the management of increasingly scarce health care resources, the issues raised by advance directives are complex. How these is-sues are understood will have practical implications for how advance direc-tives are implemented.

Advance directives originated from the Karen Ann Quinlan and Nancy Cruzan cases, which raised the issue of decision making regarding life-sustain-ing treatment when a patient has lost competence. In both cases, the focus was on making such decisions in a way that reflected the known wishes of the inca-pacitated patient rather than relying on doctors to make the decisions when the patient was no longer able to do so. In the literature, this has frequently been characterized as marking a trend toward patient autonomy as opposed to long-held Hippocratic paternalism whereby the doctor did what he presumed to be best for the patient. As in the Quinlan and Cruzan cases, loss of compe-tence for the medically ill patient is typically a chronic, irreversible condition arising from dementia, the end stages of severe illness, or a persisting vegeta-tive state.

However, there has been a growing interest in the special case of psychiatric patients, for whom loss of competence is more likely to be episodic. When pa-tients begin to decompensate as a result of a major psychiatric disorder—that

---

*Assistant Psychiatrist, Montreal General Hospital, Montreal, Quebec, Canada.

†Associate Professor, Faculty of Law, McGill University, Montreal, Quebec, Canada.

Address correspondence and reprint requests to Dr. Janet Ritchie, Department of Psychiatry, Montreal General Hospital, 1650 Cedar Ave., Montreal, Quebec, Canada, H3G 1A3.

is, become manic, psychotic, or significantly depressed—loss of competence may occur early on as insight and judgment become impaired. This can be an important obstacle to timely treatment because decisions made under these circumstances may not be what the person might have chosen at his baseline state. This includes decisions regarding hospitalization, medication, or even whether to show up for appointments. Although loss of competence can become a chronic state in psychiatric illness, more often it fluctuates with the periods of decompensation and remission that tend to characterize psychiatric illness. Advance directives therefore have the potential to be a particularly relevant and useful tool in psychiatry by allowing patients, when competent, to opt for treatment that they might refuse when their competence becomes impaired. They would be particularly useful for those patients who arrive at a point where they require treatment because their functioning has become severely impaired by their illness, who have lost the capacity to recognize this themselves, yet who have not decompensated to the point that they require civil commitment. By facilitating earlier intervention and treatment, these patients could potentially shorten the length of time they are decompensated and thereby lessen the hardship, both emotional and financial, for themselves and their families.

This specialized role for advance directives in psychiatry is captured in the name they have been given: *Ulysses* directives. This is the Latin name given to the hero of Homer's *Iliad*, who undertook a perilous 10-year voyage home with his men following the Trojan War. Their journey involved an encounter with the Sirens, notorious for their enchanted singing that had lured many an unwary sailor close, only to be shipwrecked upon the rocks on which they sang. Ulysses, longing to hear their song, sagely instructed his crew to stop up their ears with wax and to tie him firmly to the mast of his ship. Thus deafened, the crew would succumb neither to the enchantments of the Sirens nor to Ulysses's entreaties to sail toward them as he fell under their charms. Similarly, *Ulysses* directives, in the fullest sense, would allow the physician to heed the patient's prior competent instructions when these are at odds with the wishes expressed in a subsequent incompetent state.

The parallel with Ulysses's voyage is instructive in illustrating the intent of such directives: to circumvent refusal of treatment requested by a previously competent patient when this refusal is motivated by illness-induced incompetence. It also provides a metaphor for the hazards attendant on any attempt to incorporate advance directives into practice. As part of his voyage, Ulysses had to navigate his ship through a narrow strait flanked by two sea monsters, Scylla and Charybdis, who devoured whatever came within their reach. The Scylla and Charybdis of *Ulysses* directives are, paradoxically, the two concepts on which these directives are based: the principles of autonomy and competence. Most of the literature on advance directives, and all of the controversy the topic has stirred, has focused on one or both of these cardinal aspects.

Autonomy

The ideal of patient autonomy has been a driving force in the move toward advance directives. The essence of this notion is that the individual is an inde-

pendent being with the right to control his own fate by freely making choices
that pertain to his interests. The case of A. P. exemplifies this. A. P. was a 23-
year-old woman who had diagnosed herself as bipolar using the *Diagnostic
and Statistical Manual of Mental Disorders, Third Edition—Revised*. She had
never consulted a psychiatrist because her family had distrusted psychiatry
since her father's experience with insulin treatment and ECT decades ago.
However, she realized that both her hypomanic and her depressed phases
were becoming more extreme. She wanted to be able to work with a psychiatrist in such a way that she could exercise control over what happened to her.
She did not want treatment as yet, although she recognized that she was becoming depressed, but she wanted to know what was available if her depression worsened. Her fear was that her insight was becoming increasingly tenuous when she became depressed or hypomanic. She wanted her psychiatrist to
be alert to signs that she was decompensating and to intervene in ways that
would have been agreed to beforehand.

The concept of autonomy is compelling. It holds that the right to self-determination ought to be protected against infringement by others within the community based on the principle of egalitarianism. As Callahan (1984) has pointed
out, its moral precedence affords protection of fundamental values: of individual
rights and personal dignity against moral and political despotism; of minorities
against domination by majorities (p. 40). Autonomy, in a society that values
individualism and consumerism, is a forceful argument. There are, however,
potential problems in applying the concept of autonomy to advance directives.

First, the extent to which autonomy merits preeminence as a moral principle has been disputed. Wetle (1994) has wondered whether "the focus on individual autonomy in health care is both time and culture bound and may be a
luxury of modern Western economies" (p.S5). Callahan has argued that "making autonomy the central principle invites distortion; people invoke autonomy
to justify selfishness, to put their interests before others—especially if those
others are strangers" (1984, p. 41).

Underlying these observations is the fact that autonomy, and any instrument that symbolizes it including advance directives, has been championed as
a right. However, any right carries with it a concomitant responsibility even
though this may be honoured often as not in the breach. The right to vote, for
example, carries with it the responsibility to vote in an informed and rational
way. The responsibility may be incurred primarily (by the group accorded the
right) or secondarily (by those who have co-existing or interdependent rights).
Thus, the right to vote carries with it not only the primary responsibility of citizens to vote but the secondary responsibilities of politicians to conduct their
affairs openly and in accord with certain standards of behavior and decision
making (consistent with their right to seek office) and of the media to safeguard this process (consistent with their right to freedom of the press).

The "distortion" to which Callahan refers occurs not because autonomy has
been given a moral preeminence that is hypocritical or because it inherently
precludes consideration of co-existing rights but because it has been identified
solely as a right without the implied responsibility being acknowledged. The
pursuit of one person's autonomy inevitably has implications for another's autonomy. It is when this is overlooked that there is a risk of co-existing rights

being ignored. As Mappes has pointed out (Mappes & Zembaty, 1994) "the notion of autonomy as an egoistic concept is a distortion. Autonomy is neutral with respect to egoistic and altruistic concerns" (p. 30). Fundamentally, any moral value exists interdependently with other moral values and cannot be pursued exclusively without being itself undermined.

In the context of advance directives, patients' rights to autonomy are bound to be affected by and to impact upon at least three groups with whom patients have interdependent rights and duties: families or caregivers, whose needs and rights may be infringed by patients' decisions about treatment; society's duty to allocate scarce health care resources rationally; and the physician's duty to do no harm and to act in accord with standards of reasonableness. Just as in one's own life responsibilities tend to be recognized more clearly as one ages, the later literature on advance directives has been more inclined to acknowledge the presence of such co-existing rights. Brock (1994) has queried to what extent others' interests should receive direct consideration independent of whether the patient would have given weight to them. He cites both the financial and nonfinancial interests of the patient's family and of society at large. Dresser (1994) alludes to the issue of responsibility associated with advance directives when she addresses the issue that "arises when a competent patient made what now appears to be an unreasonable request for medical treatment. Even competent patients do not have an absolute right to choose treatment. No matter how strongly a patient desires it, physicians may refuse to administer ineffective treatment" (p. 634). Dresser raises the additional question of "when is treatment availability a matter of economics . . . ?" (p. 634).

These issues are particularly relevant to psychiatric treatment. For example, patients with schizophrenia, or their families, sometimes view clozapine as a "miracle drug." Such a patient may stipulate that should he decompensate, the only neuroleptic accepted would be clozapine. If this patient had a history of responding to other neuroleptics and had not been particularly bothered by their side effects, could such a stipulation be justified given the cost of clozapine and the present shape of government and hospital health care budgets?

Assume that this same patient revises his advance directive and now directs that in the event of psychosis no neuroleptic is to be used. The only treatment permitted by the revised advance directive is benzodiazepines. If such an advance directive is respected, the likelihood is that the patient's hospitalization will be significantly prolonged. Does the fact that the individual is prepared to bear the psychological cost of an extended psychosis impose on society or on the patient's family the obligation to shoulder the financial burden? If this individual is normally employed and has dependents, how are the needs and rights of his family and employer to be squared with those of the patient? Should the physician be required to give care that is less than what is indicated—that is, should a patient's wishes bind a physician to treat in a manner that the physician and/or the physician's peers would consider substandard or even negligent? What if the patient is known to be a benzodiazepine abuser? To what extent is there an obligation to make a responsible advance directive and according to what standard?

These are not easy questions to anticipate or respond to legislatively or by any institutionalized process. Any attempt to draw up guidelines would likely be extremely detailed and complicated, thus rendering advance directives inaccessible and/or tedious. To introduce a third party process to vet advance directives would be cumbersome, costly, and could arguably undermine the very autonomy that is being sought. In fact, the control will likely be exerted by the very process of completing and carrying out an advance directive. In practice, economic exigencies will be introduced whether or not the individual wishes to consider them. Hospitals and governments simply will not be able to or want to override their budgetary constraints for requests for expensive treatment that are unreasonable. Managed care has exemplified how economic considerations gain preeminence in practical terms. Patients who impose unduly on their families either financially or emotionally are likely to lose their support over time. Physicians may seek to have the advance directive overruled if the patient is already incompetent at the time this becomes an issue. While the patient is still competent, the physician can discuss with the patient the drawbacks, limitations, or benefit of treatment options. (In fact, ideally the drafting of an advance directive would be a process in which the patient involves both physician and family members.) Thus, it is unlikely that the concept of patient autonomy means that advance directives will undermine other moral principles to any significant extent in practice.

Paternalism Versus Partnership

A further difficulty with the autonomy argument is that it is not clear that autonomy in fact respects the patient. Katz (1977) observes that informed consent, the cornerstone upon which autonomy and advance directives rest, "evokes fairy-tale expectations that, once kissed by the doctrine, frog-patients will become autonomous princes." (p. 137). In essence, as Winick has so cogently put it (1994) this amounts to letting patients "rot with their rights on" (p. 99).

The autonomy argument, as it has typically been proposed, is fundamentally an adversarial argument. Autonomy faces off against what is referred to as "Hippocratic paternalism." This is evident from the literature, but it has also been reflected in the legislation. Nowhere is it clearer that advance directives are meant to protect patients from physician-as-paternalistic-entity than in Ontario's legislation, which specifically enjoins patients from appointing their physicians as their substitute decider. As the argument for advance directives has evolved, the clear implication appears to be that autonomy is morally good and paternalism is morally repugnant, serving to undermine the individual.

Again, the problem with this argument is its simplicity. There is a curious shift in nuance with the definition of "paternal" versus "paternalism." "Paternal" is defined as "of, like or characteristic of a father or fatherhood; fatherly." Rounding out this definition, "fatherly" is defined as "like, or characteristic of a father; *kindly; protective*" (italics added). Despite these benign roots, paternalism assumes a more sinister meaning: "the principle or system of governing or controlling . . . in a manner suggesting a father's relationship with his children." Gone is the sense of kindliness or protectiveness. Yet it is to the extent that we have retained the notion of kindliness and protectiveness that we endorse social programs, that we protect those among us who, for one reason or another, are unable to protect themselves. The paternalism of social programs is not always benign; the so-called paternalism of doctors is not always sinister.

Our society is consultation-oriented, and as much as it is fueled by consumerism it depends also on paternalism. We go to lawyers, doctors, plumbers seeking advice that reflects kindliness and protectiveness. We may know what we want a professional to do for us, but we depend on his advising us how and if it can be achieved with our best interests in mind. No profession is without individuals who fail to act in accord with paternal ideals. But doctors are no more likely to fall short in this regard than any other profession. Why, then, is Hippocratic paternalism regarded with so much more suspicion to the point that it is deemed preferable to allow an incompetent patient the right to overrule his prior competent wishes?

Dresser (1994) opines that "efforts to force . . . patients into the model of ourselves as autonomous decision-makers (seeking desperately to avoid their dire situations) distracts us from the real people before us. In consequence, we miss seeing who they are" (p. 612) or, perhaps, who we fear becoming. It may be that part of the deep distrust of doctors that is sometimes expressed when advance directives are advocated has to do with the near certainty that at some point in each of our lives the doctor will not be able to do our bidding—that is, make us better.

In fact, it is likely that many doctors are equally as uncomfortable with the notion of paternalism as are patients and their advocates, and that for most doctors the rewarding interactions with patients are those characterized by mutual participation in decision making. Moreover, the physician is an important source of information for the patient about the patient's illness and possible treatments and, in that sense, can act to promote the patients' autonomy. Information given defensively in an adversarial environment would be less likely to achieve this. As well, given that the person drawing up an advance directive is expected to be competent to make informed decisions about other aspects of his health care, it seems paternalistic in the most negative sense for governments—as in the example of Ontario's legislation—to assume that the person will not be competent to judge whether his physician can be trusted to fill that role. Such legislated restrictions of patient's freedom of choice are particularly relevant in psychiatry where a patient may have burned out, drifted away from, or otherwise lost family and other social supports and for whom the physician may be the most consistently present figure and the most likely to know the patient's wishes over time.

A case in point that demonstrates this, and that will be similar to what many clinicians have experienced in their practice, is that of J. L. J. L. is a 28-year-old man with a long-standing history of schizoaffective disorder, complicated by polysubstance abuse and, at best, erratic compliance with medications and follow-up. His father abandoned J. L. when he was young, and he reappears from time to time only to abandon J. L. again. J. L.'s mother is schizophrenic and has never accepted treatment. She hears voices telling her to kill J. L. Relatives have long since ended contact with both her and J. L. Although J. L. is intelligent and can be charming when he is well, he also sabotages treatment and placement plans. As he exhausts community resources, he changes cities. However, he invariably resurfaces at the hospital where his psychiatrist works.

It is his psychiatrist who has had the longest, most consistent alliance with him. J. L. has specifically stated when competent that when he decompensates he does not want either parent involved in his treatment and that he wants his psychiatrist to make all treatment decisions.

Essentially what is being described—what is implicit in the notion of advance directives and patient autonomy—is what Dresser (1984) has referred to as "self-paternalism." This concept holds "that everyone has a 'true' identity that is best equipped to make long-term decisions for the self and that an advance directive permits the state to enforce these wishes." (p. 15). It has been argued that it is difficult properly to make choices about treatment before one is in the situation where treatment is required. However, patients with major psychiatric disorders are likely to have had prior experience with their illness. Thus, their self-paternalism would be all the more informed.

Rather than being opposing values, the concepts of autonomy and paternalism have potentially complementary roles in advance directives. This is suggested by studies showing that autonomy may not necessarily be what patients want respected in health care decisions. Sehgal et al.'s survey of dialysis patients (1992) asked whether they would want their physician and surrogate to override their advance directive if this was judged to be in their best interests. Sixty-one percent said they would, with 31% saying they should have complete leeway to do so. Of those who had advance directives already completed, 40% did not want them adhered to strictly. Patients wanted several factors considered in determining their best interests: quality of life (88%); possibility of new treatment (88%); the indignity caused by continued treatment (84%); and the financial impact of continued treatment on their family (78%). Interestingly, patients with a history of severe illness other than their renal illness were particularly likely to want this leeway: Only one out of 11 patients with a history of cancer and one out of 12 patients with a history of cerebrovascular accident wanted their advance directives strictly followed.

A study by Singer, Choudry, and Armstrong (1993) shows a similar, though less marked tendency. This random telephone survey of 1,000 adult residents of Ontario showed that 77% would want their substitute decision-maker to follow their wishes exactly versus 16% who would want their substitute to do what they thought best. Women were more likely to want their wishes followed, whereas men were more likely to want substitutes to make decisions judged to be in their best interests. Given that Sehgal's population comprised individuals who were actively receiving medical treatment, it would be interesting to know whether this made them more likely to want their best interests followed than Singer's population.

Perhaps even more telling is the fact that in the United States relatively few individuals have completed advance directives despite the legislation that exists. Since 1990, the Patient Self-Determination Act requires health providers to inquire whether patients have advance directives, to inform them of their right to complete such a document, and to educate them about doing so. Nonetheless, it is estimated that only 15 to 20% of individuals in the United States have completed advance directives. Various researchers have pointed out that this is not very different from the percentage of people who have made wills (Dresser, 1984; Jacobson et al., 1994; Molloy, Clarnette, Braun,

Eisemann, and Sneiderman, 1991; Sugarman, 1994), suggesting that it is not likely to change significantly.

If advance directives are seen as a prerequisite for patient autonomy, these figures may be disappointing. However, it may be more realistic to see advance directives as part of an evolution toward patients choosing to become more involved in their health care, both having the right to participate in treatment choices and the responsibility to do so. In this context, advance directives can be viewed as facilitating a process whereby both patient and physician can, over time, arrive at mutually held treatment goals and considerations. In consequence, the physician–patient relationship is likely to become more mutually satisfying and productive. Advance directives can also facilitate this kind of discussion over time between patients and their families. Whether advance directives are actually completed, the fact that they exist and are becoming more familiar concepts is likely, at the very least, to promote "advance dialogue," which can only facilitate the process of requesting, receiving, and giving care.

Competence

Whereas autonomy has provided a philosophical context for advance directives, their practical implementation depends on notions of competence. Advance directives will be triggered when the patient is deemed incompetent. However, precisely when the line is crossed from competence to incompetence is unclear.

Definitions of Competence

One way of resolving this has been to attempt to define competence, and there are in consequence myriad definitions of competence. Appelbaum and Grisso (1988) have summarized legal standards of competence as tending to involve one or more of four capacities: the ability to communicate a choice; the ability to understand information relevant to a decision about treatment; the ability to appreciate a situation and its implications; and the ability to consider both advantages and risks associated with a decision.

In jurisprudence and legislation, competence is often defined in negative terms; that is, the question arises (in jurisprudence) or is envisaged (in legislation) in the context of a dispute over a patient's refusal of treatment. Thus, for example, Minnesota jurisprudence regarding refusal of psychiatric treatment has relied on the "Beck criteria" whereby competence is established only if the patient meets three criteria: the patient must be aware of having a mental disorder, must have sufficient knowledge about medications and mental disorder, and must not have refused treatment because of delusional beliefs (Cuca, 1993). The meaning of "sufficient" is presumably a question of jurisprudence. Whereas the Beck criteria place emphasis on reality-based knowledge and appreciation of one's state, other definitions of competence focus on how the patient's knowledge is applied to his treatment choice. In the District of Columbia, a person is considered "incapacitated" who "lacks sufficient mental capacity to appreciate the nature and implications of a health care decision, make a choice regarding the alternatives presented or communicate that choice in an unambiguous manner" (Epstein, Martins, Crowley, and Pennanen, 1994). Similarly, Ontario's Consent to Treatment Act defines a patient as "capable" if he "is able to understand the information that is relevant to making a decision concerning the treatment and able to appreciate the reasonably foreseeable consequences of a decision or lack of a decision."

Physicians Versus the Courts as Arbiters of Competence

Closely, and perhaps inextricably linked to the question of what competence (or incompetence) is, is the question of who ought to decide competence with regard to advance directives. Cuca (1993) in effect lays down the gauntlet by declaring that determination of competence to consent is the court's most important function in cases about disputed treatment decisions and is "the one the courts are least likely to surrender." Consistent with this, MacKay (1989) observes that mental health legislation reform has tended to shift authority from the psychiatrist to the legal profession. A study by Markson, Kern, Annas, and Glantz (1994) lends support to such a trend. This study surveyed various medical specialists—internists, surgeons, and psychiatrists—about an actual case of an elderly diabetic woman who refused a life-saving below-the-knee-amputation. The trial court found her incompetent based on expertise provided by a psychiatrist. The appeals court overturned this decision. Markson's survey asked medical specialists to decide for themselves the issue of competence in three stages: first, on the basis of the patient's medical history; then taking into account the patient's rationale for refusing treatment; and finally adding the psychiatrist's opinion. As well, the physicians were tested about their knowledge of standards of competence. The study found that most physicians knew the standard for competence but applied it incorrectly both at a theoretical and a practical level. Psychiatrists did not perform significantly better than other specialists, answering correctly only half the time about whether a demented patient could be considered competent. Moreover, psychiatric expertise swayed most physicians to accept the trial court's decision that was later overturned. Based on these findings, Markson et al. (1994) dispute whether competence should be considered a clinical decision and caution that in cases of competency "courts should not rely on expert opinion and perhaps should not even ask for it." Essentially, the conclusion calls into question physicians' ability to assess competence.

However, the physicians surveyed were labouring at a disadvantage. First, they were not in the court and so did not hear the information firsthand, which may have introduced a bias. It would be very difficult to make—and difficult to defend—a decision about competence made by a physician who did not actually meet with the patient. Certainly, it precluded these physicians from asking any questions they might have wanted to ask of either the patient or the psychiatrist to clarify issues. Second, it is unlikely that the physicians surveyed could have devoted the hours necessary to deliberate such a complex case removed from their own clinical practice.

These biases were largely circumvented in a study by Bean, Nishiscito, Rector, and Glancy (1996) in two ways. First, this study surveyed only health professionals and lawyers who had demonstrated a specific interest in competence issues. Second, they were all third parties to the cases under discussion. They were asked to give their opinions about the competence of five patients who had been referred for ECT and who had been evaluated both by an attending physician and by a competency evaluation scale developed by the authors (Competency Interview Schedule); one patient had also been assessed for competency by the regional review board. In the opinion of the researchers, one patient was clearly competent, one was clearly incompetent, and the competence of the remaining three was less clear. Health professionals and lawyers agreed overwhelmingly about the two clear-cut cases (over 90%). They were consistent in their assessments of two out of the remaining three patients whose competence was more questionable. With regard to one of these patients, most lawyers (75%) and health professionals (75%) agreed with the attending physician that the patient was incompetent. With regard to the second of these two patients, the majority of health professionals (67%) and lawyers (84%) disagreed with the attending physician and concluded that the patient was incompetent. The fifth patient provoked more dissension. This patient had been found incompetent both by the attending physician and the regional review board. Whereas 75% of health professionals agreed with this assessment, only 42% of lawyers agreed.

This study shows that neither physicians nor the courts are likely to prove infallible in deciding disputed cases of competence with regard to advance directives. As Ho has pointed out, it is in the "gray zone of 'marginal' capacity" where the issue of competence becomes contentious (1995); clear-cut cases are likely to be as clear-cut for physicians as for lawyers.

In contentious cases, the courts may offer the appearance of neutrality and of recourse because of the possibility that a decision can be appealed. However, the inherent delays may render the dispute moot. If a patient has an advance directive consenting to treatment, then decompensates and refuses treatment, the issue of competence must be decided in determining whether to abide by the advance directive or whether it should be overruled by the refusal. If a verdict is reached by the court and appealed by either side, the length of time that will have elapsed will likely mean that the patient will be beyond the point where treatment could offer the initially anticipated benefit.

Moreover, one of the implications of relying exclusively on the courts to decide competence in contested cases is precisely that this invites no more than the application of a standard of competence. It can be argued that by applying such a standard, the court ensures that its decision is impartial, objective, and consistent from case to case. It is not so clear, however, that this facilitates an assessment of competence that is either sufficiently comprehensive or clinically useful.

The difficulty with developing a standard of competence is reflected in the number of definitions that exist. One problem with these definitions is that in attempting to devise a standard of competence they focus on a decision made at a given point in time—that is, they adopt a cross-sectional as opposed to a longitudinal perspective. As a result, there is a loss of context that diminishes the usefulness of the standard. Appelbaum and Grisso (1988) allude to this when they point out that courts have tended to focus on outcome (the patient's disputed treatment decision) rather than on process (the way this decision has been reached).

One of the crucial aspects of process with regard to advance directives is the person's psychological state. Inasmuch as competence is essentially a cognitive capacity, reflecting the individual's ability to process, evaluate, and apply information (Epstein et al., 1994), assessment of competence must entail evaluation of the psychological status of the individual. Various authors have noted that psychiatric illness is likely to impact significantly on an individual's cognitive abilities (Appelbaum & Grisso, 1988; Epstein et al., 1994; Kapp, 1994; Sullivan & Youngner, 1994). Although the more blatant effects of psychiatric illness, such as delusions and hallucinations, may be relatively easily recognized when they are present, more subtle impairment may be obscured by decision-making that, superficially, may appear to be competent. Sullivan and Youngner (1994) have pointed out that the depressed patient may make a treatment decision that would meet criteria for competence but that may nonetheless be qualitatively different from the decision he would make if he were not depressed. Feelings of guilt, worthlessness, helplessness, or hopelessness may lead depressed patients to have a distorted perspective about themselves and their significant others. Such a patient may therefore underestimate his prognosis or the probability that he can be helped by medication. This is exemplified in the case of L. D., a health care worker who realized that she was depressed and who was able to discuss the value of medication for depression in a way that was clearly knowledgeable. Furthermore, she showed no evidence of delusional beliefs or any other psychotic symptoms. However, her depression had proven refractory to various treatment modalities and she had incorporated this refractoriness into her negative self-image. When lithium was proposed to potentiate the effect of her antidepressant, she refused because she interpreted the fact that she had not been helped by first-line treatment as further evidence of how worthless she was.

Given that psychiatric diagnosis is often subtle, and that in the majority of patients whose competence is unclear it becomes all the more important to assess psychological factors carefully, there would be a risk that patients would be ill-served by the snapshot assessment of competence that the courts afford. When competence is subject to clinical decision, assessment of competence is more likely to represent part of a process. This will invariably be the case between the patient and the treating physician, who will likely have had time to come to know the patient and to develop a therapeutic alliance that can enrich a determination of competence. A. P., the patient described earlier in the Autonomy section, illustrates this. At the present time she has opted not to receive treatment. Under the circumstances, she clearly met any standard for competence. She fulfilled Beck's criteria in that she recognized that she had an illness (so well that she had correctly diagnosed herself); she had adequate information about both the diagnosis (having both experienced and read about bipolar disorder) and the treatment options (she also knew about mood stabilizers, antidepressants, and their most common side effects); and her refusal of treatment was not based on delusional beliefs. Moreover, her decision has been consistent over successive meetings.

However, in the course of her drawing up an advance directive with her psychiatrist a therapeutic alliance developed. She revealed that her decision to refuse treatment had been based partly on a fear that she would otherwise be betraying her father, who was opposed to psychiatric intervention. Moreover, her parents had, since her father's unfortunate experience with treatment, coped with his illness by denying it existed. She had managed to keep her own illness secret as well, and one of her ways of doing so was not to seek psychiatric help.

Thus, the treating physician will, over time, gain information that would be invaluable in assessing competence in the context of advance directives. While this is not to argue that determination of competence ought to be exclusively the preserve of medicine, it is important that physicians with specific expertise be involved in the process. If there is a dispute about whether a patient is competent either to make or to retract an advance directive about treatment—and the dispute concerns a treatment issue sufficiently important to the patient's well-being that the physician feels it must be pursued—the dispute should be resolved in a forum most nearly likely to be able to pay attention to process as well as to outcome.

The other difficulty with relying on a court-imposed standard of competence is the question of its clinical usefulness. A reliance on the courts to solve competency cases could result in undue "judicialization of psychiatry" with the risk of slow, tortuous, and expensive legal procedures. Moreover, the adversarial nature of the court system could undermine whatever therapeutic alliance exists between patient and physician.

An Alternative Model

A model that could be adapted to address both definitional and therapeutic concerns raised by advance directives is provided by provincial boards of review that already exist to assess psychiatric patients who have been committed to hospital after being found unfit to stand trial for criminal charges because of their psychiatric state. These boards are required to comprise at least one lawyer and one psychiatrist, with a third position filled by either another lawyer or another psychiatrist depending on availability. Their purpose is to ascertain whether the patient, having received treatment, has become fit to stand trial or, if charges have been dropped, has ceased to be a danger to others and can be discharged from hospital. Their sources are the treating physician and the patient, as well as persons the patient may wish to have present (for example, a lawyer and/or family member). Every effort is made by the board to develop a rapport with the patient and to understand how the patient perceives his situation and to what degree the patient shows insight and reasonable judgment. Although the sessions are taped and the hearings are formal, by comparison to a court setting they are less imposing and much less adversarial. Typically, if a decision is made that runs counter to what the patient has hoped for, the tribunal discusses the reasons for this decision with the patient.

There are several advantages to implementing such a process. First, it permits both psychiatric and legal input, with both on an equal footing and each contributing to the other's understanding and assessment. Second, the setting is likely to be less intimidating for the patient. Third, the patient can avail himself of this process without necessarily having to undertake the expense of a formal court proceeding. Fourth, the onus is on tribunal members to ensure they understand the perspective of the patient; neither the patient nor the physician would be required to argue for or against the patient's stated treatment wish. The hearing would be about opposing points of view concerning competence (to request or refuse treatment) and not about opposing interests or parties. Such a process has the potential to help both patient and physician to understand their differing perspectives. There would, therefore, be less chance that the therapeutic relationship would be damaged and, in fact, a reasonable chance it might be enhanced. Fifth, the patient would have similar protections to those provided in the court system: the right to have a lawyer present and the possibility of applying to the tribunal to reconsider his or her competence.

Implications for Ulysses Directives

The question of competence is equally important, but less often discussed, at the time an advance directive is completed. This is particularly relevant in the context of psychiatric patients and *Ulysses* directives. Roth (1982) and others have pointed out that there is a legal presumption of competence for adults. Appelbaum and Grisso (1988) have shown that this presumption of competence for adults applies equally in medicine. However, given the chronicity and fluctuation of the major psychiatric disorders and the binding decision that the *Ulysses* directive would impose on the future potentially incompetent patient, it is unreasonable to presume prior competence.

There are two possible safeguards. One, suggested by Wenger and Halpern (1994), is that the physician should be required to document the patient's competence at the time an advance directive is completed, and that this should be noted on the document. The advantages of this are twofold. First, this would encourage the patient to raise the issue of an advance directive with his physician. Such a dialogue would enable the physician to be aware of the patient's wishes and to provide information about prognosis and treatment alternatives that would be useful to the patient's decision making. Second, it would ensure that the document was transportable. The patient would not feel obliged to remain with the physician to avoid future questions about his competence at the time of drafting the advance directive. The other safeguard follows from the findings of Sehgal and Singer. That is, that the advance directive form be drafted to permit the patient to stipulate whether, in the event that he or she becomes incompetent, the patient's proxy would be mandated to override the treatment decisions in the advance directive if it was judged that to do so would be in the patient's best interest.

The Limits to Incompetence

A more thorny issue arises in the situation where the patient refuses treatment, is found to be incompetent, has an advance directive or a substituted judgment consenting to treatment, but is not committable so that he can be given treatment involuntarily. If advance directives, and *Ulysses* directives in particular, are to be effective, the legislation supporting them needs to be strong enough to ensure they can provide the protection asked of them. It will otherwise prove easier to ensure that the competent wishes of the patient to refuse treatment are carried out than to treat the resistant but incompetent patient in accord with his or her competent wishes. This is demonstrated by the case of S. M., a 50-year-old divorced woman who lived alone. Her three children reported to her physician that her behavior had become increasingly odd, paranoid, and disruptive. Because of their efforts, she was admitted to hospital where she was diagnosed with delusional disorder, persecutory type. She showed no insight into her disorder and refused treatment. Her children, however, were very concerned and felt she required treatment. She was assessed by the physician and deemed incompetent to refuse treatment. Her family supported this decision. As required by the legislation in Ontario, where this occurred, S. M. was advised that she had been declared incompetent and was informed of her right to contest this. She did so but the review board concurred with her family and physician that she was incompetent. One of her daughters agreed to act as a substitute decision-maker. However, the patient refused to remain in hospital and, because she was not commitable in the traditional sense of posing a danger to herself or others, she was discharged (Hong, 1995).

One way around this would be to amend civil commitment laws to allow a patient to be hospitalized involuntarily in such a situation. To ensure that such powers are used only in clear-cut cases, patients should have to stipulate in writing in their advance directive (not merely by checking off a box) that they want this recourse used if they refuse treatment when they are incompetent.

If such a measure is not implemented, there is a very real risk that advance directives in which patients request treatment may, in practice, become largely irrelevant except for the minority of patients who become commitable because they decompensate to the point of becoming a danger to themselves or others. Patients who refuse the treatment they have previously requested when competent, but who do not decompensate to the point of being commitable, may well find that their advance directives as useful as the emperor's new clothes.

Conclusion and Recommendations

Advance directives have the potential to alter the traditional patient–physician relationship in significant and positive ways by allowing patients to exercise greater autonomy over their treatment decisions. The effect of advance directives in psychiatry may be significant financial and nonfinancial savings at an individual, family, and societal level if patients are able to opt for earlier treatment and choose to do so. The goal of advance directives is twofold: to ensure that patients are treated in accordance with their wishes and to facilitate a more informed and open dialogue between patients and their physicians. To achieve this, it is recommended that legislation regarding advance directives specifically consider the case of psychiatric patients and include the following:

1. that advance directives be signed by both patient and physician to ensure that there has been dialogue between them and that there is a mutual understanding of the patient's treatment wishes;
2. that patients indicate in their advance directive whether they wish their treatment decisions to be overridden if this is considered to be in their best interest. Their advance directive should specify who the patient entrusts with determining his best interest (e.g., substitute decision-maker, a specified health professional or quorum of family members);
3. that the physician signing the advance directive indicate whether the patient is deemed competent at the time of signing;
4. that disputes regarding competence or best interest be referred to a board. This board should comprise a psychiatrist and a lawyer, with a third member drawn from either the medical or legal profession as available. There should be a roster of tribunal members who can be called upon to ensure that those asked to decide a particular case are not directly implicated in the patient's care. As well, the composition of tribunal should be fluid—for example, changing monthly—to ensure pluralism. Cases could be resubmitted if circumstances change;
5. that patients specify in their advance directives whether they agree in advance to be hospitalized and treated involuntarily should they refuse the treatment specified in their advance directive while incompetent.

These recommendations, which are specific to the special case of advance directives in psychiatry, optimize the means for ensuring that both autonomy and competency concerns are respected.

References

Appelbaum, P. S., & Grisso, T. (1988). Assessing patients' capacities to consent to treatment. *New England Journal of Medicine, 319*, 1635–1638.

Bean, G., Nishiscito, S., Rector, N. A., & Glancy, G. (1996). The assessment of competence to make a treatment decision: An empirical approach. *Canadian Journal of Psychiatry, 41*, 85–92.

Brock, D. W. (1994). Good decision-making for incompetent patients. *Hastings Center Report, 24*, S8–S11.

Callahan, D. (1984). Autonomy: A moral good not a moral obsession. *Hastings Center Report, 14*, 40–42.

Cuca, R. (1993). Ulysses in Minnesota: first steps toward a self-binding psychiatric advance directive statute. *Cornell Law Review, 78*, 1152–1186.

Dresser, R. (1984). Bound to treatment: The Ulysses contract. *Hastings Center Report, 14*, 13–16.

Dresser, R. (1994). Missing persons: Legal perceptions of incompetent patients. *Rutgers Law Review, 46*, 609–719.

Epstein, S. A., Martins, E., Crowley, M. A., & Pennanen, M. F. (1994). The use of an advance directive in consultation-liaison psychiatry: A case report. *International Journal of Psychiatry in Medicine, 24*, 371–376.

Ho, V. (1995). Marginal capacity: The dilemmas faced in assessment and declaration. *Canadian Medical Association Journal, 152*, 259–263.

Hong, W. H. (1995, October 3). Psychiatric patient "fell through the cracks." *The Medical Post, 14*.

Jacobson, J. A., et al. (1994). Patients' understanding and use of advance directives. *Western Journal of Medicine, 160*, 232–236.

Kapp, M. B. (1994). Implications of the Patient Self-Determination Act for psychiatric practice. *Hospital and Community Psychiatry, 45*, 355–358.

Katz, J. (1977). Informed consent—a fairy tale? Law's vision. *University of Pittsburgh Law Review, 39*, 137–174.

MacKay, M. J. (1989). Financial and personal competence in the elderly: The position of the Canadian Psychiatric Association. *Canadian Journal of Psychiatry, 34*, 829–832.

Mappes, T. A., & Zembaty, J. S. (1994). Patient choices, family interests and physician obligations. *Kennedy Institute of Ethics Journal, 4*, 27–46.

Markson, L. J., Kern, O. C., Annas, G. J., & Glantz, L. H. (1994). Physician assessment of patient competence. *Journal of the American Geriatric Society, 42*, 1074–1080.

Molloy, D. W., Clarnette, R. M., Braun, E. A., Eisemann, M. R., & Sneiderman, B. (1991). Decision-making in the incompetent elderly: "The daughter from California syndrome." *Journal of the American Geriatric Society, 39*, 396–399.

Roth, L. H. (1982). Informed consent and its applicability for psychiatry. *Psychiatry: Social, Epidemiological and Legal Psychiatry, 3*, 1–17.

Sehgal, A., et al. (1992). How strictly do dialysis patients want their advance directives followed? *JAMA, 267*, 59–63.

Singer, P. A., Choudry, S., & Armstrong, J. (1993). Public opinion regarding consent to treatment. *Journal of the American Geriatric Society, 41*, 112–116.

Sugarman, J. (1994). Recognizing good decision-making for incapacitated patients. *Hastings Center Report, 24*, S11–S13.

Sullivan, M. D., & Youngner, S. J. (1994). Depression, competence, and the right to refuse lifesaving medical treatment. *American Journal of Psychiatry, 151*, 971–978.

Wenger, N. S., & Halpern, J. (1994). The physician's role in completing advance directives: Ensuring patients' capacity to make healthcare decisions in advance. *Journal of Clinical Ethics, 5*, 320–323.

Wetle, T. (1994). Individual preferences and advance directives. *Hastings Center Report, 24*, S5–S8.

Winick, B. J. (1994). The right to refuse mental health treatment. *International Journal of Law and Psychiatry, 17*, 99–117.

Advocacy

[7]

Protection and advocacy: an ethics practice in mental health

D. P. OLSEN RN PhD

Assistant Professor, Psychiatric Mental Health Nursing, Yale University School of Nursing, 100 Church Street South, PO Box 9740, New Haven, CT 06536-0740, USA

Correspondence:
D. P. Olsen
Yale University School of Nursing
100 Church Street South
PO Box 9740
New Haven
CT 06536-0740
USA

OLSEN D.P. (2001) *Journal of Psychiatric and Mental Health Nursing* 8, 121–128
Protection and advocacy: an ethics practice in mental health

This paper reports the findings of investigations into allegations of patient abuse and the implications for policy and practice. These investigations were carried out by a nurse with a background in ethics for the office of Protection and Advocacy for Individuals with Mental Illness (PAIMI), a state agency operating under a United States federal law entitling it to investigate complaints by psychiatric patients. PAIMI uses investigations both to help individuals and to provide an avenue for broader change. There are four steps in the investigation process: (1) definition of the problem; (2) gathering information; (3) synthesis; and (4) addressing the problem. Cases are presented to illustrate the investigation process and identify ethical issues arising in mental health treatment. Among the issues raised are autonomy and forced treatment, deinstitutionalization, bias against the mentally ill, privacy, and surrogate treatment decisions. Resolutions range from providing individual advice to clients or clinicians, to changes in institutional policy and the publication of guidelines for specific situations. The following lessons were learnt from the investigations: (1) tell patients what to expect; (2) pay attention to the process of giving care; (3) allow patients to feel ambivalent about treatment; and (4) work to develop good relationships; underlying every investigation has been a poor relationship.

Keywords: advocacy, ethics, humane treatment, law

Accepted for publication: 10 August 2000

Introduction

Insights into ethical and treatment issues in mental health nursing practice are revealed through the examination of investigations into allegations of poor treatment and abuse made by psychiatric patients. The process of investigation including: (1) definition of the problem; (2) gathering information; (3) synthesis; and (4) addressing the problem, is discussed and then four specific cases are presented. Finally, the four lessons that can be drawn from these and other investigations are reviewed.

The State of Connecticut, in the United States, maintains an Office of Protection and Advocacy for Persons with Disabilities administering the federal Americans with Disabilities Act (ADA) which mandates fair treatment for persons with disabilities, including appropriate workplace accommodations (House Report from the Education & Labor Committee 1990; USCS 1993) and promoting advocacy activities throughout the state. One division of this office is Protection and Advocacy for Individuals with Mental Illness (PAIMI). In addition to the ADA, PAIMI operates under a separate federal statute entitling it to investigate complaints of abuse and 'pursue administrative, legal and other appropriate remedies to ensure the protection of individuals with mental illness' (USCS 1986). This investigatory authority extends to the access of any records pertaining to the reported abuse or other treatment problems.

PAIMI assists the individuals making complaints to achieve solutions or redress, but also takes as its mission the use of these complaints as a springboard to influence practice and policy at the broadest level possible in the context of the individual case. The investigations described here were conducted by a psychiatric nurse with expertise in ethics. PAIMI refers to the persons it serves as clients rather than patients as this is more descriptive of the relationship. In this paper, the term patient is used to refer to persons receiving health care services.

The investigation process

Investigations are initiated when a complaint is filed by a patient in psychiatric treatment, a family member, or another concerned third party on behalf of a specific patient. At this point PAIMI begins working with the complainant as a client and evaluating the background and nature of the complaint with an eye towards avenues of redress.

Definition of the problem

The first task is to understand the nature of the complaint. Although clients contact PAIMI directly to report problems, the specific problem is not always obvious; frequently clients sense disrespect or poor treatment, but have trouble articulating a problem beyond these feelings.

In defining the problem, the investigator needs to balance the potential to be overly restrictive in the scope of the inquiry with the potential to be over-inclusive. If the inquiry is too restrictive, serious problems can be overlooked and if over-inclusive the inquiry can become a witch hunt. The investigator should be open to problems that extend beyond the specific complaint because clients are not privy to aspects of treatment outside the context of their interactions with providers, such as charting and policies. Clients may lack knowledge of treatment and thus be unaware of treatment techniques that were overlooked or inappropriately or poorly applied. In one of the cases discussed in this paper, the client complained of being in locked seclusion for too long. The investigation found that the client was being video monitored without her knowledge. The client was more upset about this than the original complaint. In another case, the problem was specifically presented as a possible mistaken diagnosis, but the investigation showed that the client's difficulty stemmed from deinstitutionalization.

Hospitals are rarely happy to have their clinical care investigated by an outside agency. This problem is exacerbated when the scope of the investigation is inappropriately broad, thereby threatening the possibility of finding a voluntary and equitable solution. Although PAIMI is aware that its function is to uncover problems in treatment, the organization works hard to maintain a spirit of reasonable co-operation with institutions in order to discover and correct problems. Towards this end the investigators should be aware of certain realities that experience reveals about the clinical situation:

1 Even the best treatment does not always turn out well;
2 Patient expectations can be unrealistic;
3 Sometimes forced treatment is appropriate;
4 Documentation is rarely ideal; and
5 'Good' treatment given in the context of a bad relationship may still be experienced negatively.

As an experienced psychiatric nurse, the author/investigator brings a clinical authority to distinguishing inappropriate care from care that was appropriate, but with which the client was unhappy. This is helpful in the effort to be perceived as a fair and balanced investigator.

Gathering information

There are two aspects to information about a report, defining the incident and appreciating the context. The fullest exploration of the situation comes with a broad understanding of the client, as a person, and the circumstances surrounding the complaint. In addition to reading all available records and pertinent institutional policies, investigators should talk directly with the involved parties, including the client, the client's family and friends, and the clinicians whenever possible. Touring the site of the incident can also provide experiential insight that cannot otherwise be obtained. In a typical investigation, some pieces of information will be unavailable. Some people, either providers, clients or family members may be unavailable, reluctant to talk, or unable to be interviewed for other reasons. In addition, some of the written record may be destroyed or unobtainable. Every investigation is a compromise between what is ideal and what is feasible.

In gathering information about a complaint, the first goal is to build the most objective picture possible of the situation regarding what happened and when. A written timeline can be useful when there are many separate events or events occurring over a period of time. Areas of specific disagreement between parties should be identified when sorting out the 'facts' as presented from several sources.

The clinical record is helpful to determine a timeline of events such as the medications taken, but should be interpreted as the provider's perspective and not simply an objective record. Understood to be the provider's perspective, the clinical notes reveal insights into the quality of the interaction with the client. For example, in the nurse's notes comments like, 'whines a lot' or 'almost daring us' reveal problems in the nurse–patient relationship.

Assessing the context is the second goal of information gathering. The context is defined not only by facts, such as diagnosis and prior hospitalizations, but by an appreciation of the situation from the client's perspective. The investigator's role as advocate puts great emphasis on subjective realization of the client's position. A deep appreciation of how and why the client feels wronged, outside any criteria of 'objective reasonableness', combined with a knowledge of the 'facts', is the final point of information gathering.

Synthesis

Recognizing that every complaint arises from a client's sense of being treated poorly, and regardless of other factors, constitutes a problem. A statement synthesizing the client's perception, the provider's perception, and the facts, is the task of this stage of an investigation. Potential distortions stemming from the client's pathology are considered along with clinical and institutional system problems identified in the investigation. Assessing the treatment documented in relation to clinical standards is also essential. A synthesis should also attempt to identify the sources of divergence between client and clinician accounts of the quality of care and respect shown for the client's humanity.

The endpoint of this stage is a fair statement of the problems identified in the investigation. The conclusions of the investigation should follow logically from a discussion of the information gathered. A discussion should show how the complaints evolved from the interaction of a specific client in a particular context. Specific findings may include breaches in the treatment standard, failure to follow established policies, inadequate policies, and problems in the provider–patient relationship.

At this point, it is appropriate to address the ethical principles and norms that determine the form of the problem. The investigator with a knowledge of health care ethics can go beyond listing problems to illuminating how an action or attitude enhances or diminishes the rights and humanity of the client.

Addressing the problem

Problems identified in the investigation are addressed at two levels: the specific concerns of the client, and action to prevent similar problems in the future. Investigations may offer recommendations for improving clinical care, ranging from specific treatment advice, to the suggestion that a clinical consultation is needed. Often many of the client's problems can be addressed through education. An investigator with clinical expertise may discern a destructive pattern in the therapeutic relationship and recommend a consultation from an outside expert. However, it is inappropriate to move into the role of consultant to the therapy after being an investigator.

When the findings from the investigation indicate a correctable problem within the institution, these findings are shared and the institution is invited to respond. Generally, these changes involve a change in policy or procedure. Representatives of PAIMI and clients, when appropriate, meet with members of the institution and a solution acceptable to all is negotiated.

When the problem constitutes a serious abuse where the force of law is needed to compel change, or when the client is entitled to material compensation, PAIMI assists the client in a lawsuit. PAIMI also considers legal action when existing law requires change, and initiates class action when there is the potential to improve conditions for an entire category of clients.

Examples of investigations

These case reports include a synopsis of the investigation resulting from the investigative process as described above, follow-up on the results of PAIMI's actions including the concerns sent to the hospital as appropriate, and an analysis of the issues in terms of health care ethics.

Case one: Ms B

The investigation

Ms B is a 35-year-old woman with a professional job whose depression has waxed and waned in intensity for many years. At the time of this incident she had been off her antidepressant medication for about 3 weeks as a clearance period prior to trying a new antidepressant. At that time her depression was particularly strong and worsening. A difficult employment situation had further exacerbated her feelings. On the morning of the incident Ms B called her therapist to report severe depression and suicidal feelings. Her therapist made an emergency appointment for later that morning.

Both her therapist and her psychiatrist were present when she arrived for the appointment. She spoke with them for about 15 min, reporting suicidal thoughts involving an overdose of pills saved from discontinued prescriptions. She refused hospitalization, later reporting that she felt confused about what she wanted.

Shortly afterwards the police and an ambulance arrived and Ms B was told she was being sent for psychiatric admission. Upset, confused, and angry, she resisted transport. She was physically overcome and strapped to a stretcher.

Ms B was taken to a local Emergency Department (ED) where she was placed in locked seclusion and asked to remove her clothes and put on a hospital gown. When she expressed reluctance she was told that if she did not comply her clothes would be forcibly removed. She put on a hospital gown and her clothes were taken.

She was unaware of being checked throughout her confinement and reports being unaware that she was on a video monitor which the investigator noted when touring the room. The room is obviously intended for forced containment with blank walls, a heavy door and large lock. The video monitor was viewed by the ED clerk with observations by the nursing staff documented every 15 min as required by state regulations (State of Connecticut 1993). She was in seclusion for more than 6 h.

The findings are based on a review of medical records and institutional policies, interviews with the client, ED personnel, including the medical doctor and registered nurse who treated Ms B, and a site visit.

Concerns sent to the hospital

1 Ms B was transported to the ED for a 'medical clearance' she did not need rather than going directly to the inpatient facility, even though the decision had already been made to admit her involuntarily if necessary.

2 She spent 6 h under video surveillance while in a state of near undress. Surveillance was conducted without her knowledge by persons without clinical training or credentials.

3 Her seclusion continued 2 h past the point when hospital policy requires reassessment and a new physician's order. No documentation justifying the continuation of seclusion was found.

Follow-up

At a meeting to discuss the findings, Ms B received an apology from the Medical Director of the ED. A sign was placed in the seclusion room notifying the occupant of the video monitor, which could be covered over when the monitor was not in use. The ED intensified negotiations with the local mental health centre for more timely evaluations.

On a more general level, this investigation led to the publication of a paper in the professional literature suggesting guidelines for the ethical use of video monitors in restraint situations (Olsen 1998a).

Ethical assessment

Ms B was taken to the hospital and put in seclusion against her will. Thus, her clinicians made a decision to override the usual obligation to respect her autonomy, requiring justification (Beauchamp & Childress 1994). In this case, the uncertainty about her suicidal feelings, which could have led to her being harmed, may provide a justification to bypass the usual respect for her autonomy (Alexander *et al.* 1991). However, the investigation revealed doubts about the vigour and duration of the means used to restrict her liberty, and the rigorousness of the assessment of her mental state, leading to the assessment of the possible danger. These doubts arose because of the poor documentation, which reflected a casual attitude towards the ethical duty to justify exceptions to the usual obligation to honour patients' rights.

Even when forced treatment is justified, providers have an obligation to maintain the patient's personal dignity to the maximum degree possible, including the provision of appropriate privacy. Ms B's privacy was violated by video monitoring without her knowledge. The video monitoring itself may or may not have been justified as a safety measure, but there is no justification for the lack of notification and the use of untrained personnel in the monitoring. Video monitoring also raises the possibility that human contact may have been curtailed. Persons with acute psychiatric conditions are in a highly vulnerable position; depriving them of human contact for staff convenience is ethically questionable and may be clinically undesirable.

Case two: Ms R

The investigation

Ms R, a 28-year-old mentally retarded woman, with schizophrenia and obsessive-compulsive disorder, was admitted for disruptive behaviour which could not be controlled in her group home. During the course of a month-long hospitalization she became toxic on medications, broke her leg, and had a variety of other less serious medical problems, including an infected intravenous line, thrush, a torn toenail and a serious incident of choking on her food.

While the staff might have identified the toxicity earlier, they did act appropriately in securing a medication consultation which identified the toxicity and the problem was resolved. It was shortly after the change in medications suggested by the consultation that she fell in the hallway and broke her leg. However, despite the proximity in time to the toxic reaction, her broken leg was probably not related to the toxicity. This was determined by graphing the dosage of three different medications and the need for restraint as a clinical indicator of her condition across time and then projecting blood levels of the medications at the time of the incident.

The patient's guardian, her sister, had trouble obtaining information from clinicians and was not involved in any treatment decisions. She was told that relatives were not entitled to certain information. This was the most serious ethical problem surrounding this case. There was no indication that restraints were applied inappropriately.

The findings were based on record review, and interviews with the social worker co-ordinating the client's care at the hospital, the client's guardian, and the care provider at the client's group residence. In this case, review of the client's medical record included graphing on a time chart the time in restraints, incidents of acting out behaviour, the total daily dosage of three medications, and the adverse events that occurred in the hospital.

Follow-up

Since the review of this case, hospital policy has changed to reflect the role of guardians as surrogate decision makers: 'When patients are admitted under the authorization of a guardian, a communication protocol must be established at the time of admission. This must be documented in the medical record' (Anonymous a 1998). The policy regarding investigations of abuse was also modified to include the notification of guardians.

Ethical assessment

This case illustrates the need for careful analysis of clinical details. The number and degree of problems that occurred during the hospitalization pointed to poor and possibly abusive care. However, careful review of the clinical details indicated care that was largely up to standard.

The treatment of the client's legal guardian as a 'relative' was the most significant breach of ethical practice in this case. This client was clearly incompetent to make treatment decisions. Therefore, an appropriate surrogate should have been consulted about treatment decisions. From a legal perspective, the appropriate decision maker had been determined through the assignment of guardianship. As the client's closest relative, and as a person who demonstrated ongoing concern for the client by visitation and active involvement in care, the sister was also the most ethically appropriate choice for a surrogate decision maker. The client's sister should have received full access to clinical information and been consulted about all treatment deci-

sions in the same way a competent patient would have been consulted.

Case three: Ms V

The investigation

Ms V is a 44-year-old woman who has been in psychiatric treatment since the age of 5 years. According to her record she has spent approximately 23 years of her life as an inpatient of psychiatric hospitals, including a significant portion of her childhood. In 1994 she was transferred from a large state hospital in Minnesota to one in Connecticut to be closer to her sister. When she was discharged from the Connecticut hospital after 5 months of treatment she was referred to a community mental health treatment system where she had been in treatment for 3 years at the time of the investigation. Her time in the community had been tumultuous with many inpatient admissions and over 20 trips to a psychiatric crisis service in the ED during the past year. In the ED she often reported thoughts of suicide, although the clinicians have expressed scepticism that she actually intended self-harm.

The client's sister contacted PAIMI to investigate the continuity of care and the competency of the current treating professionals. Informally she stated that she became concerned because 'so much can be done about mental illness these days and my sister's just not getting any better'.

After reviewing extensive medical records and interviewing the client and her sister, the diagnoses and treatment were found to be essentially correct. Furthermore, there was no evidence that the current clinical treatment was substandard. During the interview, the client admitted that she frequently exaggerated feelings of suicide to prolong treatment because she enjoys the social interaction. Her current entanglements with the mental health system were directly attributable to deinstitutionalization. Ms V's behaviour was consistent with having grown up in a hospital and then spending most of her adult life in an institution.

Follow-up

The client's sister had developed expectations for treatment based on the most hopeful pronouncements about the state of modern psychiatry; she took exaggerated or overly optimistic public relations rhetoric and news items far too seriously.

Expectations for treatment were discussed with the client and her sister. Suggestions were made for clinical approaches that might reduce Ms V's use of the ED for social contact. At PAIMI's last contact with Ms V she was in new, better housing, had greatly reduced her use of the ED and was more satisfied with treatment.

Ethical analysis

In this case the most pertinent ethical analysis concerned a social problem. Widely publicizing advances in mental health treatment is an appropriate way to stimulate the public's support of further work and to make those who might benefit aware of new treatments. However, such publicity should be circumspect. The mental health community is justifiably encouraged about a medication which treats a few patients or provides partial treatment when no prior medication had any efficacy. However, the author considers it morally wrong to lead patients to believe that most of these advances represent a cure in the usual sense of the word.

Regulating information about advances in mental health treatment for public dissemination is difficult as the information comes from both the provider community and the news media.

Case four: Ms L

The investigation

Ms L is a 48-year-old woman diagnosed with schizophrenia and bipolar disorder and has had several prior hospitalizations. She reported being anxious and depressed for 1 week prior to this event, due to the possibility of being evicted from her apartment.

Around 8.45 PM Ms L went to the ED with her brother. According to her brother, she contacted him by telephone and said that she was feeling suicidal with thoughts of taking an overdose. Her history, including violent behaviour, was provided by her brother. He reported infrequent contact with her, with no contact over the past year.

Ms L told the ED physician that she had some suicidal ideation and took 'several meds' and told the triage nurse that she was 'possibly suicidal' and had taken 'one extra Ativan'. The triage nurse also reported an overdose 'several years ago', but it was not clear whether this history came from Ms L or her brother. At that time the triage nurse documented that she was 'calm and co-operative'.

At 9.30 PM the nurse's notes state without elaboration that Ms L was 'placed in four-point restraints by security'. This same report states that she was 'resting quietly' and was 'quiet, alert and oriented'.

At 10.30 PM Ms L was seen for the first time by a person from the crisis intervention team. The usual ED procedure is for crisis intervention to see a patient after medical clear-

ance, but an exception was made in this case because crisis intervention leaves for the night at 11 PM and Ms L could not be medically cleared until at least 6 h of observation passed without clinical signs of toxicity, and the toxicology report returned. The crisis intervention clinician reported that Ms L denied suicidal ideation and intent. She was noted to be 'very anxious and fidgety', but speaking coherently.

Documentation on the 'Locked Restraints/Observation Flowsheet' by nursing staff began at 9.30 PM and continued every 15 min until 7.30 AM the next day. Under the behaviour column, Ms L was noted to be either quiet, co-operative or asleep in each 15-min entry. During this time period, the nurses' notes state that she denied a history of violence and reported that her brother was lying. She also denied suicidal feelings and asked that the restraints be removed.

At 7.30 AM the nurses' notes again report that she was quiet, co-operative and denying suicidal ideation. The nurses' notes state that she agreed to stay in the room if the restraints were removed and that security was called to remove the restraints.

Ms L was seen at 9 AM by the same crisis intervention person as the night before. In this interview she stated that she took one extra clonazepam and one extra respiridone for anxiety related to the potential eviction. Her outpatient psychiatrist was contacted. She was discharged to home at 11.30 AM with the telephone number of a helpline and instructions to follow-up with her outpatient psychiatrist.

Concerns sent to the hospital

1 There was no documentation justifying the initiation and later the continuation of restraint or that less restrictive means were considered. She was consistently noted to be co-operative and quiet throughout the medical record, including at the time the restraint was initiated and throughout the duration of the restraint.
2 The ED has no facility to seclude patients who should be detained but do not require restraint.
3 Ms L was detained in restraints following her medical clearance at 3 AM until 9 AM only because the crisis intervention service does not operate overnight.

Follow-up

A meeting was held with the ED personnel and representatives from the hospital's legal and quality control departments. While the legal and quality control departments were overtly co-operative, the ED personnel were openly contemptuous of having their clinical decisions questioned.

The following was agreed to in a letter from the hospital attorney: 'The nurse manager is conducting further education with staff on the use of alternative measures . . . and is re-emphasizing the use of least restrictive measures. . . . The nurse manager has been conducting monitoring and evaluation of all patients placed into restraints . . . [including] why the patients are placed in restraints, the time frame they are in restraints, the required documentation elements, and the assessment criteria to release them to less restrictive measures. . . . We will be revising our hospital restraint policy . . .' (Anonymous b 1997).

This case, in addition to others, has prompted PAIMI to initiate a broad review of ED treatment of persons with mental disorder in Connecticut. Also, these and other cases prompted the publication of ethical guidelines for the application of the least restrictive alternative standard in forced psychiatric treatment (Olsen 1998b).

Ethical analysis

The rationale documented for initiating and maintaining restraint were inconsistent with ethically acceptable justifications of apparent danger and incompetence. Instead, the client seems to have been restrained due to the hospital's lack of resources to assess and monitor the clinical situation properly. A seclusion room would have sufficed to keep a possibly suicidal but calm patient in a less restrictive manner. The clinical details of this case indicate that personal contact with the client may have contained the situation and would certainly be more desirable than spending the night in restraints. One concern arising in restraint cases where there is a marginal level of danger and lack of psychosis is that the patient is being restrained to heighten the undesirable consequences of their behaviour (Morrison 1990). This sort of impromptu behaviour modification is ethically unacceptable. This is very hard to assess because few clinicians document or admit to this rationale in a formal setting. This case has several indicators of such a situation; Mrs L's suicidality was always known to be marginal, her condition is difficult to treat leading to frequent frustrating contacts; and because she was not psychotic the behaviour might be imputed to be volitional thus angering staff.

Lessons from the investigations

Four lessons emerge from the experience of performing investigations. The first is to explain to the patient what is happening and what to expect, even if the patient is not going to like it, which is often the case in forced treatment situations. In reports about clinical experiences by PAIMI's clients, it is clear that feeling uncertainty about what is

happening or feeling deceived, greatly exacerbates negative feelings towards care givers. In investigating clinical encounters it appeared that clients were often given less than complete information without clinical justification for the omission. In the first case, the client was most disturbed about being unaware of the video monitoring. In the second case, the lack of communication with the client's guardian was a primary motivating factor in initiating the investigation. In the third case, the sister's unreasonable expectations could easily have been handled by the client's clinicians if communication had been more open.

Two temptations need to be resisted to increase patient participation in difficult decisions: first, the tendency to avoid breaking bad news, like the decision to commit; and second, the tendency to bypass discussing care with committed patients because it has already been decided that their input is not going to change the treatment decision.

The next lesson is to pay attention to the process of care. None of the investigations described involve clear examples of abuse or malicious treatment. In case four, the woman was restrained although 'calm and co-operative'; the treatment could be questioned, but was not entirely without justification. In case two, the mentally retarded woman, and case three, the woman who was deinstitutionalized, the clients asked that the appropriateness of treatment be investigated. However, questions about the appropriateness of the actual interventions arose for the clients because of a lack of attention to the process of carrying out the intervention. In all these cases the client was disturbed with the process of providing the care and this prompted the complaint.

The third lesson is to allow the patient to feel ambivalent about treatment. Individuals who report problems to PAIMI are often ambivalent about the treatment they or their relatives are receiving. The providers in these cases often seem invested in having their patients give unqualified endorsement to the treatment. In one investigation, a mother was intimately involved in her son's treatment and anxious about a particular medication. The provider never intervened with them as a family to work through the issues regarding the medication, but instead instructed the mother not to interfere with treatment. The provider correctly identified the client's dependency. However, it was likely that those dependency issues made it impossible for him to have his mother be less involved in his treatment. The client was caught in a struggle between his provider and mother and he decompensated whenever the struggle became intense. Although the choice of medication was standard treatment for this client's problem, the treatment would have been enhanced if the client and his mother had been given the opportunity to express and work through their ambivalence about treatment. Interactions with

D. P. Olsen

patients and their families must go beyond convincing them to accept the recommended treatment.

The final lesson is the relationship. The clinician's relationship with the patient determines the patient's assessment of the quality of treatment. Individuals who sense that the clinician is providing treatment based on personal knowledge of the patient coupled with a sincere desire to help rarely complain about poor treatment, even when the treatment is ineffective. At the root of every case this author has investigated so far has been a poor interpersonal relationship between a patient, or family member, and a provider. Providers who treat individuals with mental disorders must understand that difficulties with relationships are inherent, even definitional, to many mental disorders. Therefore, the onus is on the provider to understand and analyse breakdowns in communication as an essential part of treatment.

Conclusion

Every investigation should be tempered by the observation that findings are rarely black and white and almost always grey. Inevitably providers have some valid justifications and clients have some valid concerns. True 'bad guys' are rare, and when found are far easier to eliminate than bad ideas. When an aspect of treatment is labelled as a problem in an investigation, this is generally an expression of the investigator's judgement, and thus open to considerable debate and interpretation. Cases one and four both involved patients in whom the expression of suicidality represented a valid concern justifying restrictive measures in the name of safety. The investigator's analysis represents a judgement about the emphasis between safety and patient autonomy in these specific situations. The greyness of real cases teaches that ethics in health care is more often about

examining treatment to identify practices which better value humanity in patients, than about identifying deliberate immorality. Moral solutions require affecting practice standards and provider attitudes.

References

Alexander V., Bursztajn H., Brodsky A., Hamm R., Gutheil T. & Levi L. (1991) Involuntary commitment. In: *Decision Making in Psychiatry and the Law* (eds Gutheil, T., Bursztajn, H., Brodsky, A. & Alexander, V.), pp. 89–107. Williams & Wilkins, Baltimore.

Anonymous a* (1998) Communication with patients' relatives/guardian/conservator of person. Medical Administrative Procedure Manual for [Institution's Name]*, B-9.4, 9 February 1998.

Anonymous b* (1997) Letter to Maria Kahn, 25 April 1997 (Attorney for PAIMI in 1997).

Beauchamp T. & Childress J. (1994) *Principles of Biomedical Ethics*, 4th edn. Oxford University Press, New York.

House Report from the Education and Labor Committee (1990) House Report 485(II), 101st Congress, 2nd Session.

Morrison E. (1990) The tradition of toughness: a study of nonprofessional nursing care in psychiatric settings. *Image* **22**, 32–38.

Olsen D. (1998a) Ethical considerations of video monitoring psychiatric patients in seclusion and restraint. *Archives of Psychiatric Nursing* **12**, 90–94.

Olsen D. (1998b) Toward an ethical standard for coerced mental health treatment: least restrictive or most therapeutic? *Journal of Clinical Ethics* **9**, 235–246.

State of Connecticut (1993) State of Connecticut, Division of Mental Health, Commissioner's Policy Statement, no. 22a, effective 17 July 1993.

USCS (1986) Title 42 United States Codes & Statutes (USCS) 10801–109051.

USCS (1993) Title 42 United States Codes & Statutes (USCS) 12101–12213.

* Names have been withheld to maintain confidentiality. Further information can be obtained from the author if required.

[8]

Ethical Conflicts at the Interface of Advocacy and Psychiatry

Spencer Eth, M.D., Editor
Martin L. Levine, J.D., LL.D.
Martha Lyon-Levine, Ph.D.

Dr. Eth's Introduction: It is timely and appropriate for *Hospital and Community Psychiatry* to feature a column on ethics. Ethical issues related to psychiatry and mental health have never been more conspicuous or seemingly more difficult to resolve. Within the past year we have seen national controversies over a quadraplegic woman's demand to starve herself to death in a psychiatric hospital, over allegations of deceit at the core of Freudian theory, and over the withholding of surgical treatment for a severely retarded and impaired infant. Though not as widely publicized, the ethical agenda underlying every clinical practice is also of critical importance.

The column will explore a series of diverse ethical topics intrinsic to the work of mental health professionals—from consent and confidentiality to corporate control, scarce resource allocation, and medical dominance. Each article will clarify the relevant ethical issues and may argue a particular position as well.

This month's topic is mental health advocacy, which has emerged as a major force in patient care. Its reception by clinicians has been ambivalent, in part because of a perceived clash of values. Our guest columnists, Professor Levine and Dr. Lyon-Levine, address the moral difficulties generated by the role of advocacy and suggest a compromise position between two divergent ethical viewpoints. Professor Levine is the UPS Foundation professor of law, gerontology, and psychiatry and the behavioral sciences at the University of Southern California. Dr. Lyon-Levine is assistant professor of clinical psychiatry and the behavioral sciences and director of the training program in patient care advocacy at the University of Southern California.

This is the first in a series of columns on ethical issues related to psychiatry and mental health practice. The editor is Spencer Eth, M.D., assistant professor of psychiatry and the behavioral sciences at the Los Angeles County–University of Southern California Medical Center, 1934 Hospital Place, Los Angeles, California 90033. Dr. Eth invites readers to submit original manuscripts of 1,500 words or less for possible publication in the column to the *H&CP* editorial office, 1400 K Street, N.W., Washington, D.C. 20005.

The problem

Clinicians increasingly interact with advocates, sometimes supervise advocates, and may incorporate aspects of patient advocacy within their therapeutic role. The many forms advocacy takes are suggested by the different terms used: patients' rights advocate, patient care advocate, patient representative, case manager, and ombudsman. Some advocates work with individual patients, while others attempt to improve system policies or legislation (1).

Only about a fourth of mental health advocacy programs are run by lawyers. Another fourth are run by citizen volunteer groups such as mental health associations, and the remainder by mental health professionals, former patients, or the parents and families of current and former patients. About a fourth are internal advocacy programs operated within hospitals or mental health departments; the others are external. Advocacy groups differ in their emphasis; parent groups often stress enhanced treatment, while former patients often stress opposition to involuntary treatment (2).

Patient advocacy is controversial (3; Zusman J, unpublished paper, 1983). Some have criticized advocates as being unethical and have accused them of interfering with patient care, medical authority, and administrative efficiency. Simultaneously others have welcomed advocates as ethically necessary and seen them as protecting patients' rights and dignity, promoting patient rehabilitation, and facilitating effective delivery of coordinated services to patients.

Competing principles and models

Three ethical principles make competing claims in advocacy situations; they are patient autonomy, medical paternalism, and role integrity. The patient autonomy model holds that advocates' sole loyalty should be to the client. The advocates' task is to assist in achieving the client's wishes, which overrule what the advocate or therapist may perceive as the best interests of the client. The advocate thus treats the client as a person with full legal rights and of moral worth equal to that of any other individual. Furthermore, clinicians are urged to be responsive professionals and regard themselves as front-line advocates (4).

A version of the medical model suggests, by contrast, that medical paternalism is the governing consideration. Both clinicians and advocates should do what is in the best interests of the patient; treatment decisions rest within the professional domain of the clinician.

The power of clinicians is justified by their training and knowledge, together with the diminished competence of severely disturbed patients to make rational decisions. The responsible advocate (3) should properly function as part of the mental health team, and every clinician is also an advocate. Advocacy may then be seen as a type of patient care management.

An alternative version of responsible advocacy (Zusman J, unpublished paper, 1983) suggests that advocates seek to promote maximum service to patients at minimum cost in terms of intrusions on rights, balancing also the interests of other patients and of the system.

Ethical advocacy

Role integrity is given preeminence in another model, which we call ethical advocacy. Clinicians and advocates should be faithful to their role, candid to others as to the nature of their role, respectful of others' roles, and obedient to the law.

Administrators and clinicians who deal with advocates ought not to view them as inherently inimical to psychiatry or to patients' interests. Advocates must properly make a forceful exposition of why patients' wishes should be honored, or why their legal rights as declared by legislatures or courts should be observed. One should not blame the messenger for the message.

Clinicians should accept advocates' participation even if they do not agree with their conclusions. They need not concede the point at issue, however, if they believe advocates' positions are unwarranted, but may consult other experienced persons, such as senior staff, hospital authorities, or legal counsel.

Advocates for individual patients should observe several norms. If they serve the institution or clinicians as case manager or complaint representative, or if they work for organizations with their own agendas, they should make known to the patients where

their loyalty lies. If the patients are their clients, they owe loyalty to their clients' wishes and should not be "double agents" for others or for the system (5).

Advocates who are attorneys are governed by the canons of legal ethics (6); nonlawyer advocates may consider whether these norms are potentially applicable to them. For example, the lawyer owes the client "zealous" representation. The client, not the advocate, selects the goals of the representation. Since clinicians are already seeking the psychiatric best interests of the patient, the advocate's role is not to duplicate the clinician's (7), but rather to seek to achieve the client's wishes and protect his rights. The duty to the individual client is preeminent, preventing simultaneous representation of other clients with conflicting interests.

Nevertheless, the advocate's duty to clients is not unlimited, even for attorney-advocates. The advocate has substantial discretion in choosing appropriate means of representation. The advocate should also try to make sure that clients understand when their wishes conflict with recommended psychiatric treatment, interests of other patients, or needs of the system. But ultimately the decision about resolving these conflicts is the client's to make.

Overriding legal and ethical norms

Whatever the involvement of the advocates may be, and whatever model is adopted, both clinicians and advocates must accept that the ultimate locus of authority for patient care decisions is defined by society, not by medicine, and is declared in law. Generally patients have legal power to decide what is to happen to them, subject to certain restrictions for patients with impaired capabilities or those who have been declared legally incompetent.

The proper resolution of the ethical issues that advocacy raises for the clinician is often difficult. Like the resolution of other ethical

problems, such issues can be clarified through several steps, beginning with the acknowledgment that the psychiatric patient is entitled to the full rights and respect of personhood.

Other steps involve viewing the clinician as a moral actor as well as a therapeutic one; identifying the ethical concerns in patient care decisions that coexist with medical and psychiatric considerations; recognizing situations raising ethical issues; analyzing the issues, fully cognizant that the relevant ethical principles may point in different directions; giving thought to which of the appropriate ethical principles the clinician regards as holding moral priority; seeking the counsel of experienced senior colleagues or consultants with ethical or legal training; and taking personal responsibility for decisions.

Advocates and clinicians, who often operate out of diametrically opposed models, may find it difficult to accept that the other is operating ethically and in the patient's interest. But both groups should recognize that they share ethical responsibilities. Attention to the process proposed here may minimize many of the ethical conflicts generated by mental health advocacy.

References

1. Kopolow L, Bloom H: Mental Health Advocacy: An Emerging Force in Consumers' Rights. Rockville, Md, National Institute of Mental Health, 1977
2. Freddolino PP: Findings from the national mental advocacy survey. Mental Disability Law Reporter 7:416–421, 1983
3. Lamb HR: Securing patients' rights—responsibly. Hospital and Community Psychiatry 32:393–397, 1981
4. Herr SS, Arons S, Wallace RE Jr: Legal Rights and Mental Health Care. Lexington, Mass, Lexington Books, 1983
5. Lyon MA, Levine ML: Ethics, power, and advocacy: psychologists in the criminal justice system. Law and Human Behavior 6:65–85, 1982
6. Model Code of Professional Responsibility. Chicago, American Bar Association, 1983
7. Guardianships, Conservatorships, Civil Commitment, and Rights of Institutionalized Persons. Boston, New England Law Institute, 1982

The Social Construction of Madness

[9]

Psychiatry and the control of dangerousness: on the apotropaic function of the term "mental illness"

T Szasz

The term "mental illness" implies that persons with such illnesses are more likely to be dangerous to themselves and/or others than are persons without such illnesses. This is the source of the psychiatrist's traditional social obligation to control "harm to self and/or others," that is, suicide and crime. The ethical dilemmas of psychiatry cannot be resolved as long as the contradictory functions of healing persons and protecting society are united in a single discipline.

Life is full of dangers. Our highly developed consciousness makes us, of all living forms in the universe, the most keenly aware of, and the most adept at protecting ourselves from, dangers. Magic and religion are mankind's earliest warning systems. Science arrived on the scene only about 400 years ago, and scientific medicine only 200 years ago. Some time ago I suggested that "formerly, when religion was strong and science weak, men mistook magic for medicine; now, when science is strong and religion weak, men mistake medicine for magic".[1]

We flatter and deceive ourselves if we believe that we have outgrown the apotropaic use of language (from the Greek *apostropaios*, meaning "to turn away").

Many people derive comfort from magical objects (amulets), and virtually everyone finds reassurance in magical words (incantations). The classic example of an apotropaic is the word "abracadabra," which *The American Heritage Dictionary of the English Language* defines as "a magical charm or incantation having the power to ward off disease or disaster". In the ancient world, abracadabra was a magic word, the letters of which were arranged in an inverted pyramid and worn as an amulet around the neck to protect the wearer against disease or trouble. One fewer letter appeared in each line of the pyramid, until only the letter "a" remained to form the vertex of the triangle. As the letters disappeared, so supposedly did the disease or trouble.

I submit that we use phrases like "dangerousness to self and others" and "psychiatric treatment" as apotropaics to ward off dangers we fear, much as ancient magicians warded off the dangers people feared by means of incantations, exemplified by "abracadabra". Growing reliance on compulsory mental health interventions for protection against crime and suicide illustrate the phenomenon. Physicians, criminologists, politicians, and the public use advances in medicine and neuroscience to convince themselves that such interventions are "scientific" and do not violate the moral and legal foundations of English and American law. This is a serious error. There is no scientific basis whatever for preventive psychi-

atric detention, also known as involuntary mental hospitalisation or civil commitment. And the procedure is a patent violation of due process and the presumption of innocence.

We call all manner of human problems "(mental) diseases", and convince ourselves that drugs and conversation (therapy) solve such problems. Solutions exist, however, only for mathematical problems and some medical problems. For human problems, there are no solutions. Conflict, disagreement, unhappiness, the proverbial slings and arrows of outrageous fortune are challenges that we must cope with, not solve. Only after we admit that our solutions are illusions can we begin to develop more rational and more humane methods for dealing with "mental illness" and the "dangerous mental patient".

We are proud that we do not punish acts or beliefs that upset others, but do not injure them and hence do not constitute crimes. Yet, we punish people—albeit we call it "treatment"—for annoying family members (and others) with behaviours they deem "dangerous" and also for "being suicidal". To be sure, persons who exhibit such behaviours—labelled "schizophrenics", "persons with dangerous severe personality disorders," and "suicidal patients"—frighten others, especially those who must associate with them. Unable to control non-criminal "offences" by means of criminal law sanctions, how can the offended persons and society protect themselves from their unwanted fellow men and women?

One way is by "divorcing" them. However, this method of separating oneself from an unwanted companion—especially when it involves relations between disturbing and disturbed spouses or between disturbing adult children and their disturbed parents—strikes most people as an unacceptable rejection of family obligation. Psychiatrists offer to relieve the disturbed person of the burden of coping with his disturbed relative by incarcerating the latter and calling it "care" and "treatment".

How do psychiatrists do this? By allying themselves with the coercive apparatus of the state and declaring the offending individual *mentally ill and dangerous to him or herself or others*. This magic mantra allows *us* to incarcerate *him* in a prison we call a "mental hospital". Ostensibly, the term "mental illness" (or "psychopathology") names a *pathological condition* or disease, similar say to diabetes; actually, it names a *social tactic* or justification, permitting family members, courts, and society as a body, to separate themselves from individuals who exhibit, or are claimed to exhibit, certain behaviours identified as "dangerous mental illnesses". This tactic is dramatically illustrated by the following "advice" appearing on the web site of the

National Alliance for the Mentally Ill (NAMI), a mental health advocacy organisation that identifies itself as representing "more than 200 000 families, consumers, and providers across the country". As will be evident, NAMI represents the interests of mental patients the same way that the Ku Klux Klan represented the interests of black Americans.

> Sometime, during the course of your loved one's illness, you may need the police. By preparing now, before you need help, you can make the day you need help go much more smoothly. ... It is often difficult to get 911 to respond to your calls if you need someone to come & take your MI [mentally ill] relation to a hospital emergency room (ER). They may not believe that you really need help. And if they do send the police, the police are often reluctant to take someone for involuntary commitment. That is because cops are concerned about liability. ... When calling 911, the best way to get quick action is to say, "Violent EDP", or "Suicidal EDP". EDP stands for Emotionally Disturbed Person. This shows the operator that you know what you're talking about. Describe the danger very specifically. "He's a danger to himself" is not as good as "This morning my son said he was going to jump off the roof." ... Also, give past history of violence. *This is especially important if the person is not acting up.* ... When the police come, they need compelling evidence that the person is a danger to self or others before they can involuntarily take him or her to the ER for evaluation. ... While AMI/FAMI [Alliance for the Mentally Ill/Florida Alliance for the Mentally Ill] is not suggesting you do this, the fact is that some families have learned to "turn over the furniture" before calling the police.[2]

Giving false information to the police is a crime, unless it is in the cause of "mental health".

In the United Kingdom, unlike in the United States, there still are physicians, psychiatrists, and medical journals that view these developments with concern, if not alarm. The publication of a United Kingdom government white paper for a new mental health act, in 2000, that would provide for the psychiatric detention of persons diagnosed as having a "dangerous severe personality disorder" has duly alarmed some doctors in Britain.[3-5] I am afraid, however, that their lamentations are too feeble, and come too late.

THE DANGER OF THE CONCEPT OF "DANGEROUSNESS"

In *The Myth of Mental Illness*, I showed that the idea of mental illness implies dangerousness and thus requires and justifies psychiatric coercions.[6] To civilly commit a person, a psychiatrist (or physician) must certify that the subject suffers from a mental illness and is dangerous to himself and/or others. It is not by accident that when psychiatry was a young and marginalised medical specialty, its primary social function was controlling persons dangerous to others ("mad"); and that now, when it is a mature and respected medical specialty, its primary function is controlling persons who are dangerous to themselves ("suicide risks").

In his classic treatise on schizophrenia, Eugen Bleuler complained: "People are being forced to continue to live a life that has become unbearable for them for *valid reasons*. ... Even if a few more [patients] killed themselves, does this reason justify the fact that we *torture* hundreds of patients and *aggravate* their disease?" (emphasis added).[7]

Why are psychiatrists expected to prevent suicide by depriving the "suspect" of liberty? The idea of suicide makes us nervous. We cannot decide whether killing oneself is a "right" or a wrong, an element of our inalienable personal liberty or an offence of some sort that ought to be prohibited and perhaps punished. We are too uptight about suicide to recognise that killing oneself is sometimes a reasonable and right thing to do, sometimes an unreasonable and wrong thing to do, but that, in either case, it ought to be treated as an act that falls outside the scope of interference by the state.[8]

The right to kill oneself is the supreme symbol of personal autonomy. Formerly, the church allied with the state prohibited and punished the act. Now, psychiatry, as an arm of the state, prohibits the act and "treats" it as if it were a symptom of an underlying disease (typically, depression or schizophrenia). The deprivation of liberty intrinsic to such an intervention is viewed not as a human rights violation but as a human rights protection. The modern reader may be surprised, perhaps even shocked, at seeing the words "prohibition" and "suicide" bracketed. Lack of familiarity with the long history of the religious prohibition against self murder, together with unquestioning acceptance of coercive psychiatric suicide prevention as "therapy," make such a reaction a virtual certainty. This is unfortunate.

Formerly, religious doctrine defined the permissible uses of the body. Its impermissible uses—self abuse (masturbation), sex abuse (homosexuality and other "perversions"), substance abuse (drunkenness and gluttony), and self murder (suicide)—were sins, crimes, or both, punished by informal or formal sanctions. Substituting medical for religious doctrine, the modern state, in collaboration with psychiatry, transformed each of these behaviours into diseases of the mind, a view that prevailed through most of the 19th and 20th centuries. After the second world war, and more rapidly in recent decades, some of these mental maladies were divested of their disease status. In my own lifetime, masturbation ceased to be a mental disease or a cause of disease, and homosexuality became not just normal but a "right" others were legally obligated to respect. Yet, during the same period, political, psychiatric, and popular condemnation of self medication and self killing intensified. Using substances decreed to be "dangerous" and illegal is now viewed as an "international plague", justifying a worldwide "war on drugs".[9] Rejecting life and wanting to kill oneself is defined as a severe mental illness characterised by "dangerousness to self," and is treated as a quasicrime with coercions called "treatments" (especially involuntary "hospitalisation" and forced drugging). Success in committing suicide is regarded as a "waste," a preventable medical tragedy, often attributed to medical negligence.[10]

It is fundamental principle of English and American law that only persons charged with and convicted of certain crimes are subject to imprisonment. Persons who respect other peoples'

Debate

rights to life, liberty, and property have an inalienable right to their own life, liberty, and property. Having a disposition or propensity to break the law is not a crime.

Serious debate about matters regarded as mental health problems, especially suicide, is taboo. Liberals have a love affair with coercion in the name of mental health. Conservatives—fearful lest they be dismissed as not compassionate enough about the mentally ill and not scientific enough about mental illness—join in the celebration of psychiatric statism. A columnist for the conservative magazine *National Review* agrees with the psychiatric dogma that "it is *mental illness that causes most suicides*: depression, manic depression, and schizophrenia. ... The conservative critique of the therapeutic culture", he warns, "will not get a hearing until conservatives *face up to the reality of mental illness*".[11]

Speaking about, much less supporting, a right to suicide strikes most people as unimaginably uncompassionate. This opinion is the result of viewing suicide as caused by depression, and depression as a kind of unnecessary, curable unhappiness. We regard this perspective as enlightened and scientific, when in fact it is naive and conceited. Toward the end of *Brave New World*—a scientist dystopia in which all conflicts and discomforts have been eliminated—the human remnant Huxley calls the Savage, and his opponent, the "Controller" Mustapha Mond, engage in the following dialogue:

... "We prefer to do things comfortably" [said the Controller].

"But I don't want comfort. I want God, I want poetry, I want real danger, I want freedom, I want goodness, I want sin."

"In fact", said Mustapha Mond, "you're claiming the right to be unhappy."

"All right, then," said the Savage defiantly, "I'm claiming the right to be unhappy."[12]

For the person who kills himself, suicide may be the realisation of diverse aspirations and expectations. For society, suicide is, first and foremost, an act of *lese majeste* (literally, "injured majesty"). *Webster's Dictionary* defines the term as "an offense violating the dignity of a ruler as the representative of a sovereign power; detraction from the dignity or importance of a constituted authority".

For millennia, suicide was *lese majeste* against the church/state, the supreme representation of legitimate authority for people who worship a god and want a good life in the hereafter. Today, suicide is *lese majeste* against the Therapeutic State, the supreme representation of legitimate authority for people who worship health and want to stay alive as long as possible.

Regarding the issue of "dangerousness to others" as a quasicrime—once we cease to regard "it" as a "condition caused by mental illness"—there is not much to say.

In the current climate of opinion, however, things are no longer that simple. People fear, often for good reasons, persons not susceptible under our legal system for detention in prison. Persons called "sex offenders" are the most widely publicised offenders who fall into this class. In 1997, in *Kansas v Leroy Hendricks*, the US Supreme Court declared: "States have a right to use psychiatric hospitals to confine certain sex offenders once they have completed their prison terms, even if those offenders do not meet mental illness commitment criteria".[13] In February 2000, Wisconsin's oldest prison inmate, a 95 year old man, was "resentenced" as a sexual predator, after a psychologist "testified ... [that] psychological tests performed on Ellefson indicated if he was given a chance, he would commit a [sex] crime. ... After only minutes of deliberation, the jury found that Ellef J Ellefson should be committed for mental treatment under the sexual predator law."[14]

As I noted, the practice of preventive psychiatric detention has not gone unremarked by British commentators. John J Sandford, a British forensic psychiatrist, complained: "The preventive detention of those with untreatable mental disorders is already widely practised in England. Under the Mental Health Act (1983) people ... [are] detained indefinitely in hospital regardless of response to treatment and on grounds of risk to self as well as others. Secure and open psychiatric hospitals are full of such patients."[15] Derek Summerfield, also a psychiatrist, commented: "The growing pressures on them [psychiatrists] to deliver public protection was perhaps inevitable, given the rise of biopsychomedical paradigms as explanations for the vicissitudes of life in modern Western society. Psychiatrists have played their part by assuming the authority to explain, categorise, manage, and prognose in situations where well defined disease (arguably their only clear cut remit) was not present."[16]

CONCLUSION

Psychiatry is part law and part medicine. It is the psychiatrist's social mandate to function as a double agent: that is, to help voluntary patients cope with their problems in living and to help relatives and society rid themselves of certain unwanted persons, under medical auspices. The latter task requires coercing the denominated patient; the former is rendered impossible by the slightest threat of coercion, much less its actual exercise. The psychiatrist's mandate violates Jesus' injunction, "Render therefore unto Caesar the things which are Caesar's; and unto God the things that are God's".[17]

True psychiatric reform is contingent on separating the psychiatrist's two, mutually incompatible roles and functions.

REFERENCES

1 **Szasz TS**. *The second sin*. Garden City, NY: Doubleday, 1974:128.
2 **Jaffe DJ**. How to prepare for an emergency: www.nami.org and follow links for the article.
3 **Buchanan A**, Leese, M. Detention of people with dangerous severe personality disorders: a systematic review. *Lancet* 2001;**358**:1955–9.
4 **Farnham FR**, James DV. Dangerousness and dangerous law. *Lancet* 2001;**358**:1926.
5 **White SM**. Preventive detention must be resisted by the medical profession. *J Med Ethics* 2002;**28**:95–108.
6 **Szasz TS**. *The myth of mental illness*. New York: HarperCollins, 1974 (first published 1961).
7 **Bleuler E**. *Dementia praecox or the group of schizophrenias*. New York: International Universities Press, 1950:488–9 (first published 1911).
8 **Szasz TS**. *Fatal freedom: the ethics and politics of suicide*. Westport, CT: Praeger, 1999.
9 **Szasz TS**. *Our right to drugs: the case for a free market*. Syracuse: Syracuse University Press, 1996 (first published 1992).
10 **Anon**. Such a waste [editorial]. *Economist* 2001 Dec 8: www.ncpa.org and follow links for aticle.

11 **Ponnuru R**. Inner darkness. *National Review*
2000;**52**:48.

12 **Huxley A**. *Brave new world*. New York:
HarperPerennial, 1969:246. [First published in 1932.]

13 **Kansas v Leroy Hendricks**. 117 S Ct 2072. Excerpts
from opinions on status of sex offenders. *The New York
Times* 1997 Jun 24:B11.

14 **Associated Press**. Jury: 95 year old sexual predator is
still a threat. *Syracuse Herald-Journal* 2000 Feb 2:A8.

15 **Sandford JJ**. Public health psychiatry and crime
prevention [letter]. *BMJ* 1999;**318**:1354.

16 **Summerfield D**. Public health psychiatry and crime
prevention [letter]. *BMJ* 1999;**318**:1354.

17 *Holy Bible*. Matthew xxii, 21.

[10]

Dangerousness, mental disorder, and responsibility

J R McMillan

While the UK Home Office's proposals to preventively detain people with what it has called dangerous severe personality disorder (hereafter DSPD) have been subjected to debate and criticism the deeply troubling jurisprudential issues in these proposals have not yet entered into public debate in a way that their seriousness deserves.[1] It is good that a commentator as well known as Professor Szasz is speaking out on this issue.

Professor Szasz focuses upon a crucial question by calling into question the medicalisation of terms like dangerousness and mental illness.[2] There is a great temptation for legislators and the public to treat these terms as if they are purely scientific terms and to think of risk assessment as a precise science. I don't share Professor's Szasz's worry about how psychiatry is using these terms but I think there are some important questions about how these concepts function in the public sphere.

This issue is important enough to justify the use of some rhetorical claims because such claims can serve to bring out what are neglected and important issues. In raising the following objections I am not attempting to refute the message that is in Szasz's article or to say that he is not making an important point but rather to attempt to sharpen the issues and to suggest ways that we can respond to Professor Szasz's challenge.

Psychiatry has progressed in a number of ways since Professor Szasz wrote *The Myth of Mental Illness*.[3] The science is much better, we have much better medications, and psychiatrists (at least all the psychiatrists that I know) are acutely aware of the tension between treating their patient and their obligations to the public interest.

So when Professor Szasz says: "Psychiatrists offer to relieve the disturbed person of the burden of coping with his disturbed relative by incarcerating the latter and calling it 'care' and 'treatment'", this is a fairly prejudiced and outdated view of what psychiatrists do when placing a person under a compulsory treatment order. It would be more accurate to say that when care and treatment are appropriate families may be relieved of the burden of coping with a mentally unwell relative.

The major thesis of *The Myth of Mental Illness* and Professor Szasz's article is that mental illness is essentially linked with dangerousness. This link creates a huge tension within psychiatry between its obligation to heal patients and to protect the public.

While I think there are some good reasons for taking this thesis seriously when considering the history of psychiatry it is not an accurate way to describe contemporary psychiatry. I have a number of major worries about the idea that there is some intrinsic link between mental disorder and dangerousness.

While dangerousness, or perhaps more accurately social or economic disutility, was an important rationale for the incarceration of the insane[4] it is no longer the *telos* of psychiatry. Dangerousness is no longer sufficient for incarcerating the mentally ill, except in the most extreme circumstances, under British and Commonwealth mental health legislation. The wording and actual effect of these acts means that people who are a danger to other people or unable to care for themselves but who do not fall into the legally defined categories of mental disorder are routinely not placed under compulsory treatment orders. This in itself is sufficient to refute the claim that there is an essential connection between dangerousness and mental disorder in the wording and effect of the law.

Second, it's not accurate to say that dangerousness is the overriding concept when thinking about compulsory treatment. The key moral concept (in fact you could almost call it a suppressed premise) in compulsory treatment is responsibility or the lack thereof. It is because of the effect that mental illness can have upon an individual's ability to autonomously choose and act on a treatment decision when this treatment decision is related to a significant risk of harm to others or self that we might be justified in compelling people to be treated.

Not all mental health acts make this point explicit. The 1983 UK Mental Health Act requires that a person meet one of the defined categories of mental disorder, be a danger to others or not be able to care for themselves and that their condition is treatable. While the majority of people sectioned under the UK act will lack responsibility or competence there is a theoretical possibility that a person may be competent to make treatment decisions, have a treatable condition, not be able to look after themselves, and have a disorder that meets the relevant definition of mental disorder.

One interesting example of legislation that does make the link between responsibility and civil commitment explicit is the 1992 New Zealand Mental Health Act (for further discussion of this issue see Dawson).[3] The New Zealand act requires that in order for a person to placed under a compulsory treatment order it must be the case that their inability to care for themselves or their dangerousness to others results from a disorder of mood, cognition, or volition. When a disorder of mind is causally related to harm to self or others then this is a strong moral reason for not treating this behaviour as an expression of autonomy. Furthermore this impairment of autonomy is tied to a serious risk of harm to self or others and this creates an important threshold for when people can be treated against their will. So in effect both dangerousness that results from diminished autonomy and diminished autonomy are necessary for justifiable compulsory treatment in New Zealand.

RESPECTING AUTONOMY

The two classic explanations for the importance of autonomy and liberty come from Immanuel Kant and John Stuart Mill.[6,7] While Mill and Kant had different explanations for why autonomy is important, both of them thought rationality was important for the autonomy of others being binding upon us. Mill thought that a full set of liberties should only be fully extended to

. . . human beings in the maturity of their faculties. We are not speaking of children, or of young persons below the age which the law may fix as that of manhood or womanhood. Those who are still in a state to require being taken care of by others, must be protected against their own actions as well as against external injury (Mill, p 14).[7]

Mill doesn't tell us much about what constitutes a state in which a person must be protected from their own actions but it is fairly clear that he has in mind states in which the exercise of freedom would be at odds with what is important about having liberty. For Mill this would be when the exercising of a freedom does not further an individual's interests, or capacity for interests and when this results in harm to self or others. So if we turn back to one of the classic justifications for the importance of liberty, impaired autonomy can reasonably be thought of as undermining the right to a full set of liberties. While mental disorders often do not give us reason to restrict liberty they can, and in such circumstances we may be justified in treating against an individual's stated wishes.

SUICIDE

Just as considerations about diminished autonomy can underpin the morality of compulsory treatment they also furnish us with a response to Professor Szasz's position on suicide.

Rejecting life and wanting to kill oneself is defined as a severe mental illness characterised by "dangerousness to self", and is treated as a quasicrime with coercions called "treatments" (especially involuntary "hospitalisation" and forced drugging) (p 228).

While there is something to the idea that suicide becomes medicalised in psychiatry it seems very harsh to say that psychiatry views this as a quasicrime; it is more often a tragedy that we had sound moral reasons for wishing we had prevented.

Although it is foolish to ignore the history of our views about the morality of suicide this claim doesn't ring true for contemporary discussion about taking our own lives. Public opinion (at least in the UK) is, in general, sympathetic towards euthanasia and assisted suicide. Requests by an individual for help in bringing to an end an existence that has become intolerable to them (such as the request of Diane Pretty) are not treated as symptomatic of a disease nor a "quasicrime" but as reasonable requests given intolerable personal circumstances. When a person's situation is such that nothing can be done to make their life better this strengthens our conviction that this is a reasonable request.

There are, however, some crucial differences when the person who wants to commit suicide is mentally unwell. Successful suicide is irreversible so while there are instances of suicide where we should not interfere or criticise morally those who offer aid, there is an onus on being sure that an individual is not making a big mistake. Second, disturbances of mood, cognition or volition can make people want death when they would not if these disturbances were alleviated. In such cases it is reasonable for us to take their preference when not influenced by a disturbance of mind as a better indication of what they want. A third disanalogy that will hold even when a person *really* does want to take their own life is whether anything can be done to make their existence more tolerable. While the predicament faced by Diane Pretty was one that offered her no hope that her condition might improve it is much more difficult to be so sure when the predicament is related to factors such as feeling that one's life is of no value.

Professor Szasz thinks that suicide can be reasonable and that it is the ultimate expression of personal autonomy. There are some famous dissenters to this view. Kant thought that suicide, far from being an expression of self rule, was the antithesis of self rule in that it involved undertaking an action that aims at the obliteration of the self. For what it's worth I'm with Professor Szasz on this point and think that suicide is an act that exhibits the most significant amount of control over a life that an individual can exercise. But this shouldn't distract us from being certain that a person knows what they are doing, is doing what they really want, and does not want this simply because of material conditions that are in the power of another person to alter.

PREVENTIVE DETENTION

Irrespective of his views about suicide Professor Szasz is correct to question how dangerousness is used in the Home Office proposals for the preventive detention of people with DSPD.

> It is a fundamental principle of English and American law that only persons charged with and convicted of certain crimes are subject to imprisonment. Persons who respect other peoples' rights to life, liberty, and property have an inalienable right to their own life, liberty, and property. Having a disposition or propensity to break the law is not a crime (p 228).

It is important to clarify that nobody is saying that dangerousness or a disposition or propensity to break the law is sufficient for a person to be found guilty of a crime. The Home Office proposals do not recommend that preventive detention be like prison. One of the functions of imprisonment (which ought only to occur when a person

has in fact committed a crime) is punitive. For this reason conditions in prisons are designed to deprive prisoners of some of the comforts that the rest of us enjoy. If, as we have reason to believe on the basis of the Home Office report, institutions for the preventive detention of the very dangerous are to be well funded and well staffed care institutions then they will not be prisons in many of the important senses. The fact that the detained person will not, however, be guilty of any crime, means they will not be sentenced and therefore will not have a release date. So those who are deemed to continue to present risk could in effect be preventively detained indefinitely.

I've suggested that the answer to the challenge of Professor Szasz is to justify compulsory treatment on the grounds of diminished autonomy and risk to self and others. This suggestion seems to damn the Home Office proposals for managing those with DSPD. Making a case for those with DSPD having diminished autonomy is a much more difficult matter than making such a case for somebody who is in the grip of an acute schizophrenic episode. While there are often causes for the behaviour of those with the most severe personality disorders, using this as grounds for diminished autonomy places us in difficult territory where it may no longer be clear how any of us can be considered to be autonomous (for more on this idea see Elliott).[8]

The difficulty of predicting risk with the degree of accuracy that is required for preventive detention is one of the major difficulties with the Home Office proposal. If we could know with a very high probability that we were preventing a rape or murder by preventively detaining an individual then this is a compelling reason in its favour. This degree of certainty might, however, be closer to science fiction than to the reality of risk assessment. Nigel Walker has suggested that, "the harm a person has done is more than a mere indicator of what he is capable of doing. It is our only sound justification for infringing his right to be treated as harmless".[9] The thought here is that all of us should be presumed to be harmless unless we have proven otherwise. It doesn't follow from the fact that a person has performed terrible acts that the will do so again but it is the best indicator that we have.

These two major challenges must be overcome by the wording of new legislation, the way in which proposed new institutions are organised, and, crucially, how dangerousness is assessed and threshold of risk required for preventive detention.

CONCLUSION

I think that we need to tread very carefully on the issue of preventive detention. There is a risk that dangerousness becomes an all too easy justification for us to use. The deep anger and outrage at the recent abduction and murder of two young Cambridgeshire schoolgirls could easily move us towards profoundly illiberal approaches to those who may present a risk to others. If we were to ask the public about the appropriateness of preventively detaining individuals with a predisposition towards acts of that kind the reaction is likely to be quite predictable.

The decision to preventively detain a person with DSPD involves a delicate balancing of their interests, the extent to which their ability to act autonomously is impaired, and the seriousness of the danger they present to other persons. A bare minimum for whatever policy is adopted is that it is carefully underpinned by awareness of the importance of respecting and enhancing autonomy and balancing this against the probability and severity of risk.

REFERENCES

1 **The Home Office**. *Managing dangerous people with severe personality disorders: proposals for policy development*. London: The Stationery Office, 1999. http://www.homeoffice.gov.uk/cpd/persdis.htm

2 **Szasz T**. Psychiatry and the control of dangerousness: on the apotropaic function of the term "mental illness". *J Med Ethics* 2003;**29**:227–30.

3 **Szasz T**. *The myth of mental illness: foundations of a theory of personal conduct*. New York: Dell Publishing, 1961.

4 **Foucault M**. *Madness and civilization: a history of insanity in the Age of Reason* [translated by Howard R]. London: Tavistock Publications, 1967.

5 **Dawson J**. Psychopathology and civil commitment criteria. *Med Law Rev* 1996;**4**:63–83.

6 **Kant I**. *Groundwork of the metaphysics of morals* [translated by Gregor M]. Cambridge: Cambridge University Press, 1997.

7 **Mill J**. On liberty. *John Stuart Mill on liberty and other essays*. Oxford: Oxford University Press, 1998.

8 **Elliott C**. Puppetmasters and disorders: Wittgenstein on mechanism and responsibility. *Philosophy, Psychiatry and Psychology* 1994;**1**:91–100.

9 **Walker N**. Dangerousness and mental disorder. In: Griffiths AP, ed. *Philosophy, psychology and psychiatry*. Cambridge: University of Cambridge Press, 1994:10.

[11]

Sanism, Social Science, and the Development of Mental Disability Law Jurisprudence

Michael L. Perlin, J.D. and Deborah A. Dorfman, J.D.

This article examines the way that "sanist" attitudes (attitudes driven by the same kind of irrational, unconscious and bias-driven stereotypes exhibited in racist and sexist decisionmaking) lead to "pretextual" decisions (in which dishonest testimony is either explicitly or implicitly accepted) in mental disability law jurisprudence. In conjunction with these sanist ends, social science data is teleologically employed by legal decisionmakers, so that it is privileged when it supports a conclusion that the fact-finder wishes to reach but subordinated when it questions such a conclusion. The article examines recent Supreme Court cases in an effort to determine the extent of domination of such sanist behavior, and concludes by offering several prescriptions to scholars and policymakers so as to best avoid sanism's pernicious power.

I. INTRODUCTION

Any investigation of the roots or sources of mental disability jurisprudence has to factor in society's irrational mechanisms that govern our dealings with mentally disabled individuals.[1] The entire legal system makes assumptions about mentally disabled people—who they are, how they got that way, what makes them different, what there is about them that lets us treat them differently, and whether their conditions are immutable.[2] These assumptions—that reflect our fears and apprehensions about mental disability, the mentally disabled, and the possibility that *we* may

Michael L. Perlin, JD, is Professor of Law, New York Law School, and Deborah A. Dorfman, JD, is a Patient Rights Advocate at the Mental Health Advocacy Project, San Jose, CA. The authors wish to thank Joel Dvoskin, David Wexler, Keri Gould, Bob Sadoff, Mark Small, and an anonymous reviewer for their incisive comments and suggestions, and to thank Karen Cooper of the New York Law School Library for her helpful assistance. Address reprint requests and correspondence to Professor Perlin at New York Law School, 57 Worth St., New York, NY 10013, USA.

[1] *See generally* Michael L. Perlin *Unpacking the Myths: The Symbolism Mythology of Insanity Defense Jurisprudence*, 40 CASE W. RES. L. REV. 599 (1989–90).
[2] *See generally* MARTHA MINOW, MAKING ALL THE DIFFERENCE: INCLUSION, EXCLUSION AND AMERICAN LAW (1990); SANDER GILMAN, DIFFERENCE AND PATHOLOGY: STEREOTYPES OF SEXUALITY, RACE AND MADNESS (1985).

48   M. L. Perlin and D. A. Dorfman

become mentally disabled[3]—are often non-reflective, self-referential and purportedly "common sensical";[4] they reflect further the pernicious effect of heuristic reasoning and thinking (implicit cognitive devices used to simplify complex information processing tasks and which frequently lead to distorted and systematically erroneous decisions).[5] The most important question of all—why do we feel the way we do about these people?—is rarely asked.[6]

These conflicts lead us to inquire about the extent to which social science data does (or should) inform the development of mental disability law jurisprudence. After all, if we agree that mentally disabled individuals can be treated differently (because of their mental disability, or because of behavioral characteristics that flow from that disability), it would appear logical that this difference in legal treatment is—or should be—founded on some sort of empirical data base that confirms both the *existence* and the *causal role* of such difference. Yet, we tend to ignore, subordinate or trivialize behavioral research in this area, especially when acknowledging that such research would be cognitively dissonant with our intuitive (albeit empirically flawed) views.[7]

One might optimistically expect, though, that this gloomy picture is now subject to change. First, scholars such as John Monahan and Laurens Walker have constructed a jurisprudence of "social science in law," articulating coherent theories about the role of social science data and research in the trial process and outlining specific proposals for obtaining, evaluating and establishing the findings of such research.[8] Second, a recent series of social and political developments (primarily,

---

[3] *See, e.g.,* Joseph Goldstein & Jay Katz, *Abolish the "Insanity Defence"—Why Not?* 72 YALE L. J. 853, 868–69 (1963); Michael L. Perlin, *Competency, Deinstitutionalization, and Homelessness: A Story of Marginalization,* 28 HOUS. L. REV. 63, 108 (1991) (on society's fears *of* mentally disabled persons), and *id.* at 93 n.174 ("[W]hile race and sex are immutable, we all *can* become mentally ill, homeless, or both. Perhaps this illuminates the level of virulence we experience here") (emphasis in original). On the way that public fears about the purported link between mental illness and dangerousness "drive the formal laws and policies governing mental disability jurisprudence," *see* John Monahan, *Mental Disorder and Violent Behavior: Perceptions and Evidence,* 47 AM. PSYCHOLOGIST 511, 511 (1992).

[4] Richard Sherwin, *Dialects and Dominance: A Study of Rhetorical Fields in the Law of Confessions,* 136 U. PA. L. REV. 729 (1988) (discussing "ordinary common sense" (OCS). *See also,* Michael L. Perlin, *Pretexts and Mental Disability Law: The Case of Competency,* 47 U. MIAMI L. REV. (1992), manuscript at 28 n.69 ("My criticism here is not of *true* 'common sense,' but of self-referential pronouncements made under the guise of being 'common sensical,' a kind of *faux* common sense").

[5] Michael Saks & Robert Kidd, *Human Information Processing and Adjudication: Trial by Heuristics,* 15 LAW & SOC'Y REV. 123 (1980–81); Michael L. Perlin, *Are Courts Competent to Decide Competency Questions? Stripping the Facade from* United States v. Charters, 38 U. KAN. L. REV. 957, 966 n.46 (1990).

[6] *But see* Perlin, *supra* note 1; Michael L. Perlin, *Psychodynamics and the Insanity Defense: "Ordinary Common Sense" and Heuristic Reasoning,* 69 NEB. L. REV. 3 (1990).

[7] *See, generally* J. Alexander Tanford, *The Limits of a Scientific Jurisprudence: The Supreme Court and Psychology,* 66 IND. L. J. 137 (1990).

[8] *See e.g.,* Laurens Walker & John Monahan, *Social Facts: Scientific Methodology as Legal Precedent,* 76 CALIF. L. REV. 877 (1988); John Monahan & Laurens Walker, *Judicial Use of Social Science Research,* 15 LAW & HUM. BEHAV. 571 (1991). Similarly illuminating are Gary Melton's and Michael Saks' insights into "psychological jurisprudence" (the study of community and cultural norms through structures that create or sustain social behavior consistent with values that promote human welfare). *See, e.g.,* Gary Melton, *The Law Is a Good Thing (Psychology Is, Too): Human Rights in Psychological Jurisprudence,* 16 LAW & HUM. BEHAV. 381 (1992); Gary Melton & Michael Saks, *The Law as an Instrument of Socialization and Social Structure,* in 33 NEBRASKA SYMPOSIUM ON MOTIVATION: THE LAW AS A BEHAVIORAL INSTRUMENT 235 (Gary B. Melton ed. 1985).

the public awareness of psychiatric hospital deinstitutionalization and its purported link to homelessness, and a series of sensational criminal trials in which mental status defenses have been raised) have resulted in significantly increased visibility of some mentally disabled persons in often-negative ways.[9] One might expect that litigation and legislation in these areas would draw on social science data in attempting to answer such questions as, say, the actual impact that deinstitutionalization has had on homelessness, or whether experts can knowledgeably testify about criminal responsibility in so-called "volitional prong" insanity cases.[10]

And yet, when we attempt to place mental disability law jurisprudence in context, we are confronted with a discordant reality: social science is rarely a coherent influence on mental disability law doctrine.[11] Rather, the legal system selectively— teleologically—either accepts or rejects social science data depending on whether or not the use of that data meets the *a priori* needs of the legal system.[12] In other words, social science data is privileged when it supports the conclusion the fact finder wishes to reach, but it is subordinated when it questions such a conclusion.[13]

It is not enough to simply say, in an almost existential tone, that courts are teleological. What we must do next is to try to articulate exactly what ends fact finders (both trial and appellate judges) attempt to meet through their manipulation of social science data and social science reasoning.

We contend that these ends are sanist. By this we mean that decisionmaking in mental disability law cases is inspired by (and reflects) the same kinds of irrational, unconscious, bias-driven stereotypes and prejudices that are exhibited in racist, sexist, homophobic and religiously- and ethnically-bigoted decisionmaking.[14] Sanist decisionmaking infects all branches of mental disability law, and distorts mental disability jurisprudence. Paradoxically, while sanist decisions are frequently justified as being therapeutically-based, sanism customarily results in anti-therapeutic outcomes.[15]

---

[9] Perlin, *supra* note 3, at 106–08; Michael L. Perlin, *On "Sanism,"* 46 SMU L. REV. 373, 399–400 (1992). On the role of the media in the dissemination of information in such cases, *see* Thomas Grisso, *Forensic Evaluations and the Fourth Estate*, 3 FORENS. REP. 427 (1990).

[10] *See, e.g.,* Norman Finkel, *The Insanity Defense: A Comparison of Verdict Schemas*, 15 LAW & HUM. BEHAV. 533, 535 (1991); Richard Rogers, *APA's Position on the Insanity Defense: Empiricism Versus Emotionalism*, 42 AM. PSYCHOLOGIST 840 (1987).

[11] *See e.g.,* Jodie English, *The Light Between Twilight and Dark: Federal Criminal Law and the Volitional Insanity Defense*, 40 HASTINGS L. J. 1, 20–52 (1988), Perlin, *supra* note 1, at 658 n.256 (federal legislators ignored empirical evidence about the insanity defense in the debate leading to the passage of the Insanity Defense Reform Act of 1984).

[12] *See* Perlin, *supra* note 6, at 60–61; Perlin, *supra* note 4, manuscript at 75–76; Paul Appelbaum, *The Empirical Jurisprudence of the United States Supreme Court*, 13 AM. J. L. & MED. 335, 341–42 (1987); Tanford, *supra* note 7, at 157; David Faigman, *"Normative Constitutional Fact-Finding": Exploring the Empirical Component of Constitutional Interpretation*, 139 U. PA. L. REV. 541, 577 (1991).

[13] *See* Tanford, *supra* note 7, at 157; Faigman, *supra* note 12, at 581.

[14] Perlin, *supra* note 9, at 374–77. On the phobic base of these fears, *see* Deborah A. Dorfman, "Pretexts in Commitment and Medication Decisionmaking: A Psychoanalytic Perspective Through a Therapeutic Jurisprudential Filter" (unpublished manuscript, awaiting submission), manuscript at 5.

[15] *See, e.g.,* David Wexler, *Therapeutic Jurisprudence and Changing Conceptions of Legal Scholarship* (this issue) (hereinafter Wexler, *Changing*); David Wexler, *Putting Mental Health Into Mental Health Law: Therapeutic Jurisprudence*, 16 LAW & HUM. BEHAV. 27 (1992) (hereinafter Wexler, *Putting*); THERAPEUTIC JURISPRUDENCE: THE LAW AS A THERAPEUTIC AGENT (David Wexler ed. 1990) (hereinafter THERAPEUTIC JURISPRUDENCE).

50   M. L. Perlin and D. A. Dorfman

Sanist attitudes also lead to pretextual decisions. By this we mean that the legal system regularly accepts (either implicitly or explicitly) dishonest testimony in mental disability cases, and countenances liberty deprivations in disingenuous ways that bear little or no relationship to case law or to statutes.[16]

Judges are not the only sanist actors. Lawyers, legislators, jurors, and witnesses (both lay and expert) all exhibit sanist traits and sanist characteristics.[17] Until system "players" confront the ways that sanist biases (selectively incorporating or misincorporating social science data) inspire such pretextual decisionmaking, mental disability jurisprudence will remain incoherent. Behaviorists, social scientists, and legal scholars must begin to develop research agendas so as to (1) determine and assess the ultimate impact of sanism, (2) better understand how social science data is manipulated to serve sanist ends, and (3) formulate normative and instrumental strategies that can be used to rebut sanist pretextuality in the legal system. Practicing lawyers[18] must begin to articulate the existence and dominance of sanism and of pretextual legal behavior in their briefs and oral arguments so as to sensitize judges to the underlying issues.[19]

In Part II, we discuss sanism, explain its roots, demonstrate its power in all aspects of mental disability law, and show its relationship to the pretextuality of mental disability law decisionmaking. In Part III, we consider the ways that courts use social science data selectively, focusing on courts' basic suspicion and hostility toward social science, their inability to apply social science consistently and coherently, as well as the reasons why courts are threatened by its use.

In Part IV, we consider the relationship between sanism and social science, and demonstrate how the teleological use of social science data serves sanist ends. Here, we focus on cases that deal with the civil rights of mentally disabled individuals subject to the civil commitment process and the substantive and procedural rights of mentally disabled criminal defendants, and we show how sanism has poisoned

---

[16] *See generally* Perlin, *supra* note 4, manuscript at 3–7.

[17] Perlin, *supra* note 9, at 398–407; *see also*, Michael L. Perlin, *Fatal Assumption: A Critical Evaluation of the Role of Counsel in Mental Disability Cases*, 16 LAW & HUM. BEHAV. 39, 45–52 (1992). Sanism and improper use of heuristics often overlap here. Thus, legislators in one state estimated that, during a specified time period, 4400 defendants pled insanity and 1800 of those pleas were successful; in reality, only 102 defendants asserted the defense, and just one was successful. *See* 3 MICHAEL L. PERLIN, MENTAL DISABILITY LAW: CIVIL AND CRIMINAL §15 37 at 392 n. 701 (1989) (discussing findings reported in Richard Pasewark & Mark Pantle, *Insanity Plea: Legislators' View*, 136 AM. J. PSYCHIATRY 222–23 (1979)). The most recent comprehensive statistical analysis confirms that the defense is raised in one percent of all cases, and is successful just about one-fourth of the time. *See* Lisa Callahan *et al. The Volume and Characteristics of Insanity Defense Pleas: An Eight-State Study*, 19 BULL. AM. ACAD. PSYCHIATRY & L. 331 (1991).

[18] We are not limiting this to lawyers who *represent* mentally disabled individuals (as plaintiffs in civil actions or as defendants in criminal cases). *States'* attorneys have important, independent (and largely hidden) obligations in mental disability cases as well. *See* David Wexler, *Inappropriate Patient Confinement and Appropriate State Advocacy*, in THERAPEUTIC JURISPRUDENCE, *supra* note 15, at 347.

[19] *See* Perlin, *supra* note 9, at 407 (academics must "bear witness to sanist acts ... and speak up ... when sanist stereotypes are employed"). The only mention of "sanism" or "sanist behavior" in case law appears in Koe v. Califano, 573 F. 2d 761, 764 n.12 (2d Cir. 1978), and Woe v. Cuomo, 559 F. Supp. 1158, 1159 (E.D.N.Y. 1983) (subsequent citations omitted). Both cases were litigated by Morton Birnbaum, the creator of the "sanism" doctrine. *See infra* note 21.

each aspect of the law's development. In Part V, we urge scholars to confront these systemic dissonances as a means of creating a coherent framework for the use of social science data in mental disability cases. Here we also show how this confrontation will help create a mental disability jurisprudence that is truly therapeutic. Finally, we conclude with some recommendations for all participants in the mental disability law system.

II. SANISM

A. Introduction[20]

"Sanism" is an irrational prejudice of the same quality and character of other irrational prejudices that cause (and are reflected in) prevailing social attitudes of racism, sexism, homophobia and ethnic bigotry.[21] It infects both our jurisprudence and our lawyering practices. Sanism is largely invisible and largely socially acceptable. It is based largely upon stereotype, myth, superstition and deindividualization, and is sustained and perpetuated by our use of alleged "ordinary common sense" (OCS) and heuristic reasoning in an unconscious response to events both in everyday life and in the legal process.

Judges are not immune from sanism. "[E]mbedded in the cultural presuppositions that engulf us all,"[22] they express discomfort with social science[23] (or any other system that may appear to challenge law's hegemony over society) and skepticism about new thinking; this discomfort and skepticism allows them to take deeper refuge in heuristic thinking and flawed, non-reflective OCS, both of which perpetuate the myths and stereotypes of sanism.[24]

B. Sanism and the Court Process in Mental Disability Law Cases

Judges reflect and project the conventional morality of the community, and judicial decisions in all areas of civil and criminal mental disability law continue to reflect

---

[20] Much of the material *infra* text accompanying notes 21–29 is adapted from Perlin, *supra* note 4, manuscript at 79–83.

[21] The phrase "sanism" was, to the best of our knowledge, coined by Dr. Morton Birnbaum. *See* Morton Birnbaum, *The Right to Treatment: Some Comments on its Development*, in MEDICAL, MORAL AND LEGAL ISSUES IN HEALTH CARE 97, 106–07 (Frank Ayd ed. 1974); *Koe*, 573 F. 2d at 764. *See* Perlin, *supra* note 3, at 92–93 (discussing Birnbaum's insights).

[22] Anthony D'Amato, *Harmful Speech and the Culture of Indeterminacy*, 32 WM. & MARY L. REV. 329, 332 (1991).

[23] Perlin, *supra* note 6, at 59–61; Michael L. Perlin, *Morality and Pretextuality, Psychiatry and Law: of "Ordinary Common Sense," Heuristic Reasoning, and Cognitive Dissonance*, 19 BULL. AM. ACAD. PSYCHIATRY & L. 131, 133–37 (1991). The discomfort that judges often feel in having to decide mental disability law cases is often palpable. *See, e.g.*, Perlin, *supra* note 5, at 991, discussing United States v. Charters, 863 F.2d 302, 310 (4th Cir 1988) (en banc), *cert. den.*, 494 U.S. 1016 (1990).

[24] Perlin, *supra* note 6, at 61–69; Perlin, *supra* note 1, at 718–30.

and perpetuate sanist stereotypes.[25] Their language demonstrates bias against mentally disabled individuals[26] and contempt for the mental health professions.[27] Courts often appear *impatient* with mentally disabled litigants, ascribing their problems in the legal process to weak character or poor resolve. Thus, a popular sanist myth is that "[m]entally disabled individuals simply don't try hard enough. They give in too easily to their basest instincts, and do not exercise appropriate self-restraint."[28]

Rarely, if ever, is behavioral or scientific authority cited to support sanist opinions.[29] As we will show, it is not coincidental that this sort of sanist judicial behavior ignores available social science research. Through sanist thinking, judges allow themselves to avoid difficult choices in mental disability law cases; their refuge in alleged "ordinary common sense" contributes further to the pretextuality that underlies much of this area of the law.

III. SELECTIVE USE OF SOCIAL SCIENCE DATA

The use of social science data is often met with tremendous resistance by the courts, which are frequently skeptical and suspicious of and hostile toward such evidence.[30] Specifically, the skepticism toward statistical data and evidence about the behavioral sciences appears to stem directly from the belief that such data are not "empirical" in the same way that "true" sciences are and therefore are not trustworthy.[31] Social science data is seen as overly subjective and vulnerable to researcher bias.[32]

Courts are often threatened by the use of such data. Judges' general dislike of

---

[25] *See* Perlin, *supra* note 9, at 400–04. Not all judicial opinions are sanist. *See, e.g., id.,* at 403–04; Perlin, *supra* note 4, manuscript at 103–04 (citing examples). For more recent examples, *see* Riggins v. Nevada, 112 S.C+.1810 (1992) (trial court's failure to determine need for continued administration of antipsychotic medications to insanity-pleading defendant or to make inquiry about reasonable alternatives violated defendant's liberty interest in freedom from such drugs; conviction reversed); Foucha v. Louisiana, 112 S. Ct. 1780 (1992) (statute that permits continued hospitalization of insanity acquittee found to be no longer mentally ill violates due process).

[26] *See, e.g.,* Corn v. Zant, 708 F.2d 549, 569 (11th Cir. 1983), *reh. den.,* 714 F.2d 159 (11th Cir. 1983), *cert. den.,* 467 U.S. 1220 (1984) (defendant referred to as a "lunatic"); Sinclair v. Wainwright, 814 F.2d 1516, 1522 (11th Cir., 1987), *quoting* Shuler v. Wainwright, 491 F.2d 213 (5th Cir. 1974) (using "lunatic").

[27] *See, e.g.,* Commonwealth v. Musolino, 467 A.2d 605 (Pa. Super. 1983) (reversible error for trial judge to refer to expert witnesses as "headshrinkers"). *Compare* State v. Percy, 507 A.2d 955, 956 (Vt. 1986), *app'l after remand,* 595 A.2d 248 (Vt. 1990), *cert. den.,* 112 S. Ct. 344 (1991) (conviction reversed where prosecutor referred to expert testimony as "psycho-babble"), *to* Commonwealth v. Cosme, 575 N.E.2d 726, 731 (Mass. 1991) (not error where prosecutor referred to defendant's expert witnesses as "a little head specialist" and a "wizard").

[28] Perlin, *supra* note 9, at 396.

[29] *See, e.g.,* People v. LaLone, 437 N.W.2d 611, 613 (Mich. 1989), *reh.* (1989) (without citation to any authority, court found that it is less likely that medical patients will "fabricate descriptions of their complaints" than will "psychological patients"); *In re* Melton, 597 A.2d 892, 898 (D.C. 1991) (psychiatric predictivity of future dangerousness likened to predictions made by an oncologist as to consequences of an untreated and metastasized malignancy); Braley v. State, 741 P.2d 1061, 1064–65 (Wyo. 1987) (expert testimony on a homicide defendant's reactions to fear and stress rejected on grounds that such emotions are "experienced by all mankind" and thus not related to any body of scientific knowledge).

[30] Perlin, *supra* note 23, at 136–37; J. Alexander Tanford & Sarah Tanford, *Better Trials Through Science: A Defense of Psychologist-Lawyer Collaboration,* 66 N. C. L. REV. 741, 742–46 (1988).

[31] *See, e.g.,* David Faigman, *To Have and Have Not: Assessing the Value of Social Science to the Law as Science and Policy,* 38 EMORY L.J. 1005, 1010 (1989).

[32] Faigman, *supra* note 31, at 1016, 1026.

social science is reflected in self-articulated claims that they are unable to understand the data and are thus unable to apply it properly to a particular case.[33]

This dislike and distrust of social science data has led courts to be teleological in their use of this evidence. Social science that enables courts to meet predetermined sanist ends is often privileged while data that would require judges to question such ends are frequently rejected.[34] Judges often select certain proferred data that adheres to their pre-existing social and political attitudes, and use both heuristic reasoning and false OCS in rationalizing such decisions.[35] Social science data is used pretextually in many cases to rationalize otherwise baseless judicial decisions.[36]

Courts thus will take the literature out of context,[37] misconstrue the data or evidence being offered,[38] read such data selectively,[39] and/or inconsistently.[40] Other times, courts choose to flatly reject[41] this data or ignore its existence.[42] In other circumstances, courts simply "rewrite" factual records so as to avoid having to deal with social science data that is cognitively dissonant with their OCS.[43] Even when courts do acknowledge the existence and possible validity of studies

---

[33] *See, e.g.,* Perlin, *supra* note 5, at 986–93, discussing decision in United States v. Charters, 863 F.2d 302 (4th Cir. 1988) (en banc), *cert. den.,* 494 U.S. 1016 (1990) (limiting right of pretrial detainees to refuse medication). The *Charters* court rejected as incredulous the possibility that a court could make a meaningful distinction between competency to stand trial and competency to engage in medication decisionmaking:

   [Such a distinction] must certainly be of such sublety and complexity as to tax perception by the most skilled medical or psychiatric professionals ... To suppose that it is a distinction that can be fairly discerned and applied even by the most skilled judge on the basis of an adversarial fact-finding proceedings taxes credulity.

Charters, 863 F.2d at 310.

[34] Perlin, *supra* note 23, at 136–37; Appelbaum, *supra* note 12, at 341; Tanford, *supra* note 7, at 144–50; Faigman, *supra* note 12, at 581.

[35] On the courts' heuristic use of social science data, *see* Perlin, *supra* note 4, manuscript at 74–77.

[36] *See* Perlin, *supra* note 4, manuscript at 75–76, discussing decisions in Barefoot v. Estelle, 463 U.S. 880 (1983) (testimony as to future dangerousness admissible at penalty phase in capital punishment case), McCleskey v. Kemp, 481 U.S. 279 (1987) (rejecting statistical evidence offered to show racial discrimination in death penalty prosecutions), and *Charters,* (curtailing rights of criminal defendant await-ing trial to refuse antipsychotic medication).

[37] Faigman, *supra* note 12, at 577.

[38] *Id.* at 581.

[39] Katheryn Katz, *Majoritarian Morality and Parental Rights.* 52 ALB. L. REV. 405, 461 (1988) (on courts' reading of impact of parents' homosexuality in custody decisions); Tanford, *supra* note 7, at 153–54. *See, e.g.,* Holbrook v. Flynn, 475 U.S. 560, 571 n.4 (1986) (defendant's right to fair trial not denied where uniformed state troopers sat in front of spectator section in courtroom; court rejected contrary empirical study, and based decision on its own "experience and common sense").

[40] *See, e.g.,* Thomas Hafemeister & Gary Melton, *The Impact of Social Science Research on the Judiciary,* in REFORMING THE LAW: IMPACT OF CHILD DEVELOPMENT RESEARCH 27 (Gary B. Melton ed. 1987).

[41] *See, e.g.,* Barefoot, 463 U.S. at 897–902.

[42] Faigman, *supra* note 12, at 581. *See, e.g.,* Watkins v. Sanders, 449 U.S. 341 (1981) (refusal of courts to acknowledge social science research on ways that jurors evaluate and misevaluate eyewitness testimony).

[43] The classic example is Chief Justice Burger's opinion for the court in Parham v. J.R., 442 U.S. 584, 605–10 (1979) (approving more relaxed involuntary civil commitment procedures for juveniles than for adults). *See, e.g.,* Gail Perry & Gary Melton, *Precedential Value of Judicial Notice of Social Facts: Parham as an Example,* 22 J. FAM. L. 633, 645 (1984):

   The *Parham* case is an example of the Supreme Court's taking advantage of the free rein on social facts to promulgate a dozen or so of its own by employing one tentacle of the judicial notice doctrine. The Court's opinion is filled with social facts of questionable veracity, accompanied by the authority to propel these facts into subsequent case law and, therefore, a spiral of less than rational legal policy making.

54   M. L. Perlin and D. A. Dorfman

that take a contrary position from their decisions, this acknowledgement is frequently little more than mere "lip service."[44]

IV. SANISM AND SOCIAL SCIENCE

Sanist attitudes toward social science permeate all aspects of the mental disability trial process. Here, we consider specifically these attitudes in the contexts of involuntary civil commitment cases, cases involving the right to refuse antipsychotic medication, and in criminal trial determinations of incompetency to stand trial and the insanity defense.

A. Involuntary Civil Commitment

In the involuntary civil commitment process, courts often selectively use social science data in order to rationalize sanist decisions to either commit patients or deny their petitions for release. Thus, while involuntary civil commitment cases ostensibly turn on the question of whether there is clear and convincing evidence that the patient is mentally ill and, as a result of that mental illness, is dangerous to herself or others (or, in some jurisdictions, gravely disabled), other factors frequently dominate the decisionmaking process. Thus, an entirely different question—whether the patient is likely to self-medicate in the community[45]—is frequently the dispositive "swing" issue in contested commitment cases.

In deciding such cases, courts will privilege psychiatric testimony that implicitly suggests that forensic experts have the power to make this prediction in spite of an utter absence of any behavioral evidence to support either the premise that psychiatrists *can* accurately make this prediction, or whether there is any correlation between this conclusion and future dangerousness.[46] This privileging serves overtly sanist and pretextual ends; it allows courts to overcommit individuals who do not meet statutory commitment criteria where judges feel "it's the right thing to do."[47] This puts a false patina of testimonial respectability on decisions that are grounded neither in social science nor in coherent legal doctrine.

See, e.g., Washington v. Harper, 494 U.S. 210, 229–30 (1990) (prisoners retain limited liberty interest in right to refuse forcible administration of antipsychotic medications), in which the majority acknowledges, and emphasizes in response to the dissent, the harmful, and perhaps fatal, side-effects of the drugs. The court also stressed the "deference that is owed to medical professionals ... who possess ... the requisite knowledge and expertise to determine whether the drugs should be used." *Id.* at 230 n.12. *Compare id.* at 247–49 (Stevens, J., concurring in part & dissenting in part) (suggesting that the majority's side effects acknowledgement is largely illusory). *But compare* Riggins v. Nevada, 112 U.S. 1810 (1992) discussed *infra* text accompanying notes 69–78.

Scholars who recommend a critical reevaluation of the way that that social science data is received, *see, e.g.*, Monahan & Walker, *supra* note 8, at 582–83, are similarly frequently ignored. *See infra* Part IV.

[45] Perlin, *supra* note 4, manuscript at 83–95; Michael L. Perlin, *Reading the Supreme Court's Tea Leaves: Predicting Judicial Behavior in Civil and Criminal Right to Refuse Treatment Cases*, 12 AM. J. FORENS. PSYCHIATRY 37, 50–51 (1991).

[46] Perlin, *supra* note 4, manuscript at 88–89.

[47] Michael Saks, *Expert Witnesses, Nonexpert Witnesses, and Nonwitness Experts*, 14 LAW & HUM. BEHAV. 291, 293 (1990), discussing trial judge's explanation to mental health law students as to why he ordered commitment in individual cases notwithstanding a failure of proof:

> I guess you noticed that some of these people were not fit subjects for commitment under the statute. But, after all, I am a human being. I care what is best for these people, and I have to do what I think is right.

Even where courts seek to determine whether statutorily-mandated dangerousness criteria are met, dispositions inevitably turn on future dangerousness predictions, in spite of an overwhelming data base questioning the accuracy of psychiatric predictions in this area.[48] The paradox here is a pointed one: judges continue to cite approvingly observations on the state of psychiatric knowledge more than 35 years out of date[49] notwithstanding a broad array of recent and available research suggesting impressive improvement in psychiatric diagnosis and testing.[50] Yet, they doggedly endorse—and "routinely and unquestioningly accept[ ]"[51]—the continued use of psychiatric predictions of dangerousness, notwithstanding the empirical record demonstrating the inaccuracy of most such predictions. The teleological use of this paradox is demonstrated in *In re Melton*'s comparison of an oncologist's ability to predict the future prognosis of a cancer patient to a psychiatrist's ability to predict future dangerousness.[52] Here, psychiatry was placed on an equal footing with general medicine where such testimonial privileging served sanist ends.

Similarly, courts frequently teleologically ignore social science so as to justify conclusions that failure to involuntarily commit a person will lead causally to that person's future homelessness,[53] or to sustain commitments based upon legislation that broadens the scope of committability to include individuals who are "gravely disabled" and thus deemed incapable of caring for themselves.[54]

Sanist treatment of social science data is common even in cases that are generally nonpretextual. Thus, in *Zinermon v. Burch*,[55] the Supreme Court recognized that a patient's "voluntary" status is often illusory, and held that a patient could maintain a civil rights suit alleging that he had a right to a due process hearing prior to

[48] *Barefoot*, 463 U.S. at 916–19 (Blackmun, J., dissenting).

[49] *See, e.g.,* Foucha v. Louisiana. 112 S.Ct. 1780, 1789 (1992) (O'Connor, J., concurring in part & concurring in judgment) (quoting Jones v. United States, 463 U.S. 354, 365 n.13 (1983), quoting Greenwood v. United States, 350 U.S. 366, 375 (1956), on the "present state of [psychiatric] knowledge and therapy regarding mental disease"); *id.* at 1801 (Thomas, J., dissenting) (quoting *Jones'* further quotation of *Greenwood* as to the "uncertainty of diagnosis ... and tentativeness of professional judgment"). *See also* Nesbitt v. Community of South Dade, Inc., 467 So. 2d 711, 717 (Fla. Dist. App. 1985) (Jorgenson, J., dissenting), attacking the credibility of psychiatry and contrasting it to the validity of other medical evidence:
> The science of psychiatry represents the penultimate grey area ... A substantial body of literature suggests that the psychiatric field cannot even agree on appropriate diagnosis, much less recommend a course of treatment. Unlike a physician's diagnosis, which can be verified by x-ray, surgery, etc., the psychiatrist cannot verify his diagnosis, treatment, or predicted prognosis except by long-term follow-up and reporting.

[50] *See* Perlin, *supra* note 1, at 658–63 (citing developments).

[51] *See* Marilyn Hammond, *Predictions of Dangerousness in Texas: Psychotherapists' Conflicting Duties, Their Potential Liability, and Possible Solutions,* 12 St. Mary's L. J. 141, 150 n.71 (1980).

[52] 597 A.2d 892, 898 (D.C. 1991) (upholding civil commitment).

[53] *See, e.g., In re* Melton, 565 A.2d 635, 649 (D.C. 1989) (Schwalb, J., dissenting), *superseded on rehearing,* 597 A.2d 788 (D.C. 1991), discussed in Perlin, *supra* note 4, manuscript at 107–08.

[54] This category includes those unable to find and maintain housing, unable to feed themselves, or unable to effectively self-medicate for both physical as well as mental problems. *See, e.g.,* Colo. Rev. Stat. §27-10-107 (1982); Md. Health Gen. Code Ann. §§10–617, 10–805 (f) (1982 & 1987 Supp.); *see also* Mary Durham & John LaFond, *The Impact of Expanding a State's Therapeutic Commitment Authority,* Therapeutic Jurisprudence, *supra* note 15, at 121. In deciding such cases, courts frequently link a finding of "gravely disabled" to future dangerousness in order to justify commitment. *See, e.g.,* People in the Interest of King, 795 P.2d 273 (Colo. App. 1990) (even though expert testimony indicated patient was not necessarily dangerous in supervised setting, evidence sustained finding of "dangerousness" so as to sustain long-term treatment petition).

[55] 494 U.S. 113 (1990).

56   M. L. Perlin and D. A. Dorfman

his "voluntary" admission to a mental health facility.[56] Yet, in support of this decision, Justice Blackmun noted that "the very nature of mental illness" makes it "foreseeable" that such a person "*will* be unable to understand *any* proferred 'explanation and disclosure of the subject matters' of the forms that such a person is asked to sign, and *will* be unable 'to make a knowing and willful decision' whether to consent to admission."[57]

It is ironic that *Zinermon*—the first Supreme Court case to consider the multiple textures of "voluntariness"—still retains the concept of a unitary definition of the impact of mental illness on competency. Competency is not a "fixed state;" a person competent for some legal purposes may be incompetent for others at the same time; incompetency and mental illness are not identical states.[58] Although the ultimate impact of *Zinermon* on actual practice is still not clear,[59] it shows that, even in the context of a "generally sensitive" decision[60] by the member of the court with the *best* understanding of psychological concepts and constructs,[61] social science data is still misused in at least a partially sanist way.

B. The Right to Refuse Medication

The teleological use of social science data is also prevalent in decisions in cases involving the right to refuse antipsychotic medication.[62] For the past 15 years, this issue has dominated the legal-medical debate and has been seen as "the most controversial issue in forensic psychiatry today."[63] Advocates of the use of such

---

[56] *Id.* at 130–37.

[57] *Id.* at 132 (emphasis added).

[58] *See, e.g.,* Paul Appelbaum & Loren Roth, *Clinical Issues in the Assessment of Competency,* 138 AM. J. PSYCHIATRY 1462, 1465 (1981); Loren Roth, Alan Meisel & Charles Lidz, *Tests of Competence to Consent to Treatment,* 134 AM. J. PSYCHIATRY 279, 279 (1977). *See also In re* LaBelle, 107 Wash. 2d 196, 728 P. 2d 138, 146 (1986) ("the mere fact that an individual is mentally ill does not mean that the person so affected is incapable of making a rational choice with respect to his or her need for treatment").

[59] *Compare* Bruce Winick, *Competency to Consent to Voluntary Hospitalization: A Therapeutic Jurisprudence Analysis of* Zinermon v. Burch, in ESSAYS IN THERAPEUTIC JURISPRUDENCE 83, 130 (David Wexler & Bruce Winick eds. 1991) (lower courts should be "hesitant to read *Zinermon's* language broadly"), *to* 1 PERLIN, *supra* note 17, §3.69, at 60–61 (1991 pocket part) (speculating that, given the growing fear of litigation by public mental hospital staff personnel, *Zinermon* may have a "further reductive effect on state hospital admissions").

[60] 1 PERLIN, *supra* note 17, §3.69 at 60 (1991 pocket part).

[61] *See* Gary B. Melton, *Realism in Psychology and Humanism in Law: Psycholegal Studies at Nebraska,* 69 NEB. L. REV. 251, 272–73 (1990) (Justice Blackmun is "Court's scientist" and "Court's moral authority").

[62] As with involuntary civil commitment decisions, social factors play a significant role in institutional medication decisionmaking as well. *See, e.g.,* Paul Benson, *Factors Associated With Antipsychotic Drug Prescribing by Southern Psychiatrists,* 21 MED. CARE 639 (1983) (patients' race, occupation and marital status found to be significant during process of prescribing antipsychotic medications); Ira Sommers & Deborah Baskin, *The Prescription of Psychiatric Medications in Prison: Psychiatric Versus Labeling Perspectives,* 7 JUST. Q. 739 (1990) (decision to medicate mildly impaired prison inmates influenced by social factors).

[63] Michael L. Perlin, *The Right to Refuse Treatment in a Criminal Law Setting,* in FORENSIC PSYCHIATRY: A COMPREHENSIVE TEXTBOOK (R. Rosner ed. 1992) (in press), manuscript at 1, quoting, in part, Jonathan Brant, Pennhurst, Romeo, *and* Rogers: *The Burger Court and Mental Health Law Reform Litigation,* 4 J. LEG. MED. 323 (1983). *See generally* 2 PERLIN, *supra* note 17, Chapter 5; Michael L. Perlin, *Decoding Right to Refuse Treatment Law,* 16 INT'L J. L. & PSYCHIATRY (1992) (in press).

medication point to its benefits while critics point out the serious neurological side effects that can result from these drugs.[64] As a result of this debate, the courts have the opportunity to "choose sides;" thus, if they so choose, they can critically assess the empirical data, or, they can demur to the evidence and refuse to engage in a scholarly discourse over such data.[65]

Such was the case in *Washington v. Harper* in which the Court answered the question of whether a convicted prisoner could be forcibly medicated against his will. In providing defendant with a limited remedy, the majority in *Harper* selectively chose to privilege those aspects of the data available on the effects of antipsychotic drugs that discussed the benefits of such medication, while at the same time acknowledging but discounting[66] the potential harmful and debilitating effects of these drugs.[67]

Harper thus accommodated social science evidence with an important strand of the Supreme Court's penological jurisprudence: "prison security concerns will, virtually without exception, trump individual autonomy interests."[68]

The court's social science jurisprudence seemed to take a dramatic turn this term, though, in *Riggins v. Nevada*.[69] *Riggins* held that the use of antipsychotic drugs violated defendant's right to fair trial (at which he had raised the insanity defense), citing *Harper's* side-effects language, and construing *Harper* to require "an overriding justification and a determination of medical appropriateness" prior to forcibly administering antipsychotic medications to a prisoner.[70] It focused on what might be called the "litigational side-effects" of antipsychotic drugs, and discussed the possibility that the drug use might have "compromised" the substance of the defendant's trial testimony, his interaction with counsel, and his comprehension of the trial.[71]

In a concurring opinion, Justice Kennedy (the author of *Harper*) took an even bolder position. He would not allow the use of antipsychotic medication to make a defendant competent to stand trial "absent an *extraordinary* showing" on the state's part, and noted further that he doubted this showing could be made "given our

---

[64] The disagreement is seen most pointedly in United States v. Charters, 863 F.2d 302 (4th Cir. 1988) (en banc), *cert. den.*, 494 U.S. 1016 (1990), and Washington v. Harper, 494 U.S. 210 (1990).
[65] *See* Perlin, *supra* note 5, at 991 (criticizing *Charters*).
[66] *See Harper*, 494 U.S. at 240 n.5 (Stevens, J., concurring in part & dissenting in part):
    The Court relies heavily on the brief filed by the American Psychiatric Association and the Washington State Psychiatric Association ... to discount the severity of these drugs. However, medical findings discussed in other briefs support conclusions of the Washington Supreme Court and challenge the reliability of the Psychiatrists' Brief.
Compare, e.g., id. at 230 (majority relies on Psychiatrists' brief for proposition that tardive dyskinesia is found in 10–25% of hospitalized patients), *to id.* at 239 n.5 (Stevens, J., concurring in part & dissenting in part) (chances *greater* than one in four of patient developing tardive dyskinesia, and rate is increasing).
[67] In *Harper*, both the state and the defense submitted studies discussing drug side-effects. Although both sets of studies acknowledged the side-effects' seriousness, they disagreed on how pervasive they were in institutional populations. *See id.* at 229.
[68] 2 PERLIN, *supra* note 17, §5.64A, at 64 (1991 pocket part).
[69] 112 S. Ct. 1810 (1992). Even though *Riggins* might appear to be more appropriately discussed as a "criminal trial process" case, we have chosen to consider it here so as to illuminate its relationship to *Harper*. *See generally* Michael L. Perlin, *Riggins v. Nevada: Forced Medication Collides With the Right to a Fair Trial*, 16 NEWSLETTER AM. ACAD. PSYCHIATRY & L. (Dec. 1992) (in press),
[70] *Riggins*, 112 S. Ct. at 1815.
[71] *Id.* at 1816.

58   M. L. Perlin and D. A. Dorfman

present understanding of the properties of these drugs."[72] Justice Thomas dissented, suggesting (1) the administration of the drug might have *increased* the defendant's cognitive ability,[73] (2) since Riggins had originally asked for medical assistance (while a jail inmate, he had "had trouble sleeping" and was "hearing voices"), it could not be said that the state ever "ordered" him to take medication,[74] (3) if Riggins had been aggrieved, his proper remedy was a §1983 civil rights action,[75] and (4) under the majority's language, a criminal conviction might be reversed in cases involving "penicillin or aspirin."[76]

It is not clear whether *Riggins* is teleological. *Riggins* differs importantly from *Harper* in that the court treated *Harper* as a prison security case while it read *Riggins* as a fair trial case; yet, this difference in the litigants' *legal* status self-evidently has no effect on the physiological or neurological potential impact of the drugs in question. Nevertheless, the side effects language in *Harper* (subordinated there because of security reasons) is privileged in *Riggins* (where such issues are absent) by nature of the court's consideration of the question in the context of a fair trial issue. Thomas's opinion raises grave issues for defense counsel; had his position prevailed, would concerned and competent defense lawyers feel as if they were assuming a risk in *ever* seeking psychiatric help for an awaiting-trial defendant? His analogizing antipsychotic drug side effects to penicillin or aspirin may be disingenuous or it may be cynical. What *is* clear is that nowhere in the lengthy *corpus* of "right to refuse treatment" litigation is this position ever seriously raised.[77] Its use here appears, again, to reflect the sanist use of "social science."

C. The Criminal Trial Process

Courts tend to be even more sanist in their decisions in mental disability cases that arise in the criminal contexts than in civil cases.[78] Thus, the sanist use of social science in criminal cases involving the mentally ill is even more teleological than in civil matters. This selectivity is exemplified in cases involving issues such as incompetency to stand trial, insanity determinations, and post-insanity acquittal commitment and release hearings.

---

[72] *Id.* at 1817 (Kennedy, J., concurring).
[73] *Id.* at 1822–23 (Thomas, J., dissenting). Trial testimony had indicated that Riggins' daily drug regimen (800 mgs. of Mellaril) was enough to "tranquilize an elephant." *Id.* at 1819 (Kennedy, J., concurring), quoting trial record.
[74] *Id.* at 1823–24 (Thomas, J., dissenting).
[75] *Id.* at 1825–26. At his trial, Riggins had been sentenced to death.
[76] *Id.* at 1826.
[77] The only case in which a similar issue is raised is Matter of Salisbury, 524 N.Y.S. 2d 352, 354 (N.Y. Sup. Ct. 1988), holding that prior court authorization was not necessary before a state mental hospital could administer antibiotics to a patient, citing "overwhelming public policy considerations" that made it "imperative" that hospitals could perform such "routine, accepted, non-major medical treatment which poses no significant risk, discomfort, or trauma to the patient." *Salisbury* has never been cited in any subsequent case nor has it been mentioned in the law review literature.
[78] *See* Perlin, *supra* note 9, at 402–03 (criminal trial process "riddled with sanist myths and stereotypes"); Perlin, *supra* note 4, manuscript at 95–103 (discussing sanism in the incompetency to stand trial process).

Development of mental disability law jurisprudence   59

1. Incompetency to Stand Trial (IST) Determinations[79]

Courts often discourage and are hostile to pleas of incompetency based on a fear that defendants are feigning[80] in an attempt to ultimately avoid criminal responsibility.[81] This may explain why the states have been so remarkably laggard in implementing the 1972 decision in *Jackson v. Indiana*[82] in which the Supreme Court ruled that IST defendants could not be maintained in maximum security indefinitely if it were not substantially probable that they would gain their competency to stand trial within the "foreseeable future."[83]

Mentally disabled defendants are also often forcibly medicated so as to be "made competent" to stand trial, in spite of the possibility that the medications in question might cause severe side-effects and, in specific cases, a lack of evidence that the medication in question will actually serve to meet the expected end. Thus, in *United States v. Charters*,[84] the Fourth Circuit held that the "substantial professional judgment" standard[85] sufficiently protected defendant's liberty interests in seeking to refuse forced medication.[86] Although the court briefly acknowledged the possibility of side-effects, it quickly dismissed the magnitude of their potential harm by noting that they were simply "one element" to be weighed in a best-interests decision.[87] Here the court conceded that it did not do an "exhaustive analysis" of the conflicting scientific literature before it, demurring to the literature's importance:

> It suffices to observe that, while there is universal agreement in the professional discipline that side-effects always exist as a risk, there is wide disagreement within those disciplines as to the degree of their severity.[88]

In the course of its decision, the court revealed its "apprehensiveness about dealing with underlying social, psychodynamic, and political issues that form the overt and

---

[79] *See generally* Perlin, *supra* note 4, manuscript at 48–53, 68–73, 95–103; Perlin, *supra* note 5.

[80] *See* Stephen Golding *et al*, *Assessment and Conceptualization of Competency to Stand Trial: Preliminary Data on the Interdisciplinary Fitness Review*, 8 LAW & HUM. BEHAV. 321 (1984); Richard Rogers, J. Roy Gillis & R. Michael Bagby, *The SIRS as a Measure of Malingering: Cross Validation of a Correctional Sample*, 8 BEHAV. SCI. & L. 85 (1990). The best recent evidence suggests that feigning is statistically rare, and usually identifiable. *See, e.g.,* David Schretlen & Hal Arkowitz, *A Psychological Test Battery to Detect Prison Inmates Who Fake Insanity or Mental Retardation*, 8 BEHAV. SCI. & L. 75 (1990) (92–95% of all subjects correctly classified as either faking or non-faking); Dewey Cornell & Gary Hawk, *Clinical Presentation of Malingerers Diagnosed by Experienced Forensic Psychologists*, 13 LAW & HUM. BEHAV. 375, 381–83 (1989) (feigning attempted in fewer than 8% of cases studied).

[81] *See, e.g.,* State v. Evans, 586 N.E.2d 1042 (Ohio 1992); State v. Sharkey, 821 S.W.2d 544, 546 (Mo. App. 1991); Blacklock v. State, 820 S.W. 2d 882, 884–85 (Tex. App. 1991), *petit. for discret. rev. filed* (1992); State v. Drobel, 815 P.2d 724, 727 (Utah App. 1991). For the most recent example in a Supreme Court opinion in a case involving an insanity acquittee, *see* Foucha v. Louisiana, 112 S. Ct. 1780 (1992), at 1796 (Kennedy, J , dissenting), and at 1802 (Thomas, J., dissenting).

[82] 406 U.S. 715 (1972).

[83] *Id.* at 738. Thirteen years after *Jackson* was decided, it remained not implemented in almost half the states. *See* Bruce Winick, *Restructuring Competency to Stand Trial*, 32 U.C.L.A. L. REV. 921, 940 (1985).

[84] 863 F.2d 302 (4th Cir. 1988) (en banc), *cert. den.*, 494 U.S. 1016 (1990).

[85] *See* Youngberg v. Romeo, 457 U.S. 307, 322–23 (1982).

[86] *Charters*, 863 F.2d at 307–08.

[87] *Id.* at 310.

[88] *Id.* at 311. While this is certainly true, this does not excuse the court from refusing to critically analyze the scientific research in coming to its ultimate decision. *See* Perlin, *supra* note 5, at 990–92; *compare* Monahan & Walker, *supra* note 8, at 582–83 (setting out steps to be used by courts in analyzing social science evidence).

hidden agendas in any right-to-refuse case,"[89] a problem especially pointed where the right-to-refuse question arises in a criminal context. The court's decision further incorporated a broad array of heuristic devices in a way that led to the trivialization and misuse of the social science data before it.[90]

2. Not Guilty by Reason of Insanity (NGRI) Determinations[91]

In the past decade, the impact of the Hinckley acquittal has increasingly led to attacks on the insanity defense by legislators, prosecutors, the courts, and members of the general public.[92] The caselaw reflects incessant judicial disparagement of the plea, of expert testimony in support of defendants asserting the plea, and of social science data that could help illuminate the "myths" that have grown up about the insanity defense.[93]

Distrust of and selective use of social science data also surfaces in cases involving the recommitment of insanity acquittees. As a result of the use of distorted heuristic cognitive devices,[94] ego defenses,[95] and sociopolitical pressure,[96] courts are particularly sanist and teleological in their consideration of social science research in these cases.[97]

More recently, Justice Thomas's recent opinion in *Foucha v. Louisiana*[98] is a textbook case of sanist behavior in a social science setting. Dissenting from a decision holding that retention of non-mentally ill insanity acquittees in a forensic mental

---

[89] Perlin, *supra* note 5, at 966.
[90] Perlin, *supra* note 4, manuscript at 73–74.
[91] *See generally* Perlin, *supra* note 1; Perlin, *supra* note 6.
[92] Perlin, *supra* note 1, at 609–23.
[93] United States v. Lyons, 731 F.2d 243, 248–49 (5th Cir. 1984):
    A majority of psychiatrists now believe that they do not possess sufficient accurate scientific bases for measuring a person's capacity for self-control or for calibrating the impairment of that capacity ... In addition, the risks of fabrication and "moral mistakes" in administering the insanity defense are greatest when the experts and the jury are asked whether the defendant has the capacity to "control" himself or whether he could have "resisted" the criminal impulse.
Compare id., 739 F.2d 994 (5th Cir. 1984) (Rubin, J., dissenting).
[94] Perlin, *supra* note 6, at 12–22.
[95] D. Dorfman, *supra* note 14.
[96] *See, e.g., Final Report of the National Institute of Mental Health Ad Hoc Forensic Advisory Panel*, 12 MENT. & PHYS. DIS. L. RPTR. 77, 96 (1988) (in the aftermath of the Hinckley acquittal, federal government could be counted on, "in controversial cases   to oppose *any* conditional release recommendation") (emphasis added). *See also* Francois v. Henderson, 850 F. 2d 231, 234 (5th Cir. 198) (testifying doctor conceded he may have "hedged" in earlier testimony as to whether or not insanity acquittee could be released, "because he did not want to be criticized should [the defendant] be released and then commit a criminal act").
[97] *See, e.g.*, Jones v. United States, 463 U.S. 354 (1983), approving a post-commitment insanity acquittal recommitment scheme that placed the burden on the patient to prove he was no longer mentally ill or dangerous, and concluding that it was reasonable to presume that defendant's mental illness continued: "Someone whose mental illness was sufficient to lead him to commit a criminal act [at some point in the past] is likely to remain ill and in need of treatment." *Id.* at 366. No social science data base supports this assumption; the decision in *Jones* is utterly indeterminate, and reflects simply the court's "unwillingness to contradict public sentiment [soon after the Hinckley acquittal] in such a controversial area." *See* Louise Dovre, Note, Jones v. United States: *Automatic Commitment of Individuals Found Not Guilty by Reason of Insanity*, 68 MINN. L. REV. 822, 840 (1984).
[98] 112 S. Ct. 1780 (1992).

hospital violated the due process clause,[99] Thomas based his conclusion that such retention was permissible on a variety of sources, including the 1962 commentary to the Model Penal Code, a 1933 text by Henry Weihofen, and a 1956 Supreme Court case that had stressed psychiatry's "uncertainty of diagnosis."[100] He focused at some length on the possibility of "calculated abuse of the insanity defense" by defendants who might feign the plea, and speculated as to how the public might react to the specter of a "serial killer ... returned to the streets immediately after trial."[101]

Thomas's opinion is astounding for several reasons. First, he relies on legal scholarship that precedes (by 10–40 years) the Court's application of the due process clause to cases involving the institutionalization of mentally disabled criminal defendants.[102] Second, he relies on a mid-1950's characterization of psychiatric precision in diagnosis to suggest that psychiatry is so inexact that the court should discount expert testimony saying that an individual once acquitted on grounds of insanity is not mentally ill; yet—no doubt because it fits well with his *a priori* position on the case—he finds that psychiatric predictions of dangerousness are sufficiently reliable to require the acquittee's future institutionalization (although, here, the experts hedged on even this prediction).[103]

Third, Justice Thomas's twin foci on the sanist judges' worst fears about insanity acquittees—that they "faked" the insanity defense in the first place and that the improper use of the defense will allow for the speedy release of serial killers—is a profound demonstration of how sanist judges distort social science evidence. The empirical data is clear—beyond doubt—that the insanity defense is rarely feigned, that such attempts are invariably "seen through" by fact finders, and that "successful" acquittees are generally institutionalized in maximum security facilities for far longer periods of time than they would have been incarcerated in penal facilities had they been convicted of the predicate crimes.[104] His reference to "serial killers" is even more perplexing here, given the fact that Foucha's underlying charges were burglary and firearms offenses.

---

[99] Foucha had been found NGRI of burglary and weapons charges. After he spent four years in a forensic hospital, that facility's superintendent recommended that he be released since he "evidenced no signs of psychosis and neurosis" and was in "good shape mentally," notwithstanding a diagnosis of antisocial personality disorder. *Id.* at 1782. The court below had found that, because Foucha remained dangerous, he could be retained in the facility. *Id.* at 1783. The Supreme Court reversed.

[100] *See id.* at 1797 (Thomas, J., dissenting) (referring to "current provisions" of the American Law Institute's Model Penal Code); *id.* at 1801 (citing Greenwood v. United States, 350 U.S. 366, 375 (1956), for proposition that there is "uncertainty of diagnosis" in psychiatry); *id.* at 1806 (citing, *inter alia*, HENRY WEIHOFEN, INSANITY AS A DEFENSE IN CRIMINAL LAW 294–332 (1933), for proposition that there is a long history of states providing for the continued institutionalization of dangerous insanity acquittees). *Cf. Focha* at 1787 n.6 (majority opinion) (charging that sections in question "fail to incorporate or reflect substantial developments in the relevant decisional law during the intervening three decades").

[101] *Id.* at 1801–02.

[102] *See* Jackson v. Indiana, 406 U.S. 715 (1972).

[103] *See* Mary Durham & John Q. LaFond, "Responsibility or Therapy in Controlling the Mentally Ill: The Relationship Between the Insanity Defense and Involuntary Commitment," (paper presented at the annual Law & Society Meeting, May 1992), manuscript at 13: "Neoconservative law reform values psychiatric expertise only when it enhances the social control function of the law and denigrates it when it does not."

[104] *See* Perlin, *supra* note 1, at 646–55 (citing empirical studies and sources). A similar "fear of feigning" may also have been the motivating force behind Justice O'Connor's recent concurrence in Medina v. California, 112 S. Ct. 2572 (1992) (not unconstitutional to assign burden of proof to defendant in incompetency to stand trial proceeding), discussed in 3 PERLIN, *supra* note 17, §14.05A (1992 pocket part).

62   M. L. Perlin and D. A. Dorfman

D. Conclusion

Jurisprudential developments in this area still predominantly reflect sanist thinking. Although the majority opinions in *Riggins* and *Foucha* are written in nonsanist tones and demonstrate a capacity to integrate social science into mental disability law decisionmaking, courts still regularly employ heuristic cognitive devices and self-referential "common sense" in their selective use (and nonuse) of social science, leading to both sanist and pretextual outcomes. It is imperative that scholars, researchers and participants in the justice system confront this reality.

V. NEED FOR CONFRONTATION

A. Introduction

Until we articulate the roots of the legal system's sanist biases and pretextual decision-making mechanisms and subsequently demonstrate how these biases infect the legal system's "read" of social science data, we will not make any significant headway in creating a coherent framework for the consideration of social science data in mental disability law cases. A review of the caselaw reflects several specific overarching incoherences and dissonances that dominate this area of jurisprudence.

In a wide variety of jurisprudential contexts—competency determinations, civil commitments hearings, trials involving mentally disabled criminal defendants—social science is used (or *not* used) teleologically.[105] When a court wishes to avoid confronting the empirical reality known to all behavioralists that competency is a fluid state and that one can be competent for some purposes and not for others,[106] it sticks its head in the legal sand and says, basically, "This is too much for us to try to figure out."[107] When a fact-finder "knows" (because it comports with the judge's own self-referential *faux* common sense) that a rejection of a civil commitment application will exacerbate urban homelessness, he simply says that it will, without reference to any of the extensive sociological and behavioral data base that has carefully weighed this question.[108]

Other examples abound.[109] To some extent, the principle of "cognitive dissonance"—the tendency of individuals to reinterpret information or experience that conflicts with their internally accepted or publicly stated beliefs in order to avoid the inconsistent state that much inconsistencies produce[110]—may be operative here. Judges wish to avoid overt consideration of social science data that "conflicts with

---

[105] *See* Tanford, *supra* note 7, at 151 (discussing critiques of social science as a decisionmaking tool that masks the true political and ideological bases of judicial decisions).

[106] *See, e.g.*, sources cited in Perlin, *supra* note 21, manuscript at 85–87 nn.204–47.

[107] *See, e.g.*, Monahan & Walker, *supra* note 8, at 511 n.119.

[108] *See, e.g.*, Perlin, *supra* note 21, manuscript at 107–08 (discussing decision in *In re Melton*, discussed *supra* text accompanying notes 53–53; *compare* sources cited in Perlin, *supra* note 20, at 94–108.

[109] *See, e.g.*, sources cited in Perlin, *supra* note 4, manuscript at 87–91 (on the relationship between a patient's likelihood to self-medicate in the community and an involuntary civil commitment finding); David Ferleger, *Anti-Institutionalization and the Supreme Court*, 14 RUTGERS L. J. 595, 628–32 (1983).

[110] *See* Perlin, *supra* note 24, at 139; Bruce Winick, *Competency to Consent to Treatment: The Distinction Between Assent and Objection*, 28 HOUS. L. REV. 15, 46–51 & n.103 (1991). *See generally* LEON FESTINGER, A THEORY OF COGNITIVE DISSONANCE (1957); ROBERT WICKLUND & JACK BREHM, PERSPECTIVES ON COGNITIVE DISSONANCE (1976).

their internally accepted or publicly stated beliefs;" the result is a retreat to the use of sanist myths and pretextual decisions.

In this way, courts allow themselves to avoid the confrontation of the hard value choices that underlie many of the cases in question. This contributes further to the antitherapeutic quality of mental disability jurisprudence. At a time when scholars have begun to develop and refine the concept of "therapeutic jurisprudence," it is especially important that we consider its relationship to sanist case law and pretextual decisionmaking.

B. Therapeutic Jurisprudence

"Therapeutic jurisprudence" studies the role of the law as a therapeutic agent.[111] This perspective recognizes that substantive rules, legal procedures and lawyers' roles may have either therapeutic or antitherapeutic consequences, and questions whether such rules, procedures and roles can or should be reshaped so as to enhance their therapeutic potential, while not subordinating due process principles.[112]

Although an impressive body of literature has been produced,[113] there has not yet been a systematic investigation into the reasons why some courts decide cases "therapeutically' and others "anti-therapeutically."[114] Our preliminary conclusion is that sanism is such a dominant psychological force that it (1) distorts "rational" decisionmaking, (2) encourages (albeit on at least a partially-unconscious level) pretextuality *and* teleology, and (3) prevents decisionmakers from intelligently and coherently focusing on questions that are meaningful to therapeutic jurisprudential inquiries.[115]

The types of sanist decisions that we have just discussed operate in an ostensibly atherapeutic world; although some decisions are, in fact, therapeutic and others are, in fact, antitherapeutic, these outcomes seem to arise almost in spite of themselves.[116] In short, we cannot make any lasting progress in "putting mental health

---

[111] *See* THERAPEUTIC JURISPRUDENCE, *supra* note 15; ESSAYS IN THERAPEUTIC JURISPRUDENCE, *supra* note 59; Wexler, *Putting*, *supra* note 15; David Wexler & Bruce Winick, *Therapeutic Jurisprudence and Criminal Justice Mental Health Issues*, 16 MENT. & PHYS. DIS. L. RPTR. 225 (1992) hereinafter Wexler & Winick, *Criminal Justice*); Wexler, *Changing*, *supra* note 15; David Wexler & Bruce Winick, *Therapeutic Jurisprudence as a New Approach to Mental Health Law Policy Analysis and Research*, 45 U. MIAMI L. REV. 979 (1991) (hereinafter Wexler & Winick, *New Approach*).

[112] David Wexler, *Health Care Compliance Principles and the Insanity Acquittee Conditional Release Process*, 27 CRIM. L. Bull. 18, 19 n.5. *See generally* Wexler, *Putting*, *supra* note 15.

[113] *See* Wexler & Winick, *New Approach*, *supra* note 111, at 981 n.9.

[114] In two earlier papers, Perlin considered the reasons for the incoherence of insanity defense decisionmaking, and concluded that any inquiry into such a question must take into account the impact of symbolism and mythology in the unconscious ways that judges and lawmakers react to such cases, as well as the simplifying cognitive devices (heuristics) that drive such decisionmaking. *See* Perlin, *supra* note 1; Perlin, *supra* note 6. On how the relationship between heuristics and courts' reception of social science data is frequently pretextual, *see* Perlin, *supra* note 4, manuscript at 73–77.

[115] *See* M. Perlin, "Law as a Therapeutic and Anti-Therapeutic Agent," paper presented at the Massachusetts Department of Mental Health's Division of Forensic Mental Health's annual conference, Auburn, MA (May 1992) (suggesting that influence of sanism must be considered in therapeutic jurisprudence investigations).

[116] *See, e.g.*, discussions in Wexler & Winick, *New Approach*, *supra* note 111, at 990–92 (right to refuse treatment), 992–97 (treatment of incompetent death row inmates), and 997–1001 (treatment of incompetency to stand trial); Wexler & Winick, *Criminal Justice*, *supra* note 111, at 229–30 (sex offender guilty pleas). *See also*, Michael L. Perlin, *Tarasoff and the Dilemma of the Dangerous Patient: New Directions for the 1990's*, 16 LAW & PSYCHOL. REV. 29, 54–62 (1992) (duty to protect in tort law); Perlin, *supra* note 5, at 54 (right to refuse treatment). *See generally*, 1 PERLIN, *supra* note 17, §1.05A, at 4–7, and sources cited (1991 pocket part).

into mental health law"[117] until we confront the system's sanist biases and the ways that these sanist biases blunt our ability to intelligently weigh and assess social science data in the creation of a mental disability law jurisprudence.

C. Some Prescriptions for Future Behavior

First, it is essential that the issues discussed in this paper be added to the research agendas of social scientists, behaviorists and legal scholars.[118] Researchers must carefully examine case law and statutes to determine the extent to which social science is being teleologically used for sanist ends. They must also study the way that judges treat litigants who are perceived to be mentally disabled and how such litigants respond to that judicial treatment.[119] They must also study empirical inquiries into the extent of mentally disabled persons' knowledge about either their legal rights or their medication regimens.[120] These inquiries will help illuminate the ultimate impact of sanism on this area of the law, aid lawmakers and other policymakers in understanding the ways that social science data is manipulated to serve sanist ends, and assist in the formulation of both normative and instrumental strategies that can be used to rebut sanism in the legal system.

Second, lawyers representing mentally disabled individuals must familiarize themselves with this data. The track record of lawyers representing the mentally disabled has ranged from indifferent to wretched;[121] in one famous survey, lawyers were so bad that a patient had a better chance of being released at a commitment hearing if he appeared *pro se*.[122] Further, simply educating lawyers about psychiatric technique and psychological nomenclature does not materially improve lawyers' performance where underlying attitudes are not changed.[123] If counsel is to become even minimally

---

[117] *See* Wexler, *Putting, supra* note 15.

[118] *See also* Perlin, *supra* note 9, at 375–77, 406; Perlin, *supra* note 4, manuscript at 111 (same). *Compare* Perlin, *supra* note 17, at 58–59 (calling for similar scholarly inquiries into effectiveness and role of counsel in the representation of mentally disabled individuals).

[119] Recent studies thus show that judges rarely (and in some cases *never*) inform patients before them at involuntary civil commitment hearings that there is a right to counsel, a right to seek voluntary admission or a right to appeal a commitment order. Charles Parry & Eric Turkheimer, *Length of Hospitalization and Outcome of Commitment and Recommitment Hearings*, 43 HOSP. & COMMUN. PSYCHIATRY 65, 66 (1992).

[120] *See, e.g.*, Paul Wolpe et al., *Psychiatric Inpatients' Knowledge of Their Rights*, 42 HOSP. & COMMUN. PSYCHIATRY 1168 (1991) (over half of patients tested had no recollection of having heard their legal rights explained to them upon admission to hospital) (patients institutionalized in large, urban, university-affiliated hospital); Cathryn Clary et al., *Psychiatric Inpatients' Knowledge of Medication at Hospital Discharge*, 43 HOSP. & COMMUN. PSYCHIATRY 140 (1992) (more than half of patients released from similar facility did not know the name or appropriate dosage of antipsychotic medications prescribed for them, or *why* they were being asked to take these medications).

[121] *See* Perlin, *supra* note 17, at 43–45. *See also* Steven Schwartz, *Damage Actions as a Strategy for Enhancing the Quality of Care of Persons With Mental Disabilities*, 17 N.Y.U. REV. L. & SOC. CHANGE 651, 662 (1989–90) (describing "wholesale lack of legal advocacy" available to patients in public mental institutions).

[122] Elliot Andalman & David Chambers, *Effective Counsel for Persons Facing Civil Commitment: A Survey, a Polemic, and a Proposal*, 45 MISS. L. J. 43, 72 (1974). One half of the lawyers assigned to represent individuals in civil commitment cases in Dallas were unaware of the existence of either of the two treatises written specifically about Texas's mental health law. Daniel Shuman & Richard Hawkins, *The Use of Alternatives to Institutionalization of the Mentally Ill*, 33 Sw. L.J. 1181, 1193–94 (1980).

[123] Norman Poythress, *Psychiatric Expertise in Civil Commitment: Training Attorneys to Cope With Expert Testimony*, 2 LAW & HUM. BEHAV. 1, 15 (1978).

competent in this area, it is critical that the underlying issues here be confronted.[124] This is underscored by judges' lack of basic knowledge about mental disability law; in one astonishing case, a Louisiana civil commitment order was reversed where the trial court did not even know of the existence of a state-mandated Mental Health Advocacy service.[125]

Third, system decisionmakers should study the steps recently outlined by John Monahan and Laurens Walker for courts to adhere to when addressing questions concerning human behavior.[126] They should then assess the potential impact on developments in mental disability law if these steps were to be followed, as well as the extent to which adherence to these proposals could minimize teleological decisionmaking. If courts genuinely did follow these recommendations—and, for instance, began to "evaluate ... available research by determining whether the research has survived the critical review of the scientific community, has used valid research methods, ... and is supported by a body of related research"[127]—the "reasoning" in decisions such as *Barefoot*, *Jones*, and *Parham* is certainly less likely to be repeated in future litigation.

Finally, system decisionmakers must regularly engage in a series of "sanism checks" to insure—to the greatest extent possible—a continuing conscious and self-reflective evaluation of their decisions to best avoid sanism's pernicious power. We need to take what we learn from therapeutic jurisprudence to strip away sanist behavior and pretextual reasoning and provide *real* lawyers at *real* hearings (at which *real* inquiries are made as to mental status, need for commitment, availability of treatment and restrictivity of institutionalization) for mentally disabled individuals. If this were to be done, the pretextual use of social science data could be confronted in an open and meaningful way.

D. Conclusion

Sanist thinking dominates legal discourse and infects legal decisionmaking. To accommodate sanist influences, judges frequently decide mental disability cases pretextually. In doing this, they read social science data teleologically so as to confirm pre-held beliefs but so as to avoid the cognitive dissonance or psychological reactance that would be caused if they were forced to confront data or evidence that conflicted with their *faux* OCS. All of this generally operates on an unconscious level.

Mental disability is no longer—if it ever was—an obscure subspeciality of legal practice and study. Each of its multiple strands forces us to make hard social policy choices about troubling social issues—psychiatry and social control, the use of institutions, informed consent, personal autonomy, the relationship between public perception and social reality, the many levels of "competency," the role of free will in the criminal law system, the limits of confidentiality, the protection duty of mental health professionals, the role of power in forensic evaluations. These are all difficult

[124] For a rare judicial acknowledgement of the impact of lawyer incompetency in another area where inadequate counsel leads to morally intolerable results, *see* Engberg v. Meyer, 820 P.2d 70, 104 (Wyo. 1991). (Urbigkit, C. J., dissenting in part & concurring in part) ("We ... let 'chiropractors' with law degrees perform the equivalent of brain surgery in capital cases, and, predictably, the 'patient' often dies. This is intolerable.").
[125] *In re* C.P.K., 516 So. 2d 1323, 1325 (La. App. 1987).
[126] *See* Monahan & Walker, *supra* note 8, at 582–84.
[127] *Id.* at 583.

and complex questions that are not susceptible to easy, formulistic answers. When sanist thinking distorts the judicial process, the resulting doctrinal incoherence should not be a surprise.

David Wexler, Bruce Winick and others have embarked upon an important and exciting enterprise in the study of therapeutic jurisprudence. This, though, is just one step toward the reconstruction of mental disability law. We must also—simultaneously—confront the law's sanist roots and pretextual biases in all policy arenas: the courtroom, the legislature, the practicing bar, the academy. Only then, will an understanding of mental disability law jurisprudence, truly, begin.

Deinstitutionalization

[12]

The Success of Deinstitutionalization

Empirical Findings from Case Studies on State Hospital Closures

Aileen B. Rothbard* and Eri Kuno†

Introduction

The closing or "downsizing" of state and county psychiatric hospitals has had profound implications for the long-term care of the seriously mentally ill (SMI) population throughout North America, Australia, Western Europe, and Scandinavia. While there have been a host of publications on state hospital closings,[1] only a few have examined pre-post differences in mental health service utilization patterns, costs, and outcomes for state hospital populations.[2]

*Research Associate Professor, Center for Mental Health Policy and Services Research, University of Pennsylvania, Philadelphia, PA, USA.

†Research Associate, Center for Mental Health Policy and Services Research, University of Pennsylvania, Philadelphia, PA, USA.

[1]United States: Indiana (Wright, Holmes, Deb, Blunt, & Duzan, 1997), Vermont (Carling, Miller, Daniels, & Randolph, 1987; Dewees, Pulice, & McCormick, 1996; Pulice, McCormick, & Dewees, 1995); South Carolina (Deci et al., 1996); Oregon (Bigelow, Mcfarland, Gareau, & Young, 1991; Bloom, Williams, Land, Mcfarland, & Reichlin, 1998); Kansas (Rapp & Moore, 1995); Arkansas (Cuffel, Wait, & Head, 1994); Canada: (Holley, Jeffers, & Hodges, 1997; Macfarlane et al., 1997; Mercier, Renaud, & King, 1994; Sussman, 1998); United Kingdom: (Crosby, 1993; Geertshuis, Crosby, & Carter, 1995; Lawrence, Cumella, & Robertson, 1988; O'Driscoll & Leff, 1993); Ireland: (Donnelly, McGilloway, Perry, & Lavery, 1997; Farragher, Carey, & Owens, 1996; Smyth, Buckely, & Clarke, 1997); Sweden: (Dencker & Gottfries, 1991); Finland: (Honkonen, 1995; Pylkkänen, 1994); Norway: (Gråwe, Pedersen, & Widén, 1997; Salokangas & Saarinen, 1998); Australia: (Andrews, Teesson, Stewart, & Hoult, 1990); Greece: (Zissi & Barry, 1997).

[2]Amaddeo et al., 1998; Beecham et al., 1997; Fioritti, Russo, & Melega, 1996; Fisher et al., 1996; Girolamo, Mors, Grandi, Ardigo, & Munk-Jorgensen, 1988a; Girolamo et al., 1988b; Knapp et al., 1990; Leff, 1997; Leff, Dayson, Gooch, Thornicroft, & Wills, 1996; Leff, Trieman, & Gooch, 1996; Okin, 1995; Rothbard, Kuno, Schinnar, Hadley, & Turk, 1999; Rothbard, Richman, & Hadley, 1997; Rothbard, Schinnar, Hadley, Foley, & Kuno, 1998; Tansella, Balestieri, Meneghelli, & Micciolo, 1991.

We would like to thank Martin Knapp and Angela Hallam, London School of Economics, UK, for interpreting the TAPS dataset, Angelo Fioretti and Giovanni di Girolamo, University of Bologna, Italy, for providing data on the Italian psychiatric system as well as the anonymous reviewers. Support provided in part by the Pew Charitable Trusts, Effects of State Hospital Closings, 1993–1996.

Address correspondence and reprint requests to Aileen B. Rothbard, Center for Mental Health Policy and Services, 3600 Market Street, 7th Floor, Philadelphia, PA 19104-2648, USA; E-mail: abr@cmhpsr.upenn.edu

This article reviews the current status of state hospitals in the United States and abroad with respect to census and case-mix trends and summarizes the major findings from clinical and program evaluation studies of former state hospital patients living in the community. The major focus of the article is on four case studies that provide an overview of mental health service patterns, costs, and outcomes before and after state hospital closures in Pennsylvania, Massachusetts, England, and Italy. The purpose here is to summarize our knowledge to date on the status of deinstitutionalization and discuss where to go from here.

Background

Trends in Census and Case Mix of State Hospital Populations. Over the past 30 years, the process of deinstitutionalization has resulted in reductions in the number of public psychiatric hospitals and the resident patient population. The number of state psychiatric hospitals in the United States has gone from 277 in 1970 to 231 in 1996. Patient census has gone from 186 residents per 100,000 population in 1969 to 33 residents per 100,000 in 1992 (Manderscheid & Sonnenschein, 1996). The decline is primarily related to downsizing rather than closing since only 46 state hospitals have actually shut their doors (National Association of State Mental Health Program Directors, 1996). As state hospitals have downsized, the share of state mental health dollars going to community care has increased from 33 % in 1981 to 49% in 1993. A recent report shows that slightly over 50% of resources now go to community programs (National Association of State Mental Health Program Directors, 1995).

Reductions in patient populations have also occurred throughout Europe. Between 1972 and 1982, the number of large psychiatric hospitals in 21 countries decreased by 50% while the number of psychiatric beds in general hospitals increased the same amount. The number of public psychiatric beds went from 266 per 100,000 population to 168 per 100,000 population in England and Wales during that period, the extent of reduction differs by country (Freeman, Fryers, & Henderson, 1985).

Along with downsizing and census reduction, case-mix changes have also occurred in state facilities with an increased percentage of residents with a diagnosis of schizophrenia or affective disorders. The most recently published national statistics showed that 58% of the state hospital population in the United States in 1986 had a diagnosis of schizophrenia (Manderscheid & Sonnenschein, 1992). Furthermore, the proportion of residents aged 65 and older at state hospitals in the United States declined from 22% in 1984 to 15% in 1993 (Semke, Fisher, Goldman, & Hirad, 1996). Corresponding to this, the long-stay patient population (over 5 years) declined as well, while the percentage of the population with a length of stay between 1 and 5 years remained stable during the 1980s (Okin, Pearsall, & Athearn, 1990). Patients with developmental disorders, dementia, and other organic disorders, as well as elderly, long-stay patients with a diagnosis of schizophrenia or old-age depression were the first to be discharged or diverted to other programs. The degree of census reduction in these groups is, however, largely dependent on the ability to transfer them to alternative settings, such as nursing homes and residential programs (Fisher, Geller, Pearsall, Simon, & Wirth-Cauchon, 1991; Sommers, Baskin, Specht, & Shively, 1988).

Compared with the case mix of public hospitals in the United States, the United Kingdom has a greater proportion of long-stay and older persons in their psychiatric hospitals (Ford, Goddard, & Lansdall-Welfare, 1987). A study of long-stay patients in five psychiatric hospitals in the United Kingdom found that 80% of the subjects had a length of stay longer than 5 years, and 66% were age 60 and over (Clifford, Charman, Webb, & Best, 1991). Interestingly, the characteristics of "new long-stay" patients in the United Kingdom was similar to those in the United States (Lelliott, Wing, & Clifford, 1994).

Despite the trend to avoid or discharge long-stay hospitalized patients, there still remains a sizable group of individuals hospitalized more than 1 year. The estimated size of this population in the United Kingdom was about 50 per 100,000 population in 1986 (Wing & Furlong, 1986). The closest statistic in the United States is from the year-end patient census survey of county/state hospitals, which was 46.5 per 100,000 in 1986, down to 33 per 100,000 in 1992 (Manderscheid & Sonnenschein, 1996).

Summary of Patient Outcome Studies. During the first decade of deinstitutionalization, the major concern of mental health consumers, families, and psychiatric providers was related to the perceived public sector abandonment of the seriously mentally ill population and the safety net that supported them. Studies on the "discharge" population done during the 1970s and 1980s found community programs to be equally or slightly more effective than conventional long-term hospitalization, however, most of these findings came from experimental studies, where particular interventions had been mounted for a subset of the discharged population (Braun et al., 1981; Hargreaves & Shumway, 1989) rather than with deinstitutionalization as it was ordinarily carried out.

More studies continued to find that discharged patients preferred life in the community rather than an institution (Barry & Crosby, 1996; Okin, Borus, Baer, & Jones, 1995; Okin & Pearsall, 1993; Solomon, 1992). These findings are predominately based on interventions with special populations, as opposed to those individuals who received no targeted follow-up services. In contrast, a longitudinal study of formerly institutionalized patients in Vermont with no special service intervention showed that over half of the population had achieved considerable improvement after their hospital discharge (Harding, Brooks, Ashikaga, Strauss, & Breier, 1987). Except for a small group of patients with the most specialized problems (Furlong, 1996), the vast majority of long-stay patients appear to be capable of maintaining or improving their level of functioning while receiving treatment in a community system.

As characterized by Geller, Fisher, Simon, and Wirth-Cauchon (1990a), the process of deinstitutionalization has moved into its "Second-Generation." During the "First-Generation," patients with developmental disorders, dementia, and other organic disorders, as well as the elderly, long-stay patient with a diagnosis of schizophrenia or old-age depression were discharged to the community. The process of deinstitutionalization has accelerated in recent years with complete more frequent closings of state hospitals (National Association of State Mental Health Program Directors, 1996). The patients discharged during this second wave tend to be more disabled than prior cohorts and often have special behavioral problems that make them more difficult to place and maintain in community settings. However, in contrast to prior decades, the majority of state mental health agency dollars in the United States are now being allocated to outpatient and residential services versus the state hospital (National Association of State Mental Health Program Directors, 1995). Other public funding sources, predominately Medicaid, are paying for short-stay acute care psychiatric episodes in community hospitals.

Despite major changes in public policy regarding shifts in the locus of care and the funding sources for treating and maintaining individuals with serious mental illness, the cost effectiveness of deinstitutionalization has yet to be determined. Although evidence is accumulating that persons with serious mental illness can be treated in the community, the full impact of hospital downsizing and closures on patient outcomes and the mental health and social welfare systems has not been ascertained. The case studies that follow address these issues.

Case Studies on Service Use, Cost, and Outcomes Following State Hospital Closures

The four study sites we have chosen to review provide empirical findings on service use and cost for individuals in a state hospital versus a community care system. The first study in Philadelphia, Pennsylvania examines changes in service use and cost of both an admission and a long-stay cohort before and after a state hospital closed (Rothbard, Kuno, Schinnar, Hadley, & Turk, 1999; Rothbard, Schinnar, Hadley, Foley, & Kuno, 1998). The second study in Massachusetts is a cross-sectional analysis that compares service use and expenditures for the SMI in two sites; one with restricted state hospital admissions and one with traditional admission patterns (Fisher et al., 1996; Okin, 1995). The third study is a longitudinal analysis that examines service use, cost, and outcomes for multiple cohorts of long-stay patients discharged from two psychiatric hospitals in London over a 10-year period. (Beecham et al., 1997; Knapp et al., 1990; Leff, 1997). Finally, the fourth case study, in Verona, Italy, makes use of a case registry that was used to monitor the care and cost of seriously mentally ill clients over several decades in a community, where no "state" hospitals beds exist (Amaddeo et al., 1998; Tansella, Balestieri, Meneghelli, & Micciolo, 1991). The findings from these case studies are based either on a pre-post or quasi-experimental study design, where comprehensive data has been collected on case mix, services, costs, and, in some, instances outcomes. All sites also have a limited number of long-term hospital beds (e.g., 15 per 100,000 population or fewer) and a well-developed community care system.

Case Study 1: The Closing of Philadelphia State Hospital

The closure of Philadelphia State Hospital (PSH), completed in less than 3 years, provided a unique opportunity to compare the before and after effects of a total state hospital shut-down (Rothbard, Richman, & Hadley, 1997;

Rothbard et al., 1998, 1999). At the time the closing began in 1988, PSH provided psychiatric care to approximately 500 patients from Philadelphia, a city of 1.6 million people. At any time, 70% of the PSH population were residents for 1 year or more with 40% residents for 5 years or more. Acute psychiatric care was provided in both nonprofit and proprietary community hospitals prior to state hospital admission.

When PSH closed, the Philadelphia Office of Mental Health (OMH) received $50 million annually in state hospital replacement funds (~$100,000 per former PSH resident) to create an array of community-based programs. The state hospital functions were replaced by: (a) 60 extended acute care beds for stays of 90–120 days in two community hospitals; (b) 100 long-term structured residential beds with 24-hour supervision and; (c) 483 residential beds with maximum to moderate supervision in over 50 residential facilities. In addition, 200 supported living sites were created for persons with SMI and 300 low-demand housing accommodations were made available for homeless persons with SMI. Thus, residential beds for the SMI population increased from 650 in the late preclosure period (1980s) to 1,683 in the postclosure period (1990s). Furthermore, a community treatment team comprised of former state hospital employees was created to provide intensive case management services to the vast majority of discharged PSH patients (Hadley, Turk, & McGurrin, 1997; Rothbard et al., 1997)

Two groups of SMI patients were followed to assess the effects of the PSH closing. The first was a group of long-stay PSH patients that were discharged to the community because of the closing, and the second was a "divert" population (those that would have been admitted to PSH if the state hospital remained open). In a 3-year follow up of 321 "long-stay" patients discharged to the community suggested that the majority were able to live in residential settings while receiving community outpatient treatment and intensive case management services, for a reduced cost. Approximately 75% of the population lived in residential settings with 24-hour staff supervision, and only 5% returned to a long-stay hospital bed. During the 3-year period following discharge, 20–30% of the former patients required hospitalization an average of 76 to 91 days per year. Half of the patients (52%) did not use psychiatric inpatient care at all during the 3-year period. Only a few long-stay discharged patients were involved in the criminal justice system (2%) or homeless shelter system (2%). The total treatment cost per person was approximately $60,000 a year in 1992 dollars. The estimated state hospitalization cost using 1992 estimates would have been $130,000 per year had the patient remained institutionalized (Rothbard et al., 1999).

In contrast, the second group, the "divert" population, had higher costs in the post-state hospital period (Rothbard et al., 1998). Findings on hospital use showed that the postclosure group spent more days in a community hospital (103 days) than the preclosure group (61 days) and fewer days in a subacute hospital (95 days) compared to the preclosure group (132 days). In addition, the inpatient readmission rate in the year following discharge was higher for the postclosure "divert" group (63%) versus the preclosure group (47%). The increased use of acute care days at community hospitals resulted in higher annual costs for the post closure "divert" group ($66,791 vs. $48,631 for the preclosure group) using 1992 cost figures.

The PSH closing resulted in decreased cost for the long-stay patients, and increased cost for the "divert" patients. These findings suggest that when there are few long-stay hospital beds available, alternative services are required for patients requiring more intensive care following a short acute care stay in community hospitals. This problem is further exacerbated with the implementation of mandatory managed care for vulnerable populations where inpatient stays are reduced to a minimum. A sufficient number of subacute beds may be required to prevent excessive use of emergency rooms and repeated acute care inpatient admissions. A simulation analyses showed that there was a need for more subacute beds in the postclosure period to reduce the queue that developed for patients in acute care beds waiting to be admitted to the subacute unit (Schinnar, Rothbard, & Hadley, 1996).

As Okin (1995) argued, a critical element in evaluating state hospital closures is whether a comprehensive community system reduces the frequency of relapses or simply changes the location in which relapsing patients are treated. In the past, many "divert" patients had a 3–6-month stay in a state hospital but now find their care more fragmented in a system where there are few subacute stay beds available. The postclosure "divert" patients found themselves discharged quicker from extended care hospital beds and rehospitalized sooner than the preclosure PSH patients. Furthermore, they stayed longer in acute care community hospital settings (which were more expensive than community hospital settings) while waiting to be admitted to the extended care beds. Although the study findings from PSH demonstrate the feasibility of community alternatives for discharged patients whose length in the state hospital was 10 years or more, the "divert" patient who experiences shorter, more frequent episodes in the new system may require more innovative interventions if cost-effective solutions are to be found.

Case Study 2: The Closure of Northampton State Hospital in Massachusetts

Under the terms of the Northampton Consent Decree, the Commonwealth of Massachusetts was obligated to reduce the census at Northampton State Hospital (NSH) and to meet the needs of state hospital patients in least restrictive settings (Geller, Fisher, Simon, & Wirth-Cauchon, 1990a; Geller, Fisher, Simon, & Wirth-Cauchon, 1990b; Okin, 1984; Okin, 1995). The closure of Northampton provided and opportunity to compare state mental health expenditures, care patterns, and client outcomes between Western Massachusetts and other regions in Massachusetts.

The census at NSH declined from 368 in 1978 to 99 in 1991, and the hospital was finally closed in 1993 (Fisher et al., 1996; Okin, 1995). Comprehensive community services were implemented, including residential programs, day treatment, emergency services, and case management. An admission diversion program was created, which included crisis intervention, prescreening, and respite care (Fisher, Geller, Altaffer, & Bennett, 1992). By 1993, all acute cases were admitted to nine community hospitals. Thirty-two beds were allocated for subacute patients up to 120 days, and 30 long-term beds were created to treat patients who needed more than 120 days of inpatient care (Okin, 1995). In February 1993, the inpatient census was 3.4 per 100,000 population at the state hospital and 9.6 per 100,000 at the subacute facility supported by the state mental health authority, a total of 13 beds per 100,000 population.

Between 1978 and 1992, total funding for mental health services in the Western region increased from $11.8 million to $17.2 million in constant dollars. Resources devoted to noninpatient community services increased from $1.8 million to $12.7 million, while funds devoted to inpatient services declined from $10 million to $4.6 million in constant dollars (Okin, 1995). The percentage of mental health expenditure by type of service showed a different spending pattern in Western Massachusetts versus the rest of the state, for example, supported residential programs (35% vs. 20%), assertive case management and support services (16% vs. 10%), and hospital care (26% vs. 53%). Per capita expenditures in 1992 were $64.67 in Western Massachusetts, compared with $61.96 in the rest of the state. Prior to the consent decree, Western Massachusetts had fewer mental health resources than other regions. By 1993, however, total spending per capita was similar to other regions of the state but the amount of funds spent on the community-based services was greater in Western Massachusetts.

Reduction in inpatient care expenditures was largely generated by reducing the elderly and long-stay patient populations in the state facility by transferring patients to alternative programs. The inpatient case mix between 1977 and 1991 showed a decline in patients over 65 years old from 23% to 1% (Fisher et al., 1996). The largest reduction was in the long-stay population with LOS longer than 5 years, 167 (36%) to 6 (6%) patients in the same time period where nursing homes and community residential settings became alternative placements.

The number of patients whose length of stay was less than 1 year at NSH was reduced slightly from 1977 to 1986 (192 to 172), while those at a hospital serving a similar population increased from 1977 to 1986. Despite the decline in use of beds at NSH, general hospital and private psychiatric hospital service use was no higher in Western Massachusetts than in the rest of the state, dispelling the cost shifting theory (Fisher et al., 1996). Moreover, an analysis of state hospital length of stay and readmission rates showed that Northampton patients displayed no significant difference in community tenure after discharge, even though they had shorter stay in the hospital. The probability of discharge within 30 days was 51% of all admissions to NSH, compared with the statewide average of 36% (Fisher & Altaffer, 1992; Fisher et al., 1992). The probability of readmission was 11% within 30 days after discharge and 16% within 60 days for patients discharged from NSH in fiscal year 1986, which was similar to the state-wide average.

A more recent study of a randomly selected group of community clients with serious mental illness found that patients in Western Massachusetts used less inpatient care annually than those in other regions; 9 bed days for the Western region versus 12 days for Boston and 24 days for Central region subjects. There were no significant difference between regions in total expenditures for mental health and medical treatment. In contrast to the regional level analyses, which found no significant differences in the cost and outcome between groups of patients, an individual patient level cost-effectiveness analysis found the care per patient in Western Massachusetts was more cost effective than other regions. However, because of small sample sizes ($n = 35$–62), the study findings need to be interpreted cautiously (Dickey, Fisher, Siegel, Altaffer, & Azeni, 1997).

Over the 15 years, the role of state hospital in Western Massachusetts has diminished, and the largest percentage of state mental health funds are allocated to residential, case management, and other admission diversion programs, versus inpatient care. Only 13/100,000 beds per capita were used for sub-acute to long-stay patients in 1993. The experience in Western Massach - setts suggests that the long-term care function of the state hospital can be replaced by the alternative community services. However, as in the Philadelphia system, the community-based service system does not eliminate the need for repeated hospitalizations for a certain portion of the acute and intermediate client population. No differences were found in the readmission rates among the discharged NSH patients and the state hospital patients in other regions, however, the number of patients at NSH was smaller and discharged earlier than the state hospital patients in other regions. A question of whether increased resource allocation in community-based services is related to better client outcome needs further investigation.

Case Study 3: The Closure of Friern and Claybury Hospitals in London, United Kingdom

In July 1983, the North East Thames Health Authority decided to close two of the six large psychiatric hospitals in the jurisdiction. The two hospitals, Friern and Claybury, had 2,000 beds between them and served a population of about 1 million. The replacement service planning focused on the provision of residential accommodation in the community for long-stay patients. District health authorities, local-authority social service departments or voluntary organizations were involved in the development of community care, aided by the transfer payment of funds previously used to run these hospitals. The policy for the long-stay patients was to place them in normal housing in their districts of origin with staff on the premises. The discharged patients were also provided support by general practitioners, field social workers, community psychiatric nurses, as well as day-care services. The first "reprovision" patients moved to the community in 1985; Friern was closed in March 1993, and Claybury was closed in 1996 (Knapp et al., 1990; Leff, 1992; Leff, Trieman, & Gooch, 1996; O'Driscoll & Leff, 1993).

A large-scale evaluation study was conducted by The Team for the Assessment of Psychiatric Services (TAPS), established in May 1985 (Leff et al., 1996). The closures created a rare opportunity to combine a carefully planned closing process (Furlong, 1996; Wing & Furlong, 1986) with a comprehensive evaluation of the long-stay discharged patients. The study subjects were those with a length of stay of over a year, excluding patients with a diagnosis of dementia if they were over 65 years old. The long-stay patients occupied about 50% of the beds on the census day in 1985. Because the two hospitals continued to admit patients, there was an accumulation of potential new long-stay patients or the divert patient that was not admitted in the Philadelphia study. The only new patients included in the study (admitted to the hospital after 1985) were those who stayed more than 1 year. The evaluation by the TAPS project team was particularly valuable because it covered the closing process from the beginning to the end, examining the variety of outcome domains at baseline, 1 year and 5-year follow-up periods.

Over the 10-year period, patients who required less support services were discharged to the community in the earlier stages. This was followed by more dependent patients as the health districts prepared alternative residential settings with higher levels of care. The patients who left the hospital during the first 3 years of the study period were younger than the remaining patients (52.5 vs. 58.3), with shorter lengths of stay (11 years vs. 22 years), less social behavioral problems and a greater desire to leave the hospital (67% vs. 33%) (Jones, 1993).

At the final stage of its closing, 72 "difficult to place" patients were transferred to specialized care settings. These patients were younger, with a mean age of 45 years old, and with shorter lengths of stay (33 months), compared with the previously discharged patients (Trieman & Leff, 1996). Thirty-nine percent (39%) were detained legally, and 8% refused to leave the hospital. There were no differences in clinical assessment and daily living skills, but more "difficult to place" patients demonstrated hostility, destructive behavior, and inappropriate sexual behavior.

A 1-year follow-up done on 737 patients found little change in psychiatric symptoms or social behavior problems (Leff, Trieman, & Gooch, 1996). One year following discharge, 8% were in hospital settings and another 15% were transferred to hospital settings or special community residences. Approximately 14% lived independently, and 61% stayed in some kind of residential arrangement arrangements (Beecham et al., 1997; Leff, 1997).

Despite little change in clinical and social functioning, discharged patients were appreciative of their increased freedom and wished to stay in the community (Leff et al., 1996).

An analysis of the community costs of the early discharge cohorts found a 25% to 47% reduction in annualized spending per person compared to patients still residing in the hospital (Knapp et al., 1990). Because these cost figures were based on the easy to place patients who were the first to leave the hospital, Knapp et al. (1990) used a prediction model to estimate the community treatment costs for the entire long-stay population. The model predicted a much smaller cost reduction after the later cohorts were added to the case mix. Preliminary results, using the actual data from all cohorts, suggests that the cost of community care is slightly higher than institutional care. Nonetheless, TAPS investigators believe that the funds released by the closing of psychiatric hospitals are sufficient to reinvest in community replacement services (Knapp, 1996; Leff et al., 1996).

The findings from the TAPS project confirmed the findings of previous studies on discharged state hospital patients demonstrating that long-stay patients are capable of maintaining or improving their level of functioning while receiving treatment in a community outpatient and residential system with greater satisfaction. The TAPS finding is important because it shows that the community alternative works not only for selected clients but for the vast majority of resident patients, except for a small group with specialized problems. The number of psychiatric extended care beds required for this special need population was estimated at 10 to 11 per 100,000 population (Trieman & Leff, 1996).

Similar to the PSH study findings, the risk of rehospitalization was found to be higher for the younger, "new" long-stay patients who had intermittent stays, sometimes repeatedly, than for patients with a long history of hospitalization (Gooch & Leff, 1996). It should be expected that the "divert" population in the post-Friern and Claybury Hospital closure period would also make greater use of emergency and community hospital beds when compared to the long-stay patients followed in the TAPS project.

Case Study 4: Italian Experience

In 1978, the Italian Parliament passed Law 180, which prohibited first admissions to mental hospitals after May 1978 and all admissions after December 1981. The law required a comprehensive and integrated system of community psychiatric care be instituted, which included psychiatric units of up to 15 beds in general hospitals and community mental health centers to provide ambulatory psychiatric care to geographically defined areas. Consistent with other locations, the number of residents in the public mental hospital declined form 179 per 100,000 in 1965 to 44 per 100,000 in 1987 (De Salvia & Barbato, 1993).

Notwithstanding the decline in residential census of psychiatric patients, the application of the law has varied enormously from region to region because implementation of new services was locally determined (Farragher, Carey, & Owens, 1996). In progressive communities, such as Trieste and Arrezzo, community mental health services were fully implemented, and an aggressive approach resulted in the discharge of long-stay patients from the psychiatric hospital (Dell'Acqua & Dezza, 1985; Martini, Cecchini, Corlito, D'Arco, & Nascimbeni, 1985). In Trieste, most patients were discharged group homes including one for the severely disabled. In South Verona, a more gradual process of deinstitutionalization has occurred. Community services were set up in response to the law requiring no new admissions, however, less emphasis was placed on discharging long-stay patients who were in psychiatric hospital (Balestrieri, Micciolo, & Tansella, 1987). The long-stay population has declined gradually mainly from the death of aging patients. In contrast to these regions, other communities throughout Italy were slow to establish community psychiatric services and continue to admit patients to psychiatric hospitals, renamed rehabilitation centers. For example, 15% of admissions to general hospital psychiatric units in Cremona in 1986 were transferred to the former psychiatric hospital (Girolamo, Mors, Grandi, Ardigo, & Munk-Jorgensen, 1988; Girolamo, Mors, Rossi, et al., 1988).

A significant feature of communities that have genuinely implemented the law was their ability to treat patients without the backup of long-stay hospital beds. The psychiatric inpatient census per 100,000 adult population in South Verona declined from 42.6 in 1982 to 30.1 in 1988. The census in general hospital psychiatric wards during the same time period was between 13.6 and 18.7 per 100,000 adult population. The inpatient census at private hospitals did not increase during the 1980s, ranging around 6.0 to 10.5 per 100,000 adult population. Since the psychiatric reform in 1978, there was negligible build up of new long-stay patients, indicated by only 1 or 2 patients became long-stay over a 3-year follow-up period (Tansella et al., 1991).

A series of studies using the case registry data in South Verona provides insight into the Italian model of community-based care. In South Verona, an area with a population of 75,000, three multidisciplinary teams consisting of psychiatrists, psychologists, community nurses, social workers etc. were responsible for care of patients from their respective areas. The core of the system was a community mental health center, open 12 hours a day, where a drop-in approach was encouraged. The services include day care, rehabilitation, outpatient, home visit, crisis intervention, emergency room service, and psychiatric consultation for other departments of the general hospital, as well as a 15-bed inpatient unit in a general hospital (Amaddeo et al., 1998; Mosher & Burti, 1989). Sheltered apartments and 24-hour staffed hostels were also available. Except for nurses, all staff worked both in the hospital setting and in the community, ensuring continuity of care through different phases of treatment.

The characteristics of all clients with ICD-9 psychiatric diagnosis who had a contact with psychiatric services in 1992 and 1993 showed that 47% of clients were married, and 90% lived with spouse or other relatives. Only 9% lived alone, or with a child. The high percentage of clients living with family is striking. For the clients treated by South Verona community services in 1992, annualized costs of services for 136 patients with schizophrenia and other related diagnosis was 17.2 million lire at 1993 prices; 40% for inpatient care, 26% for residential services, and 34% for ambulatory and community services (Amaddeo et al., 1997). Of all clients with a diagnosis of schizophrenia, 34% received inpatient care, with an average 86.9 days per year. The mean inpatient days per client was 29.4 days. Only 4% received residential services. For the clients with affective disorders ($N = 184$), 22% received inpatient care, with an average 38 days per user, and 8.5 days per person.

Because the public psychiatric hospital was not closed in the Verona region, 81% of the total mental health annual cost (15.09 billion lira) in 1986 was spent on the public psychiatric hospital. It was claimed that failure to reallocate resources prevented the establishment of residential services where long-stay patients could be discharged (Mosher & Burti, 1989) .

It appears that the "single staff" care model in South Verona, equipped with three multidisciplinary teams and a 15-bed unit at the general hospital for 75,000 population, can treat patients without backup of the long-stay hospital. Hospitalization is not necessarily avoided, however, the hospitalization experience for South Verona may be different from the United States. For example, Geller (1991) described the disruptive admission patterns of patients at a crisis intervention service in Westfield (a population about 101,000), one of the areas served by NSH in Massachusetts. During a 1-year period, 214 admissions were made to 16 hospitals. Of 32 patients who required more than one psychiatric admission, 21 used at least two different hospitals, due to bed availability. This is not likely in South Verona. The "single staff" model is a viable possibility for improving the care of the repeated, intermediate-stay patients found in the community-based systems in the United States and United Kingdom.

Discussion

The SMI population, though small (4–5 million or 2.1% of U.S. population), consumes the vast majority of public mental health resources in all communities (Rothbard, Schinnar, & Goldman, 1994). These people are at great risk of being marginalized as institutional resources flow to individual community programs where the political power base is dispersed. Several studies have already suggested that as the share of mental health dollars to state hospitals is reduced, the total amount of resources allocated to state mental health programs, as a percent of the health and welfare budget, is smaller (Hadley, Culhane, Snyder, & Lutterman, 1992; Schinnar, Rothbard, & Yin, 1993). However, these findings were based on cross-sectional studies and require follow-up to determine whether there is a causal versus historical relationship implicit in the association.

Notwithstanding concerns around hospital closures, the trend toward hospital closures has accelerated in past years. The empirical evidence suggests that the long-stay discharge population shows an improved life satisfaction following discharge, with little or no deterioration in level of functioning. In addition, costs have generally been the same or less for discharged patients living in the community. In Philadelphia, the cost of care was substantially reduced; in Massachusetts, as well as London, costs were, on average, no higher in the community versus the state hospital, particularly after the first year following discharge. Finally, in South Verona, though there are no cost figures given for long-term psychiatric hospitals operating in contiguous regions, the data suggests that the community system is no more costly and patients appear more satisfied with community care.

There are several similarities between these case studies that may be useful in planning for systems of community-based care as long-stay psychiatric hospitals continue to downsize and close. First, it appears that the "long-stay" inpatient population is transitioned more easily into the community than might be assumed given their lengthy hospitalization histories. This may have to do with the illness trajectory associated with severe mental disorders where persons have learned over time to cope with symptoms and adjust to the functional limitations imposed by mental illness. Given that this long-stay cohort is usually the first group to be discharged, estimates of cost savings are likely to be based on the cost of residential care in the community. In Philadelphia, this care was substantially less than the cost of the state hospital, whereas in the U.K. residential care proved to be at least as costly given the support services provided in the care settings.

The challenge pointed out by several of these studies is the care of the "new" long-stay population. This population has more recently come under scrutiny as evidence accumulates that they are the ones making the greatest use of costly emergency room and community hospital beds. Increased homelessness and criminal justice involvement have not been substantiated by the data for the discharged population (Rothbard et al., 1999; Thornicroft & Bebbington, 1989) suggesting that if this is a problem, it is likely the "divert" population that is involved in such a trans-institutionalization process. The increasing co-occurring substance abuse problem is a major factor in this group. The extent to which community-based resources are targeted to this population needs to be examined. The "single staff" model in South Verona may be a viable possibility for improving the care of this "divert" population.

Despite the fact that the case study findings reported here enhance our system-level knowledge, they are not based on a common conceptual framework for evaluating state hospital closures, making it more difficult to synthesize the results (Kamis-Gould, Hadley, Rothbard, Lovelace & Eppler, 1995). What is required is a common study design, comparable patient populations, and common service and cost measures. International studies can provide a vehicle for comparing the cost effectiveness of different service delivery systems, if a conceptual framework can be determined.

The desire to create a cost-effective service system that provides care in the least restrictive setting while promoting quality of life for individuals with serious mental illness is shared by all. The relevant question, at this juncture, is what mix and level of service(s) should replace the former "state" hospital system, not whether long-stay psychiatric institutions should be eliminated.

References

Amaddeo, F., Beecham, J., Bonizzato, P., Fenyo, A., Knapp, M., & Tansella, M. (1997). The use of a case register to evaluate the costs of psychiatric care. *Acta Psychiatrica Scandinavica, 95,* 189–198.

Amaddeo, F., Beecham, J., Bonizzato, P., Fenyo, A., Tansella, M., & Knapp, M. (1998). The costs of community-based psychiatric care for first-ever patients: A case register study. *Psychological Medicine, 28,* 173–183.

Andrews, G., Teesson, M., Stewart, G., & Hoult, J. (1990). Follow-up of community placement of the chronic mentally ill in New South Wales. *Hospital and Community Psychiatry, 41*(2), 184–188.

Balestrieri, M., Micciolo, R., & Tansella, M. (1987). Long-stay and long-term psychiatric patients in an area with a community-based system of care: A register follow-up study. *The International Journal of Social Psychiatry, 33*(4), 251–262.

Barry, M., & Crosby, C. (1996). Quality of Life as an evaluative measure in assessing the impact of community care on people with long-term psychiatric disorders. *British Journal of Psychiatry, 168,* 210–216.

Beecham, J., Hallman, A., Knapp, K., Baines, B., Fenyo, A., & Asbury, M. (1997). Costing care in hospital and in the community. In J. Leff (Ed.), *Care in the community: Illusion or reality* (pp. 93–107). New York: John Wiley and Sons.

Bigelow, D. A., Mcfarland, B. H., Gareau, M. J., & Young, D. J. (1991). Implementation and effectiveness of a bed reduction project. *Community Mental Health Journal, 27*(2), 125–133.

Bloom, J. D., Williams, M. H., Land, C., Mcfarland, B., & Reichlin, S. (1998). Changes in public psychiatric hospitalization in Oregon over the past two decades. *Psychiatric Services, 49,* 366–369.

Braun, P., Kochansky, G., Shapiro, R., Greenberg, S, Gudeman, J. E., Johnson, S., & Shore, M. F. (1981). Overview: Deinstitutionalization of psychiatric patients, a critical review of outcome studies. *American Journal of Psychiatry, 138,* 736–749.

Carling, P. J., Miller, S., Daniels, L. V., & Randolph, F. L. (1987). A state mental health system with no state hospital: The Vermont feasibility study. *Hospital and Community Psychiatry, 38,* 617–624.

Clifford, P., Charman, A., Webb, Y., & Best, S. (1991). Planning for community care: Long-stay populations of hospitals scheduled for rundown closure. *British Journal of Psychiatry, 158,* 190–196.

Crosby, C. (1993). Mental health programmes. *Journal of Mental Health, 2,* 85–88.

Cuffel, B. J., Wait, D., & Head, T. (1994). Shifting the responsibility for payment for state hospital services to community mental health agencies. *Hospital and Community Psychiatry, 45,* 460–464.

Deci, P. A., Bevilacqua, J. J., Morris, J. A., & Dias, J. K. (1996). Community service development for consumers in long-stay psychiatric hospitals in South Carolina. *International Journal of Law and Psychiatry, 19,* 265–287.

Dell'Acqua, G., & Dezza, M. G. C. (1985). The end of the mental hospital: A review of the psychiatric experience in Trieste. *Acta Psychiatrica Scandinavica, 71*(Suppl. 316), 45–69.

Dencker, K., & Gottfries, C. G. (1991). The closure of a major psychiatric hospital. *Social Psychiatric and Psychiatric Epidemiology, 26,* 162–167.

De Salvia, D., & Barbato, A. (1993). Recent trends in mental health services in Italy: An analysis of national and local data. *Canadian Journal of Psychiatry, 38,* 195–202.

Dewees, M., Pulice, R. T., & McCormick, L. L. (1996). Community integration of former state hospital patients: Outcomes of a policy shift in Vermont. *Psychiatric Services, 47,* 1088–1092.

Dickey, B., Fisher, W., Siegel, C., Altaffer, F., & Azeni, H. (1997). The cost and outcomes of community-based care for the seriously mentally ill. *Health Services Research, 32*, 599–614.

Donnelly, M., McGilloway, S., Perry, S., & Lavery, C. (1997). A 3- to 6-year follow-up of former long-stay psychiatric patients in Northern Ireland. *Social Psychiatry and Psychiatric Epidemiology, 32*, 451–458.

Farragher, B., Carey, T., & Owens, J. (1996). Long-term follow-up of rehabilitated patients with chronic psychiatric illness in Ireland. *Psychiatric Services, 47*, 1120–1122.

Fioritti, A., Russo, L. L., & Melega, V. (1996). Reform said or done? The case of Emilia-Romagna within the Italian psychiatric context. *American Journal of Psychiatry, 154*, 94–98.

Fisher, W. H., & Altaffer, F. B. (1992). Inpatient length of stay measures: Statistical and conceptual issues. *Administration and Policy in Mental Health, 19*(5), 311–320.

Fisher, W. H., Geller, J. L., Altaffer, F., & Bennett, M. B. (1992). The relationship between community resources and state hospital recidivism. *American Journal of Psychiatry, 149*, 385–390.

Fisher, W. H., Geller, J. L., Pearsall, D. T., Simon, L. J., & Wirth-Cauchon, J. L. (1991). A continuum of services for the deinstitutionalized, chronically mentally ill elderly. *Administration and Policy in Mental Health, 18*(6), 397–410.

Fisher, W. H., Simon, L., Geller, J. L., Penk, W. E., Irvin, E. A., & White, C. L. (1996). Case mix in the "downsizing" state hospital. *Psychiatric Services, 47*, 255–262.

Ford, M., Goddard, C., & Lansdall-Welfare, R. (1987). The dismantling of the mental hospital? Glenside Hospital surveys 1960–1985. *British Journal of Psychiatry, 151*, 479–485.

Freeman, H. L., Fryers, T., & Henderson, J. H. (1985). *Mental health services in Europe: 10 years on.* Copenhagen: World Health Organization.

Furlong, R. C. S. (1996). Haven within or without the hospital gate: A reappraisal of asylum provision in theory and practice. In D. Tomlinson & J. Carrier (Eds.), *Aslyum in the community* (pp. 135–168). New York: Routledge.

Geertshuis, S. A., Crosby, C., & Carter, M. F. (1995). Psychiatric patients who remain in long stay hospitals. *Journal of Mental Health, 4*, 519–529.

Geller, J. L. (1991). "Anyplace but the state hospital": Examining assumptions about the benefits of admission diversion. *Hospital and Community Psychiatry, 42*, 145–152.

Geller, J. L., Fisher, W. H., Simon, L. J., & Wirth-Cauchon, J. L. (1990a). Second-generation deinstitutionalization, I: The impact of Brewster v. Dukakis on state hospital case mix. *American Journal of Psychiatry, 147*, 982–987.

Geller, J. L., Fisher, W. H., Simon, L. J., & Wirth-Cauchon, J. L. (1990b). Second-generation deinstitutionalization, II: The impact of Brewster v. Dukakis on correlates of community and hospital utilization. *American Journal of Psychiatry, 147*, 988–993.

Girolamo, D. G., Mors, O., Grandi, L., Ardigo, W., & Munk-Jorgensen, P. (1988). Admission to general hospital psychiatric wards in Italy 2: Inpatient characteristics. *The International Journal of Social Psychiatry, 34*(4), 258–266.

Girolamo, D. G., Mors, O., Rossi, G., Grandi, L., Ardigo, W., & Munk-Jorgensen, P. (1988). Admission to general hospital psychiatric wards in Italy 1: A comparison between two catchment areas with differing provision of outpatient care. *The International Journal of Social Psychiatry, 34*(4), 248–257.

Gooch, C., & Leff, J. (1996). Factors affecting the success of community placement: the TAPS project 26. *Psychological Medicine, 26*, 511–520.

Gråwe, R. W., Pedersen, P. B., & Widén, J. H. (1997). Changes in prevalence and comorbidity in a total population of patients with psychotic disorders in Norwegian psychiatric hospitals. *Nordic Journal of Psychiatry, 51*, 127–132.

Hadley, T. R., Culhane, D. P., Snyder, F. J., & Lutterman, T. C. (1992). Expenditure and revenue patterns of state mental health agencies. *Administration and Policy in Mental Health, 19*(4), 213–233.

Hadley, T. R., Turk, R., & McGurrin, M. (1997). Community treatment teams: An alternative to state hospitals. *Psychiatric Quarterly, 68*, 77–90.

Harding, C. M., Brooks, G. W., Ashikaga, T., Strauss, J. S., & Breier, A. (1987). The Vermont longitudinal study of person with severe mental illness, I: Methodology, study sample, and overall status 32 years later. *American Journal of Psychiatry, 144*, 718–726.

Hargreaves, W. A., & Shumway, M. (1989). Effectiveness of services for the severely mentally ill. In C. Taube, D. Mechanic, & A. Hohmann (Eds.), *The future of mental health services research* (pp. 253–283). Bethesda, MD: National Institute of Mental Health.

Holley, H. L., Jeffers, B., & Hodges, P. (1997). Potential for community relocation among residents of Alberta's psychiatric facilities: A needs assessment. *Canadian Journal of Psychiatry, 42*, 750–757.

Honkonen, T. (1995). Problems and needs for care of discharged schizophrenia patients. *Psychiatria Fennica, 26*, 21–32.

Jones, D. (1993). The TAPS Project. 11: The selection of patients for reprovision. *British Journal of Psychiatry, 162*(Suppl. 19), 36–39.

Kamis-Gould, E., Hadley, T. R., Rothbard, A. B., Lovelace, J., & Eppler, J. A. (1995). A framework for evaluating the impact of state hospital closing. *Administration and Policy in Mental Health, 22*, 495–509.

Knapp, M. (1996). From psychiatric hospital to community care: Reflections on the English experience. In M. Moscarelli, A. Rupp, & N. Sartorius (Eds.), *The economics of schizophrenia* (pp. 385–395). New York: John Wiley and Sons.

Knapp, M., Beecham, J., Anderson, J., Dayson, D., Leff, J., Margolius, O., O'Driscoll, C., & Wills, W. (1990). The TAPS Project 3: Predicting the community costs of closing psychiatric hospitals. *British Journal of Psychiatry, 157*, 661–670.

Lawrence, R. E., Cumella, S., & Robertson, J. A. (1988). Patterns of care in a district general hospital psychiatric department. *British Journal of Psychiatry, 152*, 188–195.

Leff, J. (1992). Problems of transformation. *The International Journal of Social Psychiatry, 38*, 16–23.

Leff, J. (1997). The outcome for long-stay non demented patients. In J. Leff (Ed.), *Care in the community: Illusion or reality?* (p. 69). New York: John Wiley and Sons.

Leff, J., Dayson, D., Gooch, C., Thornicroft, G., & Wills, W. (1996). Quality of life of long-stay patients discharged from two psychiatric institutions. *Psychiatric Services, 47*, 62–67.

Leff, J., Trieman, N., & Gooch, C. (1996). Team for the assessment of psychiatric services (TAPS) Project 33: Prospective follow-up study of long-stay patients discharged from two psychiatric hospitals. *American Journal of Psychiatry, 153*, 1318–1324.

Lelliott, P., Wing, J., & Clifford, P. (1994). A national audit of new long-stay psychiatric patients I: Method and description of the cohort. *British Journal of Psychiatry, 165*, 160–169.

Macfarlane, D., Fortin, P., Fox, J., Gundry, S., Oshry, J., & Warren, E. (1997). Clinical and human resource planning for the downsizing of psychiatric hospitals: The British Columbia experience. *Psychiatric Quarterly, 68*, 25–42.

Manderscheid, R. W., & Sonnenschein, M. A. (Eds.). (1992). *Mental Health, United States, 1992.* Center for Mental Health Services and National Institute of Mental Health, DHHS Pub. No. (SMA) 92-1942. Washington, DC: U.S. Government Printing Office.

Manderscheid, R. W., & Sonnenschein, M. A. (Eds.). (1996). *Mental Health, United States, 1996.* Center for Mental Health Services and National Institute of Mental Health, DHHS Publ. No. (SMA) 96-3098. Washington, DC: U.S. Government Printing Office.

Martini, P., Cecchini, M., Corlito, G., D'Arco, A., & Nascimbeni, P. (1985). A model of a single comprehensive mental health service for a catchment area: A community alternative to hospitalization. *Acta Psychiatrica Scandinavica, 71*(Suppl. 316), 94–120.

Mercier, C., Renaud, C., & King, S. (1994). A thirty-year retrospective study of hospitalization among severely mentally ill patients. *Canadian Journal of Psychiatry, 39*(2), 95–102.

Mosher, L. R., & Burti, L. (1989). So who said it couldn't be done: Implemenation of Law 180. In L. R. Mosher & L. Burti (Eds.), *Community mental health: Principles and practice* (pp. 204–236). New York: W.W. Norton.

National Association of State Mental Health Program Directors. (1995). *Funding sources and expenditures of state mental health agencies: Study results fiscal year 1993.* Virginia: Author.

National Association of State Mental Health Program Directors. (1996). Closing and reorganizing state psychiatric hospitals: 1996 [On-line]. Available: http://www.NASMHPD.org/nri/SHSP_RPT.htm.

O'Driscoll, C., & Leff, J. (1993). The TAPS Project. 8: Design of the research study on the long-stay patients. *British Journal of Psychiatry, 162*(Suppl. 19), 18–24.

Okin, R. L. (1984). Brewster v Dukakis: Developing community services through use of a consent decree. *American Journal of Psychiatry, 141*, 786–789.

Okin, R. L. (1995). Testing the limits of deinstitutionalization. *Psychiatric Services, 46*, 569–574.

Okin, R. L., Borus, J. F., Baer, L., & Jones, A. L. (1995). Long-term outcome of state hospital patients discharged into structured community residential settings. *Psychiatric Services, 46*, 73–78.

Okin, R. L., & Pearsall, D. (1993). Patients' perceptions of their quality of life 11 years after discharge from a state hospital. *Hospital and Community Psychiatry, 44*, 236–240.

Okin, R. L., Pearsall, D., & Athearn, T. (1990). Predictions about new long-stay patients: Were they valid? *American Journal of Psychiatry, 147*, 1596–1601.

Pulice, R., McCormick, L., & Dewees, M. (1995). A qualitative approach to assessing the effects of system change on consumers, families, and providers. *Psychiatric Services, 46*, 575–579.

Pylkkänen, K. (1994). The Finnish national schizophrenia project 1982–1992—Is a balanced deinstitutionalisation process possible? *Psychiatria Fennica, 25*, 169–183.

Rapp, C. A., & Moore, T. D. (1995). The first 18 months of mental health reform in Kansas. *Psychiatric Services, 46,* 580–585.

Rothbard, A. B., Kuno, E., Schinnar, A. P., Hadley, T. R., & Turk, R. (1999). Service utilization and cost of community care for discharged state hospital patients: A 3-year follow-up study. *American Journal of Psychiatry, 156,* 920–927.

Rothbard, A. B., Richman, E., & Hadley, T. R. (1997). "Unbundling" of state hospital services in the community: The Philadelphia State Hospital story. *Administration and Policy in Mental Health, 24,* 391–398.

Rothbard, A. B., Schinnar, A. P., & Goldman, H. (1994). The pursuit of a definition for severe and persistent mental illness. In S. Soreff (Ed.), *The seriously and persistently mentally ill: The state-of-the art treatment handbook.* Kirkland, WA: Hogrefe and Huber.

Rothbard, A. B., Schinnar, A. P., Hadley, T. R., Foley, K., & Kuno, E. (1998). Cost comparison of state hospital vs. community-based care for seriously mentally ill adults. *American Journal of Psychiatry, 155,* 523–529.

Salokangas, R. K. R., & Saarinen, S. (1998). Deinstitutionalization and schizophrenia in Finland: I. Discharged patients and their care. *Schizophrenia Bulletin, 24,* 457–467.

Schinnar, A. P., Rothbard, A. B., & Hadley, T. (1996). *Effects of state mental hospital closings.* A final report to Pew Charitable Trusts. Grant Log no. 92-01985-000, October 1996.

Schinnar, A. P., Rothbard, A. B., & Yin, D. (1993). *Size distribution of state mental hospitals: Occupancy, availability, length of stay, and functional role.* Philadelphia: University of Pennsylvania.

Semke, J., Fisher, W. H., Goldman, H. H., & Hirad, A. (1996). The evolving role of the state hospital in the care and treatment of older adults: State trends, 1984 to 1993. *Psychiatric Services, 47,* 1082–1087.

Smyth, A. M., Buckely, C., & Clarke, A. (1997). Where to? A survey of the residual population of a district mental hospital and their predicted placement needs. *International Journal of Psychiatric Medicine, 14*(3), 105–108.

Solomon, P. (1992). The closing of a state hospital: What is the quality of patients' lives one year post-release. *Psychiatric Quarterly, 63*(3), 279–296.

Sommers, I., Baskin, D., Specht, D., & Shively, M. (1988). Deinstitutionalization of the elderly mentally ill: Factors affecting discharge to alternative living arrangements. *The Gerontologist, 28,* 653–658.

Sussman, S. (1998). The first asylum in Canada: A response to neglectful community care and current trends. *Canadian Journal of Psychiatry, 43*(3), 260–264.

Tansella, M., Balestieri, M., Meneghelli, G., & Micciolo, R. (1991). Trends in the provision of psychiatric care 1979–1988. In M. Tansella (Ed.), *Psychological medicine: Community based psychiatry: Long-term patterns of care in South-Verona* (Vol. Mono Suppl. 19, pp. 5–16). Cambridge: Cambridge University Press.

Thornicroft, G., & Bebbington, P. (1989). Deinstitutionalization: From hospital closure to service development. *British Journal of Psychiatry, 155,* 739–753.

Trieman, N., & Leff, J. (1996). Difficult to place patients in a psychiatric hospital closure programme: The TAPS project 24. *Psychological Medicine, 26,* 765–774.

Wing, J., & Furlong, R. (1986). A haven for the severely disabled within a context of a comprehensive psychiatric community service. *British Journal of Psychiatry, 149,* 449–457.

Wright, E. R., Holmes, A., Deb, P., Blunt, B., & Duzan, J. (1997). *Treatment costs of the former central state hospital patients: A comparison of institutionalized and community-based care.* Indiana Consortium for Mental Health Services Research.

Zissi, A., & Barry, M. M. (1997). From Leros Asylum to community-based facilities: Levels of functioning and quality of life among hostel residents in Greece. *International Journal of Social Psychiatry, 43*(2), 104–115.

[13]

Build a Better State Hospital: Deinstitutionalization Has Failed

Alexander Gralnick, M.D.

The author cites increasing numbers of chronic, homeless, and neglected mentally ill people as evidence of the failure of deinstitutionalization and community care to live up to their promise to reduce chronicity, the need for long-term hospitalization, and even mental illness itself. He believes the state hospital system, despite having been maligned and nearly destroyed, has great therapeutic potential. It could provide extended care to acutely ill patients before they become chronically ill; restore the ability to pinpoint responsibility for patient care, which has been lost under community care; and provide a stimulating academic environment conducive to research into treatment of the mentally ill.

Deinstitutionalization is more than a policy—it is a 30-year-old social movement that appeals to the idealism and ambition of many groups, including public servants, economists, sociologists, lawyers, mental hygienists, psychiatrists, and patients and their families. But as might be expected of a movement begun with little forethought, less planning, and no advance scientific study, it has failed to live up to its promise. In its

Dr. Gralnick is medical director at High Point Hospital, Upper King Street, Port Chester, New York 10573. An opposing view of deinstitutionalization and community care is presented by Robert L. Okin, M.D., beginning on page 742.

wake the state hospital system has been maligned and effectively destroyed.

Considering the powerful social and medical forces supporting deinstitutionalization and the devastated condition of the state hospital system, is there any going back? The answer is yes; there are good reasons for attempting to revitalize the state hospital system. They in-

Deinstitutionalization: Success or Failure?

Editor's Note: The tragedy of large numbers of homeless mentally ill in America's cities has stimulated renewed debate about whether deinstitutionalization has failed and should be abandoned as a social policy. We asked Alexander Gralnick, M.D., and Robert L. Okin, M.D., to present their views on this controversial issue. Dr. Okin's commentary begins on page 742.

clude the current shortcomings of deinstitutionalization and the community care system, the therapeutic potential of the state hospital system, our society's rejection of the mentally ill in the community, humanitarian considerations, the scientific and research potential of the state hospital, the negative effects of deinstitutionalization on society and families, the plight of the mentally ill in the community, and the demedicalization of the state hospital and of psychiatry.

Historical perspective

For some 200 years, the insane in the United States lived in the com-

munity or were housed with paupers and the physically ill in jails and almshouses. The conditions under which they lived were indescribably brutal and inhumane. In the mid-19th century, Dorothea Dix began a crusade to remedy the inhumane treatment of the mentally ill, and her efforts stimulated rapid growth in the number of state hospitals (1). Although the care provided by the hospitals varied from acceptable to very poor, the state hospital system flourished. At its zenith in the 1950s, it housed more than a half million patients around the country, compared with only about 130,000 today (2).

The process of deinstitutionalization began in the mid-1950s. It followed decades of attack upon the state hospital system in movies such as *The Snake Pit* and books such as Albert Deutsch's *The Shame of the States* (3), a scathing exposé of the state hospitals that aroused great public antipathy.

The time was ripe for action for other reasons as well. There had already been public outcry about the expense of caring for the insane, and it was popular to favor saving money on their treatment. The emerging civil libertarian movement stressed individual rights. From a humanitarian point of view it was thought that patients could be better off in the community. Psychiatrists and mental hygienists trumpeted the idea that long hospitalization, particularly in the state hospitals, promoted chronicity and that community care would prevent chronicity and even mental illness itself. The success of the major tranquilizers, developed in the 1950s and 1960s, added to the conviction that community care could work.

Around the same time that the public system was under attack, efforts were made to save it. The Hill-Burton Act in 1947 provided funds to build general hospitals that included psychiatric units, thus launching the system of early intervention and short-term care of the mentally ill. The National Mental Health Study Act established the Joint Commission on Mental Illness and Health, whose 1961 report, *Action for Mental Health* (4), urged increased support for and improvement of the state hospital system.

However, the forces opposed to the state hospitals prevailed, and another committee established by President Kennedy sidetracked the Joint Commission's recommendations. In the mid-1960s the Community Mental Health Centers Act was passed, as were bills establishing Medicaid and Medicare. The deinstitutionalization process was well on its way.

Serious problems

Deinstitutionalization has failed to cure the so-called evils of the state hospital system. Community care has not lessened the incidence of mental illness or the number of mentally ill. It has not diminished the numbers of chronically ill or significantly reduced the mistreatment and suffering of the mentally ill. Under deinstitutionalization, patients do not receive better treatment and are not provided a more promising future.

Instead of reducing chronic illness, deinstitutionalization all too often has resulted in too-short, ineffective care that leads to repeated episodes of illness and chronicity. The "miracle drugs" have not been as effective in community-based psychiatry as they seemed to have been in institution-based psychiatry. The reason may be that fewer than 50 percent of discharged patients continue to take their medication (5). In addition, only 25 percent of patients participate in some form of aftercare (5).

According to Talbott (5), "moving from a single system to multiple settings in the community, our ability to pinpoint the responsibility for care of both the entire population and individual patients was lost." Assigning responsibility is critically important but not possible under the scattered community-based system.

Further, if it were possible to include all the hidden costs of community care, it would likely be shown that deinstitutionalization has not saved money. And if it has, at what cost in suffering and lost opportunity?

There is no precise measure of the failure of deinstitutionalization, but several facts give us reason to view the situation with pessimism. There are increasing numbers of the mentally ill in jails, single rooms of seedy hotels, halfway houses, and single-room-occupancy hotels. Fifty percent of nursing home residents are mentally ill (5). None of these facilities provide adequate treatment or living quarters. Many mentally ill rely on soup kitchens for food, emergency shelters for lodging, and subway tunnels for escape from the cold. At least 25 percent of the homeless are mentally ill. What would Dorothea Dix say today?

Deinstitutionalization can also be blamed for the growing numbers of young adult chronic patients in the community. They have spent little time in state hospitals, or any hospital, yet they resemble in many ways the chronic state hospital patient of old. We are puzzled about how to care for them. Had they been given good hospital attention in the earliest stages of their illness, they would not now, despite their youth, be chronically, and perhaps hopelessly, ill.

Deinstitutionalization has also placed great strain on families who are compelled to care for a mentally ill member. The mentally ill, and particularly the severely ill, are very difficult to manage even under the best of hospital conditions, let alone by a family, even if it is loving and willing to try. Extended

failure can be devastating to both family and patient. Results of home care are particularly bad if the family is not willing to try or the patient is dissatisfied with his family. If the sick family member is homeless or in constant trouble, the family is also burdened.

The ultimate breakdown in family stability may cause other family members to develop mental or physical symptoms whose treatment may pose a further financial burden to society. That expense, and increased use of the legal system by patients and family members, are among the hidden costs of community care.

The relative neglect of the acutely ill under deinstitutionalization has resulted in increased numbers of chronically ill patients. The failure to effectively treat acutely ill patients is caused by hospitalization criteria that are overrestrictive. Currently commitment laws in many states stipulate that a patient may not be hospitalized unless he is deemed harmful to himself or others. If he is hospitalized, it is usually for no more than 30 days, hardly enough time for effective treatment. Repeated exacerbations of illness and similar brief hospital stays usually follow. If the patient is schizophrenic, the disease process progresses.

If the patient becomes dangerous to himself or others one, two, or three years later, he may receive extended hospital care, now quite late, in a state hospital or, if he is fortunate, in a private hospital where he may receive better quality long-term intensive care. If he does not become dangerous, he may never reach the hospital but instead become increasingly sick, hopeless, and deteriorated.

A program that fails to provide structured and enforced care, particularly in the early stages of illness, is bound to promote chronic illness. If there is an unquestioned principle in psychiatry, it is that the mentally ill are most successfully treated if symptoms are caught early and treated promptly and adequately. Anything short of that promises failure. The longer a patient is sick, the smaller the chance that any therapy will be effective. Promotion of chronic illness may be the worst and most ominous failing of deinstitutionalization.

The demedicalization of psychiatry is another negative consequence of deinstitutionalization. State hospitals at one time were uniformly headed by physician-psychiatrists and manned by psychiatrists in all responsible posts. That is hardly the case today, as the situation in New York State illustrates. Keill (6) reported that in 1974 there were 52 psychiatrists in the New York State Department of Mental Hygiene at the level of assistant commissioner and above, including 35 hospital directors and six regional directors. Over the following ten years, 47 of the psychiatrists (90 percent) left the department. By July 1, 1984, there were 14 psychiatrists at or above the assistant commissioner level. They included 11 hospital directors, one regional director, and two officials at the central office in Albany, one of whom was the commissioner. Such a drain has resulted in an anemic system despite the fact that it cares for fewer patients.

Society's attitudes
Our society rewards competitiveness, aggressiveness, action, and accomplishment. Lately it especially seems to recognize and reward the strongest and, while professing to prevent anyone from falling through the so-called safety net, is least tolerant of its mentally ill population. Although current conduct toward the deranged is palatable when compared to the brutalities of the late 18th and early 19th centuries, if we look carefully we may see much in community psychiatry for which we should feel shame.

If we are not careful, we may slip into treating the mentally ill as they were treated in bygone days. Our society tolerates massive violence and poverty—40 million people and one in four children live below the poverty line (7). Might it not also tolerate mounting numbers of chronically ill?

The failure of community-oriented psychiatry to provide adequate housing, employment, and emotional and medical support for the mentally ill is due in large part to the community's antipathy toward, intolerance of, and rejection of the mentally ill. Compelled to receive the mentally ill into the community, the public has segregated them in seedy hotels in undesirable neighborhoods, in jails, in nursing homes, in emergency shelters, in tunnels, and on streets and highways. This fact has been overlooked by those who have pressed for deinstitutionalization.

On the other hand, the concept of hospital care of the mentally ill is acceptable to the public. However, we will need to shed the typical image of the state hospital as a facility without redeeming features if the state system is to be salvaged. Confidence and creativity will be needed to design facilities capable of reaching, diagnosing, studying, and more successfully treating the mentally ill soon after the onset of illness and treating them for periods long enough to effectively arrest or reverse the process.

Upgrading the state system
Let us try to imagine the new state system. Its main function would be to treat patients who are too sick to function in the community. Ideally the hospitals would be located centrally, and outpatient clinics would be attached to them, as suggested by the 1961 Joint Commission report. Patients would not leave the hospital until adequate arrangements had been made for their aftercare. After discharge they would be provided medical and psychiatric care and would live in supportive and satisfactory quarters. In this way they could become productive members of society. Should patients decompensate, the hospital would provide further treatment regardless of whether they were considered dangerous to themselves or others.

The revamped state hospital would be at the cutting edge of psychiatric treatment and research. It would engage in constant self-

assessment to discover how it can help patients who do not respond to available therapies. The goal of research would be the development of therapeutic advances. Acute and chronic patients would receive the latest treatments and medications. Affiliation with teaching institutions would ensure a vital academic and therapeutic atmosphere. Many of these ideas were proposed in *The Shame of the States* (3), in 1948, but rather than leading to improvements in the state system, the book was used to destroy it.

The hospital environment offers the controlled conditions required for serious study and valid research, whereas the community setting does not. The crippling and near destruction of the state hospital system has eliminated any opportunity to conduct comprehensive studies in psychiatry, especially of hospital conditions that can help the chronically ill. Relatively little research emanates from the public hospital today compared to the output years ago.

Facing facts
Some supporters of deinstitutionalization are aware of the plight of the mentally ill in the community, but instead of faulting deinstitutionalization, they condemn society for not doing more to make life livable for the chronically ill in the community. These supporters are so committed to deinstitutionalization that they do not criticize those who let the fox loose in the chicken coop but rather those who do not give the chickens adequate protection.

An example of this reasoning can be found in a fine paper by Lamb (8) outlining the terrible plight of the mentally ill. The paper stresses the criminalization and homelessness of the deinstitutionalized mentally ill, but ultimately states that those who support returning the chronically ill to the hospital are "exaggerating and romanticizing the activities and care the patients are said to have received there. To some, reinstitutionalization seems like a simple solution to the problems of deinstitutionalization such as homelessness. But activity and treatment programs geared to the needs of long-term patients can easily be set up in the community, and living conditions, structured or unstructured, can be raised to any level we choose—if adequate funds are made available."

It will remain for the reader to decide who offers, in Lamb's terms, the "simple solution" and who is "romanticizing" rather than facing the cold facts. Our society has not been willing to give patients in the community what they need. Society will be more willing to care adequately for its mentally ill in a hospital setting. Those who resist comprehensive use of the hospital insist on thinking of it only as it was, or was thought to be. They emphasize its shortcomings, minimize its attributes, and refuse to consider the possibility of superior state hospitals. Yet hospitals geared to the mentally ill can achieve what other specialty hospitals have in treatment of the physically ill. A failure to see this possibility is the result of pessimism or bias. The recommendations made by the Joint Commission on Mental Illness and Health in its report, *Action for Mental Health* (4), remain valid today.

If we fail to act

Deinstitutionalization has led psychiatry in a dismal direction. In the future, care of psychiatric patients will be frighteningly inadequate if community care continues in its current direction. Cuts in governmental spending for mental health care will seriously aggravate the situation. Unless action is taken to brake or reverse deinstitutionalization, the mental health care field will be in crisis.

Rising numbers of chronically ill, inadequately treated patients will be beyond help. The acutely ill, having been treated inadequately in the community or by brief hospitalization, will become chronically ill. Ill-equipped nursing homes will hold greater percentages of primarily elderly men-

tally ill. Prisons will hold many more acute and chronic mentally ill young people.

The numbers of the homeless mentally ill will rise as more mentally ill live in train stations and emergency shelters or wander the highways of the nation. Increasing numbers of people with bizarre behavior will be seen in our city streets, to be tolerated as everyday oddities, taunted, or laughed at. Hospital treatment will fail to achieve its potential and will continue to deteriorate, perhaps irretrievably. State hospital research will continue to diminish and will perhaps vanish. Increasing numbers of young people will commit suicide.

That scenario is not an exaggerated or privately held view of the future; it coincides with some aspects of Talbott's forecast (5). It can only be avoided by reversing the deinstitutionalization process and its excessive emphasis on community care. According to Talbott, "What we do will reveal not only our ingenuity but our ability to act

humanely in the best interests of those who do not and cannot speak effectively for themselves" (5).

References

1. Deutsch A: The Mentally Ill in America. New York, Columbia University Press, 1949
2. Redick RM, Witkin MJ: State and County Mental Hospitals, United States, 1970–1981. Mental Health Statistical Note 165. Rockville, Md, National Institute of Mental Health, 1983
3. Deutsch A: The Shame of the States. New York, Harcourt Brace, 1948
4. Joint Commission on Mental Illness and Health: Action for Mental Health; Final Report. New York, Basic Books, 1961
5. Talbott JA: The Chronic Mentally Ill: What Do We Now Know And Why Aren't We Implementing What We Know. Presented to Group Without a Name, White Plains, New York, 1984
6. Keill SL: And then there were none. Bulletin (Area II Council, American Psychiatric Association) 27:1,8, 1984
7. Reston J: The irony of poverty. New York Times, Nov 21, 1984
8. Lamb HR: Deinstitutionalization and the homeless mentally ill. Hospital and Community Psychiatry 35:899–907, 1984

Information for Contributors to *H&CP*

Hospital & Community Psychiatry is a monthly interdisciplinary journal directed to professional staff members of mental health facilities and agencies. It publishes material on all aspects of psychiatric service delivery.

H&CP reviews material for publication with the understanding that it has not been previously published and is not being reviewed for publication elsewhere. Submit manuscripts (four copies) to the editor, John A. Talbott, M.D., *Hospital and Community Psychiatry*, 1400 K Street, N.W., Washington, D.C. 20005. (Phone inquiries, 202-682-6070.) All material, including case reports and references, must be typed double-spaced on 8 1/2-by-11 inch paper with generous margins (at least 1 1/2 inches on all sides). Authors'

bylines and identifications must be typed on a separate title page.

Manuscripts submitted for publication are sent for blind review to at least three independent peer reviewers; the final decision is the editor's. Authors are usually notified of the decision about their papers within three to four months, although delays are sometimes unavoidable. Reviewers' comments will be returned with rejected manuscripts if they are considered useful to the authors.

Authors may be asked if they wish to make suggested revisions in a manuscript and resubmit it. If the revisions are substantial, the manuscript will be sent again for outside review; every effort will be made to expedite such review. All revised manuscripts must be submitted in triplicate.

---

[14]

Keeping the Mentally Ill Out of Jail

Richard Lamb

There is evidence of a "criminalization" of mentally disordered behavior, a shunting of mentally ill persons into the criminal justice system. Deinstitutionalization has led to large numbers of mentally ill persons in the community, but there are not enough community psychiatric resources, including hospital beds. Society has a limited tolerance of mentally disordered behavior, and the result is pressure to institutionalize those needing 24-hour care wherever there is room, including jail.

Problems such as criminalization and homelessness (which are often interrelated) are best understood not as a result of deinstitutionalization per se, but of the way it has been implemented. The chronically mentally ill have been provided neither a full range nor an adequate quantity of community residential placements. Aggressive case management is available to only a few. Also lacking are a stable source of income for each patient and access to acute hospitalization. Even when beds are available, many emergency room psychiatrists are reluctant to admit chronically mentally ill persons who are acutely decompensated. Many of this group are being arrested for minor criminal acts that are really manifestations of their illness, their lack of treatment, and the lack of structure in their lives. Legal restrictions on involuntary hospitalization have also made the jail the only avenue of asylum for many of the acutely mentally ill. Further, our clinical judgment tells us that a number of the chronically mentally ill need locked residential care. Deinstitutionalization is not for everyone.

Moreover, the system of voluntary mental health outpatient treatment is inadequate for many of the mentally ill found in jail; if they do agree to accept treatment, they tend not to keep their appointments, not to take their medications, and to be least welcome at outpatient facilities.

The need for more mental health services in jails is apparent. Even so, many mentally ill inmates will not accept referral for community housing or treatment even when resources are available. As a result they are released to the streets to begin anew their chaotic existences.

We must face up to our responsibilities to this vulnerable group. We must take a stand for involuntary treatment, both acute and ongoing. Such intervention should not be limited to those who can be proven to be dangerous but should be extended to gravely disabled persons who are too disorganized to avail themselves of vitally needed care. We must stop playing the public hospital emergency room game of seeing how many admissions we can avoid. And we must make an all-out effort to obtain the resources needed to serve our highest priority patients, the chronically and severely mentally ill.—H. Richard Lamb, M.D., *professor of psychiatry, University of Southern California School of Medicine*

Hospital and Community Psychiatry, established in 1950 by Daniel Blain, M.D., is published monthly by the American Psychiatric Association for staff members of facilities and agencies concerned with the care of the mentally disabled, in keeping with the association's objectives to improve care and treatment, to promote research and professional education in mental health and related fields, and to advance the standards of all mental health services and facilities.

Cross-Cultural Psychiatry

[15]

DEPRESSION, SOMATIZATION AND THE "NEW CROSS-CULTURAL PSYCHIATRY"

Arthur M. Kleinman*

Clinical Instructor, Department of Psychiatry, Harvard Medical School,
Massachusetts General Hospital, Lecturer, Department of Anthropology,
Harvard University

Abstract—Contrary to Singer's contention that the features of depressive disorders do not exhibit significant cross-cultural differences, the author uses material from field research in Taiwan and data from recent anthropological and clinical investigations to support the opposite view that such differences exist and are a function of the cultural shaping of normative and deviant behavior. Somatization amongst Chinese depressives is used as an illustration. This discrepancy reflects substantial changes in the nature of more recent cross-cultural studies by anthropologists and psychiatrists, changes which are giving rise to a new cross-cultural approach to psychiatric issues. Some features and implications of that approach are described.

INTRODUCTION

Singer's [1] review of cross-cultural studies on depressive disorders in a recent issue of this journal "concludes that there is insufficient evidence to support a prevalent view that depressive illness in primitive and certain other non-Western cultures has outstanding deviant features". Many researchers who have studied human behavior and deviance cross-culturally will find Singer's conclusion disturbing and a good number will believe it to be wrong. A careful reading of Singer's review discloses much that is amiss with what I shall call the "old transcultural psychiatry". Drawing attention to these problems also gives an opportunity to briefly introduce theory and findings from a rapidly developing interdisciplinary field which I shall call the "new cross-cultural psychiatry", and to contrast the latter with the former over the question of culture and depression.

WHAT IS WRONG WITH THE "OLD TRANSCULTURAL PSYCHIATRY"?

Like Singer's review, much of the work has involved a breathless search through large amounts of data from different societies looking for "universals". Since most findings were collected in dissimilar ways by researchers working with different methods and hypotheses, the results of such literature searches are disturbingly alike: the conclusions are superficial and most of the interesting and more depthful issues are cast aside as unproven and incomparable. Although the chief concern of transcultural psychiatry has been to determine the relative distribution and frequency of particular kinds of mental illnesses in different societies by using epidemiological methods, only a very few studies make systematic cross-cultural comparisons. The Dohrenwends [2] demonstrate the failure of most psychiatric epidemiological studies to successfully evaluate the impact of basic social and cultural factors on psychopathology, and the studies Singer reviews illustrate the same problem. The question of culturogenesis of mental illness, which has preoccupied many of these studies, remains unanswered but seems to be leading to a dead-end.

As Singer notes chief amongst the difficulties is the absence of universally accepted definitions of psychiatric disorders such as depression. Lacking that, cross-cultural studies of depression, for example, do not study a single phenomenon. Dysphoric affect, normative depressive states, and various behavioral deviances are lumped together. After calling our attention to this failing, however, it is hard to see how Singer pushes ahead to the conclusion we have already quoted. His conclusion is no more supported by the studies, given his critique of their limitations, than is its opposite. Just as Singer eliminates a wide range of other solution-frameworks that have been erected to resolve the question of culture and depression, so too must his conclusion be eliminated.

But the problems raised by Singer's article go beyond the fact that we still lack a comparative epidemiology of depression which can apply the same disease category and the same diagnostic methods in different social and cultural settings. Indeed the chief question emerging from the traditional transcultural psychiatric approach is whether the quest for such a comparative epidemology is itself an obstacle to understanding how culture affects depression.

Following Klerman [3, 4], amongst others, we can isolate a *depressive syndrome* characterized by depressive affect, insomnia, weight loss, lack of energy, diurnal mood changes, constipation, dry mouth, and an apparently limited number of related psychological complaints. Singer is right in suggesting that this syndrome appears to be present in a number of cultural settings. But he is not correct when he uses this fact in support of his conclusion. The depressive syndrome represents a small fraction of the entire field of depressive phenomena. It is a cultural category constructed by psychiatrists in the West to yield a homogeneous group of patients. By definition, it excludes most depressive phenomena, even in the West, because they fall outside its narrow boundaries.

* After 1 July 1976 Associate Professor and Head, Division of Social and Cross-Cultural Psychiatry, University of Washington School of Medicine, Seattle, WA 98195, U.S.A.

4   ARTHUR M. KLEINMAN

Applying such a category to analyze cross-cultural studies, or even in direct field research, is *not* a cross-cultural study of depression. because by definition it will *find* what is "universal" and systematically *miss* what does not fit its tight parameters. The former is what is defined and therefore "seen" by a Western cultural model: the latter. which is not so defined and therefore not "seen", raises far more interesting questions for cross-cultural research. It is precisely in the latter group that one would expect to find the most striking examples of the influence of culture on depression. Therefore, the kind of study Singer and the traditional transcultural psychiatric perspective believe to be "ideal" is systematically unable to study the influences of culture on depression. The data it is collecting are the wrong data for that purpose. Given its orientation such a study is bound to arrive at the conclusion Singer draws; it is a self-fulfilling prophecy.

Here we have evidence of a *category fallacy*, perhaps the most basic and certainly the most crucial error one can make in cross-cultural research. Having dispensed with indigenous illness categories because they are culture-specific, studies of this kind go on to superimpose their own cultural categories on some sample of deviant behavior in other cultures, as if their own illness categories were culture-free. This assumption simply cannot be made in comparative cross-cultural research as Fabrega has repeatedly shown [5–7]. Psychiatric categories are bound to the context of professional psychiatric theory and practice in the West. Psychiatry must learn from anthropology that culture does considerably more than shape illness as an experience; it shapes the very way we conceive of illness [8, 9]. A true comparative cross-cultural science of illness must begin with this powerful anthropological insight. It must make a systematic analysis and comparison of the relevant illness categories *prior to* the study of illness phenomena.

Closely connected to the category fallacy is the traditional transcultural psychiatric preoccupation with disease as an entity, a thing to be "discovered" in pure form under the layers of cultural camouflage. This assumption results in the erroneous belief that deviance can be studied in different societies independent of specific cultural norms and local patterns of normative behavior. Both are problematic. The first assumption runs counter to our most developed contemporary conceptions of disease, which argue that disease—be it biological or psychological—is an explanatory model not a thing [10]. Thus, in comparing diseases one is always comparing explanations not entities. There can be no stripping away of layers of cultural accretion in order to isolate a culture-free entity. Culture shapes disease first by shaping our explanations of disease. This is additional support for the far reaching influence of the category fallacy. Most transcultural psychiatric research, because it ignores this issue, is no more than the application of Western psychiatric categories to non-Western societies. Although this type of research may hold importance for validating professional psychiatric constructs. by no means a trivial concern. we should not delude ourselves that it is studying disease in relation to culture or that it represents real cross-cultural comparisons.

For example. the largest and most sophisticated study of this kind in the field of mental illness is the W.H.O. supported International Pilot Study of Schizophrenia (IPSS) [11]. Although that study is an important advance in our understanding of schizophrenia. it starts from a category fallacy which significantly limits its value as a study of cultural influences on mental illness. Its strength comes from reifying a narrowly defined syndrome affecting patients in nine separate cultural locations, but that is also its weakness. It is unable to systematically examine the impact of cultural factors on schizophrenia, since its methodology has ruled out the chief cultural determinants. The homogeneous patient sample in each culture represents a fraction of all cases labeled as schizophrenia in those societies, and excludes all those carrying the most extensive cultural imprint. This is obviously an appropriate way to factor out a special class of psychotic disorders probably having a major genetic component and definitely distinct from other kinds of psychoses frequently labeled schizophrenia, not an inconsiderable achievement, but it can tell us almost nothing about the relation of culture to either the group it includes or that much larger one it excludes.

The "ideal" cross-cultural study of schizophrenia or depression, on the other hand. would begin with detailed local phenomenological descriptions. Such phenomenological descriptions would enable us to compare indigenous and professional psychiatric explanations of these disorders along with the behaviors they interpret. They would elicit and compare symptom terms and illness labels independent of a unified framework. Translating between these local cultural accounts would be the basis for elaborating a comparative model and for making cross-cultural comparisons. The reverse of what usually occurs. These accounts could also be used to analyze the influence of culture on these disorders in each cultural site and later on to compare these influences between cultures. A final stage would be the testing at each site of specific hypotheses about the way culture influences these disorders, hypotheses which are generated by the phenomenological descriptions and the cross-cultural comparisons. Not only do we not possess such a study of schizophrenia or depression, but investigations of this kind represent a considerably different theoretical and research orientation from that which has become dominant in transcultural psychiatric studies [12, 13].

In summary, then, the chief failing of the "old transcultural psychiatry" is its total reliance on external, Western psychiatric categories which are applied by clinicians and epidemiologists as if they were "independent" of cultural bias. but which in fact are culture-specific categories. Moreover, they systematically disregard the key local influences on mental illness, beginning with the cultural shaping of disease models and the way we perceive, label, and valuate deviant behavior. Other weaknesses of this approach are its preoccupation with the issue of culturogenesis rather than the more sophisticated and more pervasive question of cultural shaping of illness phenomena: its inability to get beyond the most superficial assessment of cultural variables: its greater interest in "universals" than "differences": its remoteness from anthropological studies of normative behavior in the same cultural settings: its inadequate conceptualization of disease as an entity: and its reliance on traditional epidemiological methods as virtually the only way to conduct cross-cultural studies.

THE NEW CROSS-CULTURAL PERSPECTIVE ON BEHAVIOR AND DEVIANCE: THE MERGING OF ANTHROPOLOGICAL AND PSYCHIATRIC RESEARCH

As a response to these salient weaknesses with the traditional approach, a "new cross-cultural psychiatry" is emerging as an interdisciplinary framework drawing off both anthropological and more recent psychiatric investigations of culture and illness. This inchoate field has several distinct components. First, there is a much more sophisticated use of psychiatric epidemiology. The work of Leighton, Lambo *et al.* [12] and most recently Carstairs and Kapur [13] confronts the issue of indigenous cultural categories, even if the working out of an ideal comparative epidemiological paradigm remains a distant goal, and makes use of anthropological data and ethnographic methods. On the theoretical level, Singer's predecessor at Hong Kong, the late P. M. Yap [14] explored the issues requiring integration into a comparative psychiatry. Interestingly, Yap's theoretical analysis and some of his own research on Chinese patients oppose Singer's conclusion, a point we shall return to in the following section.

The past decade has witnessed an increasing convergence of anthropological and cross-cultural psychiatric research on the ways culture influences the perception, classification, process of labelling, explanation, experience of symptoms, course, decisions regarding, and treatment of sickness [15–19]. One major advance has been the development of medical anthropological studies in which biologically-based disorders are studied [9, 15, 32]. This is providing us with a broader framework for understanding illness. It is also circumventing certain difficulties that continue to plague studies of cultural influences on behavioral deviance, where cross-cultural markers are less certain or absent. Another major advance proceeds from the recognition that studies of illness in large-scale, literate non-Western societies offer more suitable comparisons with similar studies in the West than do those performed in small-scale, pre-literate societies [20, 21]. Closely related to this development is renewed interest in studying illness beliefs and behavior in the context of ethnic subgroups [22, 23] and popular (largely family-based) health care in the West [24, 25]. Finally, and perhaps most importantly, we are obtaining excellent ethnographies which focus on the relationship of normative behavior and deviance in non-Western societies [26–32]. These studies disclose the complex mechanisms by which culture affects emotions and psychopathology. Although we still lack systematic cross-cultural comparisons of depression, phenomenological descriptions from different cultures are becoming available [13, 26, 33–37] (see next section). A recent study by Rin *et al.* [38] is an example of a systematic comparison of psychopathology amongst matched patient groups in two distinct cultures (Japan and Taiwan) which attempts to relate differences to operationalized

cultural variables. We can expect more of these studies in the future, including ones focused on depression.

In the following section I report such a study. Like the other investigations I have mentioned, it makes use of both clinical and ethnographic methods. I present these findings because they differ substantially from Singer's conclusion: i.e. they support a marked cross-cultural variation in the phenomenology of depression. Furthermore, they illuminate an essential theoretical distinction which has emerged from the "new cross-cultural psychiatry". That distinction I shall use to show why the merger of anthropological and psychiatric investigations carries us beyond a critique of Singer's conclusion toward a better appreciation of the relationship of culture and illness.

DEPRESSION AND SOMATIZATION IN CHINESE CULTURE

Psychiatrists in Chinese cultural areas have noted for some time the tendency of Chinese patients with mental disorders to present somatic complaints in place of psychological complaints [14, 35, 38–42]. In one study, 70% of patients who were later documented to suffer from mental illness initially presented to the psychiatry clinic at the National Taiwan University Hospital with somatic complaints [35]. In a study carried out in the same clinic, my research assistants and I assembled a group of 25 patients with the depressive syndrome who presented consecutively at two of the daily psychiatric clinics. Twenty-two of these cases (88%) initially complained only of somatic complaints (i.e. they did not complain of dysphoric affect or report it when queried). During their subsequent treatment in the psychiatric clinic, ten patients (40%) never admitted to experiencing dysphoric affect. Seven of these patients (28%) rejected the idea that they were depressed even after they had been successfully treated (i.e. had experienced complete symptom relief) with anti-depressant medication.

Thus, 10 of 25 patients (40%) exhibited all the signs and symptoms of the depressive syndrome, and seven of those (28%) responded completely to specific treatment for depression, but none of them reported depressive affect or would accept the medical diagnosis that they were suffering from depression or mental illness. They looked upon their physical complaints as their "real" sickness, a *physical* sickness. Gaw [42], Tseng [35], and myself [9] have found much the same kind of phenomenological pattern amongst Chinese patients with depression in the U.S. The same has been reported for depressed patients in China prior to 1949 [43] and in Hong Kong [14, 44].

This finding contrasts sharply with depressed patients in the West. Amongst a parallel group of 25 patients with the depressive syndrome whom I assembled and studied in the same way at the Massachusetts General Hospital, only one (4%) presented with somatic complaints in the absence of dysphoric affect, while four others (16%) reported somatic complaints along with dysphoric affect as their chief complaint.

Somatization exists in the U.S. but to a much smaller degree than in Chinese cultural settings or amongst Chinese patients in the U.S. Somatization appears to be more common in traditional societies, but perhaps not to the same extent it is found amongst Chinese, although this remains unproven. While Singer suggests somatization may relate more to socioeconomic class and educational level than to culture, there is some evidence that this is not the case [13, 45]. For example, in our study in Taiwan patients experiencing somatization represented the full range of socioeconomic classes and educational backgrounds; while amongst the somatizing patients in Boston, two were upper middle class college graduates. Somatization in the U.S. seems to be more common amongst ethnic minorities [45, 46]. Out of the five somatizers in our Boston study, three were Italian-Americans, one was a Jewish-American, and one was Black.

Our research findings enable us to appreciate how somatization functions in relation to depression and other mental illnesses amongst Chinese. In Taiwan, we found that approx 50% of 100 patients we interviewed in the offices of indigenous healers suffered from somatization—making it the most common type of sickness they treat [47]. Roughly the same degree of somatization can be found in the clinics of Western-style doctors in Taiwan [48].

Because mental illness is very highly stigmatized amongst Chinese—e.g. in Taiwan and Boston's Chinatown its presence in a family can lead to labeling that family's offspring unfit for marriage—it is not surprising that popular labels for mental illness cover only indisputably psychotic behavior and mental retardation. Minor psychiatric problems—depression, anxiety reaction, hysteria, psychophysiological reactions, etc—most commonly are labeled as medical illnesses. That is, the secondary physical complaints accompanying the psychological disorders are labeled as medical problems, while the psychological issues are systematically left unlabeled. This provides them with a legitimated sick role, but a medical sick role. The medical sick role (as in the West) releases patients from responsibilities and obligations, sanctions failure, and affords them care. Since there is virtually no psychotherapy available in Taiwan and since indigenous healers and non-psychiatric Western-style doctors handle the vast majority of minor mental disorders, most psychiatric care for these problems is given under the guise of care for putative medical disorders. The most common medical sick role is *shen-ching shuai jo* (Mandarin, neurasthenia). The popular belief holds this to be a physical disorder, but one said to include a range of psychological symptoms and to be stress-related. The Chinese characters which make up this disorder signify "neurological" and "weakness". But most behavior labeled neurasthenia would be diagnosed by a psychiatrist as minor mental illness, psychophysiological disorders, psychosexual problems, and interpersonal or family-related problems.

As Hsu has noted, Chinese informants and patients do not commonly reveal strong normal or dysphoric affects [49]. Cultural rules governing behavior prohibit such open expression [50]. Suppression of affect is common [51]. Patients frequently use physical complaints as a legitimated metaphor to indirectly express personal and interpersonal problems. Such terms function as semantic networks [36]. They link popular beliefs about body states and illness with psychosocial experiences and social relations. Such terms are often thoroughly psychophysiological. For example, in Mandarin a common word for depression is *mên*. The character for this term is written with the radicle which represents the heart (classically and still popularly believed to be the seat of the emotions) inside a radicle representing a doorway. Most Chinese somatizers whom I have studied point to their chest when they use this term. They report a physical sensation of pressure on the chest or heart. But when they describe it by using *mên* they mean both the physical sensation of something "pressing on" or "depressing into" their chest, as well as its psychological concomitants—e.g. sadness. But they focus on the former as the chief problem. They might also relate this term to family tensions or social stresses. People interpret their depressive symptoms in these terms. They explain etiology, pathophysiology and course as well as symptoms and treatment by this popular cultural system of articulating and explaining illness. Family and friends use the same framework to interpret those symptoms. Other examples are *suan* (sourness), a painful sensation common in Chinese patients with arthritis but also used to refer to a physical sensation felt in the chest, believed to be affecting the heart, of people who are experiencing grief and actively mourning; and *huo ch'i ta* (big internal fire) which signifies a constellation of nonspecific upper gastrointestinal and oral complaints, but which also stands for certain emotional complaints. These symptom expressions have a major impact on the perception and labelling of symptoms, as well as on the experience and treatment of the disorders they manifest [47, 53].

Because they illustrate the striking difference in phenomenology between Chinese and American depressives, it is worth reviewing several brief case descriptions of somatization in Chinese patients. These cases are typical of many Chinese with depression I have studied and treated in Taiwan and Boston.

Case 1

Miss Liu is a 32-year-old unmarried Taiwanese accountant who presented to the Psychiatry Clinic at the National Taiwan University Hospital with headaches of several months duration. Besides headaches, she suffered from insomnia with early morning wakening, easy fatigability and loss of energy. She had been to Western- and Chinese-style doctors and had used self and family treatment without success. Her symptoms had begun shortly after the collapse of a love affair, one of several which her family had forced her to end over the years because the prospective husband and his family were held to be unsuitable for her in one way or another.

Following that loss, Miss Liu became despondent. She now believed, apparently for the first time, that she would never marry, owing to a combination of her age and basic disagreements with her family over what constituted a suitable husband.

During her first visit to the Psychiatry Clinic, Miss Liu denied repeatedly any deep or significant psychological problems. Slowly over a number of sessions, she admitted feeling depressed and frustrated, and entertaining suicidal thoughts. Whenever queried in detail about her "bad feelings" (the general label she used to refer to them), she would quickly change the subject to her physical complaints or social problems. Beyond defining her feelings as depressed (*mên*) she claimed she was unable to be more specific about them: but she admitted that they were intense and quite disturbing. Thinking about them made her feel much worse. She noted that talking about them "in a vague way" made them seem less severe, more distant, and less overwhelming. Minimizing or denying their existence made her feel better, as did talking about her family and somatic problems. She could see no value in talking about her feelings to a doctor, though she reported feeling better on those occasions when her feelings were most intense when she spoke to close girlfriends about them.

Miss Liu pointed out to us that the most effective method she had found for dealing with her "bad feelings" was to occupy herself completely with her work, and after she returned home to immediately eat and then go to sleep. That kept her from being preoccupied with her depressed mood. Falling asleep so early, however, resulted in her being unable to sleep throughout the entire night; instead, she would wake up quite early in the morning and then find herself unable to go back to sleep. "I was no longer tired." But as soon as she awoke she found herself preoccupied with her dysphoric affect. At such times she noted she felt better if she could distract her mind by reading, working, or performing physical activity. Not infrequently headaches would occur at this time. When they were present, she felt totally preoccupied with them, and was unable to think about anything else, she reported, including her depressed feelings. Because of her unusual sleep cycle, Miss Liu often felt tired and sleepy in the late afternoon, so that by the time she returned home she was ready to eat and then immediately go to bed, thus perpetuating this behavioral cycle.

Case 2

Mr. Hung is a 60-yr-old retired Navy Captain from the China mainland, a widower now living alone in Taipei. He has suffered from the following constellation of symptoms over the past 2 years: weakness in all extremities; tremor of hands; unsteadiness of gait; heart palpitations; easily fatigued; profound weight loss; and insomnia. Full medical and neurological work-ups revealed no organic pathology on several occasions. Medical doctors told him he had neurasthenia. Since tranquilizers did not help and since Western-style medical doctors spent very little time talking to him about his problem and led him to believe there was nothing further they could do for his condition, Mr Hung began visiting the clinic of a noted acupunturist, a friend who had retired from the Navy. There over the last 6 months he has begun to feel much better with return of strength and appetite, increase in weight, improvement in gait, and greatly improved sleep pattern. He spends three full mornings each week in this Chinese-style doctor's clinic. He receives a half hour of acupuncture therapy and some herb teas each visit, and spends the remainder of the morning sitting in the clinic talking with his friend and the patients who come there. He feels that his friend's acupuncture has benefitted him, but admits also that his friend has inspired confidence in him, helped him relax, and encouraged him to socialize—things that have been problems for him since the onset of his disorder.

Mr Hung was in good health upon retiring from the Navy 3 years ago. However, over the next year he experienced severe financial reverses in his business ventures which left him without any income other than his very small government pension. These reverses destroyed both his savings and the plans for retirement he had made. He found himself deeply disturbed and ashamed. He felt that he had failed in life and had brought shame on himself and his family. He feared his friends would ridicule him if they knew his plight, and that he would lose "face". He felt unable to express his sadness to anyone. He began to avoid his friends and his grown children. He experienced his depressive affect as a feeling of pressure on his head and chest. Whenever he felt sad or wished to cry he associated his psychological feelings with these somatic sensations. His depression came to mean not the psychological symptoms but the somatic ones:

"First the bad financial problem caused my depression on the heart and brain. (He demonstrates this with his hands as a physical pressure, a pressing on heart and brain.) Then that depression pressed further on me causing my nerves to become weak and also my heart to become weak ... Now I take tonic and get acupuncture to make my heart and brain stronger."

Mr Hung would tell me he was depressed, but then describe that in somatic terms. If I asked him about his personal feelings he would not tell me anything other than that he was getting better. He would tell me repeatedly that his financial problems caused his sickness (which he believed to be a physical disorder), but if I asked him how this made him feel, tears would come to his eyes, which his facial muscles would strain to hold back, and he would look away for minutes at a time. He would tell me that these were things that were better not talked about, that he never talked about them with anyone, *even with himself*, that after all they were getting better; and then he would politely but firmly introduce another topic. Even after 4 months, when his depression had largely subsided, Mr Hung refused to talk about what his feelings had been like. In fact, on one occasion he told me that he himself did not know what they were like since when they came to mind he felt his somatic symptoms greatly worsen and became preoccupied with the latter. He also admitted that he spent most of the time watching television, reading, collecting stamps, or playing card games in order to keep his "mind blank". Keeping his mind blank seemed to him important because he felt his physical symptoms less at such times. Even at the time of my last visit, he could talk about his financial reverses in detail but could not say how they affected him beyond that they depressed his heart and brain, thereby hurting his nerves and bringing on all of his physical symptoms.

Case 3

Mr. W. is a 33-yr-old Chinese male (Cantonese

speaking) who presented at the medical clinic at the · Massachusetts General Hospital with tiredness, dizziness, general weakness, pains in the upper back described as rheumatism, a sensation of heaviness in the feet, 20 lb. weight loss, and insomnia of 6 months duration. Patient denied any emotional complaints. Past medical history was non-contributory. Medical work-up was unrevealing, except that the patient seemed anxious and looked depressed. Mr. W. refused to acknowledge either, however. He initially refused psychotherapy, stating that talk therapy would not help him. He finally accepted psychiatric care only after it was agreed that he would be given some kind of medication. During the course of his care, Mr. W. never accepted the idea that he was suffering from a mental illness. He described his problem, as did his family, as due to "wind" *(fung)* and "not enough blood" *(m̄-kaù huèt).*

Pertinent past history included the following: Mr. W. was born into a family of educated farmers and teachers in a village in Kwantung Province. He and his family moved to Canton when he was a young child. His father died during the war with Japan, and Mr. W. remembered recurrent feelings of grief and loneliness throughout his childhood and adolescence. At age 10 he accompanied his family to Hong Kong; 10 years later they moved to the U.S. Mr. W. denied any family history of mental illness. He reported that his health problem began two years before when he returned to Hong Kong to find a wife. He acquired the "wind" disease he believes in retrospect, after having over-indulged in sexual relations with prostitutes, which resulted in loss of *huèt-hei* (blood and vital breath) causing him to suffer from "cold" *(leūng)* and "not enough blood". His symptoms worsened over the past 6 months, following his wife's second miscarriage (they have no children) and shortly after he had lost most of his savings in the stock market and in a failing restaurant business. However, he denied feeling depressed at that time, though he admitted being anxious, fearful, irritable, and worried about his financial situation. These feelings he also attributed to "not enough blood".

Mr. W. first began treating himself for his symptoms with traditional Chinese herbs and diet therapy. This involved both the use of tonics to "increase blood" *(po-huèt)* and treatment with symbolically "hot" *(ît)* food to correct his underlying state of humoral imbalance. He did this only after seeking advice from his family and friends in Boston's Chinatown. They concurred that he was suffering from a "wind" and "cold" disorder. They prescribed other herbal medicines when he failed to improve. They suggested that he return to Hong Kong to consult traditional Chinese practitioners there. While the patient was seen at the Massachusetts General Hospital's medical clinic, he continued to use Chinese drugs and to seek out consultation and advice from friends, neighbors, and recognized "experts" in the local Chinese community. He was frequently told that his problem could not be helped by Western medicine. At the time of receiving psychiatric care, Mr. W. was also planning to visit a well known traditional Chinese doctor in New York's Chinatown, and he was also considering acupuncture treatment locally. He continued taking Chinese drugs throughout his

illness, and never told his family or friends about receiving psychiatric care. He expressed gratitude, however, that the psychiatrist listened to his views about his problem and that he explained to him in detail psychiatric ideas about depression, etc. He remembered feeling badly about his care in the medical clinic where, after the lengthy work-up, almost nothing was explained to him and no treatment was given him. He had decided not to return to the clinic.

Mr. W. responded to a course of anti-depressant medication with complete remission of all symptoms. He thanked the psychiatrist for his help, but confided that (1) he remained confident that he was not suffering from a mental illness, (2) talk therapy had not been of help, (3) anti-depressants perhaps were effective against "wind" disorders, and (4) since he had concurrently taken a number of traditional Chinese herbs it was uncertain what had been effective, and perhaps the combination of both traditional Chinese and Western drugs had been responsible for his cure.

Case 3 is typical of the use of indigenous Chinese cultural categories to pattern the perception and experience of depression. Although the content of the cultural label changes, this is the commonest pattern of somatization I encountered amongst Chinese. It is different from that found amongst non-Chinese somatizers just as the labels represent distinct cultural categories and experiences. Case 2, unlike Case 3, referred to himself as depressed, but by depression meant a somatic affect and physical disorder. Case 1, who is unusual in my experience, was willing to label herself depressed and talk about it, but was unable to clearly define her psychological complaint or to communicate in a psychological idiom. She is similar in this regard to non-Chinese somatizers with the depressive syndrome whom I have studied in Boston. All three cases demonstrate that somatization leads to specific treatment approaches, so that when we talk about cultural influence on the sickness we are also talking about its impact on treatment. It is misleading to separate the two. Taken together, these cases illustrate a spectrum of somatization experiences of patients with the depressive syndrome which range from that exhibiting most extensive to that exhibiting least extensive cultural patterning. In the latter (Case 1) similarities with somatization of depression in other cultures are obvious; while in the former (Case 3) the patterning is so extensive that the sickness may appear unique (e.g. like so-called culture-bound disorders), yet it too is an instance of the depressive syndrome, as defined by the specific constellation of symptoms listed on p. 1.

CONCLUSION: CULTURE, DISEASE AND ILLNESS. SOME THEORETICAL AND METHODOLOGICAL IMPLICATIONS FOR CROSS-CULTURAL RESEARCH

It can be flatly stated that the experience of most anthropological and psychiatric researchers working in Chinese culture supports the opposite of Singer's conclusion: i.e. depression has outstanding deviant features in Chinese society [14, 35, 40–42, 44, 47, 48]. I have tried to show how this discrepancy relates to certain limitations in the traditional transcultural psychiatric approach Singer reviews and exemplifies, as well as to the elaboration of a whole new generation of anthropological. clinical. and epidemiological studies. which I have termed the "new cross-cultural psychiatry". From what I have said it can be seen that cross-cultural research on behavior and deviance is in process of changing theoretical and methodological paradigms: new problem-frameworks and solution-frameworks are being developed and used. Examining one of these changes and its implications will be an appropriate way to conclude.

Recent analyses of cross-cultural medical and psychiatric research stress the importance of distinguishing two interrelated aspects of sickness: *disease* and *illness* [15, 47, 52]. Disease can be thought of as malfunctioning or maladaptation of biological or psychological processes. Illness is the personal. interpersonal. and cultural reaction to disease. Although social and cultural factors may or may not influence the etiology, pathophysiology, and course of disease, they *always* influence illness. Illness is by definition a cultural construct. Disease may occur without illness, as in acute overwhelming disorders, like massive trauma, in which there simply is not sufficient time to generate an illness response. Illness may occur without disease. as in malingering, and also perhaps in certain problems like the non-medical aspects of drug abuse and alcoholism that are made into illness problems for political. social, and historical reasons. But in most sicknesses, especially chronic sickness, disease and illness occur together and reciprocally influence each other. In diabetes, asthma, chronic physical impairment, depression, schizophrenia. and so on. the illness reaction plays a large role in the form and meaning of the sickness. The illness response may strongly influence symptoms [53] and care [24, 25]. Just as there are disease problems so too there are illness problems. Whereas the former may respond to technological interventions. the latter frequently do not, and often require psychosocial issues be attended to. Treatment of the former we can call *cure*, while treatment of the latter we can refer to as *healing*. Cross-cultural studies suggest most traditional healing systems provide both forms of treatment. whereas modern medical care provides principally the former. Patients appear to consider both essential [9, 47]. Evidence is accumulating that patient non-compliance and dissatisfaction with care is in part a function of the absence of healing in modern health care [9, 47, 52]. Discrepancies in doctor and patient evaluations of treatment efficacy seem to support this dichotomy [54] as does patient use of alternative forms of care [55].

The depressive syndrome, as defined above, would appear to be a disease; while the degree and form of somatization in Chinese culture would appear to reflect a major discrepancy between the way this disease is shaped into illness behavior in Chinese and Western cultures. Most of the research questions we have reviewed must be distinguished as to whether they pertain to disease or illness. Singer confuses these categories. But so does most of the work he reviews. The new cross-cultural approach to behavior and deviance makes this separation so that it can study the relation of culture to both disease and illness. Yet it is already clear that the key questions facing cross-cultural studies in medicine and psychiatry lie on the illness side of the dichotomy. To focus only on the disease side. is to strip the question of culture and depression of its chief significance. Yet this is as large a failing in cross-cultural research as it is in medical research generally.

Biomedicine attends almost entirely to disease, and appears to be systematically blinded to the evaluation of illness. This holds enormous importance for health care throughout the world, and has deeply influenced medical research. Cross-cultural research in medicine and psychiatry heretofore has been under this seriously distorting influence [16, 56–58]. The major consequence of the "new cross-cultural" approach is its systematic attention to these questions which go to the heart of the relationship of culture to depression and illness in general [59].

REFERENCES

1. Singer K. Depressive disorders from a transcultural perspective. *Soc. Sci. & Med.* **9**, 289, 1975.
2. Dohrenwend B. and Dohrenwend B. Social and cultural influences on psychopathology. *Ann. Rev. Psychol.* 417, 1974.
3. Klerman G. L. Overview of depression. In *Comprehensive Textbook of Psychiatry—II* Vol. 1. pp. 1003–1011. (Edited by Freedman A. et al.). Wilkins & Wilkins, Baltimore, Md., 1975.
4. Klerman G. L. and Barrett J. E. The affective disorders: clinical and epidemiological aspects. In *Lithium: Its Role in Psychiatric Treatment and Research* (Edited by Gershon S. and Shopsin B.). Plenum, New York, 1972.
5. Fabrega H. The need for an ethnomedical science. *Science* **189**, 969. 1975.
6. Fabrega H. The study of disease in relation to culture. *Behav. Sci.* **17**, 183, 1972.
7. Fabrega H. Problems implicit in the cultural and social study of depression. *Psychosom. Med.* **36**, 377, 1974.
8. Kleinman A. The cognitive structure of traditional medical systems. *Ethnomedicine* **3**, 27, 1974.
9. Kleinman A. Explanatory models in health care relationships. In *Health of the Family* pp. 159–172. (National Council for International Health), Washington, D.C., 1975.
10. Englehardt H. T. Explanatory models in medicine. *Texas Rep. Biol. Med.* **32**, 225, 1974.
11. *Report of the International Pilot Study of Schizophrenia.* Vol. 1. W.H.O., Geneva, 1973.
12. Leighton A. et al. *Psychiatric Disorder among the Yoruba.* Cornell University Press, New York, 1963.
13. Carstairs G. M. and Kapur R. L. *Great Universe of Kota: A Study of Stress, Change and Mental Disorder in an Indian Village.* University of California Press, Berkeley, 1976.
14. Yap P. M. *Comparative Psychiatry.* University of Toronto Press. 1974.
15. Fabrega H. *Disease and Social Behavior.* M.I.T. Press. Cambridge, Mass., 1974.
16. Kleinman A. Social, cultural and historical issues in the study of medicine and psychiatry in Chinese culture. In *Medicine in Chinese Cultures: Comparative Studies of Health Care in Chinese and Other Societies* (Edited by Kleinman A. et al.). Fogarty International Center. N.I.H.. Bethesda, Md., 1976.
17. LeVine R. *Culture, Behavior, and Personality.* Aldine. Chicago, 1973.
18. Gove W. (Ed.) *The Labelling of Deviance.* Wiley, New York, 1975.
19. Young A. Some implications of medical beliefs and practices in social anthropology. *Am. Anthrop.* **78**, 5. 1976.

20. Leslie C. (Ed.) *Asian Medical Systems.* University of California Press. Berkeley. 1976.

21. Kleinman A. *et al.* (Eds.) *Medicine in Chinese Cultures: Comparative Studies of Health Care in Chinese and Other Societies.* Fogarty International Center, N.I.H., Bethesda, Md., 1976.

22. Harwood A. The hot–cold theory of disease: implications for treatment of Puerto Rican patients. *J. Am. med. Ass.* **216.** 1153, 1971.

23. Snow L. Folk medical beliefs and their implications for care of patients. *Annls intern. Med.* **81,** 82, 1974.

24. Zola I. The concept of trouble and sources of medical assistance. *Soc. Sci. & Med.* **6,** 673, 1972.

25. Zola I. Studying the decision to see a doctor. *Adv. psychosom. Med.* **8,** 216, 1972.

26. Levy R. *Tahitians: Mind and Experience in the Society Islands.* University of Chicago Press, 1973.

27. Fabrega H. and Silver D. *Illness and Shamonistic Curing in Zinacantan.* Stanford University Press, 1974.

28. Reynolds D. *Morita Psychotherapy.* University of California Press. Berkeley. 1976.

29. Rohlen T. P. The promise of adulthood in Japanese spiritualism. *Daedalus* **105, (2)** , 125, 1976.

30. Crapanzano V. *The Hamadsha: A Study in Moroccan Ethnopsychiatry.* University of California Press, Berkeley, 1973.

31. Wolf M. *Women and the Family in Rural Taiwan.* Stanford University Press, 1972.

32. Lewis G. Knowledge of illness in a Sepik society. Athlone, London, 1975.

33. Rubel A. The epidemiology of a folk illness: Susto in Hispanic America. *Ethnology* **3,** 268. 1964.

34. Young A. Why Amhara get *kureynya*: sickness and possession in an Ethiopian ZAR cult. *Am. Ethnol.* **2,** 567, 1975.

35. Tseng W. S. The nature of somatic complaints among psychiatric patients: the Chinese case. *Comprehensive Psychiat.* **16,** 237, 1975.

36. Good B. The heart of what's the matter: semantics and illness in Iran. Paper presented at the Harvard Faculty Seminar on "Cross-Cultural Studies of Illness and Clinical Care," 28 October 1975, to be published in *Culture, Medicine and Psychiatry.*

37. Fabrega H. and Manning P. K. An integrated theory of disease: Ladino-Mestizo views of disease in the Chiapas highlands. *Psychosom. Med.* **35,** 223, 1973.

38. Rin H. *et al.* Culture, social structure and psychopathology in Taiwan and Japan. *J. nerv. ment. Dis.* **157,** 296, 1973.

39. Lin T. Y. A study of the incidence of mental disorder in Chinese and other cultures. *Psychiatry* **16,** 313, 1953.

40. Rin H. *et al.* Psychophysiological reactions of a rural and suburban population in Taiwan. *Acta psychiat. scand.* **42,** 410, 1966.

41. Tseng W. S. and Hsu J. Chinese culture, personality formation and mental illness. *Int. J. soc. Psychiat.* **16,** 5, 1969.

42. Gaw A. An integrated approach in the delivery of health care to a Chinese community in America. In Kleinman *et al.* (Eds.) *op. cit.*

43. Chin R. and Chin A. *Psychological Research in Communist China,* 1949–1966. M.I.T. Press, Cambridge, 1969.

44. Topley M. Chinese and Western medicine in Hong Kong. In Kleinman *et al.* (Eds.) *op. cit.*

45. Zola I. Culture and symptoms. *Am. sociol. Rev.* **31,** 615, 1966.

46. Zborowski M. Cultural components in response to pain. *J. soc. Issues* **8,** 16, 1952.

47. Kleinman A. and Sung L. H. Why indigenous practitioners successfully heal: a follow-up study of patients treated by indigenous practitioners in Taiwan. Paper presented at the Michigan State University Medical Anthropology Workshop on "The Healing Process", 7–10 April, 1976.

48. Kleinman A. Medical and psychiatric anthropology and the study of traditional medicine in modern Chinese culture. *J. Inst. Ethnol., Academica Sinica* **39,** 107, 1975.

49. Hsu F. L. K. Psychosocial homeostasis and *jen*: conceptual tools for advancing psychological anthropology. *Am. Anthrop.* **73,** 23, 1971.

50. Hsu F. L. K. Eros, affect and *pao.* In *Kinship and Culture* (Edited by Hsu F. L. K.) Aldine, Chicago. 1971.

51. Hsu F. L. K. Suppression versus repression. *Psychiatry* **12,** 223, 1949.

52. Eisenberg L. Delineation of clinical conditions: conceptual models of "physical" and "mental" disorders. In *Research and Medical Practice.* (Ciba Foundation Symposium 44), Elsevier, North-Holland, 1976.

53. Mechanic D. Social psychological factors affecting the presentation of bodily complaints. *New Eng. J. Med.* **286,** 1132, 1972.

54. Cay *et al.* E. L. Patient assessment of the result of surgery for peptic ulcer. *Lancet* **1,** 29, 1975.

55. Kane R. *et al.* Manipulating the patient: a comparison of the effectiveness of physicians and chiropractic care. *Lancet* **1,** 1333, 1974.

56. Lumsden D. P. On "transcultural psychiatry", Africans. and academic racism. *Am. Anthrop.* **78.** 101, 1976.

57. Seijas H. An approach to the study of the medical aspects or culture. *Curr. Anthrop.* **14,** 544, 1973.

58. Waxler N. Culture and mental illness: a social labelling perspective. *J. nerv. ment. Dis.* **159,** 379, 1974.

59. Marsella A. Cross-cultural studies of depression. In *Handbook of Cross-Cultural Psychology.* Allyn & Bacon, Boston (in press).

Mental Health Law and Ethics in Transition: A Report From Japan

Paul S. Appelbaum, M.D.

The ideal of individual autonomy has had a profound impact on mental health law in the United States in the last generation. However, the power of this ideal is not limited to Western societies. Even Japan, a country with a tradition of placing the interests of the group above those of the individual, is falling under the sway of approaches to mental health law that emphasize the value of individual rights.

These thoughts were stimulated by a symposium on law and ethics in psychiatry sponsored by the Tokyo Institute of Psychiatry and held in Tokyo in November 1993. More than 160 Japanese psychiatrists and lawyers joined invited guests from around the world in exploring the changing face of legal and ethical regulation of psychiatry in Japan. What was clear from the conference—whose proceedings will be published in a forthcoming issue of the *Japanese Journal of Psychiatry and Neurology*—is the influence that events in the West are having on Japan.

Japanese mental health care has developed somewhat differently from mental health systems in the United States. The first law dealing

Dr. Appelbaum is A. F. Zeleznik professor and chair of the department of psychiatry at University of Massachusetts Medical School. Address correspondence to him at the Department of Psychiatry, University of Massachusetts Medical Center, 55 Lake Avenue North, Worcester, Massachusetts 01655.

with the treatment of the mentally ill, passed in 1900, codified the existing practice of caring for most mentally ill people at home, where they were kept locked in special rooms. In 1919 the Mental Hospital Act authorized each prefecture (roughly equivalent to an American state) to build a public psychiatric hospital, but only five were constructed. As Western approaches to psychiatric care became more widely accepted, private hospitals assumed the burden of treating most hospitalized mentally ill people. Even today, 89 percent of the 355,000 psychiatric beds in Japan are in private hospitals (1).

In 1950, in the wake of American occupation, Japan passed the Western-style Mental Hygiene Act, which outlawed the confinement of mentally ill persons in private homes. Involuntary commitment could be effected by two physicians certifying that a person was likely to harm himself or herself or others.

Since 1950 two scandals that attracted international attention have motivated major changes in mental health law and the delivery of mental health services. The 1964 assault by a mentally ill young man on U.S. Ambassador Edwin Reischauer precipitated legislation conferring broad powers on the police to monitor mentally ill persons in the community, as well as an expansion of outpatient services (2). The highly publicized deaths of two patients in 1984 at the hands of attendants in a psychiatric hospital led to widespread concern about the quality of psychiatric services and about disregard for patients' civil liberties. An investigation by the International Commission of Jurists (3), which highlighted abuse of the rights of mental patients in Japanese hospitals, stimulated passage of the Mental Health Law of 1988.

The 1988 law, currently in effect, established a psychiatric review board for each prefecture. The boards—each composed of three psychiatrists, a lawyer, and an independent member—review involuntary admissions, undertake periodic reviews of patients' status, and make recommendations to the prefectural governor concerning patients' requests for release. Patients must be informed of their rights on admission and can present their release petitions directly to the board. The law also strengthened provisions for community-based care, especially in rehabilitation facilities (1,2).

Nonetheless, many vestiges of traditional practice remain, including deference to medical authority. Although patients have the right to challenge their involuntary commitments, a survey of 1,000 commitments in Kyoto found that only three patients requested independent review (1).

Another holdover from earlier times is the *hogosha* system, a kind of conservatorship that is supposed to be applied to all mentally ill people. The *hogosha* is a family member charged with making sure that the mentally ill person receives psychiatric and medical care and that the person's assets are protected (4). As such, a *hogosha* has authority to consent to medical treatment and psychiatric hospitalization for the patient and, if the patient is found incompetent, even to abortion or sterilization. Along with this power comes the responsibility of paying for the patient's hospitalization and compensating third parties to whom the mentally ill person has caused harm.

An approach like the *hogosha* system, with its emphasis on familial responsibility and familial control of mentally ill relatives, would be unthinkable in the United States. As Western attitudes toward individual rights and responsibilities become more prevalent in Japan, however, the *hogosha* system is showing signs of stress (4). Many patients, especially those who have been hospitalized for extended periods, lack a *hogosha* because family members are unwilling to bear the burdens associated with the role. Particularly problematic in many families' eyes is the obligation to pay for whatever damage their relative causes.

Patient and family organizations, including *Zenseiren* (Japan Network of the World Federation of Psychiatric Users) and *Zenkaren* (Japanese National Federation of Families With Mentally Ill Members), have objected as well to the *hogosha's* right to consent to admission on the patient's behalf. Although only 10 percent of hospitalizations occur through this route, it is now seen as a major deprivation of patients' rights. Moreover, since a *hogosha* is required by law to follow physicians' advice, he or she cannot exercise independent judgment regarding a family member's needs, allowing treatment to proceed without informed consent of any kind.

How might the *hogosha* system be altered? Hiromi Shiraishi, M.D., a community psychiatrist who critiqued the current system at the conference, offered several suggestions (4). Removing the power from the *hogosha* to consent to hospitalization would encourage psychiatrists to work harder to get informed consent from patients. Nonconsenting patients who required hospitalization could be processed through the involuntary commitment system, where they would at least have the protection of independent oversight by the psychiatric review board. A publicly administered compensation fund could be created to indemnify victims harmed by mental patients—an idea that might have some relevance for our own tangled system of liability for harmful acts by mentally ill persons (5). Finally, public guardian offices, similar to those in many U.S. states and European countries, might be created to offer supervision of person and property to mentally ill people in need of these services.

Informed consent to psychiatric services was another focus of the conference. Whereas it was once assumed in Japan that patients would simply comply with doctors' orders,

a good deal of attention is now being paid to defining when patients are sufficiently able to make decisions that their refusals of treatment should be respected (6). A conference participant who argued that a patient's rejection of treatment should not be respected if the psychiatrist believes that the patient really desires to be treated was roundly criticized by his colleagues for attempting to undercut patients' right of choice.

For Japanese psychiatrists and mental health law experts, the question is whether to adopt Western values *in toto* or to allow them to be modified by more traditional Japanese values.

However, the extent to which these rights-oriented views are representative of Japanese psychiatry—or of Japanese medicine in general (7)—is unclear. One presenter confided privately that psychiatrists commonly slip liquid medication into the beverages of patients who express a reluctance to follow their orders.

Patients' right to give informed consent to psychotherapy was also addressed. In a discussion billed—somewhat remarkably to an American psychiatrist—as the first public presentation ever made in Japan on ethical issues in psychotherapy, one of a small number of Japanese psychoanalysts advocated efforts to obtain informed consent from patients in psychotherapy (8). He recounted the case of an adolescent girl referred for psychoanalysis without having been told about or having agreed to the process. She was stunned to find herself expected to lie on a couch and reveal her most intimate thoughts to a stranger—this in a culture in which feelings are closely held. When she expressed her embarrassment, the analyst shifted to a face-to-face mode of psychotherapy, which gave the patient a greater sense of control. But the problem could have been avoided

by seeking the patient's agreement before beginning treatment.

The presenter, Masahisa Nishizono, M.D., a professor of psychiatry at Fukuoka University School of Medicine, pointed out some of the problems in obtaining patients' consent to psychotherapy (8). Although patients usually come to treatment for relief of symptoms and for help in changing their behavior, long-term psychotherapy often aims as well at improving patients' adaptation and self-understanding, goals that patients may be not prepared to embrace at the start of treatment. In addition, although patients may understand something about the psychotherapeutic attitude, which emphasizes empathy and support, they often lack the ability to understand the details of therapeutic techniques. Nonetheless, Dr. Nishizono urged colleagues to make the effort to educate patients and to obtain their consent. He argued that children and adolescents should receive an age-appropriate explanation of therapy and the patients' agreement should be obtained to the extent possible.

Since the opening of Japan to the West by Commodore Perry in 1853, the Japanese have enthusiastically embraced Western attitudes and practices while struggling to hold on to many traditional values and to a core identity of themselves as different from the rest of the world (9). This process is now under way in mental health law. The transition was stimulated partly by embarrassment over conditions that were perceived as inhumane by outsiders (3), and the resulting "political need to make Japanese psychiatry acceptable on an international basis" (6). Theories of individual rights, however, played an important role in motivating these changes, much as they did in the United States and other Western countries.

For Japanese psychiatrists and mental health law experts, the question they must now address is whether to adopt Western values *in toto* or to allow them to be modified by more traditional Japanese values. The extent to which ideas of familial responsibility, deference to authority,

(Continued on page 644)

nify for individuals, families, and society. *Larry* will be a major contribution to the teaching of students in the various fields of mental health.

The journal *Family Process* devoted a special clinical section in its December 1993 issue to family therapy perspectives on manic-depressive disorder. A comment in that section from Moltz (2) is germane to this video: "Psychiatric illness occurs simultaneously on the biological, the individual, and the social level. The manifestations of the illness are the result of ongoing interaction between these levels. It is thus fruitless to debate whether an illness is biological, psychological, or social in etiology; it is finally and irreducibly all of these, and it is not only possible but also necessary to address each of these aspects, and their interactions, in the evaluation and treatment of the illness."

Will Harding has certainly succeeded in helping us know and understand his father the human being and his father who suffers from manic-depressive illness. The video is a cinema verité. It is powerful. It is tender. It will teach all who watch it.

Chain of Hope—produced by Leonard A. Lies. VHS videocassette, 25 minutes, color, 1993. Purchase price $39.95, plus $4 shipping and handling. Contact Lies Film & Video Productions, P.O. Box 71132, Pittsburgh, Pennsylvania 15213; telephone, 412-682-3916. (Also available, for $5, is a manual written by Chain of Hope consumers on how to set up and operate a drop-in center.)

This professionally produced video engagingly presents the story of a consumer-operated drop-in center in Pittsburgh named Chain of Hope. The viewer's interest is immediately captured by the involvement of the consumers themselves. We see some of them erecting the sign at the front of the center, and we hear the testimony of many who have found the Chain of Hope to be a crucial and central part of their lives. "I can come when I want to . . . get food or a sandwich . . . for over four years," says one woman, who is sitting in a comfortably furnished area with many other consumers.

The segments of straightforward talk by consumers explain not only the value of the services received, but also the strength the consumers gain from participating in the development and operation of the center. "Before self-help, I was a victim!" comments one woman. For more than six years, this consumer-run center has provided an unusual opportunity for people to take responsibility and to support one another through the maintenance of a place that is open when other services are not, and that can offer not only food and recreation but also support from peers, the use of computers, and the chance to foster the expansion of such facilities.

The Allegheny East Mental Health and Mental Retardation Center in Pittsburgh has provided additional support to the center in the form of accounting and management help. In addition, the Chain of Hope is part of the Pennsylvania Unified Systems Program. Consumer-members of the Chain of Hope visit hospitalized patients and welcome for trial visits consumers who are still hospitalized so that movement from hospital to community is facilitated.

The production values of the videotape are excellent. Sound and video are of good quality. The editing, with a small amount of music and some special production effects added, makes the program stimulating and easy to watch while not spoiling the genuineness so compellingly obvious in the consumers' words and actions. Special note should be made of the overvoice, which achieves excellence in its sparseness, its appropriate timing, and its easy-to-listen-to tone and quality.

This video is an excellent example of a combined educational-promotional tape, used for both education and fund raising. The core message is empowerment of consumers. The tape demonstrates that they have enormous personal resources and talents that can be realized when they have the opportunity to take charge of their own lives. The director of the Chain of Hope, Nancy Abel, emphasizes this view with her closing message to viewers: "I believe that your unselfish efforts will strengthen consumers as self-empowered individuals and help to tear down the walls of stigma."

References

1. Engel GL: The clinical application of the biopsychosocial model. American Journal of Psychiatry 137:535–544, 1980
2. Moltz DA: Bipolar disorder and the family: an integrative model. Family Process 32:409–423, 1993

Law & Psychiatry

(Continued from page 636)

and sacrifice of individual interests for group interests will prevail is not yet apparent. That Japanese psychiatry is committed to examining the alternatives, however, should not be doubted. As evidence, one need only look at the agenda for this year's international symposium, which will address issues related to death and dying, including assisted suicide. Western ethics and Japanese values will again be in the spotlight.

References

1. Oya M: Reform of mental health legislation in Japan: from the Mental Hygiene Act of 1950 to the Mental Health Act of 1988. Japanese Journal of Psychiatry and Neurology, in press
2. Koizumi K, Harris P: Mental health care in Japan. Hospital and Community Psychiatry 43:1100–1103, 1992
3. Human Rights and Mental Patients in Japan. Geneva, International Commission of Jurists, 1986
4. Shiraishi H: Some guidelines for the reform of the "caretaker (hogosha) system" and psychiatric practice in Japan. Japanese Journal of Psychiatry and Neurology, in press
5. Appelbaum PS, Greer A: Civil liability of the mentally ill. Hospital and Community Psychiatry 44:617–618, 1993
6. Kumakura N: Models of "self-determination" in psychiatric treatment. Japanese Journal of Psychiatry and Neurology, in press
7. Hadfield P: Tokyo perspective: informed consent. Lancet 341:1141, 1993
8. Nishizono M: Ethical issues in psychotherapy. Japanese Journal of Psychiatry and Neurology, in press
9. Reischauer EO: The Japanese Today: Change and Continuity. Cambridge, Mass, Harvard University Press, 1988

[17]

PSYCHIATRIC DIAGNOSIS AND RACIAL BIAS: EMPIRICAL AND INTERPRETATIVE APPROACHES

ROLAND LITTLEWOOD

Centre for Medical Anthropology, Department of Anthropology, University College London,
London WC1E 6BT, U.K.

Abstract—Understanding of psychiatric illness among Britain's Black and ethnic minority population has shifted from an emphasis on cultural difference to one on racism within psychiatric theory and practice. In spite of this apparent turn, the explanations put forward remain within an empirical framework of methodological individualism, reflecting the background and training of British psychiatrists themselves. How racism may be actually demonstrated in individual clinical practice remains elusive. The standard hypotheses are examined here through a conventional clinical vignette study: this suggests medical education does not in itself now involve any specific racist psychiatric assumptions. Fuller understanding of the exercise of social power within this particular domain requires not only more complex interactive studies, preferably derived from a variety of clinical and social contexts, but a more developed interpretation of psychiatric practice and ideology within the social system.

Key words—diagnosis, racism, psychiatry

INTRODUCTION

Cultural psychiatry in Britain has focussed almost exclusively on ethnic minority groups. The subject is essentially dominated by psychiatrists: although British social anthropology had previously considered psychological and psychopathological aspects of the peoples of its empire, the work of Seligman, Fortes and Field had always been modest in comparison with that of American 'Culture and Personality' theorists. Psychiatric research in the colonies was carried out by descriptive general psychiatrists, usually employing an evolutionary biological approach, and with close links to the colonial administration. Like psychoanalysts they employed an idiom of 'maturity' in which social, psychological and biological 'development' were simultaneous reflections of the same evolutionary process [1]. Much of their work is now considered ethnocentric in the extreme, if not explicitly racist, both in theory and practice. Only with the extensive migration to Britain from Commonwealth countries in the 1950s and 1960s did a now more liberal psychiatry begin to look at the people from its former colonies with an emphasis on their 'culture' rather than on their putative biology.

What came to be known in Britain as 'transcultural psychiatry' derived initially from traditional European psychiatry, with an emphasis on descriptive accounts of symptomatology. Serious mental illness was to be understood in individual biological terms. The core *form* of the illness was the reflection in psychological functioning of underlying physical changes, uniform across societies, which were characteristic of and directly depended on an underlying disease process. This was to be distinguished from the *content* of the illness, a variable and diagnostically

insignificant manifestation of the individual's personality, preoccupations, ethnicity and culture [2]. This biomedical focus on the individual symptoms, with its ignorance of general social theory, let alone of more specific debates on symbolisation and experience, led one British professor of social anthropology to note that while a dialogue "between those who study the culturally standardised symbolism of societies and those who study the idiosyncratic personal symbolism of individuals seems obvious...the rather limited fruits which [transcultural psychiatry] has so far produced merely provided for British social anthropologists additional confirmation of the undesirability of all liaisons of this sort" [3].

The emerging transcultural psychiatry devoted itself primarily to the statistical study of the non-White immigrants to Britain from what was euphemistically known as the 'New Commonwealth' (Africa, the Caribbean, South Asia). Of the 120 or so academic papers which have been published on the mental health of British minorities, none are concerned with migrants from the Old Commonwealth (the largely White ex-Dominions), and only four on the Irish in Britain, who actually form the largest foreign-born community. Transcultural psychiatry has remained essentially the study of 'Black' people [4].

The subject developed in two phases. Initially, concern was focussed on the difference in rates of hospitalised patients who had migrated from different countries (for example Ref. [5]). Two findings which emerged in the 1970s have dominated the debate ever since: higher rates of diagnosed schizophrenia and other psychoses among those of West Indian origin, and increased parasuicide, particularly overdoses with medical drugs, among South Asians. Attempts to explain these statistics first emphasised selective patterns of migration (the most vulnerable were those who chose to move), or later that 'the culture' of the immigrant group was itself pathogenic. This latter idea was barely elaborated beyond vague suggestions about family structure, inter-generational stress or 'culture conflict', and fitted uneasily with the biological primacy of the form/content model. The single social scientist involved in the area argued for Mertonian theories of relative deprivation but the suggestion was not developed [6]. No-one looked at the minorities' construction of self-hood, their understanding of illness, recourse to mental health agencies or indeed their attitudes to professional medicine in general. 'Pathology' is always a measure of difference, and medical understanding of 'culture' was simply one of cultural difference, easily accessible as a check list of discrete items such as religious belief, family pattern, goals and expectations in Britain, each of which could be argued to associate statistically with pathology one way or the other.

Although what may be termed the 'epidemiological' approach still continues, from the early 1980s a second and more critical set of ideas developed. It was argued that the medical diagnoses of people of non-European origin, particularly for schizophrenia, were frequently inappropriate or even 'wrong', biased by British psychiatric stereotypes about what constituted 'normality' in different groups [1]. Many West Indian immigrant patients who had been hospitalised with a diagnosis of schizophrenia were found in research studies to lack the symptoms of schizophrenia commonly regarded as of primary diagnostic significance in such studies as the World Health Organisation's cross-national project on schizophrenia, itself modelled on British descriptive psychiatry [7]. An earlier study which had showed that alcoholism was preferentially diagnosed among Irish people independently of actual symptomatology [8] was cited to suggest that popular ethnic stereotypes carried over into medical practice. Increased salience was given to these issues by repeated findings that non-White patients of quite diverse linguistic and cultural backgrounds were two to three times more likely to be involuntary patients under the Mental Health Act than were comparable groups of Whites, whether these were native Britons or non-English speaking European immigrants [9]. There was some evidence of differences in treatment. In one study Black patients were more likely to be given physical treatment [10] and it has become generally recognised that access to psychotherapy is easier for Whites [11].

The shift from '*cultural*' explanations—locating psychopathological differences within the characteristics of an individual's ethnicity—to explanations based on *race* (now the social construction of ethnicity and its articulation with social interest and medical power) was accompanied by a shift from empirical, descriptive statistics to a more critical interpretative approach. It was however supported by a study which showed that the British-born children

of West Indian immigrants were likely to have even higher rates of diagnosed schizophrenia than their migrant parents [12]. (In most situations of international migration, if a migrating group have higher rates of psychiatric illness than the population they come to live amongst, their children born in the new country have levels of morbidity intermediate between the two.) The difficulty of explaining this study (which had used the internationally recognised WHO procedures for diagnosis—the 'first-rank symptoms' and a diagnostic decision tree rather than the local hospital diagnosis) led to debate among the British mental health professionals grouped in the Transcultural Psychiatry Society: the existing type of statistical surveys was extensively criticised. No alternative explanations were offered as to the figures for British-born Afro-Caribbeans, beyond a general conviction that psychiatrists were themselves still prejudiced, consciously or unconsciously [13].

The almost complete absence of social scientists among those practically involved seems to have led to a reversal in explanation; one which was still couched in individualistic terms, but now away from the Black patient to the White psychiatrist. The diagnostic differences were now not 'real' ones but reflected explicit bias on the part of psychiatrists. They were now urged to participate in Racism Awareness Training to reduce this prejudice [13]. The minority press and some activist groups took up the issue which was rehearsed by a number of television documentaries: it became accepted by the media that British psychiatry was racist, even if few took the radical view that transcultural psychiatry itself generally was simply "a crucial . . . new operational method" of medicalising existing social controls over the Black population [14]. While this view was taken up by many social workers, it was greeted unfavourably by psychiatrists; by the 1970s, expressly racist positions were only espoused in Britain by fringe political groups, and the medical consensus was one of equal opportunity and treatment. Other doctors who had not been previously involved in the debate now published studies which argued that there was no racial bias in treatment, but rather that excessive caution had actually led to the underdiagnosis of schizophrenia among Black people [15, 16]. Biological explanations— genetic or obstetric vulnerability, nutritional disadvantage—were not widely volunteered, presumably because of a consensus that a biological position was likely to be associated with racist assumptions.

The shift within transcultural psychiatry from emphasising 'culture' to racism, similar to that described in the United States [17, 18], attempted to situate the practice of psychiatry within a social field. It remained however bound by the biomedical training of its practitioners. The non-medical explanations which were offered remained simplistic, at times conspiratorial, but still individualistic. If patterns of 'psychopathology' were no longer located within the individual attitudes, experiences and actions of the designated patient, they were now to be found in those of the psychiatrist [13]. The relativity of psychiatric categories was dramatically illustrated when a well-publicised study on the medical use of the category of 'cannabis psychosis' (diagnosed 95 times more frequently among young Afro-Caribbean men than among a comparable group of White men) was accompanied by the virtual disappearance of the diagnosis within 2 years [19, 20]. To some it appeared that the new emphasis on the culture of psychiatry itself, however welcome, instead of examining the interaction between psychiatry and patient, left the latter as a mere cypher, a palimpsest on whom psychiatric institutions simply inscribed their power [21]. The possibility that 'real' psychopathology in Black people could in part be also understood as 'resistance' (as an active, howbeit unsuccessful, appropriation of the dominant symbolic system for personal ends) was dismissed as exoticism or romanticism [14]. 'Culture' remained an attribute of individuals, not the interactive matrix in which different forms of power, representation, ideology and social action clashed, compromised or coalesced.

PATTERNS OF EXPLANATION

If it was accepted by many that, at some level, something to be understood as 'racial bias' was manifest in the psychiatric field, how did this actually occur in individual clinical practice? It has proved easier to discuss the history of post-colonial psychiatric theory using a Foucauldian perspective of power and knowledge [1, 13, 14, 22, 23] than to use empirical studies in teasing out the logic of current decision-making, medical education and perception, and patterns of psychiatric services.

The older educational goal, of simply greater 'cultural awareness' on the part of doctors and other health service personnel was discredited for many but it was still necessary for the professionals themselves, embedded as they were in day-to-day care of Black patients, continually making decisions on compulsory admission and treatment, to try to find the links between a complex of racist power/knowledge and the distinct interactions between the individual patient and the physician [22]. If 'racism' was a politico-social practice which explained a link between certain historically grounded interpretations of Black people by Whites and which continued to allocate economic and social power on a differential basis, it was presumably still identifiable in individual attitudes and decisions. These would be more amenable to the sort of empirical inquiries appropriate to social psychology and which were used in studies of medical decision-making, without this suggesting that 'racism' was to be understood as a purely psychological phenomenon [13].

Examining this continuing debate through the individual arguments which appear amenable to an empirical study gives us the following current hypotheses about the increased rates of diagnosed mental illness and compulsory treatment among Black Britons:

(a) Inaccurate population figures

Careless use of demographic data has led to serious errors in the base population figures and hence rates of illness. These population data have not been criticised because the association of insanity with the Black population subserves certain existing political needs [23, 24].

(b) The psychological consequences of racial oppression

Severe psychiatric illness is more common among ethnic minority groups because of the psychological effects of colonial and post-colonial power. A devalued identity, with an internalised expectation of poorer economic and educational achievement, is likely to develop into, or precipitate, an illness in those otherwise vulnerable. The possibility of such a social vulnerability has been underestimated by a conventional research focus on general populations who lack such stressors [13]. Minority groups in other countries who are in a similar situation—Maori in New Zealand, Native Australians and United States Blacks (and we may include the Irish) have similar elevated rates of schizophrenia [1, 17, 25–27]. These illnesses are 'real' illnesses in the sense that they can be adequately defined by conventional psychiatric criteria such as those used in the WHO study.

(c) Genetic and biological vulnerability

Certain populations are more genetically vulnerable to mental illness and mistaken liberal approaches have ignored this, thus imposing a European biological baseline on minority populations. This seems unlikely for no differences in international rates of major mental illness have been correlated with population genetics, and it would be surprising if minority groups of quite different backgrounds share a similar genetic vulnerability. There is some evidence however that Afro-Caribbean immigrants from different islands have rather different rates of schizophrenia [28], a finding arguably difficult to interpret in terms of differential experience in Britain. Another variant of the 'misplaced liberalism' hypothesis is that minority groups are at an obstetrical and nutritional disadvantage: a prolonged labour period and neurological trauma have been implicated in the aetiology of schizophrenia. Such illnesses would again be 'real' ones.

(d) Misdiagnosis

Psychiatric diagnosis is less consciously racist than ethnocentric, and White Europeans are simply not very good at understanding the experiences of people rather different from themselves. These are then 'misdiagnosed'. The category of 'abnormal personality' is seldom recognised among minority patients [1, 5], suggesting the medical perception of cultural baselines is uncertain: if in doubt doctors diagnose illness. This was basically the position of the earlier 'cultural awareness' model (e.g. Ref. [29]): better medical education would alter the situation. Rates of schizophrenia however do not correspond with anything which might be interpreted as cultural or linguistic 'distance', nor do the diagnostic practices of the large number of British psychiatrists of South Asian origin differ from those of the Whites [1, 10] (although the elevated rates of schizophrenia are found primarily among people of Afro-Caribbean origin who might be argued to be equally 'distant' for Asian doctors).

(e) Unequal access and custodial options

Racism is associated with unequal access to a variety of social facilities, independent of social class, and to differential use of custodial institutions.

Increased and compulsory admissions to psychiatric hospitals rather than to other therapies simply reflect this. Thus, there is nothing specifically racist about psychiatry relative to other British institutions. 'Cultural awareness' is perhaps unlikely to affect these patterns, while an emphasis on anti-racist practice might.

(f) The historical association between 'the Black' and 'the Other'

(i) Once in contact with psychiatrists, non-European patients are more likely to be diagnosed as schizophrenic, because of certain specific associations between the medical perception of 'the Black' and the insane as some sort of undifferentiated 'Other' [1, 30, 31], rooted in psychiatric theory albeit implicitly. Thus there is something fundamentally flawed about the very notion of schizophrenia which should be abandoned [22]. Psychiatrists would respond that schizophrenia is defined by abnormal psychological functioning alone which can be assessed in any culture and which is not associated with any social or political institutions (e.g. Ref. [12]).

(ii) Or else, more generally in Western society, ethnic stereotypes embody notions of irrationality, violence and inability to communicate [31] which are close to those which characterise mental illness and which are thus perceived clinically in the Black patient.

(g) Minority attitudes and response

In a situation of unequal power, the individual does indeed physically resist to confirm an impression of irrationality, 'lack of insight', or an unwillingness to accept stigmatising psychiatric care. Psychiatric care patterns are accordingly not dissimilar to those of court sentencing, prison seclusion and probation orders for minorities. This may be enhanced by the Black British community's understandings of psychiatric illness and treatment in the ex-colonies, derived from the colonial and post-colonial situation of punitive psychiatric care and near-ubiquitous compulsory treatment [1, 30, 32, 33].

(h) Cultural resistance

'Insanity' is itself emblematic of personal identity in a 'crazy world' of post-colonial power in which self-hood is attained through inverting the language, institutions and perceptions of the dominant group [32]. Thus personal dilemmas and cultural resistance are presented in an 'irrational' and dramatic form, particularly if there is a local conceptualisation of 'madness' as some sort of cathartic release from overwhelming pressure [33, 34]. In a 'weak' form this explanation would be allied to the earlier form/content explanations in which cultural values modify a pre-existing pattern enhancing its salience in a particular context, confounding the 'irrationality' of sub-dominance with that consequent on cerebral disease. In its 'strong' form it would argue that 'madness' in Black people is to be interpreted less as a question of pathology than as one of appropriation and resistance [35].

These various hypotheses do not seem to be discrete explanations which, if correct, characterise processes independent of each other. Rather they appear to overlap conceptually and reinforce each other to form part of the same sequence of events. Hypothesis (a), however, argues for an epidemiological error and, like (b) and (c) which presume a 'real' increase in illness, are beyond the scope of this paper, being more properly the subject of medical epidemiology. The 'strong' form of (h) excepted, the remaining explanations generally assume that the conventional biomedical definition of schizophrenia reflects something 'real': objectively measurable in different societies in accordance with the WHO studies, relatively culturally invariate and potentially independent of the perception of ethnicity by the psychiatrist. We can thus talk of 'ethnic bias': the observable tendency to link ethnicity and psychiatric practice in a way incompatible with accepted medical theory. And this may be examined in practice. If the very notions of insanity and 'Blackness' explicitly participate in a common conception of the 'Other' [hypothesis (f)(i)], this notion will be debatable, although an empirical study can demonstrate an overlap of concept not generally recognised (e.g. Ref. [31]).

If there is a specific but unarticulated bias in the psychiatric perception of Black people which is independent of lay perceptions (f)(i), we should expect medical education (both the education of medical students and the post-graduate training of psychiatrists) to enhance this tendency. If the misdiagnosis and general ethnocentricity hypotheses [(d), (f)(i)] are correct, a medical education which places some emphasis on 'cultural knowledge' of minority groups should diminish the tendency.

If bias is conceptually inherent in medical perception independent of any actual clinical situation, then one might reasonably claim that psychiatrists are unfairly biased, indeed racist. To demonstrate bias in an actual clinical context is of course difficult because one has to control for the other variables which may be significant—social context, external pressures on the clinical interview, family interventions, and so on. If a higher proportion of non-White patients are referred to the psychiatrist by the police [36, 37] than are Whites, what is the appropriate White control group? White patients brought by the police—who are not typical of White patients? Or all White patients, leaving our minority study population already perceived as more in need of social control? Clearly we need both, and similarly one has to allow for the vast number of potentially confounding variables which may be relevant, including gender, body size, particular patterns of symptoms, different consulting contexts, with patients from a variety of non-White groups, and with psychiatrists of different ethnicities, cultural awareness, political stance, and training. One needs to videotape the interviews so as to standardise assessments of body language, spatial distance, and so on. And it is impossible for these to be independent of the observer's perception of ethnicity. We need additionally to determine the doctor's subjective evaluation of the patient's symptoms, perceived hostility, dangerousness and failure to disclose, and the social context; and the patient's own understanding of illness causality and personal control in general [38, 39], and his or her interpretation of the situation. And we cannot record the interviews in this way without permission from the patient and doctor, all this in situations of crisis, frequently at night. If the response of the potential patient is to be taken into account [hypothesis (g)], the 'context' to be studied needs to be taken back earlier, to the household, to the public space, previous experiences. If we wish to particularise psychiatric perception as opposed to those of other social agencies, we need comparable studies of police, lawyers, magistrates, prison doctors and others.

Clearly, the logistics of such an empirical study are enormous, and its practical limitations might argue against attempting it and favour more general interpretative studies. In the rest of the paper I describe a more modest project which focusses on the assumptions which individual British medical students and doctors do make about Black patients; not in an actual clinical situation but in responding to a written vignette. At this level of abstraction from actual clinical contexts, can we find any implicit assumption about Black people and mental illness? If there is, is it affected by psychiatric training? More specifically, is 'disturbed behaviour' likely to be seen as psychotic or as a personal crisis? Are Black patients less likely to be perceived as mildly psychiatrically ill, as the epidemiological data might argue [5, 40]? Are psychiatrists indeed unable to determine what is 'abnormal personality' in different groups [13]?

A CLINICAL VIGNETTE STUDY

Simulated clinical situations have been extensively used both to study decision-making by mental health professionals [41], and through altering salient details in differing versions of a single vignette to examine how a variable like gender or ethnicity influences the eventual diagnosis [42, 43]. Complimentary strategies employ respondents supplying clinical data to match a given gender or other item, as in Broverman's well-known study of gender bias in personality profiles [44].

For this study, a brief clinical vignette was prepared, derived from a number of existing summaries from medical notes. It was designed to offer an equal likelihood of six diagnoses commonly used in Britain—manic-depressive psychosis, major depressive disorder, paranoid psychosis, schizophrenia, personality disorder and a composite category 'neurotic/stress reaction'. The first four are considered 'psychoses', that is as patterns of severely disturbed psychological response, qualitatively different from everyday functioning and which would generally be regarded as of biological origin while social response would be allowed as having some role in determining the course of the illness [45].

The vignette was piloted and modified with close colleagues (who took no further part in the study) so as to improve the chances of 'equal diagnostic weighting'. The case described does not then have the recognised pathognomic symptoms of any single category. The vignette and questionnaire in its final form was individually handed out to 342 health professionals: 62 psychiatrists, 42 other doctors, 32 psychiatric social workers and psychologists, 39 nurses, 116 medical students before they had taken any psychiatry, 48 medical students after their psychiatric course, 3 unspecified. As I was known to be identified with an explicitly anti-racist position in the existing debates, the majority of the vignettes were distributed by colleagues. The setting was in the teaching areas of three leading hospital medical schools within London University. Each is situated in an inner-city area with significant minority populations. Two of them have a particular teaching and clinical focus on minority groups, one with an active and well-known anti-racist advocacy service. The project was presented as one of evaluating a series of clinical vignettes to be used in psychiatric teaching. Each participant was given 10 min to read the vignette and select from the 6 diagnoses the 'single most likely'. Unknown to the responders, the vignette was randomly distributed in two forms. 175 received this version:

Case study No. 4

Mr L. J., a 24 yr old unemployed mechanic, was admitted to the psychiatric ward following an assessment in the Accident and Emergency Department of a London hospital. He had been taken there by the police after not paying his fare on a bus: he had assaulted the police who were called by the bus driver and they had decided that he was behaving bizarrely and in need of psychiatric treatment.

Clinical examination. Well built. Casually dressed. Talked rapidly and at times incoherently. Appeared sullen, at times irritated, at others distressed. Poor rapport established. Whilst his speech was at times difficult to understand, there was no apparent thought disorder. Query hallucinatory experiences? Complained that local authority officials were following him about. Objected to being brought to hospital and decided to leave: said doctors could not help. Later in the interview became angry for no apparent reason and broke a window; tried to leave. Appeared perplexed but no gross cognitive abnormalities. Physical examination NAD. Agreed eventually to come into hospital.

Personal history. No previous psychiatric history. Born locally. An elder sister and a brother, one younger sister. No family history of psychiatric illness but they are well known to local social workers. Father left the family when Mr J. was about 5. Apparently uneventful birth and early childhood. Did not do well at school where teachers and an educational psychologist reported a learning difficulty. Attended a special school from the age of 12: frequent truanting. Left without qualifications and took a series of unskilled jobs. Frequently unemployed. Many superficial friendships with boys of the same age. A few shortlived sexual relationships with girls. Neighbours reluctant to talk about him but seem to regard him as rather solitary and quarrelsome. Has twice been charged with assault, once with handling stolen goods. Poor relationship with his mother's social worker who seems a little nervous of him. Mother describes him as 'bad'. His interests seem to include television, music and fantasy comics. Attended a local church sporadically in his teens but not recently. Occasional alcohol and use of cannabis (but none detected on urine analysis). Lives alone in a council flat; sometimes it is shared by casual friends. Previously evicted from other flats for non-payment of rent. Well known to receptionists at the local social security office whom he has threatened verbally in the past.

Antecedent events. Currently unemployed for a year. A month before his admission his elder sister with whom he was close left London. His mother reported he had become more solitary. Gave up going to the pub. Always rather suspicious, he had got into an argument with a neighbour over a trivial issue. Seems to have spent the weeks preceding admission alone in his flat brooding, sleeping poorly and not watching television. Later described his mood at this time as 'depressed' but denied any mental illness. Complained that people were ganging up on him, especially his mother and the council.

Progress on the ward. On observation with no psychotropic drugs. Sat quietly for the first hour but complained bitterly when disturbed and twice verbally threatened staff. A Section of the Mental Health Act contemplated but not carried out. Appetite poor. Mental state basically unchanged. Repeat physical examination NAD. Woke early on the second day and wandered off the ward. Did not return and was found walking nearby. Was offered and accepted with reluctance chlorpromazine 50 mg per day without any obvious effect. Said he had only come into hospital to get his social security problems sorted out. Did not establish any real rapport with staff. Discharged after 2 weeks with an appointment with a community psychiatric nurse arranged: was not in when she called.

167 received the same vignette with "to Jamaican parents" inserted after "born locally" in the third paragraph. Ethnicity is usually cited in British psychiatric summaries only when the patient is not of White English origin, and it was felt that specifying White origin in the first version might highlight the focus on race. The consequence is that any difference between the responses to the two versions consequent on the perception of race would thus be minimised.

Table 1. Diagnosis and vignette ethnicity

	Neutral	Black
Manic-depressive psychosis	16	12
Major depressive disorder	7	8
Neurotic/stress reaction	26	30
Paranoid psychosis	38	42
Personality disorder	66	56
Schizophrenia	21	17
Totals:	174	165

RESULTS

There were three refusals/incomplete returns. The remaining 339 were examined for differences in response to the 'Neutral' and the 'Black' versions. There were no significant differences between the two versions: either in total (Table 1); when each professional group was considered separately; when they were collected together in broader groups (e.g. all doctors vs the rest, and so on); or when the diagnoses were grouped into broader categories (e.g. all psychoses vs the rest). The only significant finding was that the "medics" (all doctors plus all medical students) were more likely to diagnose schizophrenia in both the 'Neutral' and 'Afro-Caribbean' versions (taking both versions together, χ^2-test, schizophrenia vs other categories, $P < 0.025$). There were no differences between the hospitals.

INTERPRETING VIGNETTE STUDIES

The immediate conclusion is of course that this particular study does not demonstrate any diagnostic 'bias'. In other words, in assessing written clinical descriptions (which may be presumed to have a close relationship with formal psychiatric theorising) neither psychiatrists nor other health professionals perceive any link between stated ethnicity and a particular psychiatric category [hypotheses (d), (e), (f)]. Neither undergraduate nor post-graduate medical education seem to affect this one way or the other. Hypotheses (e), (f)(i), (g), that medical practice may reflect general racism, would appear to be potentially supported. Hypothesis (d), the 'cultural awareness' model, would argue for psychiatrists and trained medical students becoming less biased when they were offered special training; while (f)(i), specific psychiatric racism, would argue for an increase in bias with medical and psychiatric training: neither are supported.

To what extent do the respondents represent general clinical practice? In a similar study which used a postal questionnaire of senior psychiatrists alone, Lewis and his colleagues [46] also found no preference for any particular diagnosis with either 'a White' or 'an Afro-Caribbean' vignette. That the two respondent samples and the vignettes were rather different argues for some general lack of bias at this level, although 'bias' may only occur in certain, as yet unknown, clinical situations which were not represented in either vignette. Taking the two studies together, together with the finding that medical education seemed not to affect diagnostic decisions in any way, argues against any specific psychiatric theories that link insanity of one sort or another with people of West Indian origin. Stress and personality difficulties were rated equally for both ethnic groups in my vignette. Can we conclude therefore that the model of specific medical racism is inappropriate and that the existing epidemiological findings perhaps reproduce 'real' rates of illness [hypotheses (b) and (c)]?

Before the possibility of 'racial bias' is dismissed, we have to take into account the overrepresentation of Black people in the penal system: if psychiatry no longer seems to contain any specific theories linking Black people to insanity, neither does it diminish the increased numbers of blacks in custodial institutions as might be expected on the 'cultural awareness' hypothesis: if there is a general bias in society which places Blacks in these situations, White psychiatry merely reaffirms it [37, 48–50].

A more specific problem lies in the use of vignettes, modelled as they are on assumptions of rational choice and on an empirical natural science model of psychiatric disorder in which the context of the psychiatric interview can be held constant, leaving ethnicity as the single independent variable [47]. Lewis' study found that, diagnosis apart, Black patients were perceived as more violent and in need of treatment with medical drugs [46], a finding which corresponds with previous perceptions of actual patients [9, 10, 37, 48–51]. The vignette used in the current study describes a cognate pattern of 'anti-social' response which we may argue is *already* seen to be associated with the Black community, and which has been said to lead to preferential psychiatric admission, thus leading to increased numbers of Black patients who are compulsorily admitted [15, 37, 48]. There can never be a neutral vignette: virtually every item is already associated, positively or negatively, with the Black community; this alters the chances of admission and the determining medical perceptions, either in actual clinical situations or in vignette studies. To take the instance of repeated unemployment in the vignette: as this is already a more common experience for the Black community in general, it will have a greater diagnostic salience for Whites (as then more likely in those severely mentally ill). To remove it from the vignette however restricts the study to the perception of Black patients statistically unrepresentative of their community relative to Whites, and certainly not representative of Black patients in general. Similarly, schooling, class status, occupation, housing, 'poor rapport', the particular family constellation and involvement of social workers, police charges, 'aggression', use of cannabis and church membership, internal migration and poor relations with council officials are not perceived as neutrally balanced between Black and White [52].

It might appear that including more social and behavioural variables in the vignettes might lead to a

greater approximation to some empirical truth [53]. In the actual clinical instance, which such studies are trying to explicate, we have however an association of practical contingencies and theoretical models which are not easily amenable to disentangling. If Black patients in a situation of unequal power do respond with poor rapport and 'anti-social' behaviour [hypothesis (g)], then they will be diagnosed preferentially as psychotic, for these are among the symptoms of psychosis. If action is called for on the part of the doctor in the emergency room and such action requires by its very context social control, then psychiatric diagnosis is a likely option, for in situations of doubt doctors respond by offering a medical diagnosis by which alone they can legitimate their coercive measures [54].

Studies using clinical vignettes, with their assumption that psychiatric diagnosis is simply a discrete and individual cognitive process which can be isolated from the political context in which it occurs, can certainly tell us something about the implicit assumptions through which psychiatrists work. What they cannot do is to examine fully how these constructs are embedded in a social world of power. We may be thankful that psychiatrists no longer appear to have a simple conception of ethnicity which invariably links the non-European with insanity. Nevertheless, they work within a social context which relegates Black people to economic marginality and political disadvantage, a context which psychiatric practice itself appears to replicate.

The shift in British transcultural psychiatry from an emphasis on individual symptoms and 'culture' to a focus on racism within psychiatry seems likely to carry with it a certain methodological progression from empirical statistics to a critical interpretative perspective. To an extent this may be a consequence of the professional allegiances of those involved, but it is also a function of the difficulty of examining statistically a vast number of individual contingencies. Not that psychiatric practice is inherently any *more* a reflection of a complex social context than the patient's response: simply that medical practice has always found observation of the patient more convenient than observation of the doctor. A fuller understanding of the interaction between patient and doctor certainly requires a more critical perspective than transcultural psychiatry has yet developed, but this does not presuppose the redundancy of empirical studies.

Acknowledgements—I am grateful to Maurice Lipsedge and Graham Thornicroft and others for helping to distribute the vignette; to them, Parimala Moodley, Tim Rackett, John Murphy and others for assistance in piloting it.

REFERENCES

1. Littlewood R. and Lipsedge M. *Aliens and Alienists: Ethnic Minorities and Psychiatry.* Penguin Books, Harmondsworth, 1982.

2. Littlewood R. Russian Dolls and Chinese Boxes: an anthropological approach to the implicit models of comparative psychiatry. In *Transcultural Psychiatry* (Edited by Cox J.), pp. 37–58. Croom Helm, London, 1986.

3. Lewis I. M. Introduction. In *Symbols and Sentiments* (Edited by Lewis I. M.), pp. 1–24. Academic Press, London, 1977.

4. The term 'Black', which I have used in this paper, became accepted in Britain in the 1970s as the preferred term used by Britons of African and Afro-Caribbean descent. This followed a similar shift in the United States from 'Negro' to 'Black' [Gaines, A. D. Knowledge and practice: anthropological ideas and psychiatric practice. In *Clinically Applied Anthropology* (Edited by Chrisman N. and Maretzki T.), pp. 243–274. Reidel, Dordrecht, 1982; Kavanagh K. H. Invisibility and selective avoidance: gender and ethnicity in psychiatry and psychiatric nursing staff interaction. *Cult. Med. Psychiat.* **15**, 245–274, 1991]. The origin of 'Black' was of course in the racial ('biological') term used by the Europeans, and its adoption by those of African descent in Britain reflected a shift from an autonomous 'cultural' identity to one which in part ascribed self-identity to European dominance. Psychiatry in Britain has in part followed the shift in terminology, one which has been adopted in the National Census of 1991 as a term of ethnicity. The use of 'Black' to designate other non-European groups in Britain such as those of South Asian origin is variable: it is not used in this way in the Census nor by the majority of the communities themselves (Littlewood R. Glossary. In *Report of the Ethnic Issues Special Committee*. Royal College of Psychiatrists, London, 1989).

5. Cochrane R. Mental illness in immigrants to England and Wales: an analysis of mental hospital admissions. *Soc. Psychiat.* **12**, 23–35, 1977.

6. Bagley C. The social aetiology of schizophrenia in immigrant groups. *Int. J. Soc. Psychiat.* **17**, 292–304, 1971.

7. Littlewood R. and Lipsedge M. Acute psychotic reactions in Caribbean-born patients. *Psychol. Med.* **11**, 303–318, 1981. The use of 'culture' in the W.H.O. study simply as a dependent variable which was not taken into account as part of the actual illness has been extensively criticised by Arthur Kleinman (Anthropology and Psychiatry: the role of culture in cross-cultural research on illness. *B.J. Psychiat.* **151**, 447–454, 1987) and myself (Ref. [2]).

8. Bagley C. and Binitie A. Alcoholism and schizophrenia in Irishmen in London. *Br. J. Addict.* **65**, 3–7, 1970.

9. Littlewood R. Ethnic minorities and the Mental Health Act: patterns of explanation. *Bull. R. Coll. Psychiat.* **10**, 306–308, 1986.

10. Littlewood R. and Cross S. Ethnic minorities and psychiatric services. *Sociol. Hlth Illness* **2**, 194–201, 1980.

11. Kareem J. and Littlewood R. (Eds) *Intercultural Therapy: Themes, Interpretation and Practice.* Blackwell, Oxford In press.

12. Harrison G. *et al.* A prospective study of severe mental disorder in Afro-Caribbean patients. *Psychol. Med.* **18**, 643–658, 1988.

13. Littlewood R. and Lipsedge M. The development of 'transcultural psychiatry' in Britain 1982–9. In *Aliens and Alienists* (Edited by Littlewood R. and Lipsedge M.), 2nd edn, pp. 255–294. Unwin Hyman, London, 1989.

14. Black Health Workers and Patients Group, Psychiatry and the corporate state. *Race and Class* **25**, 49–64, 1983. A similar position was offered more rigorously by Kobena Mercer (Racism and transcultural psychiatry. In *The Power of Psychiatry* (Edited by Millar P. and Rose N.). Polity Press, London, 1986) who places the emphasis on ethnicity within the context of a post-war

medicine which sought to control the interaction between patient and doctor more effectively through a focus on the patient's social identity (a point developed at length by David Armstrong—The patient's view. *Soc. Sci. Med.* **18**, 737–744, 1984).

15. Dunn J. and Fahy T. A. Police admissions to a psychiatric hospital: demographic and clinical differences between ethnic groups. *Br.J. Psychiat.* **156**, 373–378, 1990.

16. Richardson E. and Hendrik-Gutt R. Diagnosis of psychiatric illness in immigrant patients. *Br.J. clin. Soc. Psychiat.* **1**, 78–81, 1981.

17. Adebimpe V. R. American blacks and psychiatry. *Transcult. Psychiat. Res. Rev.* **21**, 83–111, 1984.

18. Jones B. E. and Gray B. A. Problems in diagnosing schizophrenia and affective disorder among American blacks. *Hosp. Comm. Psychiat.* **37**, 61–65, 1986.

19. Littlewood R. Community initiated research: a study of psychiatrists' conceptualisations of cannabis psychosis. *Psychiat. Bull.* **12**, 486–488, 1988.

20. Littlewood R. Cannabis psychosis. (corr). *Psychiat. Bull.* **13**, 148–149, 1989.

21. Although I have used here a somewhat distanced style, it will be evident from the references that I remain involved in the debates, both in my writing and in clinical work.

22. Fernando S. *Race and Culture in Psychiatry.* Croom Helm, London, 1988.

23. Sashidharan S. P. Ideology and politics in transcultural psychiatry. In *Transcultural Psychiatry* (Edited by Cox J.), pp. 158–178. Croom Helm, London, 1986.

24. Until 1991 the numbers of different ethnic groups in Britain had to be calculated indirectly from the national census data by using various correction factors derived from small scale surveys: the census data only specified for a locality the number of people living in a household headed by individuals defined by country of birth. While this provides reasonably accurate information in the period immediately following large scale migrations, it becomes increasingly inappropriate as internal migration and intermarriage occur, and diverse patterns of families and households come into being. It has been suggested that using the 'corrected' census data alone gives a much lower denominator figure for calculating rates (and hence leads to inflated rates) than using figures from local social service use (S. P. Sashidharan, personal communication on data for the Birmingham area). It is difficult to argue however that this alone could decrease the reported rates to anything like parity with the White figures, for we would need at least a ten-fold error in the 'corrected' census figures.

25. Sachdev P. S. Psychiatric illness in the New Zealand Maori. *Aust. New. Z. J. Psychiat.* **23**, 529–541, 1989.

26. Robins, J. *Fools and Mad: A History of the Insane in Ireland.* Institute of Public Administration, Dublin, 1986.

27. Scheper-Hughes N. *Saints, Scholars and Schizophrenics: Mental Illness in Rural Ireland.* University of California Press, Berkeley, 1979.

28. Glover G. R. Differences in psychiatric admission patterns between Caribbeans from different islands. *Soc. Psychiat.* **24**, 209–211, 1989.

29. Rack P. *Race, Culture and Mental Disorder.* Tavistock, London, 1982.

30. Gilman S. *Difference and Pathology: Stereotypes of Sexuality, Race and Madness.* Cornell University Press, Ithaca, 1985.

31. Townsend J. M. Stereotypes and mental illness: a comparison with ethnic stereotypes. *Cult. Med. Psychiat.* **3**, 205–230, 1979.

32. Fisher R. *Colonial Madness; Mental Health in the Barbadian Social Order.* Rutgers University Press, New Brunswick, 1986.

33. Littlewood R. From vice to madness: the semantics of naturalistic and personalistic understandings in Trinidadian local medicine. *Soc. Sci. Med.* **27,** 129–148, 1988.

34. Pryce K. *Endless Pressure: A Study of West Indian Life-Styles in Bristol.* Penguin, Harmondsworth, 1979.

35. Littlewood R. Anthropology and psychiatry: an alternative approach. *B. J. Med. Psychol.* **53,** 213–225, 1980.

36. Under Section 136 of the British Mental Health Act, people believed by the police to be psychiatrically ill in a public place can be taken to "a place of safety" (usually a hospital emergency room, or sometimes a police station) to be assessed by a psychiatrist who can then admit them to hospital compulsorily. It was once thought that Section 136 was especially used by the police with Black people, but the overrepresentation of minority groups under the Mental Health Act is equal for both police and medical Sections of the Act (Ref. [9]; Fahy T., Bermingham D. and Dunn J. Police admissions to psychiatric hospitals: a challenge to community psychiatry. *Med. Sci. Law* **27,** 263–268, 1987). The question of direct referral by courts or prisons to psychiatric care is beyond the scope of this paper, but we know that Black people are overrepresented here, as they are in the Special Hospitals (for the criminally insane or patients otherwise considered especially dangerous) and in the 'secure' (locked) facilities of general psychiatric hospitals (Refs [48–50]). While I have focussed here on one particular context, we might expect similar social processes to occur in these other situations: the perception of madness and badness are likely to run together (Horwitz A. V. *The Social Control of Mental Illness.* Academic Press, New York, 1982).

37. Moodley P. and Thornicroft G. Ethnic group and compulsory detention. *Med. Sci. Law* **28,** 324–328, 1988.

38. Donovan J. *We Don't Buy Sickness: It Just Comes: Health, Illness and Health Care in the Lives of Black People in London.* Gower, London, 1986.

39. Currer C. Concepts of mental well and ill-being: the case of Pathan mothers in Bradford. In *Concepts of Health, Illness and Disease* (Edited by Currer C. and Stacey M.), pp. 183–198. Berg, Leamington Spa, 1986.

40. I have previously argued (Ref. [1]) that European psychiatry's reluctance to diagnose 'depression' among non-European populations was in part due to the practical politics of colonial psychiatry becoming codified in psychiatric texts, while also related to certain very specific notions of the 'non-psychologisation' of

Black people who were found to demonstrate 'undifferentiated' patterns of psychological distress. 'Depression' is now commonly diagnosed in the independent countries which were once European colonies.

41. For an overview, see R. E. Kendell *The Role of Diagnosis in Psychiatry*, Chaps 2, 3. Blackwell, Oxford, 1975.

42. Warner R. The diagnosis of anti-social and hysterical personality: an example of sex bias. *J. Nerv. Ment. Dis.* **166,** 839–845, 1978.

43. Loring M. and Powell B. Gender, race and DSM-111: a study of the objectivity of psychiatric diagnostic behaviour. *J. Hlth Soc. Behav.* **29,** 1–22, 1988.

44. Broverman I. D., Broverman D. M., Clarkson F. E., Rosenkrantz P. S. and Vogel S. R. Sex role sterotypes and clinical judgements of mental health. *J. Consult. clin. Psychol.* **34,** 1–7, 1970.

45. A possible confusing factor here is that the category of *paranoid psychosis* has been used to describe short-lived and 'reactive' (in Karl Jasper's sense of intelligible and psycho- or socio-genic) psychoses in Afro-Caribbean patients (see Ref. [7]).

46. Lewis G., Croft-Jeffreys C. and David A. Are British psychiatrists racist? *Br. J. Psychiat.* **157,** 410–415, 1990.

47. Littlewood R. From categories to contexts: a decade of 'the new cross-cultural psychiatry'. *Br.J. Psychiat.* **156,** 308–327, 1990.

48. Bolton P. Management of compulsorily admitted patients to a high security unit. *Int. J. Soc. Psychiat.* **30,** 77–84, 1984.

49. Royal College of Psychiatrists, *Report of the Special Committee on Ethnic Issues*, R. C. Psychiat., London, 1989.

50. Norris M. *Integration of Special Hospital Patients into the Community*, pp. 75–77. Gower, Aldershot, 1984.

51. Noble P. and Ranger S. Violence by psychiatric inpatients, *Br.J. Psychiat.* **155,** 384–390, 1989.

52. Similarly in Lewis' study (Ref. [46]), unemployment, cannabis, religious interest, father's occupation and persecutory beliefs cannot be 'neutral' elements in the history.

53. It is statistically unlikely that significance can be shown with so many discretely varied sub-groups, even in a multi-variate design as the total number of consultant psychiatrists in Britain who may be sampled is less than three thousand. Using a battery of different vignettes for each respondent is theoretically possible but is likely to affect the response rate.

54. Young A. Some implications of medical beliefs and practices for social anthropology. *Am. Anthrop.* **78,** 5–24, 1976.

[18]

Providing Culturally Appropriate Mental Health Services for Minorities

Jacqueline Wallen, Ph.D.

Abstract

Research on the use of outpatient mental health services has shown lower rates of utilization by minorities. Barriers include economic considerations, access difficulties, and cultural factors. Promoting the use of outpatient mental health services by minorities can have a positive effect on the overall cost of health and mental health care, as well as increasing access to care and quality of care for minority populations. Advantages and disadvantages of various approaches to providing culturally appropriate programming in mental health services are discussed.

Use of Mental Health Services by Minorities

Research on the use of mental health services has consistently shown lower rates of utilization of outpatient mental health care among members of racial or ethnic minorities,[1-4] even though there is often considerable evidence that their need for mental health services is high.[5,6] Differences in utilization persist even when such factors as income, level of health insurance coverage, and availability of care are controlled,[7,8] suggesting that underutilization on the part of minorities reflects cultural, as well as economic, barriers.

While there are differences among groups, when minorities do use outpatient care, they typically use less of it[7] and are more apt to terminate prematurely.[9-11] At the same time, minorities are more likely to use inpatient and emergency mental health services,[7,12] more likely to be rehospitalized after inpatient treatment,[13] and more often admitted involuntarily to mental institutions.[14]

Inpatient and emergency mental health care services are far more costly than outpatient care.[15] While the relationship between use of inpatient and outpatient mental health care is not yet fully understood, research findings suggest that the appropriate and timely utilization of outpatient mental health services reduces the need for and use of inpatient treatment.[15,16] Increasing the use of needed outpatient mental health services in underserved populations can potentially enhance the quality of mental health care while lowering its cost.

Barriers to the use of outpatient mental health services by minorities may involve economic considerations, access difficulties, or cultural factors:

Economic barriers. Because minorities in American society suffer disproportionately from economic disadvantages, they are more likely to lack health insurance and to experience the out-of-

---

Address correspondence to Jacqueline Wallen, Ph.D., Associate Professor, Department of Family and Community Development, University of Maryland at College Park, College Park, MD 20742.

pocket costs of health care as a barrier to seeking care.[7] Economic barriers have a greater effect on the use of outpatient care (which is relatively discretionary) than on the use of inpatient or emergency services (which may reflect an acute or emergency problem).[7]

Access barriers. A number of factors may limit access to community mental health services for minority individuals who are economically disadvantaged. The services which they can afford may be inconveniently located and they may have difficulty obtaining transportation to these services. Their job may not permit them the flexibility required to visit an agency or clinic during normal working hours. Knowledge of available services may not be available in their community.[8]

Cultural barriers. Green[17] has used the term "help-seeking behavior" to point to the fact that cultures differ in what they consider to be a mental health problem, what kind of care they consider appropriate, what they see the role of the care provider as being, and what they consider to be a successful outcome of treatment. Mental health services are shaped primarily by the values and beliefs of the dominant culture in a society and may not be perceived as desirable or helpful by individuals from other backgrounds. This can be especially problematic when the client does not speak the language of the dominant culture. There is also evidence that mental health care providers who lack familiarity with particular cultural subgroups may be more likely to misdiagnose their problems, referring them to emergency or inpatient care when outpatient care would have been more appropriate.[14,18,19]

Attempts to remove barriers to outpatient mental health care for minorities were stimulated by the community mental health movement in the latter half of the 1960s and advanced by the civil rights movement and grass roots community organizing. In 1978, the President's Commission on Mental Health urged renewed commitment to meeting the mental health needs of minorities. Initiatives resulting from these developments included the following: increased community representation on policy-making boards, provision of training in cultural sensitivity for providers, recruitment of minority professionals and of paraprofessionals from the community, incorporation of healers and healing practices of ethnic communities into the mental health system, development of ethnic-specific service agencies in the community, and provision of treatments and programs matched to clients' ethnic backgrounds.

Follow-up studies indicate that, where they were implemented, such programs have been effective in attracting minority clients[20,21] and keeping minority clients in treatment for a longer period of time.[12,20,22] They have also led to improved treatment outcomes.[12]

Changing Demographics in Mental Health Services

Unfortunately, planning with respect to mental health services for minorities has been neither comprehensive nor widespread. Although we are currently in an era of shrinking mental health budgets, the need for such programming is greater than ever before. Comparison of the 1980 and 1990 U.S. Census shows that the proportion of the U.S. population that can be defined as non-White, or minority, increased by 6% between 1980 and 1990, from approximately 17% to approximately 20%.[23] Demographers predict that by the year 2060, "minorities" will outnumber Whites.[24] The most recent census also reveals that, due to recent patterns of immigration, the minority population itself is becoming increasingly more diverse, with respect to national origins, and less concentrated.[23] This means that suburban and rural, as well as urban, mental health agencies are increasingly finding themselves with minority clients from a variety of diverse backgrounds.

The mental health administrator who can facilitate more appropriate use of outpatient mental health services by minority individuals and communities can have a positive effect on the overall cost of mental health care while increasing access to care and quality of care for minority populations.

Approaches to Multicultural Programming

Sue[25] has identified three strategies that can be used by a mental health agency to improve the compatibility, or fit, between minority clients and the agency's services: finding the right service outside the agency, changing the client to fit the agency's way of providing service, and changing the agency's way of providing service to fit the client. This typology provides a convenient framework for classifying multicultural programs.

Finding the Right Service Outside the Agency

Finding culturally appropriate services when they are not available within the agency may include referral to services provided by indigenous community institutions such as churches, extended families, family and ethnic associations, and credit associations or to community helpers such as elders, ministers, medicine men, curanderos, or family doctors. To do this, an agency may need to improve its referral process and knowledge about bicultural/bilingual therapists and other community resources. In-service training can be provided for staff to teach them how to consult with various agencies. Some mental health clinics train providers to refer clients to native healers from whom they also receive referrals.[26-28] Such training is particularly useful if organizations and indigeneous helpers from the targeted minority communities are first involved in the planning for workshops for agency staff.[29]

Changing the Client To Fit the Service

Changing the client to fit the service occurs when clients are trained to use the mental health system as it is currently structured. Public relations efforts to increase community awareness of available mental health services represent one such approach and can increase the willingness of targeted populations to use services. Radio and television announcements have been particularly effective in this regard.[29] Preparing clients for the service they are to receive can improve the fit between client and service, resulting in increased accessibility, lower attrition rates, and better outcomes in therapy.[30] For example, patients can be prepared for psychotherapy by watching a video or listening to a lecture about what to expect in therapy.[31] Instruction concerning the nature of psychotherapy may be given by the therapist[28] or by other staff during the intake process.[32] Or the client may be assigned an advocate other than the therapist who will explain how therapy works and encourage him or her to bring up matters of concern in therapy.[33]

Changing the Service To Fit the Client

Changing services to accommodate individuals from diverse cultures is the most innovative and responsive approach, but also the most difficult. At the more conservative end, adaptations may involve training professionals in cultural sensitivity and recruiting bilingual or bicultural personnel from the minority population without making other changes in what services are offered or how they are delivered. For example, counselors and other staff may be provided with training in "cultural sensitivity," or "cultural awareness," meaning that they are taught to recognize how their own cultural conditioning affects their attitudes and behavior and to be alert to the cultural factors that may be shaping the experience of the client. Both cultural sensitivity training[22,34] and utilization of minority personnel[3,35] have been shown to increase satisfaction and use of mental health services in minorities.

At the more innovative end, major changes may also be made in how services are structured and delivered. Successful changes of this kind have included moving a clinic to a more convenient location within the community or opening satellite clinics;[20] delivering some services with a mobile unit;[36] expanding clinic hours;[28] incorporating community representatives on the policy-making board;[29,37] or adding medical, social, or child care services.[29,37] Services may be provided in a manner that more clearly resembles indigenous or native techniques. For example, traditional healers and healing practices have been used in the treatment of alcoholism in Native Americans.[38] O'Sullivan and colleagues[29] have evaluated the long-term effects of several such changes in the delivery of community mental health services in the Seattle-King County area and have found that, compared to 10 years earlier, the number of services used had increased substantially for all minority groups (Asian, African American, Hispanic, and Native American).

Considerations

A number of considerations are relevant to decisions concerning how to provide culturally appropriate services to individuals from diverse cultural groups. Some involve administrative issues, others relate to client characteristics, and still others involve the nature of the service itself.

Administrative Issues

Planning must take into account the degree to which the target population represents a substantial proportion of the agency case load as opposed to being only a small proportion of the total population served. This may influence decisions concerning the extent to which it is practical or cost effective for the agency to redesign its services to make them more culturally appropriate.[37] When an agency serves only a small number of clients from a particular cultural minority or serves small numbers of clients from several different groups, improving referral sources may be a more realistic policy. A related factor involves the extent to which a particular minority population is concentrated in a single geographic region as opposed to being widely dispersed. In an area where a particular minority is strongly represented, alternative services for that population are more likely to be available and referrals can be made. When alternative, culturally appropriate services are not available, an agency may have to change itself or change the client to serve the client effectively. O'Sullivan et al.[20] have emphasized the value of facilitating a consortium of minority groups to provide supportive services for minority clients when no single minority is represented in large numbers.

The size of the agency or organization can also affect the strategy employed to provide services that meet the needs of cultural minorities. A larger agency may have the resources to develop alternative programs of its own or orientation programs for clients. A smaller agency may need to rely on referral. The extent to which an agency can refer clients to other organizations, however, depends on the degree of interagency cooperation that can be achieved and on the flexibility of jurisdictional boundaries.[39]

Service-Related Issues

Reimbursement issues arise when services are contracted out to native or community healers who are not recognized by credentialing bodies. Services rendered by indigenous healers or paraprofessionals recruited from the targeted community may not be reimbursable under agency regulations or health insurance plans.[40] Also, community mental health centers and other mental health agencies receive many referrals from probation departments, the courts, protective services, and other social agencies that may require that conventional mental health services be provided. All of these factors limit both the extent to which an agency can refer clients to culturally appropriate services and the extent to which they can modify their own services and strategies for delivering those services. Table 1 illustrates the advantages and disadvantages of the three approaches to providing culturally appropriate services in light of the administrative and service-related issues discussed above.

Table 1

Advantages and Disadvantages of Three Approaches to Providing Culturally Appropriate Services

	Advantages	Disadvantages
Find right service	Can empower client and community	Services may not exist in community
	Does not require much change on part of agency	Nonprofessional services may not be reimbursed
	Useful with small or diverse minority population	
Change client	Does not require change on part of agency	Least responsive to clients
		Least empowering and affirmative
		Difficult for small agencies or those with diverse populations
Change service	Most responsive, affirming, and empowering	Requires high concentration of particular minority
		Most likely to be resisted by system and stakeholders

Client-Related Issues

Members of cultural minorities vary widely with respect to their participation in the dominant culture and in their own subculture. Figure 1, adapted from a figure presented by LeVine and Padilla,[29] depicts four different categories describing clients' cultural orientations. The acculturated client is the assimilated client who has absorbed the values and practices of the dominant culture and has very little commitment to the culture of his or her ethnic or racial group. The bicultural client is one who is committed to the dominant culture yet still retains a commitment to the subculture. The unacculturated client maintains a strong commitment to the subculture and has not absorbed the dominant culture. The marginal client is one who has very little attachment to any cultural group.

LeVine and Padilla reason that, because they are comfortable with the dominant culture, acculturated and bicultural clients can benefit from mental health services shaped by the dominant culture while unacculturated clients require special programming of some kind. Marginal clients have difficulty benefiting from mental health services, generally, and may need social or other services first. Research on health and mental health services has shown that barriers to care are greater for less acculturated individuals.[8] But while it is true that acculturated and bicultural clients may often benefit from mental health services even when their cultural background is not taken into account, this is not necessarily optimal. Regardless of their commitment to the dominant culture, all minority clients can benefit from mental health services that recognize their unique position and experience in American society.[28,41,42]

Figure 1
Client Characteristics and Choice of Approach

		Commitment to dominant culture	
		High	Low
Commitment to own culture	High	"A" bicultural client	"B" unacculturated client
	Low	"A" acculturated client	"C" marginal client

A = Can benefit from conventionally designed mental health services. B = Requires special programming in mental health services. C = Has difficulty benefitting from mental health services unless other services are provided first.

Constraints on Change

Mental health services, for the most part, are provided by organizations and are shaped by the bureaucratic setting in which they are rendered. This is both an advantage and a disadvantage to clients from cultural minorities. Solomon[41] has described this fundamental paradox. Bureaucracies, by definition, have standardized policies, procedures, and regulations. Since these are designed to guarantee that all will be treated the same, it would seem that bureaucratization would counteract bias or prejudice in the treatment of clients. But if "standardization" reflects values and norms of a dominant group, then discrimination is inevitable. Multicultural, or pluralistic, approaches to providing culturally appropriate services to minorities reject the notion of standardized services and represent, in most cases, a threat to the status quo.

Some degree of conflict is inevitable when a multicultural perspective is implemented by an organization. Because individuals who do not represent the dominant majority have traditionally experienced systematic disadvantage from the rules, policies, and procedures in our major social institutions, to advocate the client is often to challenge the system.[43] It is impossible to undertake the task of making mental health services more culturally appropriate to minorities without facing the conflict between the need to change the system and the desire to preserve the status quo. Collective action may be required to bring about change.[39]

Implications for the Mental Health Administrator

Enhancing the cultural appropriateness of services to minorities can reduce overall health and mental health care costs and improve the quality of care. The modifications in mental health service delivery required to provide culturally appropriate care for minority clients depend upon the ethnic composition of the community served and on the degree of acculturation present in each subgroup.

The approach to multicultural programming that is selected must take into account the resources of the organization as well as those of the community. Efforts to provide culturally appropriate mental health services for minority clients are most effective if they encourage community input, but they may be met with resistance by individuals committed to conventional programs and may place the administrator in the position of mediating among conflicting interest groups. At the same time, the notion of cultural appropriateness, or cultural sensitivity, is one that can benefit all clients, whether or not they are minorities, because it reflects a perspective that values clients' perceptions and needs.

References

1. Sue S: Community mental health services to minority groups. *American Psychologist* 1977; 41: 373-384.
2. President's Commission on Mental Health: Volume 2. Task Panel Reports: *The Nature and Scope of the Problem.* Washington, DC: Government Printing Office, 1978.
3. Wu I, Windle C: Ethnic specificity in the relationship of minority use and staffing of community mental health centers. *Community Mental Health Journal* 1980; 16:156-168.
4. Barrera M: Raza populations. In Snowden, L (ed.): *Reaching the Underserved: Mental Health Needs of Neglected Populations.* Beverley Hills, CA: Sage Publications, 1982.
5. Neighbors HW: Professional help use among Black Americans: implications for unmet need. *American Journal of Community Psychology* 1984; 12: 551-566.
6. Leong FT: Counseling and psychotherapy with Asian Americans: review of the literature. *Journal of Counseling Psychology* 1986; 33:196-206.
7. Scheffler RM, Miller AB: Demand analysis of mental health service use among ethnic subpopulations. *Inquiry* 1989; 26: 202-215.
8. Wells KB, Golding JM, Hough RL et al.: Acculturation and the probability of use of health services by Mexican Americans. *Health Services Research* 1989; 24: 237-257.
9. Su S, McKinney H, Allen D et al.: Delivery of community mental health services to Black and White clients. *Journal of Consulting and Clinical Psychology* 1974; 42:794-801.
10. Sue S, McKinney H: Asian-Americans in the community mental health care system. *American Journal of Orthopsychiatry* 1975; 45:111-118.
11. Armstrong HE, Ishiki D, Heiman J, et al.: Service utilization by Black and White clientele in an urban community mental health center: revised assessment of an old problem. *Community Mental Health Journal* 1984; 20:269-281.
12. Snowden LR, Cheung FK: Use of inpatient mental health services by members of ethnic minority groups. *American Psychologist* 1990; 45:347-355.
13. Havassy BE, Hopkin JT: Factors predicting utilization of acute psychiatric inpatient services by frequently hospitalized patients. *Hospital and Community Psychiatry* 1989; 40: 820-823.
14. Lindsey KP, Paul GL: Involuntary commitments to public mental institutions: issues involving the overrepresentation of Blacks and assessment of relevant functioning. *Psychological Bulletin* 1989; 106:171-183.
15. Holder HD, Blose JO: Mental health treatment and the reduction of health care costs. In: McGuire TG, Scheffler RM (eds.): *Advances in Health Economics and Health Services Research.* Greenwich, Conn: JAI Press, 1987.
16. Jones KR, Vischi TR: Impact of alcohol, drug abuse, and mental health treatment on medical care utilization: a review of the research literature. *Supplement to Medical Care* 1979; 17.
17. Green JW: *Cultural Awareness in the Human Services.* Englewood Cliffs, NJ: Prentice-Hall, Inc., 1982.
18. Adebimpe VR: Overview: White norms and psychiatric diagnosis of Black patients. *American Journal of Psychiatry* 1981; 138: 279-285.
19. Snowden LR. Cheung FK: Use of inpatient mental health services by members of ethnic minority groups. *American Psychologist* 1990; 45:347-355.

20. O'Sullivan MJ, Peterson PD, Cox GB et al.: Ethnic populations: community mental health services ten years later. *American Journal of Community Psychology* 1989; 17:17-30.
21. Zane N: An evaluation of parallel outpatient services for Asian-American clients. Paper presented at American Psychological Association Annual Convention, New Orleans, LA, 1989.
22. Wade P, Bernstein BL: Culture sensitivity training and counselor's race: effects on black female clients' perceptions and attrition. *Journal of Counseling Psychology* 1991; 38:9-15.
23. Vobejda B: Asians, Hispanics giving nation more diversity. *Washington Post* July 3, 1991.
24. Duke L, Morin R: Demographic shift reshaping politics. *Washington Post* August 17, 1991.
25. Sue S: Mental health in a multiethnic society: the person-organization match. Paper presented at the American Psychological Association Convention, Toronto, Canada, September, 1978.
26. Ruiz P, Langrod J: The Role of Folk Healers in Community Mental Health Services. In: Dana RH (ed.): *Human Services for Cultural Minorities*. Baltimore: University Park Press, 1981, pp. 217-224.
27. Jilek W, Jilek-Aall L: The psychiatrist and his shaman colleague. In: Dana RH (ed.): *Human Services for Cultural Minorities*. Baltimore: University Park Press, 1982, pp. 15-26.
28. Sue S, Morishima JK: *The Mental Health of Asian Americans*. San Francisco: Jossey Bass, 1982.
29. LeVine ES, Padilla AM: *Crossing Cultures in Therapy*. Monterey, CA: Brooks/Cole Publishing Co., 1980.
30. Heitler JB: Preparatory techniques in initiating expressive psychotherapy with lower-class, unsophisticated patients. *Psychological Bulletin* 1976; 83:339-352.
31. Strupp H, Bloxom A: Preparing lower-class patients for group psychotherapy: development and evaluation of a role induction film. *Journal of Consulting and Clinical Psychology* 1973; 41:373-384.
32. Frank JD: Expectation and therapeutic outcome — the placebo effect and the role induction interview. In: Frank, JD (ed.): *Effective Ingredients of Successful Psychotherapy*. New York: Brunner/Mazel, 1978.
33. Warren NC, Rice LN: Structuring and stabilizing of psychotherapy for low-prognosis clients. *Journal of Consulting and Clinical Psychology* 1972; 39:173-181.
34. Gim RH, Atkinson DR, Kim SJ: Asian-American acculturation, counselor ethnicity, and cultural sensitivity, and ratings of counselors. *Journal of Counseling Psychology* 1991, 38:57-62.
35. Flores-Ortiz YG: Indigenous paraprofessionals. In Snowden L (ed.): *Reaching the Underserved*. Beverley Hills, Calif.: Sage Publications, 1982; pp. 259-280.
36. Hernandez AH, Schweon C: Mobile mental health team reaches minorities. *Aging* 1989; 46:12-13.
37. Wong HZ: Asian and Pacific Americans. In: Snowden L (ed.): *Reaching the Underserved: Mental Health Needs of Neglected Populations*. Beverley Hills, Calif.: Sage Publications, 1982, pp. 185-204.
38. Westermeyer J, Walker D: Approaches to treatment of alcoholism across cultural boundaries. *Psychiatric Annals* 1982; 12:434-439.
39. Zane N, Sue S, Castro FG, et al.: Service system models for ethnic minorities. In: Snowden L. (ed.): *Reaching the Underserved: Mental Health Needs of Neglected Populations*. Beverley Hills, Calif.: Sage Publications, 1982.
40. Dinges NG, Trimble JE, Manson SM, et al.: Counseling and psychotherapy with American Indians and Alaskan Natives. In: Marsella AJ, Pedersen PB (eds.): *Cross-Cultural Counseling and Psychotherapy*. New York: Pergamon Press, 1981.
41. Solomon BB: *Black Empowerment*. New York: Columbia University Press, 1976.
42. Pinderhughes E: *Understanding Race, Ethnicity, and Power*. New York: The Free Press, 1989.
43. Cloward RA, Piven FF: Notes toward a radical social work. In: Baily R, Brake M (eds.): *Radical Social Work*. New York: Random House, 1975.

Part II
The Ordinary Mind

The Psychological Underpinnings of Law

[19]

THE PSYCHOLOGICAL CONSEQUENCES OF JUDICIAL PROCEDURES: IMPLICATIONS FOR CIVIL COMMITMENT HEARINGS

*Tom R. Tyler**

A key Supreme Court decision regarding involuntary civil commit-ment hearings is *Parham v. J.R.*[1] In *Parham*, the Supreme Court ruled that minors are not entitled to a hearing prior to involuntary admission into a state mental hospital because state psychiatrists, those otherwise responsible for making the admissions decision, could act as a "neutral factfinder."[2]

The identification of "neutral factfinding" as the criterion against which to evaluate the adequacy of judicial hearings is consistent with the legal litera-ture on procedures. That literature typically focuses on issues such as bias, honesty, and expertise.[3] These aspects are regarded as important because they are believed to influence the ability of a procedure to reach an objec-tively correct outcome.[4]

An important question in determining the balance of authority in commit-ment hearings is whether the procedural safeguards can assure neutral factfinding.[5] In commitment hearings authority can be given to professional and/or to judicial decision-makers. Professional authority refers to the dis-cretion given to psychiatrists or psychologists to determine mental compe-tence, usually based on tests and interviews with the person whose competence is in question.[6] Judicial authority refers to similar discretion

* This paper is based on a presentation at the annual meeting of the American Associa-tion of Law Schools in San Antonio, Texas, on January 5, 1992. I would like to thank Don Bersoff, James Ellis, Daniel Shuman, and Chris Slobogin for helpful comments on that presen-tation. The research that forms the basis for this presentation was supported by the Law and Social Science Program of the National Science Foundation, the American Bar Foundation, and the Dispute Resolution Research Center of the Kellogg Graduate School of Management at Northwestern University.

1. 442 U.S. 584 (1979). *Parham* was not the first case to consider the therapeutic conse-quences of commitment hearings for juveniles. For a review of the history of laws governing the parental commitment of minors, see J.W. Ellis, *Volunteering Children: Parental Commit-ment of Minors to Mental Institutions*, 62 CAL. L. REV. 840-916 (1974).

2. *Parham*, 442 U.S. at 606-07.

3. *See* TOM R. TYLER, WHY PEOPLE OBEY THE LAW 6-7 (1990).

4. *Id.*

5. Donald N. Bersoff, *Judicial Deference to Nonlegal Decisionmakers: Imposing Simplis-tic Solutions on Problems of Cognitive Complexity in Mental Disability Law*, 46 SMU L. REV. 329 (1992).

6. *Id.*

given to judges, typically exercised through some form of judical hearing.[7]

If the key concern in devising commitment procedures is determining the true mental state of the person in order to make the best decision about commitment, then this balance of authority should be shaped by evaluations of the capabilities of professional and judicial decision-makers.[8] Recent research has documented many errors in clinical decision-making, suggesting that judicial decision-making might be beneficial.[9] If future studies that directly compare the relative error rates in clinical and judicial decision-making suggest that judicial hearings are more accurate, or lead to more desirable errors,[10] those findings would support the use of judicial hearings.

It is also possible to draw potential criteria for evaluating commitment procedures from a different set of criteria used for evaluating legal procedures. These alternative criteria have been articulated by the Supreme Court. In *Goldberg v. Kelley*[11] the Supreme Court argued that welfare recipients are entitled to a hearing of a particular type before their welfare benefits are terminated.[12] Although primarily concerned with issues of accuracy, the Court also recognized that termination without a hearing could be psychologically harmful, potentially damaging feelings of security, dignity, and self-worth.[13] In other cases dealing with the due process rights of students and prisoners, the Court similarly identified the possible psychological harm of experiencing unfair procedures as a reason for granting rights to a hearing.[14]

The potential consequences of the psychological harm of experiencing unfair hearings is articulated most clearly in *Morrissey v. Brewer*.[15] In *Morrissey* the Court indicated that prisoners should be given judicial hearings because denying them due process could cause them psychological harm (i.e. would be antitherapeutic) and thus undermine their rehabilitation.[16]

These decisions are important because the courts recognize the importance of considering the psychological impact of judicial procedures on those experiencing the procedures. This impact is distinct from the desire for a neutral, fact-finding expert, such as a judge or a psychiatrist, who is expected

---

7. *Id.* One important difference between these two procedures is that judicial hearings involve due process rights, while professional evaluations do not.
    8. *Id.*
    9. *See* JOHN MONAHAN & LAURENS WALKER, SOCIAL SCIENCE IN LAW: CASES AND MATERIALS (1st ed. 1985).
    10. It is important to recognize that the total amount of error in a procedure is not the only criteria for its evaluation. The legal system deems some types of error to be more unacceptable than others. For example, falsely committing a sane peson might be viewed as a more serious error than falsely releasing an insane person.
    11. 397 U.S. 254 (1970).
    12. *Id.* at 264.
    13. *Id.* at 264-66.
    14. *See, e.g.*, Morrissey v. Brewer, 408 U.S. 471, 472 (1972) (addressing whether the "Due Process Clause of the Fourteenth Amendment requires that a State afford an individual some opportunity to be heard prior to revoking his parole").
    15. 408 U.S. 471 (1972).
    16. *Id.* at 484. Some state courts have also recognized similar interests of individuals. For example, the California Supreme Court discussed those interests in People v. Ramirez, 599 P.2d 622 (Cal. 1979).

to reach accurate decisions.[17] When conceptualized this way, due process involves giving people judicial procedures that they will perceive as fair.

The law concerning the use of civil commitment hearings to determine mental competence has varied greatly in the degree that it has suggested that people are entitled to judicial hearings. In the past, such hearings, like those involving prisoners, welfare recipients, and students, were often conducted with minimal attention to issues of due process.[18] The introduction of what David Wexler labelled "libertarian commitment codes" has heightened concerns about the due process rights of those involved in involuntary commitment procedures.[19] Protection of those rights requires some form of judicial determination prior to commitment.[20]

Discussions about the appropriate degree of judicial due process that should be involved in commitment procedures raise the question of whether attention to due process rights is wise. Attention to these rights increases judicial authority at the expense of professional authority. Addressing this question involves attention to both the objective quality of professional and judicial commitment procedures and to their psychological consequences. This discussion will focus on the psychological consequences of commitment hearings—i.e. on the therapeutic effects of the commitment process.[21] One potential benefit of judicial hearings is that they result in objectively better outcomes. In addition, they may be psychologically beneficial to the person whose conduct is under review.

I. HOW PEOPLE ARE AFFECTED BY JUDICIAL HEARINGS

The first issue to be addressed is whether the type of judicial process that people experience influences them independently of the outcome of those procedures. In other words, are there things about a commitment hearing that affect people psychologically but are unrelated to the outcome of the procedure? Does the process itself have therapeutic implications? Legal psychologists have studied a wide variety of decision-making procedures, including jury trials, mediation hearings, arbitration hearings, settlement conferences, informal police-citizen interactions, and plea bargaining hearings, in an effort to understand what determines how people react to their dealings with legal authorities.[22] Unfortunately, there are currently no direct examinations of commitment hearings. Nonetheless, the findings of these other studies have important implications for such hearings.

---

17. *See* Parham v. J.R., 442 U.S. 584, 606 (1979).
18. *See* DAVID WEXLER, THERAPEUTIC JURISPRUDENCE: THE LAW AS A THERAPEUTIC AGENT (1990).
19. *Id.* at 165-87.
20. *Id.*
21. There is a large body of psychological literature dealing with the objective quality of the decisions reached through varying legal procedures, in particular the use of different types of juries. That literature will not be addressed in this paper. *See* Bersoff, *supra* note 5; JOHN MONAHAN & LAURENS WALKER, SOCIAL SCIENCE IN LAW: CASES AND MATERIALS 79 (2d ed. 1990).
22. *See* E. ALLAN LIND & TOM R. TYLER, THE SOCIAL PSYCHOLOGY OF PROCEDURAL JUSTICE (1988).

The psychological perspective on judicial hearings builds on the classic research of psychologist John Thibaut and attorney Laurens Walker.[23] Their studies examined how people evaluated the adversary and the inquisitorial trial procedures.[24] Their research focussed on procedural preferences, specifically the types of trial procedures that people wanted to use to settle their disputes.[25]

The work of Thibaut and Walker stimulated a number of studies on the psychological consequences of personal experiences with legal authorities.[26] Of particular relevance are studies on the psychological consequences of participating in various aspects of the judicial system.[27] This body of work examines how people react to legal procedures after they have experienced them.[28] It differs from the work of Thibaut and Walker in its reactive character. Instead of choosing a procedure prior to experiencing it (i.e. expressing a preference), people react to a procedure that they have already experienced. Thus, they indicate their degree of satisfaction with the procedure used to deal with their problem.

Subsequent studies also differ from the work of Thibaut and Walker by placing greater weight on the study of real disputes.[29] The original Thibaut and Walker research utilized laboratory experimentation methods that were heavily criticized by the legal community.[30] The studies that will be examined here involve either surveys of people reporting on their personal experiences with judicial procedures or field studies of variations in legal procedures. Field studies of this type also involve an examination of people who have actually experienced different types of judicial proceedings.

The first important finding of studies of people's reactions to judicial procedures is that people are not primarily influenced by the outcome of their experience, i.e. by whether they win or lose their case, whether they go to jail or go free, or whether they pay a large fine or nothing.[31] Further, studies suggest very little impact from the time it takes to resolve a case or the amount of money expended in the effort.[32] The objective characteristics of the case disposition experience have very little psychological impact.[33] An example of these findings is the study by E. Allan Lind comparing bilateral

---

23. JOHN THIBAUT & LAURENS WALKER, PROCEDURAL JUSTICE: A PSYCHOLOGICAL ANALYSIS (1975).
24. *Id.*
25. *Id.* Thibaut and Walker also dealt with the objective quality of the decisions reached using different types of legal procedure. *Id.* However, their research on that topic will not be discussed in this article.
26. LIND & TYLER, *supra* note 22, at 13.
27. Tom R. Tyler, *The Role of Perceived Injustice in Defendants' Evaluation of Their Courtroom Experience*, 18 LAW & SOC'Y REV. 51 (1984) [hereinafter, Tyler, *Role of Perceived Injustice*].
28. *See, e.g.*, TYLER, *supra* note 3 (evaluating how people react to their personal experiences with legal authorities).
29. *See* LIND & TYLER, *supra* note 22, at 13-40.
30. *Id.*
31. *See* E. Allan Lind et al., *In the Eye of the Beholder: Tort Litigants' Evaluations of Their Experiences in the Civil Justice System*, 24 LAW & SOC'Y REV. 953, 968-71 (1990).
32. *Id.* at 974.
33. *Id.* at 968-71, 975.

negotiation, mediation, settlement conferences, and trials.[34] That study found that the amount of money won or lost, the duration of the case disposition process, and the costs of the process to the litigant were all largely unrelated to judgments of fairness and satisfaction.[35]

What does influence people is their assessment of the fairness of the case disposition process. People are most strongly affected by their evaluations of the procedure by which the outcomes are reached—i.e., by their evaluations of the judicial process itself.[36] In other words, people are affected by the way in which decisions are made, irrespective of what those decisions are. People are also influenced by judgments about the fairness of the outcome itself.[37]

The relative importance of receiving a fair outcome or experiencing a fair procedure depends on the types of psychological consequence with which we are concerned. If we are concerned about personal reactions, reaction to the experience or the willingness to voluntarily accept judicial decisions, then people are affected by both the fairness of the outcome and, independently, by the fairness of the procedure.[38]

Studies suggest that if the socializing influence of experience is the issue of concern (i.e., the impact of participating in a judicial hearing on a person's respect for the law and legal authorities), then the primary influence is the person's evaluation of the fairness of the judicial procedure itself, not their evaluations of the outcome.[39] Such respect is important because it has been found to influence everyday behavior toward the law.[40] When people believe that legal authorities are less legitimate, they are less likely to be law-abiding citizens in their everyday lives.[41]

Many of the studies alluded to deal with informal police-citizen interactions,[42] and citizen experiences in small claims courts.[43] These studies focus on the experiences of ordinary citizens, whose primary interactions with the legal system typically involve informal contacts with the police and the courts.[44]

Other studies have focused more directly on judicial hearings. The first is a recent study of felony criminal case disposition.[45] That study examined

---

34. *See id.* at 953-86.
35. *Id.* at 980-84.
36. *See* LIND & TYLER, *supra* note 22.
37. *Id.*
38. *Id.*
39. TYLER, *supra* note 3, at 94-112. *See* Tom R. Tyler et al., *Maintaining Allegiance Toward Political Authorities: The Role of Prior Attitudes and the Use of Fair Procedures*, 33 AM. J. OF POL. SCI. 629 (1989) (examining "the impact of experience with the criminal justice system on defendant attitudes toward legal authorities, law, and government) [hereinafter, Tyler, *Maintaining Allegiance*].
40. TYLER, *supra* note 3, at 4-5.
41. *Id.*
42. *Id.*; Tom R. Tyler & Robert Folger, *Distributional and Procedural Aspects of Satisfaction With Citizen-Police Encounter*, BASIC & APPLIED SOC. PSYCHOL. 281-92 (1980).
43. Tyler, *Role of Perceived Injustice, supra* note 27.
44. *See* TYLER, *supra* note 3; Tyler & Folger, *supra* note 42, at 281; Tyler, *Role of Perceived Injustice, supra* note 27.
45. *See* Jonathan Casper et al., *Procedural Justice in Felony Cases*, 22 LAW & SOC'Y REV. 483 (1988).

the impact of the case disposition process on both satisfaction with the case disposition process itself and on attitudes toward law and legal authorities.[46]

Although those defendants received outcomes varying from a suspended sentence to twenty years in prison, the objective severity of the outcomes received was not found to influence overall reactions to the case-disposition experiences. Reactions to the case-disposition experience were influenced by: 1) the fairness of the sentence and 2) evaluations of the fairness of the case-disposition process. The impact of the case-disposition process on attitudes toward the legal system was found to be responsive only to evaluations of the fairness of the case-disposition process and not to judgments of distributive justice or to the objective severity of the outcome.[47]

These findings about the felony case disposition process are important for several reasons. First, the deprivation of personal liberty involved is quite substantial. Second, the people involved are marginal members of society: poor, poorly educated, minority, unemployed; those who might be expected to care the least about questions of due process and the most about the favorability of the outcomes they have received.

A second set of findings are from a series of studies of civil tort case hearings conducted by the Rand corporation.[48] These studies examine the resolution of tort cases in settlement conference hearings, mediation/arbitration hearings, and formal trial hearings.[49] The findings of Lind et al., on arbitration in the federal courts are especially striking.[50] All of the cases they studied involved lawsuits over at least $50,000 and some lawsuits involved amounts up to $2,000,000.[51] Yet they found that people's willingness to accept mediation decisions, instead of going on to have a formal trial, were affected by their evaluations of the fairness of the mediation session.[52] Similar findings were obtained by Rand studies that examined the acceptance of arbitration claims in lawsuits over automobile injuries in New Jersey.[53] These findings suggest that civil, like criminal, proceedings are strongly influenced by people's evaluations of procedures.

The findings of the studies I have outlined are very supportive of the speculations of the Supreme Court in the cases I have already noted, *Goldberg v. Kelley*[54] and *Morrissey v. Brewer.*[55] Experiencing judicial procedures that are evaluated as unfair does influence people's respect for legal authorities

---

46. Casper, *supra* note 45, at 483-507; Tyler, *Maintaining Allegiance, supra* note 39, at 629-52.

47. Casper, *supra* note 45, at 483-507; Tyler, *Maintaining Allegiance, supra* note 39, at 629-52.

48. E. Allan Lind et al., *Outcome and Process Concerns in Organizational Dispute Resolution*, AM. B. FOUND. WORKING PAPER # 9109 (1991); Robert J. MacCoun et al., *Rand Institute for Civil Justice*, ALTERNATIVE ADJUDICATION: AN EVALUATION OF THE NEW JERSEY AUTOMOBILE ARBITRATION PROGRAM (1988).

49. *See* Lind, *supra* note 48; MacCoun, *supra* note 48.

50. Lind, *supra* note 48.

51. *Id.* at 1.

52. *Id.* at 29.

53. MacCoun, *supra* note 48, at 56-57.

54. 397 U.S. 254 (1970).

55. 408 U.S. 471 (1972).

and for the law. Further, it shapes people's behavior. People who have experienced a procedure that they judge to be unfair are not only less respectful of the law and legal authorities, they are less likely to accept judicial
decisions and less likely to obey the law in the future. These findings point
to the possibility of developing exactly the type of social malaise that the
Supreme Court speculated might result from experiencing an "arbitrary"
(i.e. unfair) procedure.[56]

In their original discussion of procedural justice, Thibaut and Walker suggested that conducting a judicial proceeding using procedures that all parties
to a dispute would regard as fair facilitates efforts to "resolve conflicts in
such a way as to bind up the social fabric and encourage the continuation of
productive exchange between individuals."[57] Similar concerns underlie the
therapeutic jurisprudence movement. If people leave commitment hearings
with favorable views about the legitimacy of legal authorities, such views are
likely to facilitate the subsequent therapeutic process.

A. SUBJECTIVE NEUTRALITY

It is possible that people care about procedural justice but define it in
terms of neutrality such as lack of bias, honesty, the use of expertise, and
factual decision-making. If so, they share the concern with factors shaping
the objective decision-making quality that has influenced judicial holdings
such as *Parham v. J.R.*[58]

Studies indicate that people focus on lack of bias, honesty, and factual
decision-making.[59] Each of these aspects of a judicial procedure has some
influence on judgments of the procedure's fairness.[60] In addition, people are
more likely to indicate that a procedure is fair if it yields them a favorable
outcome.

What is interesting is not that the neutrality of a judicial procedure matters—neutrality is after all a core element of procedure that forms the central concept in most textbooks on legal procedure. What is interesting is
that there are other aspects of procedures that are more important determinants of people's judgments about procedural fairness. Three such elements
will be considered: participation, dignity, and trust.

1. Participation

Studies of people's reactions to judicial procedures consistently find that
people regard procedures in which they are allowed to participate as fairer.[61]
Participation can involve the presentation of evidence and one's own views

---

56. *Goldberg*, 397 U.S. at 265.
57. *See* THIBAUT & WALKER, *supra* note 23.
58. 442 U.S. 584 (1979).
59. *See* TYLER, *supra* note 3, at 6-7.
60. *See* Tom R. Tyler & E. Allan Lind, *A Rational Model of Authority in Groups, in* 25
ADVANCES IN EXPERIMENTAL SOCIAL PSYCHOLOGY 115, 137-66 (Mark P. Zanna ed., 1992)
(discussing existing research on characteristics that make procedures appear fair and addressing features that affect procedural justice judgments).
61. *See* LIND & TYLER, *supra* note 22.

(voice or process control), shared decision-making (decision control), or both.[62] Studies suggest that either form of participation enhances feelings of fair treatment.[63]

It is not particularly surprising that people value shared control over decisions. Such shared control gives them influence over the outcome of the procedure. It is also not surprising that people value the opportunity to present evidence and express their views. They no doubt feel that this opportunity to present evidence allows them to influence indirectly judicial decisions through persuading the mediator or judge of the validity of their perspective.

What is interesting is that people value the opportunity to present their arguments and state their views even when they indicate that what they say is having little or no influence over the third-party authority.[64] The most striking example of this effect is found in studies allowing people to present their evidence after a decision has been made.[65]

Imagine that you are invited to visit another university because you are being considered for a job. When you arrive your host says that he or she has good news and bad news. The bad news is that someone else has already been hired to fill the job. The good news is that you can still demonstrate how good you would be for the job by giving a job talk. Would you think that you were being more fairly treated than you would if you were simply told that the job had been filled? Interestingly, the answer is yes. In fact, people do place a value on the opportunity to present evidence that is not linked to the influence of that evidence on decisions.

Obviously this example is extreme. Typically the message people receive from authorities is much less straightforward. But the extremity of the example makes the point clear; people do not want to state their opinions simply because they believe that their arguments will influence third-party decisions. Presenting arguments to a third-party has value in and of itself.

2. Dignity

A second important finding of psychological research on people's reactions to their dealings with legal authorities is that people care how they are treated by legal authorities.[66] In other words, they respond to whether they are treated with respect, politeness, and dignity, and whether their rights as citizens are acknowledged.[67] People value the affirmation of their status by legal authorities as competent, equal, citizens and human beings, and they

---

62. *Id.*

63. *Id.*

64. *Id.*

65. E. Allan Lind et al., *Voice, Control, and Procedural Justice: Instrumental and Noninstrumental Concerns in Fairness Judgments*, 59 J. PERSONALITY & SOC. PSYCHOL. 952, 952-59 (1990).

66. *See* TYLER, *supra* note 3; Tyler & Folger, *supra* note 42; Tyler & Lind, *supra* note 60.

67. *See* Lind, *supra* note 31; TYLER, *supra* note 3; Tyler & Folger, *supra* note 42; Tyler & Lind, *supra* note 60.

regard procedures as unfair if they are not consistent with that affirmation.[68] To understand the effects of dignity, it is important to recognize that government has an important role in defining people's views about their value in society. Such a self evaluation shapes one's feelings of security and self-respect.[69]

3. Trust

Finally, people value evidence that the authorities with whom they are dealing are concerned about their welfare and want to treat them fairly.[70] Trust is the most important quality, but also the most elusive, because it involves a motive attribution.[71] In other words, people must infer whether an authority is or is not motivated to treat them fairly based on that authority's actions.

What influences whether people regard authorities as trustworthy? One factor is participation. People regard authorities who allow them to present evidence as more trustworthy.[72] Similarly, people regard authorities who treat them with dignity and respect as more trustworthy.[73] Finally, the efforts of authorities to explain or account for decisions heighten judgments of trustworthiness.[74]

Concerns about trustworthiness reflect a desire to understand the future actions of authorities.[75] Since people typically believe that motives are stable and unchanging over time, knowledge of the motivations of authorities allows the authorities' future actions to be predicted.[76] If people infer a benevolent disposition in some authority, they can trust that, in the long-run, an authority will behave in ways that serve their interests.[77] For this reason trust is a key component of legitimacy.[78]

The importance of trustworthiness helps to explain an important limitation to the participation effects that have been outlined. People generally feel more fairly treated if they can present evidence, even when they think their evidence does not affect the decisions made by the third party. However, this effect does not occur if people do not believe that their evidence was considered by the third party. Without considering their arguments, people believe that the authority cannot be acting benevolently, and no effect occurs.

The role of trustworthiness also leads to another important conclusion of the study of procedures. Structural features of procedures, such as the pro-

68. *See* Tyler & Lind, *supra* note 60, at 139-43.
69. Robert Lane, *Procedural Goods in a Democracy: How One is Treated v. What One Gets*, 2 SOC. JUST. RES. 177-92 (1988).
70. *See* Tyler & Lind, *supra* note 60, at 139-43.
71. *Id.*
72. *Id.*
73. *Id.*
74. *Id.*
75. *Id.*
76. *Id.*
77. *Id.*
78. BERNARD BARBER, THE LOGIC AND LIMITS OF TRUST (1983).

vision of a right to appeal, may or may not shape people's feelings about authorities. The key issue to those affected by procedures is whether the authority involved is attempting to be fair in the implementation of rules.[79] Without such a belief the simple existence of structures associated with fairness does not enhance perceived fairness.[80] On the other hand, people can experience "unfair treatment" such as sexism or racism without reporting that the procedures involved were unfair if they infer that the authorities involved are motivated to treat them fairly.[81]

B. SUMMARY

People's evaluations of the fairness of judicial hearings are affected by the opportunities which those procedures provide for people to participate, by the degree to which people judge that they are treated with dignity and respect, and by judgments about the trustworthiness of authorities. Each of these three factors has more influence on judgments of procedural justice than do either evaluations of neutrality or evaluations of the favorableness of the outcome of the hearing.

II. THE PSYCHOLOGY OF JUDICIAL HEARINGS

Why do those who experience judicial hearings react to issues of participation, dignity, and trustworthiness? The answer lies in recognizing the important role that legal and political authorities play in defining peoples' feelings of self-esteem, self-worth, and their sense of personal security.

In a study of the citizens of Chicago, people were found to recognize a widespread occurrence of injustice when citizens dealt with the police and courts.[82] Yet the same people almost universally indicated that they believed the authorities would treat them fairly if they personally dealt with them.[83] Tyler and Lind label this belief the "illusion of personal justice" because it reflects a strong belief in one's own invulnerability to unfair treatment.[84] Faye Crosby identified a similar unwillingness to recognize that one is a victim of discrimination, which she labels "comfortable ignorance."[85] In each case, people resist the belief that they are vulnerable, instead seeing themselves as linked to personally benevolent authorities.[86] When people deal with authorities, they open these beliefs to possible disconfirmation.[87]

---

79. Tom R. Tyler & Robert Bies, *Interpersonal Aspects of Procedural Justice*, *in* APPLIED SOCIAL PSYCHOLOGY IN BUSINESS SETTINGS (J.S. Carroll ed., 1990).

80. *See* Tyler & Lind, *supra* note 60, at 139-43.

81. *See* TYLER, *supra* note 3, at 91-92.

82. *See* Tyler & Lind, *supra* note 60, at 144-58.

83. *Id.*

84. *Id.* at 155.

85. Faye Crosby, *Relative Deprivation in Organizational Settings*, *in* 6 RESEARCH IN OR-GANIZATIONAL BEHAVIOR (L.L. Cummings & Barry M. Staw eds., 1984); *see also* Faye Crosby, *The Denial of Personal Discrimination*, *in* AMERICAN BEHAVIORAL SCIENTIST 371; Faye Crosby & Donna Nagata, Denying Personal Advantage (paper presented at the annual meeting of the International Society of Political Psychology, Washington, D.C.) (1990).

86. Tyler & Lind, *supra* note 60, at 155.

87. *Id.* at 155 n.19.

The importance of self-respect and self-worth is indicated by the centrality of those issues to people's reactions to their experiences with authorities. People may initially approach authorities instrumentally, but they react to their experiences by focusing on their implications for the social bond linking people to authorities.[88]

The legal system is one aspect of the larger society, so legal authorities provide people with information about their standing both in the eyes of the law and in society more generally. Research shows that people care about their status and react to their experiences in terms of their implications concerning that status.[89] In contrast, people's concerns about traditional issues such as lack of bias, honesty, factual decision-making, and obtaining favorable outcomes, while important, have less influence on people's judgments regarding the fairness of their experiences.[90]

A. COMMITMENT HEARINGS

I have discussed a number of studies examining the psychology underlying people's reactions to their dealings with legal authorities. None of these studies directly examines commitment hearings. However, they do examine a variety of legal procedures, including mediation/arbitration hearings, trials, and plea bargaining, which share many basic characteristics with commitment hearings.

The key question is what implications can be drawn from this literature regarding the therapeutic consequences of personal experiences with legal authorities. One implication is that people respond to how decisions are made—a response that is not simply linked to what decisions are. Hence, the psychological arena defined by the Supreme Court in cases such as *Goldberg v. Kelly*[91] and *Morrissey v. Brewer*[92] clearly exists.

Failure to receive due process has a number of negative consequences for people who have personal experiences with legal authorities, including reluctance to accept decisions, diminished respect for the judge, mediator, or other third party, diminished respect for the courts and the legal system, and a diminished willingness to follow legal rules.[93] These effects are completely consistent with the suggestion that experiencing arbitrary procedures leads to social malaise and decreases people's willingness to be integrated into the polity, accepting its authorities and following its rules.

Of particular relevance to the question of therapeutic implications is the issue of behavior. Enhancing respect for authorities, the willingness to voluntarily accept the decisions of authorities, and the willingness to follow social rules are core objectives of any therapeutic program. Hence, it seems likely that future studies of the therapeutic consequences of judicial hearings

---

88. *See* William Felstiner et al., *The Emergence and Transformation of Disputes: Naming, Blaming, Claiming . . .* , 15 LAW & SOC'Y REV. 631 (1973).

89. *See* Tyler & Lind, *supra* note 60, at 144-66.

90. *Id.*

91. 397 U.S. 254 (1970).

92. 408 U.S. 471 (1972).

93. *See* TYLER, *supra* note 3.

will demonstrate that commitment hearings experienced as unfair by those potentially being committed will have strongly antitherapeutic consequences.

The findings of studies about fair process have especially important implications for the study of commitment hearings. Judicial hearings in general are clearly used by people to gain information about their status as members of society. Perhaps no type of hearing more directly threatens a person's belief that they are an equal member of society than a mental commitment hearing. Given the stigma attached to "insanism,"[94] the label "mentally incompetent" is truly a threat to individual's ability to define themselves as an equal member of society.[95] Many groups affected by judicial and administrative hearings, welfare recipients, prisoners, and students are socially marginal in some respects. For those and other groups the issue of mental competence is central to issues of self-respect and security in society.

B. PROFESSIONAL VS. JUDICIAL DECISION-MAKING

The psychological perspective that has been outlined highlights the importance of conducting judicial hearings in ways that will have positive psychological consequences on those who undergo commitment hearings. In other words, it is clearly beneficial for personal experiences with judicial authorities to contribute to developing psychological and behavioral characteristics that enhance the therapeutic process. The enhancement of such attitudes and behaviors will, of course, be beneficial irrespective of the disposition of the case (i.e., whether the person involved is or is not committed to a mental institution).

It is also important to note, however, that the characteristics of a hearing that are associated with fairness can be enacted by either judicial or professional decision-makers. In other words, the psychological research reviewed suggests that people will benefit from hearings in which they can participate, in which they are treated with dignity, and in which they believe that they are dealing with trustworthy authorities who are motivated to be fair to them. It seems possible to design either judicial or professional decision-making procedures, or both, so that they will have the characteristics of "fair" decision-making procedures.

The findings outlined are consistent with the suggestion of the therapeutic jurisprudence literature that hearings which lack the characteristics which people associate with due process are likely to be experienced as unfair.[96] Such unfairness, in turn, is likely to have negative consequences for the subsequent therapeutic process. However, it does not point to judicial hearings as the only possible source of procedures that people will experience as unfair. It is also possible that professionals could develop procedures containing some of the elements that have been outlined. If they did so, then professional decision-making procedures might also be therapeutic. It is an

---

94. *See* Michael L. Perlin, *On "Sanism"*, 46 SMU L. REV. 373 (1992).
95. *Id.*
96. *See* Wexler, *supra* note 18.

empirical question, as yet unanswered, whether mental health professionals could conduct commitment proceedings in ways that would lead people to feel that their views were being considered, that they were being treated with dignity and respect, and that they were dealing with trustworthy authorities.

C. Objective and Psychological Criteria for Procedural Evaluation

There are two distinct issues that need to be considered in evaluating civil commitment procedures. The first is the ability of a procedure to make accurate decisions. Bersoff has outlined the problems, including bias, with professional decision-making in great detail.[97] If future studies indicate that professional decision-making is more subject to such biases and consequently less accurate than judicial decision-making, then accuracy concerns would favor judicial decision-making.

Distinct from accuracy issues are concerns about the psychological impact of procedures, in particular their potential impact on future therapeutic processes. If people become estranged from authority, distrusting others; believing that they are vulnerable, and hence feeling insecure; and lacking in feelings of self-worth, these consequences are disadvantageous and preferably could be avoided. Historically, many of these negative psychological consequences have occurred in the context of professional commitment hearings. Judicial hearings, which have been more sensitive to issues of due process, may have more positive psychological consequences. Ultimately, decisions about the desirability of different judicial procedures need to be responsive to both the objective quality of the decisions made and to the psychological consequences of varying types of decision-making procedure.

97. Bersoff, *supra* note 5.

[20]

Social Justice: Outcome and Procedure

Tom R. Tyler

New York University, USA

A review of recent research demonstrates that people are more willing to accept decisions when they feel that those decisions are made through decision-making procedures they view as fair. Studies of procedural justice judgements further suggest that people evaluate fairness primarily through criteria that can be provided to all the parties to a conflict: whether there are opportunities to participate; whether the authorities are neutral; the degree to which people trust the motives of the authorities; and whether people are treated with dignity and respect during the process. These findings are optimistic and suggest that authorities have considerable ability to bridge differences and interests and values through the use of fair decision-making procedures. The limits to the effectiveness of such procedural approaches are also outlined.

Une recension des recherches récentes montre que les gens sont prêts à accepter des décisions quand ils sentent que ces décisions sont prises à la suite d'une procèdure décisionnelle qu'ils considèrent équitable. De plus, les études sur les jugements dans les procèdure judiciaires suggèrent que les gens évaluent l'équité prioritairement sur la base des critères fournies à toutes les parties en conflit: possibilités de participation: neutralité des autorités; confiance dans les motifs des autorités; et procèdure qui traite les personnes avec dignité et respect. Ces résultats optimistes suggèrent que les autorités peuvent, par des procèdures équitables de prise de décision, concilier des différences, des intérêts et des valeurs. Les limites à l'efficacité de ces approches procèdurales sont aussi soulignées.

My goal is to review recent psychological research on justice. This is a good time for such a review. I believe that recent research findings about social justice can truly make a contribution to our understanding of how to resolve conflicts and promote stable and lasting peaceful relationships among individuals and groups. In this review I will focus primarily upon issues of process and procedural justice. I will both discuss this area of research and describe its implications.

In their book on procedural justice, John Thibaut and Laurens Walker (1975) prefaced their research by commenting that:

> One prediction that can be advanced with sure confidence is that human life on this planet faces a steady increase in the potential for interpersonal and intergroup conflict. The rising expectations of a continuously more numerous population in competition for control over rapidly diminishing resources create the conditions for an increasingly dangerous existence. It seems clear that the quality of future human life is likely to be importantly determined by the effectiveness with which disputes can be managed, moderated, or resolved. Procedures or methods that may be put to this task of conflict resolution therefore claim our attention.

This comment is as relevant today as it was when it was made in 1975. Although the prospects of global war may have diminished, local wars continue to flourish. Further, it is not possible to say that the threat of nuclear war has been ended, and the threat of chemical and biological war in the future seems to be increasing. There remains a considerable arena of international conflict to which the research findings of psychologists can be directed. On a more mundane level, the many interpersonal and intergroup conflicts that occur within societies and organized groups certainly continue. Now, as in the past, we need to seek ways to resolve conflicts and promote harmonious interpersonal and intergroup relationships.

One clear possible avenue for the peaceful resolution to conflicts is through an understanding of the psychology of social justice. People's views about what is just or fair are a social facilitator through which the interaction among people and groups is enabled. I think of justice as akin to the oil within an engine. It allows the many parts within the engine to interact without the friction that generates heat and leads to breakdown. Similarly, justice allows people and groups to interact without conflict and societal breakdown. Just as a car can suffer mechanical breakdown, social interactions can break down amid conflict and hostility. I will argue that social justice minimizes such breakdowns and contributes to the continuation of productive interactions among people—in the manner hoped for by Thibaut and Walker. As a consequence, it is an important topic of concern to diplomats and others who seek to prevent, contain, or end social conflicts.

The especially striking thing about social justice is that it is a social concept that exists only in the minds of the members of an ongoing interaction, a group, an organization, or a society. Hence, justice is a socially created concept that, unlike oil, has no physical reality. It exists and is useful to the degree that it is shared among a group of people. This shared idea facilitates the task of social coordination within the group that holds it or among groups with common conceptions of justice.

For justice to be effective, it is important that people's behaviour be shaped by their judgements about what is right, separately from judgements about what is personally beneficial. For justice to be effective, it must be able to gain acceptance of rules and decisions that depart from individual or group self-interest.

It is also important that people share a set of principles for defining justice. If one person regards a jury trial as the fair way to resolve a conflict, while another person thinks that trial by combat is the fair way to resolve the same dispute, both parties may be interested in having a fair procedure, but they will not be able to agree about what such a fair procedure would look like.

The basic problem that has to be solved via social cooperation is that everyone cannot have everything they want at the same time. Everyone cannot have the resources they desire for themselves and/or the groups to which they belong; they cannot live in a group, society, or organization that always follows the policies they prefer; and they cannot have their preferred status or social position for themselves and the groups to which they belong. Hence, people need to be willing to accept outcomes, policies, and status that they do not view as desirable.

Norms of social justice have evolved to regulate co-operation by specifying reasonable solutions to conflicts that arise among people trying to coordinate their behaviours. These justice principles are the rules that will govern people's coordination of their social interactions. The question is whether the rules of social coordination are effective in managing the activity of group members, that is, in resolving conflicts and disagreements when people cannot have everything that they want.

The first wave of social justice research began with the development of the concept of relative deprivation during the period following the Second World War (Tyler, Boeckmann, Smith, & Huo, 1997; Tyler & Smith, 1997). The theory of relative deprivation argues that satisfaction/dissatisfaction in social situations is not a direct function of the objective quality of the rewards or resources that people receive from others. Instead, satisfaction is socially determined through comparisons between one's own outcomes and some type of standard. The same objective outcome can be satisfying or upsetting depending upon the standard to which it is compared. The nature of these standards is socially determined. As a consequence, people shape their subjective experience through their choice of comparison standards. The roots of justice theory lie in the insights of relative deprivation theory. With justice judgements, comparisons occur, and the standards of comparison used are principles of justice.

There are two types of justice judgements that might potentially be of interest. The first are judgements about distributive justice. Distributive justice examines people's views about what is a fair outcome or distribution of resources. Norms of distributive justice effectively resolve coordination problems when people accept them and defer to decisions that give them less than they want when they think the outcomes they have received are fair. To the degree that people defer because allocation decisions are just or fair, judgements about distributive justice are an important factor in creating and maintaining peace.

DISTRIBUTIVE JUSTICE

The first important type of research on distributive justice focused upon the distributive justice norm of equity. Equity theory argues that fairness means that people's rewards should be proportional to their contributions. Equity researchers hoped to be able to resolve conflicts by making outcome allocations in response to people's sense of what constitutes a fair outcome. It was hoped that people would be willing to accept fair outcomes, as opposed to being angry if they did not receive everything they wanted. This willingness to defer to justice was seen as one way of lessening conflicts over pay and promotion within work settings.

Although research in work settings has supported the importance of outcome fairness judgements in shaping people's satisfaction with pay and promotions, equity theory based approaches have not been found to be as effective as researchers hoped they would be at resolving conflicts. The problem with applying equity concepts comes out of people's tendency to exaggerate the importance or value of their contributions to groups. Because of this tendency, it has proved difficult to provide people with the level of rewards they regard as fair, relative to their subjective sense of their own contributions. Hence, research on outcome fairness has not proved as useful in resolving social conflicts as its proponents originally thought possible.

Further, equity studies have found that issues of outcomes, such as concerns about pay and promotion, are often not the key concerns that drive unhappiness in interactions with others. For example, Messick, Bloom, Boldizar, and Samuelson (1985) asked people to list unfair behaviours others had enacted toward them. They found that respondents seldom mentioned unfair allocations. Instead, they focused upon issues such as being treated with consideration and politeness. Similarly, Mikula, Petri, and Tanzer (1990, p. 133) found that "a considerable proportion of the injustices which are reported . . . refer to the manner in which people are treated in interpersonal interactions and encounters." I will refer to these concerns about the quality of the treatment received from others, whether other people or third-party authorities, as elements of procedural justice. The findings outlined suggest that outcomes are less central to the feelings and actions of the individuals who receive those outcomes than is supposed by theories of distributive justice.

Recent distributive justice research suggests another important area within which outcome fairness judgements may be important. This is in people's willingness to help others. Here the concern is whether people will find the outcomes received by others to be unfair and, if they do, whether they will be willing to take actions to help those who are receiving too little. A key distributive justice question is when those who are advantaged are willing to redistribute resources to the disadvantaged. Montada and Schneider (1989) found that evaluations of justice and deservedness were central to emotional reactions to those who are less well off. Both moral outrage, in which society and social institutions are blamed for the disadvantaged, and existential guilt, in which people feel personal blame for the disadvantaged, led to a readiness to perform prosocial actions. Interestingly, although both existential guilt and moral outrage led people to engage in actions, such as spending money, to help the disadvantaged, political actions were shaped only by moral outrage.

As justice theory predicts, responses to the disadvantaged were not predicted by sympathy or by self-interest. That is, people are not motivated by sympathy or empathy; and they act even when it is not in their self-interest to do so. In fact, people were willing to engage in redistributive behaviours that were not in their self-interest when they felt that others were entitled to help. That entitlement was recognized when the situation of others departed from a person's sense of what was just and fair.

PROCEDURAL JUSTICE

Thibaut and Walker's hope was that people would be willing to accept outcomes because those outcomes were fairly decided upon—that is because of the justice of the decision-making procedures (procedural justice). Their work developed as a second wave of justice research, following the era of equity research.

I am pleased to say that more recent research on procedural justice suggests a much more optimistic conclusion about the utility of social justice as a mechanism for resolving social conflicts than do the results of early research on distributive justice. The results of procedural justice research are optimistic about the ability of social authorities to bridge differences in interests and values and find differences that the parties to a dispute will accept. Further, the findings of procedural justice research suggest how authorities should act to pursue such procedural justice strategies.

Thibaut and Walker (1975) performed the first systematic set of experiments designed to show the impact of procedural justice. Their studies demonstrate that people's assessments of the fairness of third-party decision-making procedures shape their satisfaction with their outcomes. This finding has been widely confirmed

in subsequent laboratory studies of procedural justice (Lind & Tyler, 1988). The original hope of Thibaut and Walker was that the willingness of all the parties to a dispute to accept decisions that they view as fairly arrived at would provide a mechanism through which social conflicts could be resolved.

Subsequent studies have found that when third-party decisions are fairly made people are more willing to accept them voluntarily (Kitzman & Emery, 1993; Lind, Greenberg, Scott, & Welchans, 1998; Lind, Kulik, Ambrose, & de Vera Park, 1993; MacCoun, Lind, Hensler, Bryant, & Ebener, 1988; Wissler, 1995). What is striking about these studies is that the procedural justice effects are found in studies of real disputes, in real settings, involving actual disputants. They confirm the earlier experimental findings of Thibaut and Walker.

Procedural justice judgements are found to have an especially important role in shaping adherence to agreements over time (Pruitt, Peirce, McGillicuddy, Welton, & Castrianno, 1993; Pruitt, Peirce, Zubek, Welton, & Nochajski, 1990). Pruitt and his colleagues studied the factors that lead those involved in disputes to adhere to mediation agreements that end those disputes. They found that the procedural fairness of the initial mediation session was a central determinant of whether people were adhering to the agreement 6 months later.

Beyond reactions to particular decisions, groups generally benefit when those within them engage in cooperative actions that help the group. As was true in the case of accepting the decisions of authorities, one way that groups can gain desired cooperative behaviours is through shaping the costs and benefits associated with cooperation. People can be made to accept decisions by threats of punishment or incentives for cooperation. However, groups benefit when the people within them voluntarily engage in actions that help their group out of internal feelings of identification with and commitment to the group. Within formal organizations such actions have been labelled "extra-role" behaviours, since they involve nonrequired actions that help the group. Research suggests that people voluntarily cooperate with groups when they judge that group decisions are being made fairly (Bies, Martin, & Brockner, 1993; Moorman, 1991; Moorman, Niehoff, & Organ, 1993; Neihoff & Moorman, 1993; Tyler, 1999). Hence, the use of fair decision-making procedures has the general effect of encouraging people to voluntarily help the groups to which they belong.

A common response of groups seeking to manage themselves is to organize by creating rules and establishing authorities and institutions to facilitate social regulation. These authorities can gain compliance with rules through the use of rewards or threats of punishment. However, such strategies are costly and unwieldly. As a consequence, authority structures based upon compliance are inefficient and ineffective. The efficiency and effectiveness of rules and authorities is enhanced when group members are willing to voluntarily support the empowerment of authorities and to willingly defer to the decisions of those authorities and to follow social rules. The willingness to defer to social rules flows from judgements that authorities are legitimate and ought to be obeyed. Studies of the legitimacy of authority suggest that people decide how legitimate authorities are, and how much to defer to those authorities and to their decisions, primarily by assessing the fairness of their decision-making procedures. Hence, using fair decision-making procedures is the key to developing, maintaining, and enhancing the legitimacy of rules and authorities and gaining voluntary deference to social rules (Fondacaro & Dunkle, 1998; Kim & Mauborgne, 1991, 1993; Sparks, Bottoms, & Hay, 1996; Tyler, 1990).

Again, procedural justice is especially important in gaining deference to rules over time. For example, Paternoster and his colleagues interviewed men who had dealt with police officers who were called to their homes because they were abusing their wives (i.e. due to domestic violence). They explored which aspects of police behaviour during the initial call predicted subsequent compliance with the law against domestic violence among the men interviewed. It was found that those men who felt fairly treated during the initial encounter with the police adhered to the law in the future. Interestingly, procedural justice judgements during this initial encounter with the police were more powerful predictors of subsequent law-abiding behaviour than were factors such as whether the police arrested the man during the initial contact, fined them, and/or took them into the police station (Paternoster, Brame, Bachman, & Sherman, 1997).

As this research on deference to authorities suggests, procedural justice also shapes people's willingness to defer to policies that are designed to help others. For example, advantaged citizens are more likely to accept policies that redistribute resources and opportunities to disadvantaged citizens if they think that the government agencies making the policies make their policies fairly (Smith & Tyler, 1996). Citizens are generally more willing to accept policies that they disagree with when they feel that government policy-making processes are fair (Ebreo, Linn, & Vining, 1996; Tyler & Mitchell, 1994).

The research outlined here has primarily been conducted within the context of organized groups that are ongoing and have existing authority structures. These authorities are typically widely viewed as legitimate and, hence, as being entitled to be obeyed. However, when people regard authorities as less legitimate, they are less willing to defer to their decisions because those decisions are fairly made. Instead, they focus upon the favourability of the decisions made (Tyler, 1997a). It is more difficult for authorities lacking legitimacy to bridge issues and problems and gain deference to common policies. When new authorities are created, for example the New Parliament in Russia, or the European Union, a central problem for authorities is how to legitimize those new political authorities. Here procedural justice also plays a key role. If people view or personally experience the authorities as making decisions fairly, they increas-

ingly view them as legitimate. Over time, this legitimacy shapes deference, which becomes increasingly independent of the favourability of policies and decisions. Similarly, studies of work organizations show that they often adopt symbols and decision-making procedures associated with justice and fairness in an effort to legitimize their authority structures and encourage employees to defer to organizational authorities and to identify with the organization.

Of course, procedural justice effects are not confined to hierarchical relationships or established groups. Studies suggest that people are influenced by issues of procedural justice across a variety of types of social settings. Barrett-Howard and Tyler (1986) systematically varied situations across the four basic dimensions which Deutsch argues represent the fundamental dimensions of social situations. They found that procedural justice concerns generally dominated people's reactions to allocations in all situations. Similarly, Sondag and Sheppard (1995) utilized the situational typology created by Fiske (1992) as a basis for identifying possible types of authority structures. They found that procedural issues were important across all types of social situations.

JUSTICE AND INTERNALIZED VALUES

Fair decision-making procedures encourage voluntary cooperation with groups because they lead to identification with and loyalty and commitment toward groups (Folger & Konovsky, 1989; Korsgaard, Schweiger, & Sapienza, 1995; McFarlin & Sweeney, 1992; Schaubroeck, May, & Brown, 1994; Taylor, Tracy, Renard, Harrison, & Carroll, 1995). Similarly, procedural justice promotes deference to social rules because it promotes the belief that authorities are legitimate (Tyler, 1997a). This internal value is important because when people feel that authorities ought to be obeyed, they take the obligation to do this on themselves, and voluntarily defer to authorities and rules.

In both of these cases, procedural justice is central to creating and maintaining internal values that support voluntary cooperative behaviour on the part of the members of groups. The importance of developing and maintaining such values is increasingly being emphasized, as social scientists recognize the limits of strategies of conflict resolution which are based upon seeking to shape the rewards and punishments received by the parties to a dispute. Recent social science thinking has been dominated by rational choice models of the person. As a consequence, command and control, deterrence, or social control strategies have dominated discussions about social regulation. These strategies focus upon the individual as a calculative actor, thinking, feeling, and behaving in terms of potential rewards and costs in their immediate environment.

Increasingly, social scientists have recognized the limits of command and control approaches to managing conflict. In political and legal settings, authorities have recognized that both social regulation (Tyler, 1990, 1999) and the encouragement of voluntary civic behaviour (Green & Shapiro, 1994) are difficult when authorities can only rely upon their ability to reward and/or punish citizens. Similarly, organizational theorists are recognizing the difficulties of managing employees using command and control strategies (Pfeffer, 1994). The alternative to such strategies is to focus on approaches based upon appeals to internal values. If people have internal values that lead them to voluntarily defer to authorities and to act in prosocial ways that help the group, then authorities need not seek to compel such behaviour through promises of reward or threats of punishment. They can instead rely upon people's willingness to engage in the behaviour voluntarily.

Research suggests that using fair decision-making procedures is central to the development and maintenance of supportive internal values. Those authorities that use fair decision-making procedures are viewed as more legitimate, and people more willingly defer to their decisions. This produces uniformity of behaviour in line with organizational rules and the decisions of organizational authorities. When authorities want people to defer their own desires in the interests of the group, they can obtain such behaviour by calling upon people's views that they are legitimate.

In addition, organizations that use fair decision-making procedures encourage commitment and identification on the part of their members, which leads to voluntary cooperative behaviour. People want the group to succeed and engage in behaviours to help achieve that objective. In other words, people willingly engage their own creative efforts and energies into efforts to advance the interests of the group. They might help others do their jobs during a crisis, help and encourage new group members, engage in activities that are nonobservable, and hence will not be rewarded, but which help the group.

In other words, the recognition of the importance of creating a "civic culture" or an "organizational culture," which supports the development and maintenance of internal values among group members, is increasing as the limits of command and control approaches to managing conflict become clearer. Procedural justice is central to both developing and maintaining judgements that authorities are legitimate and feelings of commitment and identification with groups, organizations, and societies.

These findings demonstrate that providing people with procedural justice can be an important and viable mechanism for gaining deference to decisions. This effect occurs across a variety of settings, including both hierarchical and nonhierarchical situations, in political, legal, managerial, interpersonal, familial, and educational settings, and when important issues of outcomes and treatment are involved. Hence, conflict resolution efforts can gain viability through the use of fair decision-making procedures.

WHAT IS A FAIR PROCEDURE?

There are two levels upon which we can address the question of what type of procedures people think are fair. One is to focus upon possible legal procedures, and to discuss whether people view them as fair. When we do so, it becomes clear that informal legal procedures are viewed as particularly fair. In fact, in civil cases, defendants rate mediation to be fairer than a formal trial, and it is typically rated as more satisfactory (Tyler, 1997b). In criminal cases, defendants rate plea bargaining to be fairer than a formal trial (Tyler, 1997b). In terms of procedural fairness, giving people fair procedures means putting more emphasis upon informal dispute resolution.

What characteristics lead people to associate informal justice with the procedural fairness? Studies typically find seven, eight, or even more elements that contribute to assessments of their fairness (Lissak & Sheppard, 1983; Sheppard & Lewicki, 1987; Tyler, 1988). However, four elements of procedures are the primary factors that contribute to judgements about their fairness: opportunities for participation (voice), the neutrality of the forum, the trustworthiness of the authorities, and the degree to which people receive treatment with dignity and respect.

Participation

People feel more fairly treated if they are allowed to participate in the resolution of their problems or conflicts by presenting their suggestions about what should be done. Such opportunities are referred to as process control or voice. The positive effects of participation have been widely found, beginning in the work of Thibaut and Walker (1975). These effects have been found in studies of plea bargaining (Houlden, 1980), sentencing hearings (Heinz & Kerstetter, 1979), and mediation (Kitzmann & Emery, 1993; MacCoun, Lind, Hensler, Bryant, & Ebener, 1988; Shapiro & Brett, 1993). In all of these diverse settings, people feel more fairly treated when they are given an opportunity to make arguments about what should be done to resolve a problem or conflict.

Participation effects have been found to be enhanced when people feel that the things they say are shaping the outcomes of the dispute—an instrumental influence (see Shapiro & Brett, 1993). However, voice effects have not been found to be dependent just upon having control over the actual outcomes of conflicts. People have also been found to value the opportunity to express their views to decision-makers in situations in which they believe that what they are saying has little or no influence upon the decisions being made (Lind, Kanfer, & Earley, 1990; Tyler, 1987). For example, victims value the opportunity to speak at sentencing hearings irrespective of whether their arguments influence the sentences given to the criminals involved (Heinz & Kerstetter, 1979).

People are primarily interested in sharing the discussion over the issues involved in their problem or conflict, not in controlling decisions about how to handle it. In fact, people often look to societal authorities to make decisions about which legal or managerial principles ought to govern the resolution of their dispute. In other words, they expect societal authorities to make final decisions about how to act based upon what they have said.

The finding that people value the opportunity to participate by expressing their opinions and stating their case helps to explain why people like mediation. Mediation is typically rated as providing greater opportunities for participation than formal trials (McEwen & Maiman, 1984). Similarly, defendants involved in disposing of felony charges against themselves indicate that they have greater opportunities to participate in plea bargaining than in a formal trial (Casper, Tyler, & Fisher, 1988), and they rate plea bargaining to be a fairer procedure for resolving their case.

Neutrality

People are influenced by judgements about the honesty, impartiality, and objectivity of the authorities with whom they are dealing. They believe that authorities should not allow their personal values and biases to enter into their decisions, which should be made based upon rules and facts. Basically, people seek a "level playing field" in which no one is unfairly disadvantaged. If they believe that the authorities are following impartial rules and making factual, objective decisions, they think procedures are fairer.

Trustworthiness of Authorities

Another factor shaping people's views about the fairness of a procedure is their assessment of the motives of the third-party authority responsible for resolving their dispute. People recognize that third parties typically have considerable discretion to implement formal procedures in varying ways, and they are concerned about the motivation underlying the decisions made by the authority with which they are dealing. They judge whether that person is benevolent and caring, is concerned about their situation and their concerns and needs, considers their arguments, tries to do what is right for them, and tries to be fair. All of these elements combine to shape a general assessment of the person's trustworthiness.

Interestingly, judgements about the trustworthiness of the authorities are the primary factors shaping evaluations of the fairness of the procedures used by those authorities (Tyler & Lind, 1992). The importance of trust is illustrated by a finding of the literature on participation. People only value the opportunity to speak to authorities if they believe that the authority is sincerely considering their arguments. They must trust that the authority sincerely considered their arguments, even if they were then rejected, before having had the chance to participate leads to the evaluation of procedures as fairer.

How can authorities communicate that they are trying to be fair? A key antecedent of trust is justification. When authorities are presenting their decisions to the people influenced by them, they need to make clear that they have listened to and considered the arguments made. They can do so by accounting for their decisions. Such accounts should clearly state the arguments made by the various parties to the dispute. They should also explain how those arguments have been considered and why they have been accepted or rejected.

I have already outlined the importance of neutrality to assessments of the fairness of procedures. There is considerable evidence that the basis of the authoritativeness—the ability of authorities to gain deference to their decisions—is shifting from a neutrality base to a trust base. That is, in the past authorities have often gained their authoritativeness through the neutral application of rules, i.e. through the use of facts and formal decision-making procedures that are objective and factual in character. A person, for example, can go to any police officer or judge and receive more or less equivalent treatment and outcomes, since the particular authority with whom they are dealing will be following universal rules. Having personal knowledge about the specific authority involved in an interaction is not important. On the other hand, trust is linked to judgements about particular authorities. Hence, trust is linked to particularized personal connections between citizens and authorities. For example, people might get to know a beat cop because that person patrols their neighbourhood. They might trust that person because they have dealt with them, know their motives and values, and consequently feel that they can trust them.

An organization can gain deference by having formal rules that reflect neutrality. It can also gain deference through the personal relationships that exist between employees and their own particular supervisors. The former approach reflects a neutrality model of procedural fairness, the latter approach a trust-based model. Similarly, the police can gain deference because they are viewed as following professional rules of conduct and uniform procedures, or particular police officers can be respected and known in their communities and can, through these personalized connections, gain deference.

Treatment with Dignity and Respect

People value having respect shown for their rights and for their status within society. They are very concerned that, in the process of dealing with authorities, their dignity as people and as members of society is recognized and acknowledged. Since politeness and respect are essentially unrelated to the outcomes people receive when they deal with social authorities, the importance that people place upon this affirmation of their status is especially relevant to conflict resolution. More than any other issue, treatment with dignity and respect is something that authorities can give to everyone with whom they deal.

LIMITS TO EFFECTIVENESS OF PROCEDURAL JUSTICE MECHANISMS

I have presented a generally optimistic picture of the viability of procedural strategies for resolving conflicts. However, there may be limits to the range within which such strategies will be effective. I want to discuss one type of potential limit, the impact of the nature of the society within which conflicts are being resolved.

The first issue is that of *social consensus*. There have been widespread concerns about the potential of cultural backgrounds to disrupt the viability of procedures strategies. There are two ways that such disruption might occur. First, cultural background might change the degree to which people care about whether they receive procedural justice. Second, it might change the criteria by which people define the fairness of procedures. How important are such concerns?

Research among people of varying ethnicity in the United States is fairly optimistic. Little difference is found in the importance placed upon procedural justice by the members of varying ethnic groups. Both whites and minorities are more influenced by the fairness of the procedures they experience than they are by the fairness of the outcomes they receive through third-party conflict resolution decisions (Huo & Tyler, in press). Further, studies consistently find that whites and minorities define the meaning of procedural fairness in the same way (Huo & Tyler, in press; Tyler, 1988, 1994). Hence, these findings are fairly optimistic about the ability of procedures to be robust across differences in ethnicity.

Interestingly, research also finds that procedures are robust across ideologies. That is, people who differ in their fundamental social values or political ideologies are often found to agree about whether or not a particular procedure is fair (Bierbrauer, 1997; Peterson, 1994; Tyler, 1994). This is especially striking, since ideological differences have a strong impact upon views about what constitutes a fair outcome. In this respect, procedural justice may be a better bridge across social and ideological groups than is distributive justice.

These findings do not suggest that there is some type of universal fair procedure that is appropriate in all situations. On the contrary, the same studies suggest that people view different procedural elements as being key to defining procedural fairness within particular situations. For example, in a conflict between people, the opportunity to state one's views is central to procedures that are viewed as fair. However, in other situations opportunities to participate are less important to judgements about the fairness of procedures. People differentiate among situations and apply a different model of fairness to different situations. So, we know that people are not thinking about procedural fairness in simple-minded terms. This makes it especially interesting that there is little evidence of differences linked to ethnicity or gender.

This research suggests an optimistic conclusion about the robustness of procedures. They seem to be viable mechanisms for bridging differences among people of varying ethnic and ideological backgrounds. However, it is important to note that not all research suggests that procedures are robust. For example, studies of decision making in political settings suggest that majority and minority factions often disagree about what constitutes a fair decision-making procedure for their organization (Azzi, 1993a, b).

The second issue is *social categorization*. Basically, we find that people are less concerned about justice when they are dealing with people who are outside of their own ethnic or social group (Tyler, Lind, Ohbuchi, Sugawara, & Huo, 1998). For example, when people have a dispute with someone who is not a member of their own social group, they pay more attention to the personal favourability of a proposed dispute resolution when deciding whether to accept it. If the dispute is with someone who is a member of their own social group, they pay more attention to whether they have been treated fairly when deciding whether to accept a proposed dispute resolution. Hence, group boundaries may pose a limit to the effective scope of justice.

This points to a strategy for dealing with conflict. We need to encourage people to frame their group memberships in terms of superordinate categorizations that build across subgroups. Instead of seeing two separate groups, we want people to see one common group. This suggestion develops from the prior recognition within social psychology that superordinate categorization encourages cooperation within the group (Gaertner, Dovidio, Anastasio, Bachman, & Rust, 1993). We need to focus on how people frame their group boundaries. After all, if we think of ourselves as members of the "human race" then everyone is a member of our group.

The third issue is that of *identification*. People are more likely to care about justice when they identify with the group within which their conflict is occurring, and with the authorities responsible for dealing with the conflict. Several studies support this argument by showing that people who identify more strongly with an organization or society rely more heavily on justice judgements when deciding whether to defer to the decisions of authorities (Huo, Smith, Tyler, & Lind, 1996; Smith & Tyler, 1996; Tyler & Degoey, 1995).

This also points to a strategy. We need to focus on building up people's identification with society and with social institutions. If people identify more strongly with the group that authorities represent, they are more concerned about whether or not they receive fair treatment, and less concerned about receiving favourable outcomes. How can we build positive identification? By treating those within groups in procedurally fair ways. Research suggests that procedural justice builds commitment to the group, identification with the group, and feelings of obligation to authorities and group rules.

CONCLUSIONS

As this review of justice research makes clear, there are important reasons for optimism concerning the viability of justice-based strategies for conflict resolution. In particular, approaches based upon an understanding of people's views about fair decision-making procedures have been very successful in gaining deference to decisions and to rules, authorities, and institutions more generally. This does not mean, of course, that people do not care about outcomes. They do. However, they do not care only about outcomes. On the contrary, their feelings and behaviours have an important ethical and moral component. This ethical/moral aspect to people's reactions to others in social settings provides an approach to the constructive resolution of social conflicts.

REFERENCES

Azzi, A. (1993a). Group representation and procedural justice in multigroup decision-making bodies. *Social Justice Research, 6*, 195–217.

Azzi, A. (1993b). Implicit and category-based allocations of decision-making power in majority-minority relations. *Journal of Experimental Social Psychology, 29*, 203–228.

Barrett-Howard, E., & Tyler, T.R. (1986). Procedural justice as a criterion in allocation decisions. *Journal of Personality and Social Psychology, 50*, 296–304.

Bierbrauer, G. (July, 1997). Political ideology and allocation preferences: What do Turkish immigrants in Germany deserve? Potsdam, Germany: International Network for Social Justice Research Conference.

Bies, R.J., Martin, C.L., & Brockner, J. (1993). Just laid off, but still a "good citizen:" Only if the process is fair. *Employee Responsibilities and Rights Journal, 6*, 227–248.

Casper, J.D., Tyler, T.R., & Fisher, B. (1988). Procedural justice in felony cases. *Law and Society Review, 22*, 483–507.

Ebreo, A., Linn, N., & Vining, J. (1996). The impact of procedural justice on opinions of public policy: Solid waste management as an example. *Journal of Applied Social Psychology, 26*, 1259–1285.

Fiske, A.P. (1992). The four elementary forms of sociality: Framework for a unified theory of social relations. *Psychological Review, 99*, 689–723.

Folger, R., & Konovsky, M.A. (1989). Effects of procedural and distributive justice on reactions to pay raise decisions. *Academy of Management Journal, 32*, 115–130.

Fondacaro, M., & Dunkle, M.E. (1998). *Procedural justice in resolving family disputes.* Unpublished manuscript.

Gaertner, S.L., Dovidio, J.F., Anastasio, P.A., Bachman, B.A., & Rust, M.C. (1993). The common ingroup identity model. *European Review of Social Psychology, 4*, 1–26.

Green, D.P., & Shapiro, I. (1994). *Pathologies of rational choice theory.* New Haven, CT: Yale University Press.

Heinz, A.M., & Kerstetter, W.A. (1979). Pretrial settlement conference: Evaluation of a reform in plea bargaining. *Law and Society Review, 13*, 349–366.

Houlden, P. (1980). The impact of procedural modifications on evaluations of plea bargaining. *Law and Society Review, 15*, 267–292.

Huo, Y.J., Smith, H.J., Tyler, T.R., & Lind, E.A. (1996). Superordinate identification, subgroup identification, and justice concerns: Is separatism the problem, is assimilation the answer. *Psychological Science, 7*, 40–45.

Huo, Y.J., & Tyler, T.R. (in press). Ethnic diversity and the viability of organizations: The role of procedural justice in bridging differences. In J. Greenberg & R. Cropanzano

(Ed.), *Advances in organizational justice.* San Francisco, CA: New Lexington Press.

Kim, W.C., & Mauborgne, R.A. (1991). Implementing global strategies: The role of procedural justice. *Strategic Management Journal, 12*, 125–143.

Kim, W.C., & Mauborgne, R.A. (1993). Procedural justice, attitudes, and subsidiary top management compliance with multinationals' corporate strategic decisions. *Academy of Management Journal, 36*, 502–526.

Kitzman, K.M., & Emery, R.E. (1993). Procedural justice and parents' satisfaction in a field study of child custody dispute resolution. *Law and Human Behavior, 17*, 553–567.

Korsgaard, M.A., Schweiger, D.M., & Sapienza, H.J. (1995). Building commitment, attachment, and trust in strategic decision-making teams: The role of procedural justice. *Academy of Management Journal, 38*, 60–84.

Lind, E.A., Greenberg, J., Scott, K.S., & Welchans, T.D. (1998). *The winding road from employee to complaint: Situational and psychological determinants of wrongful termination claims.* San Diego, CA: Academy of Management.

Lind, E.A., Kanfer, R., & Earley, P.C. (1990). Voice, control, and procedural justice. *Journal of Personality and Social Psychology, 59*, 952–959.

Lind, E.A., Kulik, C.T., Ambrose, M., & de Vera Park, M. (1993). Individual and corporate dispute resolution. *Administrative Science Quarterly, 38*, 224–251.

Lind, E.A., MacCoun, R.J., Ebener, P.A., Felstiner, W.L.F., Hensler, D.R., Resnik, J., & Tyler, T.R. (1989). *The perception of justice: Tort litigants' views of trial, court-annexed arbitration, and judicial settlement conferences.* Santa Monica, CA: Rand.

Lind, E.A., & Tyler, T.R. (1988). *The social psychology of procedural justice.* New York: Plenum Press.

Lissak, R.I., & Sheppard, B.H. (1983). Beyond fairness: The criterion problem in research on dispute resolution. *Journal of Applied Social Psychology, 13*, 45–65.

MacCoun, R.J., Lind, E.A., Hensler, D.R., Bryant, D.L., & Ebener, P.A. (1988). *Alternative adjudication: An evaluation of the New Jersey automobile arbitration program.* Santa Monica, CA: Rand.

McEwen, C., & Maiman, R.J. (1984). Mediation in small claims court. *Law and Society Review, 18*, 11–49.

McFarlin, D.B., & Sweeney, P.D. (1992). Distributive and procedural justice as predictors of satisfaction with personal and organizational outcomes. *Academy of Management Journal, 35*, 626–637.

Messick, D.M., Bloom, S., Boldizar, J.P., & Samuelson, C.D. (1985). Why we are fairer than others. *Journal of Experimental Social Psychology, 21*, 389–399.

Mikula, G., Petri, B., & Tanzer, N. (1990). What people regard as unjust: Types and structures of everyday experiences of injustice. *European Journal of Social Psychology, 22*, 133–149.

Montada, L. (1995). Applying social psychology: The case of redistributions in unified Germany. *Social Justice Research, 8*, 73–90.

Montada, L., & Schneider, A. (1989). Justice and emotional reactions to the disadvantaged. *Social Justice Research, 3*, 313–344.

Moorman, R.H. (1991). Relationship between organizational justice and organizational citizenship behaviours: Do fairness perceptions influence employee citizenship? *Journal of Applied Psychology, 76*, 845–855.

Moorman, R.H., Niehoff, B.P., & Organ, D.W. (1993). Treating employees fairly and organizational citizenship behaviour. *Employee Responsibilities and Rights Journal, 6*, 209–225.

Niehoff, B.P., & Moorman, R.H. (1993). Justice as a mediator of the relationship between methods of monitoring and organizational citizenship behaviour. *Academy of Management Journal, 36*, 527–556.

Paternoster, R., Brame, R., Bachman, R., & Sherman, L.W. (1997). Do fair procedures matter?: The effect of procedural justice on spouse assault. *Law and Society Review, 31*, 163–204.

Peterson, R. (1994). The role of values in predicting fairness judgements and support of affirmative action. *Journal of Social Issues, 50*, 95–116.

Pfeffer, J. (1994). *Competitive advantage through people.* Cambridge, MA: Harvard University Press.

Pruitt, D.G., Peirce, R.S., McGillicuddy, N.B., Welton, G.L., & Castrianno, L.M. (1993). Long-term success in mediation. *Law and Human Behavior, 17*, 313–330.

Pruitt, D.G., Peirce, R.S., Zubek, J.M., Welton, G.L., & Nochajski, T.H. (1990). Goal achievement, procedural justice, and the success of mediation. *The International Journal of Conflict Management, 1*, 33–45.

Schaubroeck, J., May, D.R., & Brown, F.W. (1994). Procedural justice explanations and employee reactions to economic hardship. *Journal of Applied Psychology, 79*, 455–460.

Shapiro, D., & Brett, J. (1993). Comparing three processes underlying judgements of procedural justice. *Journal of Personality and Social Psychology, 65*, 1167–1177.

Sheppard, B.H., & Lewicki, R.J. (1987). Toward general principles of managerial fairness. *Social Justice Research, 1*, 161–176.

Smith, H.J., & Tyler, T.R. (1996). Justice and power. *European Journal of Social Psychology, 26*, 171–200.

Smith, H.J., & Tyler, T.R. (1997). Choosing the right pond: The influence of the status of one's group and one's status in that group on self-esteem and group-oriented behaviours. *Journal of Experimental Social Psychology, 33*, 146–170.

Sondag, H., & Sheppard, B. (August, 1995). *Evaluating alternative models for allocating scarce resources: A relational approach to procedural justice and social structure.* Vancouver: Academy of Management.

Sparks, R., Bottoms, A., & Hay, W. (1996). *Prisons and the problem of order.* Oxford: Clarendon.

Taylor, M.S., Tracy, K.B., Renard, M.K., Harrison, J.K., & Carroll, S.J. (1995). Due process in performance appraisal: A quasi-experiment in procedural justice. *Administrative Science Quarterly, 40*, 495–523.

Thibaut, J., & Walker, L. (1975). *Procedural justice.* Hillsdale, NJ: Lawrence Erlbaum Associates Inc.

Tyler, T.R. (1987). Conditions leading to value-expressive effects in judgements of procedural justice: A test of four models. *Journal of Personality and Social Psychology, 52*, 333–344.

Tyler, T.R. (1988). What is procedural justice? Criteria used by citizens to assess the fairness of legal procedures. *Law and Society Review, 22*, 301–355.

Tyler, T.R. (1990). *Why people obey the law.* New Haven, CT: Yale University Press.

Tyler, T.R. (1994). Governing amid diversity: The effect of fair decision-making procedures on the legitimacy of government. *Law and Society Review, 28*, 809–831.

Tyler, T.R. (1997a). The psychology of legitimacy. *Personality and Social Psychology Review, 1*, 323–345.

Tyler, T.R. (1997b). Citizen discontent with legal procedures: A social science perspective on civil procedure reform. *American Journal of Comparative Law, 45*, 871–904.

Tyler, T.R. (1999). Why people cooperate in organizations: An identity-based perspective. *Research in Orgnizational Behavior, 21*, 201–246.

Tyler, T.R., Boeckmann, R., Smith, H.J., & Hou, Y.J. (1997). *Social justice in a diverse society.* Boulder, CO: Westview Press.

Tyler, T.R., & Degoey, P. (1995). Collective restraint in a social dilemma situation: The influence of procedural justice and community identification on the empowerment and legitimacy of authority. *Journal of Personality and Social Psychology, 69*, 482–497.

Tyler, T.R., & Lind, E.A. (1992). A relational model of authority in groups. In M. Zanna (Ed.), *Advances in experimental social psychology, Vol. 25* (pp. 151–191). New York: Academic Press.

Tyler, T.R., Lind, E.A., Ohbuchi, K., Sugawara, I., & Huo, Y.J. (1998). Conflict with outsiders: Disputing within and across cultural boundaries. *Personality and Social Psychology Bulletin, 24*, 137–146.

Tyler, T.R., & Mitchell, G. (1994). Legitimacy and the empowerment of discretionary legal authority: The United States Supreme Court and abortion rights. *Duke Law Journal, 43*, 703–814.

Tyler, T.R., & Smith, H.J. (1997). Social justice and social movements. In D. Gilbert, S. Fiske, & G. Lindzey (Eds.), *Handbook of social psychology* (4th ed., Vol. 2, pp. 595–629).

Wissler, R.L. (1995). Mediation and adjudication in small claims court. *Law and Society Review, 29*, 323–358.

[21]

A CRITICAL-PSYCHOLOGY APPROACH TO LAW'S LEGITIMACY

DENNIS R. FOX*

When the field of psychology and law became institutionalized three decades ago with the birth of an organization and a journal, the central goal of pioneering psychologists of law was to promote justice. That goal paralleled the effort within critical legal studies to identify and oppose law's oppressive tendencies and reshape law as an agent of human freedom and equality. Unfortunately, early efforts to expose psychological mechanisms contributing to injustice have since declined. As a consequence, today's legal psychology mainstream too often limits expectations of, and demands for, justice both within law and outside the law (Fox, 1999).

The field's reduced justice focus can be seen in legal psychology textbooks that emphasize presumed differences between psychology and law while minimizing some troubling similarities. Law is doctrinal, the writers tell us, whereas psychology is empirical. Law is adversarial, while psychology seeks a single comprehensive truth. Law is emphatic, psychology tentative and cautious. At the same time, the texts generally underemphasize some shared traits: Both fields have been used for social control and the service of elite needs. Both emphasize individualism, generally attributing responsibility and guilt to persons rather than to relationships or institutions. And both rely on and strengthen ideological defenses of an unjust status quo.

In the field of psychology more broadly, critical psychologists increasingly call on their field to alter its own status quo and embrace more liberatory alternatives (Fox & Prilleltensky, 1997; Sloan, 2000). Although many differences exist among critical psychologists inspired by disparate traditions, several propositions (resembling those common among critical legal scholars) draw widespread support:

■ Psychology's values, assumptions, and practices have been culturally and historically determined, reflecting among other things the prevailing socioeconomic setting, political affinities, responses to external pressures, and battles over power, professionalism, and turf. In contrast, mainstream psychology generally portrays itself as progressing through objective, scientific, "value–free" progress.

* Associate Professor of Legal Studies, University of Illinois, Springfield. An earlier version of much of this paper appeared in 15 *Psicología Política* 39 (1997).

■ Modern society is marked by widespread injustice, inequality, and systemic barriers to both survival and meaning. To explain the origins of the unacceptable status quo and to justify its continuation, dominant institutions inculcate a psychologized ideology and use the process of false consciousness to encourage widespread belief in unjustified assumptions about human nature. Societal elites may or may not believe the ideology they disseminate; in either case it narrows the range of institutional arrangements the society considers possible and desirable and encourages people to accept unjust outcomes. (A capitalist economic system is justified by the insistence that human beings are inherently selfish, competitive, and accumulative and that people who fall behind have only themselves to blame; people learn to expect the worst from others and from themselves. A legal and political system whose essential principles, procedures, and styles were created by white privileged men with substantial property is justified by the false claim that today everyone is treated equally; because the law is unconcerned with unjust outcomes so long as approved procedures are followed, *substantive* justice is displaced by the perception of procedural justice.)

■ In their everyday work, mainstream psychologists too often contribute to complacency at one extreme and oppression at the other. This is the case whether they are well–intentioned and avowedly apolitical helping professionals or, less commonly, conscious agents of social control. Mainstream psychologists typically overemphasize individualism, the narrow pursuit of personal goals, and either adapting to or bypassing societal norms and expectations; they de-emphasize mutuality beyond the family, justice, and the need for institutional change. Mainstream psychology and critical psychology differ, thus, in their level of analysis.

■ Critical psychology seeks to alter, and ultimately provide alternatives to, both mainstream psychology's norms and the societal institutions that those norms strengthen. Desired values such as social justice, self–determination and participation, caring and compassion, health, and human diversity must be advanced in a balanced way, with awareness that some of these culturally specific values have more potential for social transfor-mation than others. Our ultimate goal is to respect and enhance both individuality and diversity within a mutually supportive just and equal society (Fox, 2000: 25-27).

These four propositions are directly relevant to how psychologists of law might approach legal theory and legal practice. Unfortunately, as in law, psychology's mainstream is uncritical of its own assumptions, and psychology lags behind law in the visibility of critical efforts.

I. APPROACHING LEGITIMACY

To the public, the electoral ballot and the formal courtroom symbolize the superiority of a law-based civil society over authoritarian reliance on brute force. Given the degree to which dictatorial regimes resist the transition to representative democracy, this symbolism is understandable. Surely the opposition of dictators and oligarchies to the creation of autonomous legal institutions demonstrates that the use of law to maintain order and resolve disputes will benefit members of society at the expense of the old guard. The rush by Western legal experts to help authorities in the fragmented Soviet empire write new constitutions and devise independent judicial systems followed from the assumption that law is self-evidently a good thing for those seeking justice, equality, and freedom. As Silbey (1997) noted, American legal practices—often mandated by the International Monetary Fund and the World Bank—circulate around the globe, as do public images of law derived from American television.

Unfortunately, the perspective of Western mainstream psychologists parallels that of most citizens in the new democracies: Psychologists routinely endorse law as the guarantor of justice and human rights, believing that despite its shortcomings "law is a good thing" (Melton, 1990). Although relief at the downfall of authoritarian regimes makes sense, the broad endorsement of legal institutions in general, and of American legal institutions in particular, strikes me as a mistake. Silbey's (1997) caution about the globalization of American law is worth emphasizing: "I am worried about how local justice can be achieved within a supposedly universal, all-purpose, one-size-fits-all law" (222).

Unlike scholars in some other fields, psychologists pay little attention to law's potential downside even as they examine discretionary factors in legal decision-making and propose relatively minor reforms to smooth the workings of legal institutions. They rarely pose more significant questions that go to the heart of law's inherently political and often unjust nature: How might law actually make life worse for people? How does law ensure the maintenance of societal inequality and power imbalances? When does law provide the appearance of justice without the reality? To what extent does reliance on law deflect attention from other solutions to societal problems? More often, psychologists focus instead on less controversial topics that leave the legal status quo intact. Thus, system-challenging questions are typically "absent"—under emphasized, brushed aside—as are other important absences in political psychology and elsewhere (Montero, 1997). The role of *false conscious-ness* in maintaining system legitimacy is given little attention by psychologists (Jost, 1995).

The widespread endorsement of law parallels mainstream psychol-ogy's more general endorsement of society's status quo (Fox & Prilleltensky, 1997). Psychologists typically see themselves as insiders within the legal system (Melton, 1990) just as they see themselves as insiders in society's other dominant policy institutions, particularly in the United States (Herman, 1995). This insider orientation allows psychologists to propose, implement, and assess minor reforms of societal institutions and even occasionally to expose oppressive practices. However, when important social problems persist because of conflicting values and competing interests rather than because the authorities lack accurate data (Fox, 1991), any belief that being inside will lead to social change is unrealistic.

Even psychologists who are developing a psychological jurisprudence that seeks to redirect legal institutions typically mirror rather than challenge popular myths about law (Fox, 1993b, 1997, 1999). The notion that theorizing about law should be based on "the values that make up the conventional knowledge of the community of scientific psychology" (Wiener, Watts, & Stolle, 1993: 93) blocks the development of alternative approaches more suspicious of received wisdom and more amenable to fundamental societal change.

In the remainder of this article I first consider law's legitimacy, taking into account the role of myth and the relevance of conflicting views about law. I then speculate about several components of false consciousness about law. I conclude by suggesting directions for future work by critical psychologists of law.

II. LEGITIMACY AND MYTH

Especially in representative democracies, the survival of state institutions depends on their perceived legitimacy (Kairys, 1990). According to legitimacy theorists, most people obey authorities not just to avoid punishment but because they believe those authorities have the right to make demands and because they feel that complying is the right thing to do. Whether the apparently increasing political cynicism has undercut legitimacy is an open question, but to the extent that it exists, perceived legitimacy remains a significant barrier to movements for social change that confront not just the state's power but the public's endorsement of that power (Lefcourt, 1971). The state, in other words, can leave its tanks hidden except during direct (and extraordinary) challenges to the system. "Legitimacy—the feeling of obligation to follow the decisions of group authorities and group rules—works to the benefit of group authorities" (Tyler et al., 1997, 196-197). For the most part, the public polices itself.

The law claims legitimacy on two distinct grounds. On one level, legal authorities are formally granted the power to carry out state mandates. In this way, the law as an agent of the state absorbs the state's legitimacy and has the power of the state to back it up with force when necessary. This form of legitimacy flows from the political state, and is secondary to it. It is the form most relevant to cruder depictions of legal dominance that see judicial power as merely subservient to the state rather than as autonomous.

At a more central level, law is legitimate in its own right, as something different from the state. Legal authorities often proclaim the law to be

> separate from—and "above"—politics, economics, culture, and the values or preferences of judges. This separation is supposedly accomplished and ensured by a number of perceived attributes of the decision-making process, including judicial subservience to a Constitution, statutes, and precedent; the quasi-scientific, objective nature of legal analysis; and the technical expertise of judges and lawyers (Kairys, 1990, 1).

In this view, law is not really "part of" the government, as demonstrated when judges occasionally block governmental actions or demand that political authorities comply with the law. Unlike some of its regrettably flawed practitioners, and unlike political parties and social movements, the essence of law is neutral, rational, truthful, and autonomous.

Although law schools make it clear that the law is not a set of rules (especially in a common-law country such as the U.S.) and that conflicting principles and values can lead to a variety of legitimate ends, they teach the specialized artificial language that judges expect when lawyers try to demonstrate which single course of action is "correct" (Kennedy, 1990). Similarly, appellate judges overturn trial court decisions not by acknowledging they disagree or that they have different values, but by declaring the trial judge's actions wrong and then arguing that there are objective grounds for the decision. Logical connections between one case and the next are emphasized; the central role of judicial discretion is minimized; sometimes, with a deceptively straight face, it is even denied. Through these and other "fetishizing" techniques (McBride, 1974), the system enhances its legitimacy.

That legitimacy reaches mythical proportions is widely acknowledged, and even applauded, because it allows the authorities to act on behalf of a public that may not share the authorities' view of what is best: "Even if this idea of law above and beyond all politics is a myth, it is still a valuable way to appeal to people's inner voices, to motives higher than their crude self-interest" (Friedman, 1984, 275). "In a very real sense," Haney (1991) emphasized in his critique of Supreme Court decision-making, "the 'consent of the governed' depends upon such fictions" (185). Countering these myths and fictions is not easy, as "once people believe in a myth, their skeptical sense vanishes, they accept it as fact, and—most importantly—the invented reality becomes reality itself, the only reality" (Nimmo & Combs, 1990, 18).

Inaccurate assumptions about human nature enhance the public's acceptance of the system's legitimacy. According to Tapp (1974), the myth of humankind's lawlessness ignores the fact that "the search for rules and rule dependency appears early in human life and is visible across all activity from games to government and language to law" (53). "In essence," she added, "no community is truly lawless," and adherence to the myth perpetuates a law-and-order mentality. Tapp also pointed to the legality myth, with its "crippling . . . assumption that legality and its correlates of justice, obligation, and responsibility reside only in the law. . . . If [this assumption] continues . . . then the emergence of an authoritarian repressive law is more likely" (54). Tapp's (1974) concerns are widely shared, with good reason. The belief that people behave justly and responsibly only because the law requires it—that we cannot be good unless we are forced to be good (Lerner, 1982)—lowers our expectations for our own actions as well as for the actions of others.

III. CONTESTED TERRAIN

Given the centrality of the fiction that law is objective, neutral, and consensual, members of the public are often troubled when judges disagree among themselves about how to interpret the law. In a complex society, it is comforting to rely on experts who have learned through specialized training what the law really is. When the experts cannot agree, the public's faith in legal and political authorities can be shaken, as we saw recently in the wake of the U.S. Supreme Court's decision that resulted in George Bush becoming President of the United States.

Disagreement among judges echoes long-standing debates among legal scholars. More recent attacks on our conventional views of law make it clear that law is not an exercise in pure reason but a battle among contesting forces (Kairys, 1990). Although it is tempting to claim that those who agree with us are objective and those who disagree wrongly misguided, many critiques of law have gone well beyond the merely cynical. More challenging to law's official view of itself have been attacks on the central fiction of logical decision-making.

In the first third of the last century, legal realists in the United States openly acknowledged the subjective nature of legal decision-making. Lawyers and social scientists demonstrated how different judges reached very different conclusions given the same set of facts. Some judges talked about how their own political views, class position, religious beliefs, and personality affected their decisions even when they sought to remain neutral and objective. Although today such expressions of subjectivity are commonplace and unremarkable (at least outside the courtroom), in the 1920s and 30s verbalizing the notion that judges make decisions just like the rest of us was shocking. Even more shocking, the legal realists did not call upon judges to be less subjective. They recognized that subjectivity was inevitable, that judges (like prosecutors and police officers) have sometimes boundless discretion. They wanted judges to acknowledge that fact rather than hide it.

And they went even further: The realists maintained that judges, aware of the subjective nature of decision-making, should intentionally shape the law guided by a clear sense of ultimate goals. No longer should judges seek to reach some imagined correct decision regardless of the decision's effects. "There was *no such thing* as an objective legal methodology behind which judges could hide in order to evade responsibility for the social consequences of legal decision-making. Every decision they made was a moral and political choice" (Mensch, 1990, 22, emphasis in original). Consciously choosing among conflicting values would be better than letting unacknowledged social influences shape the decisions. The law could be wrong, after all. It could be unjust and immoral. Applying legal logic to oppressive assumptions had made slavery and women's subjugation and intolerable conditions in the workplace legal. It made the European appropriation of lands throughout the world legal and later made the Holocaust legal. Today, it allows the continuation of a status quo that fails to seek, let alone guarantee, fundamental justice. If the law can be so immoral, suggested the realists, judges should openly abandon the pretense and use their discretion to improve society.

Today, feminist, Marxist, communitarian, libertarian, and other movements offer competing jurisprudential theories that question law's underlying assumptions and the legal system's underlying justifications. Radical perspectives, clashing with dominant conservative and liberal ones (Lesnick, 1991), clarify how law's reality departs from the law

Legal Studies Forum

myth. From a critical perspective, it becomes clear that the purpose of the "rule of law" is not to ensure justice but to establish a rules-based social control system based on technicalities, categories, and abstract principles. Those who establish the basic assumptions and principles have the power to direct law's practice. At the policy level, judges and lawyers have the power to tell us which options are legally available, thus deflecting calls for social change—a particularly crucial role for lawyers that Tocqueville (1831/1973) long ago identified (and admired) in the United States as a substitute for the rejected European aristocracy.

IV. FALSE CONSCIOUSNESS ABOUT LAW AND JUSTICE

It is not uncommon to hear the law professor's response to the new student who exclaims "That's not fair!" upon hearing the unjust application of one legal rule or another. The apocryphal professor takes the student outside and points to the name of the building: Clearly it is "School of Law," not "School of Justice."

Law and justice are two different things, a message brought home to most law students fairly quickly even without the walk outside. The general public, though, has not assimilated this message, partly because it is not often talked about outside law school and the publicly invisible realm of legal scholarship. In public, lawyers and judges continue to talk about their role in obtaining justice, as if that is law's purpose. There is widespread awareness that the public might question the legitimacy of any legal system that doesn't consider justice primary. In theory, if a democratic public decides the system is unjust, it can vote in a new system.

To get around this conceptual and political problem, mainstream legal scholars and authorities prefer to focus not on hard-to-define substantive justice but on procedural justice. In this view, the "rule of law" is satisfied when there is a procedurally correct application of general principles regardless of unfair results in particular cases. As emphasized repeatedly in empirical psychological research (Tyler, 1990; Tyler & McGraw, 1986; Tyler & Mitchell, 1994; Tyler et al., 1997), the common belief that authorities use fair procedures enhances system legitimacy. Because people want to be treated fairly, "procedures can act as a cushion of support, allowing authorities to deliver unpopular decisions without losing support in the eyes of the public" (Tyler et al., 1997, 177). Procedural rules thus can help resolve conflicts that are inevitable not just between people with conflicting interests but even among people with similar goals and values. On the other hand, as the naive law student in the above example understands, until law school corrects the unspoiled intuition, correct procedures are not enough. "The national obsession with process has allowed us to ignore dramatic inequalities in substantive outcome" (Haney, 1991, 194). By directing attention to procedures rather than to results, legal authorities deflect justice-based demands for social change.

This deflection is an example of false consciousness, a concept long dismissed by mainstream social scientists because it was first presented as a part of Marxist doctrine (Parenti, 1996). Interestingly, Jost (1995) demonstrated that social and political psychologists have actually examined a wide variety of false-consciousness phenomena without using the terminology. Defining false consciousness as "the holding of false or inaccurate beliefs that are contrary to one's own social interest and which thereby contribute to the maintenance of the disadvantaged position of the self or the group," Jost found "a considerable amount of evidence for the proposition that people will hold false beliefs which justify their own subordination" (400, 401).

False consciousness is relevant to popular beliefs about law in at least three different ways, as a minimalist focus on reforming dishonest procedures; the strong reformist recognition that honest procedures can mask unjust law; and the anarchist critique of the rule of law's conflict with individualized justice.

The Minimalist Focus on Dishonest Procedures
Most obviously, as well as most superficially, legally mandated procedures themselves may be a sham. False consciousness exists to the extent that people expect to get a fair hearing when no such fairness is likely. For example, we may be allowed to defend ourselves before judges or government bureaucrats who merely give the appearance of paying attention to the evidence when in fact they have already made up their minds and are simply waiting for us to have our say before a decision is announced. "Government leaders may find it easier to create conditions of 'perceived fairness' than to solve problems or provide needed benefits" (Tyler, Rasinski, & Griffin, 1986, 1976).

The media focus our attention on cruder miscarriages of justice—judges who accept bribes, lawyers who lie, brutal cops who beat up suspects, bureaucrats who are pressured by superiors to reach predetermined results. But they ignore the more routine injustices carried out in the name of procedure. The popular belief that the system can be improved by weeding out a few bad actors is itself a manifestation of false consciousness that fails to take into account structural constraints on individual action. It ensures that a disproportionate amount of reformist energy goes to endlessly cleaning up the system rather than to changing the system.

The Strong Reformist Concern: Honest Procedures Mask Unjust Law

The media pay little attention to a second aspect of false consciousness more significant than the first: the belief that honest, conscientiously applied procedural protections can bring just decisions is false when legal doctrine itself is unjust. It is relatively easy to identify dishonest and biased lawyers and judges. It is harder to conceptualize an honest system that enforces biased legal principles. It's a problem when judges accept bribes to rule in favor of a landlord rather than a tenant; it's a more serious problem when an honest judge rules the same way because the law was written by legislators who themselves are landlords and interpreted by appellate judges who believe they are merely applying neutral principles about the sanctity of contracts and private property. Haney pointed out that "Even if all our due process dreams came true in psychology and law, and this mythical justice machine ground away with perfect procedural precision and accuracy, much substantive injustice would still remain" (1993: 381). As emphasized by a variety of challengers to mainstream legal thought, the law would be very different if its basic doctrines had been written by workers and poor people, by women, and by people of color.

When technically fair procedures are used to apply unfair legal principles, the unfair results seem legitimate because the gaze is focused on procedure. The role of power becomes invisible, reducing demands for justice and social change (Silbey, 1997) as procedurally correct hearings delay, but do not alter, the ultimately unjust final decision. The rare victory maintains the belief that "the system works," encouraging claimants to cling to unrealistic hopes and their lawyers to move on to the next client. Providing these procedurally correct hearings and appeals may be expensive (and thus must be fought for), but formal hearings and appointed lawyers are not nearly as expensive and disruptive as establishing a more just society.

At the same time, of course, defining and providing substantive justice is not a simple task, as recognized by psychologists who have considered distributive and retributive justice (Tyler et al., 1997). Clearly there is no consensus. Culturally-derived definitions of justice vary over space, culture, and time as well as by political perspective. In the context of psychology and law in particular, it is not clear which "independent definitions [of justice] . . . might 'make sense' from a psychological perspective" (Haney, 1993, 379). Yet a task for political psychology in particular is to assess the relationship between different political systems and different conceptions of justice. Surely we can say that oppression, inequality, and racism, for example, cannot be part of any system seeking to attain social justice (Prilleltensky & Fox, 1997). In this regard, Tyler's own early belief that "people's views about procedural justice are dysfunctional" (Tyler & McGraw, 1986: 126) and "nonrational" (123) had more reformist potential than his more recent rejection of efforts by psychologists to determine which principles of distribution are just on the grounds that this is "not a psychological question" (Tyler et al., 1997: 58).

We should be able to agree that psychologists might usefully critique the negative consequences of capitalism. As many psychologists have noted, capitalist theory is steeped in psychological assumptions about an essentially selfish human nature (Wachtel, 1983). Central to modern Western legal systems, and a central target of any effort to create social justice, is the role of the law in endorsing and protecting capitalism and class inequality. Yet psychologists of law generally ignore assumptions about the centrality of the profit motive, the relevance of economic growth to individual well-being, and the virtues of resource distribution according to social psychology's equity norm rather than by competing principles of equality and need (Fox, 1993a, 1996). There is little effort by psychologists to identify the false consciousness that helps prop up capitalism despite the literature on this topic in other fields.

An important example is seen in recent efforts to examine modern capitalism's expanding centerpiece, the business corporation. Researchers increasingly examine how executives and managers make decisions and how workers carry them out. They propose methods to reduce risky and harmful decisions and enhance corporate responsibility and ethics. These approaches fall squarely within the liberal reform tradition of trying to reduce capitalism's more blatant negative consequences by trying to make capitalism more fair. Unfortunately, as with efforts by industrial-organizational psychologists to maintain managerial control over workers (Prilleltensky, 1994), these efforts do nothing to challenge corporate dominance (Fox, 1996).

The law, in other words, has created institutions that now dominate the world economy and increasingly dominate and homogenize the world's cultures (Bonsignore, 1994; Silbey, 1997). It has done so over the past century and a half, as judges and legislators reversed earlier legal principles that restricted the scope, size, and function of corporate institutions. The public today believes that "business has rights, too," apparently accepting the law's adoption of a bizarre "group mind" theory as the basis of a legal doctrine that treats immense business organizations as if they were living individuals. Yet rather than pointing out the obvious dangers and the psychological absurdity of treating conglomerates as if they were individuals, psychologists mostly look the other way (Fox, 1996). This redirection adds to the unequally distributed negative consequences of corporate expansion around the globe that is "facilitated, organized, and protected through increasingly standard legal forms and processes" (Silbey, 1997, 223). Liberal reformers seeking to reduce capitalism's negative consequences without damaging its essence routinely seek procedural regulation rather than altered outcomes (Lesnick, 1991).

The Anarchist Critique of a System for Law, Not for People

A third form of false consciousness about law is harder to grasp than the false confidence in crooked judges and elite-dominated legal doctrine. Even with good judges, and even in the unlikely event that some future legal system is based on substantively just principles established through democratic participation, there remains the problem that the nature of law itself precludes humane, individualized decisions. As noted above, ideal law is based on the logical derivation and procedurally correct application of legal principles, devoid of subjectivity and emotion. What counts in legal decision-making are discrete provable facts to which accepted abstract principles can be applied. General rules and principles designed for categories of people are applied to particular individuals regardless of individual circumstances. Simply put, law bureaucratizes relationships. This bureaucratization is actually portrayed as one of law's strong points, distinguishing it from more "primitive" systems where individuals allegedly suffer routinely at the whim of despotic or inconsistent rulers. The common boast that we live under "a system of law, not of people" misrepresents a historical and anthropological record that makes it clear that so-called "primitive" groups resolved disputes and maintained order without legal systems—and mostly without authoritarian brutality—for most of human history (Barclay, 1982; Clastres, 1974/1977; Orbell & Rutherford, 1973). Although the results of the rule of law are often justifiable, they inevitably cause unjust hardship in many specific cases. Under the strict rule of law, however, these unjust results are merely part of the price we pay for having a system of law whose supposed benefits outweigh unjust results in individual cases.

In contrast to law, on the fringes of most legal systems, we find principles of equity. Decisions based on equity reject the legally required outcome when doing so is necessary to reach a fair outcome in a specific case. Equity has been a part of law since the earliest legal systems, and appears to be "founded on a sense of justice which is innate in human nature, however diverse may be the explanation of its presence" (Newman, 1965, 410). Menkel-Meadow (1985) identified equity with a female relationship-based response to harsher male-dominated law, paralleling Gilligan's (1982) distinction between traditionally male and female modes of moral judgment and Bakan's (1966) distinction between agency and communion. Of course, unlike the rule of law, real people take individual circumstances into account, leading to both positive and negative results shaped by structural constraints on the discretionary use of power as well as on other discoverable, and often politically manipulable, factors.

Equity-based notions are especially compatible with modern anarchist thought, which generally views the development of state legal systems not as an extension and improvement over harsh primitive custom but as the forced imposition of centralized control over societies with long-standing local norms (Diamond, 1974). Anarchists emphasize that even if modern legal systems provide certain benefits to portions of the population, dependence on state-enforced solutions brings a host of negative outcomes as well. Community psychologist Seymour Sarason (1976) called attention to the central anarchist insight that state power should be viewed suspiciously because the centralized state inhibits both individual autonomy and a psychological sense of community. From an anarchist perspective, legal institutions may bring short-term gains, but only at the expense of a greater dependency on legal authorities that causes people to lose their ability to work together to resolve conflicts. "When law is fully in command, morality itself loses relevance. Right and wrong become a specialty of professionals such as lawyers, police, and judges. Justice becomes an industry" (Black, 1989, 85). Psychologists have many reasons to take anarchist theory seriously (Chomsky, 1973; Ehrlich, 1996; Fox, 1985, 1986, 1993a, 1993c, 1999; Fromm, 1955; Goodman, 1966/1979; Maslow, 1971; Sarason, 1976).

Unlike the popular image of anarchists as bomb-throwing terrorists, anarchism does not reject social order and most anarchists do not advocate violence. Anarchists have created alternative forms of societal organization, frequently based on decentralized, autonomous, voluntary communities (Ehrlich, 1996; Taylor, 1982, 1984). Even when conceding that effective communities might sometimes require some form of peer compulsion (as occurs in non-law societies), anarchists insist that a just society requires neither formal law nor the centralized state (Fox, 1985, 1993a; Holterman & van Meerseveen, 1984). Any anarchist-approved system would have to incorporate principles such as voluntariness, cooperative consensus-driven decision-making, equality rather than hierarchy, and decentralization (van Maarseveen, 1984).

The tendency of law to drive out equity makes even a procedurally just legal system suspect, just as the belief that unfair results must stand because "that's the law" is a manifestation of false consciousness. As might be expected, judges typically construe equity principles narrowly or ignore them entirely (Fox, 1993a). Appeals to individualized justice are often dismissed on the grounds that bypassing the rule of law leads to anarchy.

V. CONCLUSION

Psychology's support of system legitimacy is significant and deserves greater attention. Paralelling other critiques of mainstream psychology by critical psychologists (Fox & Prilleltensky, 1997; Sloan, 2000), Jost (1995) called for "politicizing" psychology by addressing

> the political context of domination and subordination which surrounds most of our thinking and behaving in the social world. The phenomenon of false consciousness provides just such an opportunity. Affective and cognitive bases of human error are now well understood; virtually no attention, however, has been given to social and political circumstances (such as status, power, inequality, injustice, exploitation, and abuse) that foster negative illusions (413).

Psychologists seeking to assess the presence and consequences of false consciousness in law could usefully begin with Jost's (1995) delineation of distinct categories of false consciousness, each examined (usually in depoliticized fashion) by mainstream psychologists. Categories include the failure to perceive justice and disadvantage ("people frequently perceive situations to be fair or just, even when there are good reasons to suppose that such situations are not") (402); fatalism (including the beliefs that protest is futile, embarrassing, or exhausting); the justification of social roles (as through person perception and stereotyping); false attribution of blame (including self-blame and false other blame); identification with the aggressor (including psychological dependence and preference for the outgroup); and resistance to change (taking into account cognitive conservatism and behavioral conservatism). These categories offer a starting point for understanding the inculcation and acceptance of false beliefs about law.

Useful, too, is Sloan's (1997) discussion of how personality theories "could play a very important role in the process of social transformation and human betterment, in particular by showing how personal concerns and social injustice are intertwined" (97). Sloan pointed out that "while the emancipatory interest is relatively inoperative in mainstream psychology, it is this interest that the general public expects the field . . . to serve" (96). He added: "People do not need a set of universal principles or laws of behavior. Instead, people need to be invited by psychologists and other social scientists to participate in an ongoing process of reflection on our personal and collective problems in living meaningfully" (97).

What is there about law that such an ongoing process of reflection might encounter? As one example, the law frequently uses the fictional reasonable person as a standard for behavior the law expects. As psychologists of law have frequently pointed out, the law's view of what behavior is reasonable often conflicts with the behavior and beliefs of real human beings (Horowitz and Willging, 1984). The law's fictitious reasonable person is purely rational, a self-oriented, asocial individual motivated not at all by concern for others and unusually aware of the law's logic and assumptions. It is not surprising that the law's warped view of human nature leads to legal support for an equally warped capitalist economic system (with an equally fictitious rational actor at its core). It would not be surprising to find that real human beings recoil from the legal and economic fictions that purport to serve as behavioral ideals.

Similarly, the belief that social problems are too complicated to resolve in other than piecemeal fashion leads to a lack of support for comprehensive social change. Dominant cultural assumptions fail to take into account the intertwined nature of seemingly different problems. Unfortunately, focusing only on narrow, "manageable" problems, often at the individual level, can cause the resolution of one policy issue to actually complicate others (Fox, 1991). Thus, even when mainstream proposals for legal and policy reform do sometimes succeed, they often bring unpredicted and unintended side effects because so many seemingly separate social problems are actually related. They also fail to achieve system-wide change because they aim too low.

Yet is the public potentially amenable to more fundamental change than is commonly thought? Psychologists might consider the possibility that widespread discontent with the current system is not so much nonexistent as it is hidden: perhaps the discontented adopt cynical silence or sullen grumbling because they fail to perceive that their discontent is widely shared. Is this the case? Is there more support for fundamental social change than the dominant culture assumes, demonstrating the existence of pluralistic ignorance (Jost, 1995)? Would the public oppose fundamental change if it thought that such change was indeed possible? These are the sorts of questions that psychologists too rarely address (Montero, 1997).

Mainstream psychologists and other social scientists often reject the term false consciousness because it is associated with Marxism and other radical political perspectives (Jost, 1995; Parenti, 1996). Yet it is radical theory's insistence on system-wide change that holds the most promise for solutions that do more than merely skim the surface. Psychologists who confront the centrality of legitimacy in propping up support for the political, legal, and economic system must abandon mainstream assumptions if they are to expose the sources of power and enhance social justice. If the system creates people "whose minds work to preserve the status quo at all costs" (Jost & Banaji, 1994, 15), then psychologists must join the effort to "challenge the common sense through which we interpret the world" (Montero, 1997, 243).

REFERENCES

Bakan, D. (1966). *The Duality of Human Existence: An Essay on Psychology and Religion.* Chicago: Rand McNally.

Barclay, H. (1982). *People Without Government: An Anthropology of Anarchism.* London: Kahn & Averill.

Black, D. (1989). *Sociological Justice.* New York: Oxford University.

Bonsignore, J. J. (1994). *Law and Multinationals: An Introduction to Political Economy.* Englewood Cliffs, NJ: Prentice-Hall.

Chomsky, N. (1973). *For Reasons of State.* New York: Vintage.

Clastres, P. (1977). *Society Against the State: The Leader as Servant and the Humane Uses of Power among the Indians of the Americas.* (R. Hurley, Trans.). New York: Urizen Books. (Original work published 1974)

Diamond, S. (1974). *In Search of the Primitive.* New Brunswick, NJ: Transaction Books.

Ehrlich, H. J. (ed.) (1996). *Reinventing Anarchy, Again.* San Francisco: AK Press.

Fox, D. R. (1985). Psychology, ideology, utopia, and the commons. *American Psychologist, 40,* 48-58.

_____. (1986). Beyond individualism and centralization. *American Psychologist, 41,* 231-232.

_____. (1991). Social science's limited role in resolving psycholegal social problems. *Journal of Offender Rehabilitation, 17,* 117-124.

_____. (1993a). The autonomy-community balance and the equity-law distinction: Anarchy's task for psychological jurisprudence. *Behavioral Sciences and the Law, 11,* 97-109.

_____. (1993b). Psychological jurisprudence and radical social change. *American Psychologist, 48,* 234-241.

_____. (1993c). Where's the proof that law is a good thing? *Law and Human Behavior, 17,* 257-258.

_____. (1996). The law says corporations are persons, but psychology knows better. *Behavioral Sciences and the Law, 14,* 339-359.

_____. (1997). Psychology and law: Justice diverted. In D. Fox & I. Prilleltensky (eds.), *Critical Psychology: An Introduction* (pp. 217-232). London: Sage Publications.

_____. (1999). Psycholegal scholarship's contribution to false consciousness about injustice. *Law and Human Behavior, 23,* 9-30.

_____. (2000). The critical psychology project: Transforming society and transforming psychology. In T. Sloan (ed.), *Critical Psychology: Voices for Change.* Hampshire, England: Macmillan Press.

Fox, D., & Prilleltensky, I. (eds.). (1997). *Critical Psychology: An Introduction.* London: Sage Publications.

Friedman, L. M. (1984). *American Law: An Introduction.* New York: Norton.

Fromm, E. (1955). *The Sane Society.* New York: Holt, Rinehart.

Gilligan, C. (1982). *In a Different Voice: Psychological Theory and Women's Development.* Cambridge, MA: Harvard University Press.

Goodman, P. (1979). Reflections on the anarchist principle. In T. Stoehr (ed.), *Drawing the Line: The Political Essays of Paul Goodman* (pp. 176-177). New York: Dutton. (Original work published 1966)

Haney, C. (1980). Psychological and legal change: On the limits of a factual jurisprudence. *Law and Human Behavior, 4,* 147-200.

————. (1991). The Fourteenth Amendment and symbolic legality: Let them eat due process. *Law and Human Behavior, 15,* 183-204.

————. (1993). Psychology and legal change: The impact of a decade. *Law and Human Behavior, 17,* 371-398.

Herman, E. (1995). *The Romance of American Psychology: Political Culture in the Age of Experts.* Berkeley, CA: University of California Press.

Holterman, T., & van Maarseveen, H. (Eds.). (1984). *Law and Anarchism.* Montreal: Black Rose Books.

Horowitz, I. A., & Willging, T. E. (1984). *The Psychology of Law: Integrations and Applications.* Boston: Little, Brown.

Jost, J. T. (1995). Negative illusions: Conceptual clarification and psychological evidence concerning false consciousness. *Political Psychology, 16,* 397-424.

Jost, J. T., & Banaji, M. R. (1994). The role of stereotyping in system-justification and the production of false consciousness. *British Journal of Social Psychology, 33,* 1-27.

Kairys, D. (Ed.). (1990). *The Politics of Law: A Progressive Critique* (Rev. ed.). New York: Pantheon.

Kennedy, D. (1990). Legal education as training for hierarchy. In D. Kairys (ed.), *The Politics of Law: A Progressive Critique* (Rev. ed.) (pp. 38-58). New York: Pantheon.

Lefcourt, R. (Ed.). (1971). *Law Against the People: Essays to Demystify Law, Order, and the Courts.* New York: Vintage.

Lerner, M. J. (1982). The justice motive in human relations and the economic model of man: A radical analysis of facts and fictions. In V. J. Derlega and J. Grzelak (eds.), *Cooperation and Helping Behavior: Theories and Research* (pp. 249-278). New York: Academic Press.

Lesnick, H. (1991). The wellsprings of legal responses to inequality: A perspective on perspectives. *Duke Law Journal, 1991,* 413-454.

Maslow, A. H. (1971). *The Farther Reaches of Human Nature*. New York: Penguin.

McBride, W. L. (1974). An overview of future possibilities: Law unlimited? In J. R. Pennock & J. W. Chapman (Eds.), *The Limits of Law: Nomos XV* (pp. 28-38). New York: Lieber-Atherton.

Melton, G. B. (1990). Law, science, and humanity: The normative foundation of social science in law. *Law and Human Behavior*, 14, 315-332.

Menkel-Meadow, C. (1985). Portia in a different voice: Speculations on a women's lawyering process. *Berkeley Women's Law Journal*, 1, 39-63.

Mensch, E. (1990). The history of mainstream legal thought. In D. Kairys (ed.), *The Politics of Law: A Progressive Critique* (Rev. ed.) (pp. 13-37). New York: Pantheon.

Montero, M. (1997). Political psychology: A critical perspective. In D. Fox & I. Prilleltensky (eds.), *Critical Psychology: An Introduction* (pp. 233-244). London: Sage Publications.

Newman, R. A. (1965). The place and function of pure equity in the structure of law. *Hastings Law Journal*, 16 401-429.

Nimmo, D., & Combs, J. E. (1990). *Subliminal Politics: Myths and Mythmakers in America*. Englewood Cliffs, NJ: Prentice-Hall.

Orbell, J. M., & Rutherford, B. (1973). Can Leviathan make the life of man less solitary, poor, nasty, brutish, and short? *British Journal of Political Science*, 3, 383-407.

Parenti, M. (1996). *Dirty Truths: Reflections on Politics, Media, Ideology, Conspiracy, Ethnic Life and Class Power*. San Francisco: City Light Books.

Prilleltensky, I. (1994). *The Morals and Politics of Psychology: Psychological Discourse and the Status Quo*. Albany, NY: State University of New York Press.

Prilleltensky, I. & Fox, D. (1997). Introducing critical psychology: Values, assumptions, and the status quo. In D. Fox & I. Prilleltensky (eds.), *Critical Psychology: An Introduction* (pp. 3-20). London: Sage Publications.

Sarason, S. B. (1976). Community psychology and the anarchist insight. *American Journal of Community Psychology*, 4, 243-261.

Silbey, S. S. (1997). "Let them eat cake": Globalization, postmodern colonialism, and the possibilities of justice. *Law and Society Review*, 31, 207-235.

Sloan, T. (1997). Theories of personality: Ideology and beyond. In D. Fox & I. Prilleltensky (eds.), *Critical Psychology: An Introduction* (pp. 87-103). London: Sage Publications.

_____. (ed.), *Critical Psychology: Voices for Change*. Hampshire, England: Macmillan Press.

Tapp, J. L. (1974). The psychological limits of legality. In J. R. Pennock and J. W. Chapman (eds.), *The Limits of Law: Nomos XV* (pp. 46-75). New York: Lieber-Atherton.

Taylor, M. J (1982). *Community, Anarchy, and Liberty*. Cambridge, England: Cambridge University Press.

_____. (1984). Social order without the state. In T. Holterman & H. van Maarseveen (eds.), *Law and Anarchism* (pp. 157-189). Montreal: Black Rose Books.

Tocqueville, A. de (1973). *Democracy in America*. New York: Knopf. (Original Work Published 1831)

Tyler, T. R. (1990). *Why People Obey the Law*. New Haven: Yale University.

Tyler, T. R., Boeckman, R. J., Smith, H. J., & Huo, Y. J. (1997). *Social Justice in a Diverse Society*. Boulder, CO: Westview Press.

Tyler, T. R., & McGraw, K. M. (1986). Ideology and the interpretation of personal experience: Procedural justice and political quiescence. *Journal of Social Issues*, 42, 115-128.

Tyler, T. R. & Mitchell, G. (1994). Legitimacy and the empowerment of discretionary legal authority: The United States Supreme Court and abortion rights. *Duke Law Journal*, 43, 703-802.

Tyler, T. R., Rasinski, K. A., & Griffin, E. (1986). Alternative images of the citizen: Implications for public policy. *American Psychologist*, 41, 970-978.

van Maarseveen, H. (1984). Anarchism and the theory of political law. In T. Holterman & H. van Maarseveen (eds.), *Law and Anarchism* (pp. 85-105). Montreal: Black Rose Books.

Wachtel, P. L. (1983). *The Poverty of Affluence: A Psychological Portrait of the American Way of Life*. New York: Free Press.

Wiener, R. L., Watts, B. A., and Stolle, D. P. (1993). Psychological jurisprudence and the information processing paradigm. *Behavioral Sciences and the Law*, 11, 79-96.

The Law's Assumption of Rationality

[22]

Memories of Things Unseen

Elizabeth F. Loftus

University of California, Irvine

ABSTRACT—*New findings reveal more about the malleability of memory. Not only is it possible to change details of memories for previously experienced events, but one can sometimes also plant entirely false memories into the minds of unsuspecting individuals, even if the events would be highly implausible or even impossible. False memories might differ statistically from true ones, in terms of certain characteristics such as confidence or vividness, but some false memories are held with a great degree of confidence and expressed with much emotion. Moreover, false memories can have consequences for later thoughts and behaviors, sometimes rather serious ones.*

KEYWORDS—*memory; false memory; suggestibility*

Faulty memory has led to more than its share of heartbreak. The cases of individuals who have been released from prison after DNA evidence revealed their innocence make compelling examples. Larry Mayes of Indiana had the dubious distinction of being the 100th such person to be freed in the United States. He was convicted of raping a gas station cashier after the victim positively identified him in court. Apparently it did not matter that she had failed to identify him in two earlier lineups and did so in court only after she was hypnotized by the police. Mayes spent 21 years in prison for a crime he did not commit. Attorney Thomas Vanes had prosecuted Mayes, believing at the time that Mayes was guilty. But two decades later, after Vanes saw the result of old evidence being subjected to new DNA testing, he changed his mind. "He was right, and I was wrong," wrote Vanes (2003), in a newspaper op-ed piece arguing for the DNA testing of another individual who was awaiting execution for an ugly robbery-murder of an elderly couple. For Vanes, it was a "sobering lesson."

The DNA exonerations have taught all of us a sobering lesson, namely, that faulty memory is the major cause of wrongful convictions. Concerns about justice are but one reason why the study of memory is so important.

MEMORY DISTORTION: FROM CHANGING DETAILS TO PLANTING FALSE MEMORIES

Pick up any textbook in the field of memory or cognition, and you will invariably find mention of faulty memory. That has been true for decades. But lately, the study of memory distortion has been thriving.

Address correspondence to Elizabeth F. Loftus, 2393 Social Ecology II, University of California, Irvine, CA 92697-7085; e-mail: eloftus@uci.edu.

In the 1970s through 1990s, hundreds of studies showed the power of new information to contaminate memory reports. Stop signs became yield signs, hammers turned into screwdrivers, and broken glass got "added" to memories for accidents. The inaccuracies in memory caused by erroneous information provided after the event became known as the "misinformation effect."

In the mid 1990s, memory investigators went further. It was one thing to change a detail in memory for a previously experienced event, but quite another thing to plant an entirely false memory into the mind. Using fairly strong suggestions, investigators succeeded in getting people to incorrectly believe that when they were children, they had been lost in a shopping mall for an extended time, hospitalized overnight, or involved in an unfortunate accident at a family wedding (see Loftus, 1997). The "strong suggestion" involved enlisting the help of family members to construct scenarios describing true and false experiences and feeding these scenarios to the subjects as if they were all true. The method was later dubbed the "familial-informant false-narrative procedure" (Lindsay, Hagen, Read, Wade, & Garry, 2004), but it is easier to call it the "lost in the mall" procedure. After being fed suggestive information that ostensibly came from their relatives, a significant minority of subjects came to accept all or part of the suggestion and claimed it as their own experience.

Would people also fall sway to suggestion if the to-be-planted event was particularly horrible? The answer is yes, as revealed in one study that convinced one third of subjects that when they were children they had nearly drowned and had to be rescued by a lifeguard (Heaps & Nash, 2001). Another research group convinced about half of their subjects that they had had particularly awful experiences as children, such as being a victim of a vicious animal attack (Porter, Yuille, & Lehman, 1999).

The suggestion used in these lost-in-the-mall studies was strong. In the real world, some forms of suggestion that are used are far more subtle. Perhaps their persuasive powers would be weaker. Take *guided imagination*, a technique in which individuals are led to imagine that they have had experiences (like breaking a window) that they have previously denied. Even a minute's worth of such imagination can increase people's confidence that in the past they had an experience like the imagined one—a phenomenon called *imagination inflation*. (See Garry & Polaschek, 2000, for an excellent review.) Imagining another person engaged in an event can also increase your confidence that it happened to you. Finally, some individuals, such as those who tend to have lapses in memory and attention, are more susceptible to imagination inflation than others. The clinical implications are evident—many therapy techniques involve imagination-based interventions; their capacity for distorting autobiography (an unexpected side effect?) needs to be appreciated.

Memories of Things Unseen

PLANTING FALSE MEMORIES OR EXTRACTING TRUE MEMORIES?

When people claim, after suggestion, that they were lost in a mall, or attacked by an animal, perhaps the suggestive manipulation has extracted true memories rather than planting false ones. This quite-legitimate challenge has been met with research efforts to plant memories of events that would be highly implausible or even impossible.

In one such study, subjects evaluated advertisements under a pretense. One of the ads was for Disneyland and featured Bugs Bunny by the magic castle. The text made reference to meeting Bugs—the perfect end to the perfect day. After evaluating this ad, or a control ad, subjects were asked about their own childhood experiences at Disneyland (Braun, Ellis, & Loftus, 2002). About 16% of those who had been exposed to the fake Bugs ad later said they had personally met Bugs Bunny at Disneyland. Later studies showed that with multiple exposures to fake Disney ads that mentioned Bugs Bunny, the percentages rose even higher. Many of those subjects who fell sway to the suggestion remembered the impossible encounter in quite a bit of detail (e.g., they hugged Bugs or touched his ear). Of course, this memory is impossible because Bugs Bunny is a Warner Bros. character and would not be found at a Disney theme park. But the study shows that suggestive methods are indeed capable of leading to false beliefs or memories.

Other efforts to plant impossible or implausible memories show just how far one can go in tampering with people's autobiographies. In one case, people were led to believe that they had witnessed a person being demonically possessed as a child (Mazzoni, Loftus, & Kirsch, 2001). In the most powerful of these studies, subjects read articles that described demonic possession and were designed to increase its plausibility. One article was a testimonial from a prominent individual describing his own childhood experience with witnessing a possession. Subjects also received false feedback about causes of certain fears; they were told that witnessing a possession probably led to their particular childhood fears. Finally, they answered questions about their own childhood experiences. Relative to control subjects, those who had received the suggestion were more confident that they had witnessed possession as a child.

In yet another study, subjects were led to remember an event that never occurs in the country in which they lived, namely, "having a nurse remove a skin sample from my little finger" before age 6 (Mazzoni & Memon, 2003, p. 187). The most powerful method of suggestion in this study involved having subjects imagine that they had had the experience.

Perhaps you are thinking that these events are not sufficiently implausible—that Bugs might not be at Disneyland but other rabbits are, that demonic possession may not have been witnessed but other bizarre behavior was. Such critiques have encouraged researchers to come up with new pseudoevents that are less susceptible to these charges. Some researchers have also tried to make the false event so specific that it is unlikely to have happened to large numbers of people. So, in another study, subjects were persuaded that they had gotten in trouble with a friend for putting Slime (a brightly colored gelatinous substance manufactured as a toy) in their teacher's desk when in the first or second grade (Lindsay et al., 2004). The pseudoevent was chosen to be distinctive and memorable, and neither entirely implausible nor likely actually to have occurred. What was surprising about the findings was the sheer number of people who were led to believe that they had "Slimed" their teacher. The most powerful method of suggestion in this study involved the combination of a narrative and a photo ostensibly provided by the subject's parents. The narrative for the pseudoevent was customized for each subject by inserting the subject's name and the teacher's name into it:

> I remember when Jane was in Grade 1, and like all kids back then, Jane had one of those revolting Slime toys that kids used to play with. I remember her telling me one day that she had taken the Slime to school and slid it into the teacher's desk before she arrived. Jane claimed it wasn't her idea and that her friend decided they should do it. I think the teacher, Mrs. Smollett, wasn't very happy and made Jane and her friend sit with their arms folded and legs crossed, facing a wall for the next half hour. (Lindsay et al., 2004, p. 150)

The photo provided was the subject's actual class photo for Grade 1 or 2.

Using a fairly strict criterion for classifying a response as a pseudomemory, Lindsay and his colleagues found that when subjects returned to the lab for a second interview, more than 65% of subjects had developed such memories. Moreover, when debriefed and told their memories were false, some individuals expressed great surprise, as revealed in their verbalizations: "You mean that didn't happen to me?" and "No way! I remember it! That is so weird!" (Lindsay et al., 2004, pp. 152–153).

So (almost certainly), false memories do get planted by suggestion. Some methods are more powerful than others, leading to very high rates of false-memory reports. In the Slime study, the suggestion included a suggestive narrative ostensibly provided by an authoritative figure, namely, the subject's parent. Moreover, the class photo may have added to the authoritativeness of the suggestive narrative and increased the subject's confidence that the Slime event happened. The photo may have further encouraged speculation about the details of the pseudoevent. So, for example, a subject looking at the photo might have mused over who the co-perpetrator might have been in the Slime prank and even picked out a likely candidate. Finally, these studies indicate that rather unlikely events can be planted in the mind, and they counter the criticism that the events planted in such studies revive true memories.

CHARACTERISTICS OF FALSE MEMORIES

Can we tell the difference between true memories and false ones? Many studies show that there are some statistical differences, that true memories are held with more confidence or seem more vivid than false ones. But other studies do not demonstrate such differences. In the Slime study, for example, subjects rated their memories on a number of scales, including scales indicating their confidence that the event actually took place and the extent to which they felt their memory experience resembled reliving the event. False memories were as compelling as true memories, at least on these dimensions.

Are false memories felt with as much emotion as true ones? One answer to this question comes from research on individuals who presumably have false memories of events not planted experimentally. In a study of people who have memories of abduction by space aliens (McNally et al., 2004), physiological measures (e.g., heart rate and electrical conductance of the skin) were taken while abductees listened to tape-recorded accounts of their reported alien encounters.

146

The abductees showed greater reactivity to their abduction scripts than to other scripts (positive and neutral). Moreover, this effect was more pronounced among the abductees than among control subjects who did not have abduction memories and listened to the same accounts. Assuming no one was actually abducted, these results suggest that false memories of abduction can produce very strong physiological responses. Thus, a memory report accompanied by strong emotion is not good evidence that the memory report reflects a genuine experience (see also McNally, 2003).

CONSEQUENCES OF FALSE MEMORIES

Changing beliefs or memories can influence what people think or do later. In one study, people who were led by a fake advertisement to believe that they met Bugs at Disneyland were later asked to say how associated various pairs of characters were in their minds (e.g., How associated are Mickey Mouse and Minnie Mouse? How associated are Bugs Bunny and Mickey Mouse?). Those who fell for the fake ad and believed that they had met Bugs later on claimed that Bugs Bunny was more highly related to various Disney characters than did people who were not exposed to the fake ad. This suggests that the thought processes of ad-exposed individuals can be influenced (see Loftus, 2003, for other examples).

There are also real-world examples showing how false memories can have repercussions. Recall the Heaven's Gate cult, a group whose members had been led to believe they were in telepathic contact with aliens. Apparently the cult members had taken out an insurance policy, to insure against being abducted, impregnated, or killed by aliens. The group paid $1,000 a year for this coverage. So clearly their (presumably false) beliefs had economic consequences (Siepel, 1997). Thirty-nine members of the cult participated in the ultimate act of consequence: They partook in a mass suicide in 1997, killing themselves under the belief that to do so would free their souls.

FINAL REMARKS

There is now ample evidence that people can be led to believe that they experienced things that never happened. In some instances, these beliefs are wrapped in a fair amount of sensory detail and give the impression of being genuine recollections. Some researchers have suggested that implausible or unlikely events will be hard to plant into the minds of adults or children, but in fact people can be led to believe in experiences that are highly unlikely to be true (e.g., witnessing demonic possession, being abducted by aliens, being hugged by Bugs Bunny at Disneyland). In one recent study of false memories in children, the children came up with elaborate stories for such unlikely events as helping a woman find her lost monkey and helping a person who injured her ankle after spilling Play-Doh (Scullin, Kanaya, & Ceci, 2002). These "rich" false memories can have repercussions down the line, affecting later thoughts and behaviors.

A half century ago, Frederic C. Bartlett, the psychologist from Cambridge, England, shared his important insights about memory. He posited that remembering is "imaginative reconstruction, or construction," and "it is thus hardly ever exact" (Bartlett, 1932, p. 213). His insights link up directly with contemporary research on memory distortion, although even he might have been surprised to find out just how inexact memory can be. He might have also relished the contemporary research, which has brought us quite a ways toward understanding what it is like for people when they experience "imaginative construction" in both experimental and real-world settings. Bartlett died in 1969, just missing the beginning of a vast effort to investigate the memory processes that he so intelligently foreshadowed, and that show unequivocally how humans are the authors or creators of their own memories. They can also be the authors or creators of someone else's memory.

Recommended Reading

Lindsay, D.S., Hagen, L., Read, J.D., Wade, K.A., & Garry, M. (2004). (See References)

Loftus, E.F. (2002). Memory faults and fixes. *Issues in Science and Technology, 18,* 41–50.

Loftus, E.F. (2003). (See References)

McNally, R.J. (2003). (See References)

REFERENCES

Bartlett, F.C. (1932). *Remembering: A study in experimental and social psychology.* Cambridge, England: Cambridge University Press.

Braun, K.A., Ellis, R., & Loftus, E.F. (2002). Make my memory: How advertising can change our memories of the past. *Psychology and Marketing, 19,* 1–23.

Garry, M., & Polaschek, D.L.L. (2000). Imagination and memory. *Current Directions in Psychological Science, 9,* 6–10.

Heaps, C.M., & Nash, M. (2001). Comparing recollective experience in true and false autobiographical memories. *Journal of Experimental Psychology: Learning, Memory, and Cognition, 27,* 920–930.

Lindsay, D.S., Hagen, L., Read, J.D., Wade, K.A., & Garry, M. (2004). True photographs and false memories. *Psychological Science, 15,* 149–154.

Loftus, E.F. (1997). Creating false memories. *Scientific American, 277*(3), 70–75.

Loftus, E.F. (2003). Make-believe memories. *American Psychologist, 58,* 864–873.

Mazzoni, G., & Memon, A. (2003). Imagination can create false autobiographical memories. *Psychological Science, 14,* 186–188.

Mazzoni, G.A.L., Loftus, E.F., & Kirsch, I. (2001). Changing beliefs about implausible autobiographical events. *Journal of Experimental Psychology: Applied, 7,* 51–59.

McNally, R.J. (2003). *Remembering trauma.* Cambridge, MA: Harvard University Press.

McNally, R.J., Lasko, N.B., Clancy, S.A., Macklin, M.L., Pitman, R.K., & Orr, S.P. (2004). Psychophysiological responding during script-driven imagery in people reporting abduction by space aliens. *Psychological Science, 15,* 493–497.

Porter, S., Yuille, J.C., & Lehman, D.R. (1999). The nature of real, implanted, and fabricated memories for emotional childhood events: Implications for the recovered memory debate. *Law and Human Behavior, 23,* 517–537.

Scullin, M.H., Kanaya, T., & Ceci, S.J. (2002). Measurement of individual differences in children's suggestibility across situations. *Journal of Experimental Psychology: Applied, 8,* 233–246.

Siepel, T. (1997, March 31). Leader's health tied to deaths. *San Jose Mercury News.* Retrieved June 24, 2003, from http://www.sacred-texts.com/ufo/39dead16.htm

Vanes, T. (2003, July 28). Let DNA close door on doubt in murder cases. *Los Angeles Times,* p. B11.

[23]

False memory syndrome: Undermining the credibility of complainants in sexual offences

Fiona E. Raitt [a,*], M. Suzanne Zeedyk [b]

[a] *Department of Law, University of Dundee, Scotland DD1 4 HN, UK*
[b] *University of Dundee, Scotland DD1 4 HN, UK*

1. Introduction

Within the last 10 years the concept of false memory syndrome (FMS) has entered the legal arena. It is a label increasingly used to describe and account for adults' recollection of sexual abuse committed against them during childhood. The phenomenon first appeared in the courts in 1994 in the U.S. civil case of *Ramona* v *Isabella*,[1] and since then has appeared on numerous occasions in courts throughout the Anglo-American jurisdictions (including the United States, Canada, Scotland, and England, all of which feature in the present article). Vigorous debates have taken place within the academic and professional literatures across several disciplines (e.g., psychology, psychiatry, law) addressing the reliability of memory processes and their significance in legal testimony.

The purpose of this article is not to rehearse the claims and counterclaims concerning the validity of repressed memories or FMS, as these have been thoroughly aired in the literature (e.g., Ceci & Bruck, 1995; Conway, 1997; Lindsay & Read, 1995; Ofshe & Watters, 1994; Koocher, 1998). Instead, this article explores the extent to which this phenomenon plays an increasingly important role in the legal construction of credibility, one of the determining features of a reliable witness in the courtroom. Determining that a witness is incredible is the most effective route to dismissing their testimony. Historically, there have been numerous rules of evidence and procedure that have had the effect of rendering the testimony of women and children incredible. Although attempts have been

---

* Corresponding author.
E-mail address: f.e.raitt@dundee.ac.uk (F.E. Raitt).

[1] In this case, Gary Ramona was accused of incest by his adult daughter, Holly. He successfully sued her therapists, counsellor Marche Isabella and psychiatrist Richard Rose, for malpractice, claiming that they had falsely implanted the memories of childhood sexual abuse. For discussion, see Johnston (1997).

made (sometimes successfully) to dilute the impact of these rules, those that remain still adversely affect the manner in which testimony concerning sexual assault is received. This article contends that the courtroom use of FMS is the latest in that tradition. It argues that those who bring charges concerning childhood abuse (most of whom are women) are disadvantaged, not primarily because of unreliable memory processes about traumatic events, but more importantly because of the historical tendency to doubt women's credibility. This distrust continues to be reflected in the contemporary debate surrounding FMS and is even exacerbated by the rules of evidence that allow testimony on the phenomenon into the courtroom.

2. False memory syndrome

In order to make sense of the controversies surrounding FMS, it is necessary to understand its origins. The term "false memory" arose in the early 1990s as part of the debate surrounding child sexual abuse, particularly in the context of reports of recovered memories of childhood sexual abuse. Such reports originate from adults who have made allegations of sexual abuse, based on incidents that occurred during their childhood, the memory of which they have forgotten for a period of time and only later recalled. The phenomenon gained such attention within the psychological and psychiatric communities, as well as within society more generally, that the British Psychological Society carried out an investigation into the matter in 1995 (Andrews et al., 1995), and The Royal College of Psychiatrists did so in 1998 (Brandon, Boakes, Glaser, & Green, 1998).

These investigations revealed that recovered memories occur in response to a variety of events, such as a further trauma, media accounts of sexual abuse, reading accounts of abuse, joining an incest survivors' group, or the death of the abuser (e.g., Andrews et al., 1995; Bass & Davis, 1994; Brandon et al., 1998; Freyd, 1996; Hall & Lloyd, 1989). Memories may also be recovered during a period of therapy, and it is this route that has attracted the most controversy and attention. This is because there are concerns that poor therapeutic practice may "implant" false memories, rather than assist in the "recovery" of accurate ones (e.g., Gardner, 1992; Hochman, 1994; Pendergrast, 1998; for reviews, see Lindsay & Read, 1994; Prozan, 1997).[2] A variety of labels now exist in the literature for memories that have apparently been remembered after a period of quiescence, and the distinctions in terms are important because they embody different perspectives on the accuracy of the memories. Terms such as "repressed memories," "recovered memories," and "delayed memories" imply that the recollections are accurate, while the term "false memory" implies that the memories are fabricated, either partially or entirely.

---

[2] Interestingly, although it is this source that has raised particular controversy and professional concern, recovery during therapy has been found to be less frequent than is commonly believed. The Royal College of Psychiatrists (Brandon et al., 1998) concluded that false memories "usually but not always" occurred during a course of therapy, while the survey carried out by British Psychological Society (Andrews et al., 1995, p. 211) found that "the most common context in which memory recovery occurred was prior to any therapy."

The term "false memory" and the associated psychiatric condition of FMS are the currency of an organization called the FMS Foundation.[3] This foundation was set up in 1992 in the United States by Ralph Underwager and his wife, Holly Wakefield, following a well-publicized case of repressed memories of alleged incest. It is a highly effective lobby group with the backing of a Scientific and Professional Advisory Board of over 30 members, including many prominent academic and clinical psychologists and psychiatrists. It has a sister body within the United Kingdom, the British False Memory Society, founded in 1993 by Roger Scotford, who argued he had been wrongly accused of sexual abuse by his daughter after she recovered memories of abuse while undergoing therapy. It, too, has an Advisory Committee comprising eminent British psychologists, and it has been actively involved, among other activities, in the formal investigations into the phenomenon of recovered memories carried out by the British Psychological Society and the Royal College of Psychiatrists. The Foundation's website[4] describes their aims as seeking scientific knowledge regarding memory processes, as investigating the increasing occurrence of FMS, and as supporting those families whose lives are damaged by false memories. Critics, in contrast, maintain that the aims of these groups are partisan, alleging that their primary purpose is not to facilitate the use of scientific knowledge, but to "form an advocacy group" for those accused of abuse (Schuman & Galvez, 1996, p. 9).

It is important to acknowledge that there will be casualties of the FMS controversy, including parents who suffer as a result of their children's inaccurate claims regarding sexual abuse, whether intentional or sincerely mistaken. The painful consequences of such errors for their families' lives have been explored in detail by authors such as Pendergrast (1998) and Loftus (1993). However, given the frequency of childhood sexual abuse, our concern in this article is to draw attention to the consequences of the FMS controversy for those women (and men) who have suffered such abuse. Estimates of the occurrence of sexual abuse during childhood suggest that between 5% and 33% of girls suffer abuse, with equivalent figures for boys varying from between 3% to as much as 30% (Finkelhor, 1986; Ghate and Spencer, 1995; Hall & Lloyd, 1989; Herman, 1981). Estimates of the occurrence of repressed memories, although difficult to derive, have been found to range between 20% and 40% in samples of adults who report childhood sexual abuse (Elliot, 1997; Epstein & Bottoms, 2002; Melchert, 1996; Melchert & Parker, 1997).

FMS as yet has no formal status as a psychiatric or psychological disorder. There is no entry for it in the *Diagnostic and Statistical Manual of Mental Disorders* (DSM-IV, American Psychiatric Association, 1994) or the *International Statistical Classification of Diseases and Related Health Problems* (ICD-10, 1992), which are the two key reference manuals for mental illness throughout the world. The proponents of the syndrome would be keen to see it

---

[3] This ownership is explicitly acknowledged in the 2003 website of the False Memory Syndrome Foundation (http://www.fmsonline.org).

[4] www.fmsonline.org.

included, however. The 2003 website of the FMS Foundation, for example, supplies the following definition for the syndrome.

> [A] condition in which a person's identity and interpersonal relationships are centered around a memory of traumatic experience which is objectively false but in which the person strongly believes ... [T]he syndrome may be diagnosed when the memory is so deeply ingrained that it orients the individual's entire personality and lifestyle, in turn disrupting all sorts of other adaptive behavior.

Explicit parallels have been drawn by the Foundation between FMS and multiple personality disorder, a condition that has been included within the DSM for more than 20 years. Thus, there is a large group of informed and influential professionals who would be keen to see it acquire formal recognition. Ironically, it could be argued that such endorsement, while helpful to the groups' aims, is not essential, for the term FMS has already gained extensive societal and legal currency.

The dispute over FMS, and the choice between terms such as "false" and "recovered," has given rise to deep divisions within the therapeutic and research communities of psychology and psychiatry, with consequent confusion for professions such as law, social work, and the media. From the research perspective, the phenomenon of repressed memories is an area of scientific enquiry, to be investigated using empirical methods that produce reliable, verifiable, and objective evidence. Research outcomes have, so far, emphasized the complexities and fallibility of the memory process, with few findings obtained to support the claim that memories can be forgotten over the long periods of time that the "delayed memories" account advocates (e.g., Ceci & Bruck, 1993, 1995; Ceci & Loftus, 1994; Hochman, 1994; Lindsay & Read, 1994; Loftus, 1993; Pendergrast, 1998). From the therapeutic perspective, the dispute is essentially an epistemological one. It is argued that cognitive scientists have failed to find evidence of delayed memories because they have not asked the right research questions, searching for generalizable, objective characteristics of memory at the expense of its contextualized, subjective qualities. This group tends to see delayed memories of child sexual abuse as a credible occurrence, in part because the repression of memories is associated with posttraumatic stress disorder, an accepted psychiatric condition. Moreover, the phenomenon of delayed memories is consistent with the "continuum of violence" (Kelly, 1988) that women and children experience (e.g., Armstrong, 1978, 1996; Bass & Davis, 1994; Hall & Lloyd, 1989; Hester, Kelly, & Radford, 1996; Kelly, 1988; Russell, 1984; Schuman & Galvez, 1996). Abusers exert a considerable amount of power and psychological "conditioning" over their child victims, and that may help to explain why it is often not until individuals reach adulthood, with its attendant autonomy, that they are able to face such memories and to break their silence.

The debate generated by these two perspectives is lively and provocative (for a review, see Courtois, 1997), but our concern here is not with establishing which side has a better claim to "truth." Rather, we seek to highlight the ramifications of legal arguments that utilize the concept of FMS, given its inherent accusation that adult memories of childhood abuse are untrustworthy and should be regarded with suspicion.

3. Women, children, and credibility

One of the enduring concerns of feminist critique has been the way in which the criminal justice process devalues women's experiences, undermining and distorting their testimonial accounts within the courtroom. The prosecution of sexual offences offers compelling examples of this treatment. Attacking the credibility of a witness is the most effective route to dismissing her testimony as unreliable, and research has shown that victims of sexual violence are consistently discredited when they act as witnesses in the courtroom (Adler, 1987; Brownmiller, 1975; Estrich, 1987; Naffine, 1994; Smart, 1989; Temkin, 1987). This practice becomes relevant to the issue of delayed and false memories because sexual violence lies at the heart of such memories. The vociferous FMS debate does not pertain equally to all kinds of childhood memories and experiences (either positive or negative), but is concerned about a particular type of childhood trauma: sexual abuse.

When accusations of sexual assault are received in the courtroom, they are met with suspicion. The force of this response has been revealed most powerfully in the literature on rape, where the theme of the mendacious woman making false accusations of rape has resonated down the centuries. One of the early indicators of attitudes towards women in rape cases is recorded in the writings of the 17th century English jurist, Sir Matthew Hale (1678, p. 635) who declared:

> It must be remembered that [rape] is an accusation easily to be made and hard to be proved, and harder to be defended by the party accused, tho' never so innocent.

Even at the end of the 20th century, scholars claimed that the focus in societal and legal discourse of rape still "falsely remains on the victim as an instigator of most rapes" (Allison & Wrightson, 1993, p. 2). In legal theory and in courtroom practice, it makes little difference whether the alleged sexual assault was carried out against an adult woman or a child, for the response of the court to either is suspicion and disbelief.

This can be seen in both historical and contemporary cases (for review, see Raitt & Zeedyk, 2000). For example, in the 1887 U.S. case of *Dodson v State*, a young woman's allegations that her father had raped her were discounted on the grounds that "her reputation for truth and chastity was bad long before the birth of the child which she alleged was the result of the alleged incestuous intercourse," resulting in a finding that she was an accomplice to the crime of incest (*American Law Reports Annotated*, 1960, p. 713). In the 2002 Scottish case of *E v HM Advocate*,[5] the appeal court upheld an appeal on the ground of defective representation in regard to criminal charges against *E* for the rape of his two daughters, who were aged 3 and 5 at the time of the alleged rapes. The trial defense team had chosen what the appeal court described as a "gently, softly, softly approach" to the cross-examination of the children, and the court agreed with the appellant that he was entitled to have expected a much more vigorous attack on their credibility. One of the three

---

[5] *E v HM Advocate* 2002 SLT 715.

appeal court judges, Lord McCluskey, explained that if the defense was to succeed "there was no escape from facing up to the need to challenge the evidence of the two girls as being deliberately false." Although there was no basis for suggesting the girls had themselves concocted a story, Lord McCluskey agreed that "the defense should positively argue with as much force as the evidence would permit that the children had been manipulated by their mother" (*Scots Law Times* 715 at 732).

One of the processes by which this legal skepticism is facilitated is the use of the rules of evidence on credibility (Hunter, 1996; Lees, 1997; MacCrimmon, 1991; MacKinnon, 1987; Temkin, 1987). Credibility is a crucial feature of litigation in most legal systems, and certainly within the adversarial environment of Anglo-American jurisdictions, in which oral testimony occupies a pivotal role. The credibility of a witness is paramount to the outcome of a case. In cases of rape, for example, a complainant's failure to conform to the expected behaviors and normative standards of the "ideal" rape victim typically has harsh consequences, including debilitating and humiliating cross-examination by defense counsel. As Ellison (2000, p. 41) notes:

> Routinely, complainants are questioned extensively about their 'sexually suggestive' clothing, 'sexually provocative behaviour,' their financial situation and their role as mothers.

Tactics to discredit rape victims are a feature of adversarial litigation throughout the common law world, where the principal objective in the cross-examination process appears to be to underline a belief in the tendencies of women to mislead and prevaricate in matters relating to sex (Heenan & McKelvie, 1997; Lees, 1997; Brown, Burman, & Jamieson, 1993; Smart, 1989; Taslitz, 1999). The tactics are underpinned by a remarkably tenacious social mythology that has become embedded in legal discourse. It imposes considerable responsibility on women for rape and has led to judicial comments such as:

> Women who say no do not always mean no. It is not just a question of how she says it, how she shows and makes it clear. (Judge Wild, 1981, cited in Kennedy, 1993, p. 111)

As we have seen, children are explicitly caught up in the same mythology. The comments of Glanville Williams (1987, p. 188), a leading English academic lawyer, provide a good example of such views.

> It has been known for children to invent elaborate fantasies and tell rank falsehoods. Children can be extraordinarily precocious, well versed in sexual language and quite capable of making false accusations, especially when they believe this to be a form of self-defence.

Such constructions reveal compellingly the extent to masculinist constructions continue to shape expectations across all the Anglo-American jurisdictions about the behavior of women and children.

F.E. Raitt, M.S. Zeedyk / International Journal of Law and Psychiatry 26 (2003) 453–471   459

It is fair to say that critiques of the treatment of witnesses in cases of sexual offences have not been ignored. Reform of the prosecution of such cases has been a political aim in most jurisdictions over the past several decades. A variety of measures has been undertaken, including the introduction of screens and closed circuit television link to assist vulnerable witnesses in giving testimony, the widespread enactment of rape shield legislation, the redefinition of rape to acknowledge the possibility of male victims, and restrictions on rape defendants conducting their own defense (for reviews, see Ellison, 2001; Hunter, 1996). However, these protective measures are almost exclusively mechanistic changes that provide formalistic improvement and superficial relief. They do little to address the more fundamental problem caused by negating women's perspectives and excluding them from the courtroom (Hunter, 1996; Ellison, 2001; Matoesian, 2001). A comprehensive study of rape law reform in the United States concluded that:

> The ability of rape reform legislation to produce instrumental change is limited. In most of the jurisdictions we studied, the reforms had no impact. (Spohn & Horney, 1992, p. 173)

UK researchers (e.g., Brown et al., 1993; Temkin, 2000) have drawn similarly disappointing conclusions about the effectiveness of legislative changes. Barristers, for example, continue to be heavily influenced in their professional strategies by personal views about the propriety of women's behavior.

> I mean the silly woman is prepared to be picked up by a stranger and go back for, quotes, coffee, you know, what does she expect? If a woman does that, can she really be surprised that a jury will say that she may have consented to sex? Again a hitch-hiker or somebody like that. (Temkin, 2000, p. 225)

It is against this backdrop of long-standing doubt about women's credibility in relation to matters of sex and sexual violence that we turn to examine in more depth the phenomenon of false memories, given that it has begun to emerge as a fresh strategy for discrediting complainants of sexual violence.

However, before doing so, it is important to comment on the relevance of our argument to the distinction in civil and criminal cases. It is only in criminal cases, especially those involving sexual assault, that credibility occupies a central role. This is because, in criminal cases, the complainant is a key prosecution witness, and her credibility and status will therefore be fundamental to the success of the case. If she is not perceived as believable, then the State's case is likely to collapse. In civil cases, issues of credibility rarely arise, because this is not an issue that is usually relevant to the categories that can serve as the basis for civil suits (e.g., breach of contract, personal injury, divorce, adoption). Notably, FMS first came to public attention through the civil courts (*Ramona* v *Isabella*, 1994), and it has remained most strongly associated with civil cases, as a result of law suits filed against therapists. Within such civil cases, and in contrast to criminal cases, the contentious issues do not normally give rise to an attack on the plaintiff's credibility. However, as we shall see, the criminal courts are beginning to make increased reference to the issue of false memories (e.g., *US* v *Rouse and others*, 1997;[6] *R* v *Jenkins*, 1998;[7] for a review, see Raitt & Zeedyk, 2000). With that increase, concerns about the credibility of witnesses are given a new lease of life.

4. False memories and credibility

The accusation of "false memory" strikes at the very heart of a witness's credibility, signifying as it does that this is a person incapable of offering accurate or reliable testimony. Whether the charge relates to recollection of a specific event or to the broader psychiatric syndrome, the outcome is equally damaging. This is an observation that may seem rather obvious, given that it might have appeared predictable that the law would respond to FMS in a manner that was in keeping with its usual wary response to claims of sexual violence. However, that similarity is obscured in most of the legal literature on the topic. Indeed, it was the covert nature of that link that prompted the analysis undertaken in this article. We would argue that three factors have been central in achieving this shroud: a scientific focus on memory processes, the inherent nature of sexual violence to FMS, and the rules governing the production of evidence within the courtroom. This final section of the article examines each of these factors in turn.

4.1. FMS as a scientific debate over memory processes

Within the field of psychology, the debate about FMS has focused on scientific arguments about the nature of memory processes. Although authors stress the abhorrent nature of child sexual abuse, it is an issue that remains fairly peripheral to their theoretical inquiry. Abuse tends to be treated as background societal context, rather than as one of the components central to an understanding of the syndrome and its symptoms. The comments of Loftus (1993, p. 521), in one of the classic papers within this domain, illustrate that composition.

> There is little doubt that actual childhood sexual abuse is tragically common. Even those who claim that the statistics are exaggerated still agree that child abuse constitutes a serious social problem. I do not question the commonness of childhood sexual abuse itself but ask here about how the abuse is recalled in the minds of adults . . . Despite the confidence with which assertions [about repressed memories] are made, there are few studies that provide evidence of the extent to which repression occurs.

Such comments seek to emphasize the distinction between, rather the integration of, sexual abuse and memories of it.

The accusatory split between scientists and therapists, discussed earlier, has been encouraged by this separation of psychological processes from their context. It is not

---

[6] *United States* v *Rouse*, 111 F.3d 561 (8th circuit 1997).
[7] [1998] 4 All ER 411.

F.E. Raitt, M.S. Zeedyk / International Journal of Law and Psychiatry 26 (2003) 453–471   461

surprising to find that when the methods of investigation used by researchers and clinicians differ, it is the scientific account that the courts prefer. This is because, like science, the law esteems qualities such as rationality, generalizability, and objectivity (Raitt & Zeedyk, 2000). Crucially, it is precisely such a decontextualized account that allows historical prejudices about women's credibility to be obscured, despite the irony that taking account of such factors might be the key to understanding the phenomenon of delayed memories.

The mainstream psychological and psychiatric communities regard the issue of delayed memories and FMS as one of cognitive function. This is the reason that so much of the psychological literature on the topic makes only passing reference to the social context of child sexual abuse (e.g., Groff, 1994; Kihlstrom, 1997; Loftus & Ketcham, 1994; Memon & Young, 1997; Schacter, Norman, & Koutstaal, 1997; Yapko, 1997). Cognitive psychologists seek to understand the generalizable principles by which basic human memory processes operate, just as empirical researchers in other psychological domains usually seek to discover the universal, decontextualized principles that govern the processes they study. That emphasis is illustrated in the definitions provided in introductory psychology textbooks, such as that written by Gleitman, Fridlund, & Reisberg, 1999, p. 11, which is one of the best selling texts on the market.

> Like all other sciences, psychology looks for general principles—underlying uniformities among different events. A single event as such means little; what counts is what any one event shares with others ... [T]he science's main concern is with the discovery of the general principles.

Psychologists consider memory to be a topic on which they have preeminent expertise, given that it was amongst the issues studied by the field's forefathers. Ebbinghaus (1885) developed the method of studying patterns of forgetting through the recitation of nonsense syllables, and that is the basic paradigm still used in much contemporary cognitive work, despite advances in the technological delivery of visual and audio stimuli. These laboratory-based methods are preferred not only because they can be tightly controlled and manipulated to test theoretical hypotheses, but also because laboratories are viewed as neutral environments where contextual factors are less likely to influence experimental outcomes. In short, the appeal of laboratories for many cognitive theorists is their simplicity as decontextualized contexts.

This preference provides a good example of the ways in which researchers' perspectives contrast with those of therapists. Therapists argue that context is highly relevant to the experience of, and the recollection of, sexual abuse. They argue that adherence to the use of decontextualized methods to investigate decontextualized processes cannot provide the kinds of insights that are necessary for understanding the more complicated aspects of memory, such as autobiographical knowledge and the effect of trauma (e.g., Fivush, 2000; Freyd, 1996; Freyd & DePrince, 2001). Moreover, their professional interest lies not in reaching an objective determination of what occurred between an adult and child, but in understanding the meaning that the victim has assigned to the event(s). This explicit preference for subjectivity over objectivity leads the scientific community to have serious doubts about the usefulness of the therapeutic community's contribution to an understanding of delayed and false memories. This conflict becomes particularly sharp when such memories are subjected to the scrutiny of the courts, whose responsibility it is to determine the guilt or innocence of an accused individual.

At the core of the debate between the communities lies a difference in epistemological orientations. Therapists are not seeking a single objective truth. Memory has value for them, regardless of whether or not it meets the criteria of scientific objectivity, because the primary goal of therapists is to return patients to good health. They are comfortable with the possibility that there may be two contrasting, but equally valid, perspectives on an event. For experimental psychologists, the lack of information about the memory's veracity is precisely the problem. The data that they see as helpful in this area are those that are derived by controlled, replicable procedures, for these are regarded as objective and truthful.

Locating the issue of delayed/false memories within the experimental cognitive paradigm serves to divert attention from the issue of sexual abuse in a way that, intentionally or not, sanitizes the debate by configuring it as an internal scientific dispute that has little external context. The discussion becomes elevated in a way that would not be possible were the phenomenon located primarily in the social science lexicon within which child sexual abuse is most commonly analyzed. Just as the antiabortion lobby has promoted the medical concept of Postabortion Syndrome in a bid to make their rhetoric more palatable to a society increasingly concerned with women's health (Hopkins, Reicher, & Saleem, 1996), there is an advantage to be gained in keeping the debate defined in scientific rather than political terms. This may explain the very clear commitment on the part of the FMS societies to the scientific basis for this syndrome, and the drive for its inclusion in the DSM. Such an analysis echoes the points made by numerous theorists over the past three decades (e.g., Chesler, 1972; Downs, 1996; Herman, 1992; Lee & Gilchrist, 1997; Nicolson, 1991; Szasz, 1972) concerning the social construction of mental disorders and psychological syndromes. In short, while the debate over FMS rightly includes consideration of scientific knowledge about the memory processes, the debate is about much more than those findings. Making sense of the phenomenon and its consequences will require an explanation that extends well beyond the boundaries of cognitive science.

4.2. Memories of sexual violence

A second factor that obscures the tie between child sexual abuse and FMS is the nature of the incidents that are remembered. Memories of sexual violence are intrinsic to the concept of FMS.[8] It this therefore predictable that the law will respond to FMS in a manner that is in keeping with its customary response to charges of sexual offence, which is one of suspicion. As we have seen, individuals who bring charges of sexual assault (usually women and

---

[8] Although the relevance of repressed memories has been explored in relation to a range of traumatic experiences, including warfare, natural disasters, physical abuse, and even alien abduction, FMS is specifically concerned with memories of sexual abuse.

F.E. Raitt, M.S. Zeedyk / International Journal of Law and Psychiatry 26 (2003) 453–471   463

children) are liable to be portrayed as emotionally labile, unreliable, and disordered (Chesler, 1972; Showalter, 1987; Smart, 1992; Ussher, 1997). The concept of FMS serves to disadvantage them because it so easily feeds into the existing juridical tapestry that treats complaints of sexual abuse as incredible.

Disbelief of the frequency of sexual abuse as well as the veracity of the complainant underscores much of the reaction of the legal system to child sexual abuse. The comments of Lord Justice Salmon are frequently cited because they provide such an exemplary illustration of this view. In the 1969 case of *R v Henry and Manning*,[9] in which two men had appealed against their convictions of raping a 16-year-old girl, Lord Justice Salmon commented that:

> Human experience has shown that in these courts girls and women do sometimes tell an entirely false story which is very easy to fabricate, but extremely difficult to refute. Such stories are fabricated for all sorts of reasons, which I need not now enumerate, and sometimes for no reason at all.

The insidious nature of such views is demonstrated in the 1997 Canadian case of *R. v N.R.*[10] In that case, the court permitted a rape victim's medical records to be released to the defendant's lawyers in order to assist in the preparation of his defense. The permission was granted on the basis that the records contained details of when she had lost her virginity, a piece of information that the judges accepted would have a bearing on her credibility "in the sense that she has both a motive and a propensity to fabricate" (cited in Gotell, 2001, p. 328).

Belief in the propensity of women and children to fabricate false stories is hard to dispel. Fact construction serves as the basis for legal argument in adversarial systems. As a vehicle for ascertaining "the truth," however, this is a method that has been roundly exposed as a fallacy (Amsterdam & Bruner, 2000; Bennett and Feldman, 1981; Nicolson, 1994; Scheppelle, 1992). Fact construction may be expedient within an adversarial system, but it cannot do more than reproduce the narratives of those actors within the system who are empowered to provide the dominant version of the "truth." In regard to stories of sexual assault, the complainant's version is rarely the dominant one, and it is not just the substantive content that attracts doubt but also the manner in which that story is recounted.

> Women who delay telling their stories of abuse at the hands of men or who appear to change their stories over time about such abuse are particularly likely to be discredited as liars. The very fact of delay is used as evidence that the delayed or changed stories cannot possible be true. But women frequently have exactly this response: they repress what happened; they cannot speak; they hesitate, waver, and procrastinate; they hope the abuse will go away; they cover up for their abusers; they try harder to be "good girls"; and they take the blame for the abuse upon themselves. Such actions produce delayed or altered stories over time, which are then disbelieved for the very reason that they have been revised. (Scheppele, 1992, pp. 126–127, fns 10–19)

---

[9] *R. v Henry and Manning* [1969] 53 Cr App R 150 at 153.
[10] *R. v N.R.* [1997] O.J. No. 80 (QL)(Prov.Div).

The turn to postmodernism that has occurred within the social sciences, including law and some marginal domains of psychology, has highlighted the contextual nature of truth. Postmodernists stress that the meaning of a behavior does not lie within the behavior itself. Rather, meaning is assigned by those providing an account of the behavior, who will naturally draw on some contextual elements while ignoring other possible elements in order to ensure that the account they are providing ends up as a sensible, coherent one. The adversarial process of fact construction, in contrast, implies that facts contain their own truth, yielding no need to consider their context or the variety of meanings that might legitimately pertain to the issues under consideration.

We have already discussed the similar attachment to decontextualized fact production that exists within cognitive psychology. Freyd (1996) is among the few cognitive scientists who have sought to incorporate context within their theoretical predictions concerning memory (but see also the review by Epstein and Bottoms, 2002). Freyd argues that the memory processes associated with recall of childhood sexual abuse may differ from those associated with other memories, including those that are traumatic (e.g., the death of a loved one, natural disasters, car accidents, hospitalization). This is because, unlike most other events, sexual abuse usually involves emotional betrayal, given that it is most often perpetrated by a known and trusted adult. She suggests that coping with such betrayal may result in particular memory processes, of which we as yet have little knowledge. It may well be "normal" for the recall of trauma involving betrayal to show the fragmentation, partiality, and lack of coherence described in patients' recovered memories. However, because the experimental cognitive approach to studying memory has failed to explore the ways in which (traumatic) context may influence the generation and maintenance of memory, scientists are unable to speak to the normality or otherwise of such characteristics.

The inability of psychologists to offer detailed information concerning the extent to which childhood sexual trauma normally causes memories to be fragmented, partial, and incoherent takes an ominous turn when it is realized that such characteristics already have a preexisting meaning for lawyers: a fragmented, partial, and incoherent story is the mark of an unreliable witness.

4.3. The rules of evidence

The rules of evidence constitute one further means by which the link between FMS and sexual violence continues to be obscured. This could be viewed as a rather extreme claim, given that the rules of evidence are generally viewed as neutral legal artifacts. They are regarded as having a rational, objective, internal logic, which excludes them from critique or analysis. They have been designed to structure the legal process so that it operates consistently and fairly. However, this means that they also have the power to control and constrain the ways in which witnesses can tell their stories—indeed, they are expressly designed for that purpose (Hunter, 1996; Hunter & Mack, 1997; Kinports, 1991; Scheppele, 1992). It is therefore rules of evidence that serve as the legal mechanisms that govern which stories will (and will not) get told in court about women and children (and men), including what is reasonable and unreasonable for them to claim about their own experiences.

F.E. Raitt, M.S. Zeedyk / International Journal of Law and Psychiatry 26 (2003) 453–471   465

The law's distrust of women's credibility, especially in regard to sexual matters, owes much to the framework of evidentiary rules within which testimony can be heard. Evidence rules and discourse are modeled upon the rationalist tradition (Twining, 1990), of which J. H. Wigmore was a major advocate. The rationalist tradition remains the dominant pedagogy in law schools throughout the common law world and is the lynchpin of legal practice (Nicolson, 1994; Twining, 1985, 1990). Wigmore is regarded one of the great 19th century American jurists, with his treatise, *Wigmore on Evidence* (1937), described as "the most famous legal text ever published in [the US]" (Herman, 2000, p. 11). Wigmore ensured that the issue of credibility remained firmly embedded in the epistemology of evidence discourse, when he declared in his treatise (para. 924a) that:

> [N]o judge should ever let a sex offence charge go to the jury unless the female complainant's social history and mental make-up have been examined and testified to by a qualified physician.

This instruction neatly creates an alignment of rape victim status with that of a potential psychiatric condition. It is fatal to the presentation of a witness as credible, and it is an alignment to which the accusation of FMS commends itself.

In effect, the rules of evidence tend to endorse and perpetuate the value judgments that are made within wider societal and professional contexts. Although this insight continues to prove startling to the legal literature, it has been argued to be the case with a large number of rules, such as those concerned with hearsay (Raitt, 2000), privilege (Kinports, 2000), and character (Childs, 2000). When it comes to the issue of sexual offences against children, there are several additional rules that help to keep credibility at the forefront of the court's considerations.

The first of these is the rule on expert testimony. When experts are permitted to give opinion evidence, there is considerable scope for their testimony to be privileged over the complainant's own story. The effect is to drown the authentic voice of the complainant, or to restrict her to being "heard" only through the interpretive powers of the expert (O'Donovan, 1993). For example, in *United States* v *Rouse and others*[11] (1997), the appeal court allowed a retrial in a case involving four defendants who had been convicted of a series of sexual offences against various children. The appeal was allowed on the basis that the trial judge should have permitted expert testimony to test whether or not suggestive questioning in the investigation had tainted the children's testimony, thereby raising the possibility that false memories might have been induced by the questioning. Moreover, the appeal court criticized the trial judge for refusing to permit the defendants' request for an independent psychological examination of the children to test their credibility. If children are regarded as untrustworthy when reporting contemporaneous sexual abuse, there is a concomitant likelihood that adult women (and men) will be distrusted when recalling memories of abuse that occurred some years previously. Societal attitudes towards adults suspected of having false memories of

---

[11] *United States* v *Rouse*, 111 F.3d 561 (8th circuit 1997).

466 *F.E. Raitt, M.S. Zeedyk / International Journal of Law and Psychiatry 26 (2003) 453–471*

childhood sexual abuse risk becoming indistinguishable from the attitudes expressed towards children who complain of sexual abuse. The rules of evidence perpetuate that risk, for in introducing expert testimony on FMS into the court, those who wish to challenge accounts of childhood sexual abuse have access to a register that is regarded as more authoritative and valid than the victim's own voice.

A second rule of evidence that endorses traditional views of credibility is that of corroboration. This rule states the law's preference, if not demand, that corroborative evidence be presented before conferring credibility on certain disputed facts. Interestingly, the law's preference for corroboration is affirmed by the FMS Foundation, which states that

> [T]he professional organizations agree: the only way to distinguish between true and false memories is by external corroboration. (FMSF Website, 2003)

Corroboration is not a requirement in every type of case or in all jurisdictions, but even in those jurisdictions that have abolished the general need for corroboration in criminal cases, the testimony of children and the complainer's testimony in sexual offences are often exceptions to the rule. Such exceptions leave judges with the discretion to warn juries that they should be wary of the uncorroborated testimony of children or of a complainer in a case of sexual offence (Hunter, 1996; McEwan, 1998). Noticeably, such warnings are not applied to the testimony of complainers or witnesses in other types of crime, such as robbery, fraud, and physical assault. It is notoriously difficult to obtain corroborative evidence in cases involving only two people, where the activities concerned tend to occur in "private," as opposed to "public." This has been highlighted by Cheit (1998), who brought a well-publicized lawsuit against his abuser. Unlike most victims, he was able to supply considerable corroborative evidence of his claims, but he still found his account was met by substantial doubt. That experience prompted him to compile a database of recovered memories of childhood abuse that have been independently corroborated and that he believes can be proven to be accurate. He observed that

> The fact remains that, in 1994, it is extremely difficult to come forward with allegations of sexual abuse. And the external forces of denial are almost overwhelming. If a case as verified as mine meets with denial, I dread to think about the experience of people who don't have the kind of corroboration that I do. And I really worry that we're getting close to a point where it's going to be impossible to prosecute child molesters, because we don't believe children, and now we don't believe adults. (Cheit, 1994; quoted in Freyd, 1996, p. 59)

Cheit's experience demonstrates the suspicion with which law continues to greet certain narratives, resisting granting them credence unless they meet the more demanding standards set for them.

The rules pertaining to discovery offer a third example of those rules of evidence that foreground credibility. Discovery is the process by which one party in litigation seeks access to the private records belonging to the other party. The prosecution of sexual offences

F.E. Raitt, M.S. Zeedyk / International Journal of Law and Psychiatry 26 (2003) 453–471   467

provides rich, and contested, territory for the recovery of medical, therapeutic, educational, and child welfare records of complainants. Defense lawyers are interested in details of previous allegations of abuse and/or proof of prior abuse. The former, if unproven, demonstrates a propensity to fabricate, while the latter demonstrates a motive to fabricate. Either way, the credibility of the complainant is doomed. She is either mendacious, and thus unreliable, or else she is vindictive, and thus equally unreliable. As Busby (1997, p. 163) has observed, "Evidence of prior sexual abuse is perfect defence evidence on credibility." Utilizing the discovery process is an increasingly common strategy and, although it may sometimes be deflected as a breach of constitutional privacy provisions, it is having a measure of success due to its easy attachment to the defendant's claim for due process and a fair trial, the procurement of which requires (it is claimed) a full disclosure of the complainant's history in sexual complaints. When the application for discovery arises in a case where FMS is an issue, the route to accessing records may be eased, because lawyers can draw on the debates raging within the cognitive field to demonstrate that the medical or therapeutic records are needed to eliminate the possibility that memories have been implanted (Gotell, 2001).

The three rules highlighted here comprise a small part of the complex doctrinal framework that regulates the admissibility of facts and determines their relevance and weight. Although orthodox jurisprudence holds that the rules of evidence operate neutrally in an apolitical context, closer examination of the workings of each rule reveals a reinforcement of particular social and cultural interpretations that derive from a deep suspicion of the complainant of sexual offences.

5. Conclusion

Legislative reform has had little impact on the image of the incredible female complainant. Traditional attempts to destabilize women's credibility in cases of rape and sexual assault, which continue to typify prosecutions to the modern day, are mirrored in the recent emergence of the phenomenon of FMS in the courtroom. The introduction of evidence relating to false memories replicates the stereotyping of female behavior as untrustworthy, reinforcing the courtroom disadvantage that women and children have historically faced. That reinforcement is in large part due to the tenacious quality of the rules of evidence, whose reductive force has so successfully impeded the spirit of political and strategic change underpinning reform.

We suggest that the underlying reasons for the relative failure of law reform to effect change in this area can be explained by the influential mythology regarding the behavior of men and women in sexual violence. Despite the significant amount of critical literature (e.g., Armstrong, 1996; Brownmiller, 1975; Kelly, 1988; Ussher, 1997), this mythology has survived, albeit in shifting form. The implication of our argument is that the rules on credibility need to be reconfigured, such that credibility ceases to play such a dominant role in the fact construction of sexual abuse cases. It is not satisfactory to claim, as many legal theorists and practitioners have done, that the problems of sexual assault cases require that the

468   *F.E. Raitt, M.S. Zeedyk / International Journal of Law and Psychiatry 26 (2003) 453–471*

complainant's credibility be established via particularly robust cross-examination practices that are inspired by disbelief. The call for such measures is based on precisely the kinds of presumptions that we have examined in this article—that the woman's and the child's claims are unlikely to be creditworthy. Instead, a call should be made for measures that will dispel such presumptions from the courtroom. These measures could take various forms, including reforming the rules of evidence and contextualizing the legal training of judges and law students. Until the existing mythology is comprehensively addressed, then efforts directed at protecting the vulnerable witness through law reform will always be diluted and, ultimately, unsuccessful.

References

Adler, Z. (1987). *Rape on trial*. London: Routledge.

Allison, J. A., & Wrightson, L. S. (1993). *Rape: The misunderstood crime*. Newbury Park: Sage.

American Law Reports Annotated, 2nd series (1960). 74 ALR 2d [and supplement].

American Psychiatric Association (1994). *Diagnostic and statistical manual of mental disorders* (4th ed. revised). Washington, DC: Author.

Amsterdam, A. G., & Bruner, J. (2000). *Minding the law*. Cambridge, MA: Harvard University Press.

Andrews, B., Morton, J., Bakerian, D. A., Brewin, C. R., Davies, G. M., & Mollon, P. (1995). The recovery of memories in clinical pratice: Experiences and beliefs of British Psychological Society practitioners. *The Psychologist, 209–214 (*May).

Armstrong, L. (1978). *Kiss daddy goodnight: A speak-out on incest*. New York: Hawthorn Books.

Armstrong, L. (1996). *Rocking the cradle of sexual politics: What happened when women said incest*. London: The Women's Press.

Bass, E., & Davis, L. (1994). *The courage to heal: A guide for women survivors of child sexual abuse*. New York: Harper & Row.

Bennett, W. L., & Feldman, M. (1981). *Reconstructing Reality in the Courtroom*. London: Tavistock.

Brandon, S., Boakes, J., Glaser, D., & Green, R. (1998). Recovered memories of childhood sexual abuse: Implications for clinical practice. *British Journal of Psychiatry, 172,* 296–307.

British Psychological Society (1995). *The report of the working party of the British Psychological Society on recovered memories*. London: Author.

Brown, B., Burman, M., & Jamieson, L. (1993). *Sex crimes on trial*. Edinburgh: Edinburgh University Press.

Brownmiller, S. (1975). *Against our will: Men, women and rape*. London: Secker and Warburg.

Busby, K. (1997). Discriminatory use of personal records in sexual violence cases. *Canadian Journal of Women and the Law, 9,* 148–177.

Ceci, S. J., & Bruck, M. (1993). Suggestibility of the child witness: A historical review and analysis. *Psychological Bulletin, 113,* 403–439.

Ceci, S. J., & Bruck, M. (1995). *Jeopardy in the courtroom: A scientific analysis of children's testimony*. Washington, DC: American Psychological Association.

Ceci, S. J., & Loftus, E. (1994). 'Memory work': A royal road to false memories? *Applied Cognitive Psychology, 8,* 351–364.

Cheit, R. (1994). *Paper presented at the Mississippi Statewide Conference on Child Abuse and Neglect*. Jackson, MS, April 29.

Cheit, R. (1998). Consider this, skeptics of recovered memory. *Ethics and Behavior, 8,* 141–160.

Chesler, P. (1972). *Women and madness*. New York: Doubleday.

Childs, M. (2000). The character of the accused. In M. Childs, & L. Ellison (Eds.), *Feminist perspectives on evidence* (pp. 211–235). London: Cavendish.

Conway, M.A. (1997). *Recovered memories and false memories*. Oxford: Oxford University Press.

Courtois, C. A. (1997). Delayed memories of child sexual abuse: Critique of the controversy and clinical guide-lines. In M. A. Conway (Ed.), *Recovered Memories and False Memories* (pp. 206–229). Oxford: Oxford University Press.

Downs, D. A. (1996). *More than victims: Battered women, the syndrome society and the law.* Chicago: University of Chicago Press.

Ebbinghaus, H. (1885). *Memory.* New York: Teacher's College, Columbia University, 1913. Reprinted in 1964, New York: Dover.

Elliot, D. M. (1997). Traumatic events: Prevalence and delayed recall in the general population. *Journal of Consulting and Clinical Psychology, 65,* 811–820.

Ellison, L. (2001). *The adversarial process and the vulnerable witness.* Oxford: Oxford University Press.

Epstein, M. A., & Bottoms, B. L. (2002). Explaining the forgetting and recovery of abuse and trauma memories: Possible mechanisms. *Child Maltreatment, 7,* 210–225.

Estrich, S. (1987). *Real rape.* Cambridge, MA: Harvard University Press.

Fivush, R. (2000). Accuracy, authorship and voice: Feminist approaches to autobiographical memory. In P. Miller, & E. Scholnick (Eds.), *Towards a feminist developmental psychology* (pp. 85–106). New York: Cambridge University Press.

Freyd, J. J. (1996). *Betrayal trauma: The logic of forgetting childhood abuse.* Cambridge, MA: Harvard University Press.

Freyd, J. J., & DePrince, A.P. (Eds.) (2001). *Trauma and cognitive science: A meeting of minds, science, and human experience.* New York: Haworth Press.

Gardner, R. A. (1992). *True and false accusations of child sex abuse.* Cresskill, NJ: Creative Therapeutics.

Ghate, D., & Spencer, L. (1995). *The Prevalence of Child Sexual Abuse in Britain: A Feasibility Study for a Large-Scale National Survey of the General Population.* London: HMSO.

Gleitman, H., Fridlund, A. J., & Reisberg, D. (1999). *Psychology* (5th ed.). New York: W.W. Norton.

Gotell, L. (2001). Colonization through disclosure: Confidential records, sexual assault complainants and Cana-dian law. *Social and Legal Studies, 10,* 315–346.

Groff, S.E. (1994). Repressed memory or false memory: New Hampshire courts consider the dispute. *New Hampshire Bar Journal, 35,* 57–58.

Hale, E. (1680). In E. Sollom (Ed.), *Pleas of the crown,* vol. 1. London: Nott and Gosling, Reprinted in 1972.

Hall, L., & Lloyd, S. (1989). *Surviving child sexual abuse: A handbook for helping women challenge their past.* Lewes, UK: The Falmer Press.

Heenan, M., & McKelvey, H. (1997). *Evaluation of the Crimes (Rape) Act 1991.* Melbourne: Department of Justice.

Herman, J. (1981). *Father-Daughter Incest.* Cambridge (Mass.): Harvard University Press.

Herman, J. (1992). *Trauma and recovery: The aftermath of violence: From domestic abuse to political terror.* New York: Harper Collins.

Herman, J. (2000). *Father–daughter incest.* London: Harvard University Press.

Heste, M., Kelly, L., & Radford, J. (Eds.) (1996). *Women, violence and male power.* Buckingham: Open University Press.

Hochman, J. (1994). Recovered memory therapy and false memory syndrome. *Skeptic, 2,* 58–61.

Hopkins, N. P., Reicher, S. D., & Saleem, J. (1996). Constructing women's psychological health in anti-abortion rhetoric. *Sociological Review, 44,* 539–565.

Hunter, R. (1996). Gender in evidence: Masculine norms vs. feminist reforms. *Harvard Women's Law Journal, 19,* 127–167.

Hunter, R., & Mack, K. (1997). Exclusion and silence: Procedure and evidence. In N. Naffine, & R. Owens (Eds.), *Sexing the subject of law* (pp. 171–192). Sydney: LBC Information Services.

Johnston, M. (1997). *Spectral evidence, the Ramona case: Incest, memory, and truth on trial in Napa Valley.* Boston: Houghton Mifflin.

Kelly, L. (1988). *Surviving sexual violence.* Cambridge: Polity Press.

Kennedy, H. (1993). *Eve was framed: Women and British justice.* London: Vintage Books.

Kihlstrom, J. F. (1997). Suffering from reminiscences: Exhumed memory, implicit memory, and the return of the repressed. In M.A. Conway (Ed.), *Recovered memories and false memories*. Oxford: Oxford University Press.

Kinports, K. (1991). Evidence engendered. *Illinois University Law Review, 413*.

Kinports, K. (2000). The 'privilege' in the privilege doctrine: A feminist analysis of the evidentiary privileges for confidential communications. In M. Childs, & L. Ellison (Eds.), *Feminist perspectives on evidence* (pp. 79–103). London: Cavendish.

Koocher, G. P. (Ed.) (1998). The Science and Politics of Recovered Memory. *Ethics & Behavior, 8*(2), 99–193 (Special issue).

Lee, E., & Gilchrist, A. (1997). Abortion psychological sequelae: The debate and the research. In E. Lee, & M. Lattimer (Eds.), *Issues in pregnancy counselling: What do women need and want?*. Canterbury: Pro-Choice Forum.

Lees, S. (1997). Ruling passions: *Sexual violence, reputation and the law*. Buckingham: Open University Press.

Lindsay, D. S., & Read, D. J. (1994). Psychotherapy and memories of child sexual abuse: A cognitive perspective. *Applied Cognitive Psychology, 8*, 281–338.

Lindsay, D. S., & Read, D. J. (1995). 'Memory work' and recovered memories of childhood sexual abuse: Scientific evidence and public, professional and personal issues. *Psychology, Public Policy and Law, 1*, 845.

Loftus, E. F. (1993). The reality of repressed memories. *American Psychologist, 48*, 518–537.

Loftus, E. F., & Ketcham, K. K. (1994). *The myth of repressed memory: False memories and accusations of sexual abuse*. New York: St. Martin's Press.

MacCrimmon, M. (1991). The social construction of reality and the rules of evidence. *British Columbia University Law Review, 25*, 36.

MacKinnon, C. A. (1987). *Feminism unmodified: Discourses on life and law*. Cambridge, MA: Harvard University Press.

Matoesian, G. M. (2001). *Law and the language of identity*. Oxford: Oxford University Press.

McEwan, J. (1998). *Evidence and the adversarial process*. Oxford: Hart Publishing.

Melchert, T. P. (1996). Childhood memory and history of different forms of abuse. *Professional Psychology: Research and Practice, 27*, 438–446.

Melchert, T. P., & Parker, R. L. (1997). Different forms of childhood abuse and memory. *Child Abuse and Neglect 21*, 125–135.

Memon, A., & Young, M. (1997). Desperately seeking evidence: The recovered memory debate. *Legal and Criminological Psychology, 2*, 131–154.

Naffine, N. (1994). Possession: Erotic love in the law of rape. *Modern Law Review, 57*, 10–37.

Nicolson, D. (1994). Truth, reason and justice; epistemology and politics in evidence discourse. *Modern Law Review, 57*, 726–744.

Nicolson, P. (1991). Explanations of postnatal depression: Structuring knowledge of female psychology. *Research on Language and Social Interaction, 25*, 75–96.

O'Donovan, K. (1993). Law's knowledge: The judge, the expert, the battered woman, and her syndrome. *Journal of Law and Society, 20*, 427–437.

Ofshe, R., & Watters, E. (1994). *Making monsters: False memories, psychotherapy, and sexual hysteria*. New York: Scribner's.

Pendergrast, M. (1998). *Victims of memory: Incest accusations and shattered lives*. London: Harper Collins.

Prozan, C. K. (1997). *Construction and reconstruction of memory: Dilemmas of childhood sexual abuse*. Northvale, NJ: Jason Aronson.

Raitt, F. E. (2000). Gender bias in the hearsay rule. In M. Childs, & L. Ellison (Eds.), *Feminist perspectives on evidence* (pp. 59–77). London: Cavendish.

Raitt, F. E., & Zeedyk, M. S. (2000). *The implicit relation of psychology and law: Women and syndrome evidence*. London: Routledge.

Russell, D. E. H. (1984). *Sexual exploitation: Rape, child sexual abuse, and workplace harassment*. Newbury Park, CA: Sage.

Schacter, D. L., Norman, K. A., & Koustal, W. (1997). *The recovered memories debate: A cognitive neuroscience*

F.E. Raitt, M.S. Zeedyk / International Journal of Law and Psychiatry 26 (2003) 453–471   471

perspective. In M.A. Conway (Ed.), *Recovered memories and false memories.* Oxford: Oxford University Press.

Scheppele, K. M. (1992). Just the facts ma'am: Sexualised violence, evidentiary habits and the revision of truth. *New York Law School Law Review, 37,* 123–172.

Schuman, J., & Galvez, M. (1996). A meta/multi-discursive reading of 'false memory syndrome'. *Feminism and Psychology, 6,* 7–29.

Showalter, E. (1987). *The female malady: Women, madness, and English culture, 1830–1980.* London: Virago Press.

Smart, C. (1989). *Feminism and the power of law.* London: Routledge.

Smart, C. (1992). The woman of legal discourse. *Social and Legal Issues, 1,* 29–44.

Spohn, C., & Horney, J. (1992). *Rape law reform: A grassroots revolution and its impact.* New York: Plenum.

Szasz, T. (1972). *The myth of mental illness.* St. Albans: Paladin.

Taslitz, A. (1999). *Rape and the culture of the courtroom.* New York: New York University Press.

Temkin, J. (1987). *Rape and the legal process.* London: Sweet and Maxwell.

Temkin, J. (2000). Prosecuting and defending rape: Perspectives from the Bar. *Journal of Law and Society, 27,* 219–248.

Twining, W. (1985). *Theories of Evidence: Bentham and Wigmore.* London: Weidenfeld & Nicolson.

Twining, W. (1990). *Rethinking evidence: Exploratory essays.* Oxford: Basil Blackwell.

Ussher, J. M. (1997). *Fantasies of femininity: Reframing the boundaries of sex.* London: Penguin Books.

Wigmore, J. H. (1937). *Wigmore on evidence, volume IIIA.* Boston: Little Brown and Co. Reprinted and edited by Chadbourne in 1970.

Williams, G. (1987). Child witnesses. In P. Smith (Ed.), *Criminal Law Essays in Honour of J. C. Smith.* London: Butterworths.

Yapko, M. (1997). The troublesome unknowns about trauma and recovered memories. In M. A. Conway (Ed.), *Recovered memories and false memories.* Oxford: Oxford University Press.

[24]

Judgment under Uncertainty: Heuristics and Biases

Biases in judgments reveal some heuristics of thinking under uncertainty.

Amos Tversky and Daniel Kahneman

Many decisions are based on beliefs concerning the likelihood of uncertain events such as the outcome of an election, the guilt of a defendant, or the future value of the dollar. These beliefs are usually expressed in statements such as "I think that . . . ," "chances are . . . ," "it is unlikely that . . . ," and so forth. Occasionally, beliefs concerning uncertain events are expressed in numerical form as odds or subjective probabilities. What determines such beliefs? How do people assess the probability of an uncertain event or the value of an uncertain quantity? This article shows that people rely on a limited number of heuristic principles which reduce the complex tasks of assessing probabilities and predicting values to simpler judgmental operations. In general, these heuristics are quite useful, but sometimes they lead to severe and systematic errors.

The subjective assessment of probability resembles the subjective assessment of physical quantities such as distance or size. These judgments are all based on data of limited validity, which are processed according to heuristic rules. For example, the apparent distance of an object is determined in part by its clarity. The more sharply the object is seen, the closer it appears to be. This rule has some validity, because in any given scene the more distant objects are seen less sharply than nearer objects. However, the reliance on this rule leads to systematic errors in the estimation of distance. Specifically, distances are often overestimated when visibility is poor because the contours of objects are blurred. On the other hand, distances are often underesti-

The authors are members of the department of psychology at the Hebrew University, Jerusalem, Israel.

mated when visibility is good because the objects are seen sharply. Thus, the reliance on clarity as an indication of distance leads to common biases. Such biases are also found in the intuitive judgment of probability. This article describes three heuristics that are employed to assess probabilities and to predict values. Biases to which these heuristics lead are enumerated, and the applied and theoretical implications of these observations are discussed.

Representativeness

Many of the probabilistic questions with which people are concerned belong to one of the following types: What is the probability that object A belongs to class B? What is the probability that event A originates from process B? What is the probability that process B will generate event A? In answering such questions, people typically rely on the representativeness heuristic, in which probabilities are evaluated by the degree to which A is representative of B, that is, by the degree to which A resembles B. For example, when A is highly representative of B, the probability that A originates from B is judged to be high. On the other hand, if A is not similar to B, the probability that A originates from B is judged to be low.

For an illustration of judgment by representativeness, consider an individual who has been described by a former neighbor as follows: "Steve is very shy and withdrawn, invariably helpful, but with little interest in people, or in the world of reality. A meek and tidy soul, he has a need for order and structure, and a passion for detail." How do people assess the probability that Steve is engaged in a particular

occupation from a list of possibilities (for example, farmer, salesman, airline pilot, librarian, or physician)? How do people order these occupations from most to least likely? In the representativeness heuristic, the probability that Steve is a librarian, for example, is assessed by the degree to which he is representative of, or similar to, the stereotype of a librarian. Indeed, research with problems of this type has shown that people order the occupations by probability and by similarity in exactly the same way (1). This approach to the judgment of probability leads to serious errors, because similarity, or representativeness, is not influenced by several factors that should affect judgments of probability.

Insensitivity to prior probability of outcomes. One of the factors that have no effect on representativeness but should have a major effect on probability is the prior probability, or base-rate frequency, of the outcomes. In the case of Steve, for example, the fact that there are many more farmers than librarians in the population should enter into any reasonable estimate of the probability that Steve is a librarian rather than a farmer. Considerations of base-rate frequency, however, do not affect the similarity of Steve to the stereotypes of librarians and farmers. If people evaluate probability by representativeness, therefore, prior probabilities will be neglected. This hypothesis was tested in an experiment where prior probabilities were manipulated (1). Subjects were shown brief personality descriptions of several individuals, allegedly sampled at random from a group of 100 professionals—engineers and lawyers. The subjects were asked to assess, for each description, the probability that it belonged to an engineer rather than to a lawyer. In one experimental condition, subjects were told that the group from which the descriptions had been drawn consisted of 70 engineers and 30 lawyers. In another condition, subjects were told that the group consisted of 30 engineers and 70 lawyers. The odds that any particular description belongs to an engineer rather than to a lawyer should be higher in the first condition, where there is a majority of engineers, than in the second condition, where there is a majority of lawyers. Specifically, it can be shown by applying Bayes' rule that the ratio of these odds should be $(.7/.3)^2$, or 5.44, for each description. In a sharp violation of Bayes' rule, the subjects in the two conditions produced essentially the same probability judgments. Apparently, subjects evaluated the likelihood that a particular description belonged to an engineer rather than to a lawyer by the degree to which this description was representative of the two stereotypes, with little or no regard for the prior probabilities of the categories.

The subjects used prior probabilities correctly when they had no other information. In the absence of a personality sketch, they judged the probability that an unknown individual is an engineer to be .7 and .3, respectively, in the two base-rate conditions. However, prior probabilities were effectively ignored when a description was introduced, even when this description was totally uninformative. The responses to the following description illustrate this phenomenon:

Dick is a 30 year old man. He is married with no children. A man of high ability and high motivation, he promises to be quite successful in his field. He is well liked by his colleagues.

This description was intended to convey no information relevant to the question of whether Dick is an engineer or a lawyer. Consequently, the probability that Dick is an engineer should equal the proportion of engineers in the group, as if no description had been given. The subjects, however, judged the probability of Dick being an engineer to be .5 regardless of whether the stated proportion of engineers in the group was .7 or .3. Evidently, people respond differently when given no evidence and when given worthless evidence. When no specific evidence is given, prior probabilities are properly utilized; when worthless evidence is given, prior probabilities are ignored (1).

Insensitivity to sample size. To evaluate the probability of obtaining a particular result in a sample drawn from a specified population, people typically apply the representativeness heuristic. That is, they assess the likelihood of a sample result, for example, that the average height in a random sample of ten men will be 6 feet (180 centimeters), by the similarity of this result to the corresponding parameter (that is, to the average height in the population of men). The similarity of a sample statistic to a population parameter does not depend on the size of the sample. Consequently, if probabilities are assessed by representativeness, then the judged probability of a sample statistic will be essentially independent of

27 SEPTEMBER 1974

sample size. Indeed, when subjects assessed the distributions of average height for samples of various sizes, they produced identical distributions. For example, the probability of obtaining an average height greater than 6 feet was assigned the same value for samples of 1000, 100, and 10 men (2). Moreover, subjects failed to appreciate the role of sample size even when it was emphasized in the formulation of the problem. Consider the following question:

A certain town is served by two hospitals. In the larger hospital about 45 babies are born each day, and in the smaller hospital about 15 babies are born each day. As you know, about 50 percent of all babies are boys. However, the exact percentage varies from day to day. Sometimes it may be higher than 50 percent, sometimes lower.

For a period of 1 year, each hospital recorded the days on which more than 60 percent of the babies born were boys. Which hospital do you think recorded more such days?

► The larger hospital (21)
► The smaller hospital (21)
► About the same (that is, within 5 percent of each other) (53)

The values in parentheses are the number of undergraduate students who chose each answer.

Most subjects judged the probability of obtaining more than 60 percent boys to be the same in the small and in the large hospital, presumably because these events are described by the same statistic and are therefore equally representative of the general population. In contrast, sampling theory entails that the expected number of days on which more than 60 percent of the babies are boys is much greater in the small hospital than in the large one, because a large sample is less likely to stray from 50 percent. This fundamental notion of statistics is evidently not part of people's repertoire of intuitions.

A similar insensitivity to sample size has been reported in judgments of posterior probability, that is, of the probability that a sample has been drawn from one population rather than from another. Consider the following example:

Imagine an urn filled with balls, of which ⅔ are of one color and ⅓ of another. One individual has drawn 5 balls from the urn, and found that 4 were red and 1 was white. Another individual has drawn 20 balls and found that 12 were red and 8 were white. Which of the two individuals should feel more confident that the urn contains ⅔ red balls and ⅓ white balls, rather than the opposite? What odds should each individual give?

In this problem, the correct posterior odds are 8 to 1 for the 4 : 1 sample and 16 to 1 for the 12 : 8 sample, assuming equal prior probabilities. However, most people feel that the first sample provides much stronger evidence for the hypothesis that the urn is predominantly red, because the proportion of red balls is larger in the first than in the second sample. Here again, intuitive judgments are dominated by the sample proportion and are essentially unaffected by the size of the sample, which plays a crucial role in the determination of the actual posterior odds (2). In addition, intuitive estimates of posterior odds are far less extreme than the correct values. The underestimation of the impact of evidence has been observed repeatedly in problems of this type (3, 4). It has been labeled "conservatism."

Misconceptions of chance. People expect that a sequence of events generated by a random process will represent the essential characteristics of that process even when the sequence is short. In considering tosses of a coin for heads or tails, for example, people regard the sequence H-T-H-T-T-H to be more likely than the sequence H-H-H-T-T-T, which does not appear random, and also more likely than the sequence H-H-H-H-T-H, which does not represent the fairness of the coin (2). Thus, people expect that the essential characteristics of the process will be represented, not only globally in the entire sequence, but also locally in each of its parts. A locally representative sequence, however, deviates systematically from chance expectation: it contains too many alternations and too few runs. Another consequence of the belief in local representativeness is the well-known gambler's fallacy. After observing a long run of red on the roulette wheel, for example, most people erroneously believe that black is now due, presumably because the occurrence of black will result in a more representative sequence than the occurrence of an additional red. Chance is commonly viewed as a self-correcting process in which a deviation in one direction induces a deviation in the opposite direction to restore the equilibrium. In fact, deviations are not "corrected" as a chance process unfolds, they are merely diluted.

Misconceptions of chance are not limited to naive subjects. A study of the statistical intuitions of experienced research psychologists (5) revealed a lingering belief in what may be called the "law of small numbers," according to which even small samples are highly representative of the populations from which they are drawn. The responses of these investigators reflected the expectation that a valid hypothesis about a population will be represented by a statistically significant result in a sample—with little regard for its size. As a consequence, the researchers put too much faith in the results of small samples and grossly overestimated the replicability of such results. In the actual conduct of research, this bias leads to the selection of samples of inadequate size and to overinterpretation of findings.

Insensitivity to predictability. People are sometimes called upon to make such numerical predictions as the future value of a stock, the demand for a commodity, or the outcome of a football game. Such predictions are often made by representativeness. For example, suppose one is given a description of a company and is asked to predict its future profit. If the description of the company is very favorable, a very high profit will appear most representative of that description; if the description is mediocre, a mediocre performance will appear most representative. The degree to which the description is favorable is unaffected by the reliability of that description or by the degree to which it permits accurate prediction. Hence, if people predict solely in terms of the favorableness of the description, their predictions will be insensitive to the reliability of the evidence and to the expected accuracy of the prediction.

This mode of judgment violates the normative statistical theory in which the extremeness and the range of predictions are controlled by considerations of predictability. When predictability is nil, the same prediction should be made in all cases. For example, if the descriptions of companies provide no information relevant to profit, then the same value (such as average profit) should be predicted for all companies. If predictability is perfect, of course, the values predicted will match the actual values and the range of predictions will equal the range of outcomes. In general, the higher the predictability, the wider the range of predicted values.

Several studies of numerical prediction have demonstrated that intuitive predictions violate this rule, and that subjects show little or no regard for considerations of predictability (*1*). In one of these studies, subjects were presented with several paragraphs, each describing the performance of a student teacher during a particular practice lesson. Some subjects were asked to *evaluate* the quality of the lesson described in the paragraph in percentile scores, relative to a specified population. Other subjects were asked to *predict*, also in percentile scores, the standing of each student teacher 5 years after the practice lesson. The judgments made under the two conditions were identical. That is, the prediction of a remote criterion (success of a teacher after 5 years) was identical to the evaluation of the information on which the prediction was based (the quality of the practice lesson). The students who made these predictions were undoubtedly aware of the limited predictability of teaching competence on the basis of a single trial lesson 5 years earlier; nevertheless, their predictions were as extreme as their evaluations.

The illusion of validity. As we have seen, people often predict by selecting the outcome (for example, an occupation) that is most representative of the input (for example, the description of a person). The confidence they have in their prediction depends primarily on the degree of representativeness (that is, on the quality of the match between the selected outcome and the input) with little or no regard for the factors that limit predictive accuracy. Thus, people express great confidence in the prediction that a person is a librarian when given a description of his personality which matches the stereotype of librarians, even if the description is scanty, unreliable, or outdated. The unwarranted confidence which is produced by a good fit between the predicted outcome and the input information may be called the illusion of validity. This illusion persists even when the judge is aware of the factors that limit the accuracy of his predictions. It is a common observation that psychologists who conduct selection interviews often experience considerable confidence in their predictions, even when they know of the vast literature that shows selection interviews to be highly fallible. The continued reliance on the clinical interview for selection, despite repeated demonstrations of its inadequacy, amply attests to the strength of this effect.

The internal consistency of a pattern of inputs is a major determinant of one's confidence in predictions based on these inputs. For example, people express more confidence in predicting the final grade-point average of a student whose first-year record consists entirely of B's than in predicting the grade-point average of a student whose first-year record includes many A's and C's. Highly consistent patterns are most often observed when the input variables are highly redundant or correlated. Hence, people tend to have great confidence in predictions based on redundant input variables. However, an elementary result in the statistics of correlation asserts that, given input variables of stated validity, a prediction based on several such inputs can achieve higher accuracy when they are independent of each other than when they are redundant or correlated. Thus, redundancy among inputs decreases accuracy even as it increases confidence, and people are often confident in predictions that are quite likely to be off the mark (*1*).

Misconceptions of regression. Suppose a large group of children has been examined on two equivalent versions of an aptitude test. If one selects ten children from among those who did best on one of the two versions, he will usually find their performance on the second version to be somewhat disappointing. Conversely, if one selects ten children from among those who did worst on one version, they will be found, on the average, to do somewhat better on the other version. More generally, consider two variables X and Y which have the same distribution. If one selects individuals whose average X score deviates from the mean of X by k units, then the average of their Y scores will usually deviate from the mean of Y by less than k units. These observations illustrate a general phenomenon known as regression toward the mean, which was first documented by Galton more than 100 years ago.

In the normal course of life, one encounters many instances of regression toward the mean, in the comparison of the height of fathers and sons, of the intelligence of husbands and wives, or of the performance of individuals on consecutive examinations. Nevertheless, people do not develop correct intuitions about this phenomenon. First, they do not expect regression in many contexts where it is bound to occur. Second, when they recognize the occurrence of regression, they often invent spurious causal explanations for it (*1*). We suggest that the phenomenon of regression remains elusive because it is incompatible with the belief that the predicted outcome should be maximally representative of the input, and, hence, that the value of the outcome variable should be as extreme as the value of the input variable.

The failure to recognize the import of regression can have pernicious consequences, as illustrated by the following observation (*1*). In a discussion of flight training, experienced instructors noted that praise for an exceptionally smooth landing is typically followed by a poorer landing on the next try, while harsh criticism after a rough landing is usually followed by an improvement on the next try. The instructors concluded that verbal rewards are detrimental to learning, while verbal punishments are beneficial, contrary to accepted psychological doctrine. This conclusion is unwarranted because of the presence of regression toward the mean. As in other cases of repeated examination, an improvement will usually follow a poor performance and a deterioration will usually follow an outstanding performance, even if the instructor does not respond to the trainee's achievement on the first attempt. Because the instructors had praised their trainees after good landings and admonished them after poor ones, they reached the erroneous and potentially harmful conclusion that punishment is more effective than reward.

Thus, the failure to understand the effect of regression leads one to overestimate the effectiveness of punishment and to underestimate the effectiveness of reward. In social interaction, as well as in training, rewards are typically administered when performance is good, and punishments are typically administered when performance is poor. By regression alone, therefore, behavior is most likely to improve after punishment and most likely to deteriorate after reward. Consequently, the human condition is such that, by chance alone, one is most often rewarded for punishing others and most often punished for rewarding them. People are generally not aware of this contingency. In fact, the elusive role of regression in determining the apparent consequences of reward and punishment seems to have escaped the notice of students of this area.

Availability

There are situations in which people assess the frequency of a class or the probability of an event by the ease with

which instances or occurrences can be brought to mind. For example, one may assess the risk of heart attack among middle-aged people by recalling such occurrences among one's acquaintances. Similarly, one may evaluate the probability that a given business venture will fail by imagining various difficulties it could encounter. This judgmental heuristic is called availability. Availability is a useful clue for assessing frequency or probability, because instances of large classes are usually recalled better and faster than instances of less frequent classes. However, availability is affected by factors other than frequency and probability. Consequently, the reliance on availability leads to predictable biases, some of which are illustrated below.

Biases due to the retrievability of instances. When the size of a class is judged by the availability of its instances, a class whose instances are easily retrieved will appear more numerous than a class of equal frequency whose instances are less retrievable. In an elementary demonstration of this effect, subjects heard a list of well-known personalities of both sexes and were subsequently asked to judge whether the list contained more names of men than of women. Different lists were presented to different groups of subjects. In some of the lists the men were relatively more famous than the women, and in others the women were relatively more famous than the men. In each of the lists, the subjects erroneously judged that the class (sex) that had the more famous personalities was the more numerous (*6*).

In addition to familiarity, there are other factors, such as salience, which affect the retrievability of instances. For example, the impact of seeing a house burning on the subjective probability of such accidents is probably greater than the impact of reading about a fire in the local paper. Furthermore, recent occurrences are likely to be relatively more available than earlier occurrences. It is a common experience that the subjective probability of traffic accidents rises temporarily when one sees a car overturned by the side of the road.

Biases due to the effectiveness of a search set. Suppose one samples a word (of three letters or more) at random from an English text. Is it more likely that the word starts with r or that r is the third letter? People approach this problem by recalling words that

begin with r (road) and words that have r in the third position (car) and assess the relative frequency by the ease with which words of the two types come to mind. Because it is much easier to search for words by their first letter than by their third letter, most people judge words that begin with a given consonant to be more numerous than words in which the same consonant appears in the third position. They do so even for consonants, such as r or k, that are more frequent in the third position than in the first (*6*).

Different tasks elicit different search sets. For example, suppose you are asked to rate the frequency with which abstract words (thought, love) and concrete words (door, water) appear in written English. A natural way to answer this question is to search for contexts in which the word could appear. It seems easier to think of contexts in which an abstract concept is mentioned (love in love stories) than to think of contexts in which a concrete word (such as door) is mentioned. If the frequency of words is judged by the availability of the contexts in which they appear, abstract words will be judged as relatively more numerous than concrete words. This bias has been observed in a recent study (*7*) which showed that the judged frequency of occurrence of abstract words was much higher than that of concrete words, equated in objective frequency. Abstract words were also judged to appear in a much greater variety of contexts than concrete words.

Biases of imaginability. Sometimes one has to assess the frequency of a class whose instances are not stored in memory but can be generated according to a given rule. In such situations, one typically generates several instances and evaluates frequency or probability by the ease with which the relevant instances can be constructed. However, the ease of constructing instances does not always reflect their actual frequency, and this mode of evaluation is prone to biases. To illustrate, consider a group of 10 people who form committees of k members, $2 \leqslant k \leqslant 8$. How many different committees of k members can be formed? The correct answer to this problem is given by the binomial coefficient $\binom{10}{k}$ which reaches a maximum of 252 for $k = 5$. Clearly, the number of committees of k members equals the number of committees of $(10 - k)$ members, because any committee of k

members defines a unique group of $(10 - k)$ nonmembers.

One way to answer this question without computation is to mentally construct committees of k members and to evaluate their number by the ease with which they come to mind. Committees of few members, say 2, are more available than committees of many members, say 8. The simplest scheme for the construction of committees is a partition of the group into disjoint sets. One readily sees that it is easy to construct five disjoint committees of 2 members, while it is impossible to generate even two disjoint committees of 8 members. Consequently, if frequency is assessed by imaginability, or by availability for construction, the small committees will appear more numerous than larger committees, in contrast to the correct bell-shaped function. Indeed, when naive subjects were asked to estimate the number of distinct committees of various sizes, their estimates were a decreasing monotonic function of committee size (6). For example, the median estimate of the number of committees of 2 members was 70, while the estimate for committees of 8 members was 20 (the correct answer is 45 in both cases).

Imaginability plays an important role in the evaluation of probabilities in real-life situations. The risk involved in an adventurous expedition, for example, is evaluated by imagining contingencies with which the expedition is not equipped to cope. If many such difficulties are vividly portrayed, the expedition can be made to appear exceedingly dangerous, although the ease with which disasters are imagined need not reflect their actual likelihood. Conversely, the risk involved in an undertaking may be grossly underestimated if some possible dangers are either difficult to conceive of, or simply do not come to mind.

Illusory correlation. Chapman and Chapman (8) have described an interesting bias in the judgment of the frequency with which two events co-occur. They presented naive judges with information concerning several hypothetical mental patients. The data for each patient consisted of a clinical diagnosis and a drawing of a person made by the patient. Later the judges estimated the frequency with which each diagnosis (such as paranoia or suspiciousness) had been accompanied by various features of the drawing (such as peculiar eyes). The subjects markedly overestimated the frequency of co-occurrence of

natural associates, such as suspiciousness and peculiar eyes. This effect was labeled illusory correlation. In their erroneous judgments of the data to which they had been exposed, naive subjects "rediscovered" much of the common, but unfounded, clinical lore concerning the interpretation of the draw-a-person test. The illusory correlation effect was extremely resistant to contradictory data. It persisted even when the correlation between symptom and diagnosis was actually negative, and it prevented the judges from detecting relationships that were in fact present.

Availability provides a natural account for the illusory-correlation effect. The judgment of how frequently two events co-occur could be based on the strength of the associative bond between them. When the association is strong, one is likely to conclude that the events have been frequently paired. Consequently, strong associates will be judged to have occurred together frequently. According to this view, the illusory correlation between suspiciousness and peculiar drawing of the eyes, for example, is due to the fact that suspiciousness is more readily associated with the eyes than with any other part of the body.

Lifelong experience has taught us that, in general, instances of large classes are recalled better and faster than instances of less frequent classes; that likely occurrences are easier to imagine than unlikely ones; and that the associative connections between events are strengthened when the events frequently co-occur. As a result, man has at his disposal a procedure (the availability heuristic) for estimating the numerosity of a class, the likelihood of an event, or the frequency of co-occurrences, by the ease with which the relevant mental operations of retrieval, construction, or association can be performed. However, as the preceding examples have demonstrated, this valuable estimation procedure results in systematic errors.

Adjustment and Anchoring

In many situations, people make estimates by starting from an initial value that is adjusted to yield the final answer. The initial value, or starting point, may be suggested by the formulation of the problem, or it may be the result of a partial computation. In either case, adjustments are typically insufficient (4).

That is, different starting points yield different estimates, which are biased toward the initial values. We call this phenomenon anchoring.

Insufficient adjustment. In a demonstration of the anchoring effect, subjects were asked to estimate various quantities, stated in percentages (for example, the percentage of African countries in the United Nations). For each quantity, a number between 0 and 100 was determined by spinning a wheel of fortune in the subjects' presence. The subjects were instructed to indicate first whether that number was higher or lower than the value of the quantity, and then to estimate the value of the quantity by moving upward or downward from the given number. Different groups were given different numbers for each quantity, and these arbitrary numbers had a marked effect on estimates. For example, the median estimates of the percentage of African countries in the United Nations were 25 and 45 for groups that received 10 and 65, respectively, as starting points. Payoffs for accuracy did not reduce the anchoring effect.

Anchoring occurs not only when the starting point is given to the subject, but also when the subject bases his estimate on the result of some incomplete computation. A study of intuitive numerical estimation illustrates this effect. Two groups of high school students estimated, within 5 seconds, a numerical expression that was written on the blackboard. One group estimated the product

$$8 \times 7 \times 6 \times 5 \times 4 \times 3 \times 2 \times 1$$

while another group estimated the product

$$1 \times 2 \times 3 \times 4 \times 5 \times 6 \times 7 \times 8$$

To rapidly answer such questions, people may perform a few steps of computation and estimate the product by extrapolation or adjustment. Because adjustments are typically insufficient, this procedure should lead to underestimation. Furthermore, because the result of the first few steps of multiplication (performed from left to right) is higher in the descending sequence than in the ascending sequence, the former expression should be judged larger than the latter. Both predictions were confirmed. The median estimate for the ascending sequence was 512, while the median estimate for the descending sequence was 2,250. The correct answer is 40,320.

Biases in the evaluation of conjunctive and disjunctive events. In a recent study by Bar-Hillel (9) subjects were given the opportunity to bet on one of two events. Three types of events were used: (i) simple events, such as drawing a red marble from a bag containing 50 percent red marbles and 50 percent white marbles; (ii) conjunctive events, such as drawing a red marble seven times in succession, with replacement, from a bag containing 90 percent red marbles and 10 percent white marbles; and (iii) disjunctive events, such as drawing a red marble at least once in seven successive tries, with replacement, from a bag containing 10 percent red marbles and 90 percent white marbles. In this problem, a significant majority of subjects preferred to bet on the conjunctive event (the probability of which is .48) rather than on the simple event (the probability of which is .50). Subjects also preferred to bet on the simple event rather than on the disjunctive event, which has a probability of .52. Thus, most subjects bet on the less likely event in both comparisons. This pattern of choices illustrates a general finding. Studies of choice among gambles and of judgments of probability indicate that people tend to overestimate the probability of conjunctive events (10) and to underestimate the probability of disjunctive events. These biases are readily explained as effects of anchoring. The stated probability of the elementary event (success at any one stage) provides a natural starting point for the estimation of the probabilities of both conjunctive and disjunctive events. Since adjustment from the starting point is typically insufficient, the final estimates remain too close to the probabilities of the elementary events in both cases. Note that the overall probability of a conjunctive event is lower than the probability of each elementary event, whereas the overall probability of a disjunctive event is higher than the probability of each elementary event. As a consequence of anchoring, the overall probability will be overestimated in conjunctive problems and underestimated in disjunctive problems.

Biases in the evaluation of compound events are particularly significant in the context of planning. The successful completion of an undertaking, such as the development of a new product, typically has a conjunctive character: for the undertaking to succeed, each of a series of events must occur. Even when each of these events is very likely, the overall probability of success can be quite low if the number of events is

large. The general tendency to overestimate the probability of conjunctive events leads to unwarranted optimism in the evaluation of the likelihood that a plan will succeed or that a project will be completed on time. Conversely, disjunctive structures are typically encountered in the evaluation of risks. A complex system, such as a nuclear reactor or a human body, will malfunction if any of its essential components fails. Even when the likelihood of failure in each component is slight, the probability of an overall failure can be high if many components are involved. Because of anchoring, people will tend to underestimate the probabilities of failure in complex systems. Thus, the direction of the anchoring bias can sometimes be inferred from the structure of the event. The chain-like structure of conjunctions leads to overestimation, the funnel-like structure of disjunctions leads to underestimation.

Anchoring in the assessment of subjective probability distributions. In decision analysis, experts are often required to express their beliefs about a quantity, such as the value of the Dow-Jones average on a particular day, in the form of a probability distribution. Such a distribution is usually constructed by asking the person to select values of the quantity that correspond to specified percentiles of his subjective probability distribution. For example, the judge may be asked to select a number, X_{90}, such that his subjective probability that this number will be higher than the value of the Dow-Jones average is .90. That is, he should select the value X_{90} so that he is just willing to accept 9 to 1 odds that the Dow-Jones average will not exceed it. A subjective probability distribution for the value of the Dow-Jones average can be constructed from several such judgments corresponding to different percentiles.

By collecting subjective probability distributions for many different quantities, it is possible to test the judge for proper calibration. A judge is properly (or externally) calibrated in a set of problems if exactly II percent of the true values of the assessed quantities falls below his stated values of X_{II}. For example, the true values should fall below X_{01} for 1 percent of the quantities and above X_{99} for 1 percent of the quantities. Thus, the true values should fall in the confidence interval between X_{01} and X_{99} on 98 percent of the problems.

Several investigators (11) have ob-

tained probability distributions for many quantities from a large number of judges. These distributions indicated large and systematic departures from proper calibration. In most studies, the actual values of the assessed quantities are either smaller than X_{01} or greater than X_{99} for about 30 percent of the problems. That is, the subjects state overly narrow confidence intervals which reflect more certainty than is justified by their knowledge about the assessed quantities. This bias is common to naive and to sophisticated subjects, and it is not eliminated by introducing proper scoring rules, which provide incentives for external calibration. This effect is attributable, in part at least, to anchoring.

To select X_{90} for the value of the Dow-Jones average, for example, it is natural to begin by thinking about one's best estimate of the Dow-Jones and to adjust this value upward. If this adjustment—like most others—is insufficient, then X_{90} will not be sufficiently extreme. A similar anchoring effect will occur in the selection of X_{10}, which is presumably obtained by adjusting one's best estimate downward. Consequently, the confidence interval between X_{10} and X_{90} will be too narrow, and the assessed probability distribution will be too tight. In support of this interpretation it can be shown that subjective probabilities are systematically altered by a procedure in which one's best estimate does not serve as an anchor.

Subjective probability distributions for a given quantity (the Dow-Jones average) can be obtained in two different ways: (i) by asking the subject to select values of the Dow-Jones that correspond to specified percentiles of his probability distribution and (ii) by asking the subject to assess the probabilities that the true value of the Dow-Jones will exceed some specified values. The two procedures are formally equivalent and should yield identical distributions. However, they suggest different modes of adjustment from different anchors. In procedure (i), the natural starting point is one's best estimate of the quantity. In procedure (ii), on the other hand, the subject may be anchored on the value stated in the question. Alternatively, he may be anchored on even odds, or 50-50 chances, which is a natural starting point in the estimation of likelihood. In either case, procedure (ii) should yield less extreme odds than procedure (i).

To contrast the two procedures, a set of 24 quantities (such as the air distance from New Delhi to Peking) was presented to a group of subjects who assessed either X_{10} or X_{90} for each problem. Another group of subjects received the median judgment of the first group for each of the 24 quantities. They were asked to assess the odds that each of the given values exceeded the true value of the relevant quantity. In the absence of any bias, the second group should retrieve the odds specified to the first group, that is, 9 : 1. However, if even odds or the stated value serve as anchors, the odds of the second group should be less extreme, that is, closer to 1 : 1. Indeed, the median odds stated by this group, across all problems, were 3 : 1. When the judgments of the two groups were tested for external calibration, it was found that subjects in the first group were too extreme, in accord with earlier studies. The events that they defined as having a probability of .10 actually obtained in 24 percent of the cases. In contrast, subjects in the second group were too conservative. Events to which they assigned an average probability of .34 actually obtained in 26 percent of the cases. These results illustrate the manner in which the degree of calibration depends on the procedure of elicitation.

Discussion

This article has been concerned with cognitive biases that stem from the reliance on judgmental heuristics. These biases are not attributable to motivational effects such as wishful thinking or the distortion of judgments by payoffs and penalties. Indeed, several of the severe errors of judgment reported earlier occurred despite the fact that subjects were encouraged to be accurate and were rewarded for the correct answers (2, 6).

The reliance on heuristics and the prevalence of biases are not restricted to laymen. Experienced researchers are also prone to the same biases—when they think intuitively. For example, the tendency to predict the outcome that best represents the data, with insufficient regard for prior probability, has been observed in the intuitive judgments of individuals who have had extensive training in statistics (1, 5). Although the statistically sophisticated avoid elementary errors, such as the gambler's fallacy, their intuitive judgments are liable to similar fallacies in more intricate and less transparent problems.

It is not surprising that useful heuristics such as representativeness and availability are retained, even though they occasionally lead to errors in prediction or estimation. What is perhaps surprising is the failure of people to infer from lifelong experience such fundamental statistical rules as regression toward the mean, or the effect of sample size on sampling variability. Although everyone is exposed, in the normal course of life, to numerous examples from which these rules could have been induced, very few people discover the principles of sampling and regression on their own. Statistical principles are not learned from everyday experience because the relevant instances are not coded appropriately. For example, people do not discover that successive lines in a text differ more in average word length than do successive pages, because they simply do not attend to the average word length of individual lines or pages. Thus, people do not learn the relation between sample size and sampling variability, although the data for such learning are abundant.

The lack of an appropriate code also explains why people usually do not detect the biases in their judgments of probability. A person could conceivably learn whether his judgments are externally calibrated by keeping a tally of the proportion of events that actually occur among those to which he assigns the same probability. However, it is not natural to group events by their judged probability. In the absence of such grouping it is impossible for an individual to discover, for example, that only 50 percent of the predictions to which he has assigned a probability of .9 or higher actually came true.

The empirical analysis of cognitive biases has implications for the theoretical and applied role of judged probabilities. Modern decision theory (12, 13) regards subjective probability as the quantified opinion of an idealized person. Specifically, the subjective probability of a given event is defined by the set of bets about this event that such a person is willing to accept. An internally consistent, or coherent, subjective probability measure can be derived for an individual if his choices among bets satisfy certain principles, that is, the axioms of the theory. The derived probability is subjective in the sense that different individuals are allowed to have different probabilities for the same event. The major contribution of this approach is that it provides a rigorous

subjective interpretation of probability that is applicable to unique events and is embedded in a general theory of rational decision.

It should perhaps be noted that, while subjective probabilities can sometimes be inferred from preferences among bets, they are normally not formed in this fashion. A person bets on team A rather than on team B because he believes that team A is more likely to win; he does not infer this belief from his betting preferences. Thus, in reality, subjective probabilities determine preferences among bets and are not derived from them, as in the axiomatic theory of rational decision (12).

The inherently subjective nature of probability has led many students to the belief that coherence, or internal consistency, is the only valid criterion by which judged probabilities should be evaluated. From the standpoint of the formal theory of subjective probability, any set of internally consistent probability judgments is as good as any other. This criterion is not entirely satisfactory, because an internally consistent set of subjective probabilities can be incompatible with other beliefs held by the individual. Consider a person whose subjective probabilities for all possible outcomes of a coin-tossing game reflect the gambler's fallacy. That is, his estimate of the probability of tails on a particular toss increases with the number of consecutive heads that preceded that toss. The judgments of such a person could be internally consistent and therefore acceptable as adequate subjective probabilities according to the criterion of the formal theory. These probabilities, however, are incompatible with the generally held belief that a coin has no memory and is therefore incapable of generating sequential dependencies. For judged probabilities to be considered adequate, or rational, internal consistency is not enough. The judgments must be compatible with the entire web of beliefs held by the individual. Unfortunately, there can be no simple formal procedure for assessing the compatibility of a set of probability judgments with the judge's total system of beliefs. The rational judge will nevertheless strive for compatibility, even though internal consistency is more easily achieved and assessed. In particular, he will attempt to make his probability judgments compatible with his knowledge about the subject matter, the laws of probability, and his own judgmental heuristics and biases.

Summary

This article described three heuristics that are employed in making judgments under uncertainty: (i) representativeness, which is usually employed when people are asked to judge the probability that an object or event A belongs to class or process B; (ii) availability of instances or scenarios, which is often employed when people are asked to assess the frequency of a class or the plausibility of a particular development; and (iii) adjustment from an anchor, which is usually employed in numerical prediction when a relevant value is available. These heuristics are highly economical and usually effective, but they lead to systematic and predictable errors. A better understanding of these heuristics and of the biases to which they lead could improve judgments and decisions in situations of uncertainty.

References and Notes

1. D. Kahneman and A. Tversky, *Psychol. Rev.* **80**, 237 (1973).
2. ———, *Cognitive Psychol.* **3**, 430 (1972).
3. W. Edwards, in *Formal Representation of Human Judgment*, B. Kleinmuntz, Ed. (Wiley, New York, 1968), pp. 17–52.
4. P. Slovic and S. Lichtenstein, *Organ. Behav. Hum. Performance* **6**, 649 (1971).
5. A. Tversky and D. Kahneman, *Psychol. Bull.* **76**, 105 (1971).
6. ———, *Cognitive Psychol.* **5**, 207 (1973).
7. R. C. Galbraith and B. J. Underwood, *Mem. Cognition* **1**, 56 (1973).
8. L. J. Chapman and J. P. Chapman, *J. Abnorm. Psychol.* **73**, 193 (1967); *ibid.*, **74**, 271 (1969).
9. M. Bar-Hillel, *Organ. Behav. Hum. Performance* **9**, 396 (1973).
10. J. Cohen, E. I. Chesnick, D. Haran, *Br. J. Psychol.* **63**, 41 (1972).
11. M. Alpert and H. Raiffa, unpublished manuscript; C. A. S. von Holstein, *Acta Psychol.* **35**, 478 (1971); R. L. Winkler, *J. Am. Stat. Assoc.* **62**, 776 (1967).
12. L. J. Savage, *The Foundations of Statistics* (Wiley, New York, 1954).
13. B. De Finetti, in *International Encyclopedia of the Social Sciences*, D. E. Sills, Ed. (Macmillan, New York, 1968), vol. 12, pp. 496–504.
14. This research was supported by the Advanced Research Projects Agency of the Department of Defense and was monitored by the Office of Naval Research under contract N00014-73-C-0438 to the Oregon Research Institute, Eugene. Additional support for this research was provided by the Research and Development Authority of the Hebrew University, Jerusalem, Israel.

Overdiagnosis and Overmedication

[25]

The Need for a New Medical Model: A Challenge for Biomedicine

George L. Engel

At a recent conference on psychiatric education, many psychiatrists seemed to be saying to medicine, "Please take us back and we will never again deviate from the 'medical model.'" For, as one critical psychiatrist put it, "Psychiatry has become a hodgepodge of unscientific opinions, assorted philosophies and 'schools of thought,' mixed metaphors, role diffusion, propaganda, and politicking for 'mental health' and other esoteric goals" (*1*). In contrast, the rest of medicine appears neat and tidy. It has a firm base in the biological sciences, enormous technologic resources at its command, and a record of astonishing achievement in elucidating mechanisms of disease and devising new treatments. It would seem that psychiatry would do well to emulate its sister medical disciplines by finally embracing once and for all the medical model of disease.

But I do not accept such a premise. Rather, I contend that all medicine is in crisis and, further, that medicine's crisis derives from the same basic fault as psychiatry's, namely, adherence to a model of disease no longer adequate for the scientific tasks and social responsibilities of either medicine or psychiatry. The importance of how physicians conceptualize disease derives from how such concepts determine what are considered the proper boundaries of professional responsibility and how they influence attitudes toward and behavior with patients. Psychiatry's crisis revolves around the question of whether the categories of human distress with which it is concerned are properly considered "disease" as currently conceptualized and whether exercise of the traditional authority of

the physician is appropriate for their helping functions. Medicine's crisis stems from the logical inference that since "disease" is defined in terms of somatic parameters, physicians need not be concerned with psychosocial issues which lie outside medicine's responsibility and authority. At a recent Rockefeller Foundation seminar on the concept of health, one authority urged that medicine "concentrate on the 'real' diseases and not get lost in the psychosociological underbrush. The physician should not be saddled with problems that have arisen from the abdication of the theologian and the philosopher." Another participant called for "a disentanglement of the organic elements of disease from the psychosocial elements of human malfunction," arguing that medicine should deal with the former only (*2*).

The Two Positions

Psychiatrists have responded to their crisis by embracing two ostensibly opposite positions. One would simply exclude psychiatry from the field of medicine, while the other would adhere strictly to the "medical model" and limit psychiatry's field to behavioral disorders consequent to brain dysfunction. The first is exemplified in the writings of Szasz and others who advance the position that "mental illness is a myth" since it does not conform with the accepted concept of disease (*3*). Supporters of this position advocate the removal of the functions now performed by psychiatry from conceptual and professional jurisdiction of medicine and their reallocation to a

new discipline based on behavioral science. Henceforth medicine would be responsible for the treatment and cure of disease, while the new discipline would be concerned with the reeducation of people with "problems of living." Implicit in this argument is the premise that while the medical model constitutes a sound framework within which to understand and treat disease, it is not relevant to the behavioral and psychological problems classically deemed the domain of psychiatry. Disorders directly ascribable to brain disorder would be taken care of by neurologists, while psychiatry as such would disappear as a medical discipline.

The contrasting posture of strict adherence to the medical model is caricatured in Ludwig's view of the psychiatrist as physician (*1*). According to Ludwig, the medical model premises "that sufficient deviation from normal represents *disease*, that disease is due to known or unknown natural causes, and that elimination of these causes will result in cure or improvement in individual patients" (Ludwig's italics). While acknowledging that most psychiatric diagnoses have a lower level of confirmation than most medical diagnoses, he adds that they are not "qualitatively different provided that mental disease is assumed to arise largely from 'natural' rather than metapsychological, interpersonal or societal causes." "Natural" is defined as "biological brain dysfunctions, either biochemical or neurophysiological in nature." On the other hand, "disorders such as problems of living, social adjustment reactions, character disorders, dependency syndromes, existential depressions, and various social deviancy conditions [would] be excluded from the concept of mental illness since these disorders arise in individuals with presumably intact neurophysiological functioning and are produced primarily by psychosocial variables." Such "non-psychiatric disorders" are not properly the concern of the physician-psychiatrist and are more appropriately handled by nonmedical professionals.

The author is professor of psychiatry and medicine at the University of Rochester School of Medicine, Rochester, New York 14642.

In sum, psychiatry struggles to clarify its status within the mainstream of medicine, if indeed it belongs in medicine at all. The criterion by which this question is supposed to be resolved rests on the degree to which the field of activity of psychiatry is deemed congruent with the existing medical model of disease. But crucial to this problem is another, that of whether the contemporary model is, in fact, any longer adequate for medicine, much less for psychiatry. For if it is not, then perhaps the crisis of psychiatry is part and parcel of a larger crisis that has its roots in the model itself. Should that be the case, then it would be imprudent for psychiatry prematurely to abandon its models in favor of one that may also be flawed.

The Biomedical Model

The dominant model of disease today is biomedical, with molecular biology its basic scientific discipline. It assumes disease to be fully accounted for by deviations from the norm of measurable biological (somatic) variables. It leaves no room within its framework for the social, psychological, and behavioral dimensions of illness. The biomedical model not only requires that disease be dealt with as an entity independent of social behavior, it also demands that behavioral aberrations be explained on the basis of disordered somatic (biochemical or neurophysiological) processes. Thus the biomedical model embraces both reductionism, the philosophic view that complex phenomena are ultimately derived from a single primary principle, and mind-body dualism, the doctrine that separates the mental from the somatic. Here the reductionistic primary principle is physicalistic; that is, it assumes that the language of chemistry and physics will ultimately suffice to explain biological phenomena. From the reductionist viewpoint, the only conceptual tools available to characterize and experimental tools to study biological systems are physical in nature (4).

The biomedical model was devised by medical scientists for the study of disease. As such it was a scientific model; that is, it involved a shared set of assumptions and rules of conduct based on the scientific method and constituted a blueprint for research. Not all models are scientific. Indeed, broadly defined, a model is nothing more than a belief system utilized to explain natural phenomena, to make sense out of what is puzzling or disturbing. The more socially dis-

130

ruptive or individually upsetting the phenomenon, the more pressing the need of humans to devise explanatory systems. Such efforts at explanation constitute devices for social adaptation. Disease par excellence exemplifies a category of natural phenomena urgently demanding explanation (5). As Fabrega has pointed out, "disease" in its generic sense is a linguistic term used to refer to a certain class of phenomena that members of all social groups, at all times in the history of man, have been exposed to. "When people of various intellectual and cultural persuasions use terms analogous to 'disease,' they have in mind, among other things, that the phenomena in question involve a person-centered, harmful, and undesirable deviation or discontinuity . . . associated with impairment or discomfort" (5). Since the condition is not desired it gives rise to a need for corrective actions. The latter involve beliefs and explanations about disease as well as rules of conduct to rationalize treatment actions. These constitute socially adaptive devices to resolve, for the individual as well as for the society in which the sick person lives, the crises and uncertainties surrounding disease (6).

Such culturally derived belief systems about disease also constitute models, but they are not scientific models. These may be referred to as popular or folk models. As efforts at social adaptation, they contrast with scientific models, which are primarily designed to promote scientific investigation. The historical fact we have to face is that in modern Western society biomedicine not only has provided a basis for the scientific study of disease, it has also become our own culturally specific perspective about disease, that is, our folk model. Indeed the biomedical model is now the dominant folk model of disease in the Western world (5, 6).

In our culture the attitudes and belief systems of physicians are molded by this model long before they embark on their professional education, which in turn reinforces it without necessarily clarifying how its use for social adaptation contrasts with its use for scientific research. The biomedical model has thus become a cultural imperative, its limitations easily overlooked. In brief, it has now acquired the status of *dogma*. In science, a model is revised or abandoned when it fails to account adequately for all the data. A dogma, on the other hand, requires that discrepant data be forced to fit the model or be excluded. Biomedical dogma requires that all disease, including "mental" disease, be conceptualized in terms

of derangement of underlying physical mechanisms. This permits only two alternatives whereby behavior and disease can be reconciled: the *reductionist*, which says that all behavioral phenomena of disease must be conceptualized in terms of physicochemical principles; and the *exclusionist*, which says that whatever is not capable of being so explained must be excluded from the category of disease. The reductionists concede that some disturbances in behavior belong in the spectrum of disease. They categorize these as mental diseases and designate psychiatry as the relevant medical discipline. The exclusionists regard mental illness as a myth and would eliminate psychiatry from medicine. Among physicians and psychiatrists today the reductionists are the true believers, the exclusionists are the apostates, while both condemn as heretics those who dare to question the ultimate truth of the biomedical model and advocate a more useful model.

Historical Origins of the Reductionistic Biomedical Model

In considering the requirements for a more inclusive scientific medical model for the study of disease, an ethnomedical perspective is helpful (6). In all societies, ancient and modern, preliterate and literate, the major criteria for identification of disease have always been behavioral, psychological, and social in nature. Classically, the onset of disease is marked by changes in physical appearance that frighten, puzzle, or awe, and by alterations in functioning, in feelings, in performance, in behavior, or in relationships that are experienced or perceived as threatening, harmful, unpleasant, deviant, undesirable, or unwanted. Reported verbally or demonstrated by the sufferer or by a witness, these constitute the primary data upon which are based first-order judgments as to whether or not a person is sick (7). To such disturbing behavior and reports all societies typically respond by designating individuals and evolving social institutions whose primary function is to evaluate, interpret, and provide corrective measures (5, 6). Medicine as an institution and as a discipline, and physicians as professionals, evolved as one form of response to such social needs. In the course of history, medicine became scientific as physicians and other scientists developed a taxonomy and applied scientific methods to the understanding, treatment, and prevention of disturbances which the public first had designated as "disease" or "sickness."

Why did the reductionistic, dualistic biomedical model evolve in the West? Rasmussen identifies one source in the concession of established Christian orthodoxy to permit dissection of the human body some five centuries ago (8). Such a concession was in keeping with the Christian view of the body as a weak and imperfect vessel for the transfer of the soul from this world to the next. Not surprisingly, the Church's permission to study the human body included a tacit interdiction against corresponding scientific investigation of man's mind and behavior. For in the eyes of the Church these had more to do with religion and the soul and hence properly remained its domain. This compact may be considered largely responsible for the anatomical and structural base upon which scientific Western medicine eventually was to be built. For at the same time, the basic principle of the science of the day, as enunciated by Galileo, Newton, and Descartes, was analytical, meaning that entities to be investigated be resolved into isolable causal chains or units, from which it was assumed that the whole could be understood, both materially and conceptually, by reconstituting the parts. With mind-body dualism firmly established under the imprimatur of the Church, classical science readily fostered the notion of the body as a machine, of disease as the consequence of breakdown of the machine, and of the doctor's task as repair of the machine. Thus, the scientific approach to disease began by focusing in a fractional-analytic way on biological (somatic) processes and ignoring the behavioral and psychosocial. This was so even though in practice many physicians, at least until the beginning of the 20th century, regarded emotions as important for the development and course of disease. Actually, such arbitrary exclusion is an acceptable strategy in scientific research, especially when concepts and methods appropriate for the excluded areas are not yet available. But it becomes counterproductive when such strategy becomes policy and the area originally put aside for practical reasons is permanently excluded, if not forgotten altogether. The greater the success of the narrow approach the more likely is this to happen. The biomedical approach to disease has been successful beyond all expectations, but at a cost. For in serving as guideline and justification for medical care policy, biomedicine has also contributed to a host of problems, which I shall consider later.

Limitations of the Biomedical Model

We are now faced with the necessity and the challenge to broaden the approach to disease to include the psychosocial without sacrificing the enormous advantages of the biomedical approach. On the importance of the latter all agree, the reductionist, the exclusionist, and the heretic. In a recent critique of the exclusionist position, Kety put the contrast between the two in such a way as to help define the issues (9). "According to the medical model, a human illness does not become a specific disease all at once and is not equivalent to it. The medical model of an illness is a process that moves from the recognition and palliation of symptoms to the characterization of a specific disease in which the etiology and pathogenesis are known and treatment is rational and specific." Thus taxonomy progresses from symptoms, to clusters of symptoms, to syndromes, and finally to diseases with specific pathogenesis and pathology. This sequence accurately describes the successful application of the scientific method to the elucidation and the classification into discrete entities of disease in its generic sense (5, 6). The merit of such an approach needs no argument. What do require scrutiny are the distortions introduced by the reductionistic tendency to regard the specific disease as adequately, if not best, characterized in terms of the smallest isolable component having causal implications, for example, the biochemical; or even more critical, is the contention that designation "disease" does not apply in the absence of perturbations at the biochemical level.

Kety approaches this problem by comparing diabetes mellitus and schizophrenia as paradigms of somatic and mental diseases, pointing out the appropriateness of the medical model for both. "Both are symptom clusters or syndromes, one described by somatic and biochemical abnormalities, the other by psychological. Each may have many etiologies and shows a range of intensity from severe and debilitating to latent or borderline. There is also evidence that genetic and environmental influences operate in the development of both." In this description, at least in reductionistic terms, the scientific characterization of diabetes is the more advanced in that it has progressed from the behavioral framework of symptoms to that of biochemical abnormalities. Ultimately, the reductionists assume schizophrenia will achieve a similar degree of resolution. In developing his position, Kety makes

clear that he does not regard the genetic factors and biological processes in schizophrenia as are now known to exist (or may be discovered in the future) as the only important influences in its etiology. He insists that equally important is elucidation of "how experiential factors and their interactions with biological vulnerability make possible or prevent the development of schizophrenia." But whether such a caveat will suffice to counteract basic reductionism is far from certain.

The Requirements of a New Medical Model

To explore the requirements of a medical model that would account for the reality of diabetes and schizophrenia as human experiences as well as disease abstractions, let us expand Kety's analogy by making the assumption that a specific biochemical abnormality capable of being influenced pharmacologically exists in schizophrenia as well as in diabetes, certainly a plausible possibility. By obliging ourselves to think of patients with diabetes, a "somatic disease," and with schizophrenia, a "mental disease," in exactly the same terms, we will see more clearly how inclusion of somatic and psychosocial factors is indispensable for both; or more pointedly, how concentration on the biomedical and exclusion of the psychosocial distorts perspectives and even interferes with patient care.

1) In the biomedical model, demonstration of the specific biochemical deviation is generally regarded as a specific diagnostic criterion for the disease. Yet in terms of the human experience of illness, laboratory documentation may only indicate disease potential, not the actuality of the disease at the time. The abnormality may be present, yet the patient not be ill. Thus the presence of the biochemical defect of diabetes or schizophrenia at best defines a necessary but not a sufficient condition for the occurrence of the human experience of the disease, the illness. More accurately, the biochemical defect constitutes but one factor among many, the complex interaction of which ultimately may culminate in active disease or manifest illness (10). Nor can the biochemical defect be made to account for all of the illness, for full understanding requires additional concepts and frames of reference. Thus, while the diagnosis of diabetes is first suggested by certain core clinical manifestations, for example, polyuria, poly-

dipsia, polyphagia, and weight loss, and is then confirmed by laboratory documentation of relative insulin deficiency, how these are experienced and how they are reported by any one individual, and how they affect him, all require consideration of psychological, social, and cultural factors, not to mention other concurrent or complicating biological factors. Variability in the clinical expression of diabetes as well as of schizophrenia, and in the individual experience and expression of these illnesses, reflects as much these other elements as it does quantitative variations in the specific biochemical defect.

2) Establishing a relationship between particular biochemical processes and the clinical data of illness requires a scientifically rational approach to behavioral and psychosocial data, for these are the terms in which most clinical phenomena are reported by patients. Without such, the reliability of observations and the validity of correlations will be flawed. It serves little to be able to specify a biochemical defect in schizophrenia if one does not know how to relate this to particular psychological and behavioral expressions of the disorder. The biomedical model gives insufficient heed to this requirement. Instead it encourages bypassing the patient's verbal account by placing greater reliance on technical procedures and laboratory measurements. In actuality the task is appreciably more complex than the biomedical model encourages one to believe. An examination of the correlations between clinical and laboratory data requires not only reliable methods of clinical data collection, specifically high-level interviewing skills, but also basic understanding of the psychological, social, and cultural determinants of how patients communicate symptoms of disease. For example, many verbal expressions derive from bodily experiences early in life, resulting in a significant degree of ambiguity in the language patients use to report symptoms. Hence the same words may serve to express primary psychological as well as bodily disturbances, both of which may coexist and overlap in complex ways. Thus, virtually each of the symptoms classically associated with diabetes may also be expressions of or reactions to psychological distress, just as keto-acidosis and hypoglycemia may induce psychiatric manifestations, including some considered characteristic of schizophrenia. The most essential skills of the physician involve the ability to elicit accurately and then analyze correctly the patient's verbal account of his illness ex-

132

perience. The biomedical model ignores both the rigor required to achieve reliability in the interview process and the necessity to analyze the meaning of the patient's report in psychological, social, and cultural as well as in anatomical, physiological, or biochemical terms (7).

3) Diabetes and schizophrenia have in common the fact that conditions of life and living constitute significant variables influencing the time of reported onset of the manifest disease as well as of variations in its course. In both conditions this results from the fact that psychophysiologic responses to life change may interact with existing somatic factors to alter susceptibility and thereby influence the time of onset, the severity, and the course of a disease. Experimental studies in animals amply document the role of early, previous, and current life experience in altering susceptibility to a wide variety of diseases even in the presence of a genetic predisposition (11). Cassel's demonstration of higher rates of ill health among populations exposed to incongruity between the demands of the social system in which they are living and working and the culture they bring with them provides another illustration among humans of the role of psychosocial variables in disease causation (12).

4) Psychological and social factors are also crucial in determining whether and when patients with the biochemical abnormality of diabetes or of schizophrenia come to view themselves or be viewed by others as sick. Still other factors of a similar nature influence whether or not and when any individual enters a health care system and becomes a patient. Thus, the biochemical defect may determine certain characteristics of the disease, but not necessarily the point in time when the person falls ill or accepts the sick role or the status of a patient.

5) "Rational treatment" (Kety's term) directed only at the biochemical abnormality does not necessarily restore the patient to health even in the face of documented correction or major alleviation of the abnormality. This is no less true for diabetes than it will be for schizophrenia when a biochemical defect is established. Other factors may combine to sustain patienthood even in the face of biochemical recovery. Conspicuously responsible for such discrepancies between correction of biological abnormalities and treatment outcome are psychological and social variables.

6) Even with the application of rational therapies, the behavior of the physician and the relationship between patient and physician powerfully influence ther-

apeutic outcome for better or for worse. These constitute psychological effects which may directly modify the illness experience or indirectly affect underlying biochemical processes, the latter by virtue of interactions between psychophysiological reactions and biochemical processes implicated in the disease (11). Thus, insulin requirements of a diabetic patient may fluctuate significantly depending on how the patient perceives his relationship with his doctor. Furthermore, the successful application of rational therapies is limited by the physician's ability to influence and modify the patient's behavior in directions concordant with health needs. Contrary to what the exclusionists would have us believe, the physician's role is, and always has been, very much that of educator and psychotherapist. To know how to induce peace of mind in the patient and enhance his faith in the healing powers of his physician requires psychological knowledge and skills, not merely charisma. These too are outside the biomedical framework.

The Advantages of a Biopsychosocial Model

This list surely is not complete but it should suffice to document that diabetes mellitus and schizophrenia as paradigms of "somatic" and "mental" disorders are entirely analogous and, as Kety argues, are appropriately conceptualized within the framework of a medical model of disease. But the existing biomedical model does not suffice. To provide a basis for understanding the determinants of disease and arriving at rational treatments and patterns of health care, a medical model must also take into account the patient, the social context in which he lives, and the complementary system devised by society to deal with the disruptive effects of illness, that is, the physician role and the health care system. This requires a biopsychosocial model. Its scope is determined by the historic function of the physician to establish whether the person soliciting help is "sick" or "well"; and if sick, why sick and in which ways sick; and then to develop a rational program to treat the illness and restore and maintain health.

The boundaries between health and disease, between well and sick, are far from clear and never will be clear, for they are diffused by cultural, social, and psychological considerations. The traditional biomedical view, that biological indices are the ultimate criteria defining disease, leads to the present paradox that some people with positive laboratory findings are told that they are in need of treatment when in fact they are feeling quite well, while others feeling sick are assured that they are well, that is, they have no "disease" (5, 6). A biopsychosocial model which includes the patient as well as the illness would encompass both circumstances. The doctor's task is to account for the dysphoria and the dysfunction which lead individuals to seek medical help, adopt the sick role, and accept the status of patienthood. He must weight the relative contributions of social and psychological as well as of biological factors implicated in the patient's dysphoria and dysfunction as well as in his decision to accept or not accept patienthood and with it the responsibility to cooperate in his own health care.

By evaluating all the factors contributing to both illness and patienthood, rather than giving primacy to biological factors alone, a biopsychosocial model would make it possible to explain why some individuals experience as "illness" conditions which others regard merely as "problems of living," be they emotional reactions to life circumstances or somatic symptoms. For from the individual's point of view his decision between whether he has a "problem of living" or is "sick" has basically to do with whether or not he accepts the sick role and seeks entry into the health care system, not with what, in fact, is responsible for his distress. Indeed, some people deny the unwelcome reality of illness by dismissing as "a problem of living" symptoms which may in actuality be indicative of a serious organic process. It is the doctor's, not the patient's, responsibility to establish the nature of the problem and to decide whether or not it is best handled in a medical framework. Clearly the dichotomy between "disease" and "problems of living" is by no means a sharp one, either for patient or for doctor.

When Is Grief a Disease?

To enhance our understanding of how it is that "problems of living" are experienced as illness by some and not by others, it might be helpful to consider grief as a paradigm of such a borderline condition. For while grief has never been considered in a medical framework, a significant number of grieving people do consult doctors because of disturbing symptoms, which they do not necessarily relate to grief. Fifteen years ago I ad-

dressed this question in a paper entitled "Is grief a disease? A challenge for medical research" (*13*). Its aim too was to raise questions about the adequacy of the biomedical model. A better title might have been, "When is grief a disease?," just as one might ask when schizophrenia or when diabetes is a disease. For while there are some obvious analogies between grief and disease, there are also some important differences. But these very contradictions help to clarify the psychosocial dimensions of the biopsychosocial model.

Grief clearly exemplifies a situation in which psychological factors are primary; no preexisting chemical or physiological defects or agents need be invoked. Yet as with classic diseases, ordinary grief constitutes a discrete syndrome with a relatively predictable symptomatology which includes, incidentally, both bodily and psychological disturbances. It displays the autonomy typical of disease; that is, it runs its course despite the sufferer's efforts or wish to bring it to a close. A consistent etiologic factor can be identified, namely, a significant loss. On the other hand, neither the sufferer nor society has ever dealt with ordinary grief as an illness even though such expressions as "sick with grief" would indicate some connection in people's minds. And while every culture makes provisions for the mourner, these have generally been regarded more as the responsibility of religion than of medicine.

On the face of it, the arguments against including grief in a medical model would seem to be the more persuasive. In the 1961 paper I countered these by comparing grief to a wound. Both are natural responses to environmental trauma, one psychological, the other physical. But even at the time I felt a vague uneasiness that this analogy did not quite make the case. Now 15 years later a better grasp of the cultural origins of disease concepts and medical care systems clarifies the apparent inconsistency. The critical factor underlying man's need to develop folk models of disease, and to develop social adaptations to deal with the individual and group disruptions brought about by disease, has always been the victim's ignorance of what is responsible for his dysphoric or disturbing experience (5, 6). Neither grief nor a wound fits fully into that category. In both, the reasons for the pain, suffering, and disability are only too clear. Wounds or fractures incurred in battle or by accident by and large were self-treated or ministered to with folk remedies or by individuals who

had acquired certain technical skills in such matters. Surgery developed out of the need for treatment of wounds and injuries and has different historical roots than medicine, which was always closer in origin to magic and religion. Only later in Western history did surgery and medicine merge as healing arts. But even from earliest times there were people who behaved as though grief-stricken, yet seemed not to have suffered any loss; and others who developed what for all the world looked like wounds or fractures, yet had not been subjected to any known trauma. And there were people who suffered losses whose grief deviated in one way or another from what the culture had come to accept as the normal course; and others whose wounds failed to heal or festered or who became ill even though the wound had apparently healed. Then, as now, two elements were crucial in defining the role of patient and physician and hence in determining what should be regarded as disease. For the patient it has been his not knowing why he felt or functioned badly or what to do about it, coupled with the belief or knowledge that the healer or physician did know and could provide relief. For the physician in turn it has been his commitment to his professional role as healer. From these have evolved sets of expectations which are reinforced by the culture, though these are not necessarily the same for patient as for physician.

A biopsychosocial model would take all of these factors into account. It would acknowledge the fundamental fact that the patient comes to the physician because either he does not know what is wrong or, if he does, he feels incapable of helping himself. The psychobiological unity of man requires that the physician accept the responsibility to evaluate whatever problems the patient presents and recommend a course of action, including referral to other helping professions. Hence the physician's basic professional knowledge and skills must span the social, psychological, and biological, for his decisions and actions on the patient's behalf involve all three. Is the patient suffering normal grief or melancholia? Are the fatigue and weakness of the woman who recently lost her husband conversion symptoms, psychophysiological reactions, manifestations of a somatic disorder, or a combination of these? The patient soliciting the aid of a physician must have confidence that the M.D. degree has indeed rendered that physician competent to make such differentiations.

A Challenge for Both Medicine and Psychiatry

The development of a biopsychosocial medical model is posed as a challenge for both medicine and psychiatry. For despite the enormous gains which have accrued from biomedical research, there is a growing uneasiness among the public as well as among physicians, and especially among the younger generation, that health needs are not being met and that biomedical research is not having a sufficient impact in human terms. This is usually ascribed to the all too obvious inadequacies of existing health care delivery systems. But this certainly is not a complete explanation, for many who do have adequate access to health care also complain that physicians are lacking in interest and understanding, are preoccupied with procedures, and are insensitive to the personal problems of patients and their families. Medical institutions are seen as cold and impersonal; the more prestigious they are as centers for biomedical research, the more common such complaints (*14*). Medicine's unrest derives from a growing awareness among many physicians of the contradiction between the excellence of their biomedical background on the one hand and the weakness of their qualifications in certain attributes essential for good patient care on the other (*7*). Many recognize that these cannot be improved by working within the biomedical model alone.

The present upsurge of interest in primary care and family medicine clearly reflects disenchantment among some physicians with an approach to disease that neglects the patient. They are now more ready for a medical model which would take psychosocial issues into account. Even from within academic circles are coming some sharp challenges to biomedical dogmatism (*8, 15*). Thus Holman ascribes directly to biomedical reductionism and to the professional dominance of its adherents over the health care system such undesirable practices as unnecessary hospitalization, overuse of drugs, excessive surgery, and inappropriate utilization of diagnostic tests. He writes, "While reductionism is a powerful tool for understanding, it also creates profound misunderstanding when unwisely applied. Reductionism is particularly harmful when it neglects the impact of nonbiological circumstances upon biologic processes." And, "Some medical outcomes are inadequate not because appropriate technical interventions are lacking but because our conceptual thinking is inadequate" (*15*).

How ironic it would be were psychiatry to insist on subscribing to a medical model which some leaders in medicine already are beginning to question.

Psychiatrists, unconsciously committed to the biomedical model and split into the warring camps of reductionists and exclusionists, are today so preoccupied with their own professional identity and status in relation to medicine that many are failing to appreciate that psychiatry now is the only clinical discipline within medicine concerned primarily with the study of man and the human condition. While the behavioral sciences have made some limited incursions into medical school teaching programs, it is mainly upon psychiatrists, and to a lesser extent clinical psychologists, that the responsibility falls to develop approaches to the understanding of health and disease and patient care not readily accomplished within the more narrow framework and with the specialized techniques of traditional biomedicine. Indeed, the fact is that the major formulations of more integrated and holistic concepts of health and disease proposed in the past 30 years have come not from within the biomedical establishment but from physicians who have drawn upon concepts and methods which originated within psychiatry, notably the psychodynamic approach of Sigmund Freud and psychoanalysis and the reaction-to-life-stress approach of Adolf Meyer and psychobiology (*16*). Actually, one of the more lasting contributions of both Freud and Meyer has been to provide frames of reference whereby psychological processes could be included in a concept of disease. Psychosomatic medicine—the term itself a vestige of dualism—became the medium whereby the gap between the two parallel but independent ideologies of medicine, the biological and the psychosocial, was to be bridged. Its progress has been slow and halting, not only because of the extreme complexities intrinsic to the field itself, but also because of unremitting pressures, from within as well as from without, to conform to scientific methodologies basically mechanistic and reductionistic in conception and inappropriate for many of the problems under study. Nonetheless, by now a sizable body of knowledge, based on clinical and experimental studies of man and animals has accumulated. Most, however, remains unknown to the general medical public and to the biomedical community and is largely ignored in the education of physicians. The recent solemn pronouncement by an eminent biomedical leader (*2*) that "the emotional content of

organic medicine [has been] exaggerated" and "psychosomatic medicine is on the way out" can only be ascribed to the blinding effects of dogmatism.

The fact is that medical schools have constituted unreceptive if not hostile environments for those interested in psychosomatic research and teaching, and medical journals have all too often followed a double standard in accepting papers dealing with psychosomatic relationships (*17*). Further, much of the work documenting experimentally in animals the significance of life circumstances or change in altering susceptibility to disease has been done by experimental psychologists and appears in psychology journals rarely read by physicians or basic biomedical scientists (*11*).

General Systems Theory Perspective

The struggle to reconcile the psychosocial and the biological in medicine has had its parallel in biology, also dominated by the reductionistic approach of molecular biology. Among biologists too have emerged advocates of the need to develop holistic as well as reductionistic explanations of life processes, to answer the "why?" and the "what for?" as well as the "how?" (*18, 19*). Von Bertalanffy, arguing the need for a more fundamental reorientation in scientific perspectives in order to open the way to holistic approaches more amenable to scientific inquiry and conceptualization, developed general systems theory (*20*). This approach, by treating sets of related events collectively as systems manifesting functions and properties on the specific level of the whole, has made possible recognition of isomorphies across different levels of organization, as molecules, cells, organs, the organism, the person, the family, the society, or the biosphere. From such isomorphies can be developed fundamental laws and principles that operate commonly at all levels of organization, as compared to those which are unique for each. Since systems theory holds that all levels of organization are linked to each other in a hierarchical relationship so that change in one affects change in the others, its adoption as a scientific approach should do much to mitigate the holist-reductionist dichotomy and improve communication across scientific disciplines. For medicine, systems theory provides a conceptual approach suitable not only for the proposed biopsychosocial concept of disease but also for studying disease and medical care as interrelated processes (*10, 21*). If and when a general-systems approach becomes part of the basic scientific and philosophic education of future physicians and medical scientists, a greater readiness to encompass a biopsychosocial perspective of disease may be anticipated.

Biomedicine as Science and as Dogma

In the meantime, what is being and can be done to neutralize the dogmatism of biomedicine and all the undesirable social and scientific consequences that flow therefrom? How can a proper balance be established between the fractional-analytic and the natural history approaches, both so integral for the work of the physician and the medical scientist (22)? How can the clinician be helped to understand the extent to which his scientific approach to patients represents a distinctly "human science," one in which "reliance is on the integrative powers of the observer of a complex nonreplicable event and on the experiments that are provided by history and by animals living in particular ecological settings," as Margaret Mead puts it (23)? The history of the rise and fall of scientific dogmas throughout history may give some clues. Certainly mere emergence of new findings and theories rarely suffices to overthrow well-entrenched dogmas. The power of vested interests, social, political, and economic, are formidable deterrents to any effective assault on biomedical dogmatism. The delivery of health care is a major industry, considering that more than 8 percent of our national economic product is devoted to health (2). The enormous existing and planned investment in diagnostic and therapeutic technology alone strongly favors approaches to clinical study and care of patients that emphasize the impersonal and the mechanical (24). For example, from 1967 to 1972 there was an increase of 33 percent in the number of laboratory tests conducted per hospital admission (25). Planning for systems of medical care and their financing is excessively influenced by the availability and promise of technology, the application and effectiveness of which are often used as the criteria by which decisions are made as to what constitutes illness and who qualifies for medical care. The frustration of those who find what they believe to be their legitimate health needs inadequately met by too technologically oriented physicians is generally misinterpreted by the biomedical establishment as indicating "unrealistic expectations" on the part of the public rather than

being recognized as reflecting a genuine discrepancy between illness as actually experienced by the patient and as it is conceptualized in the biomedical mode (26). The professionalization of biomedicine constitutes still another formidable barrier (8, 15). Professionalization has engendered a caste system among health care personnel and a peck order concerning what constitute appropriate areas for medical concern and care, with the most esoteric disorders at the top of the list. Professional dominance "has perpetuated prevailing practices, deflected criticisms, and insulated the profession from alternate views and social relations that would illuminate and improve health care" (15, p. 21). Holman argues, not unconvincingly, that "the Medical establishment is not primarily engaged in the disinterested pursuit of knowledge and the translation of that knowledge into medical practice; rather in significant part it is engaged in special interest advocacy, pursuing and preserving social power" (15, p. 11).

Under such conditions it is difficult to see how reforms can be brought about. Certainly contributing another critical essay is hardly likely to bring about any major changes in attitude. The problem is hardly new, for the first efforts to introduce a more holistic approach into the undergraduate medical curriculum actually date back to Adolph Meyer's program at Johns Hopkins, which was initiated before 1920 (27). At Rochester, a program directed to medical students and to physicians during and after their residency training, and designed to inculcate psychosocial knowledge and skills appropriate for their future work as clinicians or teachers, has been in existence for 30 years (28). While difficult to measure outcome objectively, its impact, as indicated by a questionnaire on how students and graduates view the issues involved in illness and patient care, appears to have been appreciable (29). In other schools, especially in the immediate post–World War II period, similar efforts were launched, and while some flourished briefly, most soon faded away under the competition of more glamorous and acceptable biomedical careers. Today, within many medical schools there is again a revival of interest among some faculty, but they are few in number and lack the influence, prestige, power, and access to funding from peer review groups that goes with conformity to the prevailing biomedical structure.

Yet today, interest among students and young physicians is high, and where learning opportunities exist they quickly overwhelm the available meager re-

sources. It would appear that given the opportunity, the younger generation is very ready to accept the importance of learning more about the psychosocial dimensions of illness and health care and the need for such education to be soundly based on scientific principles. Once exposed to such an approach, most recognize how ephemeral and insubstantial are appeals to humanism and compassion when not based on rational principles. They reject as simplistic the notion that in past generations doctors understood their patients better, a myth that has persisted for centuries (30). Clearly, the gap to be closed is between teachers ready to teach and students eager to learn. But nothing will change unless or until those who control resources have the wisdom to venture off the beaten path of exclusive reliance on biomedicine as the only approach to health care. The proposed biopsychosocial model provides a blueprint for research, a framework for teaching, and a design for action in the real world of health care. Whether it is useful or not remains to be seen. But the answer will not be forthcoming if conditions are not provided to do so. In a free society, outcome will depend upon those who have the courage to try new paths and the wisdom to provide the necessary support.

Summary

The dominant model of disease today is biomedical, and it leaves no room within its framework for the social, psychological, and behavioral dimensions of illness. A biopsychosocial model is proposed that provides a blueprint for research, a framework for teaching, and a design for action in the real world of health care.

References and Notes

1. A. M. Ludwig, *J. Am. Med. Assoc.* **234**, 603 (1975).
2. *RF Illustrated*, 3, 5 (1976).
3. T. S. Szasz, *The Myth of Mental Illness* (Harper & Row, New York, 1961); E. F. Torrey, *The Death of Psychiatry* (Chilton, Radnor, Pa., 1974).
4. R. Rosen, in *The Relevance of General Systems Theory*, E. Laszlo, Ed. (Braziller, New York, 1972), p. 45.
5. H. Fabrega, *Arch. Gen Psychiatry* **32**, 1501 (1972).
6. ———, *Science*, 189, 969 (1975).
7. G. L. Engel, *Ann. Intern. Med.* **78**, 587 (1973).
8. H. Rasmussen, *Pharos* **38**, 53 (1975).
9. S. Kety, *Am. J. Psychiatry* **131**, 957 (1974).
10. G. L. Engel, *Perspect. Biol. Med.* **3**, 459 (1960).
11. R. Ader, in *Ethology and Development*, S. A. Barnett, Ed. (Heinemann, London, 1973), p. 37; G. L. Engel, *Gastroenterology* **67**, 1085 (1974).
12. J. Cassel, *Am. J. Public Health* **54**, 1482 (1964).
13. G. L. Engel, *Psychosom. Med.* **23**, 18 (1961).
14. R. S. Duff and A. B. Hollingshead, *Sickness and Society* (Harper & Row, New York, 1968).
15. H. R. Holman, *Hosp. Pract.* **11**, 11 (1976).
16. K. Menninger, *Ann. Intern. Med.* **29**, 318 (1948); J. Romano, *J. Am. Med. Assoc.* **143**, 409 (1950); G. L. Engel, *Midcentury Psychiatry*, R. Grin-

ker, Ed. (Thomas, Springfield, Ill., 1953), p. 33; H. G. Wolff, Ed., *An Outline of Man's Knowledge* (Doubleday, New York, 1960), p. 41; G. L. Engel, *Psychological Development in Health and Disease* (Saunders, Philadelphia, 1962).

17. G. L. Engel and L. Salzman, *N. Engl. J. Med.* **288**, 44 (1973).

18. R. Dubos, *Mirage of Health* (Harper & Row, New York, 1959); *Reason Awake* (Columbia Univ. Press, New York, 1970); E. Mayr, in *Behavior and Evolution*, A. Roe and G. G. Simpson, Eds. (Yale Univ. Press, New Haven, Conn., 1958), p. 341; *Science* **134**, 1501 (1961); *Am. Sci.* **62**, 650 (1974); J. T. Bonner, *On Development. The Biology of Form* (Harvard Univ. Press, Cambridge, Mass., 1974); G. G. Simpson, *Science* **139**, 81 (1963).

19. R. Dubos, *Man Adapting* (Yale Univ. Press, New Haven, Conn., 1965).

20. L. von Bertalanffy, *Problems of Life* (Wiley, New York, 1952); *General Systems Theory* (Braziller, New York, 1968). See also E. Laszlo, *The Relevance of General Systems Theory* (Braziller, New York, 1972); *The Systems View of the World* (Braziller, New York, 1972); Dubos (*19*).

21. K. Menninger, *The Vital Balance* (Viking, New York, 1963); A. Sheldon, in *Systems and Medical Care*, A. Sheldon, F. Baker, C. P. McLaughlin, Eds. (MIT Press, Cambridge, Mass., 1970), p. 84; H. Brody, *Perspect. Biol. Med.* **16**, 71 (1973).

22. G. L. Engel, in *Physiology, Emotion, and Psychosomatic Illness*, R. Porter and J. Knight, Eds. (Elsevier-Excerpta Medica, Amsterdam, 1972), p. 384.

23. M. Mead, *Science* **191**, 903 (1976).

24. G. L. Engel, *J. Am. Med. Assoc.* **236**, 861 (1976).

25. J. M. McGinnis, *J. Med. Educ.* **51**, 602 (1976).

26. H. Fabrega and P. R. Manning, *Psychosom. Med.* **35**, 223 (1973).

27. A. Meyer, *J. Am. Med. Assoc.* **69**, 861 (1917).

28. A. H. Schmale, W. A. Greene, F. Reichsman, M. Kehoe, G. L. Engel, *Adv. Psychosom. Med.* **4**, 4 (1964); G. L. Engel, *J. Psychosom. Res.* **11**, 77 (1967); L. Young, *Ann. Intern. Med.* **83**, 728 (1975).

29. G. L. Engel, *J. Nerv. Ment. Dis.* **154**, 159 (1972); *Univ. Rochester Med. Rev.* (winter 1971–1972), p. 10.

30. _____, *Pharos* **39**, 127 (1976).

31. This article was adapted from material presented as the Loren Stephens Memorial Lecture, University of Southern California Medical Center, 1976; the Griffith McKerracher Memorial Lecture at the University of Saskatchewan, 1976; the Annual Hutchings Society Lecture, State University of New York-Upstate Medical Center, Syracuse, 1976. Also presented during 1975 to 1976 at the University of Maryland School of Medicine, University of California–San Diego School of Medicine, University of California–Los Angeles School of Medicine, Massachusetts Mental Health Center, and the 21st annual meeting of Midwest Professors of Psychiatry, Philadelphia. The author is a career research awardee in the U.S. Public Health Service.

[26]

Somatization and Medicalization in the Era of Managed Care

Arthur J. Barsky, MD, Jonathan F. Borus, MD

Somatization, the reporting of somatic symptoms that have no pathophysiological explanation, appears to be increasing as sociocultural currents reduce the public's tolerance of mild symptoms and benign infirmities and lower the threshold for seeking medical attention for such complaints. These trends coincide with a progressive medicalization of physical distress in which uncomfortable bodily states and isolated symptoms are reclassified as diseases for which medical treatment is sought. Somatization and medicalization are likely to become more problematic in the era of managed care. Under capitation, providers will have greater incentives to reduce utilization, and somatizing patients may feel forced to express their "dis-ease" in more urgent and exaggerated terms in order to gain access to the physician. In addition, prepaid subscribers will suffer little financial disincentive to seek medical attention for relatively minor complaints; therefore, they are likely to increase the demand for physician consultation. This situation suggests an urgent need to improve the management of somatizing patients. Innovative consultative, behavioral, and educational interventions are now available. In addition, medical professionals should greet the process of medicalization with considerable caution and educate the public more about the normative presence of symptoms and bodily distress in healthy people. Additional research is needed into somatization and its relationship to the demand for medical care. In an era of managed care, increased attention should be devoted to understanding and controlling the demand for care, a large portion of which is symptom driven.

(*JAMA.* 1995;274:1931-1934)

MUCH OF general medical practice is devoted to the care of somatizing patients who are symptomatic but not seriously ill. Somatization is defined as the propensity to experience and report somatic symptoms that have no pathophysiological explanation, to misattribute them to disease, and to seek medical attention for them.[1] Somatization may be acute or chronic, and coincidental medical illness may or may not be present. Although the tendency to focus on the somatic aspects of distress is almost universal, more serious clinically significant somatization occurs in the context of psychiatric disorder, stressful life experiences, or major emotional turmoil. Somatization is distinct from malingering and factitious disorders, which involve the conscious simulation of illness, since the somatizer is truthfully reporting his or her bodily experience and not consciously manipulating or controlling others with his or her symptoms.

Social and cultural forces can lead individuals to amplify preexisting physical discomforts, misattribute them to disease, and seek medical help. One such influence is the progressive medicalization of bodily distress and physical suffering seen in contemporary Western culture. Medicalization refers to the invocation of a medical diagnosis to explain physical discomfort that is not caused by a disease and the application of a medical intervention to treat it. In this article, we suggest that the processes of somatization and medicalization reinforce each other, and together they are on a collision course with emerging trends in health care financing and delivery.

THE OLD PROBLEM OF SOMATIZATION

Magnitude of the Problem

Many patients in general medical practice have symptoms that are not due to serious disease or demonstrable organ pathology. Whether the unit of observation is the patient, the symptom, or the visit, studies over the past quarter century have consistently documented the high prevalence of somatization. Thus, 38% to 60% of the patients in primary care practice complain of symptoms that have no serious medical basis.[2-8] Only 16% of the 14 most common somatic symptoms found in 1000 general medical outpatients were ultimately shown to have an organic cause.[9] In 25% to 50% of all primary care visits, no serious medical cause is found to explain the patient's presenting symptom, and psychosocial factors appear to play the major role in prompting the visit.[10-16] Such somatization is a significant source of discomfort and disability, particularly when it is prolonged,[17-19] and somatizers' symptoms tend to be more chronic and refractory than those of medically ill patients.[9,17,19]

Somatizing patients are disproportionately high users of medical services, laboratory investigations, and surgical procedures.[18,20-25] Compared with nonsomatizing patients, somatizing patients are found to have elevated rates of ambulatory medical visits,[26-30] hospitalization,[28,31] and total health care costs.[17,26,32] Patients with somatization disorder (a severe form of somatizing considered a mental disorder) use three times the ambulatory medical services of patients who do not have somatization disorder[27] and 10 times the mean inpatient and outpatient services of the general population.[32] They have three times as many hospitalizations and sur-

From the Division of Psychiatry, Brigham and Women's Hospital; and the Department of Psychiatry and the Center to Study the Illness Experience, Harvard Medical School, Boston, Mass.

Reprint requests to the Division of Psychiatry, Brigham and Women's Hospital, 75 Francis St, Boston, MA 02115 (Dr Barsky).

gical procedures as patients with major depression,[28] and, predictably, they have unusually high rates of iatrogenic illness.[33]

In addition, most somatizing patients use medical services in particularly maladaptive and inefficient ways. They tend to obtain care from multiple providers simultaneously, fail to keep scheduled appointments, and frequently switch physicians.[34] Doctors find them to be difficult patients, "vexing," "taxing," and "frustrating" to care for.[30,35] Convinced that they are physically ill, somatizers characteristically deny that any psychosocial factors influence their symptoms,[36] remain unreassured after appropriate examination has revealed no serious disease,[36] resist psychiatric referral,[17] and are often refractory to conservative, palliative, and supportive medical management.[19,38] It follows that somatization adds substantially to the overall costs of medical care.

Somatic Distress in Everyday Life

There is a vast reservoir of benign, self-limited ailments that do not ordinarily bring people to a physician. Healthy adults commonly experience isolated symptoms, minor illnesses, and transient dysfunctions in the course of daily life. Fatigue, headaches and backaches, stiffness, rashes, upper respiratory symptoms, diarrhea, and dizziness are commonplace and only rarely caused by serious disease. Population-based surveys indicate that 86% to 95% of the general population experiences at least one symptom in a given 2- to 4-week interval,[36-40] and the typical adult has at least one somatic symptom every 4 to 6 days.[38,41] Population-based studies using symptom diaries and health logs indicate that 75% to 95% of such symptomatic episodes are managed exclusively outside the health care system and do not result in any medical consultation, either over the telephone or in person.[11,40-46] Thus, the lexicon for expressing somatization is almost always at hand since there is a constant backdrop of somatic symptoms available on which to focus, amplify, and become concerned.

The prevalence of somatization in general practice appears to have risen over the last 30 to 40 years.[47-53] Epidemiological studies of ambulatory practice, surveys of public attitudes, and historical examinations of medical practice all suggest that people are increasingly bothered by, aware of, and disabled by distress and discomforts that in the past were deemed less important and less worthy of medical attention.[47-53] There appears to be a progressive decline in our threshold and tolerance for mild and self-limited ailments; thus, back pain and upper respiratory tract symptoms are now the two most common complaints patients give as reasons for visiting general and family practitioners.[54]

THE NEW PROBLEM OF MEDICALIZATION

Medicalization fosters somatization by amplifying mild and benign bodily distress, repeatedly calling our attention to it, alarming us about its potential pathological significance, and suggesting that it deserves medical scrutiny. Over the past few decades, our society has reclassified a growing array of uncomfortable and undesirable aspects of life, which in the past were viewed as inescapable and inevitable concomitants of daily life, as diseases for which we increasingly seek medical consultation.[47-50,55] These include self-limited infirmities (upper respiratory tract infections, musculoskeletal symptoms, and digestive complaints) as well as isolated, benign symptoms (motion sickness, tinnitus, insomnia, fatigue, and jet lag) and physical characteristics (baldness, myopia, aging skin, or small breasts).

Medicalization results from a number of factors. Scientific and biomedical advances have furnished effective interventions for formerly untreatable conditions. The commercial interests of the growing "medical-industrial complex"[56] promote a medical ideology and seek to translate it into consumer demand for medical products and services. Beneficial educational campaigns to alert the public about the early warning symptoms of serious diseases such as cancer, heart disease, and stroke have also had the negative side effect of causing some people to focus on, worry about, and seek medical attention for benign symptoms.

We have recently witnessed the emergence of a growing number of conditions ("functional somatic syndromes") whose scientific status and medical basis remain unclear. These include chronic fatigue syndrome, total allergy syndrome, food hypersensitivity, reactive hypoglycemia, systemic yeast infection (*Candida* hypersensitivity syndrome), Gulf War syndrome, fibromyalgia, sick building syndrome, and mitral valve prolapse. Such conditions often assume prominence in the mass communications media and public consciousness before their scientific dimensions have been established. Portrayed by the media as major public health problems, they emerge suddenly, accompanied by a groundswell of patients, support groups, and national advocacy organizations. Patients with these functional somatic syndromes are often convinced that they have a specific occult disease and therefore arrive in the physician's office with an explana-

tory model for their symptom—a self-diagnosis.[57] This disease attribution tends to resist explanation to the contrary and appropriate reassurance from the physician. Although some of these individuals have an undiagnosed medical disorder, others are apparently relabeling preexisting bodily distress as a disease and seeking medical attention because of this new cognitive understanding of an old symptom. Thus, medicalization stimulates somatization by amplifying preexisting, benign discomfort, supplying a new disease attribution for it, and ushering these individuals into the medical care system.

THE NEW ERA OF MANAGED AND CAPITATED CARE

Somatization is likely to pose additional difficulties under managed, prepaid care and under capitated reimbursement. As costs are more stringently contained and providers' financial incentives change, the supply of medical care will be increasingly restricted. At the same time, there is likely to be an increased demand for care from patients whose symptoms are medically less serious.

Financial pressures on providers will likely lead to attempts to restrict the amount of medical care provided somatizing patients. Multiple physician visits for the same symptom and demands for tests and procedures that are unlikely to be revealing will be harder to countenance as the pressure for cost containment mounts. It will be less feasible to obtain a diagnostic study in order to reassure worried but healthy patients, and the emphasis on physician productivity may lessen the opportunity to explore the psychosocial issues so important in understanding somatizing patients, to take a personal history, develop empathy and understanding, and build a trusting relationship. When financial reimbursement is capitated and based on the covered life rather than on the procedure or service, providers find themselves in a zero-sum game in which the cost of clinical services directly offsets their income. The somatizer's disproportionately high rates of use and maladaptive patterns of care will then increasingly stand out. Although capitated systems may not discourage access to care for patients with acute and serious illnesses,[58] physicians will have a powerful incentive to switch from doing too much for the somatizer to doing too little.

As managed care systems attempt to regulate access to the physician, somatizing patients may feel they have little choice but to voice complaints that are more urgent and ominous. By discouraging physician consultation for mild somatic distress and ambiguous symptoms, managed care may induce patients to present their "dis-ease" at higher volume and in more serious and concretely medical terms to secure admission to the physician's office.

In addition, as we move away from fee-for-service medicine, patients who have prepaid a fixed amount for their medical care may feel entitled to get their "dollar's worth." When the marginal cost to the patient of seeking medical attention for minor symptoms is low, consultation for benign ailments becomes relatively attractive (depending on copayments and deductibles, which influence the use of medical services for both appropriate and not medically appropriate complaints).[59-62]

Finally, the current underdiagnosis and undertreatment of psychiatric disorder in somatizing patients is likely to increase.[63] Of primary care patients with a diagnosable psychiatric disorder, 50% to 70% initially present with somatic symptoms,[64,65] and these symptoms often obscure the underlying psychiatric distress from the physician's view. Overlooking these mental disorders is particularly serious because effective psychiatric treatments are now available for many, and the failure to recognize them leads to further disability and increased medical use.[66-69] Furthermore, the fruitless search for a medical diagnosis in these patients fosters iatrogenesis, somatization, invalidism, and disability.[70-74] Technological and procedural medical management can provide the transient somatizer with an identity as a sick patient and allow him or her to become ill without having a significant disease.[70]

REMEDIES

While managed and capitated care pose problems for the treatment of somatizing patients, they also present opportunities for innovation and improvement. The ultimate objective is not to exclude somatizers from the health care system or restrict their access to care, but rather to provide them more effective and efficient care that will reduce their suffering, disability, and medical care costs.

These new financial incentives should move us toward more integrated delivery systems, which could benefit somatizing patients. Such systems will designate a single primary care physician to serve an essential gate-keeping function, making it easier to detect and control "physician shopping," and prevent fragmented care, excessive testing, and the overuse of specialty consultations. As providers assume responsibility for the health status of defined populations of enrollees, rather than the illness episodes of designated patients, there will be greater incentives to develop health education and self-care programs. Enrollees should be taught about the process of somatization, the negative side effects of medicalization, and the range of bodily symptoms occurring in healthy people. Enrollees should also be guided in deciding which symptoms need immediate medical attention and which can safely be delayed.

In a competitive marketplace, functional status, quality of life, and patient satisfaction will receive increasing emphasis as relevant outcomes of care. This could improve the medical care of somatizing patients. Such patients could be identified early with screening instruments, permitting targeted interventions to prevent acute somatizing reactions from progressing to chronic illness behavior and invalidism. Psychiatric consultation to primary care physicians and medical practice guidelines have been shown to significantly decrease the health care costs of somatization disorder patients without compromising their medical management or satisfaction with care.[69,75,76] Cognitive, educational, and behavioral treatments may be provided to somatizing patients who do not respond to reassurance and appropriate medical evaluation. Such interventions have been found effective for patients with chronic pain, hypochondriasis, psychosomatic symptoms, and somatization disorder[76-80] and can be delivered cost-effectively in a short-term group format by nonphysicians.

The growth of managed care should also stimulate further study of somatization as a source of suffering, disability, and expenditures. Patients consult physicians, use services, and undergo or decline treatment based in large measure on their appraisal of their symptoms. While most managed care and cost-containment efforts have been directed toward limiting access to care and restricting its *supply*, less attention has been directed toward reducing the *demand* for care and modulating the public's undue expectations of medicine. The study of somatization presents an opportunity to learn more about the demand for care and the decision to visit the physician. Capitated and prepaid systems are ideal for comparing enrollees who do and do not obtain medical consultation for the same symptom and for comparing somatizers who are high and low users of care. Studies of the physician's role in perpetuating somatization, which compare physicians who are more or less effective in caring for these patients, are also needed. Because somatization is a complex and multidetermined process, it also will be important to define distinct subtypes of somatizers: those whose symptoms are self-limited and those with chronic symptoms, those who respond to reassurance and those who do not, and those who do and do not acknowledge psychosocial contributants to their distress.

Finally, the medical community might regard the medicalization of distress with greater reservations. In teaching students, talking with the public, and communicating with the media, physicians should raise cautions about medicalization. Although seductive, medicalization ultimately fuels unrealistic public expectations of physicians and medical care. Medical personnel need to remind both their patients and the public that not every symptom denotes disease, and despite modern biomedicine's stunning advances, there remains a great deal it cannot cure.

This work was supported by research grants MH-40487 from the National Institute of Mental Health and HL-43216 from the National Heart, Lung, and Blood Institute.

References

1. Lipowski ZJ. Somatization: the concept and its clinical application. *Am J Psychiatry*. 1988;145:1358-1368.
2. Garfield SR, Collen MF, Feldman R, Soghikian K, Richart RH, Duncan JH. Evaluation of ambulatory medical care system. *N Engl J Med*. 1976; 294:426-431.
3. Backett EM, Heady JA, Evans JCG. Studies of a general practice, II: the doctor's job in an urban area. *BMJ*. 1954;1:109-115.
4. van der Gagg J, van de Ven W. The demand for primary health care. *Med Care*. 1978;26:299-312.
5. Pilowsky I, Smith QP, Katsikitis M. Illness behavior and general practice utilization: a prospective study. *J Psychosom Res*. 1987;31:177-183.
6. Cummings NA, Vanden Bos GR. The twenty-year Kaiser-Permanente experience with psychotherapy and medical utilization: implications for national health policy and national health insurance. *Health Policy Q*. 1981;1:159-175.
7. Follette WT, Cummings WA. Psychiatric services and medical utilization in a prepaid health plan setting: part II. *Med Care*. 1968;6:31-41.
8. Hilkevitch A. Psychiatric disturbance in outpatients of a general medical outpatient clinic. *Int J Neuropsychiatry*. 1965;1:371-375.
9. Kroenke K, Mangelsdorff AD. Common symptoms in ambulatory care: incidence, evaluation, therapy, and outcome. *Am J Med*. 1989;86:262-266.
10. Bridges KW, Goldberg DP. Somatic presentation of DSM-III psychiatric disorders in primary care. *J Psychosom Res*. 1985;29:563-569.
11. Kroenke K, Arrington ME, Mangelsdorff AD. The prevalence of symptoms in medical outpatients and the adequacy of therapy. *Arch Intern Med*. 1990;150:1685-1690.
12. Katon W, Ries RK, Kleinman A. The prevalence of somatization in primary care. *Compr Psychiatry*. 1984;25:208-215.
13. Kleinman A, Eisenberg L, Good B. Culture, illness, and care; clinical lessons from anthropologic and cross-cultural research. *Ann Intern Med*. 1978; 88:251-258.
14. Gough HG. Doctors' estimates of the percentage of patients whose problems do not require medical attention. *Med Educ*. 1977;11:380-384.
15. Cartwright A. *Patients and Their Doctors: A Study of General Practice*. London, England: Routledge & Kegan Paul; 1967.
16. Mechanic D. *Politics, Medicine, and Social Sci-*

ence. New York, NY: John Wiley & Sons Inc; 1974.

17. Craig TKJ, Boardman AP, Mills K, Daley-Jones O, Drake H. The South London Somatization Study, I: longitudinal course and the influence of early life experiences. *Br J Psychiatry.* 1993;163:579-588.

18. Escobar JI, Golding JM, Hough RL, Karno M, Burnham MA, Wells KB. Somatization in the community: relationship to disability and use of services. *Am J Public Health.* 1987;77:837-840.

19. Escobar JI, Burnham A, Karno M, Forsythe A, Golding JM. Somatization in the community. *Arch Gen Psychiatry.* 1987;44:713-718.

20. Katon W, Von Korff M, Lin E, et al. Distressed high utilizers of medical care: DSM-III-R diagnoses and treatment needs. *Gen Hosp Psychiatry.* 1990; 12:355-362.

21. Lipowski ZJ. Somatization: a borderland between medicine and psychiatry. *Can Med Assoc J.* 1986;135:609-613.

22. Bass C. *Somatization: Physical Symptoms and Psychological Illness.* Oxford, England: Blackwell Scientific Publications Inc; 1990.

23. Regier DA, Narrow WE, Rae DS, Manderscheid RW, Locke BZ, Goodwin FK. The de facto US mental and addictive disorders service system. *Arch Gen Psychiatry.* 1993;50:85-94.

24. McFarland BH, Freeborn DK, Mullooly JP, et al. Utilization patterns among long term enrollees in a prepaid group practice health maintenance organization. *Med Care.* 1985;23:1211-1233.

25. Noyes R, Kathol R, Fisher M, Phillip B, Suelzer M, Holt C. The validity of DSM-III-R hypochondriasis. *Arch Gen Psychiatry.* 1993;50:961-970.

26. deGruy F, Columbia L, Dickinson P. Somatization disorder in a family practice. *J Fam Pract.* 1987;25:45-51.

27. Swartz M, Blazer D, George L, Landerman R. Somatization disorder in a community population. *Am J Psychiatry.* 1986;143:1403-1408.

28. Zoccolillo MS, Cloninger CR. Excess medical care of women with somatization disorder. *South Med J.* 1986;79:532-535.

29. Bass C, Murphy M. Somatization disorder in a British teaching hospital. *Br J Clin Pract.* 1991; 45:237-244.

30. Barsky AJ, Wyshak G, Latham KS, Klerman GL. Hypochondriacal patients, their physicians, and their medical care. *J Gen Intern Med.* 1991;6:413-419.

31. Fink P. The use of hospitalizations by somatizing patients. *Psychol Med.* 1992;22:173-180.

32. Smith GR, Monson R, Ray D. Patients with multiple unexplained symptoms: their characteristics, functional health, and health care utilization. *Arch Intern Med.* 1986;146:69-72.

33. Fink P. Surgery and medical treatment in persistent somatizing patients. *J Psychosom Res.* 1992; 36:439-447.

34. Beaber RJ, Rodney WM. Underdiagnosis of hypochondriasis in family practice. *Psychosomatics.* 1984;25:39-46.

35. Lin EH, Katon W, Von Korff M, et al. Frustrating patients: physician and patient perspectives among distressed high users of medical services. *J Gen Intern Med.* 1991;6:241-246.

36. Benjamin S, Bridges K. The special needs of chronic somatizers. In: Benjamin S, House A, Jenkins P, eds. *Liaison Psychiatry: Defining Needs and Planning Services.* London, England: Gaskell Press; 1994.

37. Hanney DR. *The Symptom Iceberg: A Study of Community Health.* London, England: Routledge & Kegan Paul; 1979:31-49.

38. Dunnell K, Cartwright A. *Medicine Takers, Prescribers, and Hoarders.* London, England: Routledge & Kegan Paul; 1972:8-22.

39. Wadsworth MEJ, Butterfield WJH, Blaney R. *Health and Sickness: The Choice of Treatment.* London, England: Tavistock; 1971.

40. White KL, Williams TF, Grenberg BG. The ecology of medical care. *N Engl J Med.* 1961;265: 885-892.

41. Egan KJ, Beston R. Response to symptoms in healthy low utilizers of the health care system. *J Psychosom Res.* 1987;31:11-21.

42. Verbrugge LM, Ascione FJ. Exploring the iceberg: common symptoms and how people care for them. *Med Care.* 1987;25:539-569.

43. Alonzo AA. Everyday illness behavior: a situational approach to health status deviations. *Soc Sci Med.* 1979;13A:397-404.

44. Demers RY, Altamore R, Mustin H, Kleinman A, Leonardi D. An explanation of the dimensions of illness behavior. *J Fam Pract.* 1980;11:1085-1092.

45. Roghmann KJ, Haggerty RJ. Daily stress, illness, and the use of health sources in young families. *Pediatr Res.* 1973;7:520-526.

46. Banks MH, Beresford SAA, Morrell DC, Waller JJ, Watkins CJ. Factors influencing demand for primary care in women, aged 20-44 years: a preliminary report. *Int J Epidemiol.* 1975;4:189-195.

47. Barsky AJ. *Worried Sick: Our Troubled Quest for Wellness.* Boston, Mass: Little Brown & Co Inc; 1988.

48. Shorter E. *Bedside Manners.* New York, NY: Simon & Schuster Inc Publishers; 1985.

49. Shorter E. *From Paralysis to Fatigue: A History of Psychosomatic Illness in the Modern Era.* New York, NY: Free Press; 1992.

50. Mishler EG, Amarasingham LR, Osherson SD, et al. *Social Contexts of Health, Illness, and Patient Care.* New York, NY: Cambridge University Press; 1981.

51. Harris L. *Inside America.* New York, NY: Vintage Books; 1989.

52. Veroff J, Douvan E, Fulka RA. *The Inner American.* New York, NY: Basic Books Inc Publishers; 1981.

53. Verbrugge LM. Longer life but worsening health? trends in health and mortality of middle aged and older persons. *Milbank Mem Fund Q.* 1984;62:475-519.

54. Barker LR. Distinctive characteristics of ambulatory medicine. In: Barker LR, Burton JR, Zieve PD, eds. *Principles of Ambulatory Medicine.* Baltimore, Md: Williams & Wilkins; 1982:1-15.

55. Conrad P. Medicalization and social control. *Annu Rev Sociol.* 1992;18:209-232.

56. Relman AS. The new medical-industrial complex. *N Engl J Med.* 1980;303:963-970.

57. Stewart DE. The changing faces of somatization. *Psychosomatics.* 1990;31:153-158.

58. Braverman P, Schaaf VM, Egerter S, Bennett T, Schechter W. Insurance-related differences in the risk of ruptured appendix. *N Engl J Med.* 1994; 331:444-449.

59. O'Grady KF, Manning WG, Newhouse JP, Brook RH. The impact of cost sharing on emergency department use. *N Engl J Med.* 1985;313:384-390.

60. Feldman R, Schwartz JS. *Paying Physicians: Options for Controlling Cost, Volume, and Intensity of Services.* Ann Arbor, Mich: Health Administration Press; 1992.

61. Shapiro MF, Ware JE, Sherbourne CD. Effects of cost sharing on seeking care for serious and minor symptoms. *Ann Intern Med.* 1986;104:246-251.

62. Barr JK. Physicians' views of patients in prepaid group practice: reasons for visits to HMOs. *J Health Soc Behav.* 1983;24:244-255.

63. Borus JF, Howes MJ, Devins NP, Rosenberg R, Livingston WW. Primary health providers' recognition and diagnosis of mental disorders in their patients. *Gen Hosp Psychiatry.* 1988;10:317-321.

64. Goldberg D. Detection and assessment of emotional disorders in a primary care setting. *Int J Ment Health.* 1979;8:30-48.

65. Kirmayer LJ, Robbins JM. Three forms of somatization in primary care: prevalence, co-occurrence, and sociodemographic characteristics. *J Nerv Ment Dis.* 1991;179:647-655.

66. Strain JJ, Hammer JS, Fulop G. APM Task Force on Psychosocial Interventions in the General Hospital Inpatient Setting: a review of cost-offset studies. *Psychosomatics.* 1994;35:253-262.

67. Simon G, Ormel J, Von Korff M, Barlow M. Health care costs associated with depressive and anxiety disorders in primary care. *Am J Psychiatry.* 1995;152:352-357.

68. Katon W, Von Korff M, Lin E, et al. Collaborative management to achieve treatment guidelines: impact on depression in primary care. *JAMA.* 1995;273:1026-1031.

69. Smith GR, Rost K, Kashner TM. A trial of the effect of standardized psychiatric consultation on health outcomes and costs in somatizing patients. *Arch Gen Psychiatry.* 1995;52:238-243.

70. Quill TE, Lipkin M, Greenland P. The medicalization of normal variants: the case of mitral valve prolapse. *J Gen Intern Med.* 1988;3:267-276.

71. Illich I. *Medical Nemesis.* New York, NY: Bantam Books Inc; 1976.

72. DeVries NW, Berg RL, Lipkin M. *The Use and Abuse of Medicine.* New York, NY: Praeger Publishers; 1982.

73. Macdonald LA, Sackett DL, Haynes RB, Taylor DW. Labelling in hypertension: a review of the behavioral and physiological consequences. *J Chronic Dis.* 1984;37:933-942.

74. Sox HC, Margulies I, Sox CM. Psychologically mediated effects of diagnostic tests. *Ann Intern Med.* 1981;95:680-685.

75. Kashner TM, Rost K, Smith GR, Lewis S. The impact of a psychiatric consultation letter on the expenditures and outcomes of care for patients with somatization disorder. *Med Care.* 1992;30:811-821.

76. Smith GR, Monson RP, Roy DC. Psychiatric consultation in somatization disorder: a randomized controlled study. *N Engl J Med.* 1986;314:1407-1423.

77. Barsky AJ. Hypochondriasis: medical management and psychiatric treatment. *Psychosomatics.* In press.

78. Sharpe M, Peveler R, Mayou R. The psychological treatment of patients with functional somatic symptoms: a practical guide. *J Psychosom Res.* 1992;36:515-529.

79. Salkovskis PM. Somatic problems. In: Hawton K, Salkovskis PM, Kirk JW, Clark DM, eds. *Cognitive-Behavioral Approaches to Adult Psychiatric Disorders: A Practical Guide.* Oxford, England: Oxford University Press; 1989:235-276.

80. Hellman CJC, Budd M, Borysenko J, McClelland DC, Benson H. A study of the effectiveness of two group behavioral medicine interventions for patients with psychosomatic complaints. *Behav Med.* 1990;16:165-173.

[27]

Setting Boundaries
for Psychiatric Disorders

Kenneth S. Kendler

How should a psychiatric nosology set the boundary between mental disorders and "nondisordered" psychiatric problems that occur commonly in human populations? Should a diagnostic system take a purely descriptive approach, outlining the key inclusion and exclusion criteria for important biobehavioral syndromes? Or should a diagnostic system require that a disorder have a significant impact on functioning (as described by a range of terms including disability, impairment, dysfunction, or disadvantage)? The following case vignettes illustrate the problem.

> Mr. A is a 42-year-old single man with a middle-management position in an investment firm. He reports an extensive delusional system in which he receives special vibrations from Jupiter that bounce over a near-by satellite dish and inform him of "how things will go for me that day." However, Mr. A is functioning well at work and has a small circle of friends that he sees regularly. He realizes that most people think that his ideas are "funny," and he usually remembers not to talk about his ideas with others because "it sometimes gets me into trouble."

> Ms. B is a 38-year-old schoolteacher who states that since early childhood, she has been irrationally afraid of snakes. She still gets an uncomfortable feeling when seeing pictures of snakes in a magazine or on television. However, aside from refusing to take her children into the snake house at the zoo last year, she is unable to recall any ways in which her fear has had any impact on her life. She lives in a city and has not seen a real snake for years.

I suspect that most clinicians would feel quite comfortable with the conclusion that Mr. A suffers from a psychiatric disorder. However, most would feel uncomfortable reaching the same conclusion about Ms. B. Why? Neither Mr. A nor Ms. B is significantly impaired by their symptoms. However, the nature of the psychiatric dysfunction in these two patients is quite different. Mr. A has lost his ability to accurately assess reality, whereas Ms. B is "just" afraid of snakes.

In DSM-III and DSM-III-R, modest attention was paid to the problem of setting boundaries for psychiatric illness. The descriptive approach was predominant, and specific reference to required dysfunction in the diagnostic criteria was limited to a few disorders. Although rarely read, the introduction to both editions did include statements about the definition of a mental disorder. Spitzer and Wakefield quote the relevant introductory section for DSM-IV, which is essentially unchanged from DSM-III-R. This all changed in DSM-IV. As reviewed by Spitzer and Wakefield in this issue of the *Journal*, clinical significance criteria were added to nearly half of all DSM-IV diagnostic categories. From the perspective of the criteria-oriented clinician or researcher, clinical significance criteria moved from a distal consideration to center stage. While the wording was variable, these clinical significance criteria most commonly required dysfunction or distress beyond that specified in the diagnostic criteria.

While this shift in focus was likely influenced by several factors, the relatively high rates of disorders reported in the major epidemiologic studies of psychiatric illness (the Epidemiologic Catchment Area Study [1] and the National Comorbidity Survey [2]) were particularly influential. Such high rates raised questions about the credibility of the diagnostic criteria and concerns that a substantial proportion of diagnosed

EDITORIAL

cases were false positives. In addition, the clinical significance criteria, it was argued, simply made explicit what had already been implicit in DSM-III and DSM-III-R.

Spitzer and Wakefield review the application of the clinical significance criteria in DSM-IV and conclude that it was likely misguided. I will not repeat their arguments here but, rather, wish to make seven additional comments. First, the empirical basis for the addition of the clinical significance criteria was at the time of the development of DSM-IV and remains now quite limited. Most other changes to DSM-IV were guided both by literature reviews and field trials. This was not the case for the clinical significance criteria. Even their impact on caseness was not studied systematically. This is not to claim that the issues in evaluating empirically the clinical significance criteria were simple. They were not. What external measures (or validators) would be used to determine whether the addition of the clinical significance criteria reduced the rate of false positive diagnoses and at what cost in an increase in false negatives?

Second, Spitzer and Wakefield only briefly address the core conceptual issue behind the clinical significance criteria—is a syndromal diagnosis with no requirements for dysfunction or distress sufficient to define a diagnostic category? On the one hand, this is more the rule than the exception in nonpsychiatric medicine. For Tourette's syndrome or psychosis not otherwise specified (e.g., Mr. A), it is hard to argue that individuals meeting clinical criteria should not be so diagnosed even if they are neither impaired nor distressed by their condition. On the other hand, some psychiatric symptoms are so common or normative in human populations (e.g., fear of snakes) that it seems hard to justify considering someone with those symptoms alone to be disordered. Is it possible that the requirement for additional dysfunction or distress might be appropriate only for certain psychiatric disorders for which the symptomatic criteria alone are insufficient? By what criteria might we decide whether the symptoms alone are sufficient to indicate a disorder? Our earlier examples suggest that symptoms which reflect a disruption of "fundamental" or "vital" psychological functions (e.g., reality testing) might alone constitute disorder. But if psychosis alone merits a designation of disorder, whereas an irrational fear must be accompanied by significant dysfunction, where, for example, does major depression lie on this continuum? The most strident discussion in the application of clinical significance criteria in the DSM-IV Task Force involved this diagnostic category. Are the symptomatic criteria (e.g., lowered mood, disordered appetite and sleep, loss of energy) alone sufficient to define an illness? (The reader who is interested in this important conceptual issue might wish to review the cogent article by Wakefield [3], who concludes that the concept of "disorder" implies and probably requires significant impact on the functioning of the organism.)

Third, both the framers of the clinical significance criteria and Spitzer and Wakefield appear to assume that dysfunction represents a good "validator" for "true" psychiatric disorders. This key assumption deserves thoughtful scrutiny. For example, several studies have shown that subsyndromal depressive symptoms are associated with substantial disability similar to that seen with common medical disorders (4–6). As Strauss and Carpenter proposed years ago (7), the linkage between symptoms and functioning is probably rather weak.

Fourth, as another possible approach to the problem of setting boundaries around mental illness, Spitzer and Wakefield suggest that the DSM concept of normal grief be expanded to a broader range of depressive and anxiety syndromes that occur in reaction to psychosocial stressors. Several lines of evidence indicate that this suggestion may be problematic. A quite large percentage of individuals with major depression in the general population report that the onset began in the setting of psychosocial adversity (8, 9). This proposal may then produce a marked change in base rates. Even when confronted with the most severe possible events (e.g., assault), a small minority of individuals develop major depression (10), raising critical questions about what is meant by a "normal" reaction to stressors. Finally, this approach suggests a return to an "etiologically" based approach to the diagnosis of depression and anxiety in which mental health professionals would be responsible for distinguishing between understandable reactions to stressors and endogenous disorders. While intellectually appealing, this approach has not been very successful in the past in psychiatry. It is not clear why it would be expected to fare better now.

Fifth, somewhat unexamined during the debate about clinical significance criteria was the assumption that because rates of psychiatric illness in the general population were so high, these data constitute prima facie evidence that the criteria were producing false positives. Might this reaction indicate, rather, the insecurity of our field vis à vis the rest of medicine? Would cardiologists question their definitions of hypertension or coronary artery disease because of their high population prevalence?

Sixth, Spitzer and Wakefield do not review the thorny issue of the attribution of dysfunction. While it is usually straightforward to assess social or occupational dysfunction, it is far more difficult to determine whether any observed dysfunction is "caused" by a given psychiatric disorder. (This is a significant problem because the clinical significance criteria in DSM-IV typically contain the phrase, "The disturbance causes clinically significant distress or impairment.") Given high levels of comorbidity between psychiatric disorders and between psychiatric and medical conditions, is it realistic to expect that we can assess reliably which disorder is responsible for which kind of disability? Many risk factors for psychiatric disorders are themselves associated with disability. How easy is it to determine whether dysfunction stems directly from the clinical diagnosis or results instead from prior existing risk factors such as a disturbed home environment or an abnormal personality? Last, Spitzer and Wakefield do not discuss the possibility that disorder-associated disability should be part of the diagnostic process, but on an axis separate from clinical diagnosis. The multiaxial DSM-IV system captures functioning on axis V, but there is no attempt to determine whether dysfunction is "due to" the diagnosed disorder or disorders. Is this a viable model for DSM-V?

What can we conclude from these discussions? It is unlikely that we will soon reach an internally consistent and comprehensive solution to the problem of defining the boundaries of psychiatric illness. A diverse set of factors affect this question, many of which are not fundamentally "scientific" in the way in which that term is commonly understood (11). Furthermore, many of our psychiatric syndromes may not exist in nature as highly discrete entities easily separable from subsyndromal conditions (12). Our questions about boundaries of psychiatric illness may not be solved definitively until we have a detailed understanding of the pathophysiology of the disorders that we treat.

Spitzer and Wakefield have done us a service in their thoughtful review of these problems. As we begin to move to DSM-V, it is probably best that we, as a field, confront this difficult problem head-on. We should clarify what empirical questions can be answered by further research and strive for a reasonable working definition which recognizes that the role of symptomatic criteria and disability in defining the boundary of mental illness may differ across diagnostic categories.

REFERENCES

1. Robins LN, Regier DA (eds): Psychiatric Disorders in America: The Epidemiological Catchment Area Study. New York, Free Press, 1991
2. Kessler RC, McGonagle KA, Zhao S, Nelson CB, Hughes M, Eshleman S, Wittchen H-U, Kendler KS: Lifetime and 12-month prevalence of DSM-III-R psychiatric disorders in the United States: results from the National Comorbidity Survey. Arch Gen Psychiatry 1994; 51:8–19
3. Wakefield JC: The concept of mental disorder: on the boundary between biological facts and social values. Am Psychol 1992; 47:373–388
4. Johnson J, Weissman MM, Klerman GL: Service utilization and social morbidity associated with depressive symptoms in the community. JAMA 1992; 267:1478–1483
5. Judd LL, Paulus MP, Wells KB, Rapaport MH: Socioeconomic burden of subsyndromal depressive symptoms and major depression in a sample of the general population. Am J Psychiatry 1996; 153:1411–1417

6. Olfson M, Broadhead WE, Weissman MM, Leon AC, Farber L, Hoven C, Kathol R: Subthreshold psychiatric symptoms in a primary care group practice. Arch Gen Psychiatry 1996; 53:880–886
7. Strauss J, Carpenter W: Characteristic symptoms and outcome in schizophrenia. Arch Gen Psychiatry 1974; 30:429–434
8. Brown GW, Harris TO: Social Origins of Depression: A Study of Psychiatric Disorder in Women. London, Tavistock, 1978
9. Kessler RC: The effects of stressful life events on depression. Annu Rev Psychol 1997; 48:191–214
10. Kendler KS, Karkowski L, Prescott CA: Stressful life events and major depression: risk period, long-term contextual threat and diagnostic specificity. J Nerv Ment Dis 1998; 186:661–669
11. Kendler KS: Toward a scientific psychiatric nosology: strengths and limitations. Arch Gen Psychiatry 1990; 47:969–973
12. Kendler KS, Gardner CO Jr: Boundaries of major depression: an evaluation of DSM-IV criteria. Am J Psychiatry 1998; 155:172–177

KENNETH S. KENDLER, M.D.

Address reprint requests to Dr. Kendler, Box 980126, Medical College of Virginia of Virginia Commonwealth University, Richmond, VA 23298-0126.

[28]

Are Stimulants Overprescribed for Youths with ADHD?

Daniel J. Safer[1]

Critics of stimulant treatment for youths with attention deficit hyperactivity disorder (ADHD) have increased their rhetoric of late, contending that the leading medication for it, Ritalin®, is vastly overprescribed. Additionally, they claim that Ritalin (methylphenidate) is inherently dangerous and that the entire system of the diagnosis and treatment of ADHD is seriously flawed. The critics view the underlying reason for the "epidemic" as societal, due to our modern pace of living, our competitive society, and our consumer emphasis. Rejoinders to and clarifications of the more tangible points of the critics are presented, followed by a discussion of some more practical and legitimate concerns for researchers in this area. These concerns include changes within the ADHD category, the clinical need for multiple sources of diagnostic data, infrequent teacher–physician communication, problematic ADHD/conduct disorder comorbidity in adolescence, and the limited amount of community-based research.

KEY WORDS: attention-deficit hyperactivity disorder; methylphenidate; stimulants; controversy.

ARE STIMULANTS OVERPRESCRIBED?

Vocal critics of medication treatment for hyperactive/inattentive children have been active on the American scene beginning in 1970, when their pressure led the U.S. Congress to appoint a blue ribbon panel to look into the reported overuse of stimulant treatment (1). Over the last three decades, outspoken critics of stimulant treatment have included leaders affiliated with the Church of Scientology, a number of newspaper reporters and talk show hosts, a few officials in the U.S. Drug Enforcement Administration, a handful of physicians and psychologists, and some conservative legislators (2–11).

With minor exceptions, these critics have never been intimately involved in treating or managing hyperactive children. Their ranks rarely include practicing pediatricians, research psychologists, involved parents, and teachers. Their writings are clearly polemical, their focus is exclusively negative, their philosophical positions are impressionistic, and they aim to alarm. All feel that stimulants are vastly overprescribed. To put it mildly, they do not shrink from exaggeration, even when some of their basic arguments have merit.

The major points of these critics will be presented, followed by a brief rejoinder to the more tangible of their positions. Since there are indeed a number of legitimate researchable issues and practical concerns relevant to stimulant treatment of hyperactive children, I will then present my perspective on these.

The claims of the critics can be grouped into the following major categories:

1. Prescribing physicians are haphazard in their diagnosis and treatment of attention deficit hyperactivity disorder (ADHD):

- During the initial visit, physicians diagnose ADHD in a hurried and incomplete manner and they then quickly prescribe medication without offering alternative or additional treatments (such as counseling, tutoring, etc.) (4,5,8).
- Prescription-only visits to physicians have become more common following the recent transition to HMO insurance coverage with its focus on cost cutting (4,5).

[1]Departments of Psychiatry and Pediatrics, Johns Hopkins University School of Medicine, Baltimore, Maryland; correspondence should be addressed to Daniel J. Safer, M.D., 7702 Dunmanway, Dundalk, Maryland 21222.

- Many physicians readily succumb to pressure from parents and teachers to prescribe (4–6).
- Many and possibly most children placed on stimulant medication do not have a major dysfunction (4–7,9). They are commonly placed on this treatment to competitively improve their academic level (4,8).

2. School alternative programs for ADHD are being neglected because of stimulant treatment:

- Many teachers frustrated with an underachieving and misbehaving child deal with this difficulty by simply advising the parent to go with their child to the family doctor and ask for a prescription for Ritalin® (4–7).
- Improved classroom environments, better teachers, more special education, and smaller classroom enrollments are needed to deal with student restlessness rather than medication treatment (4).

3. The causes of restlessness, inattentiveness, and impulsivity are social and cultural:

- Inattention and hyperactivity are primarily due to adverse family/school/social/cultural circumstances (3–5,9).
- Parents busy with work schedules employ the pill (as well as the TV), instead of spending more constructive time with their offspring (4,6).
- Parental permissiveness is a major cause of impulsive, hyperactive behavior (4).
- There is a societal drift to the quick fix (i.e., the pill) (4–6).
- Parents in our competitive, consumer-oriented society are aggressively pushing their children to excel and they believe that medication will accelerate that process (4).

4. Stimulant medication treatment has profound limitations:

- Treating hyperactivity and attention problems with a pill is another step in the *medicalization* of deviant behavior. It supports the *false* assumption of biological causality (3–9).
- The use of stimulant medication for its symptomatic benefit lessens the likelihood that fundamental corrective therapies will be utilized (4–7).
- Children with ADHD learn to rely on the pill rather than on themselves or other resources (4,7).

5. The medication is harmful, and abusable:

- Ritalin has potentially very serious side effects (3–6,8–11).
- Ritalin® is like cocaine and therefore highly abusable (3–6,8,9,11).

6. Ritalin is overprescribed:

- Stimulant medication—for good reasons—is rarely prescribed outside the United States, Canada, and Australia (3–6, 8). Family cohesion in many other cultures makes that treatment unnecessary (4).
- The rise in stimulant treatment in the United States since 1990 is a "massive increase," an "explosion," an "epidemic," such that "four to five million" or "six million" children were on stimulant treatment for ADHD in 1995–1997 (3–9). The eightfold rise in the methylphenidate (Ritalin) production quotas in the United States between 1990 and 1997 supports this contention (4).

7. Powerful pharmaceutical companies have profoundly influenced medical researchers and parent support groups to be pro-Ritalin (3–6).

The most vocal of the critics making these points are generally anti-psychiatry (and anti-Prozac® as well), do not take a balanced view of the voluminous scientific literature on ADHD, and have not published scientific studies on the subject in peer-reviewed professional journals. I will make a modest number of rejoinders and clarifications concerning the more tangible of these allegations.

1. Physician practice:

- Physicians—by *parent* survey reports—usually spend 1 hour or more initially in the evaluation of ADHD (12).
- HMO physicians actually prescribe stimulant medication *less* often for ADHD than fee-for-service and clinic physicians (13,14).
- Approximately 25% of children diagnosed with ADHD by physicians are not prescribed medication for that disorder (15,16).
- Physician and parent surveys indicate that most pediatricians offer or recommend non-medication treatments (12,17,18).

2. School involvement:

- In surveys, a majority of parents whose children receive stimulant treatment report that the major reason they initially brought their child to the doctor was their concern about the child's home behavior and overall adjustment—*not* because of school pressure (9,20).

- Forty-five percent (8971 of 20,050) of all public school students in the state of Maryland given methylphenidate (Ritalin) during school hours in 1998 are *officially* identified as receiving special education services, mostly because of learning disabilities (21).

3. Social theories of causation of ADHD:

- In careful, scholarly, and replicated research, *genetic* factors have been found to be the major causative factor for the expression of developmental hyperactivity in youths (22,23).

4. Limitations of medication treatment:

- In a very recent National Institutes of Mental Health-sponsored, six-site, 579-student, 14-month-duration, multimodal (medication and psychosocial) treatment study of 7-, 8-, and 9-year-old youths with ADHD, the addition of numerous psychosocial treatments did *not* improve upon the prominently beneficial *decrease* in core ADHD features produced by carefully monitored stimulant medication therapy. Furthermore, stimulant medication treatment by itself consistently yielded far superior outcomes than did psychosocial treatments. Two other 1- to 2-year studies of ADHD youths comparing psychosocial with stimulant treatment in the mid-1990s produced similar positive medication results (24).

5. Drug safety and abuse potential:

- Methylphenidate and dextroamphetamine are impressively safe stimulant medications for hyperactive/inattentive children which have been available by prescription for over 40 years. Their side effects are relatively mild, usually decrease over time, and, if problematic, are fully reversible following dose reductions and, should it be necessary, cessation of the treatment. Their use as *the* treatment of youths with ADHD has not resulted in any deaths (25).
- In annual nationwide surveys between 1991 and 1995, 1% or less of U.S. high school seniors reported the nonmedical use of methylphenidate (Ritalin) (26,27). In Maryland in 1996, an anonymous survey recorded a 2% rate of the

nonmedical use of methylphenidate by high school seniors during the previous month. It is noteworthy that the nonmedical use of methylphenidate peaks in the middle school period, whereas every other illicit drug increases in use (most doing so substantially) from the 8th to the 12th grade (28). Abuse by hyperactive/inattentive students has been extremely rare. Almost without exception, students with ADHD who have been treated with methylphenidate do not get 'high' and do not crave the drug (26). Methylphenidate does not substitute for cocaine in the treatment of cocaine addictions (29).

6. The increase in stimulant treatment:

- The number of children receiving methylphenidate treatment has increased two- to threefold between 1990 and 1996 in numerous large population-based assessments (30). [Even data from the U.S. Drug Enforcement Administration of shipments of methylphenidate to states within the United States show an increase of 180% from 1990 through 1995 (31).] The 1990–1996 rate *increase* is only slightly more than the average of the 5- to 6-year rate increases that took place between 1971 and 1987 (32). *Population-based* assessments suggest that approximately 2 million school-age youths received stimulant treatment for ADHD in 1996. Production quotas of methylphenidate (Ritalin) cannot be used to determine or estimate the number of treated individuals (30).
- Stimulant treatment of youths outside the United States and Canada is indeed uncommon, but this is largely due to legal restrictions and cultural preferences (33,34). Overall, physicians in continental Europe prescribe a good deal of neuroleptic medication to preschool and school-age children, medication that is more potentially hazardous than methylphenidate (34–36).
- The increased rate of stimulant treatment for ADHD is not uniform. Youths who have experienced the greatest increases include the following (a) Girls with ADHD. Their generally less boisterous ADHD pattern was often ignored in the past. (b) Teenagers with persisting features of ADHD. Most youths with ADHD finishing elementary school on stimulant treatment now remain on it into their secondary

school years. (c) Youths with attention deficits but *without* a notable degree of restlessness. They now represent 20–25% of Ritalin-treated youths (30,37). (d) Non-ADHD youths. Evidence suggests that they may represent one fifth of all youths receiving stimulants. This largely includes youths with conduct problems alone (38). (e) Preschool youths with ADHD. Their stimulant treatment rates have increased threefold since 1991 (39).

7. The influence of pharmaceutical companies:

- Although pharmaceutical companies would not regularly contribute hundreds of thousands of dollars to a national parent support group without some expectation of influence, a local consumer survey report found that parent satisfaction with and attitudes concerning medication for ADHD were similar for CHADD (Children and Adults With Attention Deficit Disorders) parents compared to non-CHADD parents whose children were also medicated for ADHD (40).
- Most of the research psychologists who have measured the positive effects of stimulant medication have also reported positive results using behavioral treatments (41,42).

There are of course some practical and legitimate concerns about stimulant treatment, the category ADHD, and research in this area. Those that follow I deem most important.

1. *The present primacy of inattentiveness within the ADHD category.* In 1980, the diagnostic category "hyperkinetic reaction of childhood" was replaced with "attention deficit disorder." In 1987, it became "attention deficit hyperactivity disorder (ADHD)." In 1994, ADHD was divided into three subtypes. With each of these changes, there has been a broadening and/or an expansion in the number of categorical descriptors that has resulted in an increase in the surveyed prevalence of the disorder. The broadening of the category was primarily due to the addition of, the emphasis on, and the increase in the *attention deficit dimension* of the disorder (43).

The emphasis on inattention within the category now termed ADHD has limitations compared to the prior emphasis on developmental hyperactivity. These include the following: at least one half of all inattentive youths are not hyperactive, inattention is comparatively far more often present in association with learning disorders and depression, inattention

has a different course and age of onset from hyperactivity, and inattention is a far more subjective and less specific entity than is hyperactivity (43).

The emphasis on inattention is most problematic when used to identify adults with ADHD. Adults self-report the features of ADHD and support its historic presence by a retrospective recall of childhood behavior patterns which are occasionally supported by a similar retrospective recall by their parent. Self-report of a pattern of inattention has quite limited diagnostic specificity and a retrospective recall in one's thirties of a *childhood* behavior pattern is not very reliable (44). No wonder that surveys using the 1994 version of ADHD report that 4–5% of U.S. adults now have ADHD (45).

Such difficulties could be corrected by adopting the International Classification of Diseases category "hyperkinetic disorder" and by splitting off attention deficit disorder as a separate category.

2. *Diagnosis based upon a parent or a teacher report.* The exclusive use of a parent report or a report by one teacher to diagnose ADHD has led to some problems in clinical diagnosis. It has also led to sizable variations in studies on the prevalence of ADHD. For example, studies using only a parent report to diagnose ADHD often report lower prevalence rates than studies using teacher ratings, and studies requiring both teacher and parent agreement on the ADHD pattern report still lower prevalence rates (46,47). This issue is complicated by the fact that the agreement between parent and teacher ratings is consistently low (48). Each sees the child's behavior under different circumstances and clinicians need to obtain data from both sources for a more comprehensive assessment.

The severity and the duration of the presenting complaints also need to be determined during the diagnostic workup. The hyperactive/inattentive disorder is mainly gauged by its two major adverse *consequences:* behavior problems and learning impediments. If the child is sent to the office repeatedly for misconduct in relation to undue restlessness, and/or if he or she is failing or nearly failing in school in association with prominent inattentiveness, these difficulties merit an investigation. Even more important than severity for the diagnostic process is the finding of a multiyear pattern. Detailed historical data in effect enormously aid the diagnostic process.

3. *Teacher–physician communication.* Communications directly from the classroom teacher to the physician concerning the initial degree of the child's

school problems and any changes that occurred in the child's adjustment following treatment have been the *exception* rather than the rule (49–53). Since one-page standardized teacher ratings of behavior and attention are a very valuable means of recording and evaluating types of student adjustment problems and of monitoring treatment outcome (54), this is unfortunate. This problem can be rectified by enlightened and tightened school system guidelines requiring such transfers of information once parent consent is obtained.

4. *The duration of action of stimulant medication.* Methylphenidate, dextroamphetamine, and Adderal® (an amphetamine mixture) are short-acting stimulants whose duration of clinical effect in tablet form is 3–4 hours. This duration necessitates a second and frequently a third dose to prolong the drug's effect to most of the day. A longer acting, first-line stimulant is needed.

5. *Sleep problems of ADHD children.* At least one third and probably one half of unmedicated children with ADHD have prominent sleep problems (55,56). As a result, clonidine is often prescribed for hyperactive youths at night (57). Clonidine is generally effective to assist sleep, but it has received a substantial degree of research *only* for the medical treatment of elevated blood pressure in adults. Since a few hundred thousand youngsters are now being treated with clonidine (38), it deserves substantive research in that age group.

6. *Treatment outcome.* Pediatricians see an average of four patients an hour and see youths with ADHD an average of three times a year for follow-up (18,58). Although pediatricians provide educational counseling, they have little time to provide alternative treatments. However, they do refer their less successful and more complicated cases to mental health professionals or to behavioral pediatricians (59,60).

A number of short-term studies have indicated that parent-focused, parent–teacher coordinated, and teacher-utilized *behavior* therapy can—particularly in conjunction with stimulant treatment—result in benefits for care providers dealing with youths having ADHD (61). There is nonetheless general agreement among researchers that stimulant medication provides the single most effective treatment for youths with hyperactivity and inattention associated with serious school and home difficulties. It has a more measurable impact on the obvious features of the disorder and parent follow-up is better with stimulant treatment.

Unfortunately, neither behavior management nor stimulant treatment can boast of measurable gains in *long-term* outcome studies. The results of stimulant treatment are primarily symptomatic, and preliminary outcome data suggest that it does not change the child's *future* academic level or rate of delinquency (62). Stimulant treatment does, however, substantially lessen the extent of readily observable problems during the period of drug effect (63). Combining different treatments for ADHD is quite reasonable, but research is still needed to clarify which cases and which circumstances might clearly benefit from concomitant therapies (25).

7. *Adverse teenage ADHD outcomes.* Adolescents with ADHD and *associated conduct problems* are particularly at risk for school, family, and neighborhood difficulties. Whereas stimulant medication alone (along with parent educational counseling and, when need be, educational assistance for the child) may suffice for a sizable number of youths with ADHD during their elementary school years, medication alone is usually insufficient for *teenage* youths with both ADHD and an antisocial behavior pattern (64,65). Such problems can be particularly serious in homes with depressed mothers or alcoholic fathers, where marital discord exists, and in economically disadvantaged single-parent families. Stimulant treatment may still provide some benefit for these youths during school hours, but its overall impact tends to be modest (64–67). Unfortunately, there appears to be no simple solution to these complicated conduct problems by way of the juvenile justice system or by the provision of mental health services.

8. *Research in clinics versus the community.* Studies in treatment clinics often present findings that are different from those that are community based. In *clinic* studies, between 52% and 71% of youths diagnosed with ADHD had been placed on stimulant treatment at some time prior to adulthood (18,67–69). In 1993–1994 and 1994–1995 *community* studies reporting both diagnosis and treatment (in rural Tennessee), an average of 15–26% of elementary school youths identified by teachers as having the features of ADHD were receiving stimulant treatment (70,71). Likewise, the satisfaction of parents with stimulant treatment ranges from 86% to 92% in clinic studies (12,72,73), but approximately 75% in community-based studies (40). Clinic studies simply do not account for nontreatment cases and dropout, and this

results in misleading assumptions. More community studies are thus needed because they more accurately reflect the actual state of affairs.

CONCLUSION

Obviously, there are some technical problems in research and clinical practice in relation to the treatment of youths diagnosed as ADHD. But "Are Stimulants Overprescribed"? They are of course overused or inappropriate when continued though not measurably useful, when they are more expensive and less effective than alternative interventions, and when they are more of a risk than a benefit. However, the *global* issue of overuse when applied philosophically or in relation to a *category* of youths who are experiencing substantial difficulties in adjustment is not medically germane for practicing physicians. Physicians nearly always treat individuals, and approximately 75% of the developmentally hyperactive children placed on stimulants respond with reports of improvement (45).

But is it an issue that is germane nonetheless? Does the weight of evidence indicate that teacher ratings of the features of ADHD are substantially different in different countries, that reducing class size or inducing mothers to forego work so as to spend more time with their child will reduce hyperactivity, that parental permissiveness can cause developmental hyperactivity, that our consumer culture has increased the number of youths with ADHD, that stimulant treatment limits the benefits of psychosocial interventions, that most youths treated with stimulants did *not* have major school adjustment problems beforehand, and that stimulant treatment for ADHD youths increases the risk of drug abuse in later years? Research studies do not support the above hypotheses. Therefore, those who lament stimulant treatment for ADHD need to support these social-speculative theories with scientific evidence.

Stimulant treatment certainly has limitations and its continuing increased use raises legitimate questions. Furthermore, there is a good deal of room for improvement in ADHD diagnostic and treatment methodology. Nonetheless, stimulant treatment is safe and is viewed as clearly useful by most of those involved with the immediate care of hyperactive/inattentive children. Should the critics of stimulant treatment by some chance become caretakers of youths with ADHD, they might

adopt this view and in the process become more sympathetic to the needs of these children, their parents, and their teachers.

REFERENCES

1. Report of the Conference on the Use of Stimulant Drugs in the Treatment of Behaviorally Disturbed Young School Children: Psychopharmacol Bull 1971; 7:23–29
2. Gibbs NC: The age of Ritalin. Time 11/30/98; 152(22):86–96
3. DeGrandpre R: Ritalin Nation. New York: Norton; 1999
4. Diller, L: Running with Ritalin. New York: Bantam Books; 1998
5. Walker S: The Hyperactivity Hoax. New York: St. Martin's Press; 1998
6. Breggin PR: Brain Disabling Treatments in Psychiatry. New York: Springer; 1997
7. Vatz RE, Weinberg LS: Overreacting to attention deficit disorder. USAToday Jan 1995; 123:84–85
8. Debriotner RK, Hart A: Moving Beyond ADD/ADHD. Chicago, IL: Contemporary Books; 1995
9. Armstrong T: The Myth of the ADD Child. New York: Plume; 1997
10. Citizens Commission on Human Rights: Ritalin: A Warning to Parents. Los Angeles, CA: Church of Scientology; 1987
11. Feussner G: Diversion, trafficking, and abuse of methylphenidate [abstract]. Presented at the NIH Consensus Development Conference: Diagnosis and Treatment of Attention Deficit Hyperactivity Disorder. Bethesda, MD; 1998:201–204
12. ADHD Task Force: Final Report of the Virginia Department of Education, Health Professions, Mental Health, Mental Retardation and Substance Abuse Services on the Effects of the Use of Methylphenidate to the Governor and General Assembly of Virginia. House Document No. 28; Richmond, VA: Commonwealth of Virginia; 1991
13. Kelleher KJ, Hohman AA, Larson DB: Prescription of psychotropics to children in office-based practice. Am J Dis Child 1989; 143:855–859
14. Zito JM, Safer DJ, Riddle MA, Johnson RE, Speedie SM, Fox M: Prevalence variations in psychotropic treatment of children. J Am Acad Child Adolesc Psychopharmacol 1998; 8:99–105
15. Hoagwood K: A national perspective on treatment and services for children with attention deficit hyperactivity disorder [abstract]. Presented at the NIH Consensus Conference: Diagnosis and Treatment of Attention Deficit Hyperactivity Disorder. Bethesda, MD; 1998:211–219
16. Copeland L, Wolraich M, Lindgren S, Milich R, Woolson R: Pediatricians' reported practices in the assessment and treatment of attention deficit disorders. J Dev Behav Pediat 1987; 8:191–197
17. Wolraich ML, Lindgren S, Stromquist A, Milich R, Davis C, Watson D: Stimulant medication use by primary care physicians in the treatment of attention deficit hyperactivity disorder. Pediatrics 1990; 86:95–101
18. Kwasman A, Tinsley BJ, Lepper HS: Pediatricians' knowledge and attitudes concerning diagnosis and treatment of attention deficit and hyperactivity disorders. Arch Pediatr Adolesc Med 1995; 149:1211–1216
19. Gadow KD: School involvement in pharmacotherapy for behavior disorders. J Spec Ed 1982; 16:385–399
20. Costello EJ, Janiszewski S: Who gets treated? Factors associated with referral in children with psychiatric disorders. Acta Psychiatr Scand 1990; 81:523–529
21. Safer DJ, Zito JM: Stimulant treatment in Maryland public

Are Stimulants Overprescribed for Youths with ADHD?

schools. Presented at the annual meeting of the American Psychological Association, Boston; 1999

22. Gjone H, Stevenson J, Sundet JM: Genetic influence on parent-reported attention-related problems in a Norwegian general population twin sample. J Am Acad Child Adolesc Psychiatry 1996; 35:588–596

23. Thapar A, Holmes J, Poulton K, Harrington R: Genetic basis of attention deficit and hyperactivity. Br J Psychiatry 1999; 174:105–111

24. The MTA cooperative group: A 14-month randomized clinical trial of treatment strategies for attention-deficit/hyperactivity disorder. Arch Gen Psychiatry 1999; 56:1073–1086

25. Du Paul GJ, Barkley RA, Connor DF: Stimulants. In: RA Barkley RA, ed. Attention Deficit Hyperactivity Disorder, 2nd ed. New York: Guilford; 1998:510–551

26. Goldman LS, Genel M, Bezman RJ, Slanetz PJ: Diagnosis and treatment of attention-deficit/hyperactivity disorder in children and adolescents. JAMA 1998; 279:1100–1107

27. Maurer K: Ritalin abuse on the rise among teenagers. Clin Psychiatry News 1996; 24(4):5

28. Maryland State Department of Education: Percent of students reporting substance use by grade level and time period. 1996 Maryland Adolescent Survey. Baltimore, MD: Author; 1997

29. Grabowski J, Roache JD, Schmitz JM, Rhoades H, Creson D, Korszun A: Replacement medication for cocaine dependence: Methylphenidate. J Clin Psychopharmacol 1997; 17:485–488

30. Safer DJ, Zito JM, Fine EM: Increased methylphenidate usage for attention deficit disorder in the 1990's. Pediatrics 1996; 98:1084–1088

31. Morrow RC, Morrow AL, Haislip G: Methylphenidate in the United States, 1990 through 1995. Am J Public Health 1998; 88:1121

32. Safer DJ, Krager JM: A survey of medication treatment for hyperactive/inattentive children. JAMA 1988; 260:2256–2258

33. Safer DJ, Krager JM: Trends in medication therapy for hyperactivity: National and international perspectives. In: Gadow KD, ed. Advances in Learning and Behavioral Disabilities. Greenwich, CT: JAI Press; 1984:125–149

34. Simeon JG, Wiggins DM, Williams E: World wide use of psychotropic drugs in child and adolescent psychiatric disorders: Prog Neuropsychopharmacol Biol Psychiat 1995; 19:455–465

35. Minde K: The use of psychotropic medication in preschoolers: Some recent developments. Can J Psychiatry 1998; 43:571–593

36. Rasmussen F, Smedby B: Life table methods applied to the use of medical care and of prescription drugs in early childhood. J Epidemiol Commun Health 1989; 43:140–146

37. Phillipi RH: Attention-deficit disorders among TennCare enrollees: A report of prevalence and medication. Internal memo. Bureau of TennCare, Department of Health, State of Tennessee; 1998

38. Zito JM, Safer DJ, dos Reis S, Gardner JF: Trends in psychotropic prescriptions for youths Medicaid insurance from a midwestern state: 1987–1995. Presented at the 38th annual meeting of the New Clinical Drug Evaluation Unit Program, Boca Raton, FL; 1998

39. Zito JM, Safer DJ, dos Reis S, Gardner JF, Boles M, Lynch F: Psychotropic medication trends in preschoolers. In press, JAMA, 1999

40. dos Reis S, Zito JM, Safer DJ, Soeken K: Parental knowledge, attitudes and satisfaction with medication for children with attention deficit disorder [abstract]. Presented at the 15th annual meeting of the Association for Health Services Research, Washington, D.C.; 1998:315

41. Pelham WE, Wheeler T, Chronis A: Empirically supported psychosocial treatments for ADHD. J Clin Child Psychol 1998; 27:189–204

42. Hinshaw SP: Attention Deficits and Hyperactivity in Children. Thousand Oaks, CA: Sage; 1994

43. Safer DJ: ADHD: Some problematic consequences of combining inattention with hyperactivity [abstract]. Presented at the 45th annual meeting of the American Academy of Child and Adolescent Psychiatry. Anaheim, CA. 1998:89

44. Henry B, Moffitt TE, Caspi A, Langley J, Silva PA: On the 'remembrance of things past.' Psychol Assessment 1994; 6:92–101

45. Barkley RA: Attention-Deficit Hyperactivity Disorder, 2nd ed. New York: Guilford, 1998

46. Lambert NM, Sandoval J, Sassone D: Prevalence of hyperactivity in elementary school as a function of social system definers. Am J Orthopsychiat 1999; 48:446–463

47. Gomez R, Harvey J, Quick C, Scharer I, Harris G: DSM-IV AD/HD: Confirmatory factor models, prevalence, and gender and age differences based on parent and teacher ratings of Australian primary school children. J Child Psychol Psychiat 1999; 40:265–274

48. Achenbach TM, McConaughy SH, Howell CT: Child/adolescent behavioral and emotional problems. Psychol Bull 1987; 101:213–232

49. Barbaresi NJ, Olsen RD: An ADHD educational intervention for elementary school teachers. J Dev Behav Pediat 1998; 19:94–100

50. Gadow KD: Pharmacotherapy for behavior disorders. Clin Pediat 1983; 22:48–53

51. Jerome L, Gordon M, Hustler P: A comparison of American and Canadian teachers' knowledge and attitudes towards attention deficit hyperactivity disorder (ADHD). Can J Psychiat 1994; 39:563–567

52. Jensen PS, Xenakis SN, Shervette RE, Bain MV, Davis H: Diagnosis and treatment of attention deficit disorder in two general hospital clinics. Hosp Commun Psychiat 1989; 40:708–712

53. Goldberg ID, Roghmann KJ, McInerny TK, Burke JD: Mental health problems among children seen in a pediatric practice. Pediatrics 1984; 73:278–293

54. Adkins MS, Pelham WE, Licht MH: A comparison of objective classroom measures and teacher ratings of attention deficit disorder. J Abnorm Child Psychol 1985; 13:155–167

55. Landgren M, Kjellman B, Gillberg C: Attention deficit disorder with developmental coordination disorders. Arch Dis Child 1998; 79:207–212

56. Marcotte AC, Thacher PV, Butters M, Bortz J, Acebo C, Carskadon MA: Parental report of sleep problems in children with attentional and learning problems. J Dev Behav Pediat 1998; 19:178–186

57. Wilens T, Biederman J, Spenser T: Clonidine for sleep disturbances associated with attention-deficit hyperactivity disorder. J Am Acad Child Adolesc Psychiatry 1994; 33:424–426

58. Ferris TG, Saglam D, Stafford RS, Causino N, Starfield B, Culpepper L, Blumenthal D: Changes in the daily practice of primary care for children. Arch Pediatr Adolesc Med 1998; 152:227–233

59. Epstein MA, Shaywitz SE, Shaywitz BA, Woolston JL: The boundaries of attention deficit disorder. J Learn Disabil 1991; 24:78–86

60. Bussing R, Zima BT, Belin TR: Variations in ADHD treatment among special education students. J Am Acad Child Adolesc Psychiatry 1998; 37:968–976

61. Pelham WE: Psychosocial interventions [abstract]. Presented at the NIH Consensus Development Conference: Diagnosis and Treatment of Attention Deficit Hyperactivity Disorder. Bethesda, MD; 1998:123–125

62. Weiss, G, Hechtman L: Hyperactive Children Grown Up, 2nd ed., New York: Guilford; 1993

63. Hinshaw SP, Klein RG, Abikoff H: Childhood attention deficit hyperactivity disorder: Nonpharmacological and combination treatments. In: Nelson PE, Gorman JM, eds. A Guide

to Treatments That Work. New York: Oxford University Press; 1998:26–41

64. Weiss G, Kruger E, Danielson U, Elman M: Effect of long-term treatment of hyperactive children with methylphenidate. Can Med Assoc J 1975; 112:159–165

65. Charles L, Schain R: A four year follow-up study of the effects of methylphenidate on the behavior and academic achievement of hyperactive children. J Abnorm Child Psychol 1981; 9:495–505

66. Barkley RA, Anastopoulas AD, Guevremont DC, Fletcher KE: Adolescents with ADHD: Patterns of behavioral adjustment, academic functioning and treatment utilization. J Am Acad Child Adolesc Psychiatry 1991; 30:752–761

67. Barkley RA, Fischer M, Edelbrock CS, Smallish L: The adolescent outcome of hyperactive children diagnosed by research criteria. J Am Acad Child Adolesc Psychiatry 1990; 29:546–557

68. Angold A, Costello EJ: Stimulant medication: A general population perspective. Psychopharmacol Bull 1997; 33:469 [abstract]

69. Biederman J, Faraone S, Milberger S, Guite J, Mike E, Chen L, Mennin D, Marrs A: A prospective 4-year follow-up study of attention-deficit hyperactivity and related disorders. Arch Gen Psychiatry 1996; 53:437–446

70. Wolraich ML, Hannah JN, Baumgaertel A, Feurer ID: Examination of DSM-IV criteria for attention-deficit/hyperactivity disorder in a county-wide sample. J Dev Behav Pediat 1998; 19:162–168

71. Wolraich ML, Hannah JN, Pinnock TY, Baumgaertel A, Brown J: Comparison of diagnostic criteria for attention-deficit hyperactivity disorder in a county-wide sample. J Am Acad Child Adolesc Psychiatry 1996; 35:319–324

72. Bowen J, Fenton T, Rappaport L: Stimulant medication and attention deficit-hyperactivity disorder. Am J Dis Child 1991; 145:291–295

73. Hazell PL, McDowell MJ, Walton JM: Management of children prescribed psychostimulant medication for attention deficit hyperactivity disorder in the Hunter region of NSW. Med J Aust 1996; 165:477–480

[29]

A Black-Box Warning for Antidepressants in Children?

Thomas B. Newman, M.D., M.P.H.

On September 14, 2004, a Food and Drug Administration (FDA) joint advisory committee voted 15 to 8 to recommend that a "black-box" warning label be required for antidepressant drugs, indicating that they increase the risk of suicidal thinking and behavior ("suicidality") in pediatric patients. Although, as an epidemiologist and general pediatrician, I do not have clinical experience caring for depressed patients, after reviewing the evidence, I strongly favored the black-box warning.

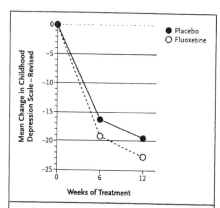

Figure. Mean Changes in Score on the Childhood Depression Scale–Revised in the Treatment for Adolescents with Depression Study.

Data are from March et al.[1] The average scores at baseline, out of a possible 113, were 58.9 in the fluoxetine group and 61.2 in the placebo group. Higher scores indicate more severe depression.

During consideration of the proposed labeling change, the committee heard a number of presentations summarizing evidence that suicidality in children and adolescents may be increased by the newer antidepressant drugs, primarily selective serotonin-reuptake inhibitors. The most convincing evidence came from an FDA analysis of randomized trials. Most of these trials had been conducted by the drug manufacturers under the Best Pharmaceuticals for Children Act, which provides companies an additional six months of patent protection for their product if they do pediatric studies. These studies need not be published and need not be of high quality. In fact, we heard that because these medications are already widely prescribed "off-label" and patents may be close to expiration, sponsors may have more incentive to do the studies quickly than to do them well. To facilitate analysis of the patchwork of pediatric studies, the FDA obtained narratives of adverse-event reports from the trials and contracted with experts on suicide at Columbia University to review them. The Columbia staff members, who were unaware of the treatment-group assignments, were asked to determine whether the adverse events represented suicidality. FDA staff members then combined the results into a meta-analysis.

The results were striking. When all the pediatric trials were pooled, the rate of definite or possible suicidality among children assigned to receive antidepressants was twice that in the placebo group. (The summary risk ratio was 2.19; 95 percent confidence interval, 1.50 to 3.19.) Although the FDA staff did not provide this information to the committee, according to my own calculations, such a dramatic result would be expected to occur by chance only 1 time in 20,000 (P=0.00005).

Nonetheless, some FDA staff and committee members expressed reservations about the data used for this analysis. For example, there was a relatively small number of events, the trials had not been designed to evaluate suicidality, and the methods of ascertainment and classification of the events in the various trials were not uniform. To me, however, these concerns only made the results more compelling. Inadequate sample size and misclassification of outcomes make it more — not less — difficult to detect differences between groups in randomized, blinded trials. The fact that an association emerged from the meta-analysis with a P value of 0.00005, for an outcome that the sponsors of the trials were not looking for, and presumably did not wish to find, was quite convincing.

Inferences from the randomized trials were supported by public testimony from people who believed that antidepressant drugs had caused their loved ones to commit suicide (or, in some cases, homicide). Several of these cases involved patients who had shown no hint of suicidality before beginning treatment with the drugs and who had been given these drugs for indications other than depression, including migraine headaches, nail biting, anxiety, and insomnia.

Several committee members spoke in favor of the antidepressants, citing either their own clinical experience or the Treatment for Adolescents with Depression Study (TADS),[1] a recently published randomized, double-blind study of fluoxetine for major depression in adolescents, which the committee reviewed in detail. However, others and I found the evidence of efficacy much less convincing than the evidence of harm. In reviewing TADS, we were struck by the small size of the difference between fluoxetine and placebo as compared with the effect of placebo alone. For example, after 12 weeks, the average decrease in the Childhood Depression Scale–Revised (scores on which were around 60 of a possible 113 at baseline in both groups, with higher scores indicating more severe depression) was 19.4 points with placebo, as compared with 22.6 points with fluoxetine (see Figure).

PERSPECTIVE   A Black-Box Warning for Antidepressants in Children?

FDA Statement on Recommendations of the Psychopharmacologic Drugs and Pediatric Advisory Committees, September 16, 2004.*

The Food and Drug Administration (FDA) generally supports the recommendations that were recently made to the agency by the Psychopharmacologic Drugs and Pediatric Advisory Committees regarding reports of an increased risk of suicidality (suicidal thoughts and actions) associated with the use of certain antidepressants in pediatric patients. FDA has begun working expeditiously to adopt new labeling to enhance the warnings associated with the use of antidepressants and to bolster the information provided to patients when these drugs are dispensed.

In summary, the members of the advisory committees:

• endorsed FDA's approach to classifying and analyzing the suicidal events and behaviors observed in controlled clinical trials and ex-

pressed their view that the new analyses increased their confidence in the results

• concluded that the finding of an increased risk of suicidality in pediatric patients applied to all the drugs studied (Prozac, Zoloft, Remeron, Paxil, Effexor, Celexa Wellbutrin, Luvox and Serzone) in controlled clinical trials

• recommended that any warning related to an increased risk of suicidality in pediatric patients should be applied to all antidepressant drugs, including those that have not been studied in controlled clinical trials in pediatric patients, since the available data are not adequate to exclude any single medication from an increased risk

• reached a split decision (15-yes, 8-no) regarding rec-

ommending a "black-box" warning related to an increased risk for suicidality in pediatric patients for all antidepressant drugs

• endorsed a patient information sheet ("Medication Guide") for this class of drugs to be provided to the patient or their caregiver with every prescription

• recommended that the products not be contraindicated in this country because the Committees thought access to these therapies was important for those who could benefit

• recommended that the results of controlled pediatric trials of depression be included in the labeling for antidepressant drugs.

*From the Food and Drug Administration, www.fda.gov/bbs/topics/news/2004/new01116.html.

It is easy to see why the personal experience of clinicians and patients would lead them to believe the drug to be effective, since they would have no way of knowing that more than 85 percent of the benefit they observed would also have occurred with placebo.

Randomized trials other than TADS have had less favorable results. The FDA indicated that only 3 of 15 trials of antidepressant use in children with depression had found a statistically significant benefit. The agency also provided us with a meta-analysis[2] that showed that the estimated effi-

cacy of antidepressants in children was minimal and likely to have been overestimated, because published studies have much more favorable results than unpublished studies. Thus, both clinical experience and published trials are likely to lead to inflated estimates of the efficacy of these drugs.

The committee members agreed that there are wide gaps in our knowledge about antidepressants. Perhaps the most important relate to their medium-term and long-term safety and efficacy. The FDA's meta-analysis suggested that the new antidepressants double the risk of suicidality, from

PERSPECTIVE　　　　　　　　A Black-Box Warning for Antidepressants in Children?

about 2.5 percent to 5 percent, in trials lasting two or three months. But what happens if you take them for a year? Does a 5 percent risk over the course of three months become a 20 percent risk over the course of a year, or does the benefit–risk balance improve over time? Does the increase in the rate of suicidality translate into an increase in the rate of completed suicide? Do additional adverse effects occur after treatment with the medications is stopped? Are there important differences among the drugs in this class? What age groups are at risk? It seems unlikely that the drugs suddenly become safe after the patient's 18th birthday. Currently, no one knows the answer to any of these questions.

There was also agreement that the experience with antidepressants illustrates serious deficiencies in the implementation of the Best Pharmaceuticals for Children Act U.S. consumers, through higher drug prices buoyed by extended market exclusivity, are paying a high price for pediatric studies that may be poorly conducted and selectively disseminated. The public is the loser, both because the availability of generic versions of the drugs is then delayed and because poor science and selective publication can lead to false conclusions about pediatric safety and efficacy. If these studies are to provide value, the requirement to do them must be changed to a requirement to do them well. Extend-

ed exclusivity should be granted only if the studies conducted in order to receive it are judged to be of high quality by independent peer review and if their results are disseminated in a timely manner.

Finally, this controversy over the use of antidepressants in children illustrates the need for a more sophisticated approach to evaluating harms and efficacy than simply seeing whether they are statistically significant at a P value of less than 0.05. Regardless of the P value, no psychotropic drug is free of potential negative effects. The best available estimates of the magnitude and nature of the effects of the drugs must be discussed with patients and families, so that they can make an informed decision about treatment. My hope is that the FDA will follow the recommendation of the advisory committee and require a black-box warning — and that doing so will make these discussions more likely to take place.

From the Departments of Epidemiology and Biostatistics and Pediatrics, University of California San Francisco, San Francisco.

1.　March J, Silva S, Petrycki S, et al. Fluoxetine, cognitive-behavioral therapy, and their combination for adolescents with depression: Treatment for Adolescents With Depression Study (TADS) randomized controlled trial. JAMA 2004;292:807-20.
2.　Whittington CJ, Kendall T, Fonagy P, Cottrell D, Cotgrove A, Boddington E. Selective serotonin reuptake inhibitors in childhood depression: systematic review of published versus unpublished data. Lancet 2004;363:1341-5.

Enhancement

[30]

Manipulating your mind

What will science discover about our brains, and how are we going to deal with it?

Holger Breithaupt and Katrin Weigmann

The Decade of the Brain, proclaimed by US President George Bush in 1990, passed without making much of an obvious impact. But it did in fact produce considerable scientific advances in neurobiology, giving scientists an exponentially increasing knowledge of how the brain works and the means to manipulate biochemical processes within and between nerve cells. This knowledge is slowly trickling down to society as well, be it in the pharmaceutical industry, to parents concerned about their child's performance in school, to students looking for chemical helpers to pass their exams, or to military researchers who have an obvious interest in keeping soldiers awake and alert.

> Unlike the many claimed applications of genetics ... diagnostic and therapeutic products from neurobiological research are already available

The ability to fiddle with the brain with ever-increasing effectiveness has also created critical questions about how to use this knowledge. Francis Fukuyama, in *Our Posthuman Future*, Leon Kass, Chairman of the US President's Council on Bioethics, and Steven Rose, a neurobiologist at the Open University, UK, are the most prominent and outspoken critics of the use of psychopharmaceuticals and other neurological techniques to analyse and interfere with human mental capabilities. Their concerns have also grasped the attention of neurobiologists, ethicists, philosophers and the lay public, who are all slowly realising the enormous potential of modern neuroscience. "People closely identify themselves with their brains, they don't with their genes," said Arthur L.

Caplan, Professor of Bioethics at the University of Pennsylvania, Philadelphia, PA, USA.

Although these debates started in the late 1990s, it took the general public a bit longer to take notice—*The New York Times* and *The Economist* did not pick up on the issue until 2002. "There is a great amount of information about the brain but no one's paying attention to the ethics," Caplan said. "The attention of ethicists went to genetics because of the Human Genome Project...so we had to jump-start the ethics [in neurobiology]." But that is rapidly changing. Unlike the many claimed applications of genetics, such as gene therapy or molecular medicine, diagnostic and therapeutic products from neurobiological research are already available. Caplan sees four major controversial areas: the definition and diagnosis of certain types of behaviour, such as aggression, terrorism or poor performance in school; the use of drugs to alter such behaviour; questions about moral responsibility—with people going to court and saying 'this man isn't responsible because his brain is abnormal'; and eventually new debates about racial and gender differences.

These controversies are not just anticipated: most are already occurring. Society's pursuit of perfection entails 'treating' whatever is not desirable—be it bad mood, aggression or forgetfulness. Many people take herbal memory enhancers, such as *ginkgo biloba*, even though they are probably no more effective than sugar or coffee. But neurobiology adds a new twist. By understanding the brain's workings at the chemical level, it paves the way for much more efficient ways to tweak brain function. And many psychopharmaceuticals already enjoy a much broader popularity beyond

treating neurological and psychiatric diseases. "When you think of the millions of pills that people take as anti-anxiety drugs, how many of these people are really anxious? Probably just a small percentage," said James L. McGaugh, Director of the Center for the Neurobiology of Learning and Memory at the University of California, Irvine, CA, USA. Millions of school children in the USA are prescribed antipsychotic drugs or are treated for depression and attention deficit and hyperactivity disorder (ADHD), and the numbers in Western Europe are also increasing (Brower, 2003). There is an epidemic of new behavioural disorders: ADHD, seasonal affective disorder (SAD), post-traumatic stress

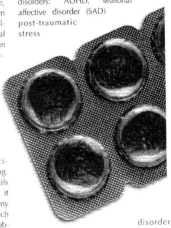

disorder (PTSD), panic disorder (PD), narcissistic personality disorder (NPD), borderline personality disorder (BPD), antisocial personality disorder (APD), histrionic personality disorder (HPD)—soon we will run out of letter combinations to abbreviate them all.

The explosive increase in prescriptions for Ritalin® for school children has already prompted questions about the apparent epidemic of ADHD. "Now it's not that Ritalin is not effective in sedating an over-active kid, it certainly is, but it's turning a complex social relationship into a problem inside the brain of a child and therefore inside the genes of a child," said Rose (see interview, in this issue).

In a way, Ritalin is neuroethics "in a nutshell", commented Wrye Sententia, co-director of the Center for Cognitive Liberty and Ethics (CCLE), a non-profit education, law and policy center in Davis, CA, USA, and head of its programme on neuroethics. The debate over the drug covers social, ethical and legal issues: who defines behaviour and behavioural disorder, who should control treatment, how should society react to drug misuse, and is it ethical to use drugs to gain an advantage over others? These are valid questions that apply equally to neuroethics in general.

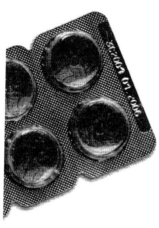

Neuropharmaceuticals have already found applications outside a medical setting. Like amphetamines before it, Ritalin is increasingly used by healthy people to help them focus their attention. Similarly, the development of new drugs to influence the biochemistry of brain function also has broad economic potential outside the medical setting. Most memory-enhancing drugs available to treat Alzheimer's, such as donezepil, galantamine or rivastigmine, inhibit cholinesterase to slow down the turnover of the neurotransmitter acetylcholine

in the synapse. New drugs in the development pipeline will act on other compounds in the biochemical pathway that encodes memory: Cortex Pharmaceuticals (Irvine, CA, USA) are studying compounds called Ampakines®, which act on the AMPA receptor. This receptor responds to glutamate, which is itself involved in memory acquisition. Another class of drugs under development acts on the cAMP responsive element-binding protein (CREB), the last step in establishing long-term memory. "What we would expect is that drugs that enhance CREB signalling would be specific to inducing long-term memory and not affect upstream events of memory, such as memory acquisition and short term memory," explained Tim Tully, Professor at Cold Spring Harbor Laboratory (NY, USA) and founder of Helicon Therapeutics (Farmingdale, NY, USA), one of two companies now working on drugs to increase CREB function.

None of these drugs, however, tackles brain degeneration itself, the cause of Alzheimer's and other neurodegenerative diseases, but instead they delay the disease by squeezing a little more out of the remaining brain material. Consequently, they will also work on healthy people. Not surprisingly, the pharmaceutical industry has a great interest in this non-medical use of memory-enhancing drugs, according to McGaugh: "The Alzheimer market is a very important one, but small. The real market is everyone else out there who would like to learn a little easier. So they take a pill in place of studying harder."

Tully warned about the dangers of this off-label use of memory enhancers. The side effects of the first generation of memory drugs are a risk that should not be taken when there is no reason, he said. And this may never become an application, due to other intrinsic side effects. "Maybe it is not a good thing to have memory enhanced chronically every day for the rest of your life. Maybe that will produce psychological side effects, like cramp your head with too many things you can't forget," Tully said.

> The strong military interest in psychopharmaceuticals also presents another conundrum: if the military allows their off-label use, it would be hard to call for a ban on their civil use…

Although memory is important, so too is the ability to forget negative experiences. As long-term memory is largely enhanced by stress hormones and emotional arousal, a horrendous event can overload the system and lead to PTSD: patients persistently re-experience the trauma. Researchers at Harvard University are now studying propranolol, a beta-blocker commonly used as a cardiac drug, as a means to decrease PTSD. Similarly, Helicon Therapeutics is working on CREB suppressors to achieve the same goal: forgetting unwanted memories. These drugs could be valuable for rape victims, survivors of terrorist attacks or young soldiers suffering from PTSD as a result of battlefield experiences. Nevertheless, an ethical debate over memory suppressors has emerged. Kass has described them as the "morning-after pill for just about anything that produces regret, remorse, pain or guilt" (Baard, 2003). But "if the soldier should be shot in the leg, he is treated. They mend the wounds. Now why wouldn't they mend the mental wounds? On what moral grounds?" countered McGaugh. "We need the right regulations and we need the right education of society so that the social acceptance of how to use such drugs is appropriate," said Tully. "Just to give the drug to every soldier that has been out in the field, that would be an abuse… A commander-in-chief, one would hope, would decide against such a use based on his education and on his advisors telling him scientists and experts have discussed this issue and it's immoral to do something like that."

> "Freedom of thought is situated at the core of what it means to be a free person"

Cognitive enhancement is of just as much military interest as the treatment of PTSD. German fighter pilots in World War II took amphetamines to stay alert during British bombing raids at night. During the war against Iraq, US fighter and bomber pilots used drugs to keep awake during the long flights to and from their targets, which with briefing and debriefing could easily exceed 24 hours. Not surprisingly, the US Air Force is carrying out research on how donepezil could improve pilots' performance. The strong military interest in psychopharmaceuticals also presents another conundrum: if the military allows their off-label use, it would be hard to call for a ban on their civil use, as Kass has suggested.

Neurological advances are not limited to new drugs. Brain imaging techniques, such as functional magnetic resonance imaging (fMRI) or positron emission tomography (PET), offer enormous potential for analysing higher behaviour. While neurologists originally used them to analyse basic sensual, motor and cognitive processes, they are now increasingly being used by psychologists and philosophers to investigate the mechanics of social and moral attitudes, reasoning and moral perceptions (Illes *et al*, 2003). Joshua Greene, a graduate student at Princeton University's Center for the Study of Brain, Mind and Behavior, put his human subjects into a fMRI scanner and presented them with hypothetical scenarios in which they had to make a decision between two more or less bad outcomes of the situation (Greene *et al*, 2001). The results of the studies show how the brain weighs emotional and rational reasoning against each other in its decision-making. Potentially, this could be used as a sophisticated lie detector to see if someone answers a question spontaneously or after considerable reasoning. Other studies showed that the brain reacts differently at first sight when seeing a person of the same or a different skin colour (Hart *et al*, 2000; Phelps *et al*, 2000). That does not necessarily mean that everyone is a racist, but refinement of such methods could unveil personal prejudices or preferences. The use of brain scans to evaluate people's talents or dispositions will therefore draw as much interest as the drugs used to manipulate them. "Parents will be falling over themselves to take these tests," Caplan said. In contrast to Kass and other conservative critics, he therefore argues that regulation will not make sense but that it should be left to the individual to make decisions about whether to undergo diagnostic tests for behaviour or take behaviour-modifying drugs. "Medicine, business and the public will have to negotiate these boundaries," Caplan said, but he remains worried that "peer pressure and advertising and marketing will make us take those pills." Rose also does not call for a ban, but wants society to take control of these new advances and their applications, based on democratic decisions.

The use of these new tests and drugs may cause another problem. Going back to Ritalin, Sententia explained that an important reason for the apparent increase in ADHD may be overcrowded classrooms and overworked teachers, who are quick to label a child with ADHD rather than call for improvements in the school. "From the top down there is a clear message to put these kids on drugs," Sententia said. Society should instead "put the parents' rights back into focus" and better educate parents about behavioural disorders. This would give them more freedom to make their own decisions for their child "so they are not at the mercy of doctors or teachers," she continued. Such "cognitive liberty", as Sententia described it, would have to rest on better public education and understanding about the risks and benefits, the potentials and myths of neurobiology. "What I think we need to do in the next five or ten years is discuss exactly what is appropriate and inappropriate in applying these things," said Tully. "Now is the time for education."

This does not, however, solve the question of who controls diagnostic tools and treatment in the case of people who are not free or able to make their own decisions—such as children, prison inmates or psychiatric patients. CCLE, for instance, filed an *amicus curiae* ('friend of the court') brief to the US Supreme Court on behalf of Charles T. Sell, to argue against a court order requiring Sell to be injected with psychotropic drugs to make him mentally competent to stand trial for insurance fraud. Sententia sees some limitations, however, to cognitive freedom. Children do not enjoy the same civil rights as adults, but it should be the parents—not teachers or schools—who make the decisions about the diagnosis and treatment of their children, she said. Prison inmates also lose some of their individual rights when they are convicted, Sententia continued, and this may include their right to refuse medication. "The legal system will have to decide how to use this knowledge about the brain," Caplan commented, in light of the "tremendous tension between brain privacy and social interest in controlling dangerous behaviour." Sententia therefore stressed that all decisions about diagnosis and treatment must at least be in accordance with the US Constitution and the United Nations Declaration of Human Rights.

Some of the most important applications of this right to privacy concern using brain scans as a sophisticated lie detector for prisoners seeking parole, foreigners applying for a visa or employers testing their employees' honesty. "What and how you think should be private," Sententia said, because "freedom of thought is situated at the core of what it means to be a free person." Caplan also

> The use of brain scans to evaluate people's talents or dispositions will therefore draw as much interest as the drugs used to manipulate them

expects more pressure from society in future to make sure that no such tests are performed without informed consent.

Equally, Caplan, Sententia and others believe that individuals should be free to use neurological technology to enhance their mental abilities outside a medical setting. This is in contrast to the prohibitive stance taken by Kass and other conservatives who argue that it would be neither 'natural' nor fair to those who choose not to use such enhancement. "It's not clear to me that all forms of enhancement are bad," commented Adina Roskies, a neuroscientist and philosopher at the Massachusetts Institute of Technology's Department of Linguistics and Philosophy (Cambridge, MA, USA). "There are all sorts of things that we do today that enhance our life prospects and that are not considered to be bad. … We're far away from the 'natural' order already." Thus, in some cases, instead of controlling or even restricting these new possibilities, it would be better if society focuses on trying to ensure that everyone has access to them, she continued. Given the increasing interest that the public is showing in the new possibilities offered by neuroscience, it may be too late for restrictions anyway. "There is no way of stopping this tide, the genie is out of the bottle," Sententia said, "so the question is: how can we navigate this sea of change?"

REFERENCES

Baard E (2003) The guilt-free soldier. *The Village Voice*, Jan 22

Brower V (2003) Analyse this. *EMBO Rep* **4**: 1022–1024

Greene JD, Sommerville RB, Nystrom LE, Darley JM, Cohen JD (2001) An fMRI investigation of emotional engagement in moral judgement. *Science* **293**: 2105–2108

Hart A, Whalen P, McInerney S, Fischer H, Rauch S (2000) Differential response in the human amygdala to racial outgroup versus ingroup stimuli. *Neuroreport* **11**: 2351–2355

Illes J, Kirschen MP, Gabrieli JDE (2003) From neuroimaging to neuroethics. *Nat Neurosci* **6**: 205

Phelps EA, O'Connor KJ, Cunningham WA, Funayama ES, Gatenby JC, Gore JC, Banaji MR (2000) Performance on indirect measures of race evaluation predicts amygdala activation. *J Cogn Neurosci* **12**: 729–738

Holger Breithaupt & Katrin Weigmann

doi:10.1038/sj.embor.7400109

[31]

Treatment, enhancement, and the ethics of neurotherapeutics

Paul Root Wolpe

Department of Psychiatry, Department of Medical Ethics, Department of Sociology, and Center for Bioethics, University of Pennsylvania, Philadelphia, PA 19104, USA

Accepted 5 August 2002

Abstract

Emerging neurotechnologies, including psychopharmaceuticals, brain stimulation, implantable brain chips, transcranial magnetic stimulation, and brain imaging raise a number of ethical questions. One of the most contentious is the proper role of these technologies in improving or increasing mental and neurological traits and skills in those with no identifiable pathology. The "enhancement" debate centers around a number of concerns and philosophical approaches to the proper role of medicine, therapeutics, and desirable human qualities. Arguements for and against neurological enhancement are reviewed, and historical and social perspectives are offered.

1. Introduction

The study of the brain has always promised more than just the cure of disease. Franz Joseph Gall's phrenology, which identified 27 faculties in the brain (such as valor, cunning, pride, ability to learn, ambition, and metaphysical perspicuity), was intended to detect the morally infirm and differentiate "higher" from "lower" races. Cesare Lombroso, the 19th Century "Father of Modern Criminology," argued that criminals were evolutionary throwbacks with "atavistic" brains and morphological features characteristic of lower races. Craniometry, the science of correlating brain size with intelligence, was used primarily to create intelligence hierarchies within and between races. Nobel Prize winning psychiatrist Antonio Egas Moniz advanced lobotomy in the late 1930s and 1940s as a means of controlling aggressive or violent behavior. These efforts, and most that came after them, were suffused with moral assumptions and visions of desirable and undesirable human characteristics, but were believed by their proponents to represent the dispassionate pursuit of objective science.

Neuroscience today is also built on a series of fundamental assumptions about human nature and worth. It is not possible, and perhaps not desirable, to purge neuroscience of moral presuppositions, dealing as it does with fundamental aspects of identity, personality, free will, and other value-wrought concepts. As in the 19th

E-mail address: wolpep@mail.med.upenn.edu

388   *P.R. Wolpe / Brain and Cognition 50 (2002) 387–395*

and early 20th centuries, our scientific inquiry is guided by culturally determined standards of what traits we think are valuable to explore and what behaviors we think are desirable to control or eradicate. For example, imaging studies that look for morphological or functional differences in the orbitofrontal cortex or the amygdala of "psychopaths" (usually defined as violent criminals with antisocial personality disorder) raise many of the same ethical and philosophical questions (if in much more sophisticated scientific packaging) as the science of earlier in the century (Abbott, 2001; Anderson, Bechara, Damasio, Tranel, & Damasio, 1999). The attempt to localize criminality and explain it as the function of a specific pathologized section of the brain is itself an agenda of a particular cultural and historical moment, and one with significant moral implications.

Perhaps the most significant moral discussion in modern neuroscience has been directed at the use of pharmaceuticals to alter the fundamental cognitive and affective functions of the brain. The human desire to induce mental states through ingestion is, of course, as old as the discovery of fermentation (if not older, with the discovery of natural hallucinogens or stimulants), and so is moral debate about it. Nineteenth century America was particularly enamored of developing nutritional philosophies of health with a moral tinge, from the botanical medicine of Samuel Thompson to the non-stimulating diets developed by Will Kellogg (corn flakes were invented as a bland breakfast to avoid stirring up the passions in the morning) or Sylvester Graham (whose now-famous cracker was designed towards the same ends as corn flakes). For centuries, lay, folk, and professional movements in both Western and Eastern medicine have prescribed foods, herbs, and potions to induce proper physical and mental functioning. We still try to "eat right" to improve mood and general mental functioning, and use stimulants (caffiene), sedatives (alcohol), and mood enhancers (chocolate), and have built nutraceuticals (St. John's Wort, Kava, *Ginkgo biloba*) into a multi-billion dollar market. Yet, the debates about the proper use of these substances show no signs of abating.

The ability of the new range of pharmaceuticals to alter or target mood states, levels of cognition, or cognitive skills such as memory is one of the most promising and challenging developments of the 21st century. Drugs developed for some of our most intractable diseases now promise us the power not only to treat pathology, but to improve or augment otherwise average or typical functioning; not only to arrest the cognitive deterioration of Alzheimer's, for example, but to improve cognitive functioning in the healthy. Drugs developed for narcolepsy entice us with amphetamine-free wakefulness (Bastuji & Jouvet, 1988); drugs developed for depression promise to elevate our spirits in general (Kramer, 1993); and drugs developed for erectile dysfunction are sold freely on the web with only a nod to medical necessity (Armstrong, Schwartz, & Asch, 1999). If history is any precedent, we will enthusiastically embrace these technologies, even as we agonize over whether or not we should do so.

Debate has already begun as to the implications of these technologies for defining the difference between treatment and enhancement. There are two fundamental questions that confront us. The first, more philosophical question of enhancement is about categorization: what do terms such as "average" or "normal" functioning, or even "disease" and "enhancement" mean when we can improve functioning across the entire range of human capability? Is the typical, occasional erectile dysfunction that most men experience a "disease" (or at least a condition worthy of medical attention) now that we have a treatment for it? If Prozac can lift everyone's mood, what then becomes "normal" or "typical" affect, and will grouchiness or sadness or inner struggle then be pathologized? And if we can all be happy and well-adjusted through Prozac, should insurance pay for everyone to reach that state of bliss? The second, related question addresses a broader social concern: should we encourage or discourage people to ingest pharmaceuticals to enhance behaviors, skills, and traits?

What are the social (and economic, religious, psychological,. . .) implications of using drugs or other neurotechnologies to micromanage mood, improve memory, to maintain attentiveness or improve sexuality?

2. Defining enhancement

The answers to these two questions are, in large measure, dependent on how we define enhancement itself. But the more closely we examine the concept, the slipperier it appears. As enhancement is a concept that defines the boundary condition between what we consider disease intervention and what we do not, by definition the term will conform to what the culture, or medical professionals, see as the proper objects of medical intervention. In other words, what medicine chooses to treat is defined as disease, while altering what it does not treat is enhancement.

The difficulty of creating a meaningful enhancement standard to use to allocate medical care or create guidelines for clinical treatment can be illustrated by looking at one proposal. The bioethicist Norm Daniels asks what kind of medical care should be covered for all citizens in a just society, and in doing so has developed probably the most detailed discussion of the enhancement issue (Daniels, 1985; Daniels, 2000; Sabin & Daniels, 1994).

Daniels is interested in determining what should be considered obligatory vs. non-obligatory provision of care in a just society. He begins by arguing *against* trying to demarcate a treatment/enhancement distinction to solve that dilemma. First, he suggests, even if we could clearly define the two, we cannot draw a clear moral line that justifies considering one the legitimate object of medical attention and not the other. Secondly, there is something ultimately arbitrary about how we draw many of our disease/non-disease distinctions. Finally, there are treatments or conditions (such as abortion or shyness) that are clearly outside disease definitions, yet that we may want to provide in our standard medical offerings.

Daniels illustrates his point by offering the following example: imagine two boys, both of whom are of short stature and are projected to grow into short stature adults of about 5 ft 3 in. (which is at the low end of the normal growth distribution for males). One is short because he has growth hormone (GH) deficiency from a brain tumor, while the other is short because, though he has normal GH secretions, he has very short parents.

Both "suffer" from the same condition, and in both the causes are fundamentally biological. Yet only one is "sick"; any intervention we design on behalf of the second is likely to be labeled "enhancement." Daniels pushes it even further: what if we find the gene(s) that cause short stature in the boy without the tumor, and discover he is short because his cells do not respond readily to GH, or because his GH levels level off faster, or because he has fewer receptors? Is he *then* "sick?" And what if the other boy has a gene that predisposes him to the tumor? Now both causes can be considered genetic, yet one boy is granted full economic and social access to medical resources, while the other may not be.

Daniels' concern is about obligatory vs. non-obligatory medical services, and its implications for social justice; what services must be provided to all citizens in a society that sees provision of basic care an inalienable right? What standards of "medical care" do we use when we desire to distribute medical care fairly and equitably in society? Why is the society ready to help the boy with the tumor reach greater stature, and not the other, and is the reasoning justified?

Daniels suggests that instead of using definitions of disease as our standard, which may lead us to treat one boy and not the other, we should instead determine for each trait, state, or behavior what he calls "species-typical functioning." The concept implies not just a statistical accumulation of some average level of functioning in a particular realm of human activity, but rather an examination of the design of the organism to determine the "natural functional organization" of its members. The "normal function model" serves as the standard of functioning that a society has an obligation to try to achieve for all its members. While a society has no obligation to provide services that raise any citizen's function above the typical level for the species as a whole, it does have an obligation to provide services that, to the degree possible, raise the level of functioning of any citizen with deficits to the species-typical level. In such a case, if short stature can be shown to cause difficulties in the lives of males of such stature (as it can, in such things as employment discrimination and mate selection), society has an obligation to try to ameliorate that departure from normal function (i.e., male-typical height) no matter what the cause. Daniels goes on to suggest that normal functioning is important as a baseline not because it is "natural" (a thorny concept philosophically) and so inviolable, but because it is a convenient baseline to determine what society should owe to its members. In addition, the approach resists the trend towards medicalizing problems, and sets stronger boundaries around what medicine should attend to. Pursuing some ideal of total physical, mental, and social well-being is beyond medicine's proper domain (Parens, 1998).

There are a number of problems with Daniels' argument. His model has been criticized as to the difficulty in determining species-typical functioning for a host of traits (e.g., what is "species-typical" happiness, or shyness, or cognition, or even erectile function?). Remember that we need to determine this not by some statistical average, but rather by a "theoretical account of the design of the organism." How happy were we, in fact, designed to be? Other critics have pointed out the model's assumption of the innateness and immutability of talents and traits; the presumption that maximization of potential is only owed the low-functioning; and the culturally and ideologically bound determination in many traits of what should be considered "typical" or "normal" (e.g., Juengst, 1998; Lachs, 2000; Silvers, 1998). Daniels' effort well illustrates the fundamental problem of drawing the lines between the kinds of physiological interventions that we conceptualize as curative or normalizing, and those we consider extraordinary or enhancing.

Other models have been proposed as well (see Juengst, 1998, for a review). Yet, ultimately, any exclusive enhancement definition must fail, in part because concepts such as disease, normalcy, and health are significantly culturally and historically bound, and thus the result of negotiated values. The provision of services under the rubric of medicine is, ultimately, somewhat arbitrary, the product of social negotiation and historical precedent. Decisions about what to fund through insurance reimbursement, what to restrict by regulating access (through physicians, for example), and how society as a whole should regard the use of "enhancing" pharmaceuticals and other technologies will be the product of a long series of conversations in the professional literature and in public fora as these technologies develop.

The enhancement/treatment conundrum can therefore be summarized as addressing three levels of inquiry:

1. *Medicine and reimbursement*: what should be the proper role of enhancement technologies in medicine and those who fund it? Can a distinction be made between therapy and enhancement that is meaningful and operationalizable? Can we defend the proposition that medicine should concern itself with, or that third party payers should only fund, "treatment" and not "enhancement?"

2. *Public policy*: in what spheres of public policy should a distinction between disease and enhancement be maintained? Should there be rules against using certain enhancement technologies in sports, for example, or among children? And conversely, should public policy encourage use of enhancement technologies among those for whom it might aid in safeguarding the public good?

P.R. Wolpe / Brain and Cognition 50 (2002) 387–395   391

3. *Normative behavior*: is there a normative recommendation for how we should think about enhancement in general? Should society promote or resist biotechnological enhancement? And whatever the normative decision, why does there seem to be such initial resistance to its uses?

3. Neurotechnologies and the enhancement question

The questions posed above are particularly trenchant when applied to emerging neurotechnologies. On one hand, human beings have always developed strategies and technologies to enhance their cognitive and affective functioning. We send our children to school, memorize poetry, develop training programs, meditate, enrich our word power, read novels, go to therapy, try to get a good night's sleep before exams, eat "brain food" such as fish, shut the door and turn off the music to study— all actions that, to one degree or another, are intended to create environments, inner states, or improved functioning that will encourage or support a desired level of neurological performance. We bang our heads, rub our temples, snap our fingers, and try to stop thinking directly about a topic to recall it to memory. In addition, we drink alcohol and caffeine, take Ritalin and Prozac, inhale nicotine, smoke marijuana, and use other pharmacological means to induce our brains to act in ways that we desire—to increase memory, stabilize mood, encourage creativity, or promote attentiveness.

The enhancement question, however, arises primarily in technologies that attempt to *directly* moderate the neurochemical, structural, or electrical components of the brain. The manipulation of brain function through learning, meditating, behavioral reinforcement, biofeedback, temple rubbing, or any other mechanism that either draws on the body's own resources, or manipulates the external environment to induce change do not raise the same ethical challenges. What characterizes the particular ethical currency of the enhancement debate today is the ability to bypass these types of activities and to change the brain directly.

Let us leaven our discussion with an example of a drug with the ability to enhance normal functioning: modafinil. Modafinil (2-(diphenylmethyl)-sulfinylacetamide) is a eugeroic (literally, "good arousal") drug that creates a wakeful, alert state in those who take it. Early reports suggest that, unlike amphetamines, modafinil does not create a "buzz," does not cycle high and low, does not increase heart rate and blood pressure, and is non-addictive (Bastuji & Jouvet, 1988; US Modafinil in Narcolepsy Multicenter Study Group, 2000). Amphetamines create a dose-dependent impairment of the sleep cycle, so that one needs more and more amphetamines to stay awake, and is ultimately more fatigued. Modafinil not only does not disturb sleep, it only seems to cause wakefulness under conditions where vigilance is sought by the person who has taken it (Legarde, Batejat, van Beers, Sarafian, & Pradella, 1995). Modafinil is generally prescribed for sleep disorders, such as narcolepsy and hypersomnia, and may be effective in the sleepiness that can accompany diseases such as Parkinson's.

Modafinil, marketed under the brand name Provigil, may eventually challenge Viagra in its appeal to off-label and black market usage. Also like Viagra, new sources have begun to tout the benefits of modafinil. A CBS News report trumpeted, "A Dream Come True? New Drug Tricks Brain To Be Awake" (CBS News, 2002). The New York Times ran an article emphasizing the drug's potential in "a chronically sleep-deprived nation" (Goode, 1998), and The New Yorker magazine ran a glowing piece asking whether "science can make regular sleep unnecessary" (Groopman, 2001). Cepahlon, the manufacturer, has done little to discourage the hype; in fact, the PDA recently cautioned Cephalon to be more careful in its claims about Provigil in its direct-to-consumer advertising (Los Angeles Times, 2002).

392   *P. R. Wolpe / Brain and Cognition 50 (2002) 387–395*

Additionally, the potential of modafinil to be used for non-therapeutic purposes has been promoted in reports citing the armed services' interest in the drug for use in pilots. One study that came out of the United States Army Aeromedical Research Laboratory examined helicopter pilots who were exposed to two 40-h periods of continuous wakefulness separated by only one night of recovery sleep. When receiving modafinil, the pilots scored higher on tests of performance and physiological arousal than they did while on placebo, and also had improved self-ratings of vigor, energy, alertness, talkativeness, and confidence (Caldwell, Caldwell, Smythe, & Hall, 2000). It is not therefore surprising that the United States army, as well as a number of European armed forces, are already using monafidil; up until now, the standard issue wakefulness drug was Dexedrine, which cause all the side effects of amphetamines. The Department of Defense Advanced Research Projects Agency (DARPA), which is funding research into modafinil, justified the research by claiming:

> As combat systems become more and more sophisticated and reliable, the major limiting factor for operational dominance in a conflict is the warfighter. Eliminating the need for sleep while maintaining the high level of both cognitive and physical performance of the individual will create a fundamental change in warfighting and force employment, (quoted in Groopman, 2001, p. 55).

The armed services are not employing the drug without at least some ethical reflection on the appropriate uses of pharmaceuticals as enhancement agents; as a United States Air Force report puts it: "The development of modafinil brings to light a crucial social question. What would be the impediment for its use, if a compound such as modafinil is more like caffeine than amphetamine in terms of safety, and yet, as effective as the amphetamines?" (Lyons & French, 1991).

The "crucial social question" of Lyons and French already confronts us. The use of Viagra, for example, is common among men who would not qualify for a diagnosis of erectile dysfunction (Armstrong et al., 1999). Ritalin sales in certain school districts exceeds any reasonable estimate of children with ADHD that meets DSM-IV criteria (Diller, 1996; Miller, Lalonde, McGrail, & Armstrong, 2001a,b). Kramer (1993) suggested that Prozac makes some patients "better than well," and prescriptions soared. Clearly, some of the top selling drugs in the world today are being used by patients who fit no traditional definition of pathology, yet still see in their own functioning a deficit that these drugs address.

Modafinil will likely follow the patterns of Viagra and Prozac, with areas of overprescribing, significant off-label usage, websites with cursory medical examination, and significant non-prescription sales. Still (or perhaps therefore?) policies need to be made, and so the enhancement question must be addressed. Should modafinil be prescribed solely as a medical drug, properly used only for those suffering from sleep pathology? If so third party payers, including government programs, should cover it. Or, should it be classified as an over-the-counter drug, available to anyone who wants it? Or, should we create a class of drugs available only to those who can show legitimate social need, those whose fatigue might put others at risk, such as airline pilots, or truck drivers? If so, we might see modafinil use as akin to reconstructive surgery, where payment is determined on perceived necessity. For those with severe injury or disfiguring birth defects, reconstructive surgery is medically justifiable and covered. For those electing to have surgery for cosmetic purposes, physicians are still free to offer it (or not), but no one is under a moral obligation to fund it. Finally, as a general social policy question, should we restrict modafinil's use in certain defined social settings, such as sports competitions (where those who use it will have an advantage), or in pediatric use (where students should be learning non-pharmaceutical attention skills), or in people in particularly high-stress jobs, such as airport traffic controllers (who might be tempted to abuse it)?

P.R. Wolpe / Brain and Cognition 50 (2002) 387–395   393

4. The problems of neurological enhancement

The difficulty in deciding the questions of the correct use of neurological enhancers is, in part, a recognition that since we do not really understand the implications of enhancing neurological function, our strategies may backfire. The idea that attention is good, so increased attention is better, or that cognition is good, so increased cognition is better, may turn out to have unexpected consequences. Let us take as an example the effort to develop drugs targeted to improving memory in human beings (e.g., Furey, Pietrini, Alexander, Schapiro, & Horwitz, 2000). The improvement of memory sounds attractive in the abstract, and certainly is desirable for those suffering from Alzheimer's or other conditions that affect memory functions. But there are many unknowns in the use of such drugs in the cognitively intact. The assumption is that memory drugs will simply increase the amount of memory we have available, leaving all other cognitive and affective processes unaffected. But in fact, memory is a selective, delicate process. There are experiences and data that our brains filters out. Our cognitive processes retain specific kinds of data, under specific circumstances, while other input is neglected. Who needs to remember the hours waiting in the Department of Motor Vehicles staring at the ceiling tiles, or to recall the transient amnesia following a personal trauma? Yet, we do not know whether memory enhancement drugs might impair our selectivity process. Might they improve our retention of all memories, even the traumatic or trivial memories that the brain tends to repress? Might we end up awash in memories that are troubling to us, unable to forget a painful past? And how might a memory drug affect associated mental processes— mood (which is closely connected to memory), or attentiveness (daydreaming is often fueled by a sudden recollection)? Perhaps evolution has stabilized at a particular level of memory capacity because more sacrifices a certain cognitive flexibility; a plastic brain may have advantages over one crammed with memory.

The concern is not only speculative. In 1999, scientists reported in *Nature* that they had genetically engineered mice with increased ability to perform learning tasks (Tang et al., 1999). The scientists inserted a gene in mouse zygotes that increased the production of the protein subunit NR2B, part of the NMDA receptor. The mice also displayed physiological changes in the hippocampus (associated with learning) when compared to non-transgenic mice. However, subsequent research seemed to indicate that the mice with enhanced NR2B seemed to have a greater sensitivity to pain (Wei et al., 2001). Though it may be that the mice do not feel the pain more acutely, just learn about pain more readily and thus seem to react to it more strongly (Tang, Shimizu, & Tsien, 2001), it is troubling that even the most preliminary research on memory enhancement has already raised the question of unexpected collateral effects. Perhaps there is a link we do not understand between memory and pain, either at the structural or behavioral level. What other unexpected linkages might be discovered in attempts to change cognitive functions through induced physiological modification?

While most of the "cognitive enhancement" discussed in the literature focuses on memory or attentiveness, the range of cognitive abilities, of course, exceeds just these two traits. Learning, language, skilled motor behaviors, and "executive functions" (such as decision making, goal setting, planning, and judgment) are all part of general cognition, and a drug that managed to enhance a greater range of function (especially executive function) may be more desirable than one that narrowly enhanced memory alone (Whitehouse, Juengst, Mehlman, & Murray, 1997). But if memory drugs alone have collateral affects, how much more so might a drug that influences a greater range of cognitive functioning?

It is not only the collateral effects of neurological enhancement that are troublesome, but also the nature of the change itself. For example, the progressive loss of cognitive function that characterizes Alzheimer's is usually described as constituting the "loss of personality" of the person with the disease. "Dad isn't Dad anymore" because his cognitive faculties as experienced by his loved ones are considered fundamental to who he is; loss of those functions are seen as loss of his essence. A general cognitive enhancement may have the same effect. Significantly improving our overall cognitive functioning may also alter aspects of our identity that are seen as fundamental to who we are. As Whitehouse et al. (1997, p. 16) write:

> Increased memory, new insights, and better reasoning could all lead to new values, new perspectives on one's relationships, and new sources of pleasure and irritation. That does not mean that the enhanced literally will lose their identities and become different people, any more than someone with Alzheimer's does. But in the figurative sense intended by caregivers of people with the disease, it may be that after some point the cognitively enhanced will no longer be recognizable by those who knew them before their enhancement.

Research on patients with frontotemporal dementia, who demonstrate often dramatic changes in well-established patterns or religion, dress, style, and political philosophy, seems to indicate that some aspects of the self are functions of the frontal lobes (Miller et al., 2001a, b). Lauren Slater, author of the memoir "Prozac Diary," writes that though Prozac relieved her of her symptoms, she no longer felt any desire to read the angst-ridden psychology and philosophy books that lined her bookshelf (Slater, 1998). Slater wonders what the loss of these books, that had once been sources of wisdom for her, meant for her sense of self: "who was I? Where was I? Everything seemed less relevant—my sacred menus, my gustatory habits, the narrative that had had so much meaning for me. Diminished." Even when she rediscovers her spiritual side later in the memoir, she now wonders if her calmer, more contemplative spirituality comes not from God, but from Prozac.

Neurological biotechnologies differ from others in that they ask us to explicitly consider the kind of "self" we want to have; or, to put it less dualistically, perhaps, the kind of self we want to be. For some, our astounding ability to manipulate our own biology is an integral part of who we are as human animals. For others, it is an affront to our humanity. This is an argument for which there are no right or wrong answers, emerging as it does from two philosophically different visions of human life. Yet therein lies the tension of the enhancement debate, and there is little doubt that the battlefield on which the debate will be waged next will be our ancient desire to control the workings of our own minds.

References

Abbott, A. (2001). Into the mind of a killer. *Nature*, **410**, 296–298.

Anderson, S. W., Bechara, A., Damasio, H., Tranel, D., & Damasio, A. R. (1999). Impairment of social and moral behavior related to early damage in human prefrental cortex. *Nature Neuroscience*, **2**(11), 1032–1037.

Armstrong, K., Schwartz, J. S., & Asch, D. A. (1999). Direct sale of sildenafil (Viagra) to consumers over the internet. *New England Journal of Medicine*, **341**(18), 1389–1392.

Bastuji, H., & Jouvet, M. (1988). Successful treatment of idiopathic hypersomnia and narcolepsy with modafinil. *Progress in Neuro psychopharmacology & Biological Psychiatry*, **12**(5), 695–700.

Caldwell, J. A., Caldwell, J. L., Smythe, N. K., & Hall, K. K. (2000). A double-blind, placebo-controlled investigation of the efficacy of modafinil for sustaining the alertness and performance of aviators: A helicopter simulator study. *Psychopharmacologia*, **150**(3), 272–282.

CBS News, A dream come true? New drug tricks brain to be awake; Military Is Interested. January 14, 2002. (http://www.cbsnews.com/now/story/0,1597,324299-412,00.shtml).

Daniels, N. (2000). Normal functioning and the treatment-enhancement distinction. *Cambridge Quarterly*, **9**(3), 309–322.

Daniels, N. (1985). *Just health care*. New York: Cambridge University Press.

Diller, L. H. (1996). The run on Ritalin: Attention deficit disorder and stimulant treatment in the 1990s. *Hastings Center Report*, **26**(2), 12–14.

Furey, M. L., Pietrini, P., Alexander, G. E., Schapiro, M. B., & Horwitz, B. (2000). Cholinergic enhancement improves performance on working memory by modulating the functional activity in distinct brain regions: A positron emission tomography regional cerebral blood flow study in healthy humans. *Brain Research Bulletin*, **51**(3), 213–218.

Goode, E. (1998). New hope for losers in the battle to stay awake. *New York Times*, November 3, F1.

Groopman, J. (2001). Eyes wide open. *The New Yorker*, December 3, 52–57.

Juengst, E. (1998). What does enhancement mean?. In E. Parens (Ed.), *Enhancing human traits* (pp. 29–47). Washington, DC: Georgetown University Press.

Kramer, P. O. (1993). *Listening to Prozac*. New York: Penguin books.

Lachs, J. (2000). Grand dreams of perfect people. *Cambridge Quarterly*, **9**(3), 323–329.

Los Angeles Times (2002). FDA reprimands 4 drug makers for misleading promotions. January 16. (http://www.latimes.com/business/la-000004018jan1 6.story?col = la-headlines-business).

Legarde, D., Batejat, D., van Beers, P., Sarafian, D., & Pradella, S. (1995). Interest of modafinil, a new psychostimulant during a sixty hour sleep deprivation experiment. *Fundamental & Clinical Pharmacology*, **9**(3), 271–279.

Lyons, T. J., & French, J. (1991). Modafinil the unique properties of a new stimulant. *USAF School of Aerospace, Brooks TX Science News Note*, **62**, 432–435.

Miller, A. R., Lalonde, C. E., McGrail, K. M., & Armstrong, R. W. (2001a). Prescription of methylphenidate to children and youth, 1990–1996. *CMAJ, Canadian Medical Association Journal*, **165**(11), 1489–1494.

Miller, M. D., Seeley, W. W., Mychack, P., Rosen, M. D., Mena, I., & Boone, K. (2001b). Neuroanatomy of the self. *Neurology*, **57**, 817–821.

Parens, E. (1998). Is better always good? The enhancement project. *Hastings Center Report*, **28**(1), S1–S15.

Sabin, J. E., & Daniels, N. (1994). Determining 'medical necessity' in mental health practice. *Hastings Center Report*, **24**(6), 5–13.

Silvers, A. (1998). A fatal attraction to normalizing, treating disabilities as deviations from "species-typical" functioning. In E. Parens (Ed.), *Enhancing human traits* (pp. 95–123). Washington, DC: Georgetown University Press.

Slater, L. (1998). *Prozac diary*. New York: Random House.

Tang, Y. P., Shimizu, E., Dube, G. R., Rampon, C., Kerchner, G. A., Zhuo, M., Liu, G., & Tsien, J. Z. (1999). Genetic enhancement of learning and memory in mice. *Nature*, **401**(6748), 63–69.

Tang, Y., Shimizu, E., & Tsien, J. Z. (2001). Do 'smart' mice feel more pain, or are they just better learners? *Nature Neuroscience*, **4**(5), 453–454.

US Modafinil in Narcolepsy Multicenter Study Group (2000). Randomized trial of modafinil as a treatment for the excessive daytime somnolence of narcolepsy. *Neurology* **54**(5), 1166–1175.

Wei, F., Wang, G. D., Kerchner, G. A., Kim, S. J., Xu, H. M., Chen, Z. F., & Zhuo, M. (2001). Genetic enhancement of inflammatory pain by forebrain NR2B overexpression. *Nature Neuroscience*, **4**(2), 164–169.

Whitehouse, P. J., Juengst, E., Mehlman, M., & Murray, T. H. (1997). Enhancing cognition in the intellectually intact. *Hastings Center Report*, May–June, 14–22.

Part III
The Therapist

Informed Consent

[32]

INFORMED CONSENT — MUST IT REMAIN A FAIRY TALE?*

Jay Katz, M.D.**

When the editors of the *Journal of Contemporary Health Law and Policy* asked me to contribute an article to their issue in honor of my friend, colleague and dean, Guido Calabresi, I accepted their invitation with pleasure. Since I had reflected about informed consent for two decades, I welcomed this opportunity to set forth my final thoughts and conclusions, however briefly and summarily, on this doctrine and its impact on physician-patient decisionmaking. This essay gives a good account of what I shall ever be able to say about informed consent.

It is appropriate that I choose this topic for this occasion because Guido has had a long standing interest in law and medicine. Twenty-five years ago, he published his remarkable paper, *Reflections on Medical Experimentation in Humans,*[1] and since then he has periodically written on issues in law and medicine. He has not, however, ever explored in depth the problematics of the legal doctrine of informed consent and, to the extent he has, only in the contexts of human experimentation and organ transplantation. If this essay will stimulate this great torts law scholar and teacher to give us his analysis and insights, we can only benefit from his wisdom.

In his article on human experimentation, Guido was mainly concerned with one crucial tension inherent in medical research: "our fundamental

---

* This essay is a revised and extended version of an address given at the Institute de droit de la santé de l'Université de Neuchâtel and the Institute universtaire Kurt Boesch (IKB) -Sion on 6 September 1993. The address was published in the Institute's proceedings under the title *Le Consentement Eclairé Doit-Il Rester un Conte de Fées?* (1993).

I wish to thank Sherwin Nulan and my research assistants Steven D. Lavine and Katherine Weinstein for their thoughtful contributions to earlier drafts of this essay. My wife, Marilyn A. Katz, as always, has commented on the many drafts and I am grateful for her critical wisdom which is reflected throughout this essay.

** Elizabeth K. Dollard Professor Emeritus of Law, Medicine and Psychiatry and Harvey L. Karp Professorial Lecturer in Law and Psychoanalysis, Yale Law School.

1. GUIDO CALABRESI, REFLECTIONS ON MEDICAL EXPERIMENTATION IN HUMANS, 98 DAEDALUS 387 (1969).

need constantly to reaffirm our belief in the sanctity of life and our practical placing of some values (including future lives) above an individual life."[2] He admonished scholars to "devot[e] themselves to the development of a workable but not too obvious control system, rather than to the spinning-out of theories of consent,"[3] because "[t]otally free consent is simply too rare an animal."[4] While I assign greater significance to consent as a mechanism of control than Guido does, I agree with him that "consent by itself is not enough."[5]

Informed consent is a hybrid concept which speaks both to physicians' disclosure obligations and patients' willingness to undergo a particular treatment. Throughout this essay I intend to give prominence to the disclosure aspect of informed consent and its implications for improving the quality of patient consent. I would go further than Guido did, when he wrote that "*some form of consent* should always be required,"[6] because I have greater faith in the crucial role that consent can play in doctor-patient decisionmaking once physicians learn to differentiate, which they have not, between acquiescence and consent. I shall have more to say about all this as I go along. In his recent, intriguing article, *Do We Own Our Bodies?*, while addressing problems of organ transplantation, Guido comes close to issues that I shall explore in this essay:

> I admit I am still an individualistic Kantian libertarian . . . I find it very hard to conceive of a situation in which the state should properly say: "Guido, you must give up that magnificent hair, blood, or marrow, to someone else regardless of your will. . . . We owe it to ourselves . . . to do more thinking about something which seems, at first glance, outlandish — like the question: Do we own our own bodies?"[7]

Guido raised his "outlandish" question with respect to state-mandated interventions. How might he answer the question, "Do we own our own bodies?" in the context of the physician-patient relationship? I shall argue that physicians take too much license with patients' bodies and that the common law doctrine of informed consent has insufficiently addressed the question of who owns our bodies. In a different vein, Guido speaks to this question in *Ideals, Beliefs, Attitudes, and the Law*:

---

2. *Id.* at 405.
3. *Id.*
4. *Id.* at 391.
5. *Id.* at 404.
6. *Id.* (emphasis added).
7. Guido Calabresi, *Do We Own Our Bodies?*, 1 HEALTH MATRIX 17-18 (1991).

Have the lives we have prolonged been, in some sense, fruitful
and rewarding (even if terribly handicapped)? Have we adhered to those beliefs, ideals and attitudes (including the ideal of
letting people hold to their own kooky ideals) which may be
dearer to us than an extra month on a life expectancy table?[8]

Physicians, as I shall argue later, have always placed greater value on
longevity than on quality of life. To resolve these and other value conflicts alone requires searching conversation between physicians and patients. Without such conversation, informed consent will remain a hollow
aspiration and preclude patients from exercising greater control over decisions which, in the end, only they can make.

Like Guido, though perhaps with modification, I too am "an individualistic Kantian libertarian," and thus I give greater weight to autonomy
and self-determination than perhaps he does. As I observed years ago:

Physicians have always maintained that patients are only in need
of caring custody. . . . The idea that patients may also be entitled
to liberty, to sharing the burdens of decision with the doctors,
was never [at least until recently] part of the ethos of medicine.
Being unaware of the idea of patient liberty, physicians did not
address the possible conflict between notions of custody and
liberty.[9]

In this essay I shall also argue that formidable problems exist which
require study and resolution before informed consent can ever safeguard
patient autonomy and self-determination. The likely outcome of such inquiries will be to return ownership of bodies to patients and to not allow
caring custody to mislead physicians and patients into believing that ownership must temporarily be transferred to doctors' "discretion." Law has
an important role to play here by prodding physicians to be more atten-
tive to patients' rights regarding decisionmaking authority. Such prodding, as I have already suggested, is necessary because the idea that
patients have rights to autonomy and self-determination has been an
alien one throughout the history of medical practice. Ultimately,
medicine and not law must formulate a doctrine of informed consent
which is responsive not only to the proddings of law but also to the realities of medical practice (i.e., to the complex caretaking and being-taken-
care-of interactions that are the essence of all interactions between patients and their physicians). Finally, I shall argue, as I have already noted,
that greater emphasis has to be given to disclosure rather than consent

---

8. GUIDO CALABRESI, IDEALS, BELIEFS, ATTITUDES, AND THE LAW 10-11 (1985).
9. JAY KATZ, THE SILENT WORLD OF DOCTOR AND PATIENT 2 (1984).

and, therefore, that the inadequacies in current disclosure practices are to begin with the greater obstacle to fashioning an informed consent doctrine which is not a charade.

Guido will soon be a judge on the United States Court of Appeals for the Second Circuit. He, of course, will often return to Yale Law School and, thus, this essay is not written in the spirit of saying farewell to him but of expressing my admiration, at a decisive moment in his professional life, to a wonderful person who over the last thirty-six years has meant so much to me and to my school. I can give him no better present than my thoughts on a topic in which we share a common interest. I hope that in the informed consent cases which will surely come before him, he will address some of my concerns about the persisting inadequacies in the physician-patient decisionmaking process.

I. THE PRE-HISTORY OF INFORMED CONSENT IN MEDICINE

The idea that, prior to any medical intervention, physicians must seek their patients' informed consent was introduced into American law in a brief paragraph in a 1957 state court decision,[10] and then elaborated on in a lengthier opinion in 1960.[11] The emerging legal idea that physicians were from now on obligated to share decisionmaking authority with their patients shocked the medical community, for it constituted a radical break with the silence that had been the hallmark of physician-patient interactions throughout the ages. Thirty-five years are perhaps not long enough for either law or medicine to resolve the tension between legal theory and medical practice, particularly since judges were reluctant to face up to implications of their novel doctrine, preferring instead to remain quite deferential to the practices of the medical profession.

Viewed from the perspective of medical history, the doctrine of informed consent, if taken seriously, constitutes a revolutionary break with customary practice. Thus, I must review, albeit all too briefly, the history of doctor-patient communication. Only then can one appreciate how unprepared the medical profession was to heed these new legal commands. But there is more: Physicians could not easily reject what law had begun to impose on them, because they recognized intuitively that the radical transformation of medicine since the age of medical science made it possible, indeed imperative, for a doctrine of informed consent to emerge.

---

10. Salgo v. Leland Stanford Jr. Univ. Bd. of Trustees, 317 P.2d 170, 181 (Cal. Dist. Ct. App. 1957).

11. Natanson v. Kline, 350 P.2d 1093 (Kan. 1960).

Yet, bowing to the doctrine did not mean accepting it. Indeed, physicians could not accept it because, for reasons I shall soon explore, the nature of informed consent has remained in the words of Churchill, "an enigma wrapped in a mystery."

Throughout the ages physicians believed that they should make treatment decisions for their patients. This conviction inheres in the Hippocratic Oath: "I swear by Apollo and Aesculepius [that] I will follow that system of regimen which according to *my* ability and judgment *I* consider for the benefit of *my* patients . . . ."[12] The patient is not mentioned as a person whose ability and judgment deserve consideration. Indeed, in one of the few references to disclosure in the Hippocratic Corpus, physicians are admonished "to [conceal] most things from the patient while attending to him; [to] give necessary orders with cheerfulness and serenity, . . . revealing nothing of the patient's future or present condition."[13] When twenty-five centuries later, in 1847, the American Medical Association promulgated its first Code of Ethics, it equally admonished patients that their "obedience . . . to the prescriptions of [their] physician should be prompt and implicit. [They] should never permit [their] own crude opinions . . . to influence [their] attention to [their physicians]."[14]

The gulf separating doctors from patients seemed unbridgeable both medically and socially. Thus, whenever the Code did not refer to physicians and patients as such, the former were addressed as "gentlemen" and the latter as "fellow creatures." To be sure, caring for patients' medical needs and "abstain[ing] from whatever is deleterious and mischievous"[15] was deeply imbedded in the ethos of Hippocratic medicine. The idea that patients were also "autonomous" human beings, entitled to being partners in decisionmaking, was, until recently, rarely given recognition in the lexicon of medical ethics. The notion that human beings possess individual human rights, deserving of respect, of course, is of recent origin. Yet, it antedates the twentieth century and therefore could have had an impact on the nature and quality of the physician-patient relationship.

It did not. Instead, the conviction that physicians should decide what is best for their patients, and, therefore, that the authority and power to do so should remain vested in them, continued to have a deep hold on the

---

12. Hippocrates, *Oath of Hippocrates, in* 1 HIPPOCRATES 299-301 (W.H.S. Jones trans., 1962).

13. 2 HIPPOCRATES 297 (W.H.S. Jones trans., 1962).

14. American Medical Association: Code of Ethics (1847), reprinted in KATZ, *supra* note 9, at 232.

15. Hippocrates, *supra* note 12, at 301.

practices of the medical profession. For example, in the early 1950s the influential Harvard sociologist Talcott Parsons, who echoed physicians' views, stated that the physician is a technically competent person whose competence and specific judgments and measures cannot be competently judged by the layman and that the latter must take doctors' judgments and measures on 'authority'.[16] The necessity for such authority was supported by three claims:

First, *physicians' esoteric knowledge, acquired in the course of arduous training and practical experience, cannot be comprehended by patients.* While it is true that this knowledge, in its totality, is difficult to learn, understand and master, it does not necessarily follow that physicians cannot translate their esoteric knowledge into language that comports with patients' experiences and life goals (i.e., into language that speaks to quality of future life, expressed in words of risks, benefits, alternatives and uncertainties). Perhaps patients can understand this, but physicians have had too little training and experience with, or even more importantly, a commitment to, communicating their "esoteric knowledge" to patients in plain language to permit a conclusive answer as to what patients may comprehend.

Second, *patients, because of their anxieties over being ill and consequent regression to childlike thinking, are incapable of making decisions on their own behalf.* We do not know whether the childlike behavior often displayed by patients is triggered by pain, fear, and illness, or by physicians' authoritarian insistence that good patients comply with doctors' orders, or by doctors' unwillingness to share information with patients. Without providing such information, patients are groping in the dark and their stumbling attempts to ask questions, if made at all, makes them appear more incapable of understanding than they truly are.

We know all too little about the relative contributions which being ill, being kept ignorant, or being considered incompetent make to these regressive manifestations. Thus, physicians' unexamined convictions easily become self-fulfilling prophesies. For example, Eric Cassell has consistently argued that illness robs patients of autonomy and that only subsequent to the act of healing is autonomy restored.[17] While there is some truth to these contentions, they overlook the extent to which doctors can restore autonomy prior to the act of healing by not treating patients as

---

16. Talcott Parsons, The Social System 464-65 (1951).

17. Eric Cassell, *The Function of Medicine*, Hastings Center Rep., Dec. 1977, at 16,
18.

children but as adults whose capacity for remaining authors of their own fate can be sustained and nourished. Cassell's views are reminiscent of Dostoyevsky's Grand Inquisitor who proclaimed that "at the most fearful moments of life," mankind is in need of "miracle, mystery and authority."[18] While, in this modern age, a person's capacity and right to take responsibility for his or her conduct has been given greater recognition than the Grand Inquisitor was inclined to grant, it still does not extend to patients. In the context of illness, physicians are apt to join the Grand Inquisitor at least to the extent of asserting that, while patients, they can only be comforted through subjugation to miracle, mystery and authority.

Third, *physicians' commitment to altruism is a sufficient safeguard for preventing abuses of their professional authority.* While altruism, as a general professional commitment, has served patients well in their encounters with physicians, the kind of protection it does and does not provide has not been examined in any depth. I shall have more to say about this later on. For now, let me only mention one problem: Altruism can only promise that doctors will try to place their patients' medical needs over their own personal needs. Altruism cannot promise that physicians will know, without inquiry, patients' needs. Put another way, patients and doctors do not necessarily have an identity of interest about matters of health and illness. Of course, both seek restoration of health and cure, and whenever such ends are readily attainable by only one route, their interests indeed may coincide.

In many physician-patient encounters, however, cure has many faces and the means selected affect the nature of cure in decisive ways. Thus, since quality of life is shaped decisively by available treatment options (including no treatment), the objectives of health and cure can be pursued in a variety of ways. Consider, for example, differences in value preferences between doctors and patients about longevity versus quality of remaining life. Without inquiry, one cannot presume identity of interest. As the surgeon Nuland cogently observed: "A doctor's altruism notwithstanding, his agenda and value system are not the same as those of the patient. That is the fallacy in the concept of beneficence so cherished by many physicians."[19]

---

18. Fyodor Dostoyevsky, The Brothers Karamazov 307 (A.P. MacAndrew trans., 1970).
19. Interview with Sherwin Nuland (1993).

76   *Journal of Contemporary Health Law and Policy* [Vol. 10:69

II. The Age of Medical Science and Informed Consent

During the millennia of medical history, and until the beginning of the twentieth century, physicians could not explain to their patients, or — from the perspective of hindsight — to themselves, which of their treatment recommendations were curative and which were not. To be sure, doctors, by careful bedside observation, tried their level best "to abstain from what is deleterious and mischievous," to help if they could, and to be available for comfort during the hours, days or months of suffering. Doing more curatively, however, only became possible with the advent of the age of medical science. The introduction of scientific reasoning into medicine, aided by the results of carefully conducted research, permitted doctors for the first time to discriminate more aptly between knowledge, ignorance and conjecture in their recommendations for or against treatment. Moreover, the spectacular technological advances in the diagnosis and treatment of disease, spawned by medical science, provided patients and doctors with ever-increasing therapeutic options, each having its own particular benefits and risks.

Thus, for the first time in medical history it is possible, even medically and morally imperative, to give patients a voice in medical decisionmaking. It is possible because knowledge and ignorance can be better specified; it is medically imperative because a variety of treatments are available, each of which can bestow great benefits or inflict grievous harm; it is morally imperative because patients, depending on the lifestyle they wish to lead during and after treatment, must be given a choice.

All this seems self-evident. Yet, the physician-patient relationship — the conversations between the two parties — was not altered with the transformation of medical practice during the twentieth century. Indeed, the silence only deepened once laboratory data were inscribed in charts and not in patients' minds, once machines allowed physicians' eyes to gaze not at patients' faces but at the numbers they displayed, once x-rays and electrocardiograms began to speak for patients' suffering rather than their suffering voices.

What captured the medical imagination and found expression in the education of future physicians, was the promise that before too long the diagnosis of patients' diseases would yield objective, scientific data to the point of becoming algorithms. *Treatment*, however, required subjective data from patients and would be influenced by doctors' subjective judgments. This fact was overlooked in the quest for objectivity. Also overlooked was the possibility that greater scientific understanding of the nature of disease and its treatment facilitated better communication with patients. In that respect contemporary Hippocratic practices remained rooted in the past.

III. The Impact of Law

The impetus for change in traditional patterns of communication between doctors and patients came not from medicine but from law. In a 1957 California case,[20] and a 1960 Kansas case,[21] judges were astounded and troubled by these undisputed facts: That without any disclosure of risks, new technologies had been employed which promised great benefits but also exposed patients to formidable and uncontrollable harm. In the California case, a patient suffered a permanent paralysis of his lower extremities subsequent to the injection of a dye, sodium urokan, to locate a block in the abdominal aorta. In the Kansas case, a patient suffered severe injuries from cobalt radiation, administered, instead of conventional x-ray treatment, subsequent to a mastectomy for breast cancer. In the latter case, Justice Schroeder attempted to give greater specifications to the informed consent doctrine, first promulgated in the California decision: "To disclose and explain to the patient, in language as simple as necessary, the nature of the ailment, the nature of the proposed treatment, the probability of success or of alternatives, and perhaps the risks of unfortunate results and unforeseen conditions within the body."[22]

From the perspective of improved doctor-patient communication, or better, shared decisionmaking, the fault lines inherent in this American legal doctrine are many:

One: The common law judges who promulgated the doctrine restricted their task to articulating new and more stringent standards of liability whenever physicians withheld material information that patients should know, particularly in light of the harm that the spectacular advances in medical technology could inflict. Thus, the doctrine was limited in scope, designed to specify those minimal disclosure obligations that physicians must fulfill to escape *legal* liability for alleged non-disclosures. Moreover, it was shaped and confined by legal assumptions about the objectives of the laws of evidence and negligence, and by economic philosophies as to

---

20. Salgo v. Leland Stanford Jr. Univ. Bd. of Trustees, 317 P.2d 170 (Cal. Dist. Ct. App. 1957).
21. Natanson v. Kline, 350 P.2d 1093 (Kan. 1960).
22. *Id.* at 1106.

78   *Journal of Contemporary Health Law and Policy* [Vol. 10:69

who should assume the financial burdens for medical injuries sustained by patients.

Even though the judges based the doctrine on "Anglo-American law['s] . . . premise of thorough-going self-determination,"[23] as the Kansas court put it, or on "the root premise . . . fundamental in American jurisprudence that 'every human being of adult years and sound mind has a right to determine what shall be done with his own body,'"[24] as the Circuit Court for the District of Columbia put it in a subsequent opinion, the doctrine was grounded not in battery law (trespass), but in negligence law. The reasons are many. I shall only mention a compelling one: Battery law, based on unauthorized trespass, gives doctors only one defense — that they have made adequate disclosure. Negligence law, on the other hand, permits doctors to invoke many defenses, including "the therapeutic privilege" not to disclose when in their judgment, disclosure may prove harmful to patients' welfare.

Two recent opinions illustrate the problems identified here. First, in a rare opinion, the Supreme Court of Pennsylvania reconfirmed its adherence to the minority view among American jurisdictions that battery, not negligence, is the appropriate cause of action whenever lack of informed consent is alleged. The court held that whenever "the patient . . . demonstrated, and the jury found, that he was not advised of . . . material facts, risks, complications and alternatives to surgery which a reasonable man would have considered significant in deciding whether to have the operation . . . the causation inquiry ends. The sole issue remaining [is] a determination of damages."[25] Earlier in its opinion, the court quoted, with approval, a prior Pennsylvania decision:

> [W]here a patient is mentally and physically able to consult about his condition, in the absence of an emergency, the consent of the patient is "a prerequisite to a surgical operation by his physician, and an operation without the patient's consent is a *technical assault.*"[26]

Second, the Court of Appeals of California, in a ground-breaking opinion, significantly reduced the scope of the therapeutic privilege by requiring that in instances of hopeless prognosis (the most common situation in which the privilege has generally been invoked) the patient be provided

---

23. *Id.* at 1104.
24. Canterbury v. Spence, 464 F.2d 772, 780 (D.C. Cir. 1972).
25. Gouse v. Cassel, 615 A.2d 331, 335 (Pa. 1992).
26. *Id.* at 333-34 (emphasis added) (quoting Moscicki v. Shor, 163 A. 341, 342 (Pa. Super. Ct. 1932)).

with such information by asking, "If not the physician's duty to disclose a terminal illness, then whose?"[27] The duty to disclose prognosis had never before been identified specifically as one of the disclosure obligations in an informed consent opinion.

Thus, the appellate court's ruling constituted an important advance. It established that patients have a right to make decisions not only about the fate of their bodies but about the fate of their lives as well. The California Supreme Court, however, reversed. In doing so, the court made too much of an issue raised by the plaintiffs that led the appellate court to hold that doctors must disclose "statistical life expectancy information."[28] To be sure, disclosure of statistical information is a complex problem, but in focusing on that issue, the supreme court's attention was diverted from a more important new disclosure obligation promulgated by the appellate court: the duty to inform patients of their dire prognosis. The supreme court did not comment on that obligation. Indeed, it seemed to reverse the appellate court on this crucial issue by reinforcing the considerable leeway granted physicians to invoke the therapeutic privilege exception to full disclosure: "We decline to intrude further, either on the subtleties of the physician-patient relationship or in the resolution of claims that the physician's duty of disclosure was breached, by requiring the disclosure of information that may or may not be indicated in a given treatment context."[29]

Two: The doctrine of informed consent was not designed to serve as a *medical* blueprint for interactions between physicians and patients. The medical profession still faces the task of fashioning a "doctrine" that comports with its own vision of doctor-patient communication and that is responsive both to the realities of medical practices in an age of science and to the commands of law. As I said years ago,

> [T]ranslating the ingredients of [the informed consent] process into legal and useful medical prescriptions that respect patients' wishes to maintain and surrender autonomy, as well as physicians' unending struggles with omnipotence and impotence in the light of medical uncertainty, is a difficult task [which the medical profession] has not pursued . . . in any depth.[30]

Thus, disclosure practices only changed to the extent of physicians dis-

---

27. Arato v. Avedon, 11 Cal. Rptr. 2d 169, 181 n.19 (Cal. Ct. App. 1992), *vacated*, 858 P.2d 598 (Cal. 1993).

28. *Arato*, 11 Cal. Rptr. 2d at 177.

29. *Arato*, 858 P.2d at 607.

30. KATZ, *supra* note 9, at 84.

closing more about the risks of a proposed intervention in order to escape legal liability.

Three: Underlying the legal doctrine there lurks a broader assumption which has neither been given full recognition by judges nor embraced by physicians. The underlying idea is this: That from now on patients and physicians must make decisions jointly, with patients ultimately deciding whether to accede to doctors' recommendations. In *The Cancer Ward*, Solzhenitsyn captured, as only a novelist can, the fears that such an idea engenders. When doctor Ludmilla Afanasyevna was challenged by her patient, Oleg Kostoglotov, about physicians' rights to make unilateral decisions on behalf of patients, Afanasyevna gave a troubled, though unequivocal, answer: "But doctors *are* entitled to the right — doctors above all. Without that right, there'd be no such thing as medicine."[31]

If Afanasyevna is correct, then patients must continue to trust doctors silently. Conversation, to comport with the idea of informed consent, ultimately requires that both parties make decisions jointly and that their views and preferences be treated with respect. Trust, based on blind faith — on passive surrender to oneself or to another — must be distinguished from trust that is earned after having first acknowledged to oneself and then shared with the other what one knows and does not know about the decision to be made. If all of that had been considered by physicians, they would have appreciated that a new model of doctor-patient communication, that takes informed consent seriously required a radical break with current medical disclosure practice.

Four: The idea of joint decisionmaking is one thing, and its application in practice another. To translate theory into practice cannot be accomplished, as the Judicial Council of the American Medical Association attempted to do in one short paragraph. The Judicial Council stated that "[t]he patient should make his own determination on treatment. Informed consent is a basic *social* policy . . . ."[32] To translate social policy into *medical* policy is an inordinately difficult task. It requires a reassessment of the limits of medical knowledge in the light of medical uncertainty, a reassessment of professional authority to make decisions for patients in light of the consequences of such conduct for the well-being of patients, and a reassessment of the limits of patients' capacities to assume responsibility for choice in the light of their ignorance about medical mat-

---

31. ALEXANDER SOLZHENITSYN, THE CANCER WARD 77 (N. Bethell & D. Burg trans., 1969).

32. JUDICIAL COUNCIL OF THE AM. MEDICAL ASS'N, CURRENT OPINIONS OF THE JUDICIAL COUNCIL OF THE AMERICAN MEDICAL ASSOCIATION 25 (1981) (*emphasis added*).

ters and their anxieties when ill. Turning now to these problems, I wish to highlight that, in the absence of such reassessments, informed consent will remain a charade, and joint decisionmaking will elude us.

IV.   BARRIERS TO JOINT DECISIONMAKING

A.   *Medical Uncertainty*

The longer I reflect about doctor-patient decisionmaking, the more convinced I am that in this modern age of medical science, which for the first time permits sharing with patients the uncertainties of diagnosis, treatment, and prognosis, the problem of uncertainty poses the most formidable obstacle to disclosure and consent. By medical uncertainty I mean to convey what the physician Lewis Thomas observed so eloquently, albeit disturbingly:

> The only valid piece of scientific truth about which I feel totally confident is that we are profoundly ignorant about nature. . . . It is this sudden confrontation with the depth and scope of ignorance that represents the most significant contribution of twentieth-century science to the human intellect. *We are, at last facing up to it.* In earlier times, we either pretended to understand . . . or ignored the problem, or simply made up stories to fill the gap.[33]

Alvan Feinstein put this in more concrete language: "Clinicians are still uncertain about the best means of treatment for even such routine problems as . . . a fractured hip, a peptic ulcer, a stroke, a myocardial infarction. . . . At a time of potent drugs and formidable surgery, the exact effects of many therapeutic procedures are dubious or shrouded in dissension."[34]

Medical uncertainty constitutes a formidable obstacle to joint decisionmaking for a number of reasons: Sharing uncertainties requires physicians to be more aware of them than they commonly are. They must learn how to communicate them to patients and they must shed their embarrassment over acknowledging the true state of their own and of medicine's art and science. Thus, sharing uncertainties requires a willingness to admit ignorance about benefits and risks; to acknowledge the existence of alternatives, each with its own known and unknown consequences; to eschew one single authoritative recommendation; to consider

---

33. LEWIS THOMAS, THE MEDUSA AND THE SNAIL 73-74 (1979).
34. ALVAN R. FEINSTEIN, CLINICAL JUDGMENT 23-24 (1967). Even though written 27 years ago, he has not changed his views. Interview with Alvan R. Feinstein (1994).

carefully how to present uncertainty so that patients will not be overwhelmed by the information they will receive; and to explore the crucial
question of how much uncertainty physicians themselves can tolerate
without compromising their effectiveness as healers.

To so conduct oneself is most difficult. For, once doctors, on the basis
of their clinical experience and knowledge, conclude which treatment is
best, they tend to disregard, if not reject, the view of other colleagues
who treat the same condition differently. Consider the current controversy over the management of localized prostate cancer: surgery, radiation or watchful waiting.[35] Some of the physicians involved in the debate
are not even willing to accept that uncertainty exists, or at least they minimize its relevance to choice of treatment. Most who advocate treatment
strongly prefer one type over another based on professional specializa-
tion (radiologists tend to recommend radiation; surgeons surgery).

Moreover, acknowledgement of uncertainty is undermined by the
threat that it will undermine doctors' authority and sense of superiority.
As Nuland put it, to feel superior to those dependent persons who are the
sick, is after all a motivating factor that often influences their choice of
medicine as a profession.[36] All of this suggests that implementation of
the idea of informed consent is, to begin with, not a patient problem but a
physician problem.

B. Patient Incompetence

Earlier, I touched on physicians' convictions that illness and medicine's
esoteric knowledge rob patients of the capacity to participate in decision-
making. Yet we do not know whether this is true. The evidence is compromised by the groping, half-hearted, and misleading attempts to inform
patients about uncertainty and other matters which can make doctors'
communications so confusing and incomprehensible. If patients then appear stupid and ignorant this should come as no surprise; nor should patients' resigned surrender to this dilemma: "You are the doctor, you
decide."

It is equally debatable, as Thomas Duffy has contended, that
"[p]aternalism exists in medicine . . . to fulfill a need created by illness."[37]
It led him to argue, echoing Cassell, that "obviously autonomy cannot

    35. Gerald W. Chodak et al., *Results of Conservative Management of Clinically Local-
ized Prostate Cancer*, 330 NEW ENG. J. MED. 242 (1994).
    36. Interview with Sherwin B. Nuland (1994).
    37. Thomas P. Duffy, *Agamemnon's Fate and the Medical Profession*, 9 W. NEW ENG.
L. REV. 21, 27 (1987).

function as the cornerstone of the doctor-patient relationship [since] the impact of disease on personal integrity results in the patient's loss of autonomy. . . . In the doctor-patient relationship, the medical profession should always err on the side of beneficence."[38] If Duffy is correct, however, then informed consent is *ab initio* fatally compromised.

C.   Patient Autonomy

Duffy's invocation of beneficence as the guiding principle is deeply rooted in the history of Hippocratic medicine. It finds expression in the ancient maxim: *primum non nocere*, above all do no harm, with "harm" remaining undefined but in practice being defined only as physical harm. Before presenting my views on the controversy over the primacy of autonomy or beneficence, let me briefly define their meaning.

In their authoritative book *Principles of Biomedical Ethics*, Thomas Beauchamp and James Childress defined these principles:

> Autonomy is a form of personal liberty of action where the individual determines his or her own course of action in accordance with a plan chosen by himself or herself. [Respect for individuals as autonomous agents entitles them] to such autonomous determinations without limitation on their liberty being imposed by others.[39]

Beneficence, on the other hand,

> [r]equires not only that we treat persons autonomously and that we refrain from harming them, but also that we contribute to their welfare including their health. [Thus the principle asserts] the duty to help others further their important and legitimate interests . . . to *confer* benefits and actively to prevent and remove harms . . . [and] to *balance* possible goods against the possible harms of an action.[40]

Beauchamp and Childress' unequivocal and strong postulate on autonomy contrasts with the ambiguities contained in their postulate on beneficence. What do they mean by "benefits" and "harms" that allow invocation of beneficence? Do they mean only benefits and harms to patients' physical integrity, or to their dignitary integrity as choice-making individuals as well? Furthermore, what degree of discretion and li-

---

38. *Id.* at 30.

39. THOMAS L. BEAUCHAMP & JAMES F. CHILDRESS, PRINCIPLES OF BIOMEDICAL ETHICS 56, 58 (1st ed. 1979).

40. THOMAS L. BEAUCHAMP & JAMES F. CHILDRESS, PRINCIPLES OF BIOMEDICAL ETHICS 148-49 (2d ed. 1983).

cense is permissible in the duty "to balance?" I have problems with balancing unless it is resorted to only as a *rare* exception to respect for autonomy. While human life is, and human interactions are, too complex to make any principle rule absolute, any exceptions must be rigorously justified.

I appreciate that mine is a radical proposal and constitutes a sharp break with Hippocratic practices. If informed consent, however, is ever to be based on the postulate of joint decisionmaking, the obligation "to respect the autonomous choices and actions of others,"[41] as Childress has put it, must be honored. Otherwise, informed consent is reduced to doctors providing more information but leaving decisionmaking itself to the authority of physicians.

As one physician once told me, echoing only an all too prevalent belief (and he was a physician allegedly deeply committed to informed consent), "I must first make the judgment which treatment alternative is best for patients, and only after I have exercised that professional judgment, will I discuss the risks and benefits of *the* recommended treatment." This story illustrates the emphasis doctors place on risk disclosures rather than alternatives. The latter, however, is more crucial to joint decisionmaking than the former. Such a view, however, again encounters the issue of disclosure of medical uncertainty inherent in any forthright discussion of treatment alternatives. Physicians remain most reluctant to acknowledge uncertainty to themselves, and even more to their patients.

V. RESPECT FOR AUTONOMY

It should be evident by now that physicians must embark on a prolonged period of self-examination about how to interact with patients in new ways in an age of medical science and informed consent. Physicians must cease to complain about lawyers forcing them "to do silly things." Whenever doctors do so, they often observe that they can easily present their disclosures in ways that lead patients to agree with what they had thought to be the best alternative in the first place. This contention is a correct assessment of what transpires in customary practices that continue to eschew joint decisionmaking. Therefore, as I have already suggested, informed consent in today's world, is largely a charade which misleads patients into thinking that they are making decisions when indeed they are not.

---

41. James F. Childress, *The Place of Autonomy in Bioethics*, HASTINGS CENTER REP., Jan.-Feb. 1990, at 12, 12-13.

Any meaningful change in Hippocratic decisionmaking practices first requires a new and revolutionary commitment to one principle: that physicians must respect patients as autonomous persons. The most crucial reason for my placing such high value on autonomy and self-determination is because doing so safeguards, as nothing else can, the recognition by the other that the person before him or her is as much a person as he or she is. Beneficence can readily reduce persons to non-persons by "taking care of them" in all of the many not only caring, but also, non-caring meanings of this phrase.

Before continuing, I must interject a few comments about my usage of the concept of autonomy. The principle of autonomy has been subjected to criticism because its invocation can so readily consign human beings to abstract categories which defy reality. I wrote about this problem in my book *The Silent World of Doctor and Patient*: "Abstract principles tend to express generalizations about conduct that are ill-suited for application to actual cases in which human capacities to exercise rights must be considered."[42] Thus, I spoke instead about "psychological autonomy," to distinguish my conception of autonomy, for example, from that of Kant who restricted it to individuals' capacities to reason without any reference to their emotional life and their dependence on the external world. Instead, I wanted to convey by psychological autonomy, or better by respect for psychological autonomy, that human autonomy is fragile and that its optimal exercise requires both physicians and patients to pay caring attention to their capacities and incapacities for self-determination. In their interactions with one another, they must therefore through obligatory conversation, support and enhance their real, though precarious, endowment for reflective thought.

My views on psychological autonomy have been criticized as reintroducing paternalism into the physician-patient relationship. In particular, critics have argued that my emphasis on the *obligation* of patients to participate in such conversations constitutes an invasion of their privacy. While the criticism has merit, without such an obligation, autonomy is reduced to an abstraction that is inattentive to the psychological reality of both the strength and fragility of the human mind.

My views have also been misunderstood to require a lengthy, even "psychoanalytic," exploration of patients' minds. This was not my intention. I merely wished to suggest that it is possible to go to some length of subjecting thoughts and contemplated actions to clarification through dia-

---

42. KATZ, *supra* note 9, at 107.

logue which, in turn, may lead to a better understanding of what is at stake in the medical decisions to be made. Doing more is impossible and doing that much may not persuade patients to choose a course of action that is "in their best interests." But, as Justice Stevens once put it, "[I]t is far better to permit some individuals to make incorrect decisions than to deny all individuals the right to make decisions that have a profound effect upon their destiny."[43]

In such conversations the principle of beneficence, often invoked as a counterpoise to autonomy, finds its rightful but delimited expression. Beneficence, in my view, requires physicians to enhance patients' capacities to arrive at the best autonomous choices they are capable of making by clearly and respectfully providing them with the information they need. The inherent tensions between the two principles, therefore, must be resolved, as I have already suggested, by giving primacy to autonomy. My reasons are twofold: (1) Autonomy assures that ultimate authority about treatment decisions resides with patients, including the decision to authorize doctors to decide for them. Since it is their bodily integrity that is at stake, no one but they can decide what should be done for them. (2) In the past, beneficence has served too unquestionably as justification for the unilateral exercise of physicians' authority to make decisions on behalf of patients. Although in rare circumstances it may trump autonomy, beneficence should only ensure that physicians will caringly assist patients to make their own choices, informed by the clarification physicians can provide about the medical consequences of the available options, particularly, of course, the consequences of patients' preferences for an option with which their doctors disagree.

Adherence to the principle of autonomy, in the ways I have defined it, demands that physicians respect patients' autonomy as choice-making individuals, and that their ultimate choices (except under the rarest and most carefully defined circumstances) be honored. It is based on the assumption that many patients are capable of comprehending what they need to know in order to decide what is best for themselves and that, therefore, they must be treated as adults possessed of the capacity for self-determination.

It is beyond the scope of this essay to explore decisionmaking between physicians and patients incompetent by virtue of severe mental illness, brain damage, or age. Throughout, I have limited my inquiry to doctors'

---

43. Thornburgh v. Am. College of Obstetricians & Gynecologists, 476 U.S. 747, 781 (1986).

interactions with *competent* patients often considered "*incompetent*" by doctors for reasons set forth above. To be sure, decisions by patients, like those of all human beings, are influenced by rational and irrational thoughts, rational and irrational emotions and rational and irrational judgments derived from the world of knowledge, experience and beliefs in which they have lived their lives. Respect for patient autonomy only postulates that patients, like human beings generally, have considerable capacity to listen, learn and reflect; that they can and must learn a great deal from doctors about the world of medicine as it affects their disease and dis-ease; and that they can choose and act better on their own behalf than doctors can act for them.

VI.   THE CURRENT STATE OF PHYSICIAN-PATIENT DECISIONMAKING

In his recent book, entitled *How We Die*, Sherwin Nuland, a distinguished surgeon, reflects with profundity and insight on his lifelong interactions with patients. In a chapter on cancer and its treatment he speaks movingly about "death belong[ing] to the dying and to those who love them."[44] Yet, that privilege is often wrested from them when,

> [d]ecisions about continuation of treatment are influenced by the enthusiasm of the doctors who propose them. Commonly, the most accomplished of the specialists are also the most convinced and unyielding believers in biomedicine's ability to overcome the challenge presented by a pathological process. . . . [W]hat is offered as objective clinical reality is often the subjectivity of a devout disciple of the philosophy that death is an implacable enemy. To such warriors, even a temporary victory justifies the laying waste of the fields in which a dying man has cultivated his life.[45]

Looking back at his work, he concludes that "more than a few of my victories have been Pyrrhic. The suffering was sometimes not worth the success. . . . [H]ad I been able to project myself into the place of the family and the patient, I would have been less often certain that the desperate struggle should be undertaken."[46]

In his view, a surgeon,

> [t]hough he be kind and considerate of the patient he treats . . . allows himself to push his kindness aside because the seduction of The Riddle [the quest for diagnosis and cure] is so strong and

---

44. SHERWIN B. NULAND, HOW WE DIE 265 (1994).
45. *Id.*
46. *Id.* at 266.

the failure to solve it renders him so weak. [Thus, at times he convinces] patients to undergo diagnostic or therapeutic measures at a point in illness so far beyond reason that The Riddle might better have remained unsolved.[47]

Speaking then about the kind of doctor he will seek out when afflicted with a major illness, Nuland does not expect him to "understand my values, my expectations for myself . . . my philosophy of life. *That is not what he is trained for and that is not what he will be good at.*"[48] Doctors can impart information, but "[i]t behooves every patient to study his or her own disease and learn enough about it. [Patients] should no longer expect from so many of our doctors what they cannot give."[49]

Nuland's views, supported by a great many poignant clinical vignettes, sensitively and forthrightly describe the current state of physician-patient decisionmaking, so dominated by physicians' judgments as to what is best. He presents many reasons for this state of affairs. One is based on doctors' "fear of failure:"

> A need to control that exceeds in magnitude what most people would find reasonable. When control is lost, he who requires it is also a bit lost and so deals badly with the consequences of his impotence. In an attempt to maintain control, a doctor, usually without being aware of it, convinces himself that he knows better than the patient what course is proper. He dispenses only as much information as he deems fit, thereby influencing a patient's decision-making in ways he does not recognize as self-serving.[50]

I have presented Nuland's observations at some length because they illustrate and support my contentions that joint decisionmaking between doctors and patients still eludes us. My critics had claimed earlier that my work on informed consent was dated because informed consent had become an integral aspect of the practice of medicine. In the paperback edition of *The Silent World of Doctor and Patient*, I argued that they have dismissed too lightly my central arguments:

> [T]hat meaningful collaboration between physicians and patients cannot become a reality until physicians have learned (1) how to treat their patients not as children but as the adults they are; (2) how to distinguish between their ideas of the best treatment and their patients' ideas of what is best; (3) how to ac-

---

47. *Id.* at 249.
48. *Id.* at 266 (emphasis added).
49. *Id.* at 260.
50. *Id.* at 258.

knowledge to their patients (and often to themselves as well) their ignorance and uncertainties about diagnosis, treatment, and prognosis; [and to all this, I now want to add, (4) how to explain to patients the uncertainties inherent in the state of the art and science of medicine which otherwise permits doctors on the basis of their clinical experience to leave unacknowledged that their colleagues on the basis of their clinical experience have different beliefs as to which treatment is best].[51]

Nuland pleads for the resurrection of the family doctor[52] because he believes that the specialist is inadequate to the task of shouldering the burdens of decision with his patients. About this I differ with him. I believe that physicians (and surgeons as well) *can*, and *must*, learn to converse with patients in the spirit of joint decisionmaking. Physicians can and must learn to appreciate better than they do now that the principle of respect for person speaks to the caring commitment of physicians in old and new ways: *Old* in that it highlights the ancient and venerable medical duty not to abandon patients, and *new* by requiring doctors to communicate with them and remain at their sides, not only while their bodies are racked with pain and suffering but also while their minds are beset by fear, confusion, doubt and suffering over decisions to be made; also *new* in that implementation of the principle of psychological autonomy imposes the obligations on physicians both to invite, and respond to, questions about the decisions to be made, and to do so by respecting patients' ultimate choices, a new aspect of the duty to care.

The moral authority of physicians will not be undermined by this caring view of interacting with patients. Doctors' authority resides in the medical knowledge they possess, in their capacity to diagnose and treat, in their ability to evaluate what can be diagnosed and what cannot, what is treatable and what is not, and what treatment alternatives to recommend, each with its own risks and benefits and each with its own prognostic implications as to cure, control, morbidity, exacerbation or even death.

The moral authority of physicians resides in knowing better than others the certainties and the uncertainties that accompany diagnosis, treatment, prognosis, health and disease, as well the extent and the limits of their *scientific* knowledge and *scientific* ignorance. Physicians must learn to face up to and acknowledge the tragic limitations of their own professional knowledge, their inability to impart all their insights to all patients, and their own personal incapacities — at times more pronounced than

---

51. JAY KATZ, THE SILENT WORLD OF DOCTOR AND PATIENT xi (1986).
52. NULAND, *supra* note 44, at 266.

others — to devote themselves fully to the needs of their patients. They must learn not to be unduly embarrassed by their personal and professional ignorance and to trust their patients to react appropriately to such acknowledgment. From all this it follows that ultimately the moral authority of physicians resides in their capacity to sort out *with* patients the choices to be made.

It is in this spirit that duty and caring become interwoven. Bringing these strands together imposes upon physicians the duty to respect patients as persons so that care will encompass allowing patients to live their lives in their own self-willed ways. To let patients follow their own lights is not an abandonment of them. It is a professional duty that, however painful, doctors must obey.

Without fidelity to these new professional duties, true caring will elude physicians. There is much new to be learned about caring that in decades to come will constitute the kind of caring that doctors in the past have wished for but have been unable to dispense, and that patients may have always yearned for.

I do not know whether my vision of a new physician-patient relationship defies medical reality. Thus, I may be wrong and I am willing to entertain this possibility as long as my critics are willing to admit that they too may be wrong. *As a profession we have never examined and tested in a committed manner what I have proposed.* It is this fact which, in conclusion, I want to highlight. For, I believe that in this age of medical science and informed consent the category of patient is in need of a radical reconceptualization. Throughout medical history, patients have been viewed as passive, ignorant persons whose welfare was best protected by their following doctors' orders, and physicians and patients were socialized to interact with one another on that basis. Throughout this essay, I have argued that such a view of the physician-patient relationship was dictated by doctors' inability to explain to themselves what was therapeutic and what was not in the practice of medicine. The advent of the age of medical science has changed all that and for the first time in medical history doctors now can distinguish better between knowledge, ignorance and conjecture. In turn, this permits physicians to take patients into their confidence.

Finally, my purpose in writing this essay is twofold: (1) To argue, notwithstanding any theories of tort law and cost containment to the contrary,[53] that patients must ultimately be given the deciding vote in matters

---

53. *See, e.g.*, Peter H. Schuck, *Rethinking Informed Consent*, 103 YALE L.J. 899 (1994).

that effect their lives; and (2) to suggest that informed consent will remain a fairy tale as long as the idea of joint decisionmaking, based on a commitment to patient autonomy and self-determination, does not become an integral aspect of the ethos of medicine and the law of informed consent. Until then, physicians, patients and judges can only deceive themselves or be deceived about patients having a vital voice in the medical decisionmaking process. Of course, there are alternatives to joint decisionmaking. One that I have briefly explored elsewhere suggested that we need a number of informed (and uninformed) consent doctrines depending on the nature of the decisions to be made, with the implication that only in certain medical contexts must informed consent rise to the rigor advanced in this essay.[54] Another alternative is to fashion an informed consent doctrine for law and medicine that is *not* based on "[t]he root premise . . . fundamental in American jurisprudence, that '[e]very human being of adult years and sound mind has a right to determine what shall be done with his own body.'"[55] It is not a road on which I would like to travel and thus, I leave that task to others. It is important that those who disagree with me set forth their premises about who decides what; otherwise physicians and patients are condemned to interact with one another, under the rubric of what is now called "informed consent," by deception of both self and the other.

---

54. Jay Katz, *Physician-Patient Encounters "On a Darkling Plain,"* 9 W. New Eng. L. Rev. 207, 221-22 (1987).
55. Canterbury v. Spence, 464 F.2d 772, 780 (D.C. Cir. 1972).

[33]

ETHICAL PERSPECTIVES ON DECISION-MAKING CAPACITY AND CONSENT FOR TREATMENT AND RESEARCH

Ron L. P. Berghmans* and Guy A. M. Widdershoven*

Abstract: Decision-making capacity for treatment and research raises complex conceptual issues. Given the fact that both considerations of respect for patient autonomy and beneficence/harm prevention have moral relevance in many cases, in the practice of health care the need exists to balance both in a moral responsible way. The moral concept of (mental) capacity or decisional capacity has a role to play in this balancing process. The current dominant approach towards the conceptualisation and assessment of decision-making capacity, which focuses on cognition and rationality, has some serious shortcomings. In order to compensate for these shortcomings of the dominant approach, a number of alternative approaches may be promising. A first alternative focuses on issues of emotion and narrative; a second on identity and identification, and a third on dialogue and deliberation.

By paying attention to the way in which people inteprete their world (not only by cognition, but also by emotion), and how they shape their lives by processes of identification and communication, a broader perspective on capacity assessment in health care can be developed. Above that, these alternative approaches are less focused on the assessment of (in)capacity and more on enabling a person to become more competent through a process of empowerment, participation, and shared decision-making.

Keywords: Ethics; decision-making capacity; treatment; research.

---

* Maastricht University, Department of Health Ethics and Philosophy, Maastricht, The Netherlands

[1] In this paper the notions of (mental) capacity, decision-making or decisional capacity, and the more legal notion of competence will be used interchangeably.

INTRODUCTION

Decision-making capacity[1] and the moral and/or legal validity of the consent of the patient for treatment or research are closely related issues. For consent in health care and health care-related research to be morally valid, a number of preconditions need to be met: ideally consent should be based on relevant information, be voluntarily given, and the patient/subject ought to have sufficient capacity[1]. It is obvious that in a number of clear-cut cases the assessment of capacity is not problematic (comatose, newborns). The issue whether a person has the capacity to decide about treatment or research generally arises in regard to patients belonging to 'vulnerable' groups: cognitively impaired elderly, the mentally handicapped, persons suffering from mental illness, and children.

In this paper conceptual issues related to decision-making capacity and its assessment are discussed from an ethical perspective. The focus is on capacity and its assessment, and not on medical and psychiatric decision-making in case a patient is considered to lack capacity. In case a patient lacks capacity, the moral and legal authority to make decisions in a medical or psychiatric context will or may be transferred to another person or persons, depending on the specific legal framework that is applicable.

The moral significance of capacity assessment

Given the fact that both considerations of respect for patient autonomy and beneficence/harm prevention have moral relevance in many cases, in the practice of health care the need exists to balance both in a morally responsible way. The moral concept of (mental) capacity or decisional capacity has a role to play in this balancing process.

A decision about a person's capacity thus serves to protect both patient autonomy and the well-being of the patient. A responsible capacity assessment should be able to prevent two possible mistakes: first the unjustifiable overruling of patient autonomy in order to safeguard patient well-being; and secondly the unjustifiable respecting of patient autonomy at the cost of the patient's well-being[2]. This means that a decision about a person's capacity is far-reaching and weighty,

---

1. Beauchamp, T.L. & Childress, J.F. *Principles of biomedical ethics. Fourth edition.* New York: Oxford University Press, 1994.

2. Buchanan, A.E. & Brock D.W. *Deciding for others. The ethics of surrogate decision making.* Cambridge: Cambridge University Press, 1989.

Medicine and Law   393

because it may imply that a person's liberty-rights may be intruded upon and that a person's wishes may be denied or overruled on paternalistic grounds.

The legal presumption and definition of capacity

From a legal perspective it is generally argued that persons ought to be considered to have decisional capacity, unless there is reason for doubt. This legal presumption applies in regard to all citizens and does not preclude specific groups within society. This presumption may be viewed as expressing a priori respect for the autonomy and dignity rights of persons[3].

This legal presumption, however, may become problematic in cases when medical interventions may not be primarily in the best interest of the patient, as can be the case in participation of patients in biomedical research[4]. The presumption of capacity may then permit patients with impaired decision-making capacity to sign consent forms they do not understand and to participate in risky and/or burdensome biomedical research protocols without being appreciative of what interests are at stake. This can be particularly problematic in case of biomedical research that involves risks and burdens to the subject, and no or little promise of benefit. A case-example is the recruitment of patients suffering from mental illness (e.g. schizophrenia) or neurological conditions (e.g. Alzheimer's disease).

The legal definition of mental capacity is generally rather vague. After the cases of Re C and Re MB, Scottish legislation and proposed legislation in England and Wales define mental incapacity as "…the inability by reason of mental disability, to make a decision on the matter in question, or to communicate that decision."[5]. In the Netherlands, capacity is defined as "the ability of a patient to evaluate his or her interests in relation to the matter in question"[6].

---

3. Carpenter, W.T., The challenge to psychiatry as society's agent for mental illness treatment and research. *American Journal of Psychiatry*, 156, 1999, 1307-10.

4. Berghmans, R.L.P., The double standard: comparison of ethical problems and standards in research and practice with demented patients. In: M. Bergener, J.C. Brocklehurst & S.I. Finkel (Eds.), *Aging, health, and healing*. Springer Publishing Company, New York, 1995, 511-21.

5. Treloar, A., Philpot, M. & Beats, B. Concealing medication in patients' food. *The Lancet*, 357, 2001, 62-4.

6. Berghmans, R.L.P., *Bekwaam genoeg? Wils(on)bekwaamheid in geneeskunde, gezondheidsrecht en gezondheidsethiek*. [Competent enough? Decision making (in)capacity in medicine, health law and biomedical ethics.] Utrecht: Nederlandse Vereniging voor Bio-ethiek, 2000.

In order to give substance to the practical assessment of capacity within existing legal frameworks, definitions, and regulations, philosophical and ethical perspectives can provide necessary guidance.

In recent years, legal definitions of (mental) capacity have moved from viewing mental capacity as a global, all-embracing condition, to a more specific condition restricted to particular realms of decision-making. This means that diagnostic categories (e.g. schizophrenia, Alzheimer's disease, depression, etc...) as such cannot decide the issue of decision-making capacity. Particular functional abilities that may be considered relevant for mental capacity (e.g. understanding, practical reasoning) are logically independent of most diagnostic and descriptive categories. This means that capacity always has to be considered in connection to a particular decision.

Assessment of decision making capacity: the current approach

As stated, the generally agreed moral and legal presumption is that persons ought to be considered to have decision-making capacity, unless the contrary can be reasonably defended.

There are no criteria or methodologies for determining capacity in a medical context that are well accepted by all disciplines. Legislatures and courts have not been consistent in the criteria they use to determine capacity, nor has there been any exhaustive legal analysis of the subject that has received judicial support[7].

In the literature, different criteria for the assessment of decision making capacity have been proposed[8]. The following four criteria or standards can be distinguished:

1. the capacity to make and express a choice;

2. the capacity to understand relevant information;

3. the capacity to evaluate the character of the situation and possible consequences; and

4. the capacity to handle information rationally.

---

7. Glass, K.C., Redefining definitions and devising instruments: two decades of assessing mental competence. *International Journal of Law and Psychiatry*, 20, 1997, 5-33.

8. Appelbaum, P.S. & Grisso, T. Assessing patients' capacities to consent to treatment. *The New England Journal of Medicine*, 319, 1988, 1635-8.

The capacity to make and express a choice is most basic and presupposed in the three other criteria. It relates to the ability of a person to express what she has decided. Hard cases are those in which it is unclear whether a person expresses a choice or decision, or whether something else motivates a person in a particular way. An example is the case of a demented patient who 'refuses' to be tube-fed. Is it the patient's wish not to be tube-fed, or is it merely so that he or she is uncomfortable (e.g. irritation of the nose)?

This standard best protects patient autonomy, in the sense that a person who is able to express a choice is considered to have capacity and authority to consent to or refuse treatment. On the other hand, it does not protect choices or actions of people that may be based on fear, misunderstanding, or psychotic experiences that may lead to potentially serious harm to the patient.

The capacity to understand relevant information emphasizes the importance of patients' comprehension of information related to the issue at hand. Obviously, this presupposes disclosure of relevant information.

In regard to this standard it is necessary to distinguish between the mere capacity to understand information, and actual understanding. Merely having the capacity to understand is not a sufficient condition for actual understanding. A person may have the intellectual capabilities to understand information, but nevertheless may misunderstand information as a result of selective attention, wishful thinking or defects in the handling of information.
The focus in this standard is on cognitive capabilities that are needed to understand information in the context of informed consent.

The capacity to evaluate the character of the situation and possible consequences differs from the mere ability to understand information in the abstract by requiring that a patient is able to apply the information to his or her own personal situation. It requires patients' recognition that information given to them about their disorder and potential treatment is significant for and applicable to their own circumstances[9]. In this context the issue of the relationship between capacity and awareness of and insight into illness can be raised. Some take the view that denial of illness implies incapacity. It is argued that patients who are required to make a decision about psychiatric treatment

---

9. Grisso, T., Appelbaum, P.S., Mulvey, E.P., & Fletcher, K. The MacArthur treatment competence study. II: Measures of abilities related to competence to consent to treatment. *Law and Human Behavior*, 19, 1995, 2, 127-48.

but who deny the existence of a psychotic state or of their severe depression cannot be considered to have capacity to decide about means of ameliorating their condition.

This view implies that a person who does not identify with the psychiatrist's view may be disqualified on the ground of lack of insight[10]. But although the patient may appreciate and evaluate his or her own condition and situation differently from the psychiatrist, this does not imply that he or she does not evaluate/appreciate her situation.

How a patient evaluates the information at least partly depends on the context in which this evaluation takes place[6]. And although different medical options (and their respective consequences) may be described objectively, the valuation of these options and consequences is related to the goals, values and norms a particular patient considers to be important in her life.

Further, evaluation and appreciation also have an affective dimension[11]. In the literature and debate on capacity, affective dimensions generally are considered to have a negative impact on capacity because they reduce cognitive performance[12]. But emotions also may play a positive role. Emotions can be considered as sources of knowledge because they provide vital information about the feelings somebody has. They also tell us what goals, values, and states of affairs a person considers important[13].

The capacity to handle information rationally refers to a patient's ability to employ logical processes to compare the benefits, burdens and risks of treatment options or interventions in biomedical research. This involves the capacity of practical reasoning[14]. Regarding this standard, confusion may take place about

---

10. Roe, D., Lereya, J., & Fennig, S. Comparing patients' and staff members' attitudes: does patient's competence to disagree mean they are not competent? *The Journal of Nervous and Mental Disease*, 189, 2001, 307-10.

11. Charland, L.C., Is Mr. Spock mentally competent? Competence to consent and emotion. *Philosophy, Psychiatry & Psychology*, 5, 1998, 68-81.

12. Bursztajn, H.J., Harding, H.P., Gutheil, T.G., & Brodsky, A. Beyond cognition: the role of disordered affective states in impairing competence to consent to treatment. *Bulletin of the American Academy of Psychiatry and Law*, 19, 1991, 4, 383-8.

13. Nussbaum, M.C., *Love's knowledge. Essays on philosophy and literature.* New York/Oxford: Oxford University Press, 1990.

14. Benn, S.I.. *A theory of freedom.* Cambridge: Cambridge University Press, 1988.

the proper meaning of the concept of rationality. A decision sometimes is considered irrational merely because the patient's choice was unconventional. Here, the irrationality to which this standard properly refers pertains to poor logic in the processing of information, not the choice that is eventually made. Thus, a patient who can understand, appreciate and communicate a decision may still be impaired because he or she is unable to process information logically, in accordance with his or her preferences[15].

This standard, which is based on rational choice theories, is highly demanding. Its focus on practical reasoning presupposes that choices are generally made according to logical procedures of rational thinking, and denies the reality and significance of choices that are made prereflectively.

In addition, this standard does not take into account the norms, values and convictions a person has and that may influence his or her reasoning. Even if somebody meets the highest standards of practical and rational thinking, one may nevertheless have doubts about his or her decision-making. Illustrative in this respect is the reasoning of a person who acts out of a paranoid delusion. He or she may have practical rationality, but lack so-called epistemic rationality[14].

The four discussed standards presuppose different (psychological) capabilities that may be relevant in the assessment of decisional capacity. Taken separately, the first criterion exclusively focuses on whether a choice is made and expressed and does not address aspects of the decision-making process. Criteria 2, 3, and 4 address specific elements of this process. A broad consensus exists that a proper and responsible way of assessing decisional capacity is by focusing on the process of decision-making, and not on the outcome of the decision being made[2]. As stated, the mere unconventionality of a choice is insufficient reason to suggest that a patient lacks capacity.

What standard is applied in assessing capacity influences the chance a patient will be considered to have or to lack decisional capacity. One study investigated the proportion of psychiatric and medical patients who were considered impaired in their decision-making capacities in relation to each of several major legal standards for determining capacity to consent to treatment. Different groups of patients were identified as impaired depending on the measure used: one

---

15. Berg, J.W. & Appelbaum, P.S. Subjects' capacity to consent to neurobiological research. In: *Ethics in psychiatric research. A resource manual for human subjects protection.* (Eds. Pincus, H.A., Lieberman, J.A., Ferris, S.) Washington, D.C., American Psychiatric Association, 1999, 81-106.

measuring understanding, another measuring reasoning, and a third measuring appreciation. The outcome of this study suggests that, other than has been suggested in the literature on decision-making capacity and legal competence, the single standards commonly used do not form a hierarchy. The authors conclude that although the standard of evidencing a choice is clearly less demanding than the three other standards, there is no clear hierarchy of rigor among the remaining three[16].

Underestimated aspects: debate and new perspectives

The current dominant approach towards issues of decisional capacity and consent can be characterised as cognitive and rational. A number of common presuppositions of the current dominant approach towards decisional capacity can be distinguished:

1. an emphasis on concrete, mostly cognitive, abilities of a person (decision-making; understanding of information; rational handling of information);

2. an emphasis on distinguishing between patients who have and patients who do not have capacity, and not on promoting capacity;

3. no attention to what actually moves a person or what a particular choice means.

In order to compensate for these shortcomings of the dominant approach, a number of alternative approaches may be promising.

A first alternative focuses on issues of emotion and narrative; a second on identity and identification, and a third on dialogue and deliberation.

Emotion and narrative

As already noted, the relevance of mood and emotion to decision-making capacity has not received much attention in the literature[17]. If emotion receives any attention at all, generally this concerns the negative impact of emotions on decisional capacity. Leaving affective and emotive aspects outside of the process of capacity assessment and focusing on cognitive abilities may unjustifiably

---

16. Grisso, T. & Appelbaum, P.S. Comparison of standards for assessing patients' capacities to make treatment decisions. *American Journal of Psychiatry*, 152, 1995, 7, 1033-7.

17. Silverman, H., The role of emotions in decisional competence. Standards of competency and altruistic acts. *Journal of Clinical Ethics*, 8, 1997, 2, 171-5.

Medicine and Law   399

deny some patients their right to participate in decision-making.

Further, it should be better recognised that interpretation is an important part of the process of capacity assessment. What is the meaning of illness and of the specific treatment decision for the patient? How can seemingly insignificant or unclear expressions be interpreted? What is the place of the actual condition and situation of the patient in his or her life-history and narrative? Paying attention to the story of the patient may safeguard that which initially may appear to be an irrational or irresponsible decision, yet becomes quite reasonable after the patient's full story becomes known[18].

Identity and identification

Processes of meaning-making are connected to notions of personal identity, self-perception, and identification. What people consider as being important and the choices and decisions they make is not always based on reflection and deliberation. This importance is what a person considers fitting within his or her own biography, as being part of his or her identity, or as something which he or she can identify with[19]. Such considerations deserve to be integrated into the process of capacity assessment. In case of a refusal of treatment one may ask whether this refusal is an authentic expression of the identity of the person, or if it reflects helplessness or embarrassment.

Dialogue and deliberation

A third alternative approach focuses attention on communicative aspects of capacity assessment. Within this perspective the primary focus is not on the issue of decisional authority, but on the fashioning of the patient-physician interaction in such a way that capacity can be promoted. Within a process of dialogue and deliberation not only information on the patient's clinical situation and treatment prospects can be discussed, but also the types of values embodied in the available options as well as the values the patient him or herself pursues[20]. From this communicative perspective the issues of mental capacity and mental

---

18. Maciunas, K.A. & Moss, A.H. Learning the patient's narrative to determine decision-making capacity: the role of ethics consultation. *The Journal of Clinical Ethics*, 3, 1992, 287-9.

19. Agich, G., *Autonomy and long-term care*. New York/Oxford: Oxford University Press, 1993.

20. Emanuel, E.J. & Emanuel, L.L. Four models of the physician-patient relationship. *Journal of the American Medical Association*, 267, 1992, 2221-6.

capacity assessment are not considered as static and fixed, but as dynamic and as being part of an ongoing process of patient-physician interaction. Ideally, patient and physician help each other to clarify preferences, norms, and values that are considered important in order to reach a good decision[21].

CONCLUSION

Decision-making capacity is a complex normative issue. The consequences of an assessment of capacity are far-reaching and there is a danger of abuse of the concept in justifying treatment against the will of the patient.

Current approaches with regard to capacity and consent are either very liberal and autonomy-focused, or very restrictive and demanding by focusing on rational decision-making. There is a strong focus on cognitive aspects of decision-making. Alternative approaches explore a middle way, by paying attention to aspects of decisional capacity that are underestimated in the current dominant approach. These approaches are critical about the model of decision-making and its presuppositions. By paying attention to the way in which people intepret their world (not only by cognition, but also by emotion), and how they shape their lives by processes of identification and communication, a broader perspective on capacity assessment in health care can be developed. Furthermore, these alternative approaches are less focused on the assessment of (in)capacity and more on enabling a person to become more competent through a process of empowerment, participation, and shared decision-making.

---

21. Berghmans, R.L.P., Capacity and consent. *Current Opinion in Psychiatry*, 14, 2001, 491-9.

[34]

INFORMED CONSENT: MYTH OR REALITY

T. Mozes*, S. Tyano**, I. Manor***, R. Mester****

Abstract: The rapidly growing awareness and respect of the social needs and legal rights of the patient in many countries is a sign of cultural maturity of society at large. However, the implementation of these achievements is especially arduous in the field of psychiatry because often mental patients have cognitive restrictions and/or emotional distress both of which may interfere with the exercise of their civil rights. One focus of this paper is the challenging process of obtaining legally valid consent from a severely ill psychiatric patient for diagnostic procedures and for treatment and also for participation in research projects.

This paper also analyzes and discusses the new developments in the health legislation in Israel and focuses on the questions that arise in its application to the field of psychiatry.

A recommendation for practical assessment of competence is presented. Systematic studies of the application of legal regulation and appropriate modifications are needed.

Keywords: Informed consent; patients' rights; competence; mental illness; research.

* Ness-Ziona Mental Health Center and Sackler Faculty of Medicine, Tel-Aviv University, Ness-Ziona, Israel.

** Geha Psychiatric Hospital and Sackler Faculty of Medicine, Tel-Aviv University, Petah Tikva, Israel.

*** Geha Psychiatric Hospital and Sackler Faculty of Medicine, Tel-Aviv University, Petah Tikva, Israel.

**** Ness-Ziona Mental Health Center and Sackler Faculty of Medicine, Tel-Aviv University, Ness-Ziona, Israel.

INTRODUCTION

A modern democracy endows all citizens with the right to make reasonable and constructive decisions regarding their self and their body within the bounds of the nation's cultural and religious laws. Consequently, informed consent is a prerequisite for all medical treatment.

Informed consent implies that the individual understands the reason for a hospitalization and/or the purpose and risks of a specific treatment.

Legal and ethical problems arise either when a patient refuses hospitalization, treatment or a medical procedure that the physician(s) consider vital to his/her well-being; or when a patient consents to hospitalization, treatment or a medical procedure, but the physician(s) cannot determine the validity of the consent. Both situations come down to the same question: Are the individual's decisions about diagnostic procedures and treatment always to be accepted?

This issue of informed consent, or lack of consent, and all its ramifications, is especially complex in psychiatry where the emotional and cognitive capacities of the patients are often seriously impaired.

The laws and regulations regarding the identification and treatment of individuals with limited cognitive abilities and the specific content of the consent form remain unclear. The problem applies to many subgroups such as nonmental geriatric patients, young patients, patients suffering from a serious physical disease, etc. This problem is even more complicated with psychiatric patients. A recent study, on the abilities of hospitalized patients to make decisions regarding participation in a research study, showed significant limitations in 52% of schizophrenic patients and in 24% of depressed patients, compared to only 12% of patients with serious medical illnesses (Grisso T. et al 1995)[1]. In two of the very few studies on consent to medical treatment, clinicians estimated that 21 of 96 patients (Bean G. et al 1994)[2] and 6 of 23 patients (Roth LH et al 1982)[3] who were referred for electroconvulsive therapy were incompetent. In

1. Grisso, T., Appelbaum, P.S.,(1995) 'The MacArthur Treatment Competence Study: III: Abilities of Patients to Consent to Psychiatric and Medical Treatment'. *Law Hum. Behav.* 19: 149-174.

2. Bean,G., Nishisato, S., Rector, N., Glancy, G.(1994) 'The Psychometric Properties of the Competency Interview Schedule'. *Can. J. Psychiatry* 39: 368-376.

3. Roth, L.H., Lidz, C.W., Meisel, A., Soloff, P.H., Kaufman, K., Spiker, D.G., Foster, F.G.,(1982) 'Competency to Decide About Treatment or Research: An Overview of Some Empirical Data'. *Int. J. Law Psychiatry.* 5:29-50.

Medicine and Law   475

neither of these studies were criteria of competence defined.

The role of emotions within the capacity to give competent consent to participate in a research study was examined by Roth (1982)[3] who found 4 of 19 depressed participants to be incompetent. Elliot (1997)[4] claimed that all the accepted criteria of competence - the ability to understand, to appreciate, to think logically and to choose – are cognitive and therefore insufficient for the evaluation of depressed patients, who may suffer from a deficiency in their "affective and motivational condition", which affects the quality of rational decision-making in two ways: first, these patients, in retrospect, often regard their decisions as not being "authentically" theirs ("it's not me"); second, as Appelbaum(1997)[5] noted, the lack of objective techniques of measuring the motivational limitations due to depression affects the evaluation of the patient's willingness to participate or not in research. The application of emotional criteria and consideration of their effect on cognitive ability would probably yield a much higher percentage of incompetent patients than previously believed. This approach should also be extended to other mental disorders apart from depression.

In light of the above mentioned dilemmas it seems that presently the question of obtaining a competent informed consent from a mental patient might be more a myth than a reality. This paper deals with the role of the legal and medical systems in preserving the rights of psychiatric patients concerning informed consent to medical treatment and research.

PSYCHIATRIC PATIENTS WHO REFUSE CONSENT

The social upheaval of the 1960s did much to advance the rights of the mentally ill. The view that involuntary hospitalization of psychiatric patients violated basic democratic principles gained support, and legal regulations were implemented to limit this practice to cases of extreme necessity, and only after other, less restrictive alternatives, had been ruled out. Nevertheless, every citizen confined to an institution which by definition limits freedom (hospital, jail), may continue to exert his/her legal rights as much as possible.

It should be emphasized that involuntary hospitalization does not necessarily

---

4. Elliott, C.(1997) 'Caring About Risk: Are Severely Depressed Patients Competent to Consent to Research'. *Arch. Gen. Psychiatry.* 54; 113-116.

5. Appelbaum, P.S.(1997) 'Rethinking the Conduct of Psychiatric Research'. *Arch. Gen. Psychiatry,* 54; 117-120.

imply total lack of competence. Incompetence in one field (hygiene, self-care, etc.) which might lead to involuntary hospitalization, need not rule out competence in other fields (working or giving testimony in court).

Involuntary psychiatric hospitalization is one way to provide needed mental treatment without appointing a guardian. It is the ultimate solution when neither a legal nor a medical solution can be found to satisfy the three basic rights: the patient's freedom, the good of the patient and the protection of society within the boundaries of constitutional tradition, national and local culture and the local health system.

Another and more complex problem in the evaluation of competence of a patient who refuses treatment or participation in a research project is related to the therapist's counter transference reactions. The patient who refuses to cooperate in a given treatment program or research often elicits intense antagonism in his/her caregivers. The antagonistic reaction of the therapist may lead him to the emotion-based conclusion that the patient is incompetent in his/her decision making and therefore unnecessary coercion may follow. Objective criteria for the evaluation of competence to give informed consent would reduce the subjective interference of the caregiver in the evaluation process.

THE CONSENTING PSYCHIATRIC PATIENT

Consenting patients are apparently easier to treat than patients who refuse treatment. They are prepared to accept the proposed treatment and to participate in different research studies. Nevertheless this kind of patient poses a serious ethical question: like the patients who refuses to consent for lack of understanding, consenting patients may consent for the same reasons. The fact that the consenting patients' behavior is more "comfortable" for the caregivers does not imply that their problem is any less severe or that they are any more competent to deal with that problem. Indeed, by complying, these patients place all responsibility for their well-being on the caregiver. This issue is even more complicated when consent is needed for research purposes.

Every research project, despite the utmost efforts to maximally protect the patients, has an inherent risk due to the researchers' interests in completing the study and their belief in its desired results. Thus, the extent of the patients' understanding of the purposes and potential dangers need to be carefully assessed to avoid "research bias".

The family: In the cases in which the patients' mental competence makes their consent questionable, it is possible to turn to their relatives for decision-making. However, this procedure may harbour ethical obstacles due to the involvement of additional people who have their own interests which may not necessarily be in the patients' best interests. On the other hand, as Applebaum(1997)[5] noted there are families who tend to assume that "their relatives with mental illness are being subjected to unfair and potentially harmful practices of research" which, realistic or not, give rise to feelings of anger and betrayal. This can affect negatively the alliance between the family and the caregivers.

The researchers. In some cases, there may be a problem of researcher awareness of the need for competent consent. The Advisory Committee on Human Radiation Experiments (1995)[6] contains the results of a survey of 125 studies on humans. Eight of the studies included cognitively limited subjects, most of them with Alzheimer's disease. The Committee found that in half of these studies there was no known advantage to the participating patients, no sufficient explanation of the possible dangers and side effects appeared in the consent form, and no attention was addressed to the question of limited competence to provide consent. This finding supports previous studies (Appelbaum, 1983)[7] showing that researchers often tend to neglect topics relating to the competence of those being tested.

The question of placebo. A controversial issue is the performance of studies that deny active drug treatment from some or all of the participants in the research by means of placebo or no treatment for purposes of comparison even when the researchers know of a treatment for their condition that is at least partially effective. In psychiatric studies, the main concern is the risk of relapse in the short and long term, especially in schizophrenic patients. Researchers tend to answer public doubts about these methods by insisting that they are legitimized by the consent of the participants, who are prepared to accept the trial procedure.

---

6. Advisory Committee on Human Radiation Experiment: *Advisory committee on Human Radiation Experiments, Final Report.* Washington DC; US Government Printing Office; October 1995.

7. Appelbaum, P.S., Roth, L.H. (1983) 'The structure of informed consent in psychiatric research'. *Behav Sci Law.* 1:9-19.

The researcher should ensure the preservation of an optimal balance between benefits and risks. Protection of the individual patient's rights is paramount to his/her well-being, but so is the use of research to advance our knowledge of the causes and treatment of mental disturbances. Bonnie(1997)[8] had recommended the establishment of a "reliable and authoritative process to re-examine and solve" these questions, namely the National Bioethics Advisory Committee. Applebaum (1997)[5] pleads that psychiatric researchers must resist the temptation to regard every doubt about their practice as an obstacle in the path of advancement. Respect of public interest, fairness and the protection of the sick should be intrinsic to medical practice and to medical research. The time has come for a widespread agreement on these questions.

INFORMED CONSENT TO PSYCHIATRIC TREATMENT-THE ISRAELI PRACTICE

The individual's right to refuse or accept medical treatment in Israel is covered by four major laws, specifically as follows:

Law of Human Dignity and Freedom (1994) states that "There shall be no violation of the life, body or dignity of any person as such" (clause 2) and "All persons are entitled to protection of their life, body and dignity" (clause 4).

Law of Legal Competency and Guardianship (1962) states that "every person is endowed with rights and obligation from birth till death" (clause 1). This law allows the appointment of a guardian for any person because of limited cognitive capacities or a specific medical condition who cannot handle his/her affairs (including giving valid consent to medical treatment).

Law of the Patient's Rights (1995) states that "no treatment will be administered to the patient if he/she has not given informed consent..." (clause 13/a). The clause includes specific directives regarding the areas in which the therapists must inform patients to enable them to reach a proper decision about the proposed treatment (such as diagnosis, prognosis and the nature, benefits and risks of the treatment).

Finally, the **Law for the treatment of the Mentally Ill (1991)** states that "A patient who requests voluntary admission to a hospital shall sign a consent to

---

8. Bonnie, R.J.(1997) 'Research With Cognitively Impaired Subjects: Unfinished Business in the Regulation of Human Research'. *Arch. Gen. Psychiatry.* 54; 105-111.

voluntary admission and to receiving treatment…" (clause 4/a) and "A patient who has been voluntarily admitted and seeks discharge from hospital shall sign a form of request for discharge and shall be discharged voluntarily within 48 hours from the time of his signature" (clause 4/b). Clause 9/a of this law defines the criteria for involuntary civil psychiatric hospitalization: a) the presence of a mental illness which severely impairs the patient's judgment or the assessment of reality; b) the risk of the patient physically endangering himself/herself or others and c) a causal connection between a) and b). The law differentiates between voluntary and involuntary hospitalization on the basis of patient competence. A serious impairment in cognitive capacities may make his/her understanding the illness, the need for treatment, the nature of the treatment and the ability to choose treatment doubtful. Of all of these, the ability to choose is the most complex. Elliot (1997)[4] claimed that even when cognitive ability is otherwise intact, the ability to choose may be impaired.

In cases of voluntary admission, Israeli psychiatric hospitals are required to ask patients to sign a form of "Consent to Voluntary Hospitalization and to Accepting Treatment". The form includes the statement that the undersigned patient consents to hospitalization "…after the medical reasons for the hospitalization, the conditions of the hospitalization and the possible treatments have been explained to me in an understandable language…". Though the patient's signature on the form fulfills the bureaucratic formality, no standardized technique is applied to ascertain his/her mental competence and his ability to give informed consent. Thus, the validity of such consent becomes questionable in two cases:

1) Patients, whose illness has not damaged or hardly damaged their thought processes, such as those with a severe but non-psychotic major depressive episode, are able to understand their condition and the need for treatment and are therefore deemed legally competent to express their true will and to give informed consent. However, as Elliot (1997) noted their consent (or their refusal) might be based on motivations heavily distorted by emotional (non-cognitive) factors.

2) Patients with an acute psychotic episode are incapable of correct judgment and reality evaluation due to severe disturbance in their thought processes and thought content. Consequently their actions, including their desire for hospitalization, are a product of their unhealthy state (for example, they may ask for hospitalization based on commanding voices). These patients often do not even understand that they are in hospital.

To be considered competent, patients need a global understanding of where they are, of the significance and consequences of hospitalization and of the alternatives to hospitalization. Otherwise, the only practical solutions in these cases are involuntary hospitalization (even if the patient is agreeable to admission) on condition that there is immediate risk of endangerment to self or others or the appointment of a guardian, if one is not already present, who will be responsible for giving consent for hospitalization. In cases of patients who do not meet criteria for competence, involuntary hospitalization is carried out based on an order from the district psychiatrist. If the patient has a legal guardian, the guardian must give his/her consent after obtaining detailed explanation of the reason for hospitalization. For a patient who does not have a guardian, the court is approached to appoint a guardian as quickly as possible or to issue appropriate orders. These may include giving medical treatment in absence of informed consent on condition that the patient constitutes an immediate physical danger to himself or others.

What the Israeli law is missing are criteria and methods for evaluating the extent of the patient's understanding of the information provided to him/her by the psychiatrist. Moreover, there is no clear definition of informed consent beyond the tautological concept that informed consent is the consent of a competent person who received the type and amount of information prescribed by the law.

RECOMMENDATIONS FOR THE PRACTICAL ASSESSMENT OF COMPETENCE

Measuring competence. Competence evaluation requires a normative analysis, which has not yet been done. Additionally, even if a "point of incompetence" was determined, does this constitute a real solution? Is there an efficient and accurate screening process for the recruitment of volunteers? Are there appropriate mechanisms to improve the decision-making abilities of patients, to enable more of them to make decisions for themselves? Does the lack of competence at a certain point in time necessarily affect the individual's competence over the long term? Can advance directives solve part of the problem for patients suffering from a recurring illness?

What is clear from these questions is that the existing knowledge regarding the extent to which a mental illness detrimentally affects the competence to consent to hospitalization, treatment or participation in a research study is limited. The present situation raises the question, as mentioned before, if evaluation of competence to participate in treatment or in research is more a myth than a reality. There is need for more empirical data on the extent of the problem, for a normative analysis of the elements of competence and for the establishment of clear new standards.

To be able to obtain a more valid consent we recommend two-stage guidelines for the examining physician for the determination of the patient's consent:

(a) assessment of competence for consenting to hospitalization, treatment or participation in research; followed by

(b) an appropriate and detailed explanation of the reason for hospitalization and the nature and risks of treatment.

A.   Assessment of Competence

The patient's consent will be considered valid only after the examining physician declares him/her competent. To be declared competent the patient must meet the following conditions:

1) In general terms the competent patient should have adequate knowledge, show the ability to comprehend something to a required standard and should be legally responsible in this regard.

2) The competent patients must be able to understand that they are being hospitalized in a psychiatric hospital. They must realize that they have a mental problem, and. the optimal place to obtain treatment for their current condition is a psychiatric setting

3) The competent patient must be able to understand that hospitalization is for the purposes of treatment and be able to understand the physician's explanations about the possible treatment choices, their benefits and their risks.

4) The competent patient must be in an emotional condition which does not interfere extensively with his cognitive capacities and with his decision making abilities.

5) The competent patient, in accordance to the Israel Mental Health Act 1991, must be able to understand that discharge is not automatic, even though hospitalization was voluntary. Discharge will be based on medical considerations and in accordance with specific guidelines. The patient must understand that in certain circumstances the head of the hospital can

recommend continued hospitalization even if the patient requests discharge.

Only after the physician is convinced that the patient has understood the whole procedure can he/she proceed to the next stage.

B.   Explanation about hospitalization and treatment

1) The explanation needs to be appropriate to the cultural, social and educational level of the patient, and must be given in a language in which the patient is fluent and in accordance with the patient's capacity to understand.

2) The explanation must include a short description of the illness or disorder, the diagnosis and the expected prognosis. It is important to include the following points: the different forms of treatment (drugs, psychotherapy, occupational therapy and so on); the different side effects of the different therapies; and the social repercussions of hospitalization in a psychiatric institute.

3) If the patient has being chosen as a candidate to participate in a research project, detailed explanations should be given about the nature of the study and its risks and benefits for him/her. The patient must be informed that he/she is free not to participate in the research and that his/her treatment needs will not be jeopardized by his/her refusal.

Most physicians today maintain that the greater the honesty and reliability of the therapist, the greater the chances of cooperation from the patient. Explanations about the treatment and their side effects should be provided in a balanced and sensible way to avoid confusion and irrational reluctance to participate.

The competency assessment and explanations are especially important in patients who are being hospitalized for the first time or who are not known to the psychiatric services. Being less familiar with the system these patients need more guidance and direction. It is often harder for them to grasp the practical implications of a psychiatric hospitalization (recording of personal and medical data, reporting to the authorities, potential withdrawal of driver's license, etc.).

Patients who do not meet the competency criteria may undergo involuntary hospitalization with or without appointment of a guardian, if this has not already been done, or enforced treatment as stipulated by Israeli Law. The lack of consent must be recorded in the patient's file. As soon the patient shows improvement the caregiver is required to redetermine competence and proceed on that basis. All competence assessment forms and consent forms are to be kept in the patient's medical file.

CONCLUSION

The laws pertaining to the mentally ill must reach a balance between the respect of their basic rights as citizens (autonomy), and paternalistic protection against endangering their own health, occupational capacities and social well-being and also the need to protect society (police principle).

Both the legal and mental communities must take care to avoid extremes. The paradox of the freedom of the mentally ill was illustrated by the work of R. Laing (R.D.Laing, A.Esterson, 1964)[9] who conceptualized the mentally ill as victims of society, not as criminals or sick people. Therefore, he demanded an overall change in the social attitude towards this subgroup, including among other things, the discharging of mentally ill patients from asylums and their placement in "shelters". Unfortunately, this would mean to imprison them in a "prison of good intentions". In some cases, idealism can turn into an immoral trap, destroying the very rights it sought to protect.

The present paper offers several social guidelines to the physician for determining patient competence, which we hope, will help to reach the necessary balance. In addition, the Israeli laws concerning psychiatric treatment have to be carefully reviewed with regard the difficult ethical problem of guardianship and involuntary hospitalization. Moreover it is essential today, when the expanding field of psychiatric research holds the promise of creating much greater understanding of the pathophysiology of many mental disturbances that the same balance will be achieved, and at the same time without interfering with the advance of science.

Systematic studies of the application of legal regulations and appropriate modifications are needed, with careful follow-up from the field. We must face and deal with the problem, not avoid it, in order to keep the medical profession a healing, not a destructive one. And to do it not in a mythical way but a realistic one.

---

9. Laing, R.D., Esterson, A.(1964) 'Sanity, Madness and Family'. *Pelican Books.*

Trust and Confidentiality

[35]

Weaving a Tangled Web:
The Deceptions of Psychiatrists

ANSAR M. HAROUN*
GRANT H. MORRIS**

I. INTRODUCTION

Our society regards deception—the act of representing as true that which is known to be false[1]—as evil. One who lies under oath can be convicted of the crime of perjury.[2] One whose intentional deceit harms another may be subjected to civil liability for the tort of fraud. "Fraud," said the California Court of Appeal, "evokes almost universal repugnance expressed with near-Biblical fervor."[3] It is, as described by the Ohio Supreme Court, "the very essence of wrong; conduct that has always been and always will be wrong, according to the common judgment of mankind; conduct that cannot be dressed up or manipulated

---

*   M.D., Supervising Forensic Psychiatrist, San Diego Superior Court; Associate Clinical Professor, Department of Psychiatry, School of Medicine, University of California, San Diego; Adjunct Professor, University of San Diego School of Law. Request for reprints should be addressed to: Ansar Haroun, M.D., Superior Court of California, Forensic Psychiatry Clinic C-537, County Courthouse, Room 1003, San Diego, CA 92101-3814.
**   Professor of Law, University of San Diego School of Law; Clinical Professor, Department of Psychiatry, School of Medicine, University of California, San Diego.

1.   The word "deceive" means to inculcate a person so that he or she "takes the false as true, the unreal as existent, the spurious as genuine . . . ." WEBSTER'S THIRD NEW INT'L DICTIONARY 584 (1964).
2.   See, e.g., CAL. PENAL CODE § 118(a) (West 1999). In California, perjury is punishable by imprisonment for two, three, or four years. Id. § 126. If, however, the perjury results in the conviction and execution of an innocent person, the perjurer is subject to a punishment of death or life imprisonment without possibility of parole. Id. § 128.
3.   In re Legeas, 256 Cal. Rptr. 117, 120 (Cal. App. 1989).

or associated so as to invest it with any element of right."[4] Our religious heritage instructs us to condemn those who would "bear false witness."[5]

Science, however, teaches us a different lesson. From evolutionary biology we learn that, throughout the plant and animal kingdom, deception is a necessary condition to survival. Organisms that fail to deceive their enemies are promptly devoured. Those of us who survived millions of years of evolution must be those who successfully deceived, and passed on genes that enabled succeeding generations to skillfully deceive. Deceptions are not rare, but rather, are ubiquitous. To deceive is to be human.

Perhaps this polar difference between biology and religious-based ethics explains our ambivalence toward deception. We are able to denounce, without even censuring, to impeach, without convicting, to revile but continue to follow, a President who lies under oath about an illicit sexual encounter with a White House intern less than half his age.

Doctors, as do most humans, also regularly practice deceptions. They may deceive the very patients who trust them,[6] the insurance companies who pay them,[7] the litigants and lawyers who seek their expertise, the judges and juries who consider their expert opinions, and even themselves. These deceptions may take several forms.[8] Sometimes doctors lie, and sometimes they merely omit to tell the truth. Sometimes they tell the truth, but they tell it falsely. Sometimes they tell the truth, but they tell only half the truth. Sometimes they betray secrets. Deception is such a broad concept that it may include some or all of the above examples.[9] Even the methods of deception vary: A doctor may

4.   Morton v. Petitt, 177 N.E. 591, 593 (Ohio 1931).
5.   The Ninth Commandment is: "Thou shalt not bear false witness against thy neighbor." *Exodus* 20:13. *But see* Bradford Wixen, *Therapeutic Deception: A Comparison of Halacha and American Law*, 13 J. LEGAL MED. 77 (1992) (suggesting that the Talmud interprets the Torah to permit therapeutic deception by physicians in disclosures to their patients).
6.   Wixen, *supra* note 5. *See also* David R. Silverman, *Narrowing the Gap Between Rhetoric and the Reality of Medical Ethics*, 71 ACAD. MED. 227, 229 (1996) (suggesting that even medical students deceive patients by representing themselves as licensed physicians).
7.   *See generally* MARC A. RODWIN, MEDICINE, MONEY, AND MORALS: PHYSICIANS' CONFLICTS OF INTEREST (1993) (suggesting that the mode of payment to physicians creates a potential conflict between the patient's interest in quality health care and the doctor's interest in maximizing personal income).
8.   *See* PAUL EKMAN, TELLING LIES: CLUES TO DECEIT IN THE MARKETPLACE, POLITICS, AND MARRIAGE 41-42 (1992).
9.   Recently, as a court-appointed psychiatrist, Dr. Haroun examined a man who was a criminal defendant in a three strikes case. He had a history of malingering seizures. He presented with an odd mental state that Dr. Haroun thought may have been malingered. After 20 minutes, the man stopped communicating with Dr. Haroun. He

[Vol. 10: 227, 1999]   *Deceptions of Psychiatrists*
THE JOURNAL OF CONTEMPORARY LEGAL ISSUES

practice any combination of evasion, suppression, euphemism, exaggeration, disguise, gesture, silence, or inaction, to successfully deceive the victim.[10]

In this article, we will discuss several examples of deceptions that Dr. Haroun has encountered in his practice as a forensic psychiatrist. The examples in Part II are unique to that practice; the examples in Part III are more generally applicable to all psychiatrists—those in clinical practice as well as those who specialize in forensic practice. In Part IV, we analyze the motives of those who deceive—why they do it—and conclude in Part V by asking whether those who deceive are morally blameworthy for their conduct.[11]

---

just muttered and chanted. When the marshal came in and informed the man that the interview was over, instead of standing up to leave, he fell to the floor and apparently had a seizure. Dr. Haroun did not know if it was a genuine seizure or a malingered seizure. It looked genuine, but Dr. Haroun had doubts because of the man's medical history of malingered seizures and his incentive to malinger a seizure to avoid punishment in the criminal case against him. When Dr. Haroun discussed the case with the man's attorney, he responded, "Yeah, doc, you're so cynical. You think everyone is malingering. I *told* him to have a seizure!" The attorney's words, taken literally, suggest that a conspiracy existed between the attorney and the defendant to malinger a seizure. But the attorney made his statement in a tone that conveyed the exact opposite, that it was preposterous for Dr. Haroun to suggest that the attorney would do such a thing. Perhaps the attorney was making a true statement, but conveying it in a way that was designed to deceive Dr. Haroun into believing that it was not true. Alternatively, perhaps the attorney was not making a true statement, but was conveying it in a way as to suggest that he was not attempting to deceive Dr. Haroun and that Dr. Haroun was not to believe his statement was a true one.

10.   J. David Newell, *The Case for Deception in Medical Experimentation, in* ETHICAL ISSUES IN SCIENTIFIC RESEARCH: AN ANTHOLOGY 141, 145 (Edward Erwin et al. eds., 1994). The Supreme Court of Oklahoma noted that deceit "includes all surprise, trick, cunning, dissembling, and any unfair way by which another is cheated." Stapleton v. Holt, 250 P.2d 451, 453 (Okla. 1952).

11.   The following sources provide insight to those who wish to pursue the topic of deception in greater detail: F.G. BAILEY, THE PREVALENCE OF DECEIT (1991); J.A. BARNES, A PACK OF LIES: TOWARDS A SOCIOLOGY OF LYING (1994); SISSELA BOK, LYING: MORAL CHOICE IN PUBLIC AND PRIVATE LIFE (1989); EKMAN, *supra* note 8; DANIEL GOLEMAN, VITAL LIES SIMPLE TRUTHS: THE PSYCHOLOGY OF SELF-DECEPTION (1985); HAROLD V. HALL & DAVID A. PRITCHARD, DETECTING MALINGERING AND DECEPTION: FORENSIC DISTORTION ANALYSIS (FDA) (1996); David M. Bersoff, *Why Good People Sometimes Do Bad Things: Motivated Reasoning and Unethical Behavior*, 25 PERSONALITY & SOC. PSYCHOL. BULL. 28 (1999); *Integrity in Biomedical Research*, 68 ACAD. MED. No. 9 Supp. (Paul J. Friedman ed., 1993). For articles discussing the relationship between psychiatry, mental disorder, and evil, *see generally Psychiatric Aspects of Wickedness*, 27 PSYCHIATRIC ANNALS No. 9 (Ansar Haroun ed., 1997).

II. DECEPTIONS THAT MAY VIOLATE FORENSIC ETHICS

Forensic psychiatrists are uniquely conflicted by issues of deception. As individuals trained in science, they are influenced by their knowledge of biology. But their very role as evaluators of defendants' mental conditions and as expert witnesses testifying as to their conclusions requires them to tell the truth. In this portion of the article, we discuss issues that raise potential violations of forensic ethics.

A. *Confidentiality*

Forensic psychiatry is a subspecialty of psychiatry, and the American Academy of Psychiatry and the Law has established ethical guidelines for that practice.[12] Confidentiality is identified as a major concern for psychiatrists performing forensic evaluations and the evaluator is required to maintain confidentiality to the extent possible.[13] Forensic psychiatrists are required to begin their evaluation by notifying the evaluee of any limitations on confidentiality.[14] The commentary to this ethical guideline states that the evaluator should explain to the evaluee that because the evaluator is not acting as a treating doctor, confidentiality that might exist in a therapeutic relationship does not exist here. Information obtained as a result of the evaluation can, and will, be disclosed. Although the evaluee may understand this "warning" at an intellectual/cognitive level, once the evaluation begins, a forensic evaluator may easily deceive the subject into believing that this examination is similar to a therapy session. By appearing empathic to the subject's statements and concerns, the evaluator may create a climate

---

12.   AMERICAN ACADEMY OF PSYCHIATRY AND THE LAW, ETHICS GUIDELINES FOR THE PRACTICE OF FORENSIC PSYCHIATRY (1995). Another source of ethical guidance for psychiatrists is AMERICAN PSYCHIATRIC ASS'N, THE PRINCIPLES OF MEDICAL ETHICS WITH ANNOTATIONS ESPECIALLY APPLICABLE TO PSYCHIATRY (1998). For scholarly discussions of ethical guidelines applicable to psychiatrists, see generally Robert Weinstock et al., *Ethical Guidelines, in* PRINCIPLES AND PRACTICE OF FORENSIC PSYCHIATRY 59 (Richard Rosner ed., 1994); ETHICAL PRACTICE IN PSYCHIATRY AND THE LAW (Richard Rosner & Robert Weinstock eds., 1990).
   Although this Article addresses ethical obligations of psychiatrists, comparable ethical obligations exist for psychologists. AMERICAN PSYCHOLOGICAL ASS'N, ETHICAL PRINCIPLES OF PSYCHOLOGISTS AND CODE OF CONDUCT (1992). In fact, these ethical principles are even more comprehensive than those established for psychiatrists.
13.   AMERICAN ACADEMY OF PSYCHIATRY AND THE LAW, *supra* note 12, Guideline II. *See also* AMERICAN PSYCHIATRIC ASS'N, *supra* note 12, § 4.
14.   AMERICAN ACADEMY OF PSYCHIATRY AND THE LAW, *supra* note 12, Guideline II. *See also* AMERICAN PSYCHIATRIC ASS'N, *supra* note 12, § 4, ann. 6.

[Vol. 10: 227, 1999]

in which the subject is "seduced" into revealing more than he or she intended to reveal. The psychiatrist may use (or abuse) therapy techniques to blur the boundaries between a forensic interview (in which the evaluee has no expectation of privacy) and a clinical interview (in which the patient has every expectation of privacy).[15]

B. *Informed Consent*

Consent is a core value of ethical psychiatric practice.[16] The ethical psychiatrist should inform the evaluee of the nature and purpose of the interview and proceed only if the individual consents.[17] In order to maximize the chances of the subject's full co-operation, the deceptive evaluator may not fully inform, or may be satisfied with the subject's behavioral assent (as opposed to psychological consent), but notify the court that informed consent to the evaluation was properly obtained. For example, the evaluator may explain the purpose of the evaluation but not suggest to the subject that if the evaluee wishes not to participate, he or she may leave. The evaluator subtly coerces the evaluee to remain for the evaluation by implying the evaluator's expectation that the examination will be conducted.

C. *Impartiality*

Forensic psychiatrists are required by the ethics of their profession to adhere to the principle of honesty and to strive for objectivity.[18]

---

15. Although no doctor/patient relationship exists, psychiatrists conducting a forensic evaluation are admonished by the American Psychiatric Association to "diligently guard against exploiting information furnished by the patient . . . ." AMERICAN PSYCHIATRIC ASS'N, *supra* note 12, § 2, ann. 2. *See generally* Michael L. Perlin, *Power Imbalances in Therapeutic and Forensic Relationships*, 9 BEHAV. SCI. & L. 111, 115-21 (1991) (explaining why the dual loyalties of forensic evaluators can lead them to misuse their power).

16. AMERICAN ACADEMY OF PSYCHIATRY AND THE LAW, *supra* note 12, Commentary to Guideline III.

17. For some forensic evaluations, for example, assessments of competency to stand trial or civil commitment, the subject's informed consent is not required. Nevertheless, the evaluator is obligated to inform the evaluee that the evaluation is legally required and that if the evaluee refuses to participate, this fact will be included in any report or testimony of the evaluator. *Id.*

18. *Id.* Guideline IV.

Nevertheless, because forensic psychiatrists may be retained by parties in adversarial proceedings, unintended bias and distortion of opinion is a real risk.[19] All humans have conscious and unconscious biases, and the conclusions reached by even the most careful doctors will be affected by such biases. Forensic psychiatrists are ethically obligated to strive to be impartial, not that they actually succeed in doing so.[20] To further their efforts, we propose that ethical doctors should not only privately note potential biases but should publicly declare them as well in written reports or in verbal testimony to the court. Currently, the community standard does not require such disclosure. Nevertheless, if, for example, a Nazi doctor is evaluating a Jewish patient, (or a Jewish doctor is evaluating a Nazi patient), and if this factor may create a bias, we believe the failure to acknowledge this potential bias is a deception.[21]

D. *Credentials and Areas of Expertise*

Ethical forensic psychiatrists will claim expertise only in the areas of their actual knowledge, skills, training, and experience.[22] Deceptive doctors may be tempted to practice outside their areas of expertise.[23] They may do so consciously by exaggerating medical credentials in order to look more credible to the fact finder. They may also do so unconsciously, not to deliberately deceive about their actual medical credentials, but to blur the boundaries between medical and non-medical knowledge. In doing so, they may then express opinions actually derived from common sense bases but that seem to rely on medical bases. For example, a doctor was asked whether an alcoholic could "control" his drinking. Presently, hard medical science does not have an

---

19.   *Id.* Commentary to Guideline IV.

20.   *Id.*

21.   For example, the authors know a doctor who is unsympathetic to drunk drivers. He considered joining Mothers against Drunk Driving, but refrained from doing so, because he feared cross-examination from a hostile attorney who would demonstrate the doctor's bias through his support of MADD. The doctor remains biased, but by not joining the organization, he has avoided creating evidence of that bias that could be used to attack him in court.

22.   AMERICAN ACADEMY OF PSYCHIATRY AND THE LAW, *supra* note 12, Guideline V. *See* Bradley J. Olson, *Physician Specialty Advertising: The Tendency to Deceive?*, 11 J. LEGAL MED. 351, 352 (1990) (suggesting that physicians who advertise to promote themselves as specialists in limited areas of practice mislead patients who do not understand the different training requirements of various specialties and certifications). Some "specialties" may only require completion of a weekend course and payment of a nominal fee. *Id.*

23.   AMERICAN PSYCHIATRIC ASS'N, *supra* note 12, § 2, ann. 3.

[Vol. 10: 227, 1999]   *Deceptions of Psychiatrists*
THE JOURNAL OF CONTEMPORARY LEGAL ISSUES

answer to this question, and the doctor should simply respond by saying so—and nothing more. But a doctor who has been qualified as a medical expert, who ventures an opinion on the issue, derived not from medical science but from some combination of philosophy or common sense, is testifying as a pseudo-expert on a matter beyond his or her professional expertise. Similarly, when a psychiatrist testifies that a man doesn't "need" prison, but rather, he "needs" rehabilitation, or visa versa, what is the expertise that supports such an opinion? Whether an individual "needs" prison is not a medical judgment. It is a legal, philosophical, or penological judgment. If a dermatologist gave an opinion in the area of psychiatry, he or she would be quickly challenged. But if a psychiatrist gives an opinion in the area of law, philosophy, or penology, the psychiatrist is rarely challenged.

E. *Data Base*

In the quest for honesty and objectivity, forensic opinions, reports, and testimony are supposed to be based on all the data available to the psychiatrist.[24] In practice, the ethical psychiatrist selects the data base from which forensic conclusions are to be drawn, and clarifies both to himself or herself and to the court the boundaries of that data base. Sometimes doctors have access to information that may or may not be reliable. Such data demands a rigorous intellectual exercise to exclude from the mind (and hence from the reasoning process) the "bad" (unreliable) data, and to form conclusions only from the "good" data. For example, Dr. Haroun was asked to give an opinion on the dangerousness of a man suspected of committing a series of sex crimes. Although the man was never convicted of these crimes, in his chart were ten-year-old newspaper articles stating that he was a suspect in a series of out-of-state sexual crimes. The articles strongly suggested that he was guilty. To reach a conclusion on the man's future dangerousness, Dr. Haroun needed to consider whether the man had or had not been dangerous in the past. As soon as Dr. Haroun read the newspaper accounts, he found it difficult to exclude from his mind, and hence from his reasoning, the likelihood that the man had acted dangerously. Dr. Haroun was tempted to conclude that the man had committed the criminal acts and was still dangerous. But was it appropriate for him to

---

24. AMERICAN ACADEMY OF PSYCHIATRY AND THE LAW, *supra* note 12, Commentary to Guideline IV.

consider, and to rely upon, the unverified newspaper accounts? If he did so, and if he testified that he did so, his expert opinion might be attacked on cross examination. How much easier for Dr. Haroun if he simply failed to mention that the newspaper accounts were a part of the data base that he relied upon in forming his opinion. He could hide his ethical dilemma, and his opinion would not be subjected to an opposing attorney's attack. But Dr. Haroun believes that he would have been guilty of deception if he failed to inform the court of his dilemma. The judge could tell him whether he could appropriately consider the newspaper accounts, and Dr. Haroun could then make a judgment using the appropriate data.

F. *Confidence Level in Medical Opinion*

We believe that an ethical psychiatrist should convey to the court not only his or her expert opinion, but also the level of confidence that the doctor has in that opinion. For example, ideally, a doctor would like to be able to tell the court: "I am fifty-two percent sure, plus or minus three percent, that there is a forty-six percent probability, plus or minus five percent, of this man re-offending." In actual practice, however, doctors do not testify with this degree of precision for two reasons. First, science does not support this degree of precision. Second, even if it did, doctors would fear the cross-examination that the above statistics would generate. Doctors are more comfortable using soft qualitative terms like "pretty sure" rather than hard quantitative numbers. Lawyers may then attempt to have the doctor translate these terms into "reasonable medical certainty."[25]

Frequently, however, the findings of forensic psychiatrists do not approach "reasonable medical certainty" or even "reasonable medical probability." If the level of confidence is actually "medical possibility," the psychiatrist should convey this degree of uncertainty to the court. Even if the doctor risks being found less credible, a failure to identify this low confidence level constitutes an act of deception.

---

25.   Bernard Diamond, M.D., a forensic psychiatrist, asserted that reasonable medical certainty "should express the psychiatrist's highest level of confidence in the validity and reliability of his opinion. This level of confidence must, necessarily, be formulated within the matrix of clinical experience and scientific knowledge. It cannot be directly translated into the legal scale of levels of proof." Bernard L. Diamond, *Reasonable Medical Certainty, Diagnostic Thresholds, and Definitions of Mental Illness in the Legal Context*, 13 BULL. AM. ACAD. PSYCHIATRY & L. 121, 123 (1985).

[Vol. 10: 227, 1999]   *Deceptions of Psychiatrists*
                              THE JOURNAL OF CONTEMPORARY LEGAL ISSUES

III. DECEPTIONS OF PSYCHIATRISTS

The American Medical Association has adopted Principles of Medical Ethics to govern the professional activities of all doctors, including psychiatrists. Those Principles are stated in very broad terms. For example, a physician is required to "deal honestly with patients"[26] and to "respect the law."[27] Nevertheless, psychiatrists in clinical (i.e., nonforensic) practice may deceive. While often such deception goes unnoticed, it may become a focus of attention if the doctor is called upon to defend his or her position in a legal proceeding.

Many of the tasks performed by psychiatrists in clinical practice are also tasks performed by forensic psychiatrists in their practice. Whether a psychiatrist is acting as a therapist in diagnosing a patient or whether the psychiatrist is acting as an evaluator in assessing whether an evaluee has a mental disorder, the process and the expertise are the same. In this portion of the article, we discuss examples of deceptive practices that are common both to psychiatrists in clinical practice and to psychiatrists in forensic practice.

A. *History Taking, Examination of Mental State, and Testing*

The ethical psychiatrist takes a history, examines the subject's mental state, orders biological or psychological tests, if necessary, and then reaches a conclusion that is maximally consistent with the history, the examination, and the test results. A doctor who wishes to reach a particular conclusion may deceive by taking only a selective history, or by selectively examining the subject's mental state, or by failing to order needed tests. In essence, by carefully manipulating the data base, the doctor will be able to reach the desired conclusion. For example, a doctor who does not want to find evidence of malingering may fail to ask the many questions that will identify the pattern of malingering and will not order tests that will detect malingering.

A common diagnostic confusion surrounds individuals who present in a psychotic state. The psychosis may be a manifestation of a primary brain disease (such as schizophrenia) or may be secondary to amphetamines, cocaine, PCP (phencyclidine), hallucinogens or other drugs (a substance-induced psychosis). The symptoms and signs are

---

26.   AMERICAN PSYCHIATRIC ASS'N, *supra* note 12, § 2.
27.   *Id.* § 3.

identical. A psychiatrist, relying on a clinical interview alone, will not be able to distinguish a primary psychosis from a secondary psychosis. The most objective method to resolve this differential is to do a urine toxicology screen. But frequently the test is not ordered. The treating psychiatrist may have a financial incentive in not knowing so that he or she maintains diagnostic flexibility. Without a urine test, the doctor can diagnose the patient with psychotic disorder not otherwise specified (NOS).[28] If a urine test is ordered and the patient tests positive, the doctor may have to report that the psychosis was drug induced—and potentially not reimbursable through the patient's insurance.[29]

A deceiving psychiatrist may also mislead the court as to the differential weight given to the history versus the examination. The patient's history is usually self reported and is therefore subjective. The doctor's examination is not self reported, and is therefore more objective. In a clinical (non-forensic) setting, doctors properly assume that their patients are telling the truth and give great weight to the patient's self report. In a forensic setting, however, the evaluee typically has a strong interest in the outcome of the evaluation and may be tempted to lie. For example, to qualify for benefits as a disabled worker under the Social Security disability insurance program[30] or as a disabled person under the supplemental security income program (SSI),[31] the individual is required to have a "physical or mental impairment" that is "demonstrable by medically acceptable clinical and laboratory diagnostic techniques."[32] Self-reported symptoms do not, of themselves, satisfy this requirement. The condition must also be manifested by signs or laboratory findings.[33] A forensic doctor should therefore give greater weight to objective findings (from the examination) and test results than to the self-reported history of the patient.

---

28.   AMERICAN PSYCHIATRIC ASS'N, DIAGNOSTIC AND STATISTICAL MANUAL OF MENTAL DISORDERS (DSM-IV) 315 (4th ed. 1994).

29.   In areas of high HMO penetration, approximately 15% of physicians surveyed reported a moderate to strong financial incentive to reduce services. Physicians experiencing this pressure experienced greater dissatisfaction with their practices than did other physicians. Their practice style was affected—they had less time to spend with patients and less ability to hospitalize, to order tests and procedures, and to make referrals. Jack Hadley et. al, *Perceived Financial Incentives, HMO Market Penetration, and Physicians' Practice Styles and Satisfaction*, 34 HEALTH SERVICES RES. 307, 307 (1999).

30.   42 U.S.C. § 401 (1991 & Supp. 1999).

31.   42 U.S.C. §§ 1381-83 (1991 & Supp. 1999).

32.   42 U.S.C.A. § 1382c(a)(3)(D) (West Supp.1999). Additionally, the impairment must result from an anatomical, physiological, or psychological abnormality. *Id.*

33.   20 C.F.R. § 416.908 (1999). Symptoms, signs, and laboratory findings are defined in 20 C.F.R. § 416.928 (1999).

Many lawyers assume, erroneously, that diagnoses of mental disorder are based on some proper combination of self report and the psychiatrist's examination. However, many diagnoses either cannot be validated by objective testing or are so difficult to validate that routine clinical practice relies solely on self report. For example, if a person claims to have post traumatic stress disorder, objective validation of the assertion is difficult, if not impossible. Can we confirm whether he was tortured twenty years ago and whether he has nightmares every time he goes to sleep? Similarly, a diagnosis of depression is almost wholly dependent on the individual's self report. For such diagnoses, the ethical psychiatrist should state not only his or her diagnostic conclusion but should also clarify that the conclusion relies heavily on the self report of a potentially biased evaluee and cannot be supported by any objective measures. The deceptive psychiatrist, seeking to have his or her opinion accepted as gospel (and not subjected to the rigors of annoying cross-examination), will delete such clarification.

B. *"Objective" Tests*

Courts are often impressed by psychiatrists who report that their clinical judgment is confirmed by the results of "objective" psychological tests such as the MMPI.[34] Judges, and lawyers as well, erroneously believe that if the test is objective, it must surely be credible. The word "objective" has two meanings, and courts are often confused by this ambiguity. In medicine, an objective test is one that is difficult, if not impossible, to falsify. If a patient self reports that his leg is broken, the doctor may give little weight to that statement. But the doctor will give great weight to an X-ray of the leg that shows the leg is broken. The X-ray is objective evidence of the break, evidence that is difficult, if not impossible, to falsify. The word "objective," when referring to standard medical tests such as X-rays or CAT scans, is contrasted with the word "subjective."

---

34. The MMPI is the common name for the Minnesota Multiphasic Personal Inventory Test, a psychological test used to assess personality and psychopathology. The MMPI "is probably the most widely used and most widely researched objective test of personality." Commonwealth v. Kappler, 625 N.E.2d 513, 517 n.5 (Mass.1993) (quoting testimony of Dr. James Carpenter). *See generally* KENNETH S. POPE ET AL., THE MMPI, MMPI-2 & MMPI-A IN COURT: A PRACTICAL GUIDE FOR EXPERT WITNESSES AND ATTORNEYS (1993); FORENSIC APPLICATIONS OF THE MMPI-2 (Yossef S. Ben-Porath et al. eds., 1995).

Psychological tests, even so-called objective psychological tests such as the MMPI, are not objective in the same sense that bio-medical tests are objective. The MMPI is scored entirely on the patient's self report. If a person claims to be depressed and answers as "true" MMPI questions asking whether he or she is unhappy or cries all the time, the MMPI will report that the person is depressed. Although the MMPI contains validity scales that attempt to identify those who deliberately malinger, psychological tests can be falsified. The word "objective," when referring to standard psychological tests such as the MMPI, is contrasted with the word "projective." In a projective test, such as the Rorschach inkblot test, the examiner analyzes and interprets a person's responses to ambiguous visual stimuli. In theory, the examinee's feeling state is projected onto the stimulus.[35] Psychiatrists deceive if they claim their diagnosis is confirmed by objective psychological testing but fail to explain how the word "objective," in this context, differs from its meaning in other, more traditional contexts. They know that without this explanation, the truth is hidden from their audience.

C. *Differential Diagnosis*

In medical school, doctors are trained to generate lists of "differential diagnoses" that account for all the various symptoms and signs of the patient. In a forensic case, however, a psychiatrist may be tempted not to generate a full differential diagnosis because each possible diagnosis invites a rigorous analysis of the evidence that confirms or disproves that diagnosis. Thus, the lazy psychiatrist, in order to save time and energy, may simply select the diagnosis that is easiest to support and not report all the possible diagnoses to the court. Similarly, the biased doctor may not report all the possible diagnoses to the court in order to avoid suggesting diagnostic possibilities that do not support the doctor's bias.

D. *Diagnostic Conclusions*

Mental disorder is difficult to define. Although the American Psychiatric Association has identified and classified mental disorders in its continuing revisions of the DSM,[36] the authors of the most recent

---

35.   ANNE ANASTASI & SUSANA URBINA, PSYCHOLOGICAL TESTING 411 (7th ed. 1997); PAUL KLINE, THE HANDBOOK OF PSYCHOLOGICAL TESTING 243 (1993).

36.   The first edition of the American Psychiatric Association's Diagnostic and Statistical Manual was published in 1952. Subsequent revisions were published in 1968 (DSM-II), 1980 (DSM-III), 1987 (DSM-III-R), and 1994 (DSM-IV).

[Vol. 10: 227, 1999]   *Deceptions of Psychiatrists*
                                          THE JOURNAL OF CONTEMPORARY LEGAL ISSUES

DSM edition acknowledged: "[A]lthough this manual provides a classification of mental disorders, it must be admitted that no definition adequately specifies precise boundaries for the concept of 'mental disorder.'"[37] The blurred boundaries of mental disorder[38] and the law's requirement of mental disorder as a prerequisite for some benefit for the patient (or insurance reimbursement for the doctor),[39] encourage psychiatrists with imaginations to find mental disorder in virtually everyone they see. Some parents of children who are lazy, but who have no mental disorder, may seek to have their children diagnosed with a learning disorder, so that they may receive tutoring or monetary benefit. Psychiatrists may be overly sympathetic to such requests. In a forensic context, psychiatrists who are sympathetic to a defendant can, with imagination, diagnose common unhappiness as major depression[40] or ordinary worry as anxiety disorder.[41] However, almost every criminal defendant is unhappy and worried. If one is charged with a crime and

---

37.   AMERICAN PSYCHIATRIC ASS'N, *supra* note 28, at xxi. The American Psychiatric Association admits: "The concept of mental disorder . . . lacks a consistent operational definition that covers all situations. . . . [D]ifferent situations call for different definitions." *Id.*

38.   *See generally* David C. Taylor, *The Components of Sickness: Diseases, Illnesses, and Predicaments*, THE LANCET, Nov. 10, 1979, at 1008-10. *See also* WHAT IS DISEASE? (James M. Humber & Robert F. Almeder eds., 1997).

39.   *See supra* note 29.

40.   Some judges and some lawyers are overimpressed by the word "major" in the diagnosis of major depression. DSM-IV identifies major depressive disorder as a mental disorder. AMERICAN PSYCHIATRIC ASS'N, *supra* note 28, at 339-45. Although dysthymic disorder, *id.* at 345-49, and depressive disorder not otherwise specified, *id.* at 350, are recognized as other diagnosable depressive disorders, "minor" depression is not.

A recent article in The Economist magazine noted that the lifetime prevalence of diagnosed major depression in the United States rose from under 5% for people born between 1936 and 1945 and for people born between 1946 and 1955, to almost 10% for people born between 1956 and 1966, and to well over 20% for people born between 1966 and 1975. *Spirit of the Age*, THE ECONOMIST, Dec. 19, 1998, at 113. The article described depression as "a malignant sadness," acknowledging use of this phrase by Lewis Wolpert. *Id.* Major depression is 200 times more prevalent in the United States than in China. *Id.* at 114.

41.   AMERICAN PSYCHIATRIC ASS'N, *supra* note 28, at 393-44. The inmate looks to the doctor for help, and the doctor, trained to diagnose illness, finds one. *See* discussion in Part IV, *infra*. Additionally, the psychiatrist, by finding and treating mental disorder, protects himself or herself from malpractice liability if the unhappy or worried inmate commits suicide. Sympathetic psychiatrists may also creatively diagnose angry or irritable jail inmates with bipolar II disorder. *Id.* at 359-63. Would imaginative psychiatrists diagnose common thieves with kleptomania? *Id.* at 612-15.

worried about the outcome of the criminal process, such unhappiness suggests good mental health, not mental illness.

Many drug-abusing criminal defendants report psychotic symptoms. Most would prefer to be diagnosed with schizophrenia,[42] which may absolve them of blame and keep them eligible for Social Security benefits, rather than with substance-induced psychotic disorder,[43] which gives neither advantage. Because the symptoms of these two conditions are identical, psychiatrists must use their judgment (or their imagination) in clarifying the diagnosis. Those who wish to deceive have the opportunity to do so.

E. *Prognosis*

In deciding on an appropriate criminal sentence, judges often ask psychiatrists whether the defendant's psychological mental state that was a risk factor for the crime can be "fixed." For example, if a man is convicted of molesting a child, the judge wants to know whether he will reoffend or whether he can be treated to reduce or eliminate that risk. If the molester is a pedophile, the man will probably remain dangerous.[44] No known "cure" exists for pedophilia.[45] Although cognitive-behavioral therapy and antiandrogen medication can, in some instances, diminish the pedophile's desire to engage in sexual misconduct and in the misconduct itself, the pedophile remains sexually attracted to children.[46] A deceptive psychiatrist misleads the judge by recommending therapy

---

42. *Id.* at 274-90.

43. *Id.* at 310-15.

44. If, however, the molestation was related only to the criminal's Alcohol Intoxication, *id.* at 196-97, the molester may be dangerous only while drinking, a condition that is less difficult to prevent.

45. *Id.* at 527-28.

46. A recent comprehensive review of the research concluded:

Although some forms of treatment for sex offenders appear promising, little is known definitively about which treatments are most effective, or for which offenders, over what time span, or in what combinations. What emerges from the literature is a strong suggestion that a comprehensive cognitive-behavioral program should involve components that reduce deviant arousal while increasing appropriate arousal and should include cognitive restructuring, social skills training, victim empathy awareness, and relapse prevention. In addition, patients should be considered for antiandrogen medication if they are at high risk for reoffending.

Linda S. Grossman et al., *Are Sex Offenders Treatable? A Research Overview*, 50 Psychiatric Services 349, 358 (1999). *See also* Howard V. Zonana & Michael A. Norko, *Sexual Predators*, 22 Psychiatric Clinics N. Am. 109, 119-23 (1999) (discussing treatment techniques for sexual predators).

for the pedophile, without clarifying the limited benefits that therapy can achieve. The doctor's pro-treatment bias results in an overly optimistic prognosis.

In contrast, sometimes a deceptive psychiatrist is excessively pessimistic in his or her prognosis. For example, a psychiatrist who wishes to help a patient obtain disability benefits may report that the prognosis is "guarded," suggesting that the patient will not or cannot improve. Although some patients will not respond to psychiatric treatment, a doctor should so conclude only after all treatments have been tried. Electroconvulsive therapy (ECT) is the most effective treatment for severe depression.[47] Clozaril is the most effective treatment for schizophrenic patients who have not responded to other neuroleptic medications.[48] Although some patients may refuse these treatments,[49] nevertheless, a psychiatrist deceives the court by asserting that the patient is incurable but omitting that not all treatment options have even been attempted.

F. *Punishment as Treatment*

Some treatments may be administered as punishments or perceived by patients as punishments. For example, some anti-psychotic medications can be dispensed orally, in a pleasant tasting orange juice, or administered by injection, which may be painful. Although electroconvulsive therapy, given appropriately under anesthesia, is actually painless, patients may be terrified of the treatment, especially if they have seen movies in which ECT was administered without anesthesia. Placing a patient in restraints may indeed be therapeutic,

---

47. Richard D. Weiner, *Electroconvulsive Therapy, in* 1 TREATMENTS OF PSYCHIATRIC DISORDERS 1237, 1241 (Glen O. Gabbard ed., 2d ed. 1995); Joan Prudic & Harold A. Sackeim, *Electroconvulsive Therapy and Suicide Risk*, 60 J. CLINICAL PSYCHIATRY 104, 104 (Supp. 2 1999).

48. Robert W. Buckman & Randy D. Malan, *Clozapine for Refractory Schizophrenia: The Illinois Experience*, 60 J. CLINICAL PSYCHIATRY 18, 18 (1999) (Supp. 1). Clozaril "has become the gold standard for treating drug-resistant patients." *Id.*

49. Patients may refuse ECT because of irrational fears of possible adverse consequences. *See* discussion in Part IIIF, *infra*. Psychiatrists may not even recommend ECT because of possible difficulties in obtaining informed consent. Psychiatrists may not recommend Clozaril because of life-threatening side effects and expense of the medication.

helping the patient gain self control. But restraints may be imposed to punish, serving only to deprive a person, perhaps unnecessarily, of liberty. Under the guise of treatment, a deceptive psychiatrist may inflict punishment.[50]

IV. WHY DO PSYCHIATRISTS DECEIVE?

Are psychiatrists malevolent people who wish to destroy society? On the whole they are not. Some, though a small minority, deliberately deceive for financial gain. These sinners bring the profession into disrepute and are appropriately described by the title of a recent book, *Whores of the Court*.[51] However, in our opinion, most deceiving psychiatrists believe that they are behaving decently, properly, ethically, and in a saintly manner. They view their deceptions not as bad deeds, performed impulsively under the stress of the moment, but rather as planned heroic measures, designed to save Western Civilization, or at least to promote Justice.

They see the Law as insensitive to the harsh realities of the psychiatric emergency room, where doctors have to quickly manage a patient who is dangerous—but perhaps not "imminently" dangerous or whatever technical level of dangerousness that the law requires to hold the patient. They know that treatment is desperately needed for a psychotic patient, but there is little time to obtain a really valid informed consent. They see the decisions of judges, not as furthering real justice, but rather as giving patients "rights" that will harm them—the right of the dangerous to endanger, the right of the psychotic to psychic pain. They fear that if they tell the truth, they will contribute not to a Great Society, but to a

---

50. For example, consider castration. Castration, whether chemical or surgical, reduces libidinal drive and may prevent sex offenders from re-offending. Some might contend that castration can be viewed as either treatment or punishment. *See generally* Pamela K. Hicks, *Castration of Sexual Offenders*, 14 J. LEGAL MED. 641, 660-66 (1993) (discussing ethical concerns in using castration). If castration is being considered as a punishment, then experts in punishment, not experts in the healing professions, should be testifying on whether its use should be authorized in an individual case. If castration is being considered as a treatment, the patient must have an illness that warrants such therapy. Most rapists do not have any such illness, and only an imaginative doctor would be able to discover one that merits such a treatment!

51. MARGARET A. HAGEN, WHORES OF THE COURT: THE FRAUD OF PSYCHIATRIC TESTIMONY AND THE RAPE OF AMERICAN JUSTICE (1997). For a discussion of the reasons why attorneys use mental health experts and the criteria they use in selecting those experts, see Douglas Mossman & Marshall B. Kapp, *"Courtroom Whores"?—or Why Do Attorneys Call Us?: Findings From a Survey on Attorneys' Use of Mental Health Experts*, 26 J. AM. ACAD. PSYCHIATRY & L. 27 (1998).

[Vol. 10: 227, 1999] *Deceptions of Psychiatrists*
THE JOURNAL OF CONTEMPORARY LEGAL ISSUES

dangerous and uncaring society.

If the deceivers sincerely believed they were doing wrong, they would not confess their actions to their peers. But they do so. They believe their deceptions are only technically or mechanistically wrong, but are warranted in order to achieve a greater good.

Doctors learn doctoring from mentors in medical school. From Day One they are taught the singular importance of helping their patients. This value predominates over all others. Just as "good" parents will lie, cheat, or bribe in order to help their children succeed in life, "good" doctors will do whatever is necessary to restore their patients' health. To achieve a desirable outcome, doctors will creatively inform patients about the risks and benefits of a physician-recommended surgical procedure or proposed medication. They will laud the curative powers of the placebo they prescribe.[52] Do they do this for their own direct benefit? No, they do this to benefit their patients. And by benefitting their patients, doctors benefit society as well. Society wants doctors to use their knowledge, their skill, their expertise to help restore patients to good health. That is why society does not allow laws, or lawyers, or even the doctors' own patients to interfere unduly with doctors' efforts.[53] In essence, by allowing doctors to practice their deceptions, society joins with them as benevolent co-conspirators.

Although students' clinical skills are continually tested in medical school, the many biases, conscious or unconscious, of medical students are not usually subjected to similar scrutiny. At the University of California, San Diego, Medical School, Dr. Haroun co-teaches a course to psychiatric residents on Law, Logic and Ethics in Medicine. In that course, students are challenged to identify and confront their biases. Dr. Haroun has even catalogued for them types of biased doctors. There is the Paternalist, who wants to help patients and who fudges findings of incompetency so that the court will order involuntary treatment. There is the Historian, who, when evaluating the patient's current mental condition, bases conclusions on the patient's past history rather than on

---

52.   *See* Walter A. Brown, *The Placebo Effect*, SCI. AM., Jan. 1998, at 90; Martin Enserink, *Can the Placebo Be the Cure?*, 284 SCI. 238 (April 9, 1999) (discussing the therapeutic effects patients sometimes experience from placebos).

53.   *See* Michael McCubbin & David Cohen, *Extremely Unbalanced: Interest Divergence and Power Disparities Between Clients and Psychiatry*, 19 INT'L J.L. & PSYCHIATRY 1, 5-11 (1996) (finding that society's assumption that the interests of psychiatrists and patients converge at therapeutic and policy levels is not justified by medical, market, or best interests models).

the patient's present mental state. There is the Puritan, who cannot tolerate disability applicants, and who fudges findings in order to deny benefits to those perceived as lazy. There is the Libertarian, who fudges findings in order to preserve all the person's rights, even those who are severely mentally disordered. There is the Social Reformer, who fudges to achieve his or her personal vision of a greater society. The social reformer's attitude—whether favorable or not—toward the death penalty, to use but one example, affects the reformer's judgment in the individual case. There is the Economist, who fudges civil commitment recommendations, calculating that it is less expensive to retain a hospitalized patient involuntarily now, rather than permit release with inevitable re-hospitalization later. There is the Policeman, who fudges society's definition of dangerousness in order to lock up anyone he or she perceives as dangerous. There is the Avenger, who, when asked if an insanity acquittee has been restored to sanity will say "no," because the psychiatrist believes that the person was never insane and should not have succeeded with an insanity plea in the criminal trial.

V. ARE PSYCHIATRISTS GUILTY OF THE "CRIME" OF LYING?

We have provided various examples of deceptions practiced by psychiatrists and motivations explaining why they deceive. The reader may be tempted to conclude that psychiatrists are indeed guilty of the crime of lying. Nevertheless, we offer three arguments to defend them. First, we assert that psychiatrists are not guilty because their conduct was justified. When a defendant engages in conduct that the criminal law does not wish to deter or prevent—a lawful arrest by a police officer, a killing in self defense—the law provides a justification defense to absolve the defendant from criminal liability.[54] When a psychiatrist lies in order to help a patient or to achieve a greater good that benefits society, do we really want to find the psychiatrist guilty? For example, do we really want the forensic psychiatrist to tell us that the insanity acquittee is not now, and never was, mentally disordered and that the judge or jury erred in finding him insane when he took someone's life a short time ago?

If the reader is not convinced by the justification defense, we offer an excuse for psychiatrists' conduct. Even if a defendant engages in conduct that is socially unacceptable, the law provides an excuse defense

---

54. PETER W. LOW, CRIMINAL LAW 165 (Rev. 1st ed. 1990). *See generally* SUZANNE UNIACKE, PERMISSIBLE KILLING: THE SELF-DEFENSE JUSTIFICATION OF HOMICIDE (1994).

[Vol. 10: 227, 1999]   *Deceptions of Psychiatrists*
                                THE JOURNAL OF CONTEMPORARY LEGAL ISSUES

if the defendant is not blameworthy for that conduct.[55] A defendant who is physically coerced to commit a criminal act or who is insane at the time of the wrongful conduct is not subject to punishment as a morally responsible person.[56] Dr. Haroun has recently identified a new mental disorder: paternalistic personality disorder. This illness is quite virulent and appears endemic to the entire medical profession. As a result of this disorder, doctors spend their entire lives zealously, perhaps overzealously, promoting their patients' well-being as they perceive it. While they understand that their deceptions on behalf of their patients may, on occasion, be legally wrong, they simply cannot understand that such conduct is morally wrong. While doctors suffering from this malady may be behaviorally guilty of lying, surely they are not criminally responsible for their conduct. If an insanity defense works to exculpate other mortals from criminal responsibility, it should not be denied to these unfortunates.

If neither justification nor excuse seems sufficiently appealing, we focus on the elements of the crime and boldly assert that the lying psychiatrist is not guilty of the crime of lying. "Lying" is defined "as a deliberate choice to mislead a target without giving any notification of the intent to do so."[57] To find the defendant guilty of the crime of lying, both elements of the crime must be proven. The first requires that the defendant deliberately choose to mislead the target, in other words, that he or she act with an intent to deceive. When a psychotic patient claims to be Jesus Christ, he may be stating an untruth, but he does not speak with an intent to deceive. If you do not accept our paternalistic personality disorder excuse for psychiatrists' actions, then we are forced to concede that when psychiatrists deceive, they do so intentionally. But wrongful intent alone is not sufficient for conviction.

The crime of lying also requires that the liar not give notification of the intent to deceive. When we go to the theater, we, the audience, pay money in order that we may be deceived by the actors. The better the acting, the more we enjoy the dramatic performance. We want to believe that the actor is actually Hamlet, and the more convincing his performance, the more pleased we are. After a worthy performance, we do not accuse the actor for deceiving us, but rather, we salute him for a job well done. Because we knowingly entered into the deception—we

---

55.   *Id.*
56.   *Id.*
57.   EKMAN, *supra* note 8, at 41.

conspired with the actor—we cannot claim that he committed the crime of lying.

And so it is with deceiving doctors. When patients make appointments with their doctors, they know their doctors are concerned with restoring their patients' health—and will say and do anything to achieve that end. Patients are not deceived when doctors exaggerate their concerns and urge their patients to immediately change their lifestyles—give up smoking, stop eating good-tasting food—in order to avoid some dire consequence. And when psychiatrists are retained as experts and testify in court, the judge, the lawyers, and the jury all know of the doctors' pro-patient, pro-treatment biases.[58] All participants in the trial are on notice, and if they are deceived, they have only themselves to blame—not the innocent, though lying, psychiatrists. If our analysis is thought to be fallacious, society must prove us wrong by holding accountable psychiatrists, and all others,[59] who deceive without obtaining the victim's consent.

58.　Although in Part IV, *supra*, we identify various types of non-paternalistic doctor biases, we note that paternalism is the most common bias encountered, especially among psychiatrists in clinical practice. "[R]eports of the demise of paternalism are premature." Frank Kee, *Patients' Prerogatives and Public Health*, 312 BRIT. MED. J. 958, 958 (1996). The author questioned whether doctors give patients sound and unbiased information about therapeutic choices and whether they communicate effectively with patients. *Id.* at 958-59. *See also* Silverman, *supra* note 6 (suggesting that medicine reinforces benign paternalism by undervaluing patient involvement in decision making.). For an interesting debate on the propriety of medical paternalism, compare Julian Savulescu, *Rational Non-Interventional Paternalism: Why Doctors Ought to Make Judgments of What is Best for Their Patients*, 21 J. MED. ETHICS 327 (1995) (rejecting the role of doctor as mere fact provider, and proposing that the doctor should argue rationally with the patient about the doctor's conception of what is best for the patient) with Hilary Madder, *Existential Autonomy: Why Patients Should Make Their Own Choices*, 23 J. MED. ETHICS 221 (1997) (asserting that Savulescu's model posits the doctor as judge of what is, all-things-considered, best for the patient thereby undermining patient choice and threatening patient autonomy).

59.　For example, police officers routinely lie to suspects during interrogations in order to secure confessions. Should society continue to countenance lying in order to achieve the greater good of truthful confessions and guilty verdicts imposed on guilty defendants? *See The Lying Game*, SAN DIEGO UNION-TRIB., May 21, 1999, at E1.

[36]

Case Studies in Confidentiality

DAVID LOWENTHAL, MD, JD

Although a fundamental principle of psychiatric practice in general and psychotherapy in particular is that interactions and communications between clinician and patient are private, there are certain instances in which there is an affirmative obligation to break confidentiality, or in which such a breach is at least legally (if not ethically) permitted. The author examines the various situations in which a psychiatrist's obligation to maintain confidentiality is modified or even completely overridden by some other competing clinical, legal, or ethical principle or obligation. He reviews the duty to protect third parties (*Tarasoff* warnings), situations in which a psychiatrist's loyalties are divided between the patient and some other entity, person, or principle (dual agency issues), the release of information in emergencies, and the reporting of abuse. He also discusses the circle of confidentiality and which individuals are deemed to be inside and outside that circle. Guidelines for the use of clinical material in presentations and publications are reviewed. The author also considers how psychiatrists should deal with knowledge of past criminal behavior that they may obtain during the course of treatment. Finally, the author discusses the need to carefully document the rationale for whatever course of action is taken. (*Journal of Psychiatric Practice* 2002;8:151–159)

KEY WORDS: confidentiality, *Tarasoff* warnings, emergency release of information, circle of confidentiality, publications, presentations, documentation

The patient is... expected to bring up all manner of socially unacceptable instincts and urges, immature wishes, perverse sexual thoughts—in short, the unacceptable, the unthinkable, the repressed.[1]

Psychiatric practice in general and psychotherapy in particular are based on the notion that interactions and communications between the clinician and patient are private.[2] Patients have come to expect that what they share with their psychiatrist or therapist is confidential and are often surprised to discover that there are exceptions to this fundamental principle of psychiatric practice. Indeed, clinicians themselves may be unaware of certain instances in which there is an affirmative obligation to break confidentiality, or in which such a breach is at least legally (if not ethically) permitted. In other cases, clinicians may in good faith not realize that issues of confidentiality are even implicated, or may misconstrue their obligation to the patient or a perceived obligation to some third party.

In this article, I examine the various situations in which a psychiatrist's obligation to maintain confidentiality is modified or even completely overridden by some other competing clinical, legal, or ethical principle or obligation. These include so-called *Tarasoff* warnings or the duty to protect, various state reporting statutes

and regulations, and clinical emergencies. Issues that generally receive less attention, such as the presentation of clinical material in an academic setting or journal, are also discussed. Each section of the article is organized around a clinical vignette that provides a context for the discussion of a particular exception to confidentiality. I have also included a section on the importance of adequate documentation, since a clear, contemporaneously recorded rationale for one's actions is probably a clinician's best protection from medicolegal problems down the road. Finally, while this paper is written for psychiatrists, many of the points also apply to other disciplines that practice psychotherapy.

State law governs the legal regulation of most aspects of psychiatric practice. While Federal law may at times be relevant (e.g., federal regulations regarding the confidentiality of patient records maintained in federally assisted substance abuse programs [42CFR2.3]), generally the

LOWENTHAL: New York State Psychiatric Institute.

Please send correspondence and reprint requests to: David Lowenthal, MD, Box 88, New York State Psychiatric Institute, 1051 Riverside Drive, New York, NY 10032.

CASE STUDIES IN CONFIDENTIALITY

statutes, agency rules and regulations, and case law of each state provide the legal parameters for a clinician's behavior with respect to his or her patients. This holds true for laws governing civil commitment, refusal of treatment, medical malpractice, and, of relevance for this paper, a clinician's obligation to maintain confidentiality. A clinician providing care to patients must be familiar with the laws of his or her jurisdiction, as the law can differ markedly from state to state. For example, while all states have statutes requiring the reporting of suspected child abuse (although the threshold for reporting may differ), as the next section indicates, not all states have adopted the *Tarasoff* duty to protect third parties. Remember that ignorance of the law does not provide protection from liability.

THE DUTY TO PROTECT THIRD PARTIES: *TARASOFF* WARNINGS

Case 1. *A patient is in a dynamically oriented psychotherapy focusing on the patient's anger towards his wife. After several months of treatment, the patient confides to his psychiatrist that he has recently been having fantasies of killing his wife. While he does not feel that he would ever actually act on these fantasies, he states that at times he is not sure. After some exploration, the psychiatrist is not confident as well.*

Case 1 concerns the psychiatrist's duty to protect third parties, which was first enunciated in 1976 by the California Supreme Court in *Tarasoff v. Regents of the University of California*.[3] Prior to that, the duty of outpatient psychiatrists to protect third parties who could be harmed by their patients' actions had not been litigated. (Inpatient psychiatrists, however, could be held liable for harm caused by discharged patients based on theories of negligence and malpractice.) The Court in *Tarasoff* found that the "special relationship" between a patient and his psychotherapist is sufficient to support such a duty. Following the *Tarasoff* decision, a psychiatrist or psychotherapist in California had an affirmative obligation to do what is reasonably necessary to protect third persons if he "determines, or pursuant to the standard of his profession should determine, that his patient presents a serious danger of violence to another."[3]

Arguably, no other legal holding has generated more discussion or anxiety among mental health professionals than the *Tarasoff* case. Dire predictions were made about the negative impact the *Tarasoff* decision would have on the practice of psychiatry and psychotherapy

because of patients' reluctance to be candid in the face of potential disclosure by the clinician.[4] However, there is little evidence that this has taken place. In fact, research suggests that most practitioners were breaking confidentiality prior to *Tarasoff* in situations in which disclosure was deemed to be ethically or clinically warranted.[5,6]

Several points about the *Tarasoff* decision should be noted.

First, the California Supreme Court initially held in 1974 (*Tarasoff I*) that the clinician had a duty to ***warn*** a third party if the clinician felt that "a warning [was] essential to avert danger arising from the medical or psychological condition of his patient."[7] This duty to warn was expanded to a duty to ***protect*** third parties when the Court reheard the case in 1976 (*Tarasoff II*).[3] The distinction, which is often lost in the confusion surrounding the implications of the Court's decision, is critical because merely warning a third party does not necessarily discharge the duty to protect that individual. On the other hand, hospitalizing the patient often does provide protection for a threatened third party and, in instances in which the patient is successfully treated, may preclude the need for a warning. In fact, the "expansion" of the duty from warning to protection has probably served to promote the maintenance of confidentiality in the long run, as clinicians can protect third parties and their patients, along with the sanctity of the therapeutic relationship, through an effective hospitalization.

Second, as emphasized above, one must remember that this is an area governed by state law. Many states have enacted statutes defining the scope of the duty to protect and specifying the method of discharging that duty (see *The Duty to Protect* by Felthous,[8] p. 140 for a table listing statutory options for discharging the duty to protect). Courts in some states have extended the duty to protect,[9] while others have limited or even held that there is no such duty.[10]

Finally, psychiatrists and other mental health professionals must be guided by good clinical practice. They should not allow the fear of potential liability to drive their actions. Indeed, I believe that, when clinicians act reflexively based on perceived medico-legal considerations with the primary aim of protecting themselves from liability, as opposed to basing decisions on their clinical judgment, this is more likely to result in a bad outcome for all parties involved, including the clinician. Accordingly, when a clinician is faced with a potentially dangerous patient, as in the example given in Case 1, he or she must make a clinical risk assessment concerning the likelihood that the patient might act on these fan-

CASE STUDIES IN CONFIDENTIALITY

tasies. In making such an assessment, the patient clearly also needs to be involved. In most instances, it is helpful for the patient to understand the dilemma facing the clinician. For example, in the case described above, the clinician should make the patient aware of the tension between the psychiatrist's legal (and presumably ethical) duty to protect his patient's wife, on the one hand, and the psychiatrist's obligation to keep his patient's communications confidential, on the other. The patient also needs to appreciate that the patient and psychiatrist are working collaboratively to ensure that the patient does not do something to his wife that he, the patient, will regret, and that protecting the patient's wife is primarily for the benefit of the patient (and obviously his wife). Ideally, the psychiatrist and patient will together make a decision to involve the patient's wife and/or to hospitalize the patient and/or undertake some other clinical intervention (such as increasing the frequency of visits or changing medication).

Hopefully, only in extreme cases would a clinician need to invoke a *Tarasoff* duty by unilaterally making a disclosure to a third party without the knowledge if not consent of the patient. Even in states in which the law is silent or in which the courts have rejected the *Tarasoff* rationale, a psychiatrist may feel ethically compelled to breach confidentiality to prevent harm to a third person, albeit it at the risk of a lawsuit by the patient for breach of confidentiality. Given the anxiety and confusion surrounding *Tarasoff*, it bears repeating that the clinician's thinking and interventions should be driven by what makes clinical sense under the circumstances.

DUAL AGENCY ISSUES

Case 2. A psychiatrist is treating a patient in a state prison, seeing him monthly and treating him with an antidepressant. The patient mentions that his cellmate has told him that he is planning to break out of prison the following week along with several other inmates, using knives constructed in prison. The psychiatrist suggests that the patient go to the prison authorities with this information, since it is seems likely that the escape attempt will place individuals at risk of serious injury or even death. The patient adamantly refuses, stating that there is no way he would consider doing that.

By dual agency, I am referring to treatment settings in which a psychiatrist's loyalties are divided between the patient and some other entity, person, or principle.

The psychiatrist is thereby faced with a conflict of interest that interferes with his duty to act solely in the best interests of his patient. When a psychiatrist's primary obligation is not solely his patient's welfare, but also involves the interests of another person or entity, clinical and ethical dilemmas can arise. This may be the case in a number of treatment venues, such as psychiatrists treating inmates in the criminal justice system, psychiatrists treating individuals on behalf of law enforcement agencies (e.g., the police), and, in some instances, even individuals being seen in settings where they work.

A patient may not be aware of the extent to which his doctor's loyalty is pulled in different directions, potentially to the detriment of the patient. In other words, when the psychiatrist must balance institutional or other concerns against what is in the best interests of his or her patient, the psychiatrist may end up taking actions that cause indirect or even direct harm to the patient. In such cases, the dictum of "do no harm" ceases to be a guiding principle, but simply one principle that must be weighed against other competing principles, usually without any clear guidance on how to reconcile the conflict.

The subspecialty of forensic psychiatry is an area of practice in which the best interests of the patient are often not even relevant. When performing a forensic evaluation, forensic psychiatrists, whose primary function is clearly not to advance a particular patient's interests, but to seek the truth with respect to an evaluee, are ethically obliged to begin evaluations by disclosing the nature of the evaluation and the limits on confidentiality.[11] Evaluees in forensic settings are entitled to what is in effect a kind of *Miranda* warning.[12] However, the possibility of conflicting loyalties in settings in which the psychiatrist's role is less clear (e.g., treating patients in correctional settings or on behalf of an employee health service) raises the issue of what patients are entitled to know about competing demands made upon their doctor, and at what point in the treatment they should be informed of this.

A psychiatrist working in a correctional setting clearly has an obligation toward his patient and a corresponding obligation to maintain his patient's confidences. However, this obligation is modified by the exigencies of working in a prison and the employer's expectation that the clinician will protect the interests of the institution. While this competing duty would, for example, presumably compel the psychiatrist to stop a prison riot if he knew one was imminent, it is less clear whether the duty subsumes alerting the prison authorities to other potentially dangerous acts where the likelihood of violence is less clear.

CASE STUDIES IN CONFIDENTIALITY

Whatever the answer to this question, it would seem that patients in settings such as correctional institutions have the right to know what are the limits to confidentiality when they enter into a treatment relationship with a clinician who may have dual loyalties.

In Case 2, the psychiatrist must first determine whether he believes that the information he received from his patient was credible. Assuming that he believes it was, he should then weigh the risks and benefits of going to the prison authorities. On the one hand, if he does nothing, there is a risk that one or more individuals could be seriously hurt or even killed. He also knows that his employer would expect him to take steps to stop an escape, even if he learned about it from one of his patients. On the other hand, if he breaks confidentiality, the psychiatrist risks significant damage to any alliance he has with the patient. While a skilled therapist may be able to manage the breach, at the very least one would expect the patient to hesitate before revealing sensitive information in any kind of subsequent treatment. Other inmates may also eventually discover that such communications are not protected and may be reluctant to accept or seek treatment in prison (perhaps based on a misunderstanding of what may prompt a therapist's disclosure). Moreover, the patient could be at risk for physical harm if his cellmate discovers he revealed the escape plan. The psychiatrist, torn by conflicting duties to both his employer and his patient, may or may not have informed his patient that, under certain circumstances, his duty to the institution may override his obligation to maintain confidentiality. Given that the risk of harm to third parties appears significant, and the fact that the psychiatrist presumably does have some obligation to his employer, revealing the information to prison authorities in a way that protects the identity of the patient would seem to be a defensible position. Of course, depending on how much weight one gives to the various risks and benefits as well as to the competing principles involved, one could reach a different conclusion.

EMERGENT RELEASE OF INFORMATION

Case 3. A psychiatrist receives a call at her office from a social worker telling her that one of her patients, a man with schizophrenia in his 50s, is in the local hospital in the midst of what appears to be an acute psychotic episode. She has not seen the patient in several months. The social worker tells her that the patient is in danger of losing his apartment because of nonpayment of rent, but that his eviction can be avoided if a psychiatric history can be documented. The social worker tells the psychiatrist that the patient is paranoid and does not want any calls made to his therapist. The social worker called the psychiatrist despite this prohibition because he did not want the patient to lose his apartment. The social worker asks for parallel history for the purpose of stopping the eviction.

In emergency situations, psychiatrists as well as other clinicians are permitted to reveal what would otherwise be confidential information that, under normal circumstances, would require the patient's consent for release. In order to justify the emergent release of information without consent, several conditions should be met:

1. The circumstances should constitute an actual emergency. One can debate what the term "emergency" means, but certainly an acute threat to the patient's health or safety would qualify.
2. The release of the information must be in the patient's best interests, a condition that is usually met when the patient's physical integrity is at significant risk.
3. The patient's refusal or inability to give consent should appear to be the result of some potentially reversible condition, in which the patient's capacity to consent is at least in question. It is this questionable capacity combined with the emergent circumstances that together override the principle of maintaining confidentiality.

The second two conditions appear to be met in Case 3. There is no reason to think that keeping his apartment is not in the patient's best interests, and it is reasonable to believe that his refusal to allow parallel history is the result of his psychotic state. The issue here is whether the potential loss of an apartment, in essence a physical asset, is the kind of emergency that merits compromising a patient's right to confidentiality. It is possible that, depending on the patient's circumstances and one's own value system, one could decide that either course of action by the psychiatrist (i.e., disclosure or refusal to disclose) is reasonable under the circumstances. Since the patient's refusal to permit contact with his psychiatrist for the purpose of keeping his apartment is in all likelihood grounded in paranoia and psychotic thinking, and the breach of confidentiality is almost certainly in the patient's interests, I believe that a limited breach of confidentiality in this situation would be justified (and probably appreciated by the patient after he is treated). This is one of those clinical situations in which alternative courses of action may be defensible, and the clinician should carefully document the reasoning behind his or her decision.

CASE STUDIES IN CONFIDENTIALITY

REPORTING OF ABUSE

Case 4. A 34-year-old single mother is in treatment for a moderately severe depressive episode. Her psychiatrist learns that the patient is dating a man with a bad temper who regularly disciplines her two children with a belt. The patient is not happy about this but is vague about the nature of the beatings and states that her children are difficult for her to handle alone. When the psychiatrist begins to probe further, the patient becomes guarded and backs off from her earlier statements.

Mental health professionals are subject to reporting requirements in virtually all jurisdictions. The specific requirements are usually mandated under state law and always include reporting of suspected child abuse or neglect; they may also include reporting of abuse of other potentially vulnerable groups such as the elderly and of communicable diseases such as HIV infection. Reporting of impaired physicians may also be required or at least permitted under state law, and the American Psychiatric Association's *Principles of Medical Ethics* state that "it is ethical, even encouraged, for another psychiatrist to intercede" when a psychiatrist jeopardizes the welfare of his patients due to mental illness.[13] Each of these situations represents an exception to the principle of confidentiality in which the clinician is usually obliged (or permitted) to make a report if the requirements of the applicable statute or regulation are met.

When faced with a clinical situation in which some kind of disclosure may need to be made, the psychiatrist should first locate and read the applicable statute or regulation, rather than relying solely on someone else's (often another clinician's) interpretation of the law. To the extent that the law is not clear, consultation with counsel would be indicated. When balancing legal risks and benefits to alternative courses of action, it may be appropriate to consult with risk management personnel as well. Finally, in complicated clinical scenarios, consultation with a colleague might be useful, and can also help insulate the treating psychiatrist from liability in the event of litigation. Whenever a reporting statute may be operative, the psychiatrist should determine who is required to make a report, what evidentiary threshold must be met to justify breaching confidentiality, whether the report is mandatory or discretionary, and precisely what information needs to be reported and to whom. As in most cases when a clinician is deciding whether to take an action that may have adverse consequences for his patient (or for a third party), he or she should carefully document the rationale for making a report, or in the event that the clinician does not believe disclosure is mandated, the reasoning behind the decision not to make a report.

In Case 4, psychiatrists in most if not all jurisdictions would need to consider whether the applicable statute protecting children from abuse and neglect required that they make a report. In all likelihood, they would feel compelled to press the patient further, explaining to her that they are obliged to report suspected abuse or maltreatment of their patients' children. If the patient continued to refuse to elaborate or in effect retracted earlier statements, depending on the threshold that triggers the reporting requirement in that jurisdiction, the psychiatrist should probably tell the patient that without further information he would have to report the case.

The extent to which this interaction, which could take place over weeks if not longer (assuming the child's physical welfare is in no immediate danger) could damage the therapeutic alliance seems obvious. (As in other scenarios, a well-managed breach may not mean the end of the therapeutic relationship but, depending on the circumstances, considerable skill may be required to repair and maintain the alliance.) Nevertheless, in this and other areas, state legislatures have made the decision that the need to protect the public or protect potentially vulnerable populations outweighs other needs of the various professionals who are required to report such matters, including the need of mental health professionals to maintain the confidences of their patients.

THE CIRCLE OF CONFIDENTIALITY

Case 5. A 21-year-old college student is hospitalized with what appears to be a psychotic illness. He is away from home at college, and one of his roommates calls his family and tells them that their son was hospitalized at one of the hospitals in the city. The patient's mother and father get on a plane and track their son down and request to speak to his doctor. The patient's doctor politely informs the parents that their son has refused to give him permission to talk about his condition with them.

The idea of "the circle of confidentiality"[14] is helpful in conceptualizing who may have access to information about a patient without that patient's consent. Again, while there may be state-to-state differences, certain parties are clearly within the circle, such as the clinical staff on an inpatient unit in a hospital or a psychiatrist

CASE STUDIES IN CONFIDENTIALITY

providing supervision to a resident for a patient in psychotherapy. However, assuming no other rationale for breaking confidentiality, such as an emergency or *Tarasoff* obligation, it is important to remember which parties are generally outside the circle. For example, not only are the police deemed to be outside the circle, but even an attorney representing the patient should not be given information without the patient's consent.

The most vexing situations often arise vis-à-vis the patient's family. Members of the patient's family are clearly outside the circle of confidentiality, yet the pull to bring the family inside the circle is strong and often supported by a good clinical rationale as well as common sense. The family is generally a source of great support for the patient, may provide much of the care for the patient, are usually the individuals most concerned about the patient, and may be in a position to first notice a deterioration in the patient's condition. Nevertheless, while clinicians are usually free to gather information *from* family members who already know that their relative is in the hospital (as there is no breach), information generally cannot be provided *to* family members, regardless of how close they seem to be to the patient, without the patient's explicit consent. Because of the importance of family to a patient's treatment, clinicians may be tempted to bypass what is often viewed as a legal formality and simply pass on information to the family. Although such an impulse is understandable, it should be resisted. Consent on the part of the patient can usually ultimately be obtained, and when a patient refuses to give consent, that patient generally is not amenable to working with the family at that time in any event.

In Case 5, it is obviously important for the treating psychiatrist to speak to the patient's family in order to obtain history and provide optimal treatment. Presumably, the patient's parents are very concerned about their son, are eager to provide information, and have many questions for the treatment team. Given the parent's knowledge of their son's hospitalization, information can and should be obtained; however, despite compelling reasons for disclosure to the parents, the vignette does not provide any clear rationale for bypassing the requirement to obtain the patient's consent to share information with his family. The patient should presumably be treated with antipsychotic medication, while at the same time the treatment team should attempt to understand and address the patient's concerns about involving his family in his treatment. Similarly, while the treatment team cannot share information with the family without the patient's consent, someone can take the time to explain to the family the

reasons behind the necessity for consent. (One need only put oneself in the position of a family member unable to obtain any information about a very sick relative to imagine the family's distress.) Hopefully, the patient will eventually give the team permission to share clinical information with his family.

I have not identified any court cases in which a psychiatrist has been held liable for revealing confidential information to a patient's family when the clinician seemed to believe that he was acting in the best interests of the patient. However, cases have arisen under other circumstances in which even the release of information to a patient's wife formed the basis for a finding of liability. In *MacDonald v. Clinger*,[15] a psychiatrist was sued by a former patient for allegedly disclosing confidential information to the patient's wife, resulting in the deterioration of the patient's marriage, the loss of his job, financial difficulty, and, not surprisingly, emotional distress and the need for more treatment. In allowing the suit to go forward, the Court stated: "Disclosure of confidential information by a psychiatrist to a spouse will be justified whenever there is a danger to the patient, the spouse or another person; otherwise information should not be disclosed without authorization."[15] While the opinion does not reveal the content of the confidential information that was disclosed to the plaintiff's wife, clinicians may not recognize in advance the potential harm that might be caused by certain disclosures to close family members. Of course, the clinician should always document the patient's consent, when it is given, or the reasoning behind an unauthorized disclosure.

USE OF CLINICAL MATERIAL IN PRESENTATIONS AND PUBLICATIONS

Case 6. *A psychiatric resident is preparing to present one of her psychotherapy patients in a clinical grand rounds. The patient is a law student at the same university, and the resident has altered biographical data in order to preclude identification of the patient. However, much of the presentation, including what has transpired in the therapy, remains factually accurate. The patient arrives at the session prior to the presentation having seen an announcement for the rounds, and states that he hopes that he is not the subject of the presentation, because "you never know who might hear it."*

In academic settings where a great deal of care is delivered, the discussion of clinical cases is routine.

CASE STUDIES IN CONFIDENTIALITY

After all, most medical professions use clinical cases as a means of training students. While many in the medical community view access to the patient by trainees as the *quid pro quo* of treatment in an academic setting, a patient nevertheless has the right to refuse such access. In situations in which the patient is present, he or she generally has the option of refusing to allow students or others in training to be privy to the clinical interaction. The practice of presenting a case in clinically oriented rounds or in a journal, while commonplace, still raises a number of issues:

- Was the patient ever informed in a general way that his case might be discussed in teaching settings?
- Was he informed about a specific presentation?
- How much can the biographical data be altered without losing essential clinical information?
- What if someone does in fact recognize the identity of the patient?

Presumably, the answer to these and other relevant questions must take into account the nature of the presentation. In other words, presenting the difficulties encountered in the removal of a patient's gall bladder during a novel surgical procedure is less problematic in terms of disclosing a patient's confidences than discussing issues raised in a psychodynamic therapy.

In discussions concerning publications and presentations by psychiatrists, the case of *Doe v. Roe*[16] is frequently cited. In *Doe*, a former patient sued her psychoanalyst 8 years after treatment for damages and to stop the publication of a book that allegedly reported "verbatim" the patient's thoughts, feelings, and fantasies. In granting relief to the plaintiff, the Court rejected the notion that the patient had consented orally during the course of treatment: "Consent was sought while the plaintiff was in therapy. It was never obtained in writing... I need not deal with the value of an oral waiver of confidentiality given by a patient to a psychiatrist during the course of treatment."[16] In other words, the Court seemed to recognize that the voluntariness of a consent given by a patient to her therapist during treatment should be scrutinized closely given the nature of the psychotherapeutic relationship and the potential power of the transference.

The psychiatrist's duty of confidentiality outweighs other considerations, however valid, when publishing or otherwise presenting information for educational or entertainment purposes. Biographical data should be altered so that even someone who knows the patient cannot identify him or her. If this cannot be done, questions then arise as to what will constitute a valid con-

sent by the patient. Some commentators question whether a blanket consent given in advance without any specific presentation or publication in mind (e.g., upon entering into treatment in an educational setting) is valid. Others (like the *Doe* Court) question whether informed consent is ever possible in a psychodynamic treatment.[17] If a clinician is planning to publish an article or book containing clinical material revealed by a particular patient, it would seem reasonable that the patient should be given the manuscript in advance and be permitted to veto its publication if he or she is uncomfortable with it.

In Case 6, the patient can refuse to give his permission to allow the presentation, particularly if there is any possibility that someone who knows him might recognize his identity despite the alteration of biographical data. If the resident believes identification is impossible, she can speak to her patient and perhaps even provide a copy of the presentation if she has reduced it to writing. However, to the extent that she is in the position of trying to persuade her patient to consent, questions about the voluntariness of the consent (including the possibility of coercion) could arise. When a patient continues to insist that the clinician refrain from publicly discussing his case, even in disguised form, the patient's wishes should be given precedence.

KNOWLEDGE OF PAST CRIMINAL BEHAVIOR

Case 7. A patient with bipolar disorder is admitted to an inpatient unit in a manic state. After he is treated and has improved, he informs his psychiatrist that prior to the admission, he robbed a clothing store with a gun and escaped with about $5,000. The psychiatrist remembers that she saw this case in the local news and that another individual was arrested and charged with the crime. The patient, who has no criminal record and a stable work history, refuses to turn himself in, stating that he does not want to risk any potential legal repercussions.

Psychiatrists in many jurisdictions have an obligation to protect victims from future harm brought about by criminal acts of their patients, even if that means breaking confidentiality. However, when a psychiatrist during treatment learns about a past crime committed by a patient, even one involving harm to third persons, the appropriate course of action is much less clear. The crime of misprision of a felony usually requires that an individual both knows about and takes active steps to

CASE STUDIES IN CONFIDENTIALITY

conceal a crime committed by some other person.[18] Other possible criminal offenses that can arise in situations in which an individual has knowledge of the commission of a criminal act, such as obstruction of justice, also generally require some affirmative act on the part of the individual being charged. Therefore, the mere knowledge of a crime committed by a patient should not make a therapist subject to potential criminal charges in most jurisdictions. However, the question would still remain whether a psychiatrist is legally and ethically permitted to make such a disclosure without the consent of the patient.

In Case 7, the psychiatrist would first have to satisfy herself that the patient indeed posed no further risk to any individual. In other words, if the psychiatrist felt that, as a result of his illness, the patient was likely to commit a crime in which he might present a significant risk to others, depending on the law in her jurisdiction, she could break confidentiality relying on a *Tarasoff* duty to protect possible victims. If the psychiatrist believed her patient posed no such risk, she might feel compelled to disclose his admission in order to limit harm to the falsely accused man. While this course of action seems reasonable, one must keep in mind that the psychiatrist presumably owes no duty to that falsely accused individual, but does have a duty to her patient. However, as a practical matter, if the psychiatrist was unable to convince her patient to confess to the crime and then disclosed the crime to law enforcement authorities, it is difficult to imagine a successful suit for breach of confidentiality under those circumstances. The outcome might be less certain, though, if the patient turned out not to have committed the crime or in a case in which no one else had been charged.

DOCUMENTATION

In all the cases described in this article, the clinician must ultimately make a choice between upholding the patient's right to have his or her confidences respected and overriding that right in the service of some competing principle. It is critical to remember that in certain instances clinicians could come to differing conclusions as to the optimal course of action. These opposing courses of action may be reasonable and defensible, since there may be no "right" or even best answer in a particular situation. This may be especially true in those cases in which a clinician feels particularly unsettled and troubled by a decision to either uphold or compromise a patient's confidentiality. The nagging doubts and second thoughts the clinician feels

reflect the virtues of the course of action the clinician chose not to take.

Given the uncertainty surrounding such decisions, it is incumbent on clinicians to carefully document the reasoning underlying their decisions. The standard of medical care for psychiatrists does not require that they make the "correct" decision in each case, but that they engage in a clinical decision-making process that is reasonable under the circumstances. Explanations offered after the fact—that is, subsequent to a bad outcome or after litigation has begun—will always appear self-serving regardless of whether such explanations truly reflect the clinician's reasoning at the time.

The case of *Abille v. U.S.*[19] highlights the importance of contemporaneous documentation. In *Abille*, a 51-year-old man was hospitalized with depression and suicidal ideation in a California military hospital. Four days after admission, following an increase in the patient's privilege level, he apparently jumped from a seventh floor landing and killed himself. There were no notes in the chart documenting the psychiatrist's rationale for increasing the patient's level of privileges. Not only did the Court hold that the failure to maintain notes fell below the applicable standard of care, but the Court stated that the plaintiff's burden to prove causation "can be readily frustrated by the doctor's self-serving testimony, in the absence of contemporary records by which to test it."[19] In other words, the Court would not accept the doctor's attempt to explain his clinical reasoning after the fact in deciding whether the plaintiffs had established a valid claim of negligence.

As in other areas of practice, there are generally no specific requirements as to what must be documented when a clinician is contemplating breaking confidentiality. However, providing more rather than less detail concerning one's rationale for taking a certain course of action is usually preferable. Many clinicians may feel they are too busy to spend much time on documentation, for which they are not reimbursed, but this is a risky and shortsighted strategy. When faced with any clinical dilemma, whether it be, for example, issuing a *Tarasoff* warning or deciding how to manage a suicidal patient, clinicians should at a minimum record the pros and cons, or risks and benefits, of each particular decision, as well as explaining how they arrived at their conclusion.

NEW DEVELOPMENTS

In the wake of the World Trade Center catastrophe in September 2001, the Justice Department announced guidelines that would permit monitoring of communica-

CASE STUDIES IN CONFIDENTIALITY

tions between individuals in federal custody and their attorneys when the attorney general concludes there is a "reasonable suspicion" that the communications are intended to further terrorist acts.[20] The confidentiality of attorney-client communications, particularly in the criminal justice setting, has traditionally been accorded the strongest protections in our legal system for various reasons, including the Constitutional guarantee of the right to counsel. It is instructive to witness what is in effect the evolution of a "national security" exception to confidentiality, regardless of whether it extends to psychiatrists and patients under certain circumstances. These decisions involve balancing extremely important yet competing principles—the need and the right to protect our country from outside threats, on the one hand, versus the right to counsel, on the other. Clearly reasonable individuals—say, for example, an Assistant U.S. Attorney and a lawyer for the American Civil Liberties Union— might hold very different views about which principle should be accorded primacy and which should be sacrificed. This is similar to the balancing that often takes place (and that should, of course, be documented) when a psychiatrist is deciding whether to break confidentiality.

CONCLUSION

The clinician's obligation to maintain confidentiality remains a cornerstone of psychiatric practice. Since state law governs much of civil practice, including the various exceptions to confidentiality, psychiatrists must remain familiar with the laws of the jurisdictions in which they practice. In deciding whether or not to compromise this fundamental principle, a psychiatrist needs to refer to the applicable law. If the law does not provide a clear answer (as is often the case), the psychiatrist then needs to balance the risks and benefits of the alternative courses of action. The decision-making process should be driven by clinical considerations, and reflexive, defensive interventions intended primarily to protect the clinician should be avoided. The psychiatrist's reasoning should be documented with a contemporaneous note; in certain situations, outside consultations may also be appropriate. Finally, we must remember that difficult decisions will often leave us feeling uneasy, but that our discomfort in large part may

reflect the importance of the competing principle that has been compromised, and does not signify that we have made the "wrong" decision.

References

1. Heller MS. Some comments to lawyers on the practice of psychiatry. Temple Law Review 1957;30:401–7.
2. Wettstein RM. Confidentiality. In: Oldham JM, Riba MB, eds. Review of Psychiatry, Volume 13, 2nd Edition. Washington, DC: American Psychiatric Press; 1994: 343–64.
3. Tarasoff v. Regents of the University of California, 551 P2d 334, , 431 (Cal 1976).
4. Anfang SA, Applebaum PS. Twenty years after Tarasoff: Reviewing the duty to protect. Harvard Rev Psychiatry 1996;4:67–8.
5. Wise TP. Where the public peril begins: A survey of psychotherapists to determine the effect of Tarasoff. Stanford Law Rev 1978;31:165–90.
6. Givelber DG, Bowers WJ, Blitch CL. Tarasoff, myth and reality: An empirical study of law in action. Wis Law Rev 1984;2:443–97.
7. Tarasoff v. Regents of the University of California, 529 P2d 553 (Cal 1974).
8. Felthous AR. The duty to protect. In: Rosner, R, ed. Principles and practice of forensic psychiatry, 2nd Edition. New York: Chapman & Hall; 1994:139–45.
9. Lipari v. Sears, Roebuck, 497 F.Supp. 185 (D Neb 1980); Petersen v. Washington, 671 P2d 230 (Wash 1983).
10. Thapar v. Zezulka, 944 S.W.2d 635 (Tex 1999).
11. American Academy of Psychiatry and the Law. Ethics guidelines for the practice of forensic psychiatry. Bloomfield, CT: AAPL; 1995.
12. Miranda v. Arizona, 384 U.S. 436 (1966).
13. American Psychiatric Association. The principles of medical ethics with annotations especially applicable to psychiatry, Section 2:4. Washington, DC: American Psychiatric Association; 1998.
14. Gutheil TG, Applebaum PS. Clinical handbook of psychiatry and the law, 3rd Edition. Philadelphia: Lippincott Williams & Wilkins; 2000.
15. MacDonald v. Clinger, 84 AD2d 482, 488 (NY App Div 1982).
16. Doe v. Roe, 93 Misc2d 201, 215 (NY Sup Ct 1977).
17. Simon RI. Confidentiality in clinical practice. In: Simon RI, ed. Clinical psychiatry and the law, 2nd Edition. Washington DC: American Psychiatric Press; 1992: 51–77.
18. Applebaum PS, Meisel A. Therapists' obligations to report their patients' criminal acts. Bull Am Acad Psychiatry Law 1986;14:221–230.
19. Abille v. United States, 482 F.Supp. 703, 709 (ND Cal 1980).
20. New York Times, Saturday, November 10, 2001: B6.

[37]

The Ethical Limits of Confidentiality in the Therapeutic Relationship

S. A. Green, M.D.

Abstract: *The author explores the moral underpinnings of psychiatric confidentiality in an attempt to define its ethical limits. Knowledge of this standard assumes growing importance as third party incursions into the patient-therapist dyad become increasingly common in day-to-day practice. The APA's AIDS policy on confidentiality and disclosure is offered as an illustrative example of the profession's ability to successfully translate moral deliberation into clinical policy.*

Introduction

Precisely what is entailed in medical confidentiality is uncertain. Growing intrusions into the presumably private environment of the patient-provider dyad which have been justified on the basis of cost containment and protecting the patient and/or third parties [1,2], in addition to long-standing statutory requirements that promote the public interest by compelling the release of certain health data (e.g., the presence of communicable disease), raise difficult ethical dilemmas for all health professionals, but particularly for psychiatrists whose clinical work is so dependent on an atmosphere of trust. It is therefore important for clinicians to clarify in their own minds the limits of confidentiality, and then articulate that standard to patients in an effort to optimally facilitate the collaborative work of therapy.

As Winslade [3] discusses, the concept of confidentiality is integrally linked to a cluster of issues, including confidence, confession, trust, reliance, respect, security, intimacy, and privacy. Because of this close affiliation with companion concepts, a precise definition of confidentiality is elusive. It can be construed in narrow or broad terms; the former perspective relates to *protection of communications* among persons in certain special relationships (e.g., patients and caregivers), the latter to a more general *right to control information* about oneself. Health providers can interpret the concept of confidentiality at many points along this axis, which can significantly affect the degree to which a patient's medical status remains private.

Most clinicians acknowledge that confidentiality is neither absolute nor an objective norm in the daily practice of medicine, but exists rather as a value-laden standard. Siegler's [4] empirical observations concerning the ease with which health care personnel access patients' charts in a general hospital led him to conclude that confidentiality was a "decrepit notion." A paradigmatic example in psychiatric practice occurs when a patient reports serious suicidal ideation, a circumstance that would likely cause a consensus of practitioners to violate confidentiality on the basis of benevolent paternalism; however, that decision is founded in judgments by the clinician that are—at least to some degree—subjective. A more debated issue in psychiatric practice concerns infringements of a patient's confidentiality in order to protect the interests of identifiable third parties, a clinical circumstance that has become increasingly common because of the AIDS pandemic. Legal obligations

Department of Psychiatry and Center for Clinical Bioethics, Georgetown University School of Medicine, Washington, D.C.

Address reprint requests to: Stephen A. Green, M.D., Department of Psychiatry, Georgetown University School of Medicine, Washington, D.C.

to notify individuals at risk for infection with human immunodeficiency virus (HIV) are limited [5] and, consequently, psychiatrists are increasingly faced with a difficult moral dilemma: they must choose between preserving patients' confidentiality and an obligation of beneficence to others, both known and unknown. Because the management of confidentiality is "much more a matter of professional ethics than of legal requirements" [2] (p 315), practitioners should be fully cognizant of the moral underpinnings of confidentiality in order to guide their decision-making in varied clinical situations.

The Ethical Basis for Medical Confidentiality

Two theoretical frameworks provide justification for medical confidentiality. First, a *principle-based ethic*, as set forth by Beauchamp and Childress [6], explores the basis of confidentiality in terms of "the consequences it produces," as well as "the moral principles it expresses." Their consequentialist arguments begin with considerations that echo Winslade's broader theoretical discussion of a world without confidentiality in which "no information about oneself would be treated as confidential . . . [and] relationships among persons would become fragmented and superficial . . . precluding the possibility of certain desirable forms of human interaction" [3] (p 196). Speculating on the effects of such compromised confidentiality within the medical environment, Beauchamp and Childress believe that patients would at least withhold relevant medical data, to the detriment of their treatment, and in the extreme, might choose never to seek needed care. This line of argument—which was specifically discussed in the *Tarasoff* dissent—suggests that the effectiveness of psychotherapy for the individual, and for society at large, would be greatly undermined by growing doubts about the privacy of the therapeutic setting. Weighing short-term, concrete gains derived from breaching confidentiality against less tangible, longer-term objectives (e.g., preserving the sanctity of the therapeutic relationship) is a demanding task. Moreover, debate about the limits of confidentiality cannot be resolved solely on the basis of considerations concerning its instrumental value, because it is a "difficult moral question from the consequentialist perspective . . . whether one rule of confidentiality is better than another rule of confidentiality in achieving the desired objectives" [5]

(p 334). Consequently, the justification of confidentiality also rests on deontologic principles—autonomy and fidelity—which are concerned with intrinsic values, not the consequences of actions.

Autonomy broadly refers to the Kantian notion of a self-legislating will, self-determined direction, as opposed to control by others. Respect for persons as autonomous agents is the accepted norm of medical practice, as patients determine (in the vast majority of instances) whether they wish to accept treatment. Beauchamp and Childress note that that principle of autonomy "carries over the idea of having a domain or territory of sovereignty for the self and a right to protect it," which is closely linked to the right of privacy. They argue that when a person voluntarily grants access to himself—either by consenting to physical interventions (e.g., surgical procedures) or relating intimate thoughts to a therapist—it is an exercise of the right to privacy, the right to control one's life in the medical environment rather than a waiver of that right, since one *chooses* to "reduce privacy with the intention of gaining other important goals through the health-care system" [5] (pp 321–322). By defining privacy in terms of the right to personal autonomy, Beauchamp and Childress argue that confidentiality is, by extension, rooted in the principle of autonomy, as it is the means for maintaining privacy within the medical setting. *Fidelity* is the obligation of health providers to keep all implicit and explicit promises to promote the welfare of patients. Certain relationships have a special moral significance that convey obligations of positive beneficence. Though the content of specific obligations varies with the promises made and the expectations that were engendered by those promises, confidentiality is considered to be a central aspect of the special relationship between patients and their caretakers, even in the absence of specific guarantees. It is conveyed, at least implicitly, by the various oaths ascribed to by health professionals and, consequently, can only be modified or disavowed overtly by practitioners when they feel compelled to delineate ethical claims that take primacy over confidentiality [3] (p 341).

On the basis of these consequentialist and deontologic principles, Beauchamp and Childress conclude that confidentiality is not an absolute condition of medical practice, but rather a *prima facie* obligation subject to infringement in order to meet a "strong conflicting moral obligation" necessitated by idiosyncratic clinical circumstances [3] (p 341). They propose a schema that weighs magni-

S. A. Green

tude of harm against probability of harm in a given situation, and suggest that when there is a high probability of major harm as defined by the number of individuals affected and/or the severity of harm for particular individuals, then the moral obligation to violate a patient's confidentiality increases.

A second theoretical framework for defining the limits of confidentiality in medical practice is a *care-based* ethic. In contrast to moral thinking based on principles of rights and justice, this approach is rooted in concepts of trust and mutual regard. An ethic of care, as discussed by Baier [7], is primarily concerned with interpersonal attachments, and the moral decision-making that emanates from those relationships. Baier objects to theories that seek to impose a general system of principles, arguing that given the diverse moral traditions characteristic of a pluralistic society, none can claim primacy. She questions why a consequentialist or deontologic ethic should prevail as normative, as opposed to simply providing moral agents with guiding precepts. Baier also objects to rationality as the exclusive basis of an ethical theory, and argues strongly that human psychology and the moral emotions play significant roles in the conduct of moral agents. Echoing Hume, she emphasizes that the passions of human nature influence moral decision-making "by positively re-inforcing our responses to the good of cooperation, trust, mutual aid, friendship, love, as well as regulating responses to the risk of evil" [7] (p 218). She suggests that a reflective process, rather than reliance on binding universal principles, more accurately expresses morality. Describing how parents transmit ethical knowledge through a developmental process which draws on psychological and social learning that complements rationality, she envisions an analogous situation of ongoing ethical reflection in the development and expression of a society's morality.

Baier believes that ethical decision-making is significantly affected by the context within which it takes place and, consequently, cannot be guided exclusively by the precepts of an ahistorical, broadly drawn theory. This seems a highly reasonable framework for the medical environment which is so focused on case-specific ethical deliberation deriving from the interaction between patient and health providers. Moreover, there is precedent for this approach in resolving fundamental issues of medical practice. Competency determinations, for example, are both task specific

and threshold dependent, two conditions heavily dependent on the idiosyncratic circumstances of the individual patient's medical condition. Informed consent is, by extension, a contextual determination, as it rests on a patient's claim to competency.

Conclusion

There is a high likelihood of concordance as to the limits of medical confidentiality whether determination of that standard derives from ethical decision-making based in care-based thinking or a principle-based method. Baier believes that society should simply decide what constitutes a permissible or unacceptable harm and act accordingly. For example, determinations about the moral limits of confidentiality of an HIV seropositive patient should rest on the degree of danger that individual imposes on others. This reasoning is highly consistent with Beauchamp and Childress' perception of confidentiality as a *prima facie* obligation, based on assessment of the magnitude and probability of harm imposed by guarantees of absolute confidentiality. Whereas a principle-based ethic emphasizes rationality over emotion, and a care-based ethic takes an opposite stance, each approach has a flexibility that provides justification to reveal confidential information related by patients when the welfare of others is significantly threatened. Establishing acceptable moral limits of confidentiality ultimately rests on that determination, regardless of the theoretical underpinning of moral reasoning employed to reach that position.

In 1987, the APA's Board of Trustees approved a report by the *ad hoc* Committee on AIDS which soon became the association's official position statement concerning confidentiality and disclosure when practitioners worked with HIV-seropositive patients [8]. The policy, which embraced the moral principle of protection from harm more strongly than respect for an individual's right of privacy, reflected long-standing historical exceptions to absolute confidentiality which have been traced back to the Hippocratic Oath, embodied in the American Medical Association's first code, and subsequently included in the Code of Ethics of varied professional groups [9]. The APA policy was strongly rooted in legal precedent, the *Tarasoff* decision; however, debate over the limits of confidentiality transcended legal arguments, and required moral deliberation that produced a nuanced policy that attempted to balance ethical claims of confidentiality against protection of welfare of identifiable third parties at risk for exposure to a fatal illness (see Appendix). The policy, which reflected influences of principle-based and care-based thinking, serves as an excellent example of the professional's ability to translate moral deliberation into guidelines for clinical practice. Its strength is in its flexibility which, in the context of a principle-based ethic, allows for a nuanced approach that offers considerable deference to the deontologic principle of respect for autonomy. There is, for example, a strong desire to obviate the need to breach confidentiality by collaboratively working with patients in an attempt to help them disclose their HIV status to at-risk third parties. Only when these measures fail does the policy advocate a reasonable weighing of autonomy against the competing bioethical principles of beneficence and nonmaleficence. Its flexibility is also reflected in a contextual (e.g., case-specific) approach which reflects the influence of a care-based ethic. The policy ultimately reduces ethical debate to a straightforward question as to whether it is permissible for clinician's to remain silent in the face of behaviors that threaten the lives of unsuspecting individuals and, like Baier, concludes that such a course is simply a moral wrong.

In sum, the APA's AIDS policy on confidentiality and disclosure combines a fundamentally consequentialist approach with a healthy respect for deontologic principles and the emotional and psychological issues inherent in all moral deliberation.

It successfully addresses the moral debate inherent in this specific clinical situation, while simultaneously advancing guidelines which, in concert, provide necessary criteria for determining the ethical limits of confidentiality in all clinical situations.

References

1. Karasu T: Ethical aspects of psychotherapy. In Bloch S, Chodoff P (eds), Psychiatric Ethics, 2nd ed. Oxford, England, Oxford University Press, 1993, pp 135–166
2. Joseph D, Onek J: Confidentiality in psychiatry. In Bloch S, Chodoff P (eds), Psychiatric Ethics, 2nd ed. Oxford, England, Oxford University Press, 1993, pp 313–340
3. William Winslade: Confidentiality. In Reich WT (ed), Encyclopedia of Bioethics. New York, Free Press, 1978, p 195
4. Siegler M: Confidentiality in medicine—a decrepit concept. N Engl J Med 307:1518–1521, 1982
5. Gostin L: Public health strategies for confronting AIDS: legislative and regulatory policy in the United States. JAMA 261:1621–1630, 1989
6. Beauchamp T, Childress J: Principles of Biomedical Ethics, 3rd ed. Oxford, England, Oxford University Press, 1989, p 333
7. Annette Baier: Theory and reflective practices. In Baier A, Postures of the Mind. Minneapolis, University of Minnesota Press, 1985
8. American Psychiatric Association: AIDS policy: confidentiality and disclosure. Am J Psychiatry 145:541–542, 1988
9. North R, Rothenberg K: The duty to warn "dilemma": a framework for resolution. AIDS Public Policy J 4:133–141, 1989

S. A. Green

Appendix
AIDS Policy: Confidentiality and Disclosure

This policy was drafted by the Ad Hoc Committee on AIDS Policy[1] ad was approved by the Board of Trustees in December 1987.

Introduction

The epidemic of acquired immune deficiency syndrome (AIDS) presents difficult and perplexing issues, many of which involve conflicts between the rights of infected individuals and the society's interest in containing the epidemic. Because these questions are highly controversial and because so many important scientific questions about the disease remain unanswered, a definitive public health strategy has not yet emerged.

Physicians have an important role in controlling human immunodeficiency virus (HIV) infection. However, for physicians, the care and treatment of individual patients is of the utmost importance. Patients must be confident that the issues discussed with their physicians are private and will not be unnecessarily divulged. Certainly, any breach of confidentiality should be a last resort, only after scrupulous attention has been given to all other alternatives.

At the present time, the operational public health strategy promotes voluntary testing while eschewing programs of contact tracing, surveillance, segregation, and other measures that could discourage people from seeking testing. Many troublesome ethical and clinical questions arise in the context of dealing with individual patients, and the purpose of this document is to provide some guidance to members of the profession as they struggle to honor their duty to preserve the confidences of their patients while taking adequate precautions to protect persons who may be at risk of contracting the disease.

Physicians should be aware that state laws may restrict some of the actions recommended in these guidelines. Where conflict exists, attempts should be made to modify the laws in accordance with the principles expressed herein.

---

[1]The committee includes Robert O. Pasnau, M.D. (chairperson), Elissa Benedek, M.D., Dorothy A. Starr, M.D., James Krajeski, M.D., Stuart E. Nichols, M.D., Howard Zonana, M.D., Francisco Fernandez, M.D., Patrick Staunton, M.D., Henry Work, M.D., and Marvin Stein, M.D.

Confidentiality

Physicians have an ethical obligation to recognize the rights to privacy, to confidentiality, and to informed consent of all patients. During the initial clinical evaluation, the physician should usually make clear the general limits of confidentiality. If the physician has reason to suspect the patient is infected with HIV (e.g., seropositive) or is engaging in behavior that is known to transmit HIV disease, the physician should notify the patient of the specific limits of confidentiality. Furthermore, if the physician intends to inquire specifically about the HIV status of a given patient, then the physician should notify the patient about the limits of confidentiality before asking such questions.

Notification of Third Parties

In situations where a physician has received convincing clinical information (the patient's own disclosure of test results or documented test records) that the patient is infected with HIV, the physician should advise and work with the patient either to obtain the patient's agreement to terminate behavior that places other persons at risk of infection or to notify identifiable individuals who may be at continuing risk of exposure. If a patient refuses to agree to change his or her behavior or to notify the person(s) at risk or the physician has good reason to believe that the patient has failed to or is unable to comply with this agreement, it is ethically permissible for the physician to notify an identifiable person who the physician believes is in danger of contracting the virus.

Disclosure to Third Parties

Most states now require physicians to report cases in which they diagnose AIDS to a public health agency; only a few require the reporting of cases of individuals who test positive for HIV. It is ethically permissible for a physician to report to the appropriate public health agency the name of a patient who has been determined by convincing clinical information (the patient's disclosure of test results or documented test records) to be infected with HIV and who the physician has good reason to believe is engaging in behavior that places other persons at risk of HIV infection. Although we recognize that public health agencies have varying responses to the problem at the present time, provision of this information will allow them to take whatever measures they regard as appropriate.

American Psychiatric Association: AIDS Policy: Confidentiality and Disclosure. American Journal of Psychiatry 145:541–542, 1988. Copyright 1988, The American Psychiatric Association. Reprinted by permission.

Boundary Violations and Dual Relationships

[38]

Managing Risk When Contemplating Multiple Relationships

Jeffrey N. Younggren
American Psychological Association Insurance Trust

Michael C. Gottlieb
Dallas, Texas

Entering into dual relationships with psychotherapy patients has been a topic of significant controversy in professional psychology. Although these types of extratherapeutic alliances have generally been considered to be unethical conduct, some authors recently have supported their development as both ethical and, in some cases, even therapeutic (A. Lazarus & O. Zur, 2002). In this article, the authors briefly review the general literature regarding dual relationships and offer the reader guidelines in applying an ethically based, risk-managed, decision-making model that could be helpful when a practitioner is considering entering into such relationships or when such relationships inadvertently develop.

One of us (Jeffrey N. Younggren) recently attended an ethics workshop where the presenter, an attorney, said, "All dual relationships in psychotherapy are unethical or at least run the risk of getting you into trouble with your licensing board." This is a common view pervading the mental health professions, although some have taken an opposing stand, arguing that dual relationships do not always cause harm and can sometimes prove helpful (e.g., Lazarus & Zur, 2002). The coexistence of these opposing arguments may cause confusion because both oversimplify a very complex area of professional practice.

Professional practice abounds with the potential for multiple relationships, and the circumstances under which these types of relationships occur are quite varied. Although psychologists frequently choose to enter into these types of relationship, many may actually be unavoidable, and in some situations one can even

JEFFREY N. YOUNGGREN received his PhD in clinical psychology from the University of Arizona. He is a clinical and forensic psychologist located in Rolling Hills Estates, California. An associate clinical professor of medical psychology at the University of California, Los Angeles, School of Medicine, he also serves as a risk management consultant for the American Psychological Association (APA) Insurance Trust. He is a past chair and member of the Ethics Committee of the APA and the Ethics Committee of the California Psychological Association and currently serves as a member of the Committee on Accreditation of the APA.

MICHAEL C. GOTTLIEB received his PhD in counseling psychology from Texas Tech University. He is a forensic and family psychologist in independent practice in Dallas, Texas. He is board certified (American Board of Professional Psychology) in family psychology, a fellow of the APA, and a clinical associate professor at the University of Texas Health Science Center, Dallas. He is a past member of APA's Committee on Professional Practice and Standards and of the Ethics Committee of the APA. His interests surround ethical decision making and the psychology–law interface.

WE EXPRESS OUR APPRECIATION to Gerald Koocher, Edward Nottingham, and Garnett Stokes for the time they took to review earlier versions of this article.

CORRESPONDENCE CONCERNING THIS ARTICLE should be addressed to Jeffrey N. Younggren, 827 Deep Valley Drive, Suite 309, Rolling Hills Estates, CA 90274. E-mail: jeffyounggren@earthlink.net

conceptualize the avoidance of the dual relationship not only as unethical but as potentially destructive to treatment itself (Campbell & Gordon, 2003). For example, consider the solo practitioner in a very small community, who must of necessity maintain some multiple relationships with his or her patients by virtue of proximity and living conditions. To avoid all contact with patients in this situation would require the practitioner to lead the life of a virtual hermit. To make matters worse, this type of unusual conduct could raise questions in the minds of other members of the community as to why the practitioner acts in such a manner. A socially isolated practitioner will attract few patients and arguably will serve them less well by failing to integrate himself or herself into the community. Such examples have forced the profession to accept the logical position that not all multiple relationships are unethical per se (American Psychological Association [APA], 2002).

The key considerations for practitioners who are faced with deciding if they should participate in a multiple relationship, or who inadvertently find themselves already in such a relationship, involve thoughtful analysis of potential hazards. Our purpose is twofold: First, we focus on how to evaluate and manage such relationships to avoid exploitation of and harm to patients, and second, we discuss how to minimize risk for the practitioner.

We do not extensively review the literature on multiple role conflicts; such overviews already exist elsewhere (e.g., Borys & Pope, 1989; Kitchener, 2000; Lazarus & Zur, 2002; Younggren & Skorka, 1992). Instead, we propose a set of questions that practitioners may use to evaluate whether they should embark upon multiple relationships with patients.

This article should not be seen as a definitive or exhaustive checklist of issues that must be addressed when dealing with multiple relationships. The complexities of professional–client relationships dictate guidance by many factors. We present a series of questions with the goal of assisting practitioners in thinking through these issues broadly and in a more systematic fashion. These questions focus on both the welfare of the patient and the practitioner's need to manage risk to both patient and therapist. We make several assumptions in addressing these issues, which are provided below.

Assumptions

1. *Engaging in multiple relationships has a high potential for harming patients and, as a general matter, should be avoided* (APA, 1992, 2002). The proscription against multiple relationships has a strong foundation in the prohibition against sexual relations with patients. Although sexual misconduct can unquestionably cause harm to patients, plainly constitutes unethical behavior, and violates the law in some states, the concept of multiple relationships extends more broadly and includes many types of nonsexual relationships that possibly may pose danger to patients or risk to the practitioner. These more ambiguous situations establish the need for the following guidelines.

2. *Psychologists have many different types of professional relationships; not all of them involve psychotherapy patients.* The range of potential professional relationships varies so much that we cannot address all such possibilities in this article. Therefore, we confine ourselves to psychotherapy relationships in which the treatment becomes more personal and intense. The issues we address may affect both short- and long-term psychotherapies.

The ethical and risk-management issues that arise in other types of professional relationships and with other types of psychotherapy do not necessarily have the same types or degrees of risk. Logically, those who engage in less intimate professional activities such as biofeedback, consultation, forensic services, and some types of assessment need to be aware of the risks associated with multiple relationships, but the relational dynamics in these situations are often different from those of psychotherapy. However, the reader should bear in mind that individuals who perform these types of functions could also ask themselves many of the same questions prior to entering into the additional relationship with a consumer and could work to resolve risks if such relationships inadvertently arise.

3. *Some multiple relationships are completely unavoidable and even obligatory, such as those that occur in the military* (Barnett & Yutrzenka, 1994). Psychologists can be placed in legally mandated dual relationships by virtue of the roles they occupy. For example, military psychologists are frequently placed in situations in which they are required to engage in administrative evaluations of individuals they treat. Because of frequent personnel limitations, combined with the unique nature of the military mission, psychologists must perform these dual functions or risk being found in violation of the Uniform Code of Military Justice. This paradox is a reality attendant to the unique role of the military psychologist, and it is only through informed consent that psychologists in the military, and others in similar situations, manage these potentially risky conflicts. Although highly problematic, such unique issues reach beyond our intended scope.

4. *Practitioners create risk for themselves and their patients when they make decisions in a vacuum.* We assume that consultation with trusted and knowledgeable colleagues should undergird all steps in the decision-making process. Those who give consideration to entering into a dual relationship should make consultation central to that process.

5. *Good risk management also means providing good care, and these notions are not viewed as mutually exclusive.* This article focuses on providing good care to the patient while also protecting the provider. Although achieving both of these objectives becomes impossible in some circumstances, we believe that they constitute realistic goals in the vast majority of the professional situations practitioners encounter. If one is to assume that good care is generally care that is satisfactory to the patient, we know that satisfied consumers become originators of litigation and disciplinary complaints far less often than those who are disgruntled clients (Hickson et al., 2002).

6. *When adjudicatory panels such as ethics committees or state regulatory boards evaluate cases alleging harmful multiple relationships, they must of necessity focus on the clinician's behavior retrospectively.* When practitioners consider entering multiple relationships, they must think prospectively to consider how professional bodies might evaluate the complaint retrospectively. Therefore, when considering whether to enter into a multiple relationship, a wise course will involve evaluating how those in the future, in an entirely different setting and circumstance, would react to the present conduct. Although a very difficult task, this commonly used risk-management strategy guides our thinking (APA Insurance Trust [APAIT], 2002a).

Questions

1. *Is entering into a relationship in addition to the professional one necessary, or should I avoid it?* Psychotherapy, by its very nature, becomes a uniquely complex interpersonal process. Diagnostic formulations may evolve as more information comes to light, causing treatment planning and goals to change. Simply speaking, one cannot know at the outset where the course of treatment will lead. Seemingly straightforward initial clinical presentations may become highly complex and difficult clinical-treatment situations that even the most experienced practitioner could not have predicted. In these circumstances, participating in dual relationships is fraught with unnecessary risk. Therefore, the best interests of the patient and the practitioner generally dictate avoiding dual relationships whenever possible.

2. *Can the dual relationship potentially cause harm to the patient?* A basic principle of biomedical ethics (Beauchamp & Childress, 1994) is that interventions should not harm patients. In addition, if some harm is a necessary component of treatment, an attempt must be made to minimize it. In this connection, any proposed relationship in addition to the therapeutic one must yield to an analysis of risk of harm (Gottlieb, 1993). That is not to say that a professional entering into a dual relationship must anticipate and prevent all risk, but that professional has a fiduciary obligation to anticipate reasonably foreseeable risks and make every effort to avoid, minimize, and manage them.

Consider the following example. A practitioner in an isolated community agrees to serve on the vestry of the local church. Subsequently, the minister's wife seeks out the practitioner for treatment. The practitioner, knowing that the prospective patient would be forced to travel great distances to obtain services elsewhere, agrees to see her. It would seem that such a decision would benefit the minister's wife, but agreeing to treat this woman has foreseeable risks. What if, sometime after treatment begins, some members of the church become dissatisfied with the minister, and the vestry must decide whether to renew his contract? Because the patient knows of the therapist's position on the vestry, the professional relationship could be seriously damaged even if the practitioner is recused from the vestry's discussions. This example only adds further emphasis to the point that what may seem to be a prudent decision at one time can create risk in the face of subsequent unpredictable events. Although the therapist did not create the problem, the situation must still be managed holding the best interest of the patient paramount.

One may argue that predicting future harm as a function of the additional relationship is an impossibility. The reality is that it is easier to believe that a multiple relationship had risk for harm after harm has occurred and a complaint has been filed. However, adjudicatory bodies will look closely at whether a practitioner considered the possibility of future harm, and if harm were a reasonably foreseeable outcome, the practitioner should assume that sanctions will follow.

3. *If harm seems unlikely or avoidable, would the additional relationship prove beneficial?* This type of dilemma occurs frequently for those who work in isolated communities. For example, what should a practitioner do about purchasing a car from the only automobile dealership in a small town when the owner is also a patient? Could making such a purchase enhance the therapeutic alliance by increasing the patient's trust of the therapist and thereby have a positive effect on the therapy? Or, does purchasing the car increase the patient's sense that the therapist trusts him or her? If the practitioner decided to buy the car from the patient, what is to be done regarding negotiating the price? Should the psychologist pay the vehicle's sticker price? Would doing so lead to resentment on the psychologist's part for being forced to pay more than necessary for the vehicle? On the other hand, would purchasing the vehicle elsewhere cause people to wonder why the therapist avoided the local dealership? This might cause particular problems for the practitioner if strong social pressures exist to support the local economy. In this example, purchasing the car elsewhere not only could raise questions among one's neighbors but also might negatively affect the therapeutic alliance. From this very plausible example, it becomes clear that assessing how patients and practitioners may benefit from additional relationships requires caution, careful thinking, and foresight.

4. *Is there a risk that the dual relationship could disrupt the therapeutic relationship?* This question not only requires careful consideration before treatment but also may require periodic re-evaluation throughout the treatment process. Given the need to minimize risk, the practitioner who chooses to enter into a dual relationship with a client must manage the relationships in such a way that the therapeutic relationship is not damaged by the additional one. Whenever possible, the practitioner has an obligation to discuss the issue of potential harm in detail with the patient prior to entering into the additional relationship. Furthermore, both therapist and client should revisit the topic regularly to prevent damage to the therapeutic alliance. In addition, the therapist has the obligation to anticipate the types of situations that could damage the therapeutic alliance, because it seems highly unlikely that the client would recognize them. This type of forethought might even benefit the therapeutic process by offering a starting point for discussion of these types of issues with the client. The client may feel more cared for and protected by the practitioner, and this may lead to enhanced therapeutic effectiveness.

Consider this example. A young, attractive female patient has symptoms that initially suggest a diagnosis of a mild, acute depression. The male practitioner finds himself in the midst of a painful divorce, and he has recently considered joining a dance group to increase his socialization opportunities. In the process of treatment, he learns that his patient loves dancing and belongs to the very club he considered joining. After obtaining consultation from a trusted colleague and discussing his own struggles with that colleague, he decides to join a different group. As therapy progresses, the practitioner begins to suspect that his patient may have borderline personality disorder.

In this example, the practitioner had no reason to believe any problem would necessarily arise if he joined the same dance club as his patient, but the consultant brought two issues to his attention. First, the practitioner's emotional state made him vulnerable and might lead to his projecting feelings onto his patient that could complicate her treatment. Second, given the relative newness of the patient, he had no way of knowing whether his diagnosis would remain unchanged once her depressive symptoms began to remit. Here the practitioner imposed a restriction on himself that many might believe unnecessary. Nevertheless, in this case the judgment proved highly prudent and preserved the professional relationship by putting the therapeutic relationship at the forefront in the decision-making process.

5. *Can I evaluate this matter objectively?* This very difficult question demonstrates a fundamental of good risk management. One must always assume that a compromise in one's objectivity might reach beyond one's awareness. However, when one is confronted with this type of problem, careful self-evaluation is always a good place to start. Standing back from a potential dual relationship and looking at it, oneself, and one's own motivation will surely help lend clarity to the matter. In addition, reviewing the available literature in this area can also improve one's objectivity and could even provide answers to questions about current professional standards of care.

The only other way to approach answering the question about objectivity begins with obtaining consultation from trusted colleagues. (It is important to note that obtaining consultation from others, such as attorneys, may also be entailed.) The inherent high level of risk associated with acting out unconscious needs, or conscious but neglected ones, makes addressing these types of professional concerns with others extremely valuable. When the answers to questions about personal objectivity are unclear, one should discuss and process them with other individuals to ensure that the answers maximize thoughtful, objective consideration; good clinical care; and sound risk management.

Risk Management

Once a practitioner has addressed the "treatment-oriented" questions above and has decided to proceed with a dual or multiple relationship, he or she should now turn to what we term the "risk-management mode." Because the decision to enter into additional relationships has risk for the patient, the therapy, and the practitioner, he or she must engage in a risk-management strategy that provides protection if charges of unprofessional conduct ever surface as a result of the choice. Although some might see such a strategy as "self-serving," the realities of a litigious society require self-protective conduct. Furthermore, in keeping with our assumptions, we contend that good risk management is also consistent with good clinical and ethical practice. Therefore, when choosing to engage in a dual or multiple relationship, the prudent practitioner should now address the following questions.

1. *Have I adequately documented the decision-making process in the treatment records?* Because the spirit of the law is "If it isn't written down, it did not happen," inadequate documentation can negate the existence and value of the entire decision-making process regardless of how comprehensive and thoughtful it may have been. No matter how well the practitioner may have addressed the questions raised earlier in this article, if the process was not documented, then the protection afforded by having done so is largely lost. Once a complaint or lawsuit is filed, efforts to explain the process without documentation will result in considerable skepticism and will be viewed as self-serving and as an effort to put one's own interests ahead of the patient's. On the other hand, good record keeping can significantly contribute to a strong defense against allegations of professional misconduct (APAIT, 2002a; Nottingham & Hertz, in press). If the record reflects a carefully considered decision-making process that led to the choice to engage in a dual relationship, it can lend great weight to one's defense, even if that choice turned out to be the wrong one.

More specifically, the record should reflect the process by which the choice evolved and demonstrate full consideration of other alternatives. Creating documentation in this manner produces a record that should lead the reader to reach the same conclusion, or at least to have a good understanding of the practitioner's thinking on the matter. To meet this standard, the practitioner should ensure that the record reflects all consultations and logically explains the rationale for the choices made.

Finally, how does the record reflect that the patient has received appropriate information and consents to the additional relationship? Ideally such documentation could take the form of a signed agreement, something that is discussed in the next section, but at the very least this type of consent should consist of a note in the patient's chart. Although a note affords weaker evidence of informed consent, it remains a testament to the fact that some agreement did, in fact, occur. If the record fails to incorporate these considerations, it may leave the practitioner as the only witness who supports the choice. A good record serves almost as a second witness to what actually occurred. If this "witness" provides data supporting the practitioner's choice, it lends great strength to the argument that the choice was a sound one.

Let us once again consider our dancing colleague and assume that he chose to join the club where his patient also danced. Before deciding to join, he spoke with a colleague and discussed his personal vulnerabilities in the situation as well as the possible harm it could cause his patient. He then reviewed the issue with the patient as a matter of informed consent. She understood and felt that his action would not pose a problem for her. After joining the club, he also periodically inquired regarding the patient's feelings in order to address potential transferential issues and documented each of these inquiries at the time. Now, because this prudent therapist created a very strong record of what happened, if the patient were to file a complaint against him, he will stand on much firmer ground when defending himself.

2. *Did the practitioner obtain informed consent regarding the risks of engaging in the dual relationship?* Patients are in relatively less powerful positions with respect to their psychotherapist (Kitchener, 1988). When a practitioner faces a difficult decision that entails the risk of a multiple relationship, he or she should make sure that the client fully understands the issues, the alterna-

tives, and the advantages and disadvantages of each as a matter of informed consent (APA, 1992, 2002; Beauchamp & Childress, 1994). Informed consent, in the era of HIPAA (the Health Insurance Portability and Accountability Act), is increasingly complex, and many consent forms and therapist–patient contracts are currently available commercially, in the published literature, and as part of free risk-management services offered by various organizations (e.g., Harris & Bennett, 1998; APAIT, 2002b; APA Practice Organization & APAIT, 2003). However, the type of informed consent being addressed here would clearly require a detailed addendum to an existing standard form or a separate agreement that clearly sets out the issues addressed in this article.

Generally, it is a good practice to allow patients time to consider these matters before making a final decision (Gottlieb, 1993). If the patient agrees to proceed with the additional relationship(s), then they may proceed.

We hasten to note that patients cannot give informed consent to something that poses severe risk to them and/or is a violation of the law, because these rights cannot be legally waived. A good example is consent to engage in a sexual relationship with a therapist. Even if attempts to use informed consent as a defense in this type of case were made, they would fail.

3. *Does the record show adequate evidence of professional consultation?* In many circumstances, consultation helps to establish that the standard of care was met. Talking with others supports the argument that the decisions made in a given matter were in accordance with the guidance of others who would have behaved in a similar fashion under comparable circumstances. This view of the standard of care can be found in the 2002 APA ethics code, where "reasonable" professional conduct is defined as "the prevailing professional judgment of psychologists engaged in similar activities in similar circumstances given the knowledge the psychologist had or should have had at the time" (APA, 2002, p. 2). Thus, adequate consultation allows the practitioner to say that he or she did what other reasonable psychologists would do under similar circumstances, creating an additional defense against criticism of his or her conduct that is founded on a violation of the standard of care.

As we noted earlier, consultation should not be limited to an exchange that occurred prior to the decision but should occur throughout the treatment process. Finally, as we have emphasized, consultation should always be documented. Too often practitioners fall into the trap of the "hallway consultation" in which neither consultant nor consultee document the conversation. The best practice is to set aside time to meet with a consultant and, for serious matters that potentially have high risk, both should document the consultation (APAIT, 2002a).

4. *Does the record reflect a patient-oriented decision-making process?* Although not an easy task, making notations that reflect a struggle on the part of the practitioner to protect the patient and to make the right choices for the benefit of the patient become a strong defense in legal and ethical proceedings. Even if the choices are arguably incorrect based on subsequent events, the visibility of the process of seeking the right, patient-oriented answer when confronted with a choice of entering into a dual relationship is a very helpful defense.

Consider a therapist who had a patient dying of terminal cancer and the patient wanted the therapist present at the time of death. Is fulfilling this request consistent with the standard of care? Should a psychologist stand a death vigil to please the patient? Is it appropriate to engage in such nontraditional conduct, given the fact that the patient is not going to recover, if it will make the patient happier? And, if the therapist chooses to be with the dying patient, is there any way that the therapist's conduct could be seen as unprofessional and reflective of a loss of objectivity? Although some might argue such conduct is inappropriate, consultation that supported the decision to be with the patient at the time of death would show an attempt to engage in some type of prudent decision-making process, even though other professionals could still question the behavior (Nottingham & Hertz, in press).

5. *Are the sources of consultation credible?* Credibility is difficult to measure as it frequently lies in the eye of the beholder. However, having consulted someone with expertise, not only in the treatment modality being utilized but also in the relevant area of ethics and mental health law, can be a very strong defense. If one does not know how to find such a consultant, contact with local or national professional associations for such a referral can frequently be of great assistance. In addition, these types of consultative services are often provided free of charge to individuals who are members of various organizations, to include the APAIT and the APA Office of Ethics. The individual with whom one consults can be quite important, and, if colleagues of this stature request payment for their consulting services, it is our view that this money is very well spent. Another benefit that comes from practicing in this fashion occurs when the psychologist is sued or his or her license is attacked. Under this circumstance, the consultant can be brought as a witness to testify and, because of being removed from the case and arguably being more objective, may be able to make a stronger argument on behalf of the psychologist than the psychologist could himself or herself.

6. *Do the diagnostic issues matter when considering a dual relationship?* In a word, yes! Logically, entering into a dual relationship with a patient who has a fear of public speaking could be viewed by other professionals as having substantially different risks from those of a patient with a complex borderline personality disorder and a history of childhood sexual abuse. In general, it is our contention that risk is inversely related to the general level of integration of the patient. Multiple relations with patients who are well integrated may present various risks, but these risks are substantially lower than those that occur when a therapist chooses to engage in the same type of relationship with a patient who is seriously emotionally compromised. Multiple relationships in the latter circumstance are almost never a good idea.

Second, there is no question that diagnosis is always provisional. The initial diagnosis is often not the diagnosis with which the patient is discharged. Although multiple relationships may be permissible under certain circumstances with some patients who are well integrated, there is no practitioner who cannot be fooled, miss a diagnosis, or simply learn more information about his or her patient later that would have led to a different decision in diagnostic formulation. Again considering our dancing colleague, much of the risk the therapist runs will depend on the developing diagnosis of the patient, and undiagnosed borderline tendencies pose substantial risk.

Finally, regardless of whether a practitioner believes a choice to enter into a dual relationship with a patient who is compromised is the correct one, he or she must consider the prevailing views of the profession regarding this type of conduct, for it is these views that

will be encountered in the courtroom and during the resolution of the complaint.

7. *Does knowledge of the patient support the establishment of a dual relationship?* How well one knows a patient has a direct impact on the choice to enter into a dual relationship. Inherent in many of the points made throughout this article is a belief that more, and accurate, information about a patient is helpful in determining whether the choice to enter into a dual relationship is a wise one. Although one might argue that this point relates to the previous one, we believe that not all knowledge impacts diagnosis. Thus, a comprehensive understanding of the patient and the complexity of the patient's life, family, and related issues would be helpful in arriving at the "right choice" in this case. In truth, when faced with the risk (to both client and therapist) that could come from being wrong, logically, more information is always helpful. For example, and simply put, knowing that a patient has a long history of litigious behavior could cause one to pause when considering whether to enter into another relationship with that individual.

8. *Does one's theoretical orientation matter when considering a dual relationship?* Theoretical orientation matters because in some cases it may increase risk. Those who practice from a more traditional, insight-oriented approach are most likely to have patients who develop transferential feelings that must be addressed in therapy. These types of treatment modalities generally call for clear boundaries and, whenever possible, the avoidance of multiple relationships. Conversely, the behavioral modalities could be seen by some as being less prone to the complexities of more traditional treatment relationships.

However, for various reasons, those who practice from a cognitive or behavioral perspective are not immune from the difficulties found in traditional therapies. First, such approaches are not always confined to symptomatic treatment. Second, the treatment itself does not preclude the possibility of perceptual distortions on the part of patients and/or therapists. Third, the type of treatment may be modified as the patient improves and his or her therapeutic needs evolve. Changing treatment modalities may also change the nature of the patient–practitioner relationship (Gottlieb & Cooper, 2002), and multiple relationships appropriate to the initial format may not be appropriate to the new one.

These points may be clarified with the following example. A man had what appeared to be a moderate reactive depression, and the psychologist treated him with a combination of behavioral and cognitive techniques. The patient responded well, but in the course of treatment the psychologist learned that her patient was having marital difficulties and offered to change format and began marital therapy. (For guidelines regarding change of format, see Gottlieb, 1995.) As the therapy progressed, it became apparent that both individuals in the marriage had family-of-origin issues that required longer term care than was first contemplated. This rather typical scenario demonstrates that it is not prudent for practitioners to assume that their therapeutic orientation will serve as sufficient protection for them. In this case, the practitioner who chose to engage in a dual relationship with the patient early in the treatment, based on the assumption that the nature of the theoretical orientation would be protective, now learns, as treatment progresses, that the choice may have created unanticipated risk and is now fraught with potential danger.

Implications for Practice

Whether one chooses to enter into a multiple relationship with a patient or inadvertently finds himself or herself in one, significant risks arise for both the patient and the professional. We acknowledge that these types of relationships are not necessarily violations of the standards of professional conduct, and/or of the law, but we know enough to recommend that they have to be actively and thoroughly analyzed and addressed, although not necessarily avoided. This process becomes extremely important in light of the aforementioned risks to both parties.

A professional finding himself or herself facing such a dilemma must address the problem based on the best interests of the client. Careful analyses of the risk for conflicts of interest, loss of objectivity, and disruption of the therapeutic alliance must be made. Following this, the professional must review and discuss the potential difficulties with the client, making the client an active part of the decision-making process. If from this analysis it appears that the relationship is appropriate and acceptable, the therapist must document the entire process and, if possible, make the client a part of that process through the use of a signed informed consent.

Following the completion of this patient-oriented evaluation of the contemplated multiple relationship, the professional must now adopt a risk-managed approach to the problem. That is, he or she must view the relationship and the decision-making process from the perspective of a regulatory or a judicial authority called upon to determine if the professional's conduct was consistent with the standard of care. The psychologist must do all that can be done to evaluate whether the decision to enter into the relationship was reasonable conduct that the public should expect from the average professional in the same or similar circumstances. This must be done through a careful review of a variety of important issues such as diagnosis, level of functioning, therapeutic orientation, local standards, and practices, and through consultation with qualified professionals who could support the decision to enter into the relationship as being consistent with the standard of care. Only after having taken all these steps can the professional consider entering into the relationship, and he or she should then do so with the greatest of caution.

References

American Psychological Association. (1992). Ethical principles of psychologists and code of conduct. *American Psychologist, 47,* 1597–1611.

American Psychological Association. (2002). Ethical principles of psychologists and code of conduct. *American Psychologist, 57,* 1060–1073.

American Psychological Association Insurance Trust. (2002a). *Legal and ethical risk management in professional psychological practice—Sequence 1: General risk management strategies* [Workshop presented nationally]. Washington, DC: Author.

American Psychological Association Insurance Trust. (2002b). *Sample Informed Consent Form.* Retrieved July 2003 from http://apait.org/download.asp?item=INF.doc

American Psychological Association Practice Organization & the American Psychological Association Insurance Trust. (2003). *HIPAA for psychologists* [CD-ROM]. Washington, DC: American Psychological Association.

Barnett, J. E., & Yutrzenka, B. A. (1994). Nonsexual dual relationships in professional practice, with special applications to rural and military communities. *The Independent Practitioner, 14*(5), 243–248.

Beauchamp, T. L., & Childress, J. F. (1994). *Principles of biomedical ethics* (4th ed.). New York: Oxford University Press.

Borys, D. S., & Pope, K. S. (1989). Dual relationships between therapists and client: A national study of psychologists, psychiatrists, and social workers. *Professional Psychology: Research and Practice, 20,* 283–293.

Campbell, C. D., & Gordon, M. C. (2003). Acknowledging the inevitable: Understanding multiple relationships in rural practice. *Professional Psychology: Research and Practice, 34,* 430–434.

Gottlieb, M. C. (1993). Avoiding exploitative dual relationships: A decision making model. *Psychotherapy, 30,* 41–48.

Gottlieb, M. C. (1995). Ethical dilemmas in change of format and live supervision. In R. H. Mikesell, D. Lusterman, & S. H. McDaniel (Eds.), *Integrating family therapy: Handbook of family psychology and system therapy* (pp. 561–570). Washington, DC: American Psychological Association.

Gottlieb, M. C., & Cooper, C. C. (2002). Ethical and risk management issues in integrative therapies. In J. Lebow (Ed.), *Comprehensive handbook of psychotherapy: Vol. 4. Integrative and eclectic therapies* (pp. 557–568). New York: Wiley.

Harris, E. A., & Bennett, B. E. (1998). Sample psychotherapist–patient contract. In G. P Koocher, J. C. Norcross, & S. S. Hill (Eds.), *Psychologists desk reference* (pp. 191–199). New York: Oxford University Press.

Hickson, G. B., Federspiel, C. F., Pichert, J. W., Miller, C. S., Gauld-Jaeger, J., & Bost, P. (2002). Patient complaints and malpractice risk. *Journal of the American Medical Association, 287,* 2951–2957.

Kitchener, K. S. (1988). Dual role relationships: What makes them so problematic? *Journal of Counseling and Development, 67,* 217–221.

Kitchener, K. S. (2000). *Foundations of ethical practice, research, and teaching in psychology.* Mahwah, NJ: Erlbaum.

Lazarus, A., & Zur, O. (2002). *Dual relationships and psychotherapy.* New York: Springer.

Nottingham, E., & Herz, G. (in press). *Promoting practice health: Risk managed documentation in clinical practice.* Sarasota, FL: Professional Resource Press.

Younggren, J. N., & Skorka, D. (1992). The nontherapeutic psychotherapy relationship. *Law and Psychology Review, 16,* 13–28.

Received June 9, 2003
Revision received December 19, 2003
Accepted January 8, 2004 ■

[39]

The Development of Dual Relationships:

Power and Professional Responsibility

Vincent J. Rinella, Jr.* and Alvin I. Gerstein**

Principle VI
"Welfare of the Consumer"

> A. Psychologists are continually cognizant of their own needs and their potentially influential position vis-à-vis persons such as clients, students and subordinates. They avoid exploiting the trust and dependency of such persons. Psychologists make every effort to avoid dual relationships that could impair their professional judgment or increase the risk of exploitation. Examples of such dual relationships include, but are not limited to, research with and treatment of employees, students, supervisees, close friends or relatives. Sexual intimacies with clients are unethical. (American Psychological Association, 1981, p. 636)

Section II

> 1. The requirement that the physician conduct himself/herself with propriety in his/her profession and in all the actions of his/her life is especially important in the case of the psychiatrist because the patient tends to model his/her behavior after that of his/her therapist by identification. Further, the necessary intensity of the therapeutic relationship may tend to activate sexual and other needs and fantasies on the part of both patient and therapist, while weakening the objectivity necessary for control. Sexual activity with a patient is

*Director, Clinical Program Development, Belmont Center for Comprehensive Treatment, Philadelphia, Pennsylvania, 19131 USA

**Director, Psychology Department, Belmont Center for Comprehensive Treatment, Philadelphia, Pennsylvania, 19131 USA.

The authors would like to thank Reba Blau for her assistance in preparing this manuscript.

The American Psychological Association continues to refine its ethical principles, and dual relationships are addressed in a number of principles (see American Psychological Association Ethics code: draft revision, 1992, *APA Monitor*, 2,3,5,38–42.

unethical. (Specifically stated in 1973). Sexual involvement with one's former patients generally exploits emotions deriving from treatment and, therefore, almost always is unethical. (American Psychiatric Association, 1989, p. 4)

Both prohibitions against sexually intimate behavior between the therapist and patient as well as prohibitions against dual relationships have received relatively scant attention until the mid-1970s (Pope & Bouhoutsos, 1986). Even then the focus was on sexual intimacies clearly prohibited for physicians by the Hippocratic Oath. The American Psychological Association did not formerly address these issues until 1981 when the Ethical Principles of Psychologists were codified and published. Standards were not codified by the American Psychiatric Association until the publication of the Principles of Medical Ethics, with annotations especially applicable to psychiatry, published in 1989.

As noted above, the Ethical Principles formulated by both of these two organizations are not explicit regarding non-sexual dual roles or dual role conflicts not involving sexual intimacy, perhaps because they are not as riddled with moral overtones. Nonetheless, even a cursory review of textbooks and guidebooks, (Keith-Spiegel & Koocher, 1985; Lakin, 1991) usually containing hypothetical questionable ethical scenarios, reveals that virtually all non-sexual dual relationships and conflicts of interest are considered unethical. These include: entering into professional relationships with close friends, family members, or employees; socializing with clients and students; accepting referrals of close friends or relations from satisfied current, or former patients, or social acquaintances; bartering psychotherapeutic services for other non-pecuniary services, (including trading psychotherapy for psychotherapy, otherwise known as engaging in peer co-counseling); accepting gifts and favors from patients or former patients; and, most recently, providing "in-situ" therapy, that is therapy conducted outside of the traditional office setting.

In almost all of these cases, while ethics case books, textbooks, and indeed, ethics committees often pay lip-service to the difficulty of establishing hard and fast rules and definitions, unvarying guidelines have evolved in these situations. For example, since it is difficult to differentiate close friends from acquaintances, the fact is that almost any case falling within this general "conflict of interest" area is almost always found to involve unethical conduct on the part of the psychotherapist (Keith-Spiegel & Koocher, 1985). Many of the distinctions which can be applied to a number of dual relationship situations rarely *make a difference* as is evidenced by the ever increasing imposition of sanctions imposed by the Association Ethics Committees on their members (usually admonishments, reprimands, suspensions, or expulsions) and the further sanctions often imposed by licensing authorities (usually suspension or revocation of the license to practice psychotherapy).

Indeed, according to a recent survey, while most causes of action in legal suits brought against psychiatrists involve breach of confidentiality or the failure to obtain informed consent, the most common increasing ethical allegation involves the existence of a dual-role relationship on the part of the psychotherapist (Stromberg, 1988). While any of the cases involving dual relationships may, of course, include cross-references to the violation of other ethical principles, there is no question that dual relationships will usually be at least one issue in an often complex clinical scenario. The current increase in dual relationship cases with concomitant decisions usually rendered in favor of the complainant may be usefully interpreted by reference to the following working hypothesis. The underlying moral and ethical rationale for prohibiting dual relationships, at least as currently articulated, is no longer tenable in view of at least three factors: (a) the rapidly changing parameters of contemporary psychotherapeutic models, (b) a shift in the view that patients have of psychotherapy and psychotherapists, (c) a change in the way psychotherapists view themselves as professionals.

It should be noted at the outset that these three rather fluid parameters are not necessarily independent of each other and that they likely serve to reinforce each other on both the theoretical and practical level. For example, the current shift from therapy based on a psychoanalytically-based model to object relations or inter-personal therapy will naturally influence the potential patients or consumers view of not only therapy (Levenson, 1983), but also his or her view of the role of the therapist. Similarly, the therapist's notion of what it means to be a contemporary psychotherapist will necessarily impact on his or her choice of what therapeutic model to espouse, and, indeed, what sorts of patients he or she is willing and competent to treat. Nonetheless, it is worthwhile to examine each of these issues separately in order to understand their total impact on the ethical principles prohibiting dual relationships.

Rationale Underlying Dual Relationships

Most statements of ethical principle do not include reference to the underlying rationale prohibiting dual relationships except, perhaps, to categorize such a principle under the general rubric of protection of the welfare of the patient. However, one cannot help but be struck by the apparently unquestioned, and always strongly stated, assumptions articulated by most authorities in the field related to the justification for a prohibition on dual relationships. For example, Lakin (1991), notes that, even in dual relationships not involving sexual or other intimate behavior, for example, relationships in which therapists have become business partners of patients whom they are supposed to be treating, or cases of therapists who barter their services to clients or 'exploit' them in various ways, we should always keep in mind the neediness, vulnerability, and dependency of the patient.

> In any of the possible dual relationships with patients, one could use one's professional status and power or influence for exploiting the person one is charged with helping. Even when the terms of a dual relationship may not actually be exploitative, the potential for exploitation renders the therapeutic intention suspect. (p. 30)

Other commentators (Keith-Spiegel & Koocher, 1985; Pope & Bouhoutsos, 1986) repeat the maxim that practitioners function in the context of relationships and, in so doing, automatically take advantage of power over their psychotherapy patients.

Historically, the prohibition against dual relationships received its specific impetus within the parameters of classical Freudian psychoanalysis, the primary tenet of which is that the patient, via the phenomenon of transference, projects onto the therapist those repressed and unconscious feelings originally directed toward parents and other early significant figures. The therapist, functioning as a "blank screen" for these projections, may necessarily be endowed with inordinate power and influence, if only as an *imago* within the patient's virtual psychic space, rather than as a real person within a therapeutic relationship. Indeed, the vulnerability and dependency of the patient resides primarily within the transferential dimensions of the relationship and the exploitative potential of the therapist also derives from this dimension, thereby, perhaps, justifying the view of the patient as a "potential victim" – a view highlighted by Lakin's (1991) somewhat tendentious description.

More recent models of psychotherapy, however, have not only transformed the working through of the transference relationship into a "learning theory" model, but have also given primacy to the interpersonal relationship between therapist and patient. Indeed, even contemporary psychoanalysis has become centered within an interpersonal context as evidenced by the growing interest in transference and counter-transference as therapeutic instruments within an interpersonal context (Levenson, 1983).

To elaborate briefly on this paradigm shift, Levenson (1983) observes that "patients are disabled not by their drives or inadequate defenses, but by an inability to read and interpret the world, to grasp nuance and to operate with sufficient skill to effect the people around them" (p. 40). Such a view of mental disability necessarily shifts the therapeutic field of inquiry from "the meaning of the symptom to the patient as a solipsistic experience to the meaning of the symptom as a social event" (p. 43).

Furthermore, as Levenson (1983) notes from an object–relations viewpoint, and following the work of Winnicott, Mahler and Kohut, psychotherapy becomes a context in which the patient is not a passive victim (as Lakin, 1991, implies) but, rather, actively learns that his perceptions are shaped *in* interaction with others, not . . . *by* the reactions of others (p. 40).

The role of the therapist within this therapeutic model also undergoes a subtle change in that he or she is no longer a blank screen but becomes, instead, a "consensual validator," in Sullivanian terms, "helping the patient distinguish between what is real and what is not . . . (and often) participating with the patient and, simultaneously examining with him their nuances of interaction" (Levenson, 1983, p. 52). This joint and structured "play" between therapist and patient which involves an exploration of messages, metamessages, and meanings, while more than a real-life contract, does demand that the therapist "experience the patient in some real way even if with contempt, disdain or total boredom" (Levenson, 1983, p. 46). And to the extent that this occurs, a "real relationship" is established which expands the parameters of what may or may not be automatically disallowed as a dual relationship.

The shift in the therapeutic paradigm, along with other social, cultural, and philosophical forces has also altered the therapists view of himself or herself as a professional. The existential psychotherapeutic caution not to "become" or identify one's authentic self with what one "does" in the world professionally has become common coinage among psychotherapists and has undercut the professional "role-playing" previously imbedded in the therapeutic relationship. Carefully gauged moments of self-disclosure and an attitude of "being with" the patient in a common quest for understanding allows the therapist to interact with the patient in ways which, again, may expand the parameters of allowable ethical behavior previously prohibited by the dual relationship barrier.

In addition, economic forces which have impacted on the formal structure of psychotherapy by, for example, limiting the allowable number of insured reimbursable sessions and foreshortening the length of the therapeutic relationship in general, have also modified the therapist's view of him or herself as a helping professional. Psychiatrists are increasingly distressed about the amount of paperwork and marketing required to sustain an active practice and their self-concept as "helpers" has slowly fused with that of at least half-time business people.

Viewing these changes from the patient's vantage point also reveals a correlative change in the patient's view of patienthood in the therapeutic relationship. For example, despite the increasing limitations imposed by employers and insurance companies on reimbursement for outpatient psychotherapy, there continues to be an increase in the number of patients seeking treatment for less severe "problems in living" than for serious and debilitating symptoms or conditions. Such patients are often less vulnerable and impaired when entering treatment and, perhaps, as a result, treatment is often scheduled with longer intervals between sessions. Indeed, many therapists see patients only when the patient has a felt need to see the therapist, not on an ongoing basis, but certainly on an "as needed" basis. Also, patient expectations of what therapy can accomplish have become less demanding and perhaps more realistic, which also may weaken the position that all patients are acutely vulnerable and easily subject to exploitation by a more powerful therapist.

In short, while at the extreme ends of the patient–therapist spectrum, there certainly exist extraordinarily dependent and vulnerable patients and potentially abusive exploitative therapists, parity and equality in the therapeutic relationship seems to be gaining acceptability. Naturally, the power dimensions of the therapeutic relationship should be continually assessed by any competent therapist and equality should never be presumed as an a priori condition. Questions such as the following should be reflexively asked by the practicing therapist, certainly when any dual relationship markers are evident: Is my self disclosure in the patient's best interest? Who am I in relation to this patient? How am I prone to abuse any power I possess? What is the extent of my power in this relationship? Furthermore, since much of the therapist's potential for abuse lies in his or her often countertransferential power to define the patient's reality in ways that suit the therapist, careful attention should be paid to the potential for exploitation in both the therapeutic and personal aspects of any relationship with a patient.

Despite these continuing cautions, however, changes in therapist and patient self-definition and in the nature of contemporary psychotherapy do, in fact, create situations where the current dual relationship rules do not adequately address specific factual contexts. And in the areas of sexual/intimate relations and the broad categories of "business relations" with patients, more flexible rules are being proffered, (Keith-Spiegel & Koocher, 1985; Appelbaum & Jorgenson, 1991). The rationale underlying current rules are being reexamined, and empirical data is being utilized to insure more rational and just decisions in dual relationship situations.

Sexual/Intimate Relationships

This past year has been extraordinary in terms of the number of sexual-dual relationship cases that have occupied mass media attention. Newsweek Magazine "Sex and Psychotherapy," (1992) recently featured a lead article on this topic subtitled, "Doctors Sleeping With Patients—A Growing Crisis of Ethical Abuse," beginning with the most authoritative available data, which reveals that 7% of male psychiatrists and 3% of female psychiatrists admitted having sexual relationships with their patients. In addition, 65% of the psychiatrists surveyed reported treating patients who had been sexually involved with their previous therapists. The article progresses to discuss a number of recent notorious cases, including the case of the Deputy Medical Director of the American Psychiatric Association, who, in March, 1992, resigned his position after it was discovered that he had conducted a 2-year sexual relationship with a female patient.

Legal Regulations of Dual Relationships

Data such as the above combined with the high profile nature of many documented cases have elicited national and international legislative and judicial responses. In the United States, some states have enacted mandatory reporting laws; civil statutes which make it easier to bring tort or malpractice suits, or pursue disciplinary actions against offending therapists, and criminal statutes which make sexual contact with patients both during and following therapy a crime (Appelbaum, 1990).

Reporting statutes, while possessing the potential for general or individual deterrence, are somewhat limited at present in their effect, since no state has mandated reporting incidents without the patient's consent. Apparently, legislatures have received input from the professional community indicating that true, mandated reporting over the patient's objections would compound any injuries felt by patients who already may feel a sense of betrayal. Wisconsin, for example, requires therapists who have reason to suspect a sexual-dual relationship involvement to request the patient's permission to report the incident without revealing patients' names, if patients so desire (Appelbaum, 1990). Even given these limitations, reporting statutes are extremely important given the fact that, as a recent national survey indicated, therapists rarely report patient's past sexual involvement with previous therapists to professional associations or legal authorities (Gartrell, 1987).

Most states have enacted civil statutes which facilitate the filing of malpractice suits by injured patients against their therapists. For example, the Minnesota statue is crafted so that "it is not a defense to the action that sexual contact occurred outside a therapy or treatment session . . . " (Appelbaum, 1990, p.

16). These new statues also often allow suits to be brought by former patients, since they define the period of illegal contact anywhere from 6 months to 2 years after the termination of therapy. Also, "Minnesota's law extends the statute of limitations, after which suits cannot be brought, to five years after the events in question" (Appelbaum, 1990, p. 16).

Other procedural aspects of these statutes, which make it more likely that a patient or former patient will file a civil action, include the provisions of both the California and Minnesota statutes which restrict discovery and introduction into evidence by the defendant of information concerning the plaintiff's sexual history unless the Court deems it relevant (Appelbaum, 1990).

Patients have begun to bring judicial legal actions against therapists who have violated the prohibition on therapist–patient intimacy and Appellate Courts have begun affirming therapist–patient sexual intimacy as a legitimate basis for malpractice or tort actions (Pope & Bouhoutsos, 1986). For example, in *Roy v. Hartogs*, (1976) the psychiatrist claimed that he had sex with a patient in order to effect a cure for her lesbianism and the Court rejected this defense. Also in *Zipkin v. Freeman*, (1968) during the course of treatment, a psychiatrist persuaded his patient to engage in nude bathing, have sexual relations with him, and leave her husband. The Court in this case found for the plaintiff on malpractice grounds, commenting that "regardless of psychiatric theories whether transference withdrawal, or otherwise this relationship (and the doctor's acts) passed the point of which anyone could logically believe that they had any reasonable connection with professional services" (Stromberg, 1988, p. 462). We might also note that while the award amounts of these civil suits has varied depending on the state in which they occur, at least a few of the judgments have been very substantial.

Sexual contact between patients and therapists has also been criminalized in the United States. Therapists have been sued for battery, for violating the prohibition on therapist–patient sexual relations, and some have also been convicted of statutory rape when they have engaged in sexual relationships with minor patients (Stromberg, 1988). In addition, at least four states—Colorado, Minnesota, North Dakota, and Wisconsin—have passed laws making patient/ therapist sex a criminal offense, usually a felony, which may carry both prison sentences and fines as penalties. A patient's consent to the sexual relationship is not allowed as a defense to the charge in any of the states mentioned, and Minnesota has also extended criminal liability to therapists who have sexual relationships with former patients who are "emotionally dependent" on them (Appelbaum, 1990).

In terms of international trends legally prohibiting sexual contact between therapist and patient, it seems clear that "some foreign countries . . . prohibit sexual conduct between therapists and patients but others ignore this very real ethical and legal problem" (Coleman, 1989, p. 578). In England, for example, the law imposes liability for damage to the patient, even in a non-sexual personal relationship. Further, the failure to follow General Medical Council regulations prohibiting sexual contact may result in criminal liability, although the regulations do not deal with a relationship "between a doctor and person whom the doctor has attended professionally in the distant past" (Coleman, 1989, p. 588). However, in these cases, liability may attach under common law apart from any violation of the regulations, as in the case of *Landau v. Werner*, (1961) where an English psychiatrist was found guilty of negligence and a breach of duty to his patient when he engaged in a social relationship that began following the termination of psychotherapy (Coleman, 1989).

Canada, Australia, New Zealand, Norway, Finland, and Brazil have not passed any specific legislation prohibiting sexual contact between patient and therapist, although all of these countries, and others, prohibit such contact in either medical or psychological codes, and such behavior is generally found to be a serious professional and ethical violation of same. Also, in Sweden, psychotherapists "are included in general legislation concerning relationships when one of the parties is in a 'dependent position' " (Coleman, 1989, p. 598), while in West Germany, general rules "governing ordinary persons" (Coleman, 1989, p. 601) are applied to psychotherapists so that civil or criminal liability may attach in certain circumstances. However, very few cases involving psychotherapists have been reported in these countries.

Finally, in the Middle East, both Saudi Arabia and Kuwait, while possessing very strict rules against sexual contact, also have no reported cases of violations in this area. In the case of Saudi Arabia where law prohibits psychiatrists from being alone with a patient of the opposite sex during a therapeutic session, the penalty for sexual intercourse, if proved, is very severe. Unmarried psychiatrists may be flogged 100 times and permanently lose their license or employment, whereas a married psychotherapist can be executed "if he confesses or if the sexual act was seen by four witnesses" (Coleman, 1989, p. 594).

Ethical Prohibition of Sexual Dual Relationships

As Appelbaum (1990) (probably the most thoughtful commentator on this thorny subject) pointed out, the "criminalization of patient–therapist sex is an indication of popular impatience with the seeming difficulty that professional associations have had in stemming the tide of cases. Unless newer educational efforts are markedly more successful, we are likely to see responsibility for the problem increasingly assumed by legislatures" (p. 16).

One year later, Appelbaum and Jorgenson (1991) spearheaded such an "educational effort" by concluding, in a controversial and well-reasoned article, that an absolute ban on sexual contact "is not essential to protecting former patients and that a 1-year waiting period after termination, during which even social contact would be precluded, should minimize problems and allow former patients and therapists to enter into intimate relationships" (p. 1466).

In addition to mounting a preemptive strike against further legislative prohibitions, this proposal utilized existing data to reexamine the rationale for prohibiting therapist–patient sexual contact after termination of treatment — thereby introducing empirical evidence into what has historically been structured as a theoretical debate.

For example, noting at the outset that the results of various surveys demonstrate a clear split between those mental health professionals who think post-termination sex might be acceptable and those who think it unethical, Appelbaum and Jorgenson (1991) carefully analyze further survey data to argue that the reasons sexual contact with current patients should be prohibited (i.e., a coercive element in the relationship and a fraudulent representation by the therapist, combined with a patient's impaired ability to make rational decisions) are much weaker when used to justify a complete prohibition on post-termination sexual contact. For example, "studies of post analysis transference suggest it is used to facilitate reality based adaptive responses to new situations" (p. 1470).

A clear conceptual analysis of the coercive component in any post-termination relation reveals that, like transference feelings, the effect on patients diminishes, although it does not altogether disappear over time. Appelbaum and Jorgenson (1991), find it even more difficult to argue for the existence of an inherent fairness in a therapist–patient post-termination sex prohibition pointing out that, for most purposes, the fiduciary relationship ends and the therapist's fiduciary obligations certainly diminish greatly when therapy is concluded. Finally, they note that, while the existing data is rare and often fragmentary, it is very uncertain to what extent former patients are likely to be harmed by sexual contact.

In sum, through a careful reexamination of the rationale prohibiting patient–therapist sex, as well as the utilization of appropriate data, they demonstrate that "the justifications for preventing sexual contact with psychotherapists after termination of treatment are weaker than for pre-termination sex" (p. 1470), and that "while valid concerns regarding impaired patient decision-making ability and some aspects of coercion remain, there are insufficient grounds to warrant an outright ban on sexual contact after termination of therapy, particularly given the general presumption that a person's choices should be respected" (p. 1471). Appelbaum and Jorgenson's argument for a 1-year waiting period is also buttressed with data reflecting the contemporary realities of clinical practice and the changing perceptions of therapists and patients. One could, of course, arbitrarily, or otherwise, disagree with the paper's conclusion. In fact, the results of an excellent study conducted by Silbertrust (1992) indicate that the longer it had been since therapy ended, the more likely it was that the client had contacted the therapist and that the frequency of the client's thoughts about their former therapist was unaffected by the length of time since termination. Silbertrust concludes, quite logically, that a "waiting period" such as Appelbaum and Jorgenson (1991) suggest may provide little protection against unethical behavior and that, in fact, the old adage "once a client always a client" may be true.

More important, one could accept Appelbaum and Jorgenson's (1991) conclusion as a general rule and reasonably argue for exceptions or "outer limits," also based on empirical data. For example, Gutheil (1991) has explored a number of commonalities found in the patient population claiming therapist sexual misconduct, including specific dynamics of vulnerability, aspects of borderline personality disorder, previous sexual abuse, and various bonding mechanisms. While not a sharply etched victim profile, such characteristics, if identified and documented prior to, or during therapy, might militate for a much longer waiting period than 1 year — perhaps forever. Similarly, Olarte (1991), drawing on admittedly unsystematic data, has attempted to investigate characteristics of sexually abusive therapists. Again, if such characteristics could be more or specifically articulated and identified, one might attempt to combine these with victim characteristics to fashion a risk management proto-col, ultimately an ethical algorithm or calculus, which might in specific in-stances determine that Appelbaum and Jorgenson's (1991) 1 year waiting pe-riod should be extended, contracted, or even abolished.

Irrespective of their conclusions, Appelbaum and Jorgenson's (1991) heuris-tic approach to the question of therapist–patient sexual contact should be adopted in examining other dual relationship issues. The utilization of empiri-cal data combined with a conceptual clarification of the justification for any ethical rule is certainly more conducive to rational decision-making than either the futile search for operational definitions of terms such as "close friend" or "acquaintance," or the equally futile attempt to answer functionally wrong-headed questions such as "when is a patient no longer a patient?" Their ap-proach also minimizes the chances that the decisions rendered by ethics com-mittees on any given case or controversy are little more than the projected collective conscious or unconscious values which committee members some-how feel violates a given ethical rule.

Non-sexual, Dual Role Relationships

A new view of the therapeutic paradigm and the roles and expectations of both therapist and patient, combined with an assessment of relevant data and a careful reexamination of the rationale underlying dual relationship prohibi-tions will also help stifle the "knee-jerk" responses of ethics committees when evaluating the exploitative potential of alleged non-sexual conflicts of interest. For example, the more egalitarian flavor of the interpersonal paradigm may bode well for the permissibility of certain therapist–patient "bartering" ar-rangements, since even the most cogent case against a flat prohibition of same rests on a series of tenuous assumptions that the patient's vulnerability will usually result in an unequal exchange of services or an agreement which has unlimited potential for abuse.

Similarly, the blanket prohibition against socializing with patients might withstand reexamination in view of the changing nature of therapist–patient expectations and interactions. Incidental, even intermittent contacts with pa-tients outside of therapy might not always be accepted as conclusive evidence that the boundaries of ethical behavior were exceeded, particularly if the ra-tionale for prohibiting dual relationships is not violated within a specific fact situation. The focus of any inquiry in these cases might be the actual parame-ters of the power relationship from the vantage of both therapist and patient, rather than a futile attempt to decide whether the degree of social contact was acceptable when measured against an ideal, often illusory, standard. The therapeutic treatment of fellow employees or even colleagues might well be ethically permissible in specific fact situations, particularly if the potential patients seek out the therapist because, for example, they want to enter treat-ment with someone they are familiar with and know to some degree. At the very least, it might be appropriate and ethical to, on occasion, attend special events in the patient's life such as a wedding, Bar Mitzvah, or piano recital.

Finally, the process by which the therapeutic relationship is established and negotiated contains critical variables that may bear heavily on whether it should be deemed unethical as violative of the rationale for prohibiting dual relationships. For example, a frank and candid sharing of the parameters and potential pitfalls of moving from a friendship to a therapeutic relationship, which sharing would likely reflect a more interpersonal therapeutic view of therapy, might comfortably create an exception to the general rule prohibiting therapy in such a situation.

The following vignette, which represents an actual dual role issue confronted by one of this paper's authors, is instructive and will serve to exemplify the flexibility proposed throughout this paper as the rationale prohibiting dual relationships is revised and reexamined in the light of contemporary therapeutic reality.

A physician contacted a psychotherapist for therapy whom he had not seen for 10 years, but who had, at one point, been his next-door neighbor when the physician was in residency training. At that time there had been a degree of socialization between the families, which included visiting back and forth. Furthermore, both the therapist and the physician/patient were graduates of the same undergraduate school and had shared reminiscences of those experiences. Although there had been no direct contact between the two for 10 years, there had been several cross-referrals of patients, indicating a business relationship. It would appear on first blush that providing psychotherapy to the physician would present a real danger to the therapist as a business relationship was already in existence, as was an acquaintance/casual friend relationship.

The therapist agreed to see this individual for a single session, the goal being to help him find a referral to a more appropriate therapist. The patient indicated: (a) that he would not go to another therapist; (b) if the therapist would not see him in therapy, he, in turn, would not seek out help and simply blunder along with his anguish; and (c) there was nothing in his history to indicate any deterioration of family relationships or his functioning in the work setting other than for mild depression and the decrease of enjoyment in his job due to a pending malpractice suit.

The therapist agreed to provide therapy to him under the following conditions; (a) both must be continually vigilant so as not to allow the therapy to slip into friendship issues, since both had enjoyed each other in social situations in the past, (b) there would be areas of concern having to do with his relationship with his father that may not be handled well since the transferences that would develop could be strongly colored by the previous friendship, (c) during this period of time no cross-referring would take place, and (d) the comfort level of working together would be reviewed in four sessions and a decision made for more extensive therapy.

The course of the therapy (40 sessions) was successful with respect to the dysthymia and guilt reduction with his demonstrating an increased capacity to be appropriately assertive. A year later the therapist received a call for a follow-up session. This was prompted by the father of the patient being diagnosed with what proved to be a fatal illness. The patient was still unable to deal effectively with his father or share his feelings with him. Yet he very much wanted to do so. Fortunately this was dealt with while the father was still alert enough to be responsive.

Following his father's death, the patient notified the therapist of the event. The therapist paid a house call to offer condolences to him and the rest of the family. Also, during the course of the therapy, the therapist and patient had been invited to a social event where seating was prearranged and, in fact, they were placed next to each other. At that time the topic of conversation dealt with social niceties appropriate to the earlier relationship as neighbors, including a sharing of pictures of their families. Fortunately, the sessions prior to and following this event were devoted to discussing the need to shift from a therapeutic to a social relationship and back.

It is clear, with this patient that three separate aspects of what are usually and traditionally viewed as dual relationships took place, all of which seemed not to have intruded negatively upon the therapeutic relationship, primarily because of the relative emotional strength of the patient and the guidelines and concerns that were clearly stated prior to any shift of relationship. Five years following the situation, the former patient and therapist have returned to cross-referring professionally.

Conclusion

In non-sexual dual relationships, great flexibility can be considered, even in the context of ongoing therapy as there are significant social and therapeutic factors which militate against a total prohibition of such dual relationships. However, one must be ever vigilant of the potential power relationship between a therapist and a client.

Within the domain of sexual activity, it is generally agreed that while therapy is in progress such activity should be forbidden. With great caution, a sexual relationship at least 1 year post-termination of therapy can be considered.

References

American Psychological Association. (1989). *The principles of medical ethics with annotations especially applicable to psychiatry.*

American Psychiatric Association. (1981). Ethical principles of psychologists. *American Psychologist, 36,* 633–638.

Appelbaum, P. S. (1990). Statistics regulating patient–therapist sex. *Hospital & Community Psychiatry, 41,* 15–16.

Appelbaum, P. S., & Jorgenson, L. (1991). Psychotherapist–patient sexual contact after termination of treatment: An analysis and a proposal. *American Journal of Psychiatry, 148*(11), 1466–1472.

Coleman, P. G. (1989). Sexual relationships between therapist and patient–different countries, different treatment. *The Journal of Psychiatry and Law,* Winter, 577–623.

Gartrell, N., Herman, J., Olarte, S., Feldstein, M., & Localio, R. (1987). Reporting practices of psychiatrists who knew of sexual misconduct by colleagues. *American Journal of Orthopsychiatry, 57,* 287–295.

Gutheil, T. G. (1991). Commonalities in the profile of a victim of sexual misconduct. *Psychiatric Annals, 21*(11), 661–667.

Keith-Spiegel, P. G., Koocher, G. P. (1985). *Ethics in psychology: Professional standards & cases.* New York: Random House.

Lakin, M. (1991). *Coping with ethical dilemmas in psychotherapy.* New York: Pergamon Press.

Levenson, E. A. (1983). *The ambiguity of change.* New York: Basic Books.

Olarte, S. W. (1991). Characteristics of the sexually abusive therapist and potential for treatment and rehabilitation. *Psychiatric Annals, 21*(11), 657–660.

Pope, K. S., & Bouhoutsos, J. C. (1986). *Sexual intimacy between therapist and patients.* New York: Praeger.

Sex and Psychotherapy (1992, April). *Newsweek*, pp. 53–57.

Silbertrust, D. (1992, January). *When is a client no longer a client: An examination of post-termination dual relationships*. The Law-Psychology Bulletin, p. 7.

Stromberg, C. D. (1988). *The psychologist's legal handbook*. Washington, DC: The Council for the National Register of Health Services Providers in Psychology, 277, 279.

This Couldn't Happen to Me: Boundary Problems and Sexual Misconduct in the Psychotherapy Relationship

Donna M. Norris, M.D.
Thomas G. Gutheil, M.D.
Larry H. Strasburger, M.D.

Drawing on their own consultative experience illustrated by case vignettes and with support from the professional literature, the authors discuss the perennial problematic issue of boundary violations and sexual misconduct, aiming at an audience of both experienced and novice clinicians. The authors review the difference between boundary crossings and boundary violations and stress the therapist's responsibility to maintain boundaries. Therapist risk factors for violations include the therapist's own life crises, a tendency to idealize a "special" patient or an inability to set limits, and denial about the possibility of boundary problems. Factors exacerbating patient vulnerability, such as overdependence on the therapist, seeking therapy to find an intense relationship or even "true love," and the acceptance by childhood abuse victims of an abusive therapy relationship, are discussed. Consultation and education—for students and for clinicians at all levels of experience—and effective supervision are reviewed as approaches to boundary problems. (*Psychiatric Services* 54:517–522, 2003)

A board-certified psychiatrist saw a woman in individual psychotherapy for ten years. During the course of the therapeutic relationship, he negotiated with her to sell his two of his boats, sight unseen. Additional transactions involved sales of her personal property to him: Waterford crystal, china, and a silver service, the last of which was appraised at $1,600 but was purchased by the psychiatrist for $200. In the same year he accepted a refrigerator and a dining table with six chairs as gifts. During the course of these commercial transactions, the patient had run up a significant bill with the psychiatrist. She sold her father's coin collection to the psychiatrist for $1,000 as a means of get-

ting one of the boats into the water. Within a year, the bank repossessed the boat and the patient declared bankruptcy.

This vignette is just one among many cases in the spectrum of behaviors in boundary problems with patients. The last quarter century has produced an extensive literature aimed at clarifying the nature of the psychotherapy relationship and the variety and complexity of possible boundary difficulties in the therapeutic dyad (1–12). Television and movie dramas have portrayed boundary dilemmas in various ways, humorous and straight; consider the television program *The Sopranos* and the film *Analyze This*. Despite broad agreement in psychiatry that sexual

misconduct and other boundary violations can cause notable harm to patients, some of our most senior and accomplished practitioners and teachers continue to find themselves embroiled in these difficulties. Next to suicide, boundary problems and sexual misconduct rank highest as causes of malpractice actions against mental health providers. Nevertheless, psychiatric training about boundary issues has continued to be ineffective despite today's wider awareness of these caveats, increased recognition of the severe dangers to patients, threats to psychiatrists' licensure from complaints to boards of registration, and professional ostracism. We speculate that these deficits of modern psychiatric training and practice may reflect the additional pressures of managed care—fostering a paradigm shift in psychiatry away from psychotherapy and toward pharmacology and excessively brief psychotherapies—but that the result is the same: We continue to see a steady stream of boundary violations, both sexual and nonsexual, in all psychiatric contexts (13).

We believe that, despite wide publicity, denial—"This couldn't happen to me"—must also play a significant role in the persistence of the problem.

Intensifying the complexity of boundary dilemmas is a form of backlash, expressed as strong criticism of boundary theory by a few scholars (14–16). These authors chide proponents of boundary theory for promoting technical therapeutic rigidity, excessive concerns with risk management, stultification of flexible inno-

The authors are affiliated with the program in psychiatry and the law at the Massachusetts Mental Health Center of Harvard Medical School, 74 Fenwood Road, Boston, Massachusetts 02115 (e-mail, dmnorris@aol.com).

vation, and proposals of procrustean prescriptions of proper performance. Nonetheless, among the vast majority of practitioners, sensitivity to boundary issues remains an essential element of good clinical work that merits attention in training and practice.

Despite growing awareness of boundary issues and possible harms of boundary violations, the problem of maintaining boundaries obviously continues, as shown by the case vignette above. In this overview of the topic we aim to clarify, particularly for novices in clinical work, the theory behind boundary maintenance and the related pitfalls commonly encountered in the therapist-patient relationship. We examine therapist factors that make the development of boundary problems more likely, patient factors that make responding to the problems more difficult, and common issues in the dyad. We also provide suggestions for resolving these conflictual issues while preserving the efficacy of the therapy.

Basic concepts

A boundary is the edge of appropriate professional behavior, a structure influenced by therapeutic ideology, contract, consent, and, most of all, context (1). Additional information about boundary theory may be found elsewhere (2,3,5,17). Boundary violations differ from boundary crossings, which are harmless deviations from traditional clinical practice, behavior, or demeanor. Examples of crossings include helping up a patient who has fallen, giving a patient an emergency taxi fare in a snowstorm, or accepting an invitation to attend a wedding. Neither harm nor exploitation is involved. Boundary violations, in contrast, are typically harmful and are usually exploitive of patients' needs—erotic, affiliative, financial, dependency, or authority. Examples include having sex or sexualized relations with patients, exploiting patients to perform menial services for the treater, exploiting patients for money or for financial demands beyond the fee, and generally using patients to feed the treater's narcissistic, dependent, pathologic, or sexual needs (1).

Although intentional breaches of

boundaries clearly focus on exploiting the patient, violators are often not aware that any exploitive action has occurred—for example, employing a student patient, rationalized as helping the patient with the cost of the therapy. However, this boundary violation creates dual roles, and thus confusion, in the relationship. Patients are governed by no professional code; therefore, maintenance of boundaries is always the responsibility of the clinician. Thus if a patient requests, demands, provokes, or initiates a boundary violation—as many do—the clinician must refuse to participate in that behavior and then must explore the underlying issues,

---

Next

to suicide,

boundary problems

and sexual misconduct

rank highest as causes of

malpractice actions

against mental

health

providers.

---

aided by consultation as indicated. Repeated demands to breach boundaries should prompt personal and consultative review about the viability of the treatment relationship, especially if the boundary issues become the only subject the patient can discuss. As always, documentation in clinical notes of the patient's refusal to discuss other subjects—coupled with the therapist's seeking consultation before, during, and after taking any action that impinges on boundaries—is the best protection against even inadvertent harm to the patient and against liability resulting from one's interventions (17).

Therapist risk factors

This discussion of therapist factors is accompanied by three caveats. First, a therapist's personal problems do not mean a release from responsibility for setting and maintaining therapeutic boundaries; the therapist always bears the professional burden in this regard. Second, discussions of boundary problems sometimes focus on the "bad apple" model: boundary problems and sexual misconduct occur only with a few bad apples, and the simple solution is to kick those persons out of the field (18). This simplistic view misses a central point of our discussion: boundary issues arise in all therapies and for all clinicians, apparently irrespective of the number of years of experience, and even for those practicing only psychopharmacology. The relevant question is whether the difficulties can be successfully surmounted. Third, repeated boundary challenges by a particular patient should lead to a review of whether the treatment relationship is a wise one.

Therapists must learn to recognize the following trouble spots as risk factors for developing boundary difficulties.

Life crises

Empirically, midlife and late-life crises in therapists' development appear repeatedly as common precipitants of boundary problems with patients, although early-career practitioners are not immune from boundary difficulties. For this last group, the challenges include difficulty establishing a practice; an excessive need to please patients, associated with filling empty hours in the schedule; and balancing the demands of family and professional life. For therapists in general, the effects of aging, career disappointments or unfulfilled hopes, marital conflict or disaffection, and similar common stress points are often associated with a therapist's turning to a patient for solace, gratification, or excitement (3,18).

Transitions

Retirement, job loss, job change—even promotion—or job transfer may produce predictable anomie that makes a therapist susceptible to crossing the line with patients. In addition, financial reversals, working with managed care, stock market declines, envy of patient wealth, greed, and other factors may increase clinicians' susceptibility to fiscal exploitation. Indeed, the authors' consultations with other clinicians suggest that some cases of financial exploitation outnumber the sexual ones.

Illness of the therapist
Therapists' illness appears to increase their vulnerability to turning inappropriately to a patient for solace and support, although this topic has been relatively underexplored (personal communication, Duckworth K, April 1990). The authors' consultations with other clinicians suggest that death anxiety and fears of mortality play a role in a therapist's turning to a patient for comfort.

Loneliness and the impulse to confide
A therapist encountering some life difficulty and seeking a "sympathetic" ear may struggle with the need to confide in a patient about financial reversals, marital or sexual problems, professional setbacks, problems with his or her children, and the like. This lapse may precipitate a role reversal in which the patient takes care of the therapist. Indeed, many patients have been someone's "therapist" in their family of origin and may slip with familiar ease into this inappropriate role. In other cases the otherwise laudable desire to find common ground with a patient may miscarry if the therapist indulges a need to self-disclose.

Self-disclosure, one of the most controversial boundary issues, is an issue that often leads to confusion and uncertainty among therapists, ethics committees, and boards of registration (19). Demanding patients at times insist that the therapist disclose personal data to restore symmetry to the therapeutic situation, to demonstrate the therapist's commitment to the patient and the therapy, or to dispel or confirm a fantasy about the therapist that is so preoccupying to the patient that it interferes with treatment. In part, therapists' uncertainty stems from

the empirical observation that self-disclosure is often the final boundary excursion before sexual relations, even though self-disclosure does not in itself lead inevitably to that outcome. Furthering the confusion are the different approaches that different ideologies assign to the role of self-disclosure in clinical work; for example, it may be common in reality therapy but eschewed in psychoanalysis. In the name of "honesty," therapists may slip into countertransference-based interventions, such as "When you say such things, I become sexually aroused; how can we understand that?"

▬

Midlife

and late-life

crises in therapists'

development appear

repeatedly as common

precipitants of boundary

problems with patients,

although early-career

practitioners are

not immune.

▬

Self-disclosure may cause no problems in the therapy, but even in response to seemingly innocent queries, it may intrude on the patient's psychic space or replace a patient's rich and clinically useful fantasy with dry fact, stripped of meaningful affect. To use a perhaps extreme example, a patient who hears that a therapist is Catholic may have greater trouble or discomfort discussing her abortion. Similarly, "Are you married?" may stand in for "Are you gay? Are you available? Have you failed in past relationships?" The point here is that the therapist's in-

ner awareness of longing to self-disclose to or confide in a particular patient may serve as an alert to potential boundary difficulty to come.

Idealization and the "special patient"
Therapists must be alert for early harbingers of trouble in certain of their own countertransference attitudes toward patients (15,20). Typical views commonly associated with problems in maintaining boundaries include viewing the patient as "special"—for example, because of beauty, youth, intellect, artistic creativity, fame or status in the community, or therapeutic challenge. Unsophisticated therapists experiencing erotic feelings toward a patient may find these common, if not universal, feelings highly threatening, creating anxiety that may distort clinical judgment.

Such feelings are an excellent stimulus to seeking consultation or supervision but not to terminating therapy with patients or abandoning them, as some clinicians seem to believe. Sexual feelings, hostile feelings, and boredom are all responses to patients that therapists must handle within the process of treatment unless these reactions become unmanageable or are unresponsive to supervision and consultation. Clues to these attitudes may lie in the therapist's tendency to treat the patient as an exception to the usual rules of the therapist's practice: scheduling excessive or excessively long sessions, especially at the end of the day; giving permission to run up a high unpaid balance; making special allowances for the patient; and having nonemergency meetings outside the office. Therapists seeking consultation on such cases often begin the request with "I don't usually do this with my patients, but in this case. . . ."

Pride, shame, and envy
Therapists with intact self-esteem systems are entitled to take pride in their work, but self-esteem—like all traits—can miscarry through excess and denial: "This couldn't happen to me." One would think that this problem is an especially common one for

the younger, inexperienced therapist, and this is often the case. However, a pitfall that is especially relevant to very senior therapists, who are often sought out for consultation, is their inclination to brush aside the need to seek consultation themselves. Seasoned practitioners may believe that, given their level of experience, they can take risks in this area: "I have good control and I know what I'm doing." We knew of one such therapist, who resisted undergoing such a review on the grounds that he knew the consultant would tell him the relationship with the patient was wrong and should be terminated. In its extreme form, this narcissistic difficulty supports the belief that one is above the law and that the usual rules do not apply.

Problems with limit setting

Some patients—who cannot be blamed for the impulses—tend to press for boundary breaches for a variety of psychological reasons (21). The question then becomes, Can the therapist set appropriate limits on this intrusion? A common barrier to appropriate limit setting is the therapist's countertransference conflicts about aggression or sadism when the prospect of the patient's expected distress, discomfort, or frustration at being told "no" is intolerable to the therapist. When caught in such conflicts, therapists often feel that they cannot refuse patients' requests to violate a boundary. These therapists report feeling pressed or intimidated by patients' unrestrained rage.

"Small town" issues

Closed communities pose another sort of boundary problem. They may be small towns; isolated institutions like schools, convents, and communes; or subcultures with a restricted social compass, such as some gay or lesbian subcultures in urban settings. When there is only one store (or gym, pool, or post office) in town, one cannot avoid the possibility of encountering patients outside the office in nonprofessional settings. Such conditions require more circumspection and care about boundaries, not less. Simon and Williams (22) have provided an excellent discussion of this issue.

Denial

Finally, denial about early problematic situations, which can lead to their evolving into full-fledged boundary disasters, is another common factor in clinical misadventures—particularly with more seasoned and experienced therapists. Evasion, externalization, and rationalization may be used by the therapist to help maintain the pretense that boundary problems are not serious, not harmful, or even not occurring at all. Here, consultation can be extremely useful in gaining perspective, but all too often the need for a consultation is also rationalized away.

> *A small percentage of patients enter treatment specifically to have an intense emotional experience in a relationship of some kind, even a paid one.*

Factors exacerbating patient vulnerability

Patients generally expect that physicians will treat them with respect and act in their best interests. Despite widespread coverage of therapist misconduct in various media, sexual misconduct and its common precursor, boundary violations, are sometimes hard for patients to recognize, or to report if recognized. Moreover, patients with some disorders appear to have more trouble with boundaries than those with other disorders (21). A number of factors may account for these vulnerabilities.

Enmeshment

Patients in psychotherapy may seek dependency rather than autonomy. With some patients, an intensely enmeshed, symbiotic relatedness may result, making it difficult for the patient either to break away or, later, to report the matter. In one case we know of, a patient described feeling tied to a former therapist in part because she was aware there was "something wrong" with what was going on in therapy, but she also felt that it was a basis for closeness with the therapist: "We were in this together." This condition may lead to the patient's clinging tighter to the image of the protective therapist.

Changing roles: from victim to actor

Initially a patient comes to treatment seeking help and, in part through transference, imbues the therapist with healing powers and intent. The patient may then seek a dependent position that precludes questioning or challenging the therapist's decisions or actions. To challenge the therapist would mean altering one's role and identifying with the therapist's aggression to become more aggressive and less dependent. In one case, a patient sought therapy after the traumatic loss of her husband and became involved in an exploitive relationship with a therapist. She was unable to report this relationship to professional boards for some time after the therapy—and the relationship—ended. Once she did so, however, she became more assertive and instituted support groups for abused patients.

Retraumatization

Some patients enter therapy to deal with the effects of previous, often childhood, trauma. For such patients, boundary violations and even outright abuse by the therapist may recapitulate this early experience, including felt helplessness to enact any escape or remedy. The familiarity of the victim role may increase the likelihood of repetition, a condition described by one clinician as the sitting duck syndrome (23,24). Tragically, such repetition of childhood patterns may recur with a subsequent treater.

Shame and self-blame

Patients involved in boundary violations or sexual misconduct often struggle with self-blame, accusing themselves of failure to know better, failure to recognize abuse, having made foolish choices, and so on. Others fault themselves for causing the therapist to lose control or cross the line or for being "too seductive" or believe they bear full responsibility for the misconduct. None of these views, of course, captures the true picture.

"True love"

Though perhaps owing much of its force to the transference, intense feeling can develop in therapy, if only because of the inherent intimacy of the situation, especially if the patient has few or no other relationships on which to draw. The relationship with the therapist may appear the only or the last chance for "true love" in the patient's sphere. Indeed, a small percentage of patients enter treatment specifically to have an intense emotional experience in a relationship of some kind, even a paid one. In one legal case, a patient tearfully told an expert witness that, although she knew that the misconduct was wrong and that she had been taken advantage of, she despaired of ever having such an exciting relationship again.

Dependency

Most boundary violations occur in the context of a helping relationship the patient depends on. It is difficult for the therapist to discern what is help and what is overinvolvement, and it can be very difficult for the patient to give up the relationship. Psychoanalyst Peter Fleming, speaking on a panel on boundaries, noted that a long-term patient who had entered a nursing home began to call him "honey" and "dear" rather than "Dr. Fleming" and to touch him a good deal when he got up to leave her room. He became concerned and raised his concern with her, which led to the patient's sobbing that she had lost her memory and could not recall his name. Had he not dealt with this boundary change, he would not have discovered the problem.

Approaches to boundary problems

Education

One stimulus for this article was our increasing awareness that the changing focus on the economics of health care delivery in this country has altered the nature and content of training for mental health professionals. Psychodynamic theory, with its central discussion of the role of transference, is now taught less and, not surprisingly, requested more by trainees to enhance their understanding of the psychotherapeutic relationship. A psychodynamically naive therapist who becomes the focus of idealization by a patient or who is placed on the positive side of a good doctor–bad doctor split by a patient with borderline personality disorder may feel that the patient is experiencing true love—a situation that must be acted upon. Whatever the current attitudes toward psychoanalysis, our professional schools have an obligation to teach trainees about transference and boundary issues.

Especially for younger clinicians and trainees, concerns are often expressed about the possible stifling of novel, innovative approaches to treatment of a patient or treatment in general. In designing these new approaches, the clinician can avoid both the Scylla of too little attention to boundaries and the Charybdis of too rigid an approach to them by keeping in mind the critical issue of maintaining sensitivity without exploiting the patient. Training techniques using films and videotapes and including presentations by victims and offending psychiatrists provide for more innovative approaches (25,26).

Supervision

Important aspects of the supervisory relationship are the dynamic learning opportunities for all participants, both trainees and supervisors. In another case, a senior forensic psychiatrist was asked to consult about the dangerousness of a former patient who was a possible stalker. Unraveled, the case proved to be one of a patient who began to experience erotic feelings for his female therapist—feelings that she did not know how to handle. Two successive layers of sen-

ior supervisors could not deal with this issue either, and the therapist terminated the psychotherapy on their recommendation. In reality, the baffled patient had taken to hanging about the clinic trying to get a straight answer about what had happened—hence, he was a "stalker."

This vignette underscores the importance of having supervisory resources able to handle dynamic issues at different points in the course of treatment. Supervision provides the ideal setting for emphasizing and clarifying to the trainee how boundary issues inevitably arise in clinical work and how they may be managed successfully. Boundary questions commonly evoke countertransference issues, which may also be profitably explored in the protected supervisory context, as well as in the clinician's personal therapy. Supervisors' openness to seeking consultation presents another learning opportunity for trainees about the complexities of the work.

Consultation

In a grim paradox, consultation—which would often make possible the solution of a therapeutic boundary problem—is all too often scanted, for reasons deriving from the same therapeutic knot that first produced the boundary problem. As noted above, therapists should consistently maintain a low threshold for seeking consultation and should respond positively when a patient requests it and welcome the occasion for both clinical and risk-management reasons. Therapists may refuse consultation because they "know" the consultant would urge them to stop treatment and get out of the relationship—an outcome they could not tolerate. Obviously, this is an inappropriate view of consultation. This individual problem is heightened by denial and resistance on the part of training institutions, especially when the boundary-violating practitioner is a senior clinician who may have trained many in the professional community (27).

The apparent challenges for the field are two. First, lower the threshold for nonjudgmental consultation with peers or specialists at early stages of difficulty. Second, heighten clinicians' awareness about issues and stages of the work that particularly present boundary risks; thus, clinicians will be likely to seek consultation early enough to benefit.

What guideposts can therapists employ to identify the need for consultation? Some have already been discussed as therapist risk factors: illness or changing life circumstances, feelings of specialness about the patient or the tendency to make exceptions, early boundary incursions and crossings, and so on. Other signs of boundary problems may include the feeling of being solely responsible for the patient's life; the feeling of being unable to discuss the case with anyone because of guilt, shame, or the fear of having one's failings acknowledged; and the realization that one has let the patient take over the management of his or her own case. Finally, noting that a patient is provoking the therapist to cross boundaries would be an excellent trigger for consultation.

Conclusions

Boundary problems are universal concerns, not merely the character defects of bad apples in the professional barrel; nor are they relevant only to those doing psychoanalytically oriented psychotherapy; nor are they confined to the offices of the private practitioner. We have presented an overview of characteristics of the patient and of the psychotherapist that may predispose to serious disruptions of the therapy process. Clinicians young and old, and in all settings, must overcome their understandable but damaging reluctance to fully examine this topic in every setting—didactic, training, consultative, and supervisory. Here we have tried to initiate that process and provide an overview for trainees and early-career and senior practitioners. We have done so because history teaches the hard lesson that this matter must be reviewed and revisited at least as often as the *Physicians' Desk Reference*, and for the same reason: the welfare of the patient and the serious and often tragic consequences of missteps in this area for both patient and practitioner (28–30). ♦

Acknowledgment

The authors are indebted to Archie Brodsky, B.A., for critical review.

References

1. Gutheil TG, Gabbard GO: The concept of boundaries in clinical practice: theoretical and risk management dimensions. American Journal of Psychiatry 150:188–196, 1993

2. Simon RI: Treatment boundary violations: clinical, ethical, and legal considerations. Bulletin of the American Academy of Psychiatry and the Law 20:269–288,1992

3. Epstein RS, Simon RI: The exploitation index: an early warning indicator of boundary violations in psychotherapy. Bulletin of the Menninger Clinic 54:450–465, 1990

4. Gabbard GO, Lester EP: Boundaries and Boundary Violations in Psychoanalysis. New York, Basic Books, 1995

5. Gorton GE, Samuel SE: A national survey of training directors about education for prevention of psychiatrist-patient sexual exploitation. Academic Psychiatry 20:92–98, 1996

6. Epstein R: Keeping Boundaries: Maintaining Safety and Integrity in the Psychotherapeutic Process. Washington, DC, American Psychiatric Press, 1994

7. Frick DE: Nonsexual boundary violations in psychiatric treatment, in Review of Psychiatry, Vol 13. Edited by Oldham JM, Riba MB. Washington, DC, American Psychiatric Press, 1994

8. Garfinkel PE, Dorian B, Sadavoy J, et al: Boundary violations and departments of psychiatry. Canadian Journal of Psychiatry 42:764–770, 1997

9. Garfinkel PE, Bagby M, Waring EM, et al: Boundary violations and personality traits among psychiatrists. Canadian Journal of Psychiatry 42:758–763, 1997

10. Hedges LE, Hilton R, Hilton VW, et al: Therapists at Risk. Northvale, NJ, Aronson, 1997

11. Enbom JA, Thomas CD: Evaluation of sexual misconduct complaints: the Oregon board of medical examiners, 1991–1995. American Journal of Obstetrics and Gynecology 176:1340–1346, 1997

12. Schoener GR, Milgrom JH, Gonstorek JC, et al: Psychotherapists' Sexual Involvement With Clients: Intervention and Prevention. Minneapolis, Walk-In Counseling Center, 1989

13. Peterson MR: At Personal Risk: Boundary Violations in Professional-Client Relationships. New York, Norton, 1992

14. Lazarus AA: How certain boundaries and ethics diminish therapeutic effectiveness. Ethics and Human Behavior 4:255–261, 1994

15. Martinez R: A model for boundary dilemmas: ethical decision-making in the patient-professional relationship. Ethical Human Sciences and Services 2:43–61, 2000

16. Kroll J: Boundary violations: a culture-bound syndrome. Journal of the American Academy of Psychiatry and the Law 29: 274–283, 2001

17. Gutheil TG, Appelbaum PS: Clinical Handbook of Psychiatry and the Law, 3rd ed. Baltimore, Lippincott Williams & Wilkins, 2000

18. Gutheil TG: Patient-therapist sexual relations. Harvard Mental Health Letter 6:4–6, 1989

19. Psychopathology Committee of the Group for the Advancement of Psychiatry: Reexamination of therapist self-disclosure. Psychiatric Services 52:1489–1493, 2001

20. Gutheil TG, Simon RI: Between the chair and the door: boundary issues in the therapeutic "transition zone." Harvard Review of Psychiatry 2:336–340, 1995

21. Gutheil TG: Borderline personality disorder, boundary violations and patient-therapist sex: medicolegal pitfalls. American Journal of Psychiatry 146:597–602, 1989

22. Simon RI, Williams IC: Maintaining treatment boundaries in small cities and rural areas. Psychiatric Services 50:1440–1446, 1999

23. Kluft RP (ed): Incest-Related Syndromes of Adult Psychopathology. Washington, DC, American Psychiatric Press, 1990

24. Luepher EL: Effects of practitioners' sexual misconduct: a follow-up study. Journal of the American Academy of Psychiatry and the Law 27:51–63, 1999

25. Schoener G: Preventive and remedial boundary training for helping professionals and clergy: successful approaches and useful tools. Journal of Sex Education and Therapy 24:209–217, 1999

26. Gorton GE, Samuel SE, Zebroski SM: A pilot course for residents on sexual feelings and boundary maintenance in treatment. Academic Psychiatry 20:43–55, 1996

27. Gabbard GO, Peltz ML: Speaking the unspeakable: institutional reactions to boundary violations by psychoanalysts. Journal of the American Psychoanalytic Association 49:659–673, 2001

28. Noel B, Watterson K: You Must Be Dreaming. New York, Poseidon, 1992

29. Duberman M: Cures: A Gay Man's Odyssey. New York, Dutton, 1991

30. Committee on Sexual Misconduct: Crossing the Boundaries. Vancouver, BC, College of Physicians and Surgeons of British Columbia, 1992

[41]

Psychotherapist-Patient Sexual Contact After Termination of Treatment: An Analysis and a Proposal

Paul S. Appelbaum, M.D., and Linda Jorgenson, J.D.

Controversy over the legitimate extent, if any, of sexual contact between psychotherapists and former patients remains intense. In this paper the authors review current approaches to controlling posttermination sexual contact, offer a conceptual framework within which the problematic aspects of therapist-patient sex both during and after treatment can be understood, and develop a set of recommendations for policies that balance the goals of protecting former patients and avoiding unnecessary interventions into consensual relationships. Review of ethical, legal, and administrative controls on posttermination sex revealed considerable heterogeneity of approaches, which appeared to be based on confusion concerning the rationale for restriction. An analysis of the problems with therapist-patient sexual contact suggests four areas of concern: impaired decision making, coercion, fraud, and exploitation of a fiduciary relationship. The nature and magnitude of these problems differ in pre- and posttermination sexual relationships. The authors conclude that clarity of restrictions on posttreatment sex is important, but an absolute ban is not essential to protecting former patients. Rather, a 1-year waiting period after termination, during which even social contact would be precluded, should minimize problems and allow former patients and therapists to enter into intimate relationships. The authors discuss the advantages and disadvantages of this approach over other approaches.
(Am J Psychiatry 1991; 148:1466–1473)

All major mental health organizations condemn psychotherapists' sexual contact with patients in treatment (1–4). However, debate still rages over the ethics of posttermination psychotherapist-patient sexual contact. In a national survey of psychiatrists (5), approximately one-third of those responding thought that sex with a former patient might be appropriate. Two studies of psychologists (6, 7) reflected the same split between those who thought posttermination sex might be acceptable and those who thought it unethical.

One study of psychotherapists on the faculty of the department of psychiatry of a major medical school (8) found that only 29.6% believed that marrying a patient after proper termination of long-term therapy was unethical.

Given this diversity of opinion, it is not surprising that the major medical and mental health organizations have been unable to agree on how to deal with posttermination sexual contact. In 1988, the American Psychiatric Association amended its ethics code to read, "Sexual involvement with one's former patient generally exploits emotions deriving from treatment and therefore almost always is unethical" (1). Two years later, the American Medical Association branded as unethical only relationships in which the physician "uses or exploits trust, knowledge, emotions, or influence derived from the previous professional relationship" (9). In contrast, the American Association for Marriage and

Received Feb. 20, 1991; accepted April 29, 1991. From the Law and Psychiatry Program, Department of Psychiatry, University of Massachusetts Medical School, and Spero & Jorgenson, Cambridge, Mass. Address reprint requests to Dr. Appelbaum, Department of Psychiatry, University of Massachusetts Medical Center, Worcester, MA 01655.

Family Therapy amended its ethics code in 1988 to prohibit sexual contact with former patients only for 2 years after termination (10). Other mental health organizations continue to consider the issue (11, 12); the American Psychological Association recently proposed a draft standard that would require the psychologist to demonstrate that a relationship was not exploitative, and an optional section would add a flat ban on sexual contacts for 1 year after termination (13).

As with the general problem of psychotherapist-patient sex, however, the initiative for dealing with posttermination sexual contact is being taken out of the hands of the mental health professions (14). Given what is generally perceived as the professions' failure to respond adequately to the phenomenon, courts are beginning to establish their own common law approaches to cases involving psychotherapists' sexual contact with former patients, and legislatures are moving to enact statutory penalties, both civil and criminal. Administrative bodies, such as boards of licensure, also are imposing sanctions more frequently for posttermination sexual contact.

These rapidly developing regulatory efforts are marked by the same diversity of approaches that characterizes mental health professionals' reactions to the problem. Even more troublesome, the rules that have been formulated are frequently unclear, leaving patients, therapists, and regulators uncertain as to whether the behavior they are about to initiate or sanction has violated the applicable standards. We believe that a large part of the difficulty stems from a lack of conceptual clarity about why psychotherapist-patient sexual contact after termination is undesirable. Without a sound theoretical basis, regulatory responses have a random quality.

In this paper we review current approaches to controlling posttermination sexual contact. We then offer a conceptual framework within which the problematic aspects of therapist-patient sex, both during treatment and after termination, can be understood. We believe this approach unifies, in a manner consistent with established law, the major reasons offered for rejecting sexual contact with former patients. From this understanding, we develop a set of recommendations for reasonable policies that achieve the goal of protecting former patients while avoiding unnecessarily paternalistic interventions in consensual relationships.

CURRENT APPROACHES

Criminal Law

Legislation criminalizing posttermination sexual contact illustrates the diversity of current approaches to the problem. Statutes making psychotherapist-patient sexual contact a crime have been passed in seven states—California (15), Colorado (16), Florida (17), Maine (18), Minnesota (19), North Dakota (20), and Wisconsin (21). Only three of the states—California, Florida,

and Minnesota—have addressed posttermination sexual contact. Both California and Florida criminalize sexual contact with former patients if the therapist terminates the therapeutic relationship primarily for the purpose of engaging in sexual acts with the patient. In California, however, a therapist may avoid criminal liability even if the relationship is terminated primarily for sex, if the therapist refers the patient to "an independent and objective psychotherapist, recommended by a third-party psychotherapist." The statute appears not to require that the consultation actually take place, as long as the referral is made.

Minnesota provides much more stringent restrictions. Criminal penalties apply if the therapist has sexual contact with a former patient who is "emotionally dependent" on the psychotherapist or if there has been any "therapeutic deception" of the patient. (Therapeutic deception is defined as a claim by the therapist that sexual contact is "consistent with or part of the patient's treatment.") The statute does not limit the period of time covered. Thus, if a patient is emotionally dependent on the therapist even 10 years after the termination of therapy, a criminal complaint may still be made. However, the only case brought under this statute to date failed, as the patient's emotional dependence on the therapist could not be proved beyond a reasonable doubt (22).

Criminalization represents one end of the spectrum of possible sanctions for sexual contact between former patients and psychotherapists. Adoption of criminal statutes has been inhibited by concern that it may not be possible to formulate the elements of the offense clearly enough to pass constitutional muster, e.g., to determine whether the patient is still under the influence of a positive transference (23). As a result, four of the seven states that criminalize sexual contact with current patients have opted to avoid criminal sanctions for posttermination sexual contact. A legislatively authorized committee in Massachusetts, one of the states now considering criminal measures for sexual contact with current patients, has also chosen not to include a provision for former patients (24). Members of the group believed that civil law and administrative boards are better suited for regulation of posttermination sexual relationships.

Civil Statutes

While most civil actions are brought under common law, four states have passed statutes providing a civil cause of action for sexual exploitation of patients by their psychotherapists, whether licensed or unlicensed. All four states—California (25), Illinois (26), Minnesota (27), and Wisconsin (28)—cover posttermination sexual contact between therapist and patient. California and Minnesota prohibit sexual contact with a former patient for 2 years. California makes this an absolute prohibition, whereas Minnesota requires, as it does under its criminal statute, that the patient prove emotional dependence on the psychotherapist at the time of the sexual contact or that the sexual contact resulted from therapeutic deception. Illinois has a statute identical to that of Minnesota except the prohibition extends for only 1 year.

The most far-reaching statute is that of Wisconsin. Wisconsin covers any person who suffers an injury as a result of sexual contact with a therapist who is rendering or has rendered psychotherapy to that person. This covers former patients if harm can be shown. In effect, this statute adopts the rule that, if harm occurs, posttermination sexual relations between a therapist and patient are never acceptable. Thus, prospective determination of the legal status of a relationship between a therapist and former patient is impossible.

Common Law

Most psychotherapist-patient sex cases in which the patient seeks compensation through the courts are brought as malpractice actions, alleging the negligent treatment of a patient (e.g., 29, 30), although actions for negligent infliction of emotional distress (31), intentional infliction of emotional distress (32), and breach of contract (33) have also been successful. Compared with the large number of cases involving claims against therapists for sexual contact with current patients, few appellate cases involving posttermination sex have been reported. In *Noto v. St. Vincent's Hospital and Medical Center of New York* (34), one of the more egregious cases, the court held that the patient had a valid cause of action against a psychiatric resident for a sexual relationship that began after the termination of therapy. The plaintiff had sought inpatient treatment for drug and alcohol dependency and "seductive behavior." After her discharge, the resident who had treated her smoked marijuana and drank alcohol with her and commenced a sexual relationship that resulted in a pregnancy. The court found that the resident's actions constituted malpractice and intentional infliction of emotional distress. Even though the therapy time was brief, the court particularly noted that the doctor's actions were intended to exploit the plaintiff's specific vulnerabilities.

It appears that the courts, at least in some cases, are willing to construe posttermination sexual contact as a negligent act by the psychotherapist that violates an ongoing duty to the former patient. The extent of acceptable contact with a former patient under the common law, however, remains to be determined. *Noto* suggests that egregious exploitation of the patient's illness is particularly likely to result in liability. The same may be true when actions by the therapist during the course of therapy set the stage for posttermination sex (35).

Administrative Board Regulations

Administrative boards have grants of power from the state legislature to perform various functions, such as licensing and regulating professions. Boards regulating the same profession may have different regulations in

different states, and boards overseeing different professions may have different regulations even in the same state. In Florida, the difference between regulations for psychologists and psychiatrists is especially acute. The Board of Psychology provides that "for purposes of determining the existence of sexual misconduct . . . the psychologist-client relationship is deemed to continue *in perpetuity*" (emphasis added) (36). However, psychiatrists in Florida are bound by the regulations of the medical board, which allows sexual contact between psychiatrist and patient *immediately after termination* (37).

A board may either set standards for a profession or leave decisions to be handled on a case-by-case basis. A recent decision by the Massachusetts Board of Registration in Medicine (38) illustrates some of the problems that may arise if a board decides to avoid setting standards. The case involved disciplinary actions against a psychiatrist for posttermination sexual contact. The patient had entered "focused therapy" with the psychiatrist concerning her mother's illness. When her mother died, the patient terminated therapy and began repeatedly phoning the psychiatrist, requesting a personal relationship. Approximately 2 months after the termination of therapy, the psychiatrist met with the patient, put his arm around her, and kissed her but told her that he could not have sex with her. For 3 more months, the psychiatrist met with the patient; the sexual contact went no further than kisses and, on one occasion, a back massage given by the patient to the psychiatrist.

The patient reported this activity to a subsequent therapist and, within 2 weeks of the patient's reporting, the psychiatrist's employment was terminated, even though there were no other allegations of substandard care rendered to any other patients. At the board's hearing, the psychiatrist was found to be "guilty of misconduct within the practice of medicine" and "guilty of conduct which undermines confidence in the integrity of the medical profession and for conduct which shows lack of good moral character." The board sanction included a reprimand, a $5,000 fine, required coursework on transference, and mandatory personal psychotherapy.

The psychiatrist argued in his own defense that he had researched what his ethical role was in relation to a former patient and claimed to have read that "a limited social relationship with a former patient would fall within ethical standards." The board's ethical standards were not clearly set forth, yet the cost of violating them was the loss of the psychiatrist's job and the imposition of disciplinary sanctions.

Professional Societies

Professional societies or associations, such as the American Psychiatric Association or the American Psychological Association, are voluntary groupings of people. Membership is not compulsory, and the governing board has limited power over the members. However, professional societies issue codes of ethics that bind their members and may be highly influential in the de-

PAUL S. APPELBAUM AND LINDA JORGENSON

cisions of other bodies, such as administrative boards. To date, only the American Psychiatric Association (1), the American Medical Association (9), and the American Association for Marriage and Family Therapy (10) have included guidelines for sexual contact with former patients.

In one case brought before the ethics committee of the American Psychiatric Association (39), a psychiatrist who had had sexual contact with a former patient was expelled from the organization. The reviewing committee's decision stated that "the psychiatrist's sexual involvement with the patient constituted exploitation of the 'knowledge, power and unique position that [the doctor] held in the patient's mental life.'" The failure of most professional groups to report their ethics actions publicly makes it difficult to ascertain the frequency with which actions are being taken against therapists for sexual contact with former patients or the point at which an ethical transgression is deemed to have occurred.

WHY SEXUAL CONTACT WITH PATIENTS SHOULD BE RESTRICTED

Current regulatory efforts aimed at posttermination sexual contact are so diverse as to bespeak a lack of consensus on when sexual contact with former patients should be prohibited. Confusion is apparent over whether sexual contact should be prohibited indefinitely or only for a period of time. Some jurisdictions taking the latter approach set a fixed period of time, while others vary the interval according to the characteristics of a particular case. In some cases, sexual intercourse alone is deemed worthy of sanction, while in others behavior that stops short of actual sexual contact may be prohibited.

What is needed to resolve this divergence of approaches is greater conceptual clarity about the critical question concerning this issue: in a society strongly disposed to allow competent adults to enter freely into consensual relationships (40), why should sexual relationships between psychotherapists and former patients be treated differently? Once it is understood why it may be undesirable to honor the decisions of former patients to enter into such relationships, reasonable and consistent rules regulating the behavior can be constructed. We begin by considering the grounds for the existing consensus that we should not respect the decisions of patients to engage in sexual contact with their current therapists and then ask to what extent the arguments apply to sexual contact after termination of treatment.

Psychotherapist-Patient Sexual Contact

Although it is true that our society generally respects its members' decisions, this is not universally the case. Despite our commitment to individual choice, we do not respect choices made when a person's decision-making capacity is substantially impaired, the person is coerced into making the decision, or the decision is based on fraudulent representations by one of the interested parties (41). The co-occurrence of two or more of these factors, even if no one of them is by itself sufficiently pronounced to justify disregard of a person's choice, increases the likelihood that we will not respect the decision (42).

These considerations provide a basis for understanding our unwillingness to respect the decisions of patients to engage in sexual contact with their psychotherapists during treatment. A patient who becomes involved in such a relationship (in the vast majority of cases, the patients are women involved with male therapists [43]) is likely to have a significantly impaired ability to decide whether to have sexual contact with the therapist. This impairment may result from two causes: the underlying distress that brought the patient into treatment, which may continue to cloud the patient's judgment, and the transference toward the therapist that develops (44). The latter is often characterized by an idealization of the therapist, including fantasies of gratifying infantile sexual desires, which compromise the patient's ability to weigh the risks and benefits of sexual involvement (45).

Added to these problems with decision making is the presence of a coercive element in the relationship. The patient has arrived in distress, lodging trust and hope in the therapist's ability to relieve pain. The therapist promises to help but instead seeks the patient's sexual favors, either by requesting sexual contact or by responding affirmatively to the patient's sexualization of the relationship. Even when not stated overtly (e.g., "Have sex with me or I will reject you"), there exists an implicit threat that the patient who decides against sexual contact will be abandoned, thereby suffering additional psychic pain and losing what she believes is the prospect of alleviating the underlying condition. Therapists may also have access to information concerning patients' vulnerabilities that makes it easier to pressure patients into sexual activity (44). Commentators on this subject frequently refer to a "power imbalance" between patient and therapist that impairs the patient's ability to choose (5, 46), but it is the manner in which the power is being exercised, not the mere fact of an imbalance, that is the problem.

There is, moreover, often a fraudulent aspect to the therapist's presentation of the possibility of sexual involvement with the patient during treatment. Although reported cases suggest it is becoming less frequent for sexually involved psychotherapists to claim that sexual contact is part of the patient's treatment, another misleading claim is inherent in the situation: "I can still treat you effectively even if you have sex with me." It is difficult to imagine a case in which this would be true, given the conflict in roles between being a lover and a therapist (47, 48). To encourage patients to believe they can gratify sexual desires with their therapists and continue to receive the treatment they need is to deceive them.

Persons who oppose flat bans on therapist-patient sex often argue that the elements just outlined occur regularly in sexual relationships outside the therapeutic set-

POSTTERMINATION SEXUAL CONTACT

ting. People "in love" have notoriously bad judgment about the qualities of their lovers, differentials in power are common and may even be considered erotic, and only a minority of relationships begin without the telling of a few lies (48). Why should psychotherapist-patient sexual relationships be treated differently?

The answer lies in the unfairness of allowing the psychotherapist to benefit from the patient's compromised decision process while the patient risks substantial harm. A therapist enters into a fiduciary relationship with a patient; that is, the therapist assumes a responsibility to act in the patient's best interests, not against them. This duty is inherent in all physician-patient and therapist-patient relations (49). Yet, while the therapist's sexual desires may be gratified, the available data and clinical experience suggest that many women who become involved in sexual relationships with their therapists suffer harm as a result (50).

Taken as a whole, these factors explain why we will not allow patients to agree to engage in sexual contact with their therapists. The quality of their decisions is likely to be affected by their impaired capacity, the coercive aspects of their situation, and fraudulent representations by the therapists. Further, the very persons who are charged with advancing their interests—their therapists—stand to benefit from the situation at their expense. This also explains why, in rejecting a patient's choice to engage in sexual contact, we place the burden on the psychotherapist to ensure that the undesirable conduct does not occur, at risk of civil or criminal liability should the therapist fail to live up to this responsibility.

The one element of our current policies that remains to be justified is the blanket nature of the prohibition of therapist-patient sex. To be sure, not every sexual relationship in therapy will be characterized by the factors discussed. Some patients may make unimpaired decisions, in the absence of coercion, with a clear understanding of the likely consequences, and without subsequent ill effects. As a society, however, we have reached the conclusion that this combination of events is so unlikely and the converse so probable that an absolute ban on psychotherapist-patient sex during treatment is warranted.

Posttermination Sexual Contact

To what extent does this rationale apply after treatment has ended? We believe that there are still reasons for restricting sexual contact but that it is difficult to justify as sweeping a rejection of patients' choices to have sex with their previous therapists. The major factors that lead to an absolute proscription of sexual contact with current patients are all, to a greater or lesser extent, modified in the posttermination context.

Certainly, the decision-making ability of former patients may continue to be impaired, either because of their primary disorders (recall the facts in *Noto*) or residual transference. The magnitude of that impairment, however, is in question. There is a good deal of contro-

versy about the degree to which transference is maintained after termination and the extent to which a "proper" termination attenuates the phenomenon (48). The existing data on this question (see studies cited in reference 39) are fragmentary, methodologically problematic, often based on single case reports, and in several instances susceptible to interpretations supporting both sides of the debate. Moreover, although some data suggest that patients may retain feelings about their therapists for considerable periods of time (51), it is unclear whether these feelings are of the type or magnitude that would interfere with competent decision making. In fact, some studies of postanalysis transference (52, 53) suggest it is used to facilitate reality-based, adaptive responses to new situations. Given the state of the empirical data, we find it reasonable to assume both that some transference continues after the patient leaves the consulting room for the final time (39) and that for most patients the effect diminishes as time passes.

As far as the therapist's potential for coercing the patient into sexual contact is concerned, that should decrease substantially after therapy is over. The implicit threat that treatment will be withheld if the patient refuses sex is now defused. An unscrupulous therapist might threaten to reveal embarrassing information conveyed during therapy, but, according to reported cases, that is uncommon. On the other hand, personal information revealed in the course of therapy might still be used to manipulate the former patient into agreeing to sexual contact (9). The therapist's potential for coercive influence on the patient has diminished but has not disappeared altogether.

Fraudulent characterization of sexual contact as therapeutic also is less likely once treatment has ended. Similarly, the concern that the therapist might mislead the patient into believing sexual relations will not interfere with the therapy loses much of its force. It may be argued that sex which begins after a properly conducted and terminated course of treatment can retroactively undermine the gains that have been achieved (39). To our knowledge, there are no data addressing this question.

Finally, it is more difficult to make an argument for the inherent unfairness of sex between therapist and patient after the therapy has terminated. For most purposes, the fiduciary relationship ends when therapy is concluded. Therapists, for example, are not obligated to resume therapy at the request of former patients (54). Although some residual obligations remain—confidentiality is the best example—as a whole, the fiduciary duties are not of the same magnitude as during therapy. Further, it is uncertain to what extent former patients are likely to be harmed by sexual contact (55). The published literature is devoid of empirical studies on the effects of relationships begun after termination of treatment, and even anecdotal reports are rare.

In sum, the justifications for preventing sexual contact with psychotherapists after termination of treatment are weaker than for pretermination sex. Valid concerns remain, however, with regard to possible impairment of decision making and some aspects of coer-

Am J Psychiatry 148:11, November 1991

PAUL S. APPELBAUM AND LINDA JORGENSON

cion. The question of the degree of harm suffered by former patients involved in sexual relationships remains unanswered. This analysis suggests that, given the general presumption that persons' choices should be respected, there are insufficient grounds to warrant an outright ban on sexual contact after termination of therapy. Rather, more selective interventions are justified to minimize the likelihood that impaired decisions will be made or adverse effects occur.

A PROPOSAL FOR REGULATING PSYCHOTHERAPIST-PATIENT SEXUAL CONTACT AFTER TERMINATION OF TREATMENT

An absolute ban on posttermination sex—now embodied in some statutes (28), argued for by some commentators (5, 12, 39, 55), and approached in the American Psychiatric Association's position (1)—appears to us to be unnecessary, given the nature and magnitude of the problem. Instead, the concerns about allowing patients to enter into sexual relationships with former therapists can be addressed by precluding the initiation of therapist-patient sexual contact until a substantial period of time has elapsed after the end of treatment. We suggest 1 year as a period that appropriately balances the interests involved, although we recognize that any line drawing is largely arbitrary (56). During this 1-year period, no social contact or communication at all (other than incidental contact) would be permitted between therapists and patients who later begin sexual relations. If social contacts occur and the parties later desire to begin an intimate relationship, a 1-year interval would still be mandatory before sexual contact took place.

How would a waiting period eliminate the problems that are likely to arise if sexual contact is permitted shortly after the end of treatment? As already noted, sex between a therapist and former patient most resembles sex during the therapeutic relationship in the possibility that the patient's decision-making ability will be impaired as a result of the transference. Although transference may never disappear, experience suggests that its force diminishes when therapist and patient are separated for a period of time (56). Patients thereby are afforded an opportunity for reflection on their attraction to their therapists and are likely to be free of possible coercive pressures. Therapists too are given a substantial period to consider the desirability of involvement with their former patients.

The extent to which sexual contact is the product of a hasty infatuation on the part of patients and/or therapists is suggested by data from a study indicating that when therapist-patient sex occurred during therapy, it began during the first 6 months in 55% of the cases and within the first year in 77% of the cases (47). A study of sexual contact beginning after the termination of therapy (57) showed that it began in the first month after termination in 18% of the cases and in the first 6 months in 63% of the cases. The likely effectiveness of

a waiting period in diminishing this impetus toward sexual contact is illustrated by our experience: in our combined experience of more than 100 cases of sexual contact between therapists and patients or former patients on which we have been consulted, we have seen only one case in which sexual contact with a former patient began more than 1 year after the termination of treatment. The Minneapolis Walk-In Counseling Center, which has evaluated more than 2,000 cases of therapist-patient sexual contact, reported that fewer than 1% of the cases seen there involved contact begun more than 1 year after termination (G. Schoener, personal communication, Jan. 15, 1991). Additional systematic data on this point would be desirable, but in their absence a blanket rule prohibiting contact for at least 1 year appears to provide an adequate buffer.

A substantial waiting period should also mitigate other problems associated with sexual contact soon after termination. Therapists will be less tempted to terminate treatment solely to engage in sex, a frequently voiced concern (39), or to use the therapy itself for the purpose of seduction. It has been suggested that posttermination sex might in itself cause patients to distort their presentations to make themselves appear more attractive as future partners, but this seems quite unlikely if they have to wait a year to begin the relationships (39).

Is a fixed waiting period, such as the one we propose, superior to a more flexible approach, such as that suggested by the AMA (9) or embodied in the Minnesota statutes (19, 27) (the latter permit sexual contact only when it is clear that the patient is no longer "emotionally dependent" on the therapist)? We believe it is superior in several respects. First, therapists and patients who wish to initiate social relationships will know clearly in advance when they will be free of sanctions for doing so. That clarity is now lacking in many approaches, including the American Psychiatric Association's annotations to the code of medical ethics (1, 11). Second, it appears to us nearly impossible to determine retrospectively, when a legal or administrative action is brought, whether a former patient was acting primarily from transference-based or autonomous motivations. The fixed waiting period eliminates the battle of the experts, in which neither side is able to offer reliable data, that would inevitably accompany an attempt to establish emotional dependence.

A different kind of flexible approach has also been suggested. Some experts have recommended that therapists who desire sex with their patients terminate treatment, refer the patients to other therapists, and perhaps enter into therapy themselves (58). The implicit rationale appears to be to encourage both parties to "work through" the presumably neurotic basis for their attraction. But the end point is unclear. If the desire for a relationship on both sides remains, after how much therapy can it be initiated? Can the parties continue social contact in the meantime? Therapy may be useful in these cases, but without a definite, substantial waiting period or a clear idea of how much therapy is enough, the decision to enter into a sexual relationship remains susceptible to the transferential, coercive, and fraudulent influences we seek to avoid.

As we envision it, our proposal would cover all treatment provided by psychiatrists and nonmedical psychotherapists. Two objections can be raised to such a uniform approach. First, it might be argued that psychiatrists in particular engage in a variety of relationships with patients and that it is unfair to treat them all the same. The nature of the psychiatrist-patient relationship may differ markedly from case to case, particularly in regard to the crucial issues of transference and the capacity for coercion, depending on whether the psychiatrist is offering psychoanalysis, ongoing prescription of medication, or brief consultation. Greater leniency in initiating posttermination relationships might be permitted when factors that would distort patients' decision making have been minimized. We recognize the force of this contention but believe distinguishing among psychiatrists' functions in this way would be extremely difficult. At what point, for example, does a psychiatrist who officially only prescribes medication, but talks sympathetically with the patient whenever they meet, cross the line into a psychotherapeutic relationship? We favor the simplicity of a uniform rule, while leaving open the possibility that future research on variations in psychiatrist-patient relationships might allow meaningful distinctions.

A second objection might be that by dealing with all patients similarly we are ignoring the special vulnerability of particular groups. Some commentators (46) have argued that certain classes of patients should be excluded permanently from the possibility of posttermination sexual relationships. These might include patients who have been involved in long-term dynamic psychotherapy, psychotic patients, or those who have come for help in dealing with such problems as promiscuity or the consequences of past sexual abuse. This argument seems particularly potent regarding the latter categories. Individual jurisdictions might well want to experiment with creating an absolute ban for groups of patients whose vulnerability is less likely to diminish over time.

Is an absolute ban for all patients a simpler and more desirable approach? Several authors (5, 39) have analogized therapist-patient sex to parent-child incest, maintaining that, just as the latter is not justified after the child has left the home, so the former ought to be precluded forever. This comparison seems to us to be misguided. Treatment and the obligations it imposes on the therapist are time limited; parenthood is not. As much as psychodynamic theory suggests comparisons between therapist and parent, it is important to recognize, as we encourage our patients to do, that in reality they are not the same. Although an absolute ban, if observed, would afford complete protection from the negative consequences of sexual relationships between therapists and former patients, it would do so at the cost of precluding relationships that may involve no more problems than many relationships routinely sanctioned in our society. A mandatory waiting period

should provide many of the protections of an absolute ban without contradicting our usual respect for people's right to choose with whom they will associate, as embodied in our Constitution and upheld by the courts (40, 59).

This approach could be embodied in the law in several ways. Criminal sanctions, which imply that society has concluded the action in question is morally reprehensible in all circumstances, are, from our perspective, unwarranted for posttermination sexual contact. Civil sanctions would be more appropriate; specific statutes would create a cause of action for a former patient who could demonstrate harm as a result of sexual contact with a licensed or unlicensed therapist that occurred within 1 year of termination of therapy. Licensing boards could implement administrative sanctions for violations of the 1-year rule without a showing of harm to the former patient. They might also promulgate regulations regarding documentation of the termination of therapy and the 1-year waiting period. This approach would not preclude them from experimenting with additional requirements, such as referrals for both former patient and therapist to independent therapists of their own for minimum periods of time.

Professional societies could include the requirement of a strict waiting period in their ethics codes. They also provide an ideal forum for working out the fine points of such a system. Among the questions they might address are, How should the end of treatment be defined? How can waiting periods be monitored? Is therapy helpful for the former patient and/or the therapist during the waiting period? Can different rules be developed for different types of treatment? Should there be some patients with whom sexual contact is absolutely prohibited, e.g., those seeking treatment for promiscuity or past sexual abuse?

Our goal in offering this proposal is not to encourage sexual contact between psychotherapists and former patients. Even when it is not sufficiently objectionable as a matter of social policy to warrant prohibition, it is not likely to be an ideal choice for either party (39). Recognizing, however, that such episodes will occur, we are compelled to consider what policies might be most consonant with the usual approach of our society to consensual sexual relations and yet responsive to legitimate concerns about harm and unfairness to former patients. We believe the system we suggest achieves a reasonable balance of interests in this difficult area.

REFERENCES

1. American Psychiatric Association: Principles of Medical Ethics With Annotations Especially Applicable to Psychiatry. Washington, DC, American Psychiatric Association, 1989
2. American Psychological Association: Ethical Principles of Psychologists. Washington, DC, American Psychological Association, 1980
3. National Association of Social Workers: Code of Ethics of the National Association of Social Workers. Washington, DC, NASW, 1980
4. American Psychoanalytic Association: Principles of Ethics for Psychoanalysis and Provisions for Implementation of the Princi-

PAUL S. APPELBAUM AND LINDA JORGENSON

ples of Ethics for Psychoanalysis. New York, American Psychoanalytic Association, 1983

5. Herman JL, Gartrell N, Olarte S, Feldstein M, Localio R: Psychiatrist-patient sexual contact: results of a national survey, II: psychiatrists' attitudes. Am J Psychiatry 1987; 144:164–169

6. Pope KS, Tabachnik BG, Keith-Spiegal P: Ethics of practice: the beliefs and behaviors of psychologists as therapists. Am Psychologist 1987; 42:993–1006

7. Akamatsu TJ: Intimate relationships with former clients: national survey of attitudes and behaviors among practitioners. Professional Psychology: Research and Practice 1988; 19:454–458

8. Conte H, Plutchik R, Picard S, Karasu TB: Ethics in the practice of psychotherapy: a survey. Am J Psychotherapy 1989; 43:32–42

9. American Medical Association: Report of the Council on Ethical and Judicial Affairs on Sexual Misconduct in the Practice of Medicine. Chicago, AMA, 1990

10. American Association for Marriage and Family Therapy: AAMFT Code of Ethical Principles for Marriage and Family Therapists. Washington, DC, AAMFT, 1988

11. Schoener GR: Sexual involvement of therapists with clients after therapy ends: some observations, in Psychotherapists' Sexual Involvement With Clients: Intervention and Prevention. Edited by Schoener GR, Milgrom JH, Gonsiorek JC, Luepker ET, Conroe RM. Minneapolis, Walk-In Counseling Center, 1989

12. Vasquez MJT: Sexual intimacies with clients after termination: should a prohibition be explicit? Ethics & Behavior 1991; 1:45–61

13. Draft of APA ethics code published. APA Monitor 1991; 22(6): 30–35

14. Appelbaum PS: Statutes regulating patient-therapist sex. Hosp Community Psychiatry 1990; 41:15–16

15. Cal Bus Prof Code, Sec 729 (West Supp 1989)

16. Colo Rev Stat, Sec 18-3-405.5(4)(c) (Supp 1988)

17. 1990 Fla Sess Laws Serv 490.0112, Sec 1(1) (tentative assignment) (West 1990)

18. Me Rev Stat, Title 17-A, Sec 253(2)(I) (Supp 1989)

19. Minn Stat, Sec 609.341 et seq (Supp 1990)

20. ND Cent Code 12-1-20-06.1(1) (Michie Supp 1989)

21. Wis Stat Ann, Sec 940.22(2) (1983)

22. Schoener GR: The new laws, in Psychotherapists' Sexual Involvement with Clients: Intervention and Prevention. Edited by Schoener GR, Milgrom JH, Gonsiorek JC, Luepker ET, Conroe RM. Minneapolis, Walk-In Counseling Center, 1989

23. Jorgenson L, Randles B, Strasburger L: The furor over patient-psychotherapist sexual contact: new solutions to an old problem. William and Mary Law Review 1991; 32:645–732

24. Mass HR No 5697, 2d Sess, 176 Gen Court (1990)

25. Cal Bus Prof Code, Sec 43-93 (West Supp 1989)

26. Ill Stat Ann, Chap 70, Sec 801 (Smith-Hurd Supp 1989)

27. Minn Stat, Sec 148A (West 1985)

28. Wis Stat Ann, Sec 895.70(2) (West 1988)

29. Simmons v US, 805 F 2d 1363 (9th Cir 1986)

30. Zipkin v Freeman, 436 SW 2d 753 (Mo 1968)

31. Rowe v Bennett, 514 A 2d 802 (Me 1986)

32. DeStefano v Grabrian, 763 P 2d 275 (Colo 1988)

33. Anclote Manor Foundation v Wilkinson, 263 So 2d 256 (Fla Dist Ct App 1972)

34. Noto v St Vincent's Hospital and Medical Center of New York, 537 NYS 2d 446 (Sup Ct 1988)

35. Doe v Samaritan Counseling Center, 791 P 2d 344 (Alaska 1990)

36. Fla Admin Code, Sec 21U-15.004(5)(a) (1986)

37. Fla Admin Code, Sec 21R-19.002(13) (1986)

38. Massachusetts Board of Registration in Medicine, Adj Case No 90-11-xx (Dec 20, 1989)

39. Gabbard GO, Pope KS: Sexual intimacies after termination: clinical, ethical, and legal aspects, in Sexual Exploitation in Professional Relationships. Edited by Gabbard GO. Washington, DC, American Psychiatric Press, 1989

40. Note: constitutional barriers to civil and criminal restrictions on pre- and extramarital sex. Harvard Law Review 1991; 104: 1660–1680

41. Feinberg J: Harm to Self. New York, Oxford University Press, 1986

42. Green MD: Fraud, undue influence and mental incompetency: a study in related concepts. Columbia Law Review 1943; 43:176–205

43. Pope KS: Therapist-patient sexual involvement: a review of the research. Clin Psychol Rev 1990; 10:477–490

44. Feldman-Summers S: Sexual contact in fiduciary relationships, in Sexual Exploitation in Professional Relationships. Edited by Gabbard GO. Washington, DC, American Psychiatric Press, 1989

45. Smith S: The seduction of the female patient. Ibid

46. Gonsiorek JC, Brown LS: Post therapy sexual relationships with clients, in Psychotherapists' Sexual Involvement With Clients: Intervention and Prevention. Edited by Schoener GR, Milgrom JH, Gonsiorek JC, Luepker ET, Conroe RM. Minneapolis, Walk-In Counseling Center, 1989

47. Bouhoutsos J, Holroyd J, Lerman H, Forer B, Greenberg M: Sexual intimacy between psychotherapists and patients. Professional Psychology: Research and Practice 1983; 14:185–196

48. Coleman P: Sex between psychiatrist and former patient: a proposal for a "no harm, no foul" rule. Oklahoma Law Review 1988; 41:1–52

49. Frankel T: Fiduciary law. California Law Review 1983; 7a:795–836

50. Pope KS, Bouhoutsos JC: Sexual Intimacy Between Therapists and Patients. New York, Praeger, 1986

51. Buckley P, Karasu TB, Charles E: Psychotherapists view their personal therapy. Psychotherapy: Theory, Research and Practice 1981; 18:299–305

52. Pfeffer AZ: The meaning of the analyst after analysis: a contribution to the theory of therapeutic results. J Am Psychoanal Assoc 1963; 11:229–244

53. Norman H, Blacker K, Oremland J, Barrett WG: The fate of the transference neurosis after termination of a satisfactory analysis. J Am Psychoanal Assoc 1976; 24:471–498

54. Appelbaum PS, Gutheil TG: Clinical Handbook of Psychiatry and the Law, 2nd ed. Baltimore, Williams & Wilkins, 1991

55. Shopland SN, VandeCreek L: Sex with ex-clients: theoretical rationales for prohibition. Ethics & Behavior 1991; 1:35–44

56. Firestein SK: Problems of termination in the analysis of adults. J Am Psychoanal Assoc 1969; 17:222–237

57. Gartrell N, Herman J, Olarte S, Feldstein M, Localio R: Psychiatrist-patient sexual contact: results of a national survey, I: prevalence. Am J Psychiatry 1986; 143:1126–1131

58. Stone AA: Law, Psychiatry, and Morality: Essays and Analysis. Washington, DC, American Psychiatric Press, 1984

59. Roberts v US Jaycees, 104 S Ct 3244 (1984)

Divided Loyalties

[42]

Abuses of Law and Psychiatry in China

Paul S. Appelbaum, M.D.

Psychiatry's utility as a device for suppressing political dissent has not been lost on totalitarian regimes. The best-known example occurred in the Soviet Union during the post-Stalin era (1,2). Khrushchev and his successors, no longer comfortable with the widespread use of overt repression, looked to confine dissidents in psychiatric facilities instead of labor camps. Psychiatric hospitalization, in addition to its "gentler" face, offered the advantage of discrediting the dissidents and their causes as "crazy" and thus unworthy of world support.

The latest allegations about the systematic misuse of psychiatry for political purposes come from China. They have recently been catalogued by Robin Munro, formerly director of the Hong Kong office of Human Rights Watch and now senior research fellow at the Centre of Chinese Studies of the University of London (3). As was the case when word of Soviet psychiatric abuses first reached the West, most of the available reports come from dissident religious and political groups, and independent verification is lacking. Nonetheless, Munro has assembled an impressive analysis of the ways in which Chinese law facilitates the misuse of psychiatry as well as a collection of individual cases. The description that follows is drawn from his account.

Munro suggests that the political use of psychiatry in China has passed through three stages. It began in the 1950s as Chinese psychiatry was reconstructed on the Soviet model after the communist takeover. Although

Dr. Appelbaum, who is editor of this column, is A. F. Zeleznik professor and chair in the department of psychiatry at the University of Massachusetts Medical School, 55 Lake Avenue North, Worcester, Massachusetts 01655 (e-mail, appelbap@ ummhc.org).

psychiatric abuses were not extensive in this era, perhaps because the psychiatric system itself was so rudimentary—there were reportedly only 50 to 60 psychiatrists in China immediately after the revolution—some dissidents were apparently diagnosed under broad Soviet standards and subjected to confinement. For example, they were said to have "sluggish schizophrenia," the diagnosis of which did not require psychotic symptoms.

During the decade of the Cultural Revolution, which began in the late 1960s, a strange inversion of this process took place. With Maoist ideologues attributing behavioral abnormalities to an incorrect appreciation of the class struggle, the reality of mental illness was denied, and study of Mao's works was substituted for other forms of therapy. Persons with genuine mental disorders whose delusional ideation manifested a political component found themselves taken from psychiatric facilities and incarcerated in labor camps and prisons for "counterrevolutionary" offenses. Only with the ascension of Deng Xiaoping in 1979 was the cruelty of this practice acknowledged and a majority of its victims freed.

In contrast, from the 1980s to the present, China has again seen persons who challenge the political and cultural hegemony of the Communist Party being labeled as mentally ill and being confined, often for substantial periods, in psychiatric facilities. Recent cases appear to fall into two groups: political dissenters and members of the quasi-religious Falun Gong movement. The former tend to be confined in special forensic hospitals—known as Ankang, which means "peace and health"—operated by the Ministry of Public Security, and the latter have been reported to be hospitalized primarily in ordinary public facilities.

Chinese criminologic and psychi-

atric writings provide evidence of the theoretical underpinnings that facilitate the misuse of psychiatry to crush dissent. For example, a contemporary Chinese textbook of forensic psychiatry offers the following discussion of the symptoms of one disorder: "Paranoid psychosis manifests itself . . . [in one of two ways, including] 'political mania,' where a dominant role is played by 'political delusions.' The content of delusions in 'political mania' concerns the line and policies of the State; those afflicted do avid research into politics and put forward a whole set of original theories of their own, which they then try to peddle by every means possible. . . . For this reason, such people are sometimes viewed as being political dissidents" (3). It is easy to imagine how any dissident could fall afoul of the psychiatric system if behaviors such as these are the sole basis on which a diagnosis is made.

Another example with a particularly pernicious twist is drawn from the work of a prominent Chinese forensic psychiatrist, who discusses crimes committed by persons with schizophrenia: "Among the cases under discussion . . . the person would often display absolutely no sense or instinct of self-preservation, for example by openly mailing out reactionary letters or pasting up reactionary slogan-banners in public places—and even, in some cases, signing his or her real name to the documents . . . " (3). By these criteria, political dissenters who openly attempt to build a democratic structure in China, rather than conspiratorially trying to undermine the communist state, are especially susceptible to being called mentally ill.

In a review of ten Chinese psychiatric journals from 1976 to 1995, Munro found reports of the forensic psychiatric evaluations of nearly 4,000 persons, 3.8 percent of whom were classified as having committed "political" crimes. Extrapolating conservatively to the entire country over the past decade, he estimated that no fewer than 3,000 political cases have been referred for forensic evaluation and that the great majority of those individuals were subjected to "some form and duration of forced psychiatric custody and treatment."

Munro cites an example from the previously mentioned textbook of forensic psychiatry (3). A 57-year-old former coal miner, referred to as Zhu, who had been an enthusiastic participant in Mao's Cultural Revolution, began to write extensively on political matters after he retired. He spoke to local political leaders and sent his writings to political journals, always signing his own name. His speech was logical, his behavior polite, and his lifestyle orderly. However, when subjected to psychiatric evaluation he was found to be suffering from paranoid psychosis on the basis that his theories were "conceptually chaotic" and in conflict with the principles laid down by the Central Committee. Moreover, "Zhu's views and utterances were incompatible with his status, position, qualifications, and learning; the great disparities here clearly demonstrated his divorcement from reality."

In the past two years, reports of actions against members of the Falun Gong movement, which is being aggressively persecuted by Chinese authorities, have been publicized widely in the Western media. Some of these accounts indicate that members of the sect are being taken to psychiatric facilities, where three of them allegedly have died. One judge who practiced Falun Gong and who apparently was hospitalized on that basis reported that he was told, "Let us see which is stronger, Falun Gong or our medicines" (3). Of particular concern is that these confinements are said to be taking place in general psychiatric hospitals, not in the special hospitals that are more directly under the authority of the state security apparatus. This observation suggests that the propensity to misuse psychiatric diagnosis and treatment is spreading to the broader psychiatric system.

To his credit, Munro forthrightly acknowledges that it is nearly impossible to determine, on the basis of the fragmentary data available in the West, whether any of the dissidents—political or religious—who have been confined to Chinese psychiatric facilities are genuinely mentally ill. A definitive conclusion would require the same kind of direct examination by impartial psychiatrists that ultimately was conducted in the Soviet Union shortly before its fall (4). However, published descriptions of Chinese diagnostic practices—only a small number of which have been quoted here—and the absence of firm legal controls over detention for forensic purposes are certainly compatible with this suspicion. With regard to the latter, for example, police and prosecutors can request forensic evaluations of persons thought to have committed crimes in the absence of standards that regulate how long such persons can be detained without trial (3).

However, even if they have not been misdiagnosed, both political and religious dissenters clearly are being arrested, hospitalized, or incarcerated for behaviors that under international standards are neither crimes nor indications for involuntary commitment. Indeed, persons detained by the police for "counterrevolutionary activities" or participation in banned religious groups face a no-win situation. If diagnosed as mentally ill, they face indefinite confinement in psychiatric facilities; if deemed not mentally ill and thus responsible for their behavior, they are likely to be sentenced to the penal system.

Assuming that the allegations Munro has assembled are valid, how are we to understand the role that at least some Chinese psychiatrists have played in these abuses? Are they deliberately engaging in what Munro terms hyperdiagnosis—knowing their patients to be mentally healthy—or honestly applying politically tinged diagnostic criteria to political and religious dissidents whom they believe to be ill? At least some of the evidence cited by Munro suggests deliberate use by psychiatrists of diagnoses of mental disorders to facilitate the system's efforts to crush challenges to its social and political domination of the populace.

Western psychiatrists are understandably concerned when their discipline is used for political purposes. To condone such abuses anywhere is to give credence to the claim that all psychiatric diagnoses are suspect and that involuntary commitment is nothing more than a transparent effort to confine those who give voice to ideas that the dominant members of society would prefer not to hear. Thus, with the encouragement of the American Psychiatric Association and comparable organizations in other countries, the World Psychiatric Association is seeking China's permission for a delegation of foreign psychiatrists to visit the country and examine persons who claim they have been subjected to unjustified detention and treatment.

At this writing, the World Psychiatric Association's efforts have not met with success. The Soviet Union's acquiescence in a visit by Western psychiatrists in 1989 came only when the leaders perceived it as being in their interests to rein in the hard-liners who were then in control of the psychiatric system. China's leaders today, at the helm of an economically vigorous nation, are in a very different political position from that of the heads of the tottering Soviet state. Nonetheless, should they become persuaded that international concern about allegations of psychiatric abuse is harming their long-term interests, they too may either permit an investigatory body to visit China or order a halt to the use of psychiatry for repressive purposes. ◆

References

1. Bloch S, Reddaway P: Psychiatric Terror: How Soviet Psychiatry Is Used to Suppress Dissent. New York, Basic Books, 1977

2. Appelbaum PS: Law and psychiatry, Soviet style. Hospital and Community Psychiatry 32:601–602, 1981

3. Munro R: Judicial psychiatry in China and its political abuses. Columbia Journal of Asian Law 14:1–125, 2000

4. Bonnie R: Soviet psychiatry and human rights: reflections on the report of the US delegation. Law, Medicine, and Health Care 18:123–131, 1990

[43]

Ethics, Power, and Advocacy

Psychologists in the Criminal Justice System*

Martha A. Lyon† and Martin L. Levine‡

I. INTRODUCTION

Psychologists long defined their role essentially as that of scientist, engaged in research or in the applied work of psychometrist; later the role of therapist assumed prominence. In recent years, psychologists have increasingly assumed new professional roles in institutional settings. The criminal justice system is one of those new settings for psychological intervention, and the ethical questions generated there have sparked a debate within the psychology profession. A recent publication of the American Psychological Association, "Who is the Client?" (Monahan, 1980) surveys the ethical questions involved in psychologists' criminal justice work.

This essay–review discusses both the new volume and the underlying topic. First, a brief summary of the study and survey which led to the book, and the task force report which is its heart will be set out. Background papers which accompany the task force report will not be discussed separately, but instead will be dealt with in connection with appropriate substantive topics. Second, two issues which cut across all the chapters of the book will be surveyed: the psychologist's divided loyalty, and the psychologist's limited competence to perform the tasks required. Finally, three concepts will be highlighted as a suggested focus for ongoing ethical debate—the psychologist's multiple roles, his or her relation to power, and the psychologist as advocate. Psychological research involving prisoners, although of considerable importance, will not be dis-

*Preparation of this manuscript was supported in part by NIMH Training grant No. 5 T24 MH 15901-02.
†Department of Psychiatry and the Behavioral Sciences, University of Southern California, Los Angeles, California.
‡Law Center, Department of Psychiatry and the Behavioral Sciences, and School of Gerontology, University of Southern California, Los Angeles, California.

cussed. The task force generally relies on the recommendations of the National Commission for the Protection of Human Subjects of Biomedical and Behavioral Research (1977). Moreover, Federal agencies have increasingly opposed research with prisoners.

A. The Study

In late 1975, the American Psychological Association (APA) Board of Social and Ethical Responsibility for Psychology was confronted with a number of requests concerning criminal justice issues. Apparently, the existing APA *Ethical Standards for Psychologists* (1963) were not thought to give sufficient guidance by those submitting the requests. It seems that the standards were also not thought sufficient by the Board itself, for it created a Task Force on the Role of Psychology in the Criminal Justice System, chaired by John Monahan, a psychologist who is now a professor at the University of Virginia School of Law. The task force was assigned to undertake a comprehensive study, with funding from the National Science Foundation's program in Ethical and Human Value Implications of Science and Technology.

Concrete ethical problems in this area have, in the past, been formally raised infrequently—though perhaps no less frequently than in other areas. During a three-year period preceding the task force report, psychologists filed only seven complaints of unethical behavior against criminal justice agencies to be heard by the APA Committee on Academic Freedom and Conditions of Employment. Furthermore, only one charge against a psychologist working in the justice system was filed before the APA Committee on Scientific and Professional Ethics and Conduct (Task Force, 1980). After reading the survey results and background papers (Monahan, 1980), one concludes that many important ethical issues must have existed though few were formally raised.

The task force's study went through several stages. The psychologists who had responded on the 1975 APA Manpower Survey by listing the criminal justice system as their primary employment setting were surveyed, in order to guide the task force's selection of topics for debate and to provide case material. Four background papers were commissioned, organized by setting; they concerned ethical issues for psychologists in police agencies, court, corrections, and the juvenile justice system. These papers, together with the survey results, are published for the first time in this volume (Monahan, 1980). The background papers were considered by the task force at four meetings held over the space of a year, with invited groups of psychologists and others working in the justice system providing input. After these meetings, the task force's report was prepared and first published separately in 1978; it is reprinted in this volume.

The task force did not relate its discussion and recommendations in any point-by-point way to the findings of the study, or to the reasoning of the background papers it had commissioned. Its decision not to do so is understandable. It would have been helpful, however, if the published volume, ''Who is the Client?,'' had been treated as a single-theme anthology and supplied with the usual editorial apparatus of comments on the several chapters. Such editorial commentary could have compared the task force recommendations with the survey report and background papers, and compared the background papers with one another, highlighting areas of disagreement. The structure of the published volume—background papers dealing with discrete settings in which psychologists work—has resulted in repetition; the work is less a unified whole than it could have been. The organization of this essay–review is guided by the contention that the published volume would have benefitted if its chapters had had a thematic organization.

There are additional related matters not covered in the Monahan book which would be interesting to consider. One could question to what extent a psychologist, or any professional, has ethical obligations as a professional different from the ethical obligations of any person (Goldman, 1980). A survey could also be conducted of psychologists who have a regular though not primary professional role in criminal justice, such as those who conduct court-ordered examinations; forensic psychologists can be identified as a group and have now formed their own specialty board (Psychiatrists and Psychologists, 1979). Moreover, a study could be undertaken of psychologists whose work influences the criminal justice policy-making decisions of legislatures, administrative agencies, or courts, through service on legislative staffs, advocacy and lobbying (Sadoff & Kopolow, 1977; Davidson & Rappaport, 1978; Zusman, Note 1), expert testimony in precedent-setting litigation (Tapp & Levine, 1977; Suggs, 1979; Perlin, 1980), or research on the scientific foundation of familiar legal rules or practices (Loftus, 1979; Yarmey, 1979). Another potential role of psychologists in criminal justice that could be considered involves hostage negotiation with terrorists, among the most visible of situations for mental health professional consultation in the justice system. Furthermore, attention could be given to persons in criminal justice who can be seen as psychological "paraprofessionals": the probation officer, parole agent, juvenile officer, prison corrections counselor, and policeman. The policeman, for example, provides advice to the troubled (as do the pharmacist, clergyman, and bartender); some police have been trained in mediation and other crisis management techniques (Bard & Berkowitz, 1967), and police are an important access to psychiatric treatment for the poor (Hollingshead & Redlich, 1958).

B. The Report

The culmination of the study was the task force's report, which offers twelve recommendations grouped under several headings. While some of the task force's recommendations refer directly to the APA *Ethical Standards*, it does not always make clear the relation its recommendations have to those standards, nor whether changes in the *Ethical Standards* are recommended.

Under the category "ethical issues the criminal justice system creates for psychologists," the task force makes recommendations in two subcategories: "questions of loyalty," including issues of confidentiality and research ethics, and "questions of competence," e.g., the requirement that mental health professionals working in criminal justice understand the system. A second category of recommendations involves "ethical issues psychologists create for the criminal justice system." The task force emphasizes the distinction between its two categories—psychologists' ethical issues, and the justice system's ethical issues—but the categorization remains somewhat arbitrary; among issues grouped under the latter category, prediction, for example, can be seen as involving issues of competence, and the rejection of involuntary treatment a question of loyalty, both issues listed under the former category.

A final group of recommendations on "implementation" calls for education in applied ethics, increased awareness of the APA's ethical enforcement process, and improved capacity to offer prompt advisory opinions on ethical questions.

The task force maintains that the psychologist who treats offenders is primarily the agent of the individual (1980, p. 5). Conclusions are drawn for the psychologist as therapist, psychometrist, and predictor. Therapy should "only be given on a truly voluntary basis" and should not be used to pursue "administrative ends, such as release" (p. 5). The administration of batteries of tests to prisoners to assess suitability for treatment programs is condemned by the task force when in fact no treatment programs exist (p. 7). It recommends that psychologists be extremely cautious in offering predictions of criminal behavior. Moreover, the task force recommends that psychologists not offer conclusions on matters of law, such as whether an individual is "too dangerous" to be released (p. 9); in principle, even if prediction skills increase, the most a psychologist would be able to say is "how dangerous" an individual is, not whether he is "too dangerous" to go free.

The task force implicitly rejects the suggestion of a background paper (Brodsky, 1980) that a legalistic ethical model for psychology be employed. Brodsky recommended a "due process model" for psychological services in institutions, seeking to have the psychologist afford to imprisoned clients the "same kinds of protections that due process affords in the courts" (p. 91). The suggestions included the "opportunity to confront psychological . . . accusers," and a right to appeal treatment decisions to "professional and citizen committees." The Task Force Report's implicit rejection of the due process model as a guide to the psychologist's behavior seems sound. Convicts by definition have already been sentenced to substantial, though of course not total, loss of autonomy. Moreover, courts are devoted to fact-finding and normative judgment; they are highly structured and staffed by lawyers; their decisions can deprive a defendant of life or freedom. Therapy is different in all these respects. Formal hearings are not a necessary mechanism for a therapist committed to be fair, and the values of due process can be sought without having psychologists replicate trial procedures. "The allure of due process hearings is indeed powerful and seductive," but nonformal procedures can be made to work (Kimp, 1976, p. 873). The appropriate locus for formal due process hearings is not within the treatment, but as an external judicial check on treatment abuses.[1]

Notwithstanding the reservations expressed above, the task force's report is professional and sensitive, worthy of commendation by colleagues. It analyzes in a rich and complex fashion a range of issues only hinted at by the volume's title, "Who is the Client?" The task force has asked good questions, grappled with problems too seldom faced, and encouraged an important debate.

C. The Survey

Valuable data are presented in the report of the survey of 349 psychologists working in the criminal justice system (Clingempeel, Mulvey & Reppucci, 1980). These psychologists are conscious of four categories of ethical dilemmas. First, "Who

---

[1] *See* Mackey v. Procunier, 477 F.2d 877 (9th Cir. 1973); Knecht v. Gillman, 488 F.2d 1136 (8th Cir. 1973).

is the client?''—the puzzle which gives a title to the overall volume—which can be seen as a role confusion engendered by competing demands of "custody versus treatment." Second, confidentiality, identified by three-quarters of the psychologists as among their major ethical dilemmas, and often involving the *Tarasoff* [2] issue of the client who reveals in confidence a danger to another person. Third, a series of problems in psychological assessment and treatment—having to do with the indeterminate sentence, prediction of dangerousness, and use of behavior modification techniques in prison settings. Fourth, the twin issues of the existence of a right to receive treatment and right to refuse treatment.

The major virtue of the survey (Clingempeel et al., 1980) is that it usefully identifies three sources of these ethical dilemmas: First, there is a role conflict for the prison psychologist who acts as evaluator for purposes of punishment and custody, and as diagnostician and confidant for purposes of treatment. Second, the psychologist observes that what he or she does in the name of treatment "to help the individual" may have little treatment efficacy, but may rather serve primarily to promote the punishment or custody values of the system. Third, there are problems of the psychologist's competence to perform the tasks assigned. Predictions of dangerousness, for example, are relevant to recommendations for initial sentencing, to recommendations to release under an indeterminate sentence, and to *Tarasoff* dilemmas; there is, however, little empirical verification of the capacity to predict dangerousness with substantial accuracy.

Psychologists are often called upon to treat offenders, but such a duty also involves competency problems. Psychologists surveyed were troubled by the "absence of efficacious treatment programs, the invalidity of assessment paradigms, the inadequacy of evaluation strategies, and the difficulties in distinguishing rehabilitation from 'pseudo-rehabilitation' '' (p. 148), as well as "the paucity of research showing generalization of treatment gains beyond the prison environment'' (p. 149). Despite these doubts about treatment, however, three-fourths of the psychologists surveyed were in favor of the use of behavior modification (while being concerned with prisoners' rights to informed consent and to refuse treatment). Several felt that dangerous prisoners could properly be forced to accept medication. "Many psychologists'' (p. 141) recognized a right of society to protect itself by imposing longer sentences for treatment refusal. There seemed to be "overall'' agreement (p. 141) that treatment could be imposed in the "best interests'' of unwilling but incompetent clients. It was not clear from the survey results whether prison psychologists fully comprehended the implications for these issues of the present absence of generally efficacious treatment methods.

II. CONFIDENTIALITY

To turn to the substantive areas emphasized throughout the Monahan volume (1980), a major ethical issue dealt with repeatedly is that of confidentiality. According to Principle 5 of the APA *Ethical Principles* (1981): ''Where appropriate, psycholo-

---

[2]*Tarasoff* v. Regents of University of California, 13 C.3d 177, 529 P.2d 553, 118 Cal. Rptr. 129 (1974).

Mental Illness, Medicine and Law

gists inform their client of the legal limits of confidentiality.'' Nevertheless, as Fersch points out in a background paper, psychologists working in court settings ''[v]iewing themselves as therapeutic figures . . . generally do not warn clients about the problems of confidentiality'' (1980b, p. 59). Clearly, these psychologists have ''a far different relationship to the confidence of persons they talk with than that of psychologists employed by individuals'' (p. 54). Although some psychologists assure involuntary clients that only the conclusions drawn from the interviews will be reported to the court, there is ''a wide variety in what psychologists actually say'' to clients and then how they respond to the court when questions about details are asked (p. 54).

In *Estelle v. Smith*,[3] the Supreme Court has recently sided in one major context with Fersch's stand that defendants must be informed if everything they say as involuntary clients may be reported to the court. In *Estelle*, an examining psychiatrist went beyond reporting to the court on the issue of competence to stand trial and testified for the prosecution as to the defendant's dangerousness at the death penalty phase of the trial. At that point, the defendant's Fifth Amendment right to be silent attaches as, the Supreme Court continued, the psychiatrist's ''role changed and became essentially like an agent of the State.''[4] Like the police interrogation ruled on in *Miranda*, ''[d]uring the psychiatric evaluation, [defendant] assuredly was 'faced with a phase of the adversary system' and was 'not in the presence of [a] person[ ] acting solely in his interest.''[5] Thus a *Miranda*-type warning is mandated in such situations. The Supreme Court is open to a distinction that Fersch (1980b) does not make; if the psychiatrist in *Estelle* had testified only as to the defendant's competency to stand trial and not at his sentencing hearing, the Court would not have required that a warning be given. The Court also differentiated court-ordered examinations by the ''prosecution's psychologist'' when the defendant has raised the insanity issue and introduced his own psychiatric evidence. While the defendant in the latter situation might not have a *Miranda* right to keep silent, notwithstanding the Court's dictum there is ethically no excuse even then for failure to clarify to the defendant the psychiatrist's role.

In addition to the *Estelle* situation of court-ordered examination, confidentiality issues arise when therapy is offered in a prison setting. Three examples discussed in Brodsky's (1980) background paper reveal different sorts of dilemmas. The clearest is where prison officials demand to be able to hear and see whatever is going on during therapy; many psychologists refuse to conduct therapy under such conditions (Corsini, 1956), though others may think that provision of some service is better than providing none at all. A second situation is where a client reports an imminent escape attempt, but pleads that the therapist not reveal the plan. Here Brodsky (1980) suggests that revelation of the confidence can be made only when *Tarasoff*-type conditions have been met *and* the client has been initially informed of the limits of confidentiality. His conclusion seems open to counter-argument. Of course the client should be told in advance of the limits of confidentiality. Nevertheless, even if the client has not been so told, where there is ''a clear and substantial risk of death'' (Brodsky, 1980, p. 69) if

---

[3]Estelle v. Smith, 451 U.S. 454 (1981).

[4]451 U.S. at 467.

[5]*Id., quoting* Miranda v. Arizona, 384 U.S. 436, 469 (1966).

the psychologist doesn't breach confidentiality, then confidentiality probably has to yield. A third example is a client's revelation of a past criminal act. Brodsky (1980, p. 69) says that "deciding if the confidence should be retained in this case is harder." Others who are used to confidential communications, lawyers or priests, are committed to protect such confidences.

When a psychologist faces a confidentiality dilemma, there are no easy answers; whether he protects the confidence or reveals it, someone may be hurt. Though advance warning and client consent may meet the psychologist's *legal* duty under *Estelle* or otherwise, it may be too easy a way out of the *ethical* dilemmas of confidentiality merely to use the concept of "informed consent." The task force's (1980, p. 5) first recommendation is that all parties should be informed in advance of any exceptions to confidentiality, preferably in writing: they assume that the individual being treated or evaluated then has the option of deciding what information to reveal. The announced goal is the achievement of the same standards of confidentiality as exist in "free world" therapy; the task force's example is the privately consenting client who can request to have information revealed to an insurance company. The task force thus uses a model of disclosure, rational consideration by the client, and consent. The model may not, however, fully meet the ethical complexities of the situation. Advance disclosure by psychologist and apparent consent by clients are necessary, but not sufficient, for the psychologist to meet ethical norms. The therapist's disclosure of the limits of confidentiality may not be meaningful to the patient: it may occur too long in advance of the revelation of a confidence, or be too general to strike home. The client's consideration may not be fully rational or logical. The client may wish to appear committed to the process, or may not want to defy the therapist (Katz, 1972). Consent may be given under "hard choices": the police applicant who does not consent may not get the job, just as the private patient who fails to consent may lose insurance benefits. Even if a patient "requests" disclosure to the insurance company or police personnel department, the therapist should hesitate, for example, before feeding into the system details of a client's sexual problems that may be disclosed to other parties, perhaps years later, causing unpredictable damage to the client. The patient's "consent" does not remove from the psychologist's shoulders the ethical issues. The psychologist should consider—usually jointly with the patient—holding back details the psychologist believes should remain private, even though the patient has given a blanket "consent."

III. LIMITS OF COMPETENCE

In addition to questions of confidentiality, a second group of ethical issues discussed throughout the Monahan (1980) volume concerns the limits of psychologists' competence. For some of the tasks the psychologist is asked to perform, the research is discouraging, and "for the great majority of tasks there are no data at all" (Task Force, 1980, p. 9). According to Rappaport, Lamiell, and Siedman's background paper (1980, p. 95), "psychologists have contributed useless 'diagnoses,' behavioral predictions with high error rates, naive theories of prevention and rehabilitation, and ineffective treatments."

A. Prediction

Issues of the psychologist's competence are raised dramatically in relation to prediction, such as in the *Estelle* situation of predicting the dangerousness of a criminal up for sentencing. It is important for the psychologist to respond as accurately as possible in such situations. Much is at stake: individual prisoners have important interests both in liberty and in rehabilitation; society will be injured if dangerous, unrehabilitated criminals go free; the psychologist is personally concerned with professional success and legal involvement; and one should avoid waste of a scarce and expensive societal resource—prison space—which could be made available for another, more dangerous, offender.

Psychologists are thus often consulted for answers concerning crucial prediction decisions in the criminal justice system. Those with the authority to make decisions may, however, be asking "experts" for "scientific" answers to questions which are more appropriately viewed as moral or policy issues, which should be decided by authorized representatives of society (Morse, 1978). The task force (1980) refers to courts asking psychologists such questions in "an attempt to evade their responsibility to deal with difficult issues" (p. 9) and recommends depriving the criminal justice system of the opportunity to "launder" difficult ethical and policy questions as matters of scientific acumen (p. 14). Conscious "evasion" of duty must, however, be a rare phenomenon. Courts, though, may have been oversold as to what is scientifically known. Courts may also unconsciously want to ease a burden of decision that is hard to bear alone (Burt, 1979). Reliance on experts may reduce the anxiety of officials and of society in general.

Aside from questions of the proper responsibility for decision making, and considered just as a matter of professional competence, the psychologist's expertise may not be up to the tasks assigned: there may be no answers to give (Morse, 1978; forthcoming). Psychologists and psychiatrists may lack the ability to make predictions of violent behavior that are sufficiently accurate to serve as a fair basis for sentencing and release decisions (Dershowitz, 1969; American Psychiatric Association, 1974; Stone, 1975). There is a widespread tendency to overpredict dangerousness, creating more false positives than false negatives (Type II error), thus producing unnecessary and unfair deprivation of liberty.

A similar difficulty in predicting specific behavior also underlies the confidentiality dilemma of a *Tarasoff* situation. Moreover, the prison psychologist, unlike most other therapists, has a clientele of convicts, many with long records of violence, who live in a violent setting. Their threats of violent acts must be much more frequent than the typical patient group, and the occasion for the professional to make a prediction of dangerousness much more common. The correctional psychologist is thus more frequently faced than his colleagues outside with the dilemma of evaluating dangerousness. And like them he or she is often without an adequate scientific basis to make an individualized prediction (though if the base rate of prisoner violence is high enough, the correctional psychologist's most accurate prediction may just be an across-the-board one).

The Supreme Court, informed in part by the brief for the American Psychiatric Association in *Estelle,* has now recognized that

some in the psychiatric community are of the view that clinical predictions as to whether a person
would or would not commit violent acts in the future are "fundamentally of very low reliability"
and that psychiatrists possess no special qualifications for making such forecasts.[6]

Psychologists, no doubt, would be similarly regarded by the Court. Just as there
appears, however, to be growing consensus on this negative judgment, one should note
that Monahan (1981) is not totally pessimistic in his most recent work on the clinical
prediction of violent behavior. Though starting with the position "why you can't do
it," and presenting no new evidence, he reports that by the time he was finished with
his review of the literature, he was toying with the subtitle "how to do it and when to
do it" (p. v). Monahan (1981) nevertheless emphasizes the statistical rather than
purely clinical component of prediction, and still believes that legal authorities must
retain responsibility for the ultimate sentencing or release decision.

The psychologist may deal with requests for prediction and treatment by taking a
stance of scientific purity and refusing to perform requested tasks because of the
limitations on expertise. The psychologist who does so, however, is unlikely to remain
employed in the criminal justice system. The individual psychologist thus may confront both an ethical dilemma and personal financial distress. Moreover, without
psychologists and other professionals, prediction decisions are likely to be made by lay
people who are no better qualified and who have no more data. As the Supreme Court
recognized in its 1976 *Jurek* decision, "prediction of future criminal conduct is an
essential element in many of the decisions rendered throughout our criminal justice
system."[7] Some psychologists will find little improvement, other than their own clean
hands, in relegating such decisions to prison wardens and lay boards; others regard
such renunciation of the task to be politically and societally preferable.

B. Treatment

Treatment, along with prediction, is an area in which competence is at issue. Not only
is the psychologist's competence to predict behavior problematic, it is also not clear that the
treatment modalities available to psychologists are efficacious. The background paper by
Rappaport et al. (1980, pp. 103–104) argues, for example, that no treatments have proven
effective for "delinquents" in general. If there is no effective treatment then, as the
Juvenile Justice Standards Project of the Institute of Judicial Administration–American Bar
Association (1976) has suggested, there should be a reduction of the court jurisdiction to
declare juveniles delinquent, which is often exercised now on a treatment rationale.
Moreover, as the task force declares (1980, p. 13), adults should be imprisoned no longer
than they would be on a nontreatment punishment rationale.

Even if treatment were effective, there are inadequate evaluation strategies to know
when it succeeds. Since the rewards for apparent improvement are so great—such as early
release—"pseudorehabilitation" will often be difficult to distinguish from true rehabilitation. Furthermore, it is not clear that rehabilitation in the prison context is generalizable to
improvement in functioning outside the prison (Rappaport et al., 1980).

While psychologists may define their task as providing psychological assessment and

---

[6]Estelle v. Smith, 451 U.S. at 472.
[7]Jurek v. Texas, 428 U.S. 262, 275 (1976) (joint opinion).

treatment services to individual clients, the scientific, testing, or therapeutic justification of their activities may thus be relatively unsure. Psychological assessment and treatment may have dubious long-range or real-world therapeutic relevance (Rappaport et al., 1980). What is certain, though, is that such activities often contribute to continued custody or punishment, the primary concern of the correctional institution. Some prison psychologists and judges have suggested that behavior modification techniques and vocabulary serve a cosmetic function to mask punishment as "treatment." Thus dilemmas arise for psychologists who adhere to an ethos of helping the individual.

IV. THE MULTIPLE ROLES OF THE PSYCHOLOGIST

Many of the ethical issues for psychologists in criminal justice, including those of loyalty and competence, can usefully be considered in the context of the psychologist's multiple roles. Psychologists function in a variety of roles with a variety of orientations, reflected in part by the 40 divisions officially recognized by the APA. One role which is important to a psychologist's self-image is that of scientist—though in fact few psychologists do any scientific research and, it is distressing to note, the clinical research of scientific psychology appears to have little or no impact on the actual clinical practice of most psychologists (Barlow, 1981). Another important role is of direct provider of client service, originally as psychometrist, increasingly as therapist or counselor. The activities of psychologists who work in the criminal justice system span all these areas: research, assessment, and treatment, as well as training and consultation (Twain, McGee, & Bennett, 1973). In the criminal justice system, psychologists deal with individuals who are involuntary clients as well as those who are voluntary; their role is sometimes as expert, sometimes as advocate, and sometimes as adversary (Fersch, 1980a). Seventy percent of the psychologists surveyed work in prisons or jails—about three out of four provide assessment and treatment of offenders—and the most personally troubling ethical dilemmas were reported by these correctional psychologists (Clingempeel et al., 1980).

This multiplicity of roles and functions may be at the heart of the task force's (1980) work. Within the model of private practice with an adult, the consumer of mental health services is the psychologist's only perceived client. Psychologists working in the criminal justice system, however, serve constituencies on several levels: the individual consumer (who may be a prisoner, but may also be a police officer or other official) with whom the psychologist directly deals; the organization that encompasses that individual and employs the psychologist (generally represented by a judge, lawyer, police chief, or warden); the larger organization that encompasses that entity (represented by a city council or other official body); and the general public (dealt with perhaps through a newspaper). The different sets of obligations the psychologist has to each underlies the question of "Who is the client?" It clearly represents what role theorists term "role conflict" (Parsons, 1951; Biddle & Thomas, 1966). This confusion of roles is a significant factor in the genesis of ethical dilemmas relating to questions of both competence and loyalty.

Psychologists, like other mental health professionals, presently lack an effective means to clarify these conflicting roles and obligations (Task Force Report, 1980). Actions should be taken on three levels. Psychologists as individuals should raise into consciousness the existence of these dilemmas and inform the individuals and organizations with whom they work of the limitations and conflicts inherent in their roles (Fersch, 1980a, p. 57; *Ethical Principles,* 1981, Principle 6). Training (both preservice and continuing education) should include a consideration of the applied ethics of psychological intervention and research (Task Force Report, 1980). Finally, psychology as a profession must face the need for more explicit ethical standards of conduct for psychologists in the criminal justice system and in other organizations than is available in the new *Ethical Principles* (1981). The task force's report does not fully meet this need as it "does not represent the official policy" of the APA (Monahan, 1980, p. v).

A. Comparisons to Other Settings and Other Professions

Psychologists in the criminal justice system are not the only ones facing similar ethical issues. Brief attention to four kinds of comparisons may suggest why they would be fruitful ones to pursue.

First, an additional dimension to the moral analysis of treating prisoners would be provided by fuller comparison with the ethical dilemmas of the child psychologist. The task force implicitly takes as a model the provision of psychological services to the usual adult. It recognizes, however, that troublesome moral issues of autonomy are present even in voluntary outpatient treatment. Those who treat children, in particular, have a familiar dilemma that the child who is for some purposes the client is also, like a prisoner, not recognized in our society as having full authority over his or her own life. Therefore the parent is for other purposes the client, and has authority recognized both legally and morally to govern the child, to hire and discharge treating professionals, to set goals for them and ask them for reports. Child psychologists, like prison psychologists, thus suffer from multiple claims for loyalty.

As a second comparison, other issues faced by the task force are not limited to the psychologist or to criminal justice, but have to do with conflicts engendered whenever a professional works within an organization (Task Force, 1980, p. 2). Sociologists working in applied settings, for example, warn that the professional cannot rest on the maxim *caveat emptor,* since the buyer lacks the knowledge to evaluate what is provided (Angell, 1967). Megargee (1977, cited in Brodsky, 1980) suggests that it is overblown to think that prisons present confidentiality issues much different from those in factories, the army, or mental hospitals.

A third comparison psychologists might be interested in is how "whistle-blowing" problems have been faced by others (see Bok, 1980; Stone, 1975). Lawyers, for example, have considered many similar ethical problems, and while they may not have solved the dilemmas, their experience may be helpful (Developments, 1981). In some situations, a lawyer hired by an organization is expected to serve an individual client just as if the client had hired the lawyer directly in a private practice relationship, with full protection of confidentiality, e.g., defendants' counsel employed by auto insurance companies, the Judge Advocate General and public defender offices. The usual lawyer employed by a corporation or similar entity is, however, in a different situation, and ethically owes his allegiance to the entity and not to any individual.[8] For example, if a corporation's lawyer

---

[8]American Bar Association, Code of Professional Responsibility, Ethical Consideration 5–18 (1969); ABA Opinion 86 (1932).

Mental Illness, Medicine and Law

learns from a corporate officer of his or her thefts from the company, the prohibition against divulging client confidences generally prevents the lawyer from disclosing that knowledge; nevertheless, according to legal ethics, the corporation itself is the client, and so the lawyer ethically "should"[9] or at least "may"[10] report the facts to the board of directors (Developments, 1981, p. 1544).

What about disclosures past the organization itself to its own "client" or "superior?" Lawyers for government agencies are ethically required to report wrongdoing to the heads of their agency or, if that person is involved, to the Justice Department.[11] Legal ethical opinion is split over whether a corporation's attorney may disclose wrongdoing to the shareholders.[12] There have been pressures by the Securities and Exchange Commission to regard the lawyers who prepare securities registration statements as sources of information to the authorities or the investing public about their clients' wrongdoing. These pressures, however, have been resisted by the bar.[13]

On the general question of exceptions to confidentiality, lawyers had established an ethical norm long before *Tarasoff*: while a client's admissions of *past* misconduct are considered confidences to be kept secret by the attorney, the profession recognized that the lawyer had an ethical duty in certain circumstances to inform persons defrauded by the client[14] and a right to inform authorities of a continuing or *future* crime.[15] Lawyers are currently debating the traditional ethical norm's balance between duties to individual client and to society (American Bar Association, 1981; Roscoe Pound, 1980).

A fourth comparison, and most salient to this topic, would be to kindred treatment professionals. Psychiatrists, for example, have also been concerned with their exercise of power, which for them comes with the apparent imprimatur of medicine as well as of science (Robitscher, 1980). They worry over their paternalism (Thompson, 1980) as well as the trend that they become "agents of social control" or "agents of the state" (Beigler, 1978, p. 8). Nursing also provides interesting comparisons, where common professional activities—report writing and such—may be carried on for ritualistic reasons (Walker, 1967), just as observers of prisons have noted that psychological assessment may become ritualistic and pointless (Brodsky, 1977, p. 65), misused, or carried on as an end in itself and not used at all (Corsini, 1956, p. 22).

---

[9]ABA Opinion 202 (1940).

[10]ABA Informal Opinion 1349 (1975).

[11]28 U.S.C. §535; "Code of Ethics for Government Service," House Concurrent Resolution, 72 Stat. B12 (1958), 5 C.F.R. §735.10; *The Government Client and Confidentiality*, Federal Bar Association Opinion 73-1, reprinted in N. Redlich, Professional Responsibility: A Problem Approach (1976).

[12]*Compare* ABA Informal Opinion 1349 (1975) *with* Garner v. Wolfinbarger, 430 F.2d 1093 (5th Cir. 1970), cert. denied, 401 U.S. 974 (1971); See ABA Rules of Professional Conduct Rule 1.12(c) (Working Draft, February 22, 1981).

[13]Statement of Policy Adopted by American Bar Association Regarding Responsibilities and Liabilities of Lawyers in Advising with Respect to the Compliance by Clients with Laws Administered by the Securities and Exchange Commission, *reprinted in* 61 A.B.A.J. at 1085 (1975); Committee on Counsel Responsibility and Liability, *The Code of Professional Responsibility and the Responsibility of Lawyers Engaged in Securities Law Practice*, 30 Business Lawyer 1289 (1975).

[14]Compare ABA Code of Professional Responsibility, Disciplinary Rule 7-102(B) (1) (1969) (duty to disclose fraud) *with id.* (1974 amendment) (protecting client's privileged communication).

[15]ABA Code of Professional Responsibility, Disciplinary Rule 4-101(C) (3) (1969).

BOOK REVIEW

Ethical issues thus often cut across disciplinary lines. There must be, neverthe-less, an additonal contribution to perceived ethical distress by the psychologist's role definition as scientist, with its implicit norms of accuracy and objectivity that place special demands on the psychologist's conscience.

V. THE PSYCHOLOGIST AND POWER

In addition to role issues, another theme underlying much of the Monahan (1980) volume is the psychologist's conflictual relation to power.

A. Proximity to Power

Much of the ethical debate cited in the background papers reflects a concern with the potential for abuse of "the considerable power that exists in psychology for controlling and shaping individuals' behavior" (Brodsky, 1980, p. 74). We are told, moreover, that "a great deal of *decision-making power*" is located at discretionary points in the system where "psychologists are often called upon to aid in the decision-making process" (p. 96). Thus some psychologists apparently feel anguish about how to exercise two significant powers—to shape prisoners' behavior and to influence official decisions—that they believe they exercise in the criminal justice setting.

Psychologists may not always recognize, however, that they hold comparatively limited power. As to power to modify behavior, the capacities of correctional psychologists are a far cry from those of Anthony Burgess' *A Clockwork Orange* (1963) and, indeed, have been criticized as insufficient (Wexler, 1975). As to decision-making power, the role of psychologist in sentencing and release decisions is by definition one of staff rather than line, making recommendations to judges or parole boards that are considered by them along with recommendations of probation officers, correctional counselors, prosecutors, friends of the accused, and others. Actual power is in the hands of the officials.

Psychologists campaigned for years to be recognized alongside psychiatrists as experts to whom the courts would look (Perlin, 1980)—a landmark is the 1965 *Jenkins* decision.[16] It is somewhat ironic that now that they have largely succeeded, some psychologists have concluded they should not be pressured to answer the questions courts often want to ask (Task Force, 1981, p. 9).

B. The Radical and "Rethinking" Stances

Psychologists may be critical, not only of the psychologist's power in the justice system, but of the very exercise of power by that system. Such criticisms stem from a broad range of positions, of which some but not all reflect a radical stance.

Sociologists of criminal justice identify two contrasting perspectives, a consensus model, in which criminal laws are taken as expressing the shared values of society (Friedmann, 1964, p. 143), and a conflict model, in which the criminal justice system

---

[16]Jenkins v. United States, 307 F.2d 637 (D.C. Cir. 1962); Annotation, *Qualifications of Non-medical Psychologist to Testify as to Mental Condition or Competency*, 78 A.L.R. 2d 919 (1961).

is seen as an apparatus for maintaining control by one group over another—"the tool of the ruling class" (Quinney, 1974, p. 8). Some of the discussion in the Monahan (1980) volume reflects the conflict model and, within that perspective, sides with the outgroup rather than the governors, to criticize the criminal justice system as a whole.

Thus developments in the 1960s are said to have brought police to the attention of psychologists, and contributed to "a view of the police as a forceful, sometimes unjust, embodiment of the power of the dominant majority" (Mann, 1980, p. 18). There is a refusal to "accept blindly" the criminal justice system as it presently exists, "since it is obvious that what is legal can be immoral . . ." (Task Force, 1980, p. 4). Some accuse psychologists of being "tools of an oppressive correctional establishment and an intolerant society" (see Brodsky, 1980, p. 89). Some psychologists "feel that their presence in court settings would validate a system they consider inadequate, if not immoral," and thus they do not participate (see Fersch, 1980b, p. 49).

Many consider it problematic for professionals to use an offender-blame model (Ryan, 1970; Brodsky & Hobart, 1978), and behavior therapies have even been labeled "genocidal" for using the offender-blame orientation rather than blaming the social and economic systems of which the prisoners are "victims" (Clemons, 1975). One discussion of the juvenile justice system (Kelman, 1968) regards it as "_ipso facto_ ethically problematic" to limit individual freedom by intervening in the life of a person to impose some group's values (Rappaport et al., 1980, p. 93). Similarly, some regard it as unethical for a psychologist to treat with the goals of "imposing the community's norms" or "enforcing conformity" (Lourens, 1973–74, pp. 436–37).

Brodsky's (1980) background paper distinguishes between therapists who accept compliance and self-control as appropriate treatment goals for confined persons ("system-professionals"), and those who challenge the legitimacy of agency objectives by taking a prisoner-first activist stance ("system-challengers"). Similarly, "[m]any find the use of recidivism as a psychotherapy criterion unacceptable, seeing it as using treatment in the service of social control and custody" (Brodsky, 1980, p. 74; Kaufman, 1973).

Some of the discussion supports an orientation of "radical nonintervention" rather than of individual treatment or "liberal reform." A role for correctional psychologists is mentioned in which they serve as "mediators between opposing political forces, never taking sides" between client and correctional system (Brodsky, 1980, p. 74).

Using an analysis quite different from the radical critics, Fersch (1980b) advocates a "rethinking" model that reaches similar conclusions limiting the psychologist's activities in the criminal justice system. Fersch recommends that the criminal justice system deal with mentally ill defendants basically through its usual procedures for the non–ill: abolish the insanity defense, deal with mental incompetency to stand trial much like physical illnesses that might delay proceedings temporarily, and eliminate the indeterminate sentence which focuses on the convict's rehabilitation. "A rethinking approach, then, would eliminate the forced use of psychologist's services and leave psychologists free to continue in the roles where they simply function as willing suppliers of services to willing consumers" (p. 58). The task force (1980, p. 5) similarly recommends that "therapy should only be given on a truly voluntary basis."

C. Responses to the Radical Stance

In analyzing the radical critique, four distinctions may usefully be made. First, while the background paper of Rappaport et al. (1980, p. 101) tells us that "[a]ny distinction between delinquents and nondelinquents relies on a set of norms that are ultimately and irreducibly subjective," the authors do distinguish from other offenders those guilty of assault, burglary, or rape—for whom they state the designation "delin- quent" would be widely regarded as appropriate. Outside the Rappaport chapter, however, much of the other discussion quoted above fails to make a similar distinction that designation as "criminal" is widely regarded as appropriate for adults convicted of violent felonies. Those who take a radical stance seem to reject the possibility that a broad consensus does exist condemning at least some crimes (e.g., wanton murder, rape).

Some radicals reject the possibility that it is legitimate for society to impose major deprivations on those convicted of serious crimes. Those convicted and sent to prison, however, are by definition persons over whom society has made an authoritative judgment that state representatives will have control over their life decisions. One meaning of the criminal law is that, if an individual is convicted, the state may under some circumstances execute him, deprive him of liberty, impose forced labor and other punishments, and generally supersede his own decisions on most daily and long-range life choices. The task force recognized that the criminal justice system is the principal locus of "legitimate" force in American society (1980, p. 2). Even if the prison regime has aspects which are "restrictive and even harsh, they are part of the penalty that criminal offenders pay for their offenses against society," as the Supreme Court has recently declared in the *Rhodes* case.[17] Some who oppose forced treatment of prisoners may basically be challenging not the treatment, but the legitimacy of impris- onment in our society—a stance which may be more political than ethical. "Some observers see imprisonment (a) as an essentially political rather than legal action, designed to oppress the powerless, and (b) as a continuation of a long American tradition of repressive racial policies" (Brodsky, 1980, p. 82).

Second, a related distinction rests on one's judgment as to the general political situation in America. Both "correctional psychology and the prisons have been ac- cused of being tools of worldwide political repression for applying labels such as evil and crazy to those who disagree with government policies and express unpopular opinions" (Brodsky, 1980, p. 73). While a paper recently presented in Moscow at the 7th All-Union Congress of Soviet Neuropathologists and Psychiatrists (Serebryakova, cited in Gillette, 1981) provides new documentation for such labeling by the KGB, for some psychologists to fail to distinguish the American situation from the Russian can be more a political than a scientific judgment.

A third needed distinction is that between treatment designed to "institution- alize" an inmate (Ennis & Emery, 1978, p. 94)—such as medication to render him passive within the prison[18]—and treatment designed to socialize the inmate by enhanc-

---

[17]Rhodes v. Chapman, 431 U.S. 337 (1981).

[18]*See* Nelson v. Heyne, 491 F.2d 352 (7th Cir.), *cert. denied* 417 U.S. 976 (1974) (tranquilizing drug used, not as part of ongoing psychotherapy, but to control).

Mental Illness, Medicine and Law

ing his capacity to function in the general society outside a criminal career—to hold a job, live in a family, and resist criminal peer influence and aggressive urges. One of the goals of the penal function, the Supreme Court recently reaffirmed, is "to return imprisoned persons to society with an improved chance of being useful, law-abiding citizens."[19] Even if treatment actually existed which could reduce the propensity to commit criminal acts, some regard forced treatment as a *sui generis* intrusion on the individual and reject the possibility that society is acting legitimately in imposing treatment on convicted criminals to promote socialization.

A fourth distinction is between treatments which "rehabilitate" prisoners, and those so harsh as to "demolish" them (Spece, 1972). Courts have been sympathetic to the argument that some involuntary treatments are so extreme as to constitute "cruel and unusual punishment" or otherwise violate the civil rights of prisoners.[20] Different ethical problems are raised by use of aversive conditioning verging on physical torture, or withdrawal of the requisites of a minimal living standard, than are raised by psychotherapy—quite apart from the question of consent.

Brodsky (1980) also supplies a response to some radical critics. He points out that rejection of conformity goals is itself hardly value-free, but reflects certain social or political values. He concludes that proposals concerning research with prisoners are more often matters of political views held on faith than scientific conclusions (p. 83). His point applies to treatment also: some of the failure to draw these four distinctions may be politically based.

Given the political implications of these issues, the appearance of impartiality of those considering them has a special importance. The APA's 12-member task force included one member designated as from a "prisoners' union." Such an appointment would make some sense within a medical model (one might include a patient in a study of a hospital) and even more sense within nonmedical psychological models (consumers are now included on many regulatory boards). Within a criminal justice model, however, such a decision would be unusual. (In a study of the death penalty, would a murderer be appointed a commission member?) More surprising is that no task force member was designated alongside the "prisoners' union" member to be explicit representative of judges, parole boards, wardens, police, prosecutors, defense lawyers, or others who have rival claims to be seen as the clients for whom psychologists work in criminal justice. Nor were there explicit representatives of the victims of crime, who might be thought of as the ultimate clients for the criminal justice system. Perhaps the psychologists on the task force who had experience working in the criminal justice system (though primarily academics) were thought to be adequate proxies for these groups, or perhaps it was thought that these other groups were adequately represented in the invitees who met to consider the background papers. Nevertheless, the inclusions and omissions in designation of the task force members may give the appearance of prejudgment on the question of "who is the client?"

D. Response to Prison Conditions

In at least one aspect the task force's (1980) report is not radical enough. There is

---

[19] Rhodes v. Chapman, 431 U.S. at 375.
[20] See note 1, *supra*.

only passing mention that "*nothing* an offender has done could 'deserve' the physical and sexual violence rampant in American 'correctional' institutions . . ." because of "the horrendous human degradation that is part of many prisons" (p. 13). As a former attorney general has said, we could hardly devise a more traumatic social experience than the prison (Clark, 1970). Prisoners are subject to widespread violence (Cohen, Cole & Bailey, 1976) and, in some institutions, to homosexual rape (Davis, 1968, cited in Buffum, 1972).

Because of these conditions, some believe that professionals are ethically obliged not to work in substandard prisons. Their position is similar to the recommendations of the National Commission for the Protection of Human Subjects of Biomedical and Behavioral Research (1976) which in its report on "Research Involving Prisoners" spelled out as a precondition of such research a detailed set of requirements on prison living conditions. Others would feel required to provide services to prisoners no matter what the prison conditions. The task force (1980) explicitly did "not suggest that psychologists . . . avoid serving in imperfect organizations . . ." (p. 3). At the least, the ethical standards for all professionals working within prisons should reinforce their efforts as advocates seeking to reform and abolish inhumane conditions (Halleck, 1971).

VI. ADVOCACY

Advocacy is still another theme—along with role conflict and power—underlying several of the ethical dilemmas of the psychologist in criminal justice. Besides the traditional role of expert, and the role of adversary to the individual, there is a new trend among psychologists and other mental health professionals toward functioning as advocate (Sadoff & Kopolow, 1977; Zusman, Note 1). While the survey reported a "tone of helplessness" among those who tried to remedy abuses of offenders' rights, or to change organizational policies (Clingempeel et al., 1980, p. 26), a variety of advocacy approaches exist through which to make such efforts.

Davidson and Rappaport (1978) identify a 3 × 3 typology of advocacy: the focus can be on the individual, administrative, or policy level and the style can be positive, neutral, or negative. (An example of what is defined as "negative" "individual" advocacy is "whistle-blowing" that exposes the denial of benefits to an individual; an example of "positive" "policy level" advocacy would be lobbying with state legislators.) There are variations on these advocacy styles. Thus, correctional counselors have been found to be particularly effective serving as mediators between prisoners and the prison bureaucracy (Brodsky & Horn, 1973). There are also additional important dimensions, such as internal vs. external advocacy. Among psychologists working with school districts, for example, different forces operate on those who are employees of the district and those who work for outside agencies (Lambert, 1963). Other examples of psychologist advocacy roles were mentioned above, including working on legislative staffs, serving as expert witness in legislative hearings or in precedent-setting cases, and doing policy-oriented research.

Viewing the psychologist as advocate requires a redefinition of professional role. Brodsky (1972; 1980) similarly supports a "Promethean" model of sharing professional power and knowledge with the client. His recommendation commendably accepts the idea of the client as active coparticipant, rather than a passive recipient as in the older medical model (Katz, 1977). Lawyers too have suggested that clients actively participate in decision making on their own cases (Rosenthal, 1974), and some have suggested a complex doctor–patient relationship in which neither patient nor physician rules (Burt, 1979).

Working together with those they seek to aid, psychologists as advocates may have an ethically important role participating in efforts seeking to remedy abuses, reform organizations, protect legal rights, and assure to individuals appropriate treatment by the system in which they function.

VII. CONCLUSIONS

Psychological ethics have several foundations: ethical implications flow from each of the psychologist's roles. As a professional, the psychologist seeks to act according to norms, not merely to earn a wage. As one grounded in science, the psychologist is committed to empirically based truth. As a participant in a formal institution, as a citizen in a democracy, as one dedicated to helping, and as a moral individual, the psychologist has multiple ethical claims upon him or her. Often these claims lead to role conflicts and subsequent ethical dilemmas.

Working in the nation's criminal justice system creates special conflicts: the psychologist is used to dealing with free individuals, while the justice system is used to commanding. Much of the psychologist's usual ethical precepts have to do with respecting the autonomy of the individual consumer (cf. Goldman, 1980), allowing each person free choice over his or her own life, and regulating social interaction by the free consent of all participants. The criminal justice system operates on a different principle. The procedural and substantive rules of criminal law designate conditions and situations wherein representatives of society exercise power over the individual. Thus when psychologists work within the criminal justice system it is often difficult for them to determine which principle morally should be operative.

Psychologists are not alone, however, in coping with these conflicting demands. Many of the psychologist's ethical responsibilities are shared with others who have similar roles, such as other professionals in criminal justice and institutional settings, and others with helping responsibilities. The psychologist can profitably engage in shared ethical discussions with others (Chalk, Frankel, and Chafer, 1980). Consideration of these ethical issues also leads to a broadened definition of the psychologist's professional role. Within the criminal justice system, as in every institution, the professional with ethical concerns can utilize advocacy as one way to express them.

Psychology can be proud of the professionalism and ethical sensitivity manifested by the task force and its collaborators in considering these issues. The discussions sparked by this important volume (Monahan, 1980) may do much to raise the ethical consciousness of psychologists working on the fringes of power in the nation's criminal justice system. The agenda for future discussion and action has been well planned by the task force. A useful next step would be for the APA to reflect the task force's recommendations as official policy for psychologists, by amending its new *Ethical Principles* (1981) or by adopting "specialty guidelines" for the delivery of services by psychologists in criminal justice.

REFERENCE NOTES

1. Zusman, J. *Responsible case advocacy for the mentally ill.* Manuscript submitted for publication, 1981.

REFERENCES

American Bar Association. *Model rules of professional conduct.* Chicago, Illinois: American Bar Association, 1980. (Discussion draft; also appears as Working draft, 1981.)

American Psychiatric Association. *Clinical aspects of the violent individual.* Washington, D.C.: American Psychiatric Association, 1974.

Angell, R. C. The ethical problems of applied sociology. In P.F. Lazarsfeld, W. H. Sewell, & H. L. Wilensky, eds., *The uses of sociology.* New York: Basic Books, 1967.

Bard, M., & Berkowitz, B. Training police as specialists in family crisis intervention: A community psychology action project. *Community Mental Health Journal,* 1967, **3,** 315–317.

Barlow, D. H. On the relation of clinical research to clinical practice: Current issues, new directions. *Journal of Consulting Psychology,* 1981, **49,** 147–156.

Beigler, J. S. Psychiatry and confidentiality: A position paper prepared for submission to The President's Commission on Mental Health. *American Psychoanalytic Association Newsletter,* July 1978, **12,** 7–8. (Summary)

Biddle, B. J., & Thomas, E. J. *Role theory: Concepts and research.* New York: Wiley, 1966.

Bok, Sissela. Whistleblowing and professional responsibilities. In Daniel Callahan & Sissela Bok, eds., *Ethics teaching in higher education.* New York: Plenum Press, 1980. (Hastings Center series on ethics)

Brodsky, S. L. Shared results and open files with the client. *Professional Psychology,* 1972, **4,** 362–364.

Brodsky, S. L. Go away; I'm looking for the truth: Research utilization in corrections. *Criminal Justice and Behavior,* 1977, **4,** 1–9.

Brodsky, S. L. Ethical issues for psychologists in corrections. In J. Monahan, ed., *Who is the client? The ethics of psychological intervention in the criminal justice system.* Washington, D.C.: American Psychological Associaiton, 1980.

Brodsky, S. L., & Hobart, S. Blame models and assailant research. *Criminal Justice and Behavior,* 1978, **5,** 379–388.

Brodsky, S. L., & Horn, C. L. The politics of correctional treatment. In A. A. Roberts, ed., *Correctional treatment of the offender.* Springfield, Illinois: Charles C. Thomas, 1973.

Buffum, P. C. *Homosexuality in prisons.* Washington, D.C.: U.S. Department of Justice, 1972.

Burgess, A. *A clockwork orange.* New York: Norton, 1963.

Burt, R. A. *Taking care of strangers: The rule of law in doctor–patient relations.* New York: Free Press, 1979.

Chalk, R., Frankel, M.S., & Chafer, S. B. *AAAS professional ethics project: Professional ethics activities in the scientific and engineering societies.* Washington, D.C.: American Association for the Advancement of Science, 1980.

Clark, R. *Crime in America.* New York: Simon & Schuster, 1970.

Clemons, R. Proposed legal regulation of applied behavior analysis in prisons: Consumer issues and concerns. *Arizona Law Review,* 1975, **17,** 127–131.

Clingempeel, W. G., Mulvey, E., & Repucci, N. D. A national study of ethical dilemmas of psychologists in the criminal justice system. In J. Monahan, ed., *Who is the client? The ethics of psychological intervention in the criminal justice system.* Washington, D.C.: American Psychological Association, 1980.

Cohen, A. K., Cole, G. F., & Bailey, R. G. *Prison violence.* Lexington, Massachusetts: Heath & Co., 1976.

Corsini, R. J. Two therapeutic groups that failed. *Journal of Correctional Psychology.* 1956, **1,** 16–22.

Davidson, W. S., & Rappaport, J. Toward a model for advocacy: Values, roles and conceptions from community psychology. In G. H. Weber & G. J. McCall, eds., *Social scientists as advocates: Views from the applied disciplines.* Beverly Hills, California: Sage, 1978.

Dershowitz, A. The psychiatrist's power in civil commitment. *Psychology Today,* February 1969, pp. 43–47.

Developments in the law—Conflicts of interest in the legal profession. *Harvard Law Review,* 1981, **94,** 1244–1503.

Ennis, B. J., & Emery, R. D. *The rights of mental patients: The revised edition of the basic ACLU guide to a mental patient's rights.* New York: Avon Books, 1978.

84

Ethical standards of psychologists. Washington, D.C.: American Psychological Association, 1963. (Previous version 1953)

Ethical principles of psychologists. Washington, D.C.: American Psychological Association, 1981. (Previous versions, Ethical standards of psychologists, 1979, 1973)

Fersch, E. A. *Psychology and psychiatry in courts and corrections: Controversy and change.* New York: Wiley, 1980a.

Fersch, E. A. Ethical issues for psychologists in court settings. In J. Monahan, ed., *Who is the client? The ethics of psychological intervention in the criminal justice system.* Washington, D.C.: American Psychological Association, 1980b.

Friedman, P. Legal regulation of applied behavior analysis in mental institutions and prisons. *Arizona Law Review,* 1975, **17**, 75–104.

Friedmann, W. *Law in a changing society.* Harmondsworth, England: Penguin Books, 1964.

Gilette, R. Dissenters hospitalized, Soviet doctor confirms: Citizens get psychiatric treatment for making ''groundless complaints,'' scientific paper says. *Los Angeles Times,* May 31, 1981, pp. 1, 32.

Goldman, A. H. *The moral foundation of professional ethics.* Totowa, New Jersey: Rowman and Littlefield, 1980.

Halleck, S. L. *The politics of therapy.* New York: Science House, 1971.

Hollingshead, A. B., & Redlich, F. C. *Social class and mental illness.* New York: Wiley, 1968.

Institute of Judicial Administration–American Bar Association Joint Commission on Juvenile Justice Standards. *Standards relating to juvenile delinquency and sanctions: Tentative Draft.* Cambridge, Massachusetts: Ballinger, 1976.

Katz, J. Informed consent—A fairy tale? Law's vision. *University of Pittsburgh Law Review,* 1977, **39**, 137–174.

Katz, J. *Experimentation with human beings.* New York: Russell Sage, 1972.

Kaufman, E. Can comprehensive mental health care be provided in an overcrowded prison system? *Journal of Psychiatry and Law,* 1973, **1**, 243–262.

Kelman, H. *A time to speak: On human values and social research.* San Francisco: Jossey-Bass, 1968.

Kirp, D. L. Proceduralism and bureaucracy: Due process in the school setting. *Stanford Law Review,* 1976, **28**, 841–876.

Lambert, N. *Variants of consultation service to schools and implications for training.* Washington, D.C.: American Psychological Association, 1963.

Loftus, E. F. *Eyewitness testimony.* Cambridge, Massachusetts: Harvard University Press, 1979.

Lourens, P. J. D. Skinner versus freedom: Concurrence and dissent. *Cumberland-Sanford Law Review,* 1973–1974, **4**, 425–439.

Mann, P. A. Ethical issues for psychologists in police agencies. In J. Monahan, ed., *Who is the client? The ethics of psychological intervention in the criminal justice system.* Washington, D.C.: American Psychological Association, 1980.

Monahan, J. *The clinical prediction of violent vehavior.* Washington, D.C.: U.S. Department of Health and Human Services, 1981. (Crime and delinquency issues)

Monahan, J. (ed.) *Who is the client? The ethics of psychological intervention in the criminal justice system.* Washington, D.C.: American Psychological Association, 1980.

Morse, S. J. Crazy behavior, morals, and science: An analysis of mental health law. *Southern California Law Review,* 1978, **51**, 527–654. Abbreviated version, Law and mental health professionals. *Professional Psychology,* 1978s, **9**, 389–399.

Morse, S. J. Mental health law: Governmental regulation of disordered persons and the role of the professional psychologist. In B. D. Sales, ed., *The professional psychologist's handbook.* New York: Plenum Press, forthcoming.

National Commission for the Protection of Human Subjects of Biomedical and Behavioral Research. *Research involving prisoners: Report and recommendations.* Washington, D.C.: Department of Health, Education and Welfare, 1976.

Parsons, T. *The social system.* New York: Free Press, 1951.

Perlin, M. L. The legal status of the psychologist in the courtroom. *Mental Disability Law Reporter,* 1980, **4**, 194–200.

Psychiatrists and psychologists to be boarded as specialists in forensic area. *Forensic Issues,* 1979, **1**, 4.

Quinney, R., ed. *Criminal justice in America: A critical understanding.* Boston: Little, Brown & Co., 1974.

Rappaport, J., Lamiell, J. T., & Seidman, E. Ethical issues for psychologists in the juvenile justice system: Know and tell. In J. Monahan, ed., *Who is the client? The ethics of psychological intervention in the criminal justice system*. Washington, D.C.: American Psychological Association, 1980.

Robitscher, J. B. *The powers of psychiatry*. Boston: Houghton-Mifflin Co., 1980.

Roscoe Pound-American Trial Lawyers Foundation, Commission on Professional Responsibility. *The American lawyer's code of conduct*. Washington, D.C.: Roscoe Pound–American Trial Lawyer's Foundation, 1980. (Public discussion draft)

Rosenthal, D. E. *Lawyer and client: Who's in charge?* New York: Russell Sage Foundation, 1974.

Ryan, W. *Blaming the victim*. New York: Vintage, 1970.

Sadoff, R. L., & Kopolow, L. E. The mental health professional's role in patient advocacy. In L. E. Kopolow & H. Bloom. *Mental health advocacy: An emerging force in consumer's rights*. Washington, D.C.: U.S. Department of Health, Education and Welfare, 1977.

Schur, E. M. *Radical non-intervention: Rethinking the delinquency problem*. Englewood Cliffs, New Jersey: Prentice-Hall, 1973.

Seidman, E. Justice, values, and social sciences: Unexamined premises. In R. J. Simon, ed., *Research in law and sociology: An annual compilation of research*, Vol. 1. Greenwich, Connecticut: JAI Press, 1978.

Shapiro, M. H., & Spece, R. G. *Cases, materials and problems on bioethics and law*. St. Paul, Minnesota: West Publishing Co., 1981.

Spece, R. G. Conditioning and other technologies used to "treat?" "rehabilitate?" "demolish?" prisoners and mental patients. *Southern California Law Review*, 1972, **45**, 616–684.

Stone, A. *Mental health and law: A system in transition*. Washington, D.C.: U.S. Government Printing Office, 1975.

Stone, C. D. *Where the law ends*. New York: Harper & Row, 1975.

Suggs, D. L. The use of psychological research by the judiciary: Do the courts adequately assess the validity of the research? *Law and Human Behavior*, 1979, **3**, 135–148.

Tapp, J. L., & Levine, F. J., eds. *Law, justice and the individual in society: Psychological and legal issues*. New York: Holt, Rinehart & Winston, 1977.

Task Force on the Role of Psychology in the Criminal Justice System Report. In John Monahan, ed., *Who is the client? The ethics of psychological intervention in the criminal justice system*. Washington, D.C.: American Psychological Association, 1980. (Earlier version in *American Psychologist*, 1978, **33**, 1099–1113.)

Thompson, Dennis F. Paternalism in medicine, law, and public policy. In Daniel Callahan & Sissela Bok, ed., *Ethics teaching in higher education*. New York: Plenum Press, 1980. (Hastings Center series on ethics)

Twain, D., McGee, R., & Bennett, L. A. Functional areas of psychological activity. In S. L. Brodsky, ed., *Psychologists in the criminal justice system*. Urbana: University of Illinois Press, 1973.

Walker, V. H. *Nursing and ritualistic practice*. New York: Macmillan Co., 1967.

Wexler, D. B. Reflections on the legal regulation of behavior modification in institutional settings. *Arizona Law Review*, 1975, **17**, 132–143.

Yarmey, A. D. *The psychology of eyewitness testimony*. New York: Free Press, 1979.

[44]

Conflicting Loyalties in the Practice of Psychiatry: Some Philosophical Reflections

James Dwyer, Ph.D.

Although Aristotle was a student and friend of Plato's, he came to disagree with Plato about a very important issue: the nature of the good. Thus Aristotle found himself in a difficult position when, in the course of his own teaching, he began to criticize Plato's idea of a universal good. He felt torn between his loyalty to Plato and his loyalty to truth. Although he loved both his friend and the truth, he concluded that his duty as a philosopher, a lover of wisdom, was to value truth above friendship (1).

More poignant is a conflict portrayed in *Fiddler on the Roof* (2). Tevye, the father, has five daughters. The first daughter wants to marry the tailor, a young man she loves. The father reluctantly accepts this, even though he must renege on an agreement he made with the butcher, an older and wealthier man. The second daughter wants to go off with a radical. The father reluctantly accepts this, too. Then the third daughter, Chava, marries a Gentile. When Tevye learns the news, he says that his family should consider Chava dead and try to forget her. But Chava comes to see him, to ask him to accept her and her husband. Tevye hesitates. He looks up to heaven and says: "Accept them? How can I accept them? Can I deny everything I believe in? On the other hand, can I deny my own child?" Torn between his loyalty to his daughter and his loyalty to his faith and his people, Tevye sees his beliefs and loyalties not merely as valuable things, but as constituents of the very person he is. He says that if he bends far enough to accept his daughter, he will break. So he decides to reject his own daughter, although in the last scene he does show some affection for her.

Few of us have faced predicaments exactly like Tevye's or Aristotle's, but most of us have found ourselves in situations where our loyalties seem to pull us in different directions. This common experience raises a number of basic questions: How do we come to have several loyalties? Why do our loyalties sometimes conflict? How are we to resolve conflicts of loyalties? Even more basic: What is loyalty and why is it a good thing? I want to consider all these questions with respect to an area of special concern: the practice of psychiatry.

The practice of psychiatry may place people, whether or not they realize it, in a variety of situations where loyalties will conflict. For example, I can imagine myself faced with the following conflicts.

1. I am seeing a young man who threatens a woman he has talked about before. I assess that there is a real danger. Still, I hesitate to warn the woman or to commit my patient. I feel torn between my loyalty to my patient and my loyalty to society, between my desire to maintain confidentiality and trust and my duty to prevent harm and protect people.

2. In discussions with a new patient, I learn that she became sexually involved with her previous therapist. She feels she was exploited by him and seems mistrustful of me. I am convinced that the previous therapist acted unethically and harmed the patient. I feel I should report his conduct and encourage my patient to bring charges against him. I don't want him to exploit and harm other patients. But I also feel I should maintain trust with my new patient and not press her to pursue a course of action she feels ambivalent about. A legal process might prove very difficult for her.

3. I lead an ethics discussion group for third-year medical students. During a discussion of informed consent, several students give examples of how a particular physician at our hospital fails to inform patients of reasonable treatment options. After the discussion I feel troubled. Loyal to my ethical standards, I want to see that patients' rights are respected. But I feel loyal to those students who discussed their experiences with me in an atmosphere of learning and who might suffer repercussions if I take action.

4. A colleague of mine has begun to drink more heavily. I fear that his drinking is now beginning to impair his work at the hospital. I have talked to him about the problem but there has been no positive response; in fact, he continues to deny the problem. Loyal to my colleague, I want to give him a chance to come to terms with his problem. But I don't want his impaired work to harm patients or the reputation of the hospital.

5. I designed a research project to compare the effectiveness of two alternative treatments. The study was approved by the IRB and uses only subjects who give their informed and free consent. Yet when I talk to prospective subjects I sometimes hesitate. Sometimes my intuitive clinical sense suggests that one of the treatments would be better for a particular patient. As a clinician, I feel loyal to my patients and want to tell them my opinion when my patients asked which treatment is better. But as a researcher, I feel loyal to the integrity of the study and want to tell them that we won't know which treatment is more effective until the study is completed.

6. I work at a private, non-profit hospital that serves a poor and working class population. The hospital has been losing money and will be forced to close if the trend continues. Because of the diagnosis-related group (DRG) payment system, the administration is pressuring the staff to discharge Medicare and Medicaid patients quickly. I feel loyal to and responsible for my patients and will not discharge them prematurely. But often there is room for judgment, for example, when patients would feel more comfortable staying an extra day but would not be endangered by early discharge. In these cases I begin to think about my duty to help the hospital and the community it serves.

7. A schizophrenic man is brought to the psychiatric emergency room. Since he is delusional and highly agitated, he is placed on hold, treated with psychotropic drugs, and scheduled for a hearing. His past pattern of hospitalization resembles a revolving door. His disease is manageable with proper medication, but after he is discharged from the hospital, he stops taking all medication, his condition deteriorates, and soon he is back in the hospital and placed on hold. I am asked to testify at this patient's hearing. I hesitate because I feel loyal to both the patient's rights and his health. I feel I should respect civil liberties and tell the truth: when the patient is taking his medication, he is not a threat to himself or others. But I also feel that I should work for the benefit of the patient: he needs a longer period in a controlled environment if he is to have any chance of managing his disease and life.

8. I am working on a routine case in forensic psychiatry. I know that my report will influence whether the person I am seeing is sent into the mental health system or the criminal justice system, and I am aware of the flaws in each system. I feel that my loyalty as a physician is to see that the person gets help and treatment. But my loyalty as a court evaluator is to provide an accurate assessment and to see that justice is done.

Reflection on examples like these may suggest quick answers to two of the basic questions. How do psychiatrists come to have several loyalties? Answer: by occupying several roles. When psychiatrists act as healers, physicians, professionals, teachers, researchers, cost controllers, social protectors, and advisers to the courts, they may have different loyalties. How are psychiatrists to resolve conflicts of loyalties? Answer: by restricting themselves to one role in order to prevent conflicts from ever arising. Before I discuss whether these quick answers are adequate, I want to discuss what loyalty is and why it is a good thing.

We can begin by thinking of loyalty as an attachment or allegiance to a person or cause. Loyalty is more than intellectual agreement based on our cognitive judgment; it is a response of our whole being, unconscious as well as conscious (3). Indeed, we may have loyalties whose depths and directions we are not aware of. A further difference is that intellectual agreement is usually a commitment to an idea or proposition whose content is more or less determined, whereas loyalty is a commitment to a person or cause whose future is not completely determined or specified.

But loyalty is not love. After all, psychiatrists can be loyal to patients they do not love, even to patients they dislike. Loyalty is more closely connected to the idea of service and duty than is love. To be loyal is to be willingly faithful to the obligations that connect us to the person or cause that is the object of our loyalty. These obligations and duties are not experienced as externally imposed; they are willingly accepted. Indeed, they are seen as part of our relationship to the person or cause. The loyal friend, for example, is willingly faithful to the commitments of friendship and sees those commitments as part of the relationship.

What good is this fidelity to obligations, this commitment to a somewhat undetermined future, this allegiance to a person or cause? What good is loyalty?

No one doubts that loyalty is good for the *object* of loyalty. Patients benefit by having psychiatrists who exemplify characteristic qualities of loyalty—devotion and sensitivity, self-control and good judgment. The loyalty of psychiatrists to their patients has important benefits for those patients: timely and appropriate treatment, as well as a sense of confidence and trust.

But how, if at all, is loyalty good for the *subject* of loyalty? We could view the loyalty of psychiatrists as part of an exchange: in return for their willing devotion to patients, psychiatrists are compensated, accorded professional privileges, and held in public esteem. Yet something is wrong with this view. Actions performed merely for their exchange value do not express loyalty, and the good of loyalty is deeper than money, privileges, and esteem. The deep value and chief benefit of loyalty has to do with meaning and the maintenance of relationships. Loyalty expresses a coherent meaning that unifies one's personal and professional conduct (3). But how?

To engage in a profession such as psychiatry commits one to certain courses of action and certain relations to various people—to patients, colleagues, and the public. There is nothing new about this idea. The Latin word *officium*, the root of the English word office, meant performance of duty. One has certain duties because of the office one holds. The office, nature, and function of the psychiatrist impose duties. Even without specifying exactly what those duties are, I see two important functions of loyalty. As an expression of the meaning of one's professional commitment, loyalty gives form and content to one's professional life and provides a unity of purpose that ties various actions together. To float aimlessly about a swimming pool may be a pleasant recreation, but to drift through life, pulled only by passing and vacillating desires, is not meaningful. To have direction and coherence in life is a great good. Fidelity to commitments is an important source of direction, coherence, and meaning. Loyalty, then, is a good thing for the subject of loyalty.

Conflicting loyalties endanger the good for both psychiatrists and patients, undermining a clear sense of the overall direction and meaning of a psychiatrist's commitment. When the rights of patients to timely and appropriate treatment are balanced against other considerations, the patients' trust and confidence may be undermined. There is then a great need to find some way of approaching the problem of conflicting loyalties, some way of unifying disjunctive commitments in a coherent way.

Before I discuss how conflicts of loyalties can be resolved and the good of loyalty reestablished, I want to look at the source and formation of these conflicts. Obviously, conflicts can arise only if psychiatrists come to have several loyalties. How does that happen? Loyalties develop with the assumption of roles and relationships inside as well as outside professional practice. Because of their roles as family members, friends, citizens, religious believers, and concerned human beings, psychiatrists relate to people in certain ways. Each role carries commitments to certain people. Psychiatrists are also committed to certain people in certain ways because of agreements, promises, and contracts they have made. They may also develop a variety of loyalties within as well as outside professional life. Each professional role they are asked to assume—therapist, teacher, researcher, cost controller, advisor to the court, employee—

brings with it certain commitments. With variety of commitments comes potential for conflict.

Often there may be no actual conflict. After all, many psychiatrists manage quite well to be family members, friends, therapists, teachers, researchers, and more. Yet conflicts arise, in two different forms. Psychiatrists may become so overextended that the amount of time and devotion they have available is not adequate for them to fulfill all their commitments in a caring way. Or they may experience a conflict because they are extended in incompatible ways, because the commitments they want to fulfill are at odds. It seems clear (at least in theory) how psychiatrists should deal with conflicts of the first kind, but how are they to avoid or resolve conflicts of the second kind? I will discuss two approaches.

One possibility is to try to prevent conflicts from ever arising. Psychiatrists taking this approach would restrict their roles and commitments so that their loyalties never become divided, taking care not to combine being clinicians with being researchers, cost controllers, court evaluators, and so on. Psychiatrists should also try to avoid treating members of their own families, treating more than one person from another family, acquiring a financial interest in drug companies and hospitals, and pursuing other courses of conduct that are similarly fraught with the potential for conflict. This approach is often expressed as the principle that psychiatrists should be loyal to their patients above all, that they should be advocates for their patients.

This approach is certainly very appealing. It would help psychiatrists to avoid conflicts, unify their allegiance, maintain their sense of purpose, and simplify the moral universe in which they work. But there are problems with the simplifying approach. Such an approach is, after all, a solution by restriction, and that in itself should raise some suspicion. Although I believe that some combinations of roles and commitments should be avoided, I do not believe that it is always desirable to restrict one's role, nor do I believe that a restricted role will always avoid conflict. For example, even if psychiatrists devote themselves exclusively to the good of the patient and show no allegiance to other persons and causes, conflicts may arise over what is good for the patient, between, say, securing effective treatment for the patient and respecting the patient's right of self-determination. Both may benefit the patient, but they may sometimes be at odds.

There is another problem with the simplifying approach. If one believes that there is a plurality of goods, a plurality of people and causes worthy of loyalty, then the solution by restriction does not seem very promising. It is a good thing to provide effective treatment, to respect patients' rights to refuse treatment, to maintain confidentiality, to prevent harm to innocent people, to see that children are placed with a loving and competent parent, to prevent impaired physicians from practicing, to pursue research, to be truthful, to control costs, to respect civil liberties, to see that justice is done. To single out one *specific* good as the absolute and exclusive object of loyalty seems like fanaticism. Truth is important, but is it wrong to tell a lie to save an innocent person from religious persecution? Confidentiality is important, but is it wrong to restrict it in order to prevent child abuse?

Very few people are fanatics, but some people believe in a radical division of moral labor: they admit that there is a plurality of important moral concerns and that each concern should have its loyalists, but they believe that no loyalist should have more than one concern. Each cause should have advocates, but no advocate should be loyal to more than one cause. But what social system or mechanism will coordinate, balance, and reconcile the separate loyalties? Perhaps a radical division of moral concerns could be combined with a system modeled on an economic market or an adversarial legal proceeding. But how would such a system work? To say that psychiatrists should respect confidentiality and that social workers should prevent child abuse is fine, but to make psychiatrists and social workers into adversaries or competitors does nothing to ensure a sensible balance and reconciliation of loyalties. Furthermore, it is not clear whether, much less why, psychiatrists should adopt a legal or an economic model of professional responsibility.

Some division of moral concern makes sense. Psychiatrists should not have the same concerns in the same degree as social workers, police officers, judges, or ministers. But a radical division of moral concerns is neither possible nor desirable. Most psychiatrists recognize a plurality of goods and feel committed to a plurality of causes. In fact, the APA's code of ethics (4) lists a number of commitments, among them: to provide competent care, to respect patients' rights, to honor confidentiality, to protect the community from danger, to expose incompetent physicians, to be compassionate, to avoid participation in executions, and to improve the community. Given this variety of commitments, the pressing problem is how to order them into a coherent practice. Sometimes the law will dictate a particular solution—as in *Tarasoff* or in the statutes for the reporting of suspected child abuse—but often psychiatrists will need to make their own ethical judgments to reconcile their commitments.

Psychiatrists need an approach to the problem of conflicting loyalties that will help them to become more aware of their various allegiances and to reconcile their various commitments. Another approach they can take is to try to articulate and reflect on the meaning of their commitments in order to determine how these commitments should be ordered or reconciled in a particular case. This approach is not new; indeed, it may be just a restatement of ordinary moral practice. Consider the conflict that Aristotle faced and the way he resolved it. Torn between his loyalty to truth and his loyalty to Plato, he decided that his commitment as a philosopher included a duty to criticize false accounts of the good, and that his loyalty as a friend did not entail withholding sincere criticism of philosophical views. Although Aristotle said that a philosopher must value truth above friendship, that formulation of the resolution is misleading. I can well imagine Aristotle telling a lie to help his friend escape unjust persecution. What his resolution amounts to is a further specification of the meaning of his loyalties. Loyalty is not simply an attachment to a person or cause, but an allegiance qualified by a meaning: I am loyal to a person as a friend, colleague, psychiatrist. Yet the meaning of a relationship is not completely determined in advance. What needs to be determined when conflict arises is the nature of the conflicting relationships and the commitments they entail. Aristotle made such a determination in order to resolve his conflict. Psychiatrists can try to make similar determinations by reflecting on the history, purpose, and consequences of their relationships and commitments.

Consider how this approach might work in cases where there is a conflict between a commitment to maintain confidentiality and a commitment to protect the public. The duty to maintain confidentiality goes to the very nature of the role and function of psychiatrists. Confidentiality enhances trust between patient and therapist, facilitates disclosure of information needed for effective treatment, and protects the patient against social prejudice. Although the psychiatrist's commitment to confidentiality is for the benefit of the patient, the purpose was never to further the patient's plans and desires uncritically. This reflection may begin to suggest a limitation. The duty to protect the public must similarly be examined. Psychiatrists are not police officers; their role is different and their duty to protect is much more specific. But their role brings with it a special responsibility when the danger is connected to the psychiatric disorders of their patients. Further reflection and specification will probably be needed to resolve a particular case. Is the patient in some way asking for help in controlling impulses? Could setting and discussing a limit on confidentiality increase trust and communication? Could a warning be seen as in the best interest of the patient? Does respect for the patient's right of self-determination include allowing conduct that may harm others? Are other people and professionals in a better position to protect the public? These and other questions may need to be considered in order to reach a resolution that will be workable in practice.

When psychiatrists specify the meaning of their loyalties, are they discovering duties and limits that were implicit in their roles and practices? Or are they inventing new duties and limits? If that is a metaphysical question, I do not know the answer. If it is a phenomenological question, the answer is that psychiatrists may be doing either. Sometimes they will have the experience of discovering and clarifying what was always their duty: "When I committed myself to maintain confidentiality, I never meant to abet a murder." Sometimes they will have the experience of adopting a new duty or setting a new limit: "Here is where I am going to draw the line; from now on I am going to limit my commitment to confidentiality at this point."

Whatever the phenomenological status of the resolution, the process of reaching it requires reasoning, though not necessarily the application of a ready-made ethical theory to a concrete case. Applying a theory is only one form of reasoning in moral life and may not be the form best suited to the problem of conflicting loyalties. The approach I describe is closer to the model of reasoning that John Rawls describes in his discussion of the search for a conception of justice (5). Rawls says that the task of this form of moral reasoning is as follows:

> . . . to articulate a public conception of justice that all can live with who regard their person and their relation to society in a certain way. And though doing this may involve settling theoretical difficulties, the practical social task is primary. What justifies a conception of justice is not its being true to an order antecedent to and given to us, but its congruence with our deeper understanding of ourselves and our aspirations, and our realization that, given our history and the traditions embedded in our public life, it is the most reasonable doctrine for us. (p. 519)

Instead of urging us to search for a theory of justice that corresponds to some divine or natural order, Rawls suggests that we take a humbler, more practical approach: that we look for a conception of justice that articulates and fits our conception of ourselves, our aspirations, and our public traditions.

Similarly, psychiatrists can look for ethical resolutions that are congruent with their conception of themselves as moral subjects, their social relations as professionals, their aspirations as healers, and their traditions of public service. Central to their overall conception of themselves as psychiatrists will probably be the idea of restoring the patient to health and a good life. This conception needs to be articulated, examined, and used in the process of resolving conflicts of loyalties. Any deep examination must consider critics like Michel Foucault and Thomas Szasz who suggest that psychiatrists have not been true to their self-conception, that in practice they have become the agents and instruments of social control (6,7). When commitments are not congruent with how psychiatrists conceive of themselves, psychiatrists should eschew the commitments or change their self-conception. When conflicting commitments seem compatible with how psychiatrists conceive of themselves, psychiatrists will need to specify their commitments and their self-conception in order to determine the meaning that fits with a deeper understanding of themselves and the practice of psychiatry.

Our experience of loyalties and our reflective response to conflicts of loyalties demonstrate two of the most characteristic abilities of ethical life. Loyalties to people and causes are so characteristic of ethical life that the complete absence of such loyalties is seen as a sign of antisocial personal disorder. Also characteristic of ethical life is the attempt to resolve conflicts of loyalties by some form of reflection. The ability to examine our commitments and our conceptions of ourselves is what allows ethical life to go beyond convention and custom. Periodic self-examination and an abiding sense of loyalty are not only characteristic of ethical life, they are also characteristic of the good practice of psychiatry.

Notes

1. Aristotle: Nichomachean Ethics. Indianapolis, IN, Hackett, 1985
2. Stein J: Fiddler on the Roof. New York, Crown, 1964, p 103
3. Royce J: The Philosophy of Loyalty. New York, Hafner, 1971
4. American Psychiatric Association: The Principles of Medical Ethics with Annotations Especially Applicable to Psychiatry. Washington, DC, American Psychiatric Association, 1986
5. Rawls J: Kantian constructivism in moral theory. J Philosophy 9:515–572, 1980, p 519
6. Foucault M: Madness and Civilization: A History of Insanity in the Age of Reason. New York, Vintage, 1973
7. Szasz T: Ideology and Insanity. Garden City, NY, Doubleday, 1970

The Psychiatrist as Expert

[45]

The Parable of the Forensic Psychiatrist: Ethics and the Problem of Doing Harm

Paul S. Appelbaum*

In his presidential address to the American Psychiatric Association, Alan Stone (1980) told a story he called "the parable of the black sergeant." The sergeant, who was being court-martialed for stealing government property, had been sent to an Army psychiatrist to determine whether his behavior had been driven by kleptomaniacal impulses. After a thorough examination, the psychiatrist "concluded that the sergeant did not have kleptomania or any other mental disorder that should excuse him from responsibility," and so testified.

Nonetheless, at trial, the psychiatrist—who we discover at the end of the parable was Alan Stone himself—was deeply disturbed about his testimony. As he faced the court, he averted his eyes from the sergeant, "who sat there in his dress uniform with his medals, his wife, and their small children." When the court passed its sentence of five years at hard labor, the powerful feeling that something terrible had happened overcame Stone, a feeling so potent that "[e]ach time my mind takes me back to that occasion I have a sense of dismay that will not be dissipated."

Why this intense reaction? In the course of evaluation, the sergeant revealed that the roots of his crime lay not in kleptomania, but in his bitterness over the fate of a black man in a discriminatory society. In Stone's words, "[H]e stole with a sense of entitlement and reparation in protest of the racist world that had deprived him of his hopes." Yet, Stone apparently chose not to describe these motives to the court, relying on a narrowly psychopathological model of explanation. His courtroom analysis was restricted to a consideration of the presence or absence of the syndrome of kleptomania. Though information about the social origins of the sergeant's actions would not have been exculpatory in a legal sense, Stone believes that it might have induced leniency in sentencing by the Army judges, and faults himself for omitting it. This parable forms the basis for an important discussion by Stone of the difficulties modern, eclectic psychiatry has in integrating its conceptual models.

I believe, however, that there is more to learn from this story. It might equally well have been entitled "the parable of the forensic psychiatrist," since either of

*Department of Psychiatry, University of Massachusetts Medical School, Worcester, MA 01655.

Dr. Appelbaum is the A. F. Zeleznik Professor of Psychiatry and Director, Law and Psychiatry Program, University of Massachusetts Medical School.

The author is grateful for the comments of Richard Bonnie, Thomas Grisso, and William Winslade on an earlier draft of this paper.

its protagonists could have served as tragic hero. The tale of the black sergeant driven to take revenge on a racist society is no more poignant than the description of an anguished psychiatrist haunted by the spectre of the harm to which he contributed. In fact, if my colleague and friend will permit me to speculate on his reactions, I think it probable that the infliction of harm, as much as the more abstract problem of selecting among conceptual models, lies at the core of Alan Stone's discomfort, both past and present.

Stone's visceral response to the court's verdict, his sympathetic descriptions of the defendant and his family, and his subsequent publicly avowed unwillingness to become involved in court proceedings are all understandable as the reaction of a morally sensitive man to a situation that confounded his ethical intuitions. How could a psychiatrist—whose calling is to help humanity—contribute to a process that resulted in an already abused person being sentenced to five years at hard labor? How could he have done harm to that man?

Three years later, in his address to the American Academy of Psychiatry and the Law, Stone elaborated on his concerns regarding these issues, particularly the justification of doing harm (Stone, 1984):

> The crucial word for me is 'justify': when the psychiatrist's goal is to do the best he/she can to ease the patient's suffering, he/she has a powerful justification. It is the justification for every physician who did not wait for science and theory to be perfected. Do whatever you can to help your patient and *primum non nocere*, first of all do no harm . . . [A]s physicians we know what the ethical struggle is. We know the boundaries of the ethical debate. When we turn our skills to forensic psychiatry, when we serve the system of justice, we can no longer agree on the boundaries of the debate.

Stone's parable is important because it reflects more than just the ethical struggles of a single psychiatrist. It describes the central ethical enigmas of forensic psychiatry. If psychiatrists are committed to doing good and avoiding harm, how can they participate in legal proceedings from which harm may result? If, on the other hand, psychiatrists in court abandon medicine's traditional ethical principles, how do they justify that deviation? And if the obligations to do good and avoid harm no longer govern psychiatrists in the legal setting, what alternative principles come into play?[1]

Psychiatric Ethics versus Forensic Ethics

A prior question must be addressed before considering these dilemmas. Are psychiatrists in general bound by the principles of beneficence and nonmalefi-

---

[1] I have chosen to focus this paper on *psychiatric* ethics, while recognizing that other mental health professions, especially psychology, have come to play as significant a role as psychiatry in forensic work. Nonetheless, psychologic ethics differ in history and in particulars from psychiatric ethics. It may be that an argument identical to the one that I make in this paper could be applied to forensic psychology. Alternatively, it may be that the origin of psychology as an academic discipline derived from philosophy, rather than as a clinical art and science, presents a very different ethical perspective. To distinguish between these possibilities would require a detailed effort that I make no attempt here to undertake.

cence — doing good and avoiding harm — as Stone assumed? A decade ago the question might have seemed strange. From the time of the Hippocratic oath, these two values have been seen as central to the practice of medicine. Most commentators today continue to give them primary importance in their ethical schemata (see e.g., Beauchamp & Childress, 1979). But the most recent revision of the American Medical Association's *Principles of Medical Ethics* makes no reference to these principles (AMA, 1980). Instead, the AMA emphasizes what one ethicist characterizes as a "contractual" approach to doctor-patient relationships (Veatch, 1981). Would Stone have seen things differently today in light of the current "Principles?"

I think not. The "Principles" themselves consist of a concise preamble and seven single-sentence statements of "conduct which define the essentials of honorable behavior for the physician." This brief exposition of medical ethics cannot be seen as exhaustive, nor can it be read out of historical context. When the AMA (1980) says, as it does in the first section of the "Principles," "A physician shall be dedicated to providing competent medical service with compassion and respect for human dignity," that statement can only be understood, in the framework of two millenia of medical ethics, as incorporating the principles of beneficence and nonmaleficence. Certainly, if one asked the majority of physicians about the ethical values that guide their behavior, those two would almost always be endorsed. If one asked most patients what they expect of their physicians, the answer would be the same.

Thus, our original questions are valid. We must be concerned with the applications of these principles to forensic psychiatry. Can a case be made that beneficence and nonmaleficence are not central to forensic ethics, that is, that the ethical principles guiding forensic psychiatrists differ from those adhered to by their clinical colleagues? Not only do I believe it can, but as we shall see, that the failure clearly to make this distinction leads to untold mischief.

Beneficence and nonmaleficence have the status of goods in themselves regardless of context. Like other goods, however, they often need to be balanced against competing values, and sometimes against each other. When goods conflict, the decision rules used to determine which, if any, takes precedence, are context specific. In the doctor-patient relationship, beneficence and nonmaleficence are given primacy (though even here they may be modified by other values, such as respect for persons (Burt, 1979)) because they form an intrinsic basis for the healing relationship. Physicians, often explicitly but always implicitly, promise to adhere to these values as a means of encouraging persons in need of medical care to entrust their bodies and well-being to them. In the absence of a belief that physicians will act to benefit patients and attempt to avoid harm, only foolish patients indeed would seek medical care.

Although the status of beneficence and nonmaleficence as moral goods in themselves is not dependent on this implicit medical promise, they become obligatory, primary goals for physicians when doctor-patient relationships are established with the presumption that they will control. Nor has the modern practice of informed consent, with its contract-like procedures, altered the importance of these principles. Patients remain dependent on physicians for the information and advice on which their choices depend. If patients in general come to doubt that physicians are offering information and advice solely with the intent of seeking their benefit and avoiding harm to them, even our consent-based medical system will rapidly fall apart.

But does such an analysis apply to the forensic setting, that is, where the task is not healing, but evaluation for the purpose of testimony in court to advance the general interests of justice? Beneficence and nonmaleficence remain goods, of course, but in the absence of a promise that they will govern the relationship, they do not attain primacy for the forensic psychiatrist. To give such a promise would undermine the very basis of the forensic process, dependent as it is on the psychiatrist's revelation of the data from his evaluation and the resulting conclusions, regardless of the consequences. Even in the absence of a promise to adhere to those values that predominate in therapeutic contexts, were a psychiatrist to seek to aid or avoid harm to an evaluee as primary goals, the evaluation process would lose its value for the justice system. The possibility that a result harmful to the evaluee might flow from the evaluation is the very feature that endows it with value. Of course, if it is possible to aid the evaluee in ways that are compatible with the primary purpose of the evaluation (e.g., by recommending psychiatric treatment, when that is indicated) that remains a good — as it does for all people in all situations. So, too, does the avoidance of gratuitous harm, (e.g., avoiding disclosure of irrelevant information obtained from an evaluee that may be embarrassing or harmful). But these goals must be subordinated to the purpose of the evaluation.

Is there something intrinsically wrong with a physician participating in a function in which beneficence and nonmaleficence are not the obligatory primary duties? Certainly physicians as human beings enter into a variety of relationships outside the medical setting where doing good and avoiding harm are not the major principles guiding their behavior. Negotiating the sale of a house, for example, is a situation in which no one could quarrel with the right of a physician to seek to maximize his own gain rather than others'. Even nonmaleficence might legitimately fall by the wayside when a physician seeks to undercut the fees of a competitor, though knowing that to do so will deprive him of income or perhaps drive him out of business. In short, we have no basis for objecting to physicians foregoing primary adherence to the principles of beneficence and nonmaleficence when they act other than as physicians.

Although not usually conceptualized in this way, the forensic psychiatrist in truth does not act as a physician either. If the essence of the physician's role is to promote healing and/or to relieve suffering, it is apparent that the forensic psychiatrist operates outside the scope of that role. To say this is not to denigrate the evaluative function that forensic psychiatrists perform. Society values highly — and in many respects increasingly — the application of psychiatric expertise in legal contexts. But to apply that expertise is not to practice psychiatry, at least not in any ethically meaningful sense of the term. Perhaps it would be better if we even used a different term to denote the role played by the evaluator who applies knowledge of psychiatric diagnosis and psychological functioning to assist the legal system in reaching legally useful conclusions. Were we to call such a person a "forensicist," or some similar appellation, it might more easily be apparent that a different — nonmedical — role with its own ethical values is involved.

The existing, sparse, but growing literature on the ethics of forensic psychiatry reveals an occasional but unclear and sometimes ambivalent recognition of these differences. The major ethical code for psychiatrists, the American Psychiatric Association's "Annotations" to the AMA's "Principles," neglects the forensic realm almost completely (APA, 1989). Recognizing this, the largest organization of American forensic psychiatrists, the American Academy of Psychiatry and the Law (1987) adopted "Ethical Guidelines for the Practice of Forensic Psychiatry." The four substantive sections of these "Guidelines" address confidentiality, consent, impartiality and objectivity, and the qualifications of forensic psychiatrists. No attempt is made, however, to develop principles underlying these guidelines, much less to distinguish them from those governing therapeutic encounters. While the existence of a separate set of guidelines in itself may suggest some recognition that the ethical underpinnings of forensic psychiatry differ from those of general psychiatry, the final section of the "Guidelines" undercuts that presumption. It states that complaints against forensic psychiatrists will be referred to the American Psychiatric Association (APA) for adjudication, though the APA relies exclusively in ethics complaints on its own "Annotations."[2]

The unofficial literature on ethics in forensic psychiatry has gone a bit further in drawing distinctions between forensic and clinical psychiatric ethics. Rappeport (1981, 1982), for example, has considered the differences between general and forensic psychiatrists (or more properly between psychiatrists filling clinical and forensic roles) based on the absence of doctor-patient relationships in the latters' work (see also, Modlin, 1984). He does not, however, directly address the implications of this distinction for the ethical principles to which forensic psychiatrists should adhere. Rather, like most other writers in this area (see e.g., Watson, 1984; Zonana, 1984), he foregoes an explicit discussion of principles, moving instead to address rules that govern in circumstances peculiar to forensic settings.

Questions of the relative primacy of ethical principles were considered most directly in two sources. First, the 1984 report of the APA Task Force on the Role of Psychiatry in the Sentencing Process recognized the potential conflict between seeking information to promote justice, and adhering to beneficence and nonmaleficence, but argued that neither set of principles ever exists in pure culture.[3] "Since some compromise between these two [sets of values] is inevitable, the only question is at what point to strike the balance" (APA, 1984, p. 8). The Task Force answered the question by giving priority to the need to promote justice. Once having satisfied this obligation to society, however, it concluded that the psychiatrist should then seek the good of and avoid harm to the evaluee. This statement of the ethics of forensic work comes close to the argument of this paper, but does not quite bite the bullet: it fails to acknowledge

---

[2]Ethics complaints against forensic psychiatrists are, as far as I can determine, infrequent. This may be because the kinds of behaviors that would serve as a focus of complaint are simply unaddressed in the APA's ethical code. Perhaps this omission represents a tacit acknowledgement that forensic evaluation lies outside the usual scope of psychiatric practice. Should the APA attempt to formulate ethical standards for forensic psychiatrists? My argument suggests that confusion would be avoided between the ethics of clinical and forensic roles were that task left to another, subspecialty group. Efforts on the part of the latter to avoid responsibility in this regard are unfortunate.

[3]I served on the Task Force and was a coauthor of the report.

openly that forensic evaluation and testimony may cause harm that cannot be ameliorated. Instead, it stresses the residual role of the principles of beneficence and nonmaleficence. For example, at a later point in the report, the Task Force falls back on nonmaleficence as a basis for urging psychiatrists to avoid direct recommendations for disposition to the court, since this might place the psychiatrist in the position of doing harm to an evaluee for whom he believes incarceration is appropriate.

The Criminal Justice Mental Health Standards formulated by the American Bar Association (1989) also come close to embracing the approach to forensic ethics presented here:

> When professionals function as either evaluators or consultants, they establish no therapeutic or habilitative relationships with defendants and thus owe them no loyalty. However, if a treatment or habilitative relationship commences, a professional owes loyalty to the person undergoing treatment or habilitation. (p. 13)

Although the meaning of the term "loyalty" is obscure in this statement, and the basis for the conclusion is uncertain, the conclusion appears to echo the one advanced above.

The issue of a qualitatively different basis for forensic ethics, although approached in some sources, has been largely unaddressed and unjustified in the literature on the ethics of psychiatry, and its implications are wholly unexplored.

The Implications of a Distinct Forensic Ethics

Before considering some of the implications of this analysis, it might be beneficial to recognize the artificiality of examining two ethical principles, as I have done so far, in isolation from the many other values relevant to forensic psychiatry. To place the discussion in an adequate context, however, would require the development of a comprehensive theory of forensic ethics, a task yet to be undertaken and well beyond my objectives here. Nonetheless, I believe that there is value in this narrower focus, both because the question at issue is a pivotal one, and because this argument may offer some stimulus to the formulation of a more complete theory.

It is fair to ask at this point, therefore, about the implications of the lack of primacy of beneficence and nonmaleficence in forensic psychiatry. Consider the question, for example, whether it is legitimate for psychiatrists to participate in criminal proceedings, especially on behalf of the prosecution, when their testimony may result in a defendant being convicted of a crime and punished. This question arises most directly when the forensic psychiatrist presents negative evidence concerning an individual's defense of not guilty by reason of insanity, as in the parable. It may also be implicated, however, when psychiatrists assess and testify about defendants' competence to have waived their rights (e.g., in giving a confession or allowing a search to take place); competence to stand trial; history and prognosis as they relate to considerations in sentencing; and post-trial competencies (e.g., competence to waive appeal). Many psychiatrists feel this issue with particular acuity in capital cases, where the punishment that may result is death.

Some psychiatrists avoid criminal courtroom work altogether in an effort to avoid doing harm. Others will work only for the defense, in the hope that their testimony will thereby never be harmful to the defendant. Given the difficulty of determining the likely effect of testimony on juries, however, it may be difficult to guarantee that even evidence the psychiatrist believes is helpful will not redound to the detriment of the defendant (Bonnie, 1990). The possibility that adverse information will be elicited on cross-examination further increases the possibility that harm will result. In some jurisdictions, psychiatrists who have examined a defendant for the defense but are not called by the defense at trial — presumably because they discovered information adverse to the defendant — can be subpoenaed by the prosecution and compelled to testify. As a strategy to comport with the principles of nonmaleficence, a decision to work only for the defense is imperfect at best.

If taken seriously, therefore, the duty of nonmaleficence would appear to preclude psychiatrists from involvement in almost all aspects of criminal trials. Courts would be forced to make determinations involving questions of defendants' mental states without any psychiatric input. The principles can also be recruited selectively, as some authors do, to denounce participation in particular forensic roles, such as predictions of dangerousness to establish aggravating circumstances at death penalty hearings (Ewing, 1982). Such a technique allows an advocate to argue for the exclusion of psychiatrists from almost any forensic function, without having to consider the general implications of the argument.

For persons who believe that psychiatric expertise has little to offer to the criminal courts, loss of these functions would not be mourned (Morse, 1982). On the other hand, if diagnostic and psychodynamic formulations are viewed as having some value, as they are increasingly in criminal law, (*Ake v. Oklahoma*, 1985; Bonnie & Slobogin, 1980) this is a serious loss to the pursuit of justice. It is also, as our analysis makes clear, an unnecessary loss. The intuition of many forensic psychiatrists that their participation is not ethically problematic because their role in court differs from their therapeutic functions is supported by the recognition that nonmaleficence and beneficence do not have a primary claim on their ethical loyalties in forensic settings.

This is not to say, of course, that no behavior of forensic psychiatrists in court can be called unacceptable, an argument ironically advanced by Stone (1984), who sees in the fall from primacy of beneficence and nonmaleficence a slide into ethical chaos. ("[F]orensic psychiatrists seem to be without any clear guidelines as to what is proper and ethical." p. 58) In so far, for example, as witnesses' behavior is incompatible with the principle of truthfulness (e.g., the psychiatrist lies about the data derived from his examination, or misrepresents existing psychiatric knowledge (Appelbaum, 1984b)), it violates the ethical framework of the courtroom. Thus, prediction of long-term propensities for violence is ethically problematic not because it may lead a jury to impose the death penalty — though that consequence may call for extra caution — but because it cannot be done in an accurate fashion, and to pretend otherwise is to falsify one's testimony (Appelbaum, 1984a).

The problem of nonmaleficence is not limited to criminal contexts. Most civil litigation involves two or more competing parties, one of whom will be harmed by an unfavorable judgment; these include claims of psychic trauma and disputes over civil competencies. If no distinction were to be drawn between thera-peutic and forensic ethics, nonmaleficence as a primary value would preclude psychiatrists' testimony in those cases as well.

A second set of controversies to which our analysis can be applied may be the most difficult ethical conundra facing psychiatrists today: the questions of whether to participate in proceedings related to the assessment of persons thought incompetent to be executed and in the treatment of those found incom-petent. Like the insanity defense, competence to be executed is an issue that may be more important for its heuristic value than for the frequency with which it is raised. Since the right not to be executed while incompetent was given new prominence and constitutional status by the U.S. Supreme Court in 1986 (*Ford v. Wainwright*), the best estimates are that only a handful of death-row prison-ers have been assessed for competence. Nonetheless, the legal and ethical prob-lems have stimulated a steady flow of papers on the subject, and the issue has also attracted the attention of the lay press (see e.g., Finkel, 1986; Radelet & Barnard, 1986, 1988; Salguero, 1986; Ward, 1986).

One set of positions on psychiatric participation argues for abstention from assessment and treatment of incompetence on the grounds that to take part would violate the principles of beneficence and nonmaleficence (Ewing, 1987; Sargent, 1986). It is argued that the ultimate purpose of both assessment and treatment, even if a finding of incompetence as a result of the former may postpone execution, is to remove an obstacle to the prisoner's death. This violates general proscriptions against doing harm: "[A] physician should not engage voluntarily in behavior that will bring about the death of a patient who does not want to die and who, but for the physician's intervention, would not" (Sargent, 1986). Sometimes this argument is linked more directly to a provision of the AMA's "Principles" that applies the principle of nonmaleficence to the death penalty context: "A physician, as a member of a profession dedicated to preserving life when there is hope of doing so, should not be a participant in a legally authorized execution" (AMA, 1980). Both assessment and treatment are deemed to violate this prohibition.[4]

In contrast, there are those who argue that participation in neither function is precluded by psychiatric ethics. Mossman (1987), for example, appeals to Kant's justification of punishment: "[W]hen responsible individuals commit crimes, they thereby commit themselves to suffer the consequences of not obey-ing the law." This leads to the conclusion that a psychiatrist who removes obstacles to a prisoner's execution is actually effectuating his wishes. Relying next on Hegel, Mossman (1987) argues that execution may even constitute a benefit to prisoners, since permitting execution to proceed "allows them to receive the punishment to which their humanity entitles them."

Neither of these extreme positions is defensible once we begin to separate therapeutic from forensic contexts and to apply the appropriate ethical analysis to each. The assessment of competence to be executed is quintessentially a forensic function. To use Pollack's (1974) classical definition of forensic psychi-atry, its involves "the application of psychiatry to legal issues for legal [not

---

[4]In the early stages of thinking through this problem, this was precisely the position that I held and argued for in the media and public debates (Appelbaum, Bonnie, Dietz, & Thorup, 1987; *Nightline*, 1986).

therapeutic] ends." As such, the argument that the principle of nonmaleficence will be violated if harm results to the evaluee is irrelevant. As long as the psychiatrist conducts and reports an evaluation in keeping with other applicable ethical standards (e.g., truthfulness, respect for persons, etc.), the assessment itself does not raise ethical concerns.

How then do we account for the disquiet that many psychiatrists feel about such evaluations? One psychiatrist reported to me his experience of being called to another state to evaluate a prisoner's competence to be executed. Only after disembarking from the airplane did he focus on the consequences that would ensue if he reached the conclusion that the prisoner was likely to be competent. At that point, he refused to perform the evaluation and returned home. Surely a good deal of anxiety about this issue relates to mistaken attempts to apply the principle of nonmaleficence. Beyond that, however, the immediacy and degree of harm to which the prisoner is subject heighten ethical concerns. But this may simply be a case of being closer to the consequences of one's actions. As Bonnie (1990) has argued:

> [I]f we focus on the outcome-effect of the clinician's opinion, rather than on its timing, the case against participation in a capital sentencing evaluation would seem to be stronger than the case against participation in an execution competency evaluation. (p. 80)

Treatment of prisoners found incompetent to be executed, however, is a different matter. As a treating physician, the psychiatrist's therapeutic ethics are implicated. Treatment should not be undertaken unless the demands of beneficence and nonmaleficence can be satisfied. Sargent's (1986) belief that treatment of an incompetent death row prisoner carries overwhelmingly negative consequences holds much greater weight here. Successful treatment will result in the prisoner/patient's death. Although it can be argued that a condemned prisoner has the right to have a competent request for such treatment honored — on the basis that he prefers relief of the immediate pain of psychosis, even if that hastens his death, to indefinite continuation of the psychotic state (Bonnie, 1990) — it is difficult to find an ethical basis for the treatment of unwilling prisoners or those incapable of making competent judgments.

This argument against treatment is not free of problems, foremost among them the question of whether an injunction against treatment of incompetent prisoners means that no psychiatric therapy can be offered on death row. The problem here is that any severe psychiatric disorder holds the potential for rendering the prisoner incompetent if it remains untreated. Does not any effort at treatment then remove a potential obstacle to execution? I think this argument fails since the evidence suggests that only a tiny percentage of prisoners will become severely ill enough to meet the generally strict standards for incompetence. Thus, the balance of risks and benefits is very different for a prisoner for whom the question of incompetence has not been raised, but who may be in need of psychiatric care. Whether or not this response is sufficient to support the position of those who oppose involvement in treatment, the basis on which the question of treatment must be decided is clear: does treatment satisfy the demands of beneficence and nonmaleficence?

Mossman's position is inadequate in this context. It may be philosophically tenable to argue that prisoners will their punishment by means of an implicit social contract. However, it does not follow that physicians legitimately can or must become the agents of that punishment. Mossman fails to recognize that societal role differentiation involves ethical differentiation as well. Although some person or profession may be justified in inflicting punishment, physicians — whose ethics are based on doing good and avoiding harm — are not.

The Parable Reconsidered

What then of the psychiatrists who agonize over the harms their testimony may cause the persons they have evaluated? Although their anguish is understandable, particularly when the harms are severe, it cannot justifiably be ascribed to a failure to conform to ethical norms. For psychiatrists operate outside the medical framework when they enter the forensic realm, and the ethical principles by which their behavior is justified are simply not the same. Concern over violating the principles of beneficence and nonmaleficence is misplaced. There may be other reasons for anguish, including the failure to portray the results of their evaluations as best they can in the difficult quest for truth, perhaps a legitimate basis for Alan Stone's regrets about the case of the black sergeant. But the possibility of failing to do good and of contributing to harm — while serving other, valid ends — is an inherent and justifiable element of forensic work. Attempts to fashion a comprehensive theory of the ethics of forensic psychiatry must begin here.

References

Ake v. Oklahoma, 105 S. Ct. 1087 (1985).

American Academy of Psychiatry and the Law (1987). *Ethical Guidelines for the Practice of Forensic Psychiatry*. Baltimore: Author.

American Bar Association (1989). *ABA Criminal Justice Mental Health Standards*. Washington, DC: Author.

American Medical Association (1980). *Principles of Medical Ethics*. Chicago: Author.

American Psychiatric Association (1989). *The Principles of Medical Ethics, with Annotations Especially Applicable to Psychiatry*. Washington, DC: Author.

American Psychiatric Association (1984). *Psychiatry in the Sentencing Process: A Report of the Task Force on the Role of Psychiatry in the Sentencing Process*. Washington, DC: Author.

Appelbaum, P. S. (1984a). Hypotheticals, psychiatric testimony and the death sentence. *Bulletin of the American Academy of Psychiatry and the Law, 12*, 169–177.

Appelbaum, P. S. (1984b). Psychiatric ethics in the courtroom. *Bulletin of the American Academy of Psychiatry and the Law, 12*, 225–231.

Appelbaum, P. S., Bonnie, R. J., Dietz, P. E., & Thorup, O. A. (1987). The death penalty: Dilemmas for physicians and society — a panel discussion. *Pharos, 50* (3), 23–27.

Beauchamp, T. L., & Childress, J. F. (1979). *Principles of Biomedical Ethics*. New York: Oxford University Press.

Bonnie, R. J. (1990). Dilemmas in administering the death penalty: Conscientious abstention, professional ethics, and the needs of the legal system. *Law and Human Behavior, 14*, 67–90.

Bonnie, R. J., & Slobogin, C. (1980). The role of mental health professionals in the criminal process: the case for informed speculation. *Virginia Law Review, 66*, 427–522.

Burt, R. A. (1979). *Taking Care of Strangers: The Rule of Law in Doctor-Patient Relations*. New York: Free Press.

Ewing, C. P. (1982). "Dr. Death" and the case for an ethical ban on psychiatric and psychological predictions of dangerousness in capital sentencing proceedings. *American Journal of Law and Medicine, 8*, 407–428.

Finkel, D. (1986). Dilemmas abound in hospital for inmates. *St. Petersburg Times*, July 27, p. B-1.

Ewing, C. P. (1987). Diagnosing and treating "insanity" on death row: legal and ethical perspectives. *Behavioral Sciences and the Law, 5*, 175–187.

Ford v. Wainwright, 106 S. Ct. 2595 (1986).

Modlin, H. C. (1984). The ivory tower v. the marketplace. *Bulletin of the American Academy of Psychiatry and the Law, 12*, 233–236.

Morse, S. J. (1982). Failed explanations and criminal responsibility: experts and the unconscious. *Virginia Law Review, 68*, 971–1084.

Mossman, D. (1987). Assessing and restoring competency to be executed: should psychiatrists participate? *Behavioral Sciences and the Law, 5*, 397–409.

Nightline (1986). Catch-22: Curing prisoners . . . to die. ABC television broadcast, March 6.

Pollack, S. (1974). Forensic psychiatry—a specialty. *Bulletin of the American Academy of Psychiatry and the Law, 2*, 1–6.

Radelet, M. L., & Barnard, G. W. (1986). Ethics and psychiatric determination of competency to be executed. *Bulletin of the American Academy of Psychiatry and the Law, 14*, 37–53.

Radelet, M. L., & Barnard, G. W. (1988) Treating the mentally incompetent death row inmate: ethical chaos with only one solution. *Bulletin of the American Academy of Psychiatry and the Law, 16*, 297–308.

Rappeport, J. R. (1981). Ethics and forensic psychiatry. In S. Bloch & P. Chodoff (Eds.), *Psychiatric Ethics* (pp. 255–276). New York: Oxford University Press.

Rappeport, J. R. (1982). Differences between forensic and general psychiatrists. *American Journal of Psychiatry, 139*, 331–334.

Salguero, R. G. (1986). Medical ethics and competency to be executed. *Yale Law Journal, 96*, 167–186.

Sargent, D. A. (1986). Treating the condemned to death. *Hastings Center Report, 16*(6), 5–6.

Stone, A. A. (1980). Presidential address: Conceptual ambiguity and morality in modern psychiatry. *American Journal of Psychiatry, 137*, 887–891.

Stone, A. A. (1984). The ethical boundaries of forensic psychiatry: a view from the ivory tower. *Bulletin of the American Academy of Psychiatry and the Law, 12*, 209–219.

Veatch, R. (1981). *A Theory of Medical Ethics.* New York: Basic Books.

Ward, B. A. (1986). Competency for execution: problems in law and psychiatry. *Florida State University Law Review, 14*, 35–107.

Watson, A. S. (1984). Response from a straw man. *Bulletin of the American Academy of Psychiatry and the Law, 12*, 221–224.

Zonana, H. (1984). Forensic psychiatry: critique of a critique. *Bulletin of the American Academy of Psychiatry and the Law, 12*, 237–241.

[46]

Revisiting the Parable:

Truth Without Consequences

Alan A. Stone*

Introduction

In "The Parable of the Forensic Psychiatrist: Ethics and the Problem of Doing Harm,"[1] Paul Appelbaum offers an interpretation of my "Parable of the Black Sergeant."[2] The "Parable" was part of my formal Presidential Address to the American Psychiatric Association, in which I attempted to demonstrate the complex relationship between psychiatry and morality as manifested in psychiatry's approach to racism, homosexuality, and female psychology. Briefly, the "parable" was an account of an experience I had while an officer in the military years ago. I had performed a psychiatric evaluation of a Black sergeant accused of theft. In the course of evaluation we developed a positive transference/countertransference relationship which led to unguarded and incriminating disclosures on his part. My testimony at his court martial proceeding was instrumental in proving his guilt. He was sentenced to five years at hard labor, and was deprived of all military benefits. My goal in the Presidential Address was to impress on my colleagues that psychiatry, as theory and in practice, inescapably involves human values and should neither claim nor aspire to be "value free science." There was no opportunity in such a paper to explore the ethical dimensions of my testimony in the Black sergeant's court-martial.

Appelbaum speculates that because of my adherence to medical ethics I was primarily concerned about the harm that my testimony at the court martial caused the patient. Appelbaum's opinion is that my understandable concern is a misleading and mistaken basis for drawing any conclusions about the ethics of forensic psychiatry. Appelbaum shares my view that forensic ethics are in a state of disarray, but makes the startling and provocative proposal that the ethics of forensic psychiatrists should not be based on the ethical principles of the medical profession. He allies himself with previous writers[3] who instead propose adherence to the principle of truthfulness.

Appelbaum is correct in stressing my remorse about harming the Black

*Touroff-Glueck Professor of Law and Psychiatry, Harvard Law School, Langdell Hall 327, 1545 Massachusetts Avenue, Cambridge, MA, 02138, U.S.A.

sergeant. However, I was equally concerned about the "double agent" problem of betraying his trust. Appelbaum also minimizes my explicit concerns about the conceptual ambiguity of psychiatry. I believe that these oversights in Appelbaum's analysis are crucial limitations both in his interpretation of my ideas concerning the ethical chaos of forensic psychiatry and in his own approach to this subject. Moreover, Appelbaum is simply wrong in his theory that my subsequent paper criticizing forensic psychiatry can be understood as originating in my concerns about causing harm. Nevertheless, it seems to me that it may be possible to avoid a zero sum debate. I have tried instead to find in our interchange of ideas some practical guidance for the ethical quandaries surrounding the issue of capital punishment that currently face forensic psychiatry. I shall first, however, deal with what I consider to be the limitations of Appelbaum's interpretation and his own proposal.

Therapeutic Encounter and Forensic Evaluation

The task of evaluating the sergeant had been one of my assigned duties as a military officer, and once I had reported my psychiatric findings I was literally ordered to testify at the court-martial. Although, as required under military law, I had warned the sergeant that anything he told me could be used against him, we established the kind of psychiatric rapport that leads to unguarded disclosure. Thus, although legally and technically the sergeant had been warned and had given informed consent, my own feeling was that I had unwittingly used my therapeutic skills to extract from him damaging personal revelations. The forensic evaluation had developed into a therapeutic encounter and I had become a "double agent." This clinical problem is one of the potential ethical quagmires of forensic psychiatry as has long been recognized by every responsible practitioner.[4]

Human Values and Diagnostic Evaluation

Less well recognized are the deeper conceptual problems raised by my parable about the Black sergeant. The parable was intended to be more than a case history; it was an attempt to portray a complex human encounter with moral overtones.

The accused, who was in fact a supply sergeant, had confiscated a very large amount of government property, but he was being court-martialed on the specific charge of stealing deodorant from the PX. He had been evaluated by a civilian psychiatrist who was prepared to testify that his behavior had been driven by unconscious kleptomaniacal impulses. The diagnosis of kleptomania[5] and the psychodynamic formulation about the determinism of the childhood on which it was based served to exculpate the sergeant, a result that infuriated the military authorities. They decided the sergeant should be evaluated by military psychiatrists.

When the sergeant and I first met he was suitably wary, and my countertransference, as a newly trained psychiatrist doing his 2 years of required military service, was probably not unusual. I wanted to demonstrate my capacity to empathize across the barriers of race and to find a way to communicate with this Black man. We had, as it turned out, a great deal of common cultural ground. He had gone to a small liberal arts college, majored in literature, and, after a prolonged unsuccessful search for employment appropriate to his learning, had been drafted into the Korean War. Because of his bleak employment prospects in civilian life, he decided that when the war ended he would serve out his 20 years in the Army. His experience was that the United States Army was profoundly racist. He was unable to advance beyond the rank of sergeant while he was forced to serve and pay deference to the less educated and less intelligent White men, most of them Southerners, who were his officers. Bitter about his situation, he stole from the Army whatever and whenever he could, with a sense of entitlement, as reparation for the racial injustices done to him. Psychiatry has no diagnosis and no exculpatory theory of socio-economic determinism for the victims of such racism. The sergeant's case history and clinical picture were subsequently reviewed by the authors of the *DSM-III-R casebook*, who concluded that he had no mental disorder.[6]

I believed the sergeant's description of the racism he had experienced and I shared his sense of outrage, yet the narrative that emerged from more than ten hours of interviewing could not have been more incriminating to him. Ironically, as the army psychiatrist who had established emotional rapport across the racial divide, I was to be the principal witness against him. After the trial, I was informed that because of my testimony the sergeant was sentenced to five years at hard labor and dishonorable discharge. He lost his pension and everything else of value he had accumulated in his lifetime.

"The Parable of the Black Sergeant" was specifically intended to draw attention to the moral ambiguity of a discipline that accepts the psychic determinism of the Oedipal family but rejects the psychic determinism of lifelong racism. This moral ambiguity, which infects many aspects of psychiatry, is particularly relevant at every juncture of law and psychiatry.

These deeper problems of moral and conceptual ambiguity are also what I emphasized in my subsequent paper on the ethics of forensic psychiatry.[7] Epistemological problems briefly discussed in my earlier paper were: the fact-valued distinction, freewill–determinism, the deconstruction of the self or agency, the mind–brain problem, and the science–morality gap. My purpose was to demonstrate that even the forensic psychiatrist, who resists all of the everyday adversarial inducements to take his testimony to the edge of dishonesty or beyond, proceeds through a further minefield of unrecognized moral hazards. The paper drew responses from a number of distinguished experts,[8] including Appelbaum.[9] Appelbaum later published the paper[10] now under discussion, in which he interpreted my views about the ethics of forensic psychiatry as deriving from a physician's concern about causing harm and expanded on his own ideas about the centrality of truthfulness. In what follows I shall argue that although Appelbaum's principle of truthfulness, as set out in his two papers, might help check some of the arrant dishonesty, it fails to resolve the three problems I have presented.

Moral Sentiments and Professional Ethics

Appelbaum, focusing on my remorseful reaction to the harm I caused, stresses the paragraph in which I wrote, "Do whatever you can to help your patient" and "primum non nocere" (first of all do no harm).[11] These contradictory imperatives constitute the "ethical dialectic of the physician's practice."[12] This dialectic, I suggested, shapes the practical "boundaries" of our struggle to be ethical physicians. However "when we turn our skills to forensic psychiatry, when we serve the system of justice, we can no longer agree on the boundaries of the debate."[13] This "lack of boundaries" was characterized more vividly by Appelbaum as a "slide into ethical chaos."[14]

Appelbaum's thesis is that I have mistakenly assumed that the ethical dialectic (which he refers to as the traditional ethical principles of benevolence and non-maleficence) should apply to the courtroom. He writes, "Can a case be made that beneficence and non-maleficence are not central to forensic ethics, that is, that the ethics guiding forensic psychiatrists differ from those adhered to by their clinical colleagues? Not only do I believe it can, but as we shall see, the failure clearly to make this distinction leads to untold mischief."[15]

Thus, according to Appelbaum, a psychiatrist can and should comfortably wear two hats and keep those hats ethically distinct. In his clinical garb, the psychiatrist is bound by the principles of beneficence and non-maleficence. But as the forensic psychiatrist, that same individual is required to adhere to only the principle of *truthfulness*. In this latter garb, the forensic psychiatrist should not be troubled as I was by the fact that harm may occur as a result of his expert testimony since the dictate primum non nocere does not apply in this context.

Appelbaum understands that as a moral human being I felt profound remorse about the consequences of my testimony. His claim is only that such feelings are not relevant to the ethical imperatives under which the forensic psychiatrist operates. "[P]sychiatrists operate outside the medical framework when they enter the forensic realm, and the ethical principles by which their behavior is justified are simply not the same."[16]

Physicians often confront conflicts between their moral convictions and their professional ethics and in those conflicts we seldom conclude, as Appelbaum has, that we should ignore our moral convictions. Many philosophers and theologians would suggest that our moral obligations generally trump our more narrow professional ethical guidelines.[17]* Thus, I am not convinced that Appelbaum's basic premise of the irrelevance of moral concerns can be ac-

---

*Appelbaum's position exhibits what could be termed *hyperpositivism* or *autopoesis*[18]. It asserts a radical division between disciplines in which values from one discipline simply make no sense and are therefore not applicable in another. However, traditional ethical approaches tend to assert the interrelatedness of interdisciplinary ethics through the medium of an individual's overarching moral scheme; an individual is taken as subscribing to one general moral system, and is not allowed to chop and change his or her ethical preferences at will, or even as the situation demands.[19] This is the view propounded by philosophers from Aristotle,[20] through Aquinas[21] and Kant[22] right up to J. L. Austin. This last was keen to argue that promises (and this would include implied promises arising from the doctor-patient relationship[23]) are not merely objective records of an inward, subjective, spiritual intention to be bound which we can modify inwardly as we move from one discipline (the therapeutic) to another (the forensic). Rather, promising as an institution stands above and apart from those disciplines. When we promise, it is the morality of the institution of promising which obligates us, and "[a]ccuracy and morality alike are on the side of the plain saying that our word is our bond."[24] To subsequently and subjectively modify our promise—that is, to transmogrify the principles of beneficence and non-maleficence into one of truthfulness—would render our professed act of promising hollow, and put it into Austin's category of abuses of promising.

cepted. Furthermore, I believe that the apparent clarity of Appelbaum's argument is purchased at the price of misunderstanding the nature of my moral sentiments. In reality I was concerned that my professional obligations and my unquestioned professional ideology had led me to betray my Black patient and to confirm his worst fears about racism.

Appelbaum recognizes that the physician's principles of beneficence and non-maleficence are binding because of the promises implicit in the doctor-patient relationship.[25] He argues that without a doctor–patient relationship physicians are not bound by those promises. He drives home his point by asking whether the doctor is bound by his professional ethics in selling his house. But the sale of a house does not begin with the doctor examining the patient. And subsequent adherence to the principle of truthfulness does not mitigate the problem of harm that arises when a doctor-patient relationship, with its implicit promises, has developed unexpectedly. Forensic psychiatrists who are well aware of this problem provide formulaic warnings to patients and carefully try to avoid conveying any promises so that they will not be bound by the principles of beneficence and non-maleficence.[26] This is particularly important when the expert has been retained by the adverse side. Specific warnings are also legally required in any situation in which the Fifth Amendment is applicable. The American Psychiatric Association has emphasized in its ethical guidelines the importance of informing patients about the purpose of any psychiatric evaluation.

However, I am not convinced that such procedures are always sufficient to negate the transference/countertransference of the psychiatrist/patient relationship that leads to unguarded disclosure. Moreover, once the forensic examiner has decided that his or her testimony will be helpful to the evaluee, it is not unusual to permit the relationship to become an intensely therapeutic encounter. Thus the expert often enters the deposition or the courtroom deeply involved in a transference/countertransference, wearing both hats and bound by both kinds of ethics, but without any sense of the conflict between them. The experts believe they are serving justice and helping their patients at the same time. This is the forensic psychiatrist's version of being on the "side of the angels." This *over involvement*, I believe, contributes to the "untold mischief" about which Appelbaum complains.

Situational Ethics and Betrayal

If Appelbaum's conception allowed the psychiatrist to gather all information from a patient in the medical situation, while bound by the principles of beneficence and non-maleficence, and then allowed that psychiatrist to serve in the courtroom, while bound only by truth, it would be the ultimate caricature of situational ethics.[27]** Unfortunately, although Appelbaum clearly rec-

---

**Situational (or act-oriented) ethics require that an act be justified through its direct relation with the situation from which the action arises, rather than a relation mediated through general rules. On this view, general moral rules do not prescribe actions by firmly establishing what is right or wrong, good or bad, obligated or prohibited. Rather, the unfolding demands of the situation are paramount. The standard of justification is a direct appeal to the consequences of a particular action, or a direct perception of one's duty (thought intuition or grace), in a particular situation. General rules, then, would not be determinative or

ognizes the "double agent" problem, including the version I have described, neither of the papers in which he discussed these ideas explicitly confronts it. Because in actual practice the line between a forensic evaluation and a therapeutic encounter is never unambiguous, the problem of broken promises may be incorrigible. In any event, I believe, Appelbaum's failure to confront directly the practical problem of the "Double Agent" constitutes a weakness in the basic premise of his theoretical argument that quite different rules can apply to the different situations. Nonetheless, his willingness to found a different ethics for forensic psychiatrists on the different contexts has convinced me that forensic psychiatrists must even more scrupulously avoid any intermingling of their dual roles. I shall, therefore, propose a more draconic ethical principle in the hope that it will prompt further discussion of these difficult matters.

Based on the above analysis I now believe that it was *ethically as well as morally wrong* for me to have testified at the sergeant's court martial. I am now prepared to argue that, regardless of whether appropriate ethical and legal warnings have been given, whenever an evaluation turns into a therapeutic encounter and produces unguarded disclosures, the psychiatrist should disqualify him- or herself from submitting expert testimony. Before expanding on this idea, I shall further consider the principle of truthfulness as an ethical guideline.

Truthfulness and the Slide into Chaos

According to Appelbaum, the principle of truthfulness that applies in the courtroom situation will serve to prevent any "slide into ethical chaos." As proof that this principle can be effectively applied, he offers (without mentioning names) the example of Dr. Grigson, whose "predictions of dangerousness" helped Texas courts to sentence scores of criminals to death.[28] Appelbaum would say that Grigson's ethical misconduct was in offering untruthful testimony—claiming that he knew with medical certainty that a particular defendant would be dangerous in the future when in fact this is not something an ethical psychiatrist should claim to know. These and other much discussed criticisms of Dr. Grigson's testimony in *Barefoot v. Estelle*[29] were presented to the Supreme Court in an American Psychiatric Association Amicus brief.[30]

Unlike Appelbaum, I have no confidence in the guiding principle of truth as an effective means of preventing the slide into ethical chaos. The standard of truthfulness, as I have said before,[31] has always been imposed by the law on all expert witnesses, who, like all other witnesses, are "sworn to tell the truth, the whole truth, and nothing but the truth."

If truth in psychiatry were a simple and straightforward matter-of-fact rather than a complex question of informed opinion, then Dr. Grigson per-

---

correct standards of action; they may assist deliberation, but can be set aside at any time as the situation demands. Beauchamp and Childress give the example of a doctor, employing a situation, ethic from whom I have extracted a promise about my future treatment. In their example, the physician would only keep her word if she thought, whether by revelation or balancing the consequences, that what was best, given the situation, was keeping her promise. But since I know that the physician will not necessarily keep her promise, she will know that it matters that much less if she does break it, and so the promise tends to become an idle one, with no obligatory force whatsoever. This holds generally for all moral rules. Moral rules, on this model, can never be absolute; they can be set aside whenever the, in this case, physician decides.

jured himself and for his obvious dishonesty he could be sanctioned by a court. Instead, a majority of the Supreme Court, fully aware of the American Psychiatric Association brief on which the dissent relied, ruled in *Barefoot v. Estelle* that Dr. Grigson's opinion was quite acceptable and expressed doubt about the credibility of the American Psychiatric Association's contradictory opinions. Justice White, writing for the majority, described the American Psychiatric Association as trying to "disinvent the wheel." This ruling was given despite the fact that Appelbaum's views, which were carefully spelled out in the brief, had accurately summarized the professional consensus about predicting future violent behavior.

Perhaps in recognition of this and other similar examples of what is thought to be judicial ignorance about scientific truth, Appelbaum has proposed that the Supreme Court avail itself of a scientific consultant.[32] The legal complications of allowing such an influential scientific insider to advise the court "ex parte" and "in camera" are monumental. The proposal runs contrary to the established norms and traditions of judicial decision-making under our adversarial system of justice. Moreover, Appelbaum's conviction that the Court needs an adviser on the subject demonstrates how arcane and complicated he, himself, believes any scientific criterion of truthfulness can be. That complexity would also be problematic for every other tribunal called on to decide whether an expert's professional opinions were ethical or not. Like Kant's categorical imperative, Appelbaum's criterion of truthfulness is convincing in theory but difficult to apply in practice.

Fully aware of these criticisms, Appelbaum has proposed a definition of truth for ethical purposes that he believes can be applied by the psychiatric profession to expert testimony. Again, although no names are mentioned by him, this formulation also seems to have been inspired by the example of Dr. Grigson, who in *Barefoot* testified in response to hypothetical questions and expressed certainty about his answers without ever having examined the defendant.

Defining Truth in Forensic Psychiatry: Subjective Truth

Appelbaum's definition of truth has a subjective and an objective component. The subjective side of truth is the expert witness's genuine belief in his testimony. It also entails the psychiatrist gathering the maximum possible amount of relevant data in order to be able to have such a genuine belief. I known no reason why Appelbaum would doubt that Dr. Grigson genuinely believed in his testimony. But Grigson had made no attempt to gather his own clinical data. If he had tried to conduct a thorough psychiatric examination, he would have been legally required to warn the defendant, Barefoot, that he was evaluating him for the prosecution in its efforts to secure a death penalty.[33] Instead of pursuing this uncertain course, Grigson answered hypothetical questions put to him by the prosecutor at the sentencing phase of the trial. This alternative strategy, which according to the Supreme Court violates no legal norms, was apparently urged on Grigson by the prosecutor.

Appelbaum may or may not be correct in assuming that Grigson can be faulted ethically for not obtaining the maximum possible information under these circumstances. However, in light of the double agent arguments made in this paper, it may have been more ethical for Dr. Grigson to answer hypothetical questions rather than to provide the necessary warning and then present himself empathetically to Mr. Barefoot and perhaps win his confidence as I had done with the Black sergeant.

Objective Truth

The objective component of Appelbaum's approach to truth requires an "acknowledgement" of limitation. When the expert presents a minority opinion, he has an ethical obligation to justify his deviation from the consensus. Presumably, in obedience to this obligation, Grigson should have informed the fact finder that most psychiatrists believe it is impossible to make the kind of predictions he was making.

Gerald Klerman[34] made similar arguments about ethical standards of care in psychiatric treatment. The essence of both their proposals is to move the psychiatric profession toward authoritative "consensus" and away from divergent schools of thought. Klerman and Appelbaum are both prepared to use emerging "scientific" research to control what is and is not ethical. As a recent paper by Grisso and Appelbaum demonstrates, this approach means that it becomes necessary to make periodic adjustments in our ethical standards in keeping with the changing scientific consensus.[35] Similar "consensus" standards are of course being hammered out in the arena of "Managed Care." These problems have been much discussed elsewhere.[36] It is sufficient for present purposes to indicate that Appelbaum's definition of objective truth is part of the growing trend in the medical profession toward "truth by consensus." There is danger, in my opinion, that such authoritative truth will be indistinguishable from authoritarian truth.

It is important to recognize that our legal system has its own traditional approach to these matters as enshrined in the Law of Evidence. Since divergent expert testimony is often critical for litigation, trial lawyers in particular would be hostile to any systematic effort by the medical profession to exercise quality control over expert testimony in the name of either science or ethics.

The incorporation of professional and scientific norms into the legal standard for admitting expert testimony in epidemiological matters is currently a matter of intense interest in the federal courts. The case of *Daubert v. Merrell Dow*[37] concerns the admissibility of the expert testimony of a plaintiff's witness. The expert was prepared to submit his own non-peer reviewed and unpublished meta-analysis of several studies. The meta-analysis contradicted the findings of the peer-reviewed and published studies.

The Good Clinician and the Truthful Expert

Appelbaum argues that his truth standard converges with the standard of "good clinical practice." The latter standard is based on the premise that whatever is good clinical practice in the office is the basis for good expert testimony in the court. He believes that I have failed to demonstrate any inadequacies in the good clinical practice standard or truth standard as a basis for ethical practice in forensic psychiatry.

It is worth noting that Dr. Andrew Watson, the principal defender of the good clinical practice standard, disagreed with Appelbaum's belief that the prediction of future dangerousness in court would be unethical. Dr. Watson argued that psychiatrists all make and act upon predictions of dangerousness in their offices and therefore should have no compunction about making such predictions in the courtroom.[38] He was therefore in less than total agreement with the criticisms of Dr. Grigson. It should also be noted that the scientific literature on prediction has also taken a discernible shift away from the extreme agnosticism reflected in the American Psychiatric Association brief in *Barefoot*. Appelbaum has, himself, concluded that subsequent research indicates that predictions of future dangerousness might be ethical in some circumstances but not in the Barefoot situation.[39] The quality of research dealing with prediction of future dangerousness is less than an exacting methodology would demand. Attempts to draw scientific conclusions from that research are therefore fraught with difficulty. The subsequent attempt to use those shaky conclusions as the basis for fine tuning the ethics of psychiatry is a fortiori unlikely to have lasting value.

Putting this matter aside, I believe that Applebaum is able to reach his conclusion about the utility of the truth standard only because he deals inadequately with the double-agent dilemma and discounts all of the epistemological problems inherent in the discipline of psychiatry when it presents itself as a value-free science. These problems are certainly not solved in the therapeutic context but they can at least be excused because our intentions are beneficent and non-maleficent. Paternalistic physicians in their ignorance have caused great iatrogenic harm.[40] The moral significance of this harm is mitigated only because we thought that we were doing our best to help our patients. The same mitigation is not available when we cause harm outside the therapeutic sphere in the name of scientific truth and in the service of justice. Appelbaum either ignores these arguments or finds them unpersuasive.

However, he readily acknowledges that I am correct in arguing that neither his truth standard nor the good clinical practice standard provides "true answers" to the "legal and moral questions posed by the law."[41] He explicitly agrees that psychiatrists should not be making moral judgments. But, he believes that this means only that an expert should not respond to ultimate legal questions such as, is this man legally insane? If one thinks, as I do, that many matters in psychiatry, including diagnosis, involve both unrecognized value judgments and moral assumptions, then the problem of making moral judgments arises well before we answer the law's ultimate questions.[42] For example, the sergeant's diagnosis of kleptomania with its determinist theory of uncontrollable impulses involved all of the the moral judgments contained in any answer to the ultimate question. Similarly, if less obviously, the absence of a diagnosis about the effects of life-long subjugation in a racist society is in itself a moral judgment.

Social Perceptions About the Physician's Ethics

Even if Appelbaum is correct in his thesis about a different ethical standard for the legal context, I think that public and even professional perceptions fail to recognize the distinction as one that makes a difference. For example, I see in the American Psychiatric Association's ethical sanctioning of Dr. Grigson, and in the media's bestowing upon him the epithet "Dr. Death," more than a response to his perceived violation of the principle of truthfulness. I believe that the outpouring of criticism stems from the fact that Grigson, a physician, was successfully helping the prosecution send individuals to their deaths. Had Grigson been stretching scientific truth on behalf of clemency for defendants in capital punishment cases, I do not believe that any professional censure would have ensued.

There have been many notorious instances since Grigson's testimony in *Barefoot* in which forensic psychiatrists have given outrageous expert testimony on behalf of defendants and have not been ethically sanctioned. The singling out of Dr. Grigson for ethical sanctions can only be explained by something other than his alleged violation of the truthfulness criterion. It is reasonable to assume that professional and lay observers alike believe that Dr. Grigson was still meant to be wearing the medical mantle of beneficence and non-maleficence in the courtroom. Such a belief may demonstrate no more than that these social perceptions of the role of the physician and the physician's ethical obligations are incorrect and need to be changed, as Appelbaum's scheme requires. But, right or wrong, these social perceptions would have important professional consequences if forensic psychiatrists were to adopt Appelbaum's approach.

Forensic Psychiatry's Negative Public Image

Appelbaum's standard of objective truth would require each expert witness to acknowledge the limitations of his or her testimony. Clearly the profession has never had a reputation for adhering to such a standard.[43] Over the years, forensic psychiatrists who take extreme positions and claim to be medically certain of their opinions have commanded the highest fees and enjoyed the greatest demand for their services among the trial lawyers who retain them. One veteran attorney summed up his experience as follows, "You don't need to pay that much money to get honest opinions." Equally troubling, it is also commonplace for highly principled non-forensic psychiatrists to lose their clinical balance in the courtroom and become partisan advocates of highly tenuous clinical or scientific opinions. Too often they testify because they have their own axe to grind, e.g., to obtain the court's imprimatur of their own self interest.

Although most experienced forensic psychiatrists pride themselves on avoiding the temptations of dishonesty on one side and the partisanship of inexperienced forensic experts who have some personal axe to grind on the other side, they do not always succeed. Even the impressive expert testimony that was provided in the trial of John Hinckley was far from Appelbaum's standard of modesty as incorporated into the objective dimension of truth.[44]

I am not alone in these observations. Most forensic psychiatrists and most trial lawyers acknowledge the widespread problem of forensic psychiatrists as "hired liars."[45] To the extent that Appelbaum's standard of truth requires the expert to be modest in his claim, it seems to have been honored only in the breach. Indeed it was this apparent lack of truthfulness, and not my concern about harm, that prompted my remark that psychiatrists do not even know the boundaries of the ethical debate when they enter the courtroom. Appelbaum clearly recognizes the problem and has been a leading proponent of peer review of forensic testimony. It remains to be seen whether that approach can be effective and what the legal system's response to such oversight would be. But, if any remedy is to be effective, it is important to understand why "the slide into ethical chaos" of untruthfulness happens so frequently.

There is much empirical evidence demonstrating that the socio-psychological context is at least as important to ethical behavior as is a person's character or ethical principles.[46] When physicians are treating patients, the human realities of that socio-psychological context usually help to reinforce the dialectic of beneficence and nonmaleficence. Although ethical abuses certainly occur, there is a synergy between being a good doctor and being ethical in clinical settings. Turn the physician into a scientific researcher with a different agenda and the socio-psychological context differs. The reinforcement of beneficence and non-maleficence weakens accordingly and patients have been systematically exploited to further scientific goals.[47] The scientific community has painfully learned this lesson and consequently now requires higher ethical standards and external review processes to insure ethical behavior toward patient/subjects during clinical research.

Now consider the physician in a legal setting being led or attacked by zealous advocates, each seeking to manipulate the expert to his own ends. Here the expert's economic and narcissistic self-interest may reinforce the tendency to take extreme positions. The norm of consensus that prevails in the clinical conference room vanishes on the witness stand. If there is any sense of clinical accountability to a patient it usually pushes even further in the extreme direction reinforcing the expert's sense of being on the "side of the angels."

Certainly the courtroom context and the adversarial system routinely induce psychiatrists and other expert witnesses to violate the principle of truth. The ethics of beneficence and non-maleficence may well contribute to the mischief. Whether it is because they themselves want to be helpful witnesses or to beat the lawyers at their own game, or because they have brought their own private agenda to the courtroom,[48] psychiatrists all too frequently fail Appelbaum's test and claim to possess more objective certainty and subjective conviction than they could possibly justify in a clinical context. This writer is certainly not alone in concluding that these powerful incentives induce many psychiatrists to behave in the courtroom as if they had no sense of ethical boundaries. The occupational disease of forensic psychiatry is the tendency to become a zealous and partisan advocate rather than to remain an impartial expert. The search for truth may be the most important goal of justice, but after-the-fact peer review applying Appelbaum's standard of truth seems unlikely to remedy these intense contextual pressures.

Reprising the Double Agent Problem

The foregoing interchange with Appelbaum has led me, as noted above, to believe that forensic psychiatrists should as a first principle eschew any overlap between their clinical and evaluative functions. I would therefore propose that forensic psychiatrists have an ethical duty to excuse themselves from testifying whenever an evaluation for a criminal tribunal has turned into a therapeutic encounter. The fact that the evaluee has been warned, as required by law, is not sufficient to satisfy the ethical requirement. Although the parable of the Black sergeant emphasizes harm, the ethical duty should apply whether or not the resulting testimony would benefit or harm the evaluee.

This more radical rule is particularly necessary for psychiatrists in the criminal justice context because many of the conceptual and epistemological problems of psychiatry cause ethical difficulty only when we move from the therapeutic encounter to the passing of the legal/moral judgments of the criminal courts. A radical rule is also justified by Appelbaum's own advocacy of different ethics for different settings. Finally, a radical rule might help to limit the countertransference pressures that lead experts to stretch the truth. This radical rule, unlike the attempt to fine tune professional ethics, is a return to and reemphasis of the Hippocratic tradition, specifically its dictate, "In every house where I come I will enter only for the good of my patients. . . . All that may come into my knowledge in the exercise of my profession or outside of my profession in daily commerce with men, which ought not to be spread abroad, I will keep secret and will never reveal."[49] In what follows I shall attempt to demonstrate how such a "traditional" approach, that would alter forensic practice as well as forensic ethics, might help to alleviate some of the ethical problems associated with capital punishment.

Capital Punishment and Psychiatric Ethics

A number of difficult ethical problems have surfaced as a result of new developments in the law of capital punishment. Dr. Grigson's questionable testimony was in fact an example of one such legal development. Much has been written about this new statutory and constitutional law and no attempt can be made here to summarize that literature. Stated in an oversimplified way, there have been two major strands in legal-moral objections to capital punishment in the United States. One strand of objections is premised on the idea that execution has become cruel and unusual punishment in contemporary society. The second major strand argues that although capital punishment is in theory acceptable, in our racist society the death sentence is in practice dispensed in a discriminatory fashion and therefore should be abolished.

Many physicians are morally opposed to capital punishment on these or other grounds. Although Dr. Joseph Guillotine might be considered a noteworthy counter-example, physicians have traditionally avoided assisting the state in the performance of executions. Even though a physician-assisted execution might be less painful for the victim, the ethical principle that has come down to us bars such participation. When states adopted lethal injection as the legally prescribed form of execution, the medical profession had little difficulty concluding that it would be unethical for a physician to administer the injection.[50]

The professional objectives behind this ethical principle have not been precisely articulated, but presumably physicians are convinced that they outweigh any countervailing obligation to serve justice or to ease the suffering. In short, the medical profession has decided that the executioner should not be a "man in a white coat."[51]

There are, however, a variety of other legal functions provided by psychiatrists that arguably facilitate the imposition of capital punishment. These include evaluating and restoring competence to be executed. Those issues have produced a great deal of interesting commentary.[52] Psychiatrists who are morally opposed to capital punishment would prefer to limit the profession's involvement in such activities. But most of the recent arguments against such involvement, like those made against Dr. Grigson, have been made on other narrower and supposedly independent ethical and scientific grounds.[53]

The moral condemnation of Dr. Grigson and of other such involvements by abolitionists is more comprehensible than the supposedly neutral professional criticisms. However, neither of these types of criticism is at the center of my own concerns about psychiatry's role in capital punishment. My concerns are centered on the previously mentioned moral and conceptual ambiguity of our supposed medical science. The decision to impose the sentence of execution is an awesome human responsibility. The retributive taking of a life in the name of justice forces the law-givers to reexamine the very concept of justice. Judges and juries should not be led to believe that the discipline of psychiatry has a scientific shoulder on which their terrible burden of decision can rest. I would, therefore, urge psychiatrists, on the grounds of humility if not truth, to inform courts that we have no professional or scientific basis for participating in a capital sentencing hearing. However, as my debate with Appelbaum indicates, I have been unable to convince my colleagues that our epistemological problems create an unbridgeable abyss in the criminal courtroom.

Without some such radical measure, the efforts of psychiatrists to decide what can and cannot be done ethically in the capital punishment area continue to be fraught with difficulty. The bright line between our therapeutic and forensic roles may help us resolve one of the intraprofessional disputes that has arisen in connection with capital punishment. The dispute centers around the psychiatrist's participation in the restoration of competency to be executed by the administration of antipsychotic medication. Leaders of the psychiatric establishment pushed for severe restrictions on the psychiatrist's involvement in restoration of competency to be executed. Their reasoning was based on a complicated extrapolation from the traditional "Do No Harm" ethical grounds prohibiting professional involvement in execution.[54]

Quite unexpectedly, African American psychiatrists within the American Psychiatric Association took a contradictory stance. These minority psychiatrists were "morally" concerned about an ethical rule which even if technically correct might result in the therapeutic neglect of death row inmates. Whatever the establishment's justification for such an ethical rule, for them it came too close to self righteously validating the widespread medical neglect of prisoners among whom African Americans are overrepresented.[55]

The debate quickly went in many other directions. As summarized by Heilbrun et al.,[56] some took the view that once a condemned prisoner became incompetent to be executed, he or she should be given clemency. Others deployed arguments in favor of attempts to restore competency in every case. Finally, there was an intermediate group opposed to absolute rules. The debate proceeded on moral, ethical, and legal grounds and stimulated important discussion about the role of psychiatry in the criminal justice system.

Recently the Supreme Court of Louisiana, in *Louisiana v. Perry*,[57] decided some of the legal questions relevant to this ethical/moral dispute. The Perry Court rejected the so-called "medicate to execute" scheme on state constitutional grounds. The court's discussion of the relevant ethical issues followed the line of analysis set out by the psychiatric establishment's extrapolation from the principle of "Do No Harm" and other recent commentary taking a similar view.[58] The majority thought that the psychiatrist, as an agent of the prosecutorial arm of the state, would, by medicating Perry, become directly involved in preparing the condemned insane prisoner for execution in violation of medical ethics. Thus, according to the court, once medicated, Perry could never be executed. However, if Perry were to recover his sanity without such medication the Court indicated that he might be executed. Although the decision points in the direction staked out by the advocates of clemency, it does not reach that conclusion in all cases.

Unfortunately, the facts of the Perry case did not require the court to resolve the more complicated ethical issues that are of importance to psychiatrists. Perry's treatment had been ordered by a court for legal purposes, i.e., to restore and maintain his competency to be executed. Furthermore, the Louisiana Supreme Court assumed that the medication ordered by the judge was given over Perry's objection and without an independent medical judgment about the appropriateness of the treatment. The Louisiana Supreme Court did not reach the question of what would be the fate of a patient/prisoner like Perry where treatment was instituted on the initiative of psychiatrists because it was deemed medically necessary.

As the ethical dispute demonstrates, many psychiatrists would be deterred from attempting to treat any patient with medication or by any other means if they believed it would lead directly to execution.[59] But, as the African American psychiatrists pointed out, it is also troubling to withhold medically necessary treatment from a psychotically deteriorating patient.

The facts of the Perry case have led commentators to analyze the problem from a particular perspective, which seems to make the ethical issues more insoluble. They imagine court-ordered treatment of a patient with antipsychotic medication. The hypothetical patient achieves a social recovery and is marched off to execution. This scenario imagines the psychiatrist being told what to do by a judge. But, judges do not have a license to practice medicine and no psychiatrist should allow a lay person to order her or him to give a particular treatment. Once the psychiatrist is free of legal coercion the ethical problems are easier to resolve.

The following ethical principles, which are based on suggestions by others[60] as well as on this paper's attempt to separate the domain of treatment from the forensic realm, might then help us find a way through this supposed dilemma. (a) No psychiatrist *treating* a prisoner should provide forensic reports to a court for either the defense or the prosection; (b) no psychiatrist should administer medication or any other treatment to a prisoner solely pursuant to a court order; (c) psychiatrists should provide medically necessary antipsychotic medications to an incompetent prisoner/patient who is under an order of execution only if the court grants a stay of execution sufficient to complete a medically appropriate course of treatment; and (d) during the course of such treatment the psychiatrist must attempt to explain to the patient the medical and non-medical ramifications of accepting treatment — in the case of the death row inmate the consequences of competency being execution. The course of medically appropriate treatment would not be considered complete until the patient is capable of making an informed medical decision about accepting or rejecting medication. By following such guidelines, the treating psychiatrist will build a "Chinese Wall" against judicial incursions. Such an approach would ensure both professional autonomy and will prevent psychiatrist's treatment relationships from being exploited by the interests of the prosecutorial arm of the state.

This solution is not entirely satisfactory. For the psychiatrist who a priori opposes the death penalty, it may not go far enough. Furthermore, there are those who would argue that by requiring the prisoner/patient to choose between endless psychosis and the death penalty, the psychiatrist is still in an ethical quandary. But informed consent, on which this approach depends, always requires that a patient assess the advantages and drawbacks of choosing a particular treatment — in this instance, the consequence of successful treatment is execution.

Such guidelines do not guarantee that all death row inmates who become incompetent to be executed will, with absolute certainty, avoid execution. But they do guarantee both the autonomy of the patient and the professional autonomy necessary to make medical treatment decisions. These ethical proposals, if followed by psychiatrists and respected by the courts, should lead to more opportunity for the psychiatrist to offer medical care unencumbered by drastic legal consequences while the prisoner retains his or her right to accept or reject such care.

Some patients who have been restored to competency through medication may remain competent even if they then exercise their choice to refuse treatment. The psychiatrist-initiated treatment of such prisoners might therefore result in their execution. According to the reasoning here, that result may not be unethical. Such a result may, however, raise State constitutional questions if *Perry v. Louisiana* is followed as a precedent in other jurisdictions.

The Victim Impact Statement

Another ethically troubling situation in capital punishment has arisen out of the Supreme Court's reversal of its prior case law to allow victim impact statements to be introduced at the sentencing phase of trial. In *Payne v. Tennessee*,[61] the court held in a 6–3 decision that the Eighth Amendment's prohibition against cruel or unusual punishments did not act as a per se bar to the admission of victim impact statements during the sentencing phase of trial.

In the wake of *Payne v. Tennessee*, psychiatrists have a potentially substantial role to play in capital sentencing.[62] The victim impact statement is tailor-made for psychiatry's diagnosis of Post-Traumatic Stress Disorder.[63] Every murder victim's family meets the trauma criterion for Post-Traumatic Stress Disorder and most are said to suffer from the condition.[64]

A psychiatrist's testimony or deposition will give scientific weight to the prosecution's argument that the evil deed is worthy of capital punishment. Although this situation fills me with moral trepidation, I recognize that most forensic psychiatrists will have no ethical objections to participating in capital punishment in this manner. Furthermore, unlike the prediction of dangerousness, the psychiatric profession has demonstrated no scientific discomfort with the diagnosis of Post-Traumatic Stress Disorder. Thus, there will be no ethical prohibition against providing such "truthful" testimony which "helps" the victim but "harms" the victimizer. Nonetheless, the approach described in this paper may at least have the minimal value of clarifying the transference/countertransference issues that can complicate expert testimony.

The Ethical Problem of the Victim Impact Statement

Recently I received a letter from a psychiatrist who wanted my advice on this very issue. He was treating a woman whose husband was murdered during an armed robbery. The woman believed that participating in a victim impact statement would help her work through the trauma and have other personal benefits. She wanted her psychiatrist's help and testimony. He had no doubt that his patient suffered from Post-Traumatic Stress Disorder but he wanted to know from me if there were any ethical principles that should keep him from participating in the legal process.

Appelbaum would presumably reason in such a case that neither my conceptual concerns, nor beneficence and nonmaleficence principles, nor the principle of truthfulness would bar this psychiatrist's participation in the legal process. Nonetheless, he and I might agree to the principle that psychiatrists should not intermingle their different roles in the different contexts. I would, therefore, urge the psychiatrist to tactfully inform his patient that, because he was treating her, his professional ethics made it necessary to refer her to a forensic psychiatrist who could do an independent objective evaluation and testify on her behalf.

None of the rules or guidelines proposed here will fully resolve the ethical problems that confound forensic psychiatrists. Nor is any claim intended that these proposals are new or rest on some new foundation. Quite the contrary, they reemphasize our ethical traditions. I believe that this reassertion of our traditional approach may help us to distinguish our therapeutic and forensic roles and, thereby, benefit our patients and our profession. The suggestions made here are expressly directed at the role of the forensic psychiatrist in the criminal courts. It is my impression that the intermingling of the roles of expert and therapist in other legal contexts requires separate consideration but might lead to similar conclusions.***

***A discerning reader has asked how such ethical guidelines might be enforced. Professionals charged with the enforcement of ethical principles have long recognized that there is a general problem. Ethical principles often embrace aspirations of the profession and are not formulated as statutes to be enforced. At a more conceptual level it is possible, following Lon L. Fuller (The Morality of Law 1964) to identify two different ethical standards that an individual should follow. The first marks the threshold of competence; what, if all else fails, we must (are under a duty to) do. This, Fuller termed a 'morality of duty.' However, beyond this threshold, there are a range of acts promoting beneficial outcomes, the omission of which will

Footnotes

[1]Paul S. Appelbaum. *The Parable of the Forensic Psychiatrist: Ethics and the Problem of Doing Harm*, 137 Int'l J. L. & Psychiatry 249 (1990).

[2]Alan A. Stone. *Presidential Address: Conceptual Ambiguity and Morality in Modern Psychiatry* 137 Am. J. Psychiatry 887 (1980).

[3]Halleck, Seymour L., *Psychiatry and the Dilemmas of Crime; A Study of Causes, Punishment, and Treatment*, Berkeley: University of California Press (1971); *See also*, Seymour L. Halleck, *Law in the Practice of Psychiatry: a Handbook for Clinicians*, New York: Plenum Medical Book Company (1980).

[4]Id.

[5]*See, e.g.*, M. J. Goldman, *Kleptomania: Making Sense of the Nonsensical*, 8 Am. J. Psychiatry 986 (1991).

[6]R. Spitzer et al., *DSM-III-R Casebook: A Learning Companion to the Diagnostic and Statistical Manual of Mental disorders* (3rd ed. rev. 1989).

[7]Alan A. Stone *The Ethical Boundaries of Forensic Psychiatry: A View from the Ivory Tower*, 12 Bull. Am. Acad. Psychiatry & L. 209 (1984).

[8]Jonas R. Rappeport. *Editorial: Is Forensic Psychiatry Ethical*, 12 Bull. Am. Acad. Psychiatry & L. 205 (1984); Andrew S. Watson, *Response from a Straw Man*, 12 Bull. Am. Acad. Psychiatry & L. 221 (1984); Herbert C. Modlin. *The Ivory Tower and the Marketplace*, 12 Bull. Am. Acad. Psychiatry & L. 233 (1984); Robert L. Sadoff, *Practical Ethical Problems of the Forensic Psychiatrist in Dealing with Attorneys*, 12 Bull. Am. Acad. Psychiatry & L. 243 (1984); Barbara A. Weiner, *Ethical issues in Forensic Psychiatry: From an Attorney's Perspective*, 12 Bull. Am. Acad. Psychiatry & L. 253 (1984); J. Richard Ciccone and Colleen D. Clements, *The Ethical Practice of Forensic Psychiatry: A View From the Trenches*, 12 Bull. Am. Acad. Psychiatry & L. 263 (1984): Seymour L. Halleck, *The Ethical Dilemmas of Forensic Psychiatry: A Utilitarian Approach*, 12 Bull. Am. Acad. Psychiatry & L. 279 (1984).

[9]Paul S. Appelbaum, *Psychiatric Ethics in the Courtroom*, 12 Bull. Am. Acad. Psychiatry & L 225 (1984).

[10]Appelbaum, *supra* note 1.

[11]This dictate comes from the Hippocratic Oath. *Dorland's Illustrated Medical Dictionary* 767–768 (27th ed., 1988).

[12]Alan A. Stone, *The Ethics of Forensic Psychiatry: A View from the Ivory Tower*, in *Law Psychiatry and Morality*, 57–75, 7 (1984).

[13]Id.

[14]Appelbaum, *supra* note 1 at 255.

[15]Id. at 251.

[16]Id. at 258.

[17]*See, e.g.*, Simon Yeznig Balian, *Personal Responsibility for Professional Actions* 32 Cath. Law. 337 (1988).

[18]*See, e.g.*, Gunther Teubner, *Autopoiesis in Law and Society: A Rejoinder to Blankenburg* 18 Law and Society Review 291 (1984).

[19]*See* Footnote 27.

[20]Aristotle, *Nicomachean Ethics* VI, 5: 1140b6-8.

---

not result in sanction, but the commission of which will result in more or less praise. While we do not see fit to punish the omission of these acts, we do recognize that they act as a guide for appropriate action to which we should all aspire; Fuller terms this standard the 'morality of aspiration' (ibid.). Some professional ethical standards are much more readily expressed as aspirational standards than ones imposing a direct duty. One example is §2 of the Principles of Medical Ethics of the American Medical Association: "Physicians should strive continually to improve medical knowledge and skill . . . " However, the difference between the two standards of aspiration and duty, Fuller points out, is not qualitative, but quantitative; it is a matter of where on the scale of morality the act in question is placed that determines which sanction is appropriate, in much the same way as the maker of a test determines what is to count as an unacceptable and, therefore, failing mark, what is a pass, and what is a distinction. To set a standard which requires that once an examination has passed from the realms of evaluation into those of a therapeutic encounter, the physician should refrain from testifying against the patient, is thus simply to determine that although failing to do so is not criminal, it is unethical. This may require some precise criteria determining when 'the therapeutic' begins, or rely on professional judgment in scrutinizing such criteria, but so do most professional negligence requirements. It is certainly no more difficult a standard than that which requires us to "improve medical knowledge and skill." And any difficulties in policing this standard may be eased by the fact that it is anticipation of the move from the therapeutic to the forensic — from one "ethic" to another — that would count as a criterion triggering consideration of the standard in the first place.

Mental Illness, Medicine and Law

ALAN A. STONE

[21]Aquinas, *Summa Theologiae* II-II, q 47, aa. 1–7. For Aquinas, knowledge of how to act in a given situation depends upon rationally discovering the correct general principles and rules of action — these apply universally — and then learning to apply them correctly in concrete situations.

[22]Kant *Foundations of the Metaphysics of Morals* 47 (1959). Kant tests the validity of every action by inquiring whether the reason (or "maxim") for action can be conceived and willed without contradiction as universal law. This is one of his versions of the "categorical imperative."

[23]*See* text at foot note 25.

[24]J. L. Austin, *How to do Things With Words* 10, Cambridge, MA: Harvard University Press (2nd ed. 1975).

[25]Appelbaum, *supra* note 1 at 251–252.

[26]Douglas Mossman, *Assessing and Restoring Competency to Be Executed: Should Psychiatrists Participate*, 5 Behav. Sci. & L. 397 (1987).

[27]*See, e.g.*, T. Beauchamp & J. Childress, *Principles of Biomedical Ethics* 25–66 (1989).

[28]Stone, *supra* note 12 at 69–71.

[29]*Barefoot v. Estelle*, 463 U.S. 880 (1983). *See also* Gerald T. Bennett and Arthur F. Sullwold, *Qualifying the Psychiatrist as a Lay Witness: a Reaction to the American Psychiatric Association Petition in Barefoot V. Estelle* 30, Journal of Forensic Sciences 462 (1985).

[30]Brief for American Psychiatric Association as *Amicus Curriae*, in *Barefoot v. Estelle*, 463 U.S. 880 (1983); *See also* American Psychiatric Association, *The Principles of Medical Ethics: With Annotations Especially Applicable to Psychiatry* 10–17 at § 1, Annot. 4 (rev. ed. 1989).

[31]Stone, *supra* note 12 at 70.

[32]Paul S. Appelbaum, *The Empirical Jurisprudence of the United States Supreme Court* (Justice Henry A. Blackmun: *The Supreme Court and the Limits of Medical Privacy*) 13 Am. J. L. & Med. 335 (1987).

[33]Stone, *supra* note 12 at 69–71.

[34]Gerald L. Klerman, *The Psychiatric Patient's Right to Effective Treatment: Implications of Osheroff v. Chestnut Lodge*, 147 Am. J. Psychiatry 409 (1990).

[35]Thomas Grisso & Paul Appelbaum, *Is it Unethical to Offer Predictions of Future Violence?* 16 L. & Hum. Behav. 621 (1992).

[36]M. Goodman *et al.*, *Managing Managed Care* (1992).

[37]In *Daubert v. Merril Dow Pharmaceuticals*, 61 U.S.L.W. 4805 Decided on June 28, 1993, the Supreme Court held that "general acceptance is not a necessary precondition to the admissibility of scientific evidence under the Federal Rules of Evidence, but the Rules of Evidence — especially Rule 702 — do assign to the trial judge the task of ensuring that an expert's testimony both rests on a reliable foundation and is relevant to the task at hand. Pertinent evidence based on scientifically valid principles will satisfy those demands."

[38]Watson, *supra* note 8.

[39]Grisso & Appelbaum, *supra* note 28.

[40]Elliot S. Valenstein, *Great and Desperate Cures: The Rise and Decline of Psychosurgery and other Radical Treatments for Mental Illness*, New York: Basic Books (1986).

[41]Appelbaum, *supra* note 9 at 228.

[42]*See* Alan A. Stone, *The Trial of John Hinckley*, in *Law Psychiatry and Morality*, 77–98 (1984).

[43]Id.

[44]Id.

[45]S. J. Morse, *Reforming Expert Testimony*, 6 L. & Hum. Behav. 39 (1982); D. Faust & J. Ziskin, *The Expert Witness in Psychology and Psychiatry*, 241 Sci. 31 (1988).

[46]*See, e.g.*, Philip G. Zimbardo & Michael R. Leippe, *The Psychology of Attitude Change and Social Influence* (1991); Lawrence Kohlberg, Charles Levine, & Alexangra Hewer, *Moral Stages: A Current Formulation and a Response to Critics* (1983); David Rosenhan, *Moral Character*, 27 Stan. L. Rev 925 (1975); David Rosenhan, *On Being Sane in Insane Places*, 179 Science 250 (1973).

[47]Jay Katz, *Experimentation with Human Beings: The Authority of the Investigator, Subject, Professions, and State in the Human Experimentation Process*, New York: Russell Sage Foundation (1972).

[48]Alan A. Stone, *Law, Science, and Psychiatric Malpractice: A Response to Klerman's Indictment of Psychoanalytic Psychiatry*, 147 Am. J. Psychiatry 419 (1990).

[49]*See* the Hoppocatic Oath, *supra* note 11.

[50]Curran and Cascells, *The Ethics of Medical Participation in Capital Punishment by Intravenous Injection*, 302 New Eng. J. Med. 226, 227 (1980) (*quoting from Ethics in Medicine: Historical Perspectives and Contemporary Concerns* 5 (S. Reiser, A. Dyke, & W. Curran eds., 1977).

[51]Council of Ethics and Judicial Affairs, American Medical Association, Current Opinions § 2.06 (1986). The APA has interpreted this opinion as a prohibition against psychiatrists participation in such proceedings. *See* David L. Katz, *Perry v. Louisiana: Medical Ethics on Death Row—Is Judicial Intervention Warranted?* 4 Geo. J. Legal Ethics 707, 714n.65 (1991) (*citing* Brief for American Psychiatric Association and American Medical Association as *Amici Curiae* at 17).

[52]*See, e.g.,* Richard J. Bonnie, *Dilemmas in Administering the Death Penalty,* 14L. & Hum. Behav. 67 (1990); Katz, *supra* note 44; Mossman, *supra* note 19.

[53]K. Heilbrun, M. Radelet, & J. Dvoskin, *The Debate on Treating Individuals Incompetent for Execution,* 149 Am. J. Psychiatry 596 (1992).

[54]*See* Katz, *supra* note 44 at 714.

[55]Personal communications with the APA committee of Black Psychiatrists.

[56]Heilbrun *et al., supra* note 46 at 598.

[57]*Louisiana v. Perry,* No. 91-KP-1324, 1992 LEXIS 3170 (La. Oct. 19, 1992).

[58]Katz, *supra* note 44; G. Linn Evans, *Perry v. Louisiana: Can a State Treat an Incompetent Prisoner to Ready Him for Execution?* 19 Bull. Am Acad. Psychiatry & L. 249 (1991; Michael L. Radelet & George W. Barnard, *Treating Those Found Incompetent for Execution: Ethical Chaos With Only One Solution,* 16 Bull. Am. Acad. Psychiatry & L. 297 (1988); Charles Patrick Ewing, *Diagnosing and Treating Insanity on Death Row: Legal and Ethical Perspectives,* 5 Behav. Sci. & L. 175 (1987); Rochelle Graff Salguero, *Medical Ethics and Competency to be Executed,* 96 Yale L. J. 167 (1986).

[59]Heilbrun *et al., supra* note 45.

[60]*See supra* note 51. *See also* Heilbrun, *supra* note 45; Mossman *supra* note 19; Bonnie *supra* note 44; Stanley L. Brodsky, *Professional Ethics and Professional Morality in the Assessment of Competence for Execution: A Response to Bonnie,* 14 L. & Human Behav. 91 (1990); Michael L. Gadelet and George Barnard, *Ethics and the Psychiatric Determination of Competency to be Executed,* 14 Bull. Am. Acad. Psychiatry & L. 37 (1986).

[61]*Payne v. Tennessee,* 111 S. Ct. 449 (1990).

[62]Alan A. Stone, *Report on the Supreme Court Decision in Payne V. Tennessee,* 16 Am. Acad. Psychiatry & L. Newsletter 79 (1991).

[63]Alan A. Stone, *Post-traumatic Stress Disorder and the Law: Critical Review of the New Frontier,* 21 Bull. Am. Acad. Psychiatry & L. (April 1993).

[64]Arthur J. Lurgio, Wesley G. Skogan, & Robert C. Davis, (eds) *Victims of Crime: Problems, Policies, and Programs,* Newbury Park, CA: Sage Publications (1990).

[47]

Liability for the Psychiatrist Expert Witness

Renée L. Binder, M.D.

Objective: An increasing number of general psychiatrists are acting as expert witnesses in the legal system. The purpose of this article is to help psychiatrists who are interested in doing forensic work by informing them of the risks entailed.

Method: The author reviews the medical and legal literature about expert witness immunity.

Results: The author explains the traditional concept of expert witness immunity and shows how a variety of factors have led to the erosion of this immunity. These factors include the proliferation of experts, the inadequacy of traditional safeguards of potential prosecution for perjury and cross-examination, the growth of attorney malpractice, the lack of protection of the injured party from unscrupulous witnesses, and the ineffectiveness of *Daubert v. Merrell Dow Pharmaceuticals*. Examples are given of how expert witnesses are being held accountable by professional associations and state medical boards and through tort liability.

Conclusions: The author provides risk-management strategies and guidelines for psychiatrists who are considering engaging in forensic work.

(Am J Psychiatry 2002; 159:1819–1825)

An increasing number of general psychiatrists are acting as expert witnesses in the legal system. As Dr. Paul Appelbaum, president of the American Academy of Psychiatry and the Law, stated, "With managed care reducing both the pleasure and the remuneration to be derived from clinical practice, a growing number of clinicians are augmenting their practices by spending some of their time doing forensic work"(1). A more quantitative measure of this statement is demonstrated by the fact that the membership of psychiatrists in the subspecialty organization the American Academy of Psychiatry and the Law has increased from approximately 1,500 in 1992 to more than 2,200 in 2002 despite a general decrease in membership in professional organizations such as APA and the American Medical Association (AMA). Most psychiatrists who join the American Academy of Psychiatry and the Law work as expert witnesses or are interested in doing so.

Traditionally, expert witnesses have been granted legal immunity for their forensic work; i.e., they cannot be sued and have charges of negligence or defamation brought against them. The argument has been that expert witnesses are an important part of the legal system and in the interest of justice, expert witnesses need to be protected from liability. This is changing for all expert witnesses, including psychiatrists. Psychiatrist expert witnesses are beginning to be held accountable for their testimony by being subject to sanctions by both professional associations and state medical boards and through tort liability actions.

The purpose of this article is to review the changing doctrine of witness immunity as it pertains to expert witnesses. The intent is to help general psychiatrists who are interested in doing forensic consultations by informing them of the risks of this work.

Role of the Expert Witness

The use of expert witnesses is favored in our legal system, and the rules of evidence reflect this belief. Rule 702 of the Federal Rules of Evidence states that "if scientific, technical or other specialized knowledge will assist the trier of fact to understand the evidence or to determine a fact in issue, a witness qualified as an expert by knowledge, skill, experience, training or education may testify thereto in the form of an opinion or otherwise"(2). This federal rule is reflected in the rules governing the admissibility of expert testimony in state jurisdictions around the country. Thus, the testimony of expert witnesses is often used to clarify, explain, and assist with the understanding of many important issues.

Concept of Witness Immunity

The witness immunity doctrine originated hundreds of years ago in English common law for broad public policy reasons. The intent of witness immunity has been to encourage open and honest testimony without fear of a subsequent lawsuit related to the testimony. In 1585, one of the courts in England opined that without immunity, "those who have just cause for a complaint would not dare to complain for fear of infinite vexation" (3). Also, in 1859, another court in England held that immunity was important to ensure that witnesses would speak freely when giving testimony (4).

In American courts, a similar principle was adopted (e.g., reference 5). In fact, the issue of witness immunity has been considered to be so important by courts that it has been maintained even when there might be negligence. For example, in *Clark v. Grigson* (6), the Texas Appeals Court stated "that no civil liability exists on the part of an expert witness who forms an opinion and states that opinion in the course of his testimony in a judicial proceeding, even though he may have been negligent in the process." The court applied the immunity doctrine on the basis of the public policy that it is in the public's interest to permit expert testimony without the threat of subsequent lawsuits.

The United States Supreme Court confirmed the importance of witness immunity in two cases in the 1980s. In *Briscoe v. LaHue* (7), a convicted man brought action against the police officers who gave perjured testimony against him. The majority opinion held that "witnesses might be reluctant to come forward to testify" if they were liable for the testimony, and "a witness who knows that he might be forced to defend a subsequent lawsuit, and perhaps to pay damages, might be inclined to shade his testimony in favor of the potential plaintiff, to magnify uncertainties, and thus to deprive the finder of fact of candid, objective, and undistorted evidence" (7). In a second case, the U.S. Supreme Court reasoned that witness immunity is important because "the judicial process is an arena of open conflict, and in virtually every case, there is, if not always a winner, at least one loser. It is inevitable that many of those who lose will pin the blame on...witnesses and will bring suit against them in an effort to relitigate the underlying conflict" (8).

State courts have also affirmed the concept of witness immunity for reasons of public policy. One example comes from Washington state, where in 1989, the Washington Supreme Court opined that without immunity, there would be a loss of objectivity and that experts could take the most extreme positions favorable to their clients. The court also argued that it feared that the imposition of liability would discourage anyone who was not a full-time professional expert witness from testifying. Additionally, concerns that one-time or infrequent experts would not carry the necessary insurance to cover the liability risk in testifying also played a part in the court's decision to provide witness immunity. The Washington State Supreme Court acknowledged that the main argument supporting expert witness liability is that the threat of liability would encourage experts to be more careful, resulting in more accurate, reliable testimony. The court stated, "While there is some merit to this contention, possible gains of this type have to be weighed against the threatened losses of objectivity described above. We draw that balance in favor of immunity" (9).

A Shift in the Concept of Immunity

Proliferation of Experts

One of the factors leading to the desire to increase the accountability of experts is the fact that the use of experts in the legal system has proliferated in the past 30 years (10). Many commercial services offer experts for hire to assist with litigation, and some of these services have thousands of experts on file. Magazines such as *Trial*, the magazine of the Association of Trial Lawyers, contain numerous experts' advertisements that claim that they can bring in the highest monetary judgments possible. Experts are known to influence the outcome of trials. A poll conducted by the *National Law Journal* and LexisNexis (11) found that paid experts were thought believable by 89% of recent criminal and civil jurors. Many of these experts are not considered to be impartial. In fact, many lawyers frankly admit that they do not want any semblance of impartiality in their expert witnesses. For example, Melvin Belli, a well-known plaintiff's attorney, once said, "If I got myself an impartial witness, I would think I was wasting my money." One former president of the American Bar Association said, "I would go into a lawsuit with an objective, uncommitted independent expert about as willingly as I would occupy a foxhole with a couple of noncombatant soldiers" (10).

The Fifth Circuit Court of Appeals expressed its concern about the testimony of many expert witnesses who are members of the academic community and who supplement their teaching salaries with consulting work: "We know from our judicial experience that many such able persons present studies and express opinions that they might not be willing to express in an article submitted to a refereed journal of their discipline or in other contexts subject to peer review. We think that is one important signal, along with many others, that ought to be considered in deciding to accept expert testimony" (12). The court also opined, "Experts whose opinions are available to the highest bidder have no place testifying in a court of law before a jury and with the imprimatur of the trial judge's decision that he is an expert" (12).

Inadequate Safeguards

There is also concern that the safeguards cited by courts to ensure honest expert witness testimony—i.e., potential prosecution for perjury and cross-examination—are not effective (13). The Illinois Supreme Court recognized that "it is virtually impossible to prosecute an expert witness for perjury....The opinion and the opinion is the result of reasoning, and no one can be prosecuted for defective mental processes. The field of medicine is not an exact science" (14). In addition, the Wyoming Supreme Court stated, "A witness is not guilty of perjury simply because his testimony is inconsistent" (15). The court reasoned that "internal inconsistencies in testimony or an insufficient foundation for the basis of an expert's opinion...may

RENÉE L. BINDER

provide sufficient contradiction to allow the jury to disregard the opinion rendered," but does not provide a basis for perjury (15).

The second primary safeguard, cross-examination, is also not an effective means of monitoring expert witness testimony. The Louisiana courts have acknowledged this and state that cross-examination "seldom is of adequate value when thrust against the broadside of the litigation expert who can so gracefully stiff-arm his unprepared cross-examiner" (16). Others have stated that many experts are "repeat performers" who have gained from past experience an ability to remain calm and focused in the midst of an attack on their opinions and credibility. As a result, the expert witness usually remains consistent in his or her testimony: "Searching cross-examination may not yield any other result than to provide an opportunity for the expert witness to repeat his already damaging testimony" (10).

Attorney Malpractice

Another factor leading to the movement to hold experts more accountable for their testimony is that attorneys are now being sued for malpractice. A lawyer can be held liable for practicing below the standard of care for failure "to exercise the skill and knowledge ordinarily possessed by attorneys under similar circumstances." The test is not whether there was an unfavorable result or whether the defendant attorney acted in good faith but whether a reasonably prudent attorney would have made that decision in the same or similar circumstances (17). Some courts have opined that an expert's act of consulting on a case is analogous to an attorney's act of trying a case (e.g., references 18, 19). Thus, if attorneys can be sued, an argument can be made that expert witnesses can also be sued (10).

Attorneys are now given guidelines to protect themselves from malpractice liability. These include guidelines related to fee setting, confidentiality, taking cases within one's area of expertise, and accurate advertising (10). Psychiatrists and other experts need to pay attention to similar guidelines.

Intent of Tort Law

One of the goals of tort law is to compensate an injured party when the cause of the loss can be ascribed to other parties for sound reasons. Tort law's secondary intent is to deter future harm by providing incentives to prevent misconduct. Therefore, one measure of the witness immunity doctrine is whether granting immunity helps to achieve the intent of tort law (10). Some courts have stated that granting immunity to expert witnesses is actually counterproductive to these goals and unfair to the injured party. The argument is that expert witnesses might be harming a plaintiff or defendant by negligent performance and that they should assume responsibility for this harm (19).

Ineffectiveness of Daubert and Kumho

In order to try and keep misleading and unscientific testimony from the courtroom, the U.S. Supreme Court looked at the issue of admissibility of evidence in the *Daubert v. Merrell Dow Pharmaceuticals* (20) and *Kumho Tire Company v. Carmichael* (21) decisions. In these decisions, the court gave the trial judge a gate-keeping function to determine whether evidence was reliable and should be allowed into or excluded from the courtroom. However, these cases have not effectively prevented the admission of scientifically questionable expert witness testimony. Some states have not adopted *Daubert*. Even in the federal courts and in the states that follow *Daubert*, courts have generally erred on the side of allowing testimony to be heard (22, 23). In fact, exclusion of medical expert testimony has constituted grounds for reversible error (23). The general jurisprudential rule is that bias does not preclude a witness from being qualified as an expert; rather, it is only to be viewed as a factor that should be considered by the fact finder in deciding how much weight to give to the testimony. Some legal scholars believe that the "let-it-all-in" approach is alive and well in post-*Daubert* proceedings (22).

Expanding Arenas for Accountability and Liability

Discipline by Professional Associations

In June 2001, the 7th U.S. Circuit Court of Appeals held that a professional society could discipline a member for improper testimony. The case involved a neurosurgeon who was suspended by the American Association of Neurological Surgeons after he testified as an expert witness for the plaintiff in a medical malpractice suit. The neurosurgeon expert witness sued the American Association of Neurological Surgeons for suspending him. The suspension was upheld by the district court and by the appellate court. The appellate court decision held that the neurosurgeon expert witness's testimony was irresponsible and violated the ethical code of the association to "provide the court with accurate and documentable opinions on the matters at hand" (24).

The field of expert witness ethics, however, is still undeveloped, and many professional societies do not have specific codes related to forensic work, besides the general principles of honesty and avoidance of conflicts of interest (25). The most comprehensive guideline for ethical conduct by forensic psychiatrists has been developed by the American Academy of Psychiatry and the Law (26). All American Academy of Psychiatry and the Law members must also have membership in the APA or the American Academy of Child and Adolescent Psychiatry. When the American Academy of Psychiatry and the Law receives reports of unethical or unprofessional conduct of its members, it refers the complainant to the appropriate district branch ethics committee of the APA or to the American Academy of Child and Adolescent Psychiatry. If there has been a breach of ethics, the member will be subject to censure by the APA or the American Academy of Child and Adolescent Psychiatry.

Discipline by State Licensing Boards

In 1997, the Washington State Supreme Court ruled that disciplinary proceedings by the state Board of Psychology were allowed against a psychologist who was alleged to have failed to meet professional ethical standards in work that formed the basis of his expert testimony in several child custody cases. It said that witness immunity did not extend to professional disciplinary hearings (27).

Physician expert witnesses may be sanctioned by their medical licensing boards. The AMA's House of Delegates passed a resolution in the late 1990s stating that the provision of expert testimony is the practice of medicine. One of the intents of this resolution was to make testimony by physicians subject to peer review (28). If their testimony is negligent, physicians may be reported to their state medical boards and disciplined. More recently, the AMA's Reference Committee asked the Board of Trustees to suggest remedies to the problem of physicians giving false testimony against their colleagues, including reporting to and sanctioning by state licensing boards (29).

Tort Liability

In addition to experts being at risk for discipline by professional societies and state medical boards, various courts have allowed lawsuits to be brought against expert witnesses (30). Although, to date, I know of no successful lawsuits related to allegations about actual testimony, there have been successful lawsuits related to other aspects of an expert's forensic work. The following are five examples of cases that have set precedents in different jurisdictions for holding experts accountable for work done in the forensic context.

Precedent-Setting Cases

New Jersey Supreme Court, 1984. In *Levine v. Wiss and Co.* (31), the court allowed a lawsuit to be brought against a court-appointed expert, an accountant, for alleged substandard performance. The accountant argued that he was entitled to witness immunity and that he was not liable for any negligence in the performance of his professional duties on behalf of the parties. The court concluded that as an accountant, the defendant had a duty to "exercise reasonable care in preparing reports, verifying underlying data, and examining the methods employed in arriving at financial statements" (31).

Although this case did not involve a psychiatrist witness, it is possible to see how the principles elucidated by the court might apply to a psychiatrist who is retained to do an evaluation and arrive at a diagnosis and treatment recommendations in a forensic case. If the diagnosis is not arrived at by practices consistent with the standards of care,

it is certainly conceivable that a psychiatrist expert witness might also be liable.

California Court of Appeals, 1992. In *Mattco Forge Inc. v. Arthur Young & Co.* (18), the court of appeals allowed a claim of negligence against an accounting firm retained as an expert witness in legal proceedings. The complaint against the accounting firm alleged professional malpractice as well as fraudulent representation of its employees' expertise. For example, the allegation was that the accounting firm's brochure had fraudulently represented the firm's litigation support personnel as having special training in California procedures. The complaint further alleged that an inexperienced certified public accountant was used by the accounting firm and that he had no training or experience in litigation services.

The trial court dismissed the lawsuit against the accounting firm on the grounds of expert witness immunity. The California Court of Appeals reversed the dismissal.

Although *Mattco* did not involve psychiatrist expert witnesses, it is relevant to psychiatrists because it allowed a retaining party to sue expert witnesses with the allegations that they had misrepresented their expertise and that their work was below the standards of practice. The retaining party claimed to have lost its lawsuit as a result of the alleged actions of the expert. It is certainly conceivable that this same principle could be used to bring a case against psychiatrist expert witnesses who misrepresent their forensic experience or whose performance as experts is alleged to be substandard.

Missouri Supreme Court, 1992. In *Murphy v. A.A. Matthews* (19), the Missouri Supreme Court held that witness immunity does not bar lawsuits against professional expert witnesses for alleged negligence in reaching opinions. The complaint was against engineers who had been retained as experts and alleged that the engineers' incompetence and carelessness had led to an inability by the plaintiff to obtain appropriate compensation in the legal action. The primary defense against the allegations was that witness immunity protected the engineers from liability. The trial court dismissed the case on the basis of the witness immunity doctrine, and the Missouri Supreme Court reversed the dismissal.

The Missouri Supreme Court opined that witness immunity should be limited in scope. The court held that witness immunity should continue to be limited to defamation or to retaliatory cases against adverse witnesses. The court felt that the imposition of liability would encourage experts to be careful and accurate. It opined that since professional experts are subject to negligence liability in their other work, it is not out of line to expect that services related to litigation should be treated in a similar manner.

The *Murphy* court also discredited the notion that expanding witness liability would result in difficulty in retaining experts by stating, "There is no reason to believe

RENÉE L. BINDER

that professionals will abandon the area of litigation support merely because they will be held to the same standard of care applicable to their other areas of practice" (19). Responding to the criticism that expert witness liability may result in a never-ending cycle of litigation, the *Murphy* court acknowledged that withholding immunity would lengthen the litigation process for yet one more lawsuit. Despite this concern, the court reasoned that an increase in the number of trials was already allowed for trial attorneys who allegedly commit malpractice and indicated that experts should receive consistent treatment.

In the view of the court, experts act as advisors and advocates, as opposed to being objective and independent witnesses. The court stated that the engineering firm charged a hefty fee to provide expert services to assist the claim of the plaintiff. By charging this fee and voluntarily agreeing to provide services, it assumed the duty of care of a professional; therefore, witness immunity did not bar the lawsuit from being heard by the court.

In this case, as in *Mattco*, we can see the evolution of thinking regarding expert witness immunity. The *Murphy* court supported the right of aggrieved parties to bring a lawsuit against a witness that they retained if they feel that the services of that witness were performed negligently. This right could also be extended to parties who retain psychiatrist expert witnesses. For example, a psychiatrist who undertakes expert witness work without receiving adequate training in how to do this type of work and who does not understand the standards of practice for forensic evaluations, report writing, and testimony might be subject to a claim that the psychiatrist expert witness performed his work negligently and was responsible for any unfavorable judgment.

California Court of Appeals, 1996. In *Pettus v. Cole et al.* (32), the court ruled that two psychiatrists violated the California Confidentiality of Medical Information Act when they disclosed to an employer details of psychiatric disability evaluations they had performed on behalf of the employer. Rather than negligence, this case involved allegations of inappropriate disclosure based on specific statutory confidentiality requirements. The case also redefined the physician-patient relationship as including the relationship between evaluator and evaluee.

Mr. Pettus requested time off from work because of disabling stress. His employer's short-term disability policy required that he undergo a medical examination that would be arranged and paid for by the employer. Two psychiatrists evaluated Mr. Pettus and submitted detailed reports to the employer, including statements that Mr. Pettus's condition might be linked to an alcohol abuse problem. As a result of these evaluations, Mr. Pettus's employer required him to receive alcohol treatment as a condition of continued employment. Mr. Pettus was terminated when he refused to enter an alcohol treatment program. He complained that he never authorized the doctors to disclose the full contents of their evaluations to his employer. Neither psychiatrist had obtained a written authorization for disclosure of all the information.

The California Confidentiality of Medical Information Act has a specific provision that was the basis of this lawsuit. This subsection states that when an employer requests and pays for employment-related health care services, the "provider of health care" may not disclose the medical cause of functional limitations. It states that the information disclosed should only include the functional limitations of the patient that may entitle the patient to leave work or to limit the patient's fitness to perform employment. The California Confidentiality of Medical Information Act states that a "provider of health care" may not disclose medical information without a written authorization from the patient.

The psychiatrists claimed that there was no physician-patient relationship, and therefore, they had no obligation of confidentiality. The court of appeals found that professional services were performed, and therefore, there was a relationship with a duty of confidentiality. The court of appeals held that the information released to the employer was far more than the employer needed to have to accomplish its legitimate objective. The psychiatrists were not being sued for malpractice. They were being sued for a breach of the duty of confidentiality, as specified in the California Confidentiality of Medical Information Act.

The psychiatrists were subsequently involved in a prolonged lawsuit over the next several years that included another review by the court of appeals. The case was finally resolved in November 2000. The court affirmed that the psychiatrists had violated the statute but had not caused the plaintiff any damage.

This case demonstrates that psychiatrists need to know statutory and legal requirements in their jurisdictions if they plan on undertaking forensic work. These requirements are generally not taught in medical school or in residencies.

Colorado Court of Appeals, 1999. In *Dalton v. Miller* (33), the court ruled that a psychiatrist could be sued for alleged misconduct of a forensic examination. The facts of the case are as follows: The plaintiff, Patricia Dalton, sued her insurance company for refusing to renew her health insurance policy. Since she alleged resulting emotional distress, the insurer requested an independent psychiatric examination of the plaintiff to determine her emotional and psychological condition. Dr. Miller examined the plaintiff, prepared a written report, and testified in a videotaped deposition. The insurance company settled the claim. The plaintiff then sued the psychiatrist for his conduct during the examination and for alleged discrepancies between his written report to the insurer and his videotaped deposition testimony. The trial court dismissed the claim against the psychiatrist, reasoning that the defendant, Dr. Miller, was entitled to immunity for his activities conducted pursuant to the psychiatric evaluation. The court of appeals upheld the portion of the trial court's decision that said that witness immunity protected the statements of the physician witness in his report and deposition. However, the court of appeals reversed another part of the lower court's decision. It stated that the case could proceed on the issue of whether the psychiatrist's conduct during his *examination* caused the plaintiff harm. The plaintiff claimed that the psychiatrist's questions were overly intrusive and that he forced her to take psychological tests. With this issue, the case against the psychiatrist was allowed to proceed.

This case demonstrates how physicians can be sued for their conduct during an examination even if they are immune from claims of negligent testimony. This is an area of potential liability for psychiatrists to be aware of if they choose to undertake forensic evaluations.

Recent Unpublished Cases

Neither of the following recent cases set a precedent, as did the previously discussed cases, because they are not cases that have reached the level of the state appellate or supreme courts. However, they both serve as examples of cases in which psychiatrists have been sued on the basis of the allegation that their forensic work was negligent and caused harm to the plaintiff. (Identifying information has been disguised in these cases.)

Case 1. A psychiatrist was asked by an employer to perform a "fitness-to-duty" evaluation of an employee. The concern was that the employee often misconstrued actions or conversations to be about himself when they were not. There was also concern about potential violence by the employee. The psychiatrist did an evaluation and diagnosed the employee as having a paranoid personality. Subsequently, the employee was suspended; he brought a lawsuit against the psychiatrist. The employee retained an "expert witness" who wrote a report discrediting the basis of the diagnosis. This "expert" stated that the diagnosis of paranoid personality was inaccurate and opined that the employee's thoughts of conspiracy were related to cultural ideas rather than to a psychiatric diagnosis. The employee represented himself in this lawsuit against the psychiatrist. Possibly partially because the courts give great leeway to pro se plaintiffs (i.e., those who represent themselves), the court refused to dismiss several of the allegations against the psychiatrist and allowed the lawsuit to proceed. Causes of action included the allegation that the psychiatrist fabricated the diagnosis to please the employer and that the diagnosis was without merit. Thus, the psychiatrist was put in the position of needing to retain a malpractice attorney to hire experts (including myself) to determine whether or not the diagnosis of paranoid personality was reasonable. These causes of action were eventually dismissed after several years of aggravation and stress for the psychiatrist/defendant.

Case 2. A psychiatrist was asked to evaluate a disability claim brought by a 45-year-old man with recurrent depression. She interviewed the man and wrote a report stating that his complaints were consistent with a major depressive disorder and supported his claim of disability. Subsequent to the writing of the report, the man's insurance company showed the psychiatrist a surveillance videotape that it had made of this businessman. The videotape showed that after leaving the psychiatrist's office, the man was laughing and conversing with an acquaintance as he went shopping in the neighborhood. This was in contrast to what the man had reported to the psychiatrist. He had told the psychiatrist that he was barely able to move and could not engage in pleasurable activities. On the basis of this brief surveillance videotape, the psychiatrist wrote a supplemental report in which she stated that she was changing her diagnosis to "malingering." As a result of this supplemental report, the man's disability claim was denied. He brought a lawsuit against the evaluating psychiatrist, and three causes of action were set forth: defamation, intentional infliction of emotional distress, and conspiracy. The psychiatrist's attorney requested a consultation to determine whether the psychiatrist's diagnosis of malingering was reached within the standards of practice for forensic psychiatrists. The attorney tried to have the defamation cause of action dismissed on the basis of the fact that psychiatrists have a qualified privilege related to their opinions; however, the court allowed this cause of action to proceed in its demurrer. This case is currently in litigation.

Guidelines for Psychiatrist Expert Witnesses

The concept of legal immunity for psychiatrists who work as expert witnesses is eroding. Psychiatrist experts are being held accountable by professional associations, state licensing boards, and tort liability actions. Being an expert witness can be challenging and rewarding for general psychiatrists. It is important, however, to be aware of the potential liabilities involved in this work. The following guidelines will help psychiatrists who are considering engaging in forensic practice defend themselves successfully against claims of negligence.

Psychiatrists should have training regarding the conduct of forensic evaluations before undertaking such work. Clinical evaluations and reports differ from forensic ones. Psychiatrists need to understand the relevant legal issues, including statutory requirements; civil and criminal procedures; how to prepare for and conduct evaluations; how to interact with the evaluee, attorneys, and judges; how to write forensic reports; and how to give depositions and court testimony. Psychiatrists should also be aware of ethical codes related to forensic work, such as the ethical guidelines of the American Academy of Psychiatry and the Law.

Psychiatrists need to be certain that they have the time to meet court deadlines and requirements. Forensic work can be flexible in the sense that records can be reviewed at

RENÉE L. BINDER

the convenience of the psychiatrist, e.g., during cancelled patient appointments or in the evenings. However, at times forensic work is inflexible, e.g., when reports need to be submitted by a discovery deadline or when a psychiatrist is called to appear in court or to give a deposition.

Psychiatrists should be aware of risk-management techniques for doing forensic work to protect themselves from malpractice liability. These are similar to those taught to attorneys and include the following:

1. Not specifying a likely result or opinion and/or advertising how your services will achieve that result.
2. Arranging fees and expenses, including retainers, at the outset of consultation.
3. Maintaining strict records, including audiotaping or videotaping interviews when appropriate.
4. Keeping the attorney informed of your opinion as it develops.
5. Not overstating your opinions.
6. Not taking cases beyond your ability and expertise.
7. Preserving the attorney's and client's confidence, as specified in the legal proceedings in which you are involved.

Psychiatrists should be certain that they have malpractice coverage that will support their defense in the event that they are sued in reference to forensic work.

Received Feb. 22, 2002; revision received April 22, 2002; accepted May 13, 2002. From the Psychiatry and the Law Program, University of California, San Francisco. Address reprint requests to Dr. Binder, 401 Parnassus Ave., San Francisco, CA 94143-0984; renee@itsa.ucsf.edu (e-mail).

References

1. Appelbaum PS: Liability for forensic evaluations: a word of caution. Psychiatr Serv 2001; 52:885–886
2. Fed R Evid 702
3. Cutler v Dixon, 76 Eng Rep 886 (QB 1585)
4. Henderson v Broomhead, 157 Eng Rep 964, 967–968 (Ex 1859)
5. Restatement (Second) of Torts 584, 588 (1977)
6. Clark v Grigson, 579 SW 2d 263 (Tex 1978)
7. Briscoe v LaHue, 460 US 325 (1983)
8. Mitchell v Forsyth, 472 US 511 (1985)
9. Bruce v Byrne-Stevens & Assoc Engineers Inc, 776 P2d 666, 667 (Wash 1989)
10. Jensen EG: When "hired guns" backfire: the witness immunity doctrine and the negligent expert witness. University of Missouri at Kansas City Law Rev 1993; 62:185–210
11. Cheever JM, Naiman J: The view from the jury box. National Law J, Feb. 22, 1993
12. In re Air Crash Disaster, 795 F2d 1230, 1234 (5th Cir 1986)
13. McDowell CM: Authorizing the expert witness to assassinate character for profit: a re-examination of the testimonial immunity of the expert witness. University of Memphis Law Rev 1997; 28:239–269
14. Sears v Rutishauser, 466 NE 2d 210, 212 (Ill 1984)
15. Little v Kobos, 877 P2d 752 (Wyo 1994)
16. Rowe v State Farm Mut Auto Ins Co, 670 So 2d 718, 726 (La App 3rd Cir) writ denied 673 So 2d 611 (1996)
17. Masterson LR: Witness immunity or malpractice liability for professionals hired as experts? University of Texas at Austin Rev Litigation 1998; 17:393–413
18. Mattco Forge Inc v Arthur Young & Co, 6 Cal Rptr 2d 781 (Cal Ct App 1992)
19. Murphy v AA Mathews, 841 SW 2d 671 (Mo 1992)
20. Daubert v Merrell Dow Pharmaceuticals, 113 S Ct 2786 (1993)
21. Kumho Tire Company v Carmichael, 119 S Ct 1167 (1999)
22. Alford WR: The biased expert witness in Louisiana tort law: existing mechanisms of control and proposals for change. Louisiana Law Rev 2000; 61:181–221
23. McAbee GN: Improper medical testimony: existing and proposed mechanisms of oversight. J Legal Med 1998; 19:257–272
24. Austin v American Association of Neurological Surgeons, 253 F3d 967 (7th Circuit 2001)
25. Lubet S: Expert witness: ethics and professionalism. Georgetown J Legal Ethics 1999; 12:465–487
26. American Academy of Psychiatry and the Law: Ethical Guidelines for the Practice of Forensic Psychiatry, adopted May 1987; revised 1989, 1991, and 1995. Atlanta, AAPL, 1995
27. Deatherage v State of Washington Examining Board of Psychology, 948 P2d 828 (Sup Ct of Washington 1997)
28. Weintraub MI: Medical expert witnesses (letter). Lancet 1999; 353:2076
29. Zonana H: AMA examines expert testimony. AAPL Newsletter, Jan 2002
30. Moore MV, Johnson GG, Beard DF: Liability in litigation support and court testimony: is it time to rethink the risks? J Legal Economics 1999; 9:53–63
31. Levine v Wiss and Co, 478 A2d 397, 399 (NJ 1984)
32. Pettus v Cole et al., 49 Cal App 4th 402 (1996)
33. Dalton v Miller, 984 P2d 666 (Colo App 1999)

[48]

Forensic ethics and capital punishment: is there a special problem?

ALAN A. STONE

The American forensic psychiatrist of the twenty-first century has reinvented the profession and is a truth seeker, not a physician. Consider the recent virtuoso performance of the forensic psychiatrist who testified in the Texas trial of Andrea Yates. Using PowerPoint and videotape of his interviews to explain and document his state-of-the-art testimony, the expert set out to persuade the jury that Mrs. Yates, though psychotic when she killed her five children, was not insane under Texas law. By most accounts his testimony played a decisive role in the jury's rejection of her insanity defense. Explaining his forensic role to the *New York Times*, he later said that in searching for the truth he had to put aside his sympathies.[1] He chided colleagues who let their clinical sympathies interfere with their forensic search for truth. Obviously the expert was defending himself against critics but he was correctly describing the professional ethics of forensic psychiatry. If his testimony had a devastating affect on this unfortunate woman, that is the price of the 'truth ethos' of forensic psychiatry. The *New York Times* failed to ask this expert how, given all of the current scientific uncertainty in psychiatry, he discerned the truth of this matter and why it was that the expert for the defense, in his search for truth, reached all the opposite conclusions.

More than 20 years ago in an invited lecture to the American Academy of Psychiatry and Law the current writer questioned the ethical standards of psychiatrists who testify in court.[2] Although the profession has grown in academic and professional stature, to my mind the forensic psychiatrists of the twenty-first century have solved none of the problems that I then outlined. My lecture emphasized the ambiguity of both the intellectual and ethical boundaries of forensic psychiatry. It touched on the scientific and epistemological standing of psychiatric evidence and the tensions the adversary system imposed on the doctor's fiduciary obligation to the patient and the traditional injunction to do no harm. I emphasized then that having abandoned medical ethics, the forensic psychiatrist has no meaningful guidelines as to what is proper and ethical in navigating through these ambiguities and the pressures of the adversary system. The Yates case, in my opinion, demonstrates that the new forensic psychiatrist has not solved these problems.

However, a considerable literature has since been produced that touches on those and other arguments.[3] Some of the writing in this field has turned to a narrower question. In 1980 the American Medical Association (AMA) and the American Psychiatric Association (APA) responded to new state laws that authorized lethal injections as the method of execution. Facing the prospect that physicians would become executioners, organized medicine declared it unethical for a physician to participate in capital punishment. The traditional principle 'Do No Harm' was given as justification.[4] The prohibition, which focused on lethal injection, did not consider the parameters of participation for forensic psychiatrists. Bloche, in an important article in 1993, reviewed the set of problems I had described, but focused on the roles of forensic psychiatrists that, in his opinion, constituted unethical participation in capital punishment.[5]

Forensic psychiatrists may play several roles in capital punishment. First, they testify at the sentencing phase of a capital punishment trial. Their opinions on dangerousness, remorse, or mitigating factors will help determine whether the death penalty is imposed. Second, they may evaluate a death row inmate to determine whether the prisoner is competent to be executed or not. Third, they may evaluate a prisoner who has previously been declared incompetent to be executed. Forensic expertise in these three situations may facilitate or impede the death penalty.

Bloche drew his line between the first and second roles I have given above. Forensic psychiatrists could offer expert testimony for the death penalty but should not participate on either side of a competency-to-be-executed evaluation. Physicians for Human Rights (PHR) and others who oppose capital punishment now condemn forensic psychiatrists who evaluate competence to be executed.[6]

Bloche in justifying his cut-off line explored a complicated set of arguments that are intended to delineate participation.[7] These include proximity to capital punishment of the forensic psychiatrists' intervention and also the

extent to which the expert's opinion is 'insulated' by intervening delibera-
tions by the court. Thus in the first role above, testimony for the prosecution that helps to convince the jury that the defendant deserves execution, is
not considered proximate enough to be unethical participation. On the other
hand, in the second and third roles the prisoner is closer to execution and
there is less court involvement.

Forensic psychiatrists disagree with Bloche. They make a sharp distinction
between their clinical/therapeutic and their legal/testimonial roles.[8] That distinction is crucial to the ethics of forensic psychiatrists as set forth by Appelbaum.[9, 10] Bloche's 1993 article was a critique of Appelbaum's views, which,
as the Yates case demonstrates, have become the prevailing ethical tenets of
American forensic psychiatry.[11]

Appelbaum's basic premise is that traditional medical ethics do not apply
to a psychiatrist offering expert testimony to a court. The forensic psychiatrist on the witness stand is not practising medicine; he is bound by a different
ethos – that of honesty. On that ground he rejects ethical criticisms connected
with all allegations that forensic psychiatrists unethically cause harm. As the
Yates expert's statements to the *New York Times* demonstrate, this is a clarifying and compelling approach and one that has liberated doctors from
ethical restraints in other situations. For example, physicians who ration
mental health care for managed care companies insist that they are making
business decisions and, although they are MDs, should not be held to the
ethical and practice standards of physicians.[12] State legislatures that favor
capital punishment have established by statute that physicians who administer injections are not practising medicine.[13] Bloche and many other critics are
understandably troubled by Appelbaum's version of 'situational' ethics. The
doctor, bound by the traditional ethos of physicianhood, steps through the
courthouse door and becomes something else. But, if one accepts Appelbaum's premise, the forensic psychiatrist is not bound by medical ethics. To
claim that a physician is participating in capital punishment when a forensic
psychiatrist evaluates competency to be executed is to confuse the apple of
the forensicist with the orange of the physician.

Thus, as I understand Appelbaum's approach and the ethical guidelines of
the AAPL, a forensic psychiatrist who has no doctor–patient relationship,
who carefully explains the purpose of his evaluation and who testifies honestly, would be able to provide testimony to a court in all of the roles I
describe. The AMA endorsed this position in 1993, rejecting Bloche's arguments.[14]

Capital punishment and the AMA–APA prohibition against participation
do not present a special ethical case for the Appelbaum school of forensic
psychiatry. Appelbaum in a subsequent published debate on the question
adds that the prohibition is futile because, if forensic psychiatrists did not
participate, forensic psychologists would replace them.[15]

My own view is that the testimonial practice of forensic psychiatry is ethically and epistemologically problematic. And those problems seem to me incorrigible and cannot be side-stepped by situational ethics. They are particularly acute in the criminal justice system and are not solved by the truth-seeking of experts who have no rules or accepted criteria for the determination of truth. Forensic psychiatry still struggles with all of the conceptual problems: fact vs. values, free will vs. determinism, mind vs. brain, and the relationship between 'normal' science and morality.[16] To seek the truth is admirable, but to testify as though one has found it, is overreaching. There is no basis in science, philosophy or morality for a claim of forensic truth. And the pragmatic reality is that experts are paid, not by some measure of objective truth, but by their ability to persuade juries and judges. No code of professional ethics can smooth away the ethical and moral pitfalls of forensic psychiatry. That being said, I agree with neither side about the ethics of forensic psychiatry's participation in capital punishment. I do not accept Appelbaum's situational side-stepping ethics and I disagree with Bloche's reasons for drawing the line defining participation at the second role.

It is difficult to believe, as Appelbaum has pointed out, that physicians, based on their 'do no harm' ethics, would bar a forensic psychiatrist from evaluating an obviously insane prisoner and testifying that he had become incompetent to be executed. In some jurisdictions, once the court holds an inmate incompetent, the death penalty will never be imposed.[17] Bloche, I believe, mistakenly discounts this scenario in his 1993 paper. Since there are real instances of insanity saving the life of an inmate, Bloche's cut-off entails a draconian calculation: better to let this man be executed than to involve the medical profession in a way that might lend some sort of medical aura to capital punishment.

Appelbaum has claimed, I think, correctly that critics of forensic psychiatry's participation in execution are really concerned about abolishing capital punishment.[18] Bloche and PHR want to rally the moral authority of the medical profession against capital punishment. In the 1960s, it seemed that the so-called civilized world was about to abolish capital punishment. The European nations did so, but in the 1970s the US Supreme Court reversed the direction it had taken and permitted execution under certain legal constraints. Abolition in Europe was soon followed by the important step of making abolition a central human rights issue. Capital punishment in America was condemned by human rights advocates and, along with them, the doctors who participated. My own review of the history of the prohibition against medical participation in capital punishment suggests that it was part of a tactic in the campaign to get organized medicine to lend its professional authority to the abolition of capital punishment.[19] The tactic, however, never succeeded. In 1980, the AMA declared that its members were free to favor or oppose capital punishment; the only prohibition was against participation. Ironically, a recent survey found that 19% of general physicians would perform a lethal injection and only 3% knew of the ethical prohibition.[20] Recently, the AMA tried to pass a resolution in favor of a moratorium on capital punishment; it failed.[21] Medical opinion, like public opinion in the USA, favors capital punishment.

Even if one opposes capital punishment, the narrow argument against forensic psychiatry makes no ethical sense either on consequentialist or on deontological-medical grounds. It is time for abolitionists to make allies of forensic psychiatrists. A way for this collaboration seems to have opened. In 1986 the Supreme Court ruled that it was unconstitutional to carry out the death penalty on someone who was incompetent to be executed.[22] (This decision intensified the debate that I have been discussing.) The Supreme Court recently took a new step and declared that, in light of emerging standards, it was unconstitutional to execute the mentally retarded including those who were competent to be executed.[23] This suggests that abolitionists, many of whom are forensic psychiatrists, should be documenting the mental disorders of the almost 4,000 death row inmates and laying the groundwork to argue that it is also cruel and unusual to execute the mentally ill.

Alan A. Stone, MD, Touroff-Glueck professor of law and psychiatry, Faculty of Law and Faculty of Medicine, Harvard Law School 1563, Massachusetts Avenue, Cambridge MA 02138, USA

NOTES

1 Toufexia, 2002: F5.
2 Stone, 1984: 57–75.
3 Rosner, 1994.
4 Baum, 2001.
5 Bloche, 1993.
6 Physicians for Human Rights: *www.phrusa.org/research/methics/cp_policy.html*
7 Bonnie, 1990.
8 Appelbaum, 1997.
9 Appelbaum, 1984.
10 Appelbaum, 1990.
11 See the 'Ethical Guidelines for the Practice of Forensic Psychiatry', adopted May 1987 by the American Academy of Psychiatry and the Law; last revised 1995.
12 Stone, 1999.
13 Keyes, 2001.
14 Council on Ethical and Judicial Affairs, American Medical Association (1993).
15 Appelbaum and Hartmann, 1998.
16 Stone, 1984: 57–75.
17 See, for instance, *Louisiana* v *Perry* (1992).

18   Council on Ethical and Judicial Affairs, AMA (1993).
19   Curran, 1980.
20   Farber, 2001.
21   Baum, 2001.
22   *Ford* v *Wainwright* (1986).
23   *Atkins* v *Virginia* (2002).

BIBLIOGRAPHY

Appelbaum, Paul A. (1984) 'Psychiatric Ethics in the Courtroom'. *Bulletin of the American Academy of Psychiatry and Law* 12: 225–231.

Appelbaum, Paul A. (1990) 'The Parable of the Forensic Psychiatrist: Ethics and the Problems of Doing Harm'. *International Journal of Law and Psychiatry* 13: 249–259.

Appelbaum, Paul A. (1997) 'Ethics in Evolution: the Incompatibility of Clinical and Forensic Functions'. *American Journal of Psychiatry* 154(4): 445–446.

Appelbaum, Paul A. (point) and Hartmann, Lawrence (counterpoint) (1998) 'Is it Ethical for Psychiatrists to Participate in Competency-to-be-Executed Evaluations?' *Psychiatric Times* 15(1): 28–29.

Baum, Kenneth (2001) ' "To Comfort Always : Physician Participation in Executions'. *NYU Journal of Legislation and Public Policy*: 47–82.

Bloche, M. Gregg (1993) 'Psychiatry, Capital Punishment and the Purposes of Medicine'. *International Journal of Law and Psychiatry* 16: 301–57.

Bonnie, R. (1990) 'Dilemmas in Administering the Death Penalty: Conscientious, Professional Ethics and the Needs of the Legal System'. *Law and Human Behavior* 14: 67–90.

Council on Ethical and Judicial Affairs, American Medical Association (1995) 'Physician Participation in Capital Punishment'. *Journal of the American Medical Association* 270 (21 July): 223–225.

Curran, William J. (1980) 'The Ethics of Medical Participation in Capital Punishment by Intravenous Drug Injection'. *New England Journal of Medicine* 302 (24 January): 226–30.

Farber, Neil J., Aboff, Brian M., Weiner, Joan, Davis, Elizabeth B., Gil Boyer, E. and Ubel, Peter A. (2001) 'Physicians' Willingness to Participate in the Process of Lethal Injection for Capital Punishment'. *Annals of Internal Medicine* (20 November): 884–8.

Keyes, W. Noel (2001) 'The Choice of Participation by Physicians in Capital Punishment'. *Whittier Law Review* (Spring): 809–40.

Rosner, Richard (ed.) (1994) *Principles and Practice of Forensic Psychiatry*. New York: Chapman and Hall.

Stone, Alan (1984) *The Ethics of Forensic Psychiatry from Law, Psychiatry and Morality*. Washington, DC: American Psychiatric Press.

Stone, Alan A. (1999) 'Managed Care, Liability and ERISA'. *Psychiatric Clinics of North America* 1: 17–29.

Toufexia, Anastasia (2002) 'A Conversation with Park Dietz: a Psychiatrist's Eye View of Murder and Insanity'. *New York Times*. 23 April 2002.

LAW REPORTS

Atkins v *Virginia* (2002) 536 US 122 S. Ct. 2242.
Ford v *Wainwright* (1986) 477 US 399.
Louisiana v *Perry* (1992) 610 So.2d 746.

Practicing in a Flawed System

[49]

Is Managed Care Ethical?

Stephen A. Green, M.D., M.A.

Abstract: *The author identifies ethical dilemmas inherent in fee-for-service medicine (grounded in patients' autonomous decision making) and managed care (grounded in the principle of efficiency). He argues that the moral legitimacy of the latter system of health care is more in question, and suggests a methodology for assessing its ethical status.* © 1999 Elsevier Science Inc.

Introduction

Shortly after joining a new HMO, Mr. JB. was informed that his current antidepressant medication (an SSRI agent which yielded clear therapeutic benefit with minimal side effects) was not included in the pharmacy's formulary, and that he would be changed to a tricyclic (TCA) agent. Mr. B. objected, reporting that he had experienced disturbing anticholinergic side effects when originally treated with a different TCA. Moreover, he argued that prior to joing the HMO he had been informed that coverage included ongoing pharmacotherapy for his previously diagnosed dysthymic disorder. An internal review of HMO policy, triggered by the patient's appeal, concluded that tricylic medications were as effective as newer agents in relieving depressive symptoms and a more economical form of treatment. Mr. B. was informed that if he wished to continue his usual medication he would have to pay for it out of pocket.

Managed Care Efficiency vs Fee-For-Service Autonomy

Situations like Mr. B.'s are all too common in today's environment of managed care (MC)—hence

Department of Psychiatry, Georgetown University School of Medicine, Washington, DC

Address reprint requests to: Stephen A. Green, M.D., M.A., Department of Psychiatry, Georgetown University School of Medicine, 3850 Reservoir Road, N.W., Washington, D.C. 20007

the cheers of moviegoers across the country when HMOs are profanely criticized in *As Good As It Gets.* However, the American fee-for-service (FFS) system of health care is also subject to justified criticism, primarily because of its obvious inefficiency. Health costs increased from $41 billion in 1965 to $750 billion by the 1990s (now accounting for more than 14% of the gross national debt), though 42 million Americans remain uninsured or underinsured. A significant factor contributing to the rise in health expenditures has been the cost of treating mental and substance abuse disorders, particularly during the 1980s when psychiatry increasingly fell under the control of market forces [1–3]. This growing commercialization was accompanied by clear concern about the ethical implications of some prevailing practices, such as utilizing inpatient facilities when other levels of treatment could have sufficed, subjecting patients to inappropriately lengthy hospitalizations, and rationing the availability and intensity of psychiatric care largely on the basis of insurance coverage. Moreover, legal settlements suggested that some treatment was unnecessary and/or fraudulent [4]. In sum, the growing influence of market forces on psychiatric care during the 1980s failed to contain costs or improve access to treatment, and had a questionable impact on quality of care—consequences strongly implicated in the shift of financing and delivery of mental health services to an MC model grounded in the principle of efficiency.

Proponents of MC argue that it promotes a fundamental moral goal, namely, conserving scarce health care resources by insuring their cost-effective distribution. Opponents of managed care criticize this philosophy of efficiency because, in an effort to balance individual needs against welfarist concerns of society, it undermines basic moral commitments of medical practice by diminishing the practitioner's autonomy and increasing the role of managed care organizations (MCOs) in clinical decision making. They believe managed care greatly reduces a clinician's ability to advocate for the individual patient, with the result that efficiency can readily and systematically disadvantage particular groups by denying them an equal claim to health resources. Harris [5,6], for example, believes that health policy based in efficiency suffers from "economism," a bias favoring treatments and illnesses that require the least amount of resources.

Concerns about ethical shortcomings of the MC and the FFS systems of health care are valid. Efficiency-based policies, as Daniels [7] observes in a discussion of the British National Health Service, are ethically acceptable when "considerations of justice are explicit in [the] design and in decisions about allocation of resources." However, managed care companies set policy according to internal bureaucratic standards (as in the case of Mr. B.), and not in response to the public debate required in considerations of justice. As a result, managed care has too often advanced welfarist concerns of society at the cost of an individual's need, thereby diminishing a sense of fairness in the distribution of health resources. And, as long as FFS medicine remains an essentially unregulated system, primarily governed by patients' autonomous decision making, it invites provision of unnecessary care with a potential for clinicians to act irresponsibly or with intentional avarice, thereby wasting needed health resources. These observations raise disturbing questions about the ethical principles that justify either system of health; however, there are several reasons why the burden rests on proponents of efficiency to demonstrate its moral legitimacy as a guiding principle for allocating health services. First, whereas FFS medicine has been guilty of providing excess care, which both wastes resources and subjects patients to unnecessary morbidity and mortality, the propensity of MC to limit benefits seems a more questionable ethical position for several reasons. These include the potential for eliminating marginal care, thereby denying patients real benefits, as well as compromising the bioethical principle of fidelity, by obliging physicians to do less for an individual patient in order to distribute resources over a broader population of patients. Moreover, because of existing federal legislation, the ERISA statute, MC avoids responsibility for adverse consequences resulting from the denial of care, which seems fundamentally unfair. Second, many believe that health care is not a commodity in the traditional sense of a market good and, consequently, that principles of market economy (e.g., efficiency) are inappropriate standards for medical practice. Finally, even if health care is considered a commodity, it is doubtful that patients qualify as educated consumers, given the extent and complexity of information required for medical decision making and the proprietary behaviors of MCOs which often keep patients uninformed about therapeutic options.

Unfortunately, critics of MC are sometimes too dismissive of *any* benefit the efficiency principle might convey to a health care system continually stressed by diminishing resources. Their stridency is based more in emotion than analysis and, consequently, their conclusions are more opinion than fact [8]. Determining whether or not a managed system of health care is ethical requires a more objective assessment of the legitimacy of efficiency as a guiding principle for the delivery of medical services. That can be accomplished by determining whether adherence to efficiency by particular managed care systems supports or undermines established bioethical principles. To illustrate, I return to the plight of Mr. B. and examine how his treatment compromised one fundamental aspect of medical practice, i.e., informed consent.

Informed Consent

Informed consent, the degree to which patients understand and agree to a proposed treatment, is concerned with the protection and facilitation of autonomous choice. As Beauchamp and Childress [9] comment, informed consent is a complex process consisting of several distinct elements, including the patient's mental capacity for decision making, the disclosure and understanding of pertinent medical information, and the active, voluntary authorization for treatment. Adequate understanding requires sufficient opportunity for patients to discuss and reflect on medical data so that they have justified beliefs about the nature and consequences of their actions; authorization rests on individuals being free of coercive influences that may undermine the independence of their actions (e.g., presenting information in a way that alters the understanding of a situation).

MCOs employ several overt and covert practices that interfere with patients obtaining relevant information, thereby limiting their autonomous choice. First, research on HMOs shows that the quality of the communication between clinician and patient is lower in prepaid settings for general medical care

S.A. Green

compared with FFS arrangements [10,11]. In particular, the organizational structure of managed care (e.g., imposing time constraints on the clinical interaction or failing to provide patients with the same caretakers over time) disrupts the communication necessary for patients to obtain information required to reach an informed decision. In addition, some MCOs impose "gag rules," thereby preventing discussion of treatments that are not included in services provided by their plan. Third, before patients join a health plan they judge the worth of its available services; however, like Mr. B., they may be unaware of the criteria of "medical necessity" that must be met in order to access those services. Because many MCOs consider these parameters proprietary, patients entering a health plan cannot know the circumstances under which they will be eligible for specific treatments. Moreover, they are often denied a forum to discuss eligibility since they do not communicate with the clinical reviewers who make those determinations.

In sum, managed health care can deny patients an adequate understanding of the treatments available to them both at the time of entry into a health plan and at the point of clinical service, thereby undermining the fundamental bioethical principle of informed consent. In these circumstances adherence to the efficiency principle imposes harm; the degree to which it does so determines whether or not the practices of a particular MCO are ethical.

Conclusion

The legitimacy of claims to limited health resources depends on circumstances that tug at our emotions and reason, particularly when we attempt to resolve difficult choices with rigid application of principles, such as efficiency and autonomy. Efficiency may be intuitively disturbing and discriminatory in ways that are morally unacceptable [6,7]. However, as Kapp [12] notes, there is a rationality to the "utilitarian, statistically based guidelines of managed care plans" because "most patients fall within an average range" of treatment. The pivotal issue, therefore, concerning the moral legitimacy of efficiency concerns the degree to which it can serve as a guiding principle for allocating health resources and the degree to which it must be tempered by patients' claims of autonomous choice.

Establishing guidelines concerning when efficiency imposes unquestionable harm is a pressing task of the medical profession—and a situation that is neither theoretical nor unique. Confidentiality,

another fundamental bioethical principle, was deemed not to be inviolate when clinicians acceded to the demands of insurance companies to reveal information concerning patients' diagnoses and, subsequently, aspects of their treatment. More recently, the profession has worked to limit the amount of medical data available to third parties, largely prompted by disturbing consequences due to serious violations of patient confidentiality [13]. In this same way we must establish the degree to which efficiency conforms with ethical norms of medical practice; this requires determinations concerning when efficiency-based policies violate fundamental bioethical principles and, if so, whether or not the degree to which they do so is morally acceptable. The process rests in public debate and political activity similar to that which culminated in the Oregon Plan [14,15]; it calls for increased responsibility on the part of patients, who must become informed about policies affecting their health care, and on the part of physicians, who have a duty to educate and advocate for patients. The net outcome is heightened public awareness about aspects of managed health care that advance or detract from the welfare of individuals and/or society at large.

A growing backlash against managed care in the United States has already been translated into legislation that increases portability of health insurance, as well as administrative decisions by MCOs, like ending the appalling policy of performing mastectomies as outpatient procedures. The moral legitimacy of managed care ultimately rests on the degree to which the fundamental principles of medical practice (e.g., fidelity, confidentiality, informed consent) are, in this manner, preserved in an environment of efficiency.

References

1. Jellinek M, Nurcombe B: Two wrongs don't make a right: managed care, mental health, and the marketplace. JAMA 14(270):1737–1739, 1993
2. Oss M, Krizsy J: Industry statistics: psychiatric room rates continue to increase faster than average hospital rates. Open Minds 2:1 Newsletter, 1991
3. McCue M, Clement J: Relative performance for for-profit psychiatric hospitals in investor-owned systems and nonprofit psychiatric hospitals. Am J Psychiatry 150:77–82, 1992
4. Kerr P: Charter and Texas settle a case. New York Times, January 1, 1993:D3
5. Harris J: QALYfying the value of life. J Med Ethics 13:117–123, 1987

6. Harris J: More and better justice. In Bell J, Mendus S (eds), Philosophy and Medical Welfare. Cambridge, Cambridge University Press, 1988, pp 75–96
7. Daniels N: Why saying no to patients in the United States is so hard. N Eng J Med 314(21)1380–1383, 1986
8. Eist H: "Managed care": Where did it come from? What does it do? How does it survive? What can be done about it? Psychoanalytic Inquiry (Suppl) 162–181, 1997
9. Beauchamp T, Childress J: Principles of Biomedical Ethics, 4th ed. New York, Oxford University Press, 1994, pp 142–170
10. Luft H: Health Maintenance Organizations: Dimensions of Performance. New York, John Wiley, 1981
11. Rogers W, Wells K, Meredith L, Sturm R, et al: Outcomes for adult outpatients with depression under prepaid or fee-for-service financing. Arch Gen Psychiatry 50:517–525, 1993
12. Kapp M: Can managed care be managed? Pharos, Spring: 15–17, 1998
13. Questions of privacy roil arena of psychotherapy. New York Times, 22 May, 1996, A1
14. Pollack D, McFarland B, George R, et al: Prioritization of mental health services in Oregon. Milbank Q 72: 515–550, 1994
15. Boyle P, Callahan D: Minds and hearts: priorities in mental health services. Hastings Cent Rep (Suppl) 23:1–23, 1993

Working in a Flawed Mental Health Care System:
An Ethical Challenge

Stephen A. Green, M.D., M.A.

Sidney Bloch, M.D., Ph.D.

Objective: Psychiatrists are under immense ethical pressure when practicing in circumstances that reasonable, informed colleagues would regard as not "good enough" in that they do not adequately meet the needs of patients and patients' families. This article is an examination of the ethical quandaries that ensue and options for response.

Method: The authors explore the ways in which mental health systems may become flawed and compare philosophical arguments that deal with the predicament of working in such systems.

Results: The principle of fidelity to the patient is compromised in flawed systems, thus threatening professional integrity. Arguments for efficiency or the greater good in the provision of mental health care fail as remedies since they both lead to harms for particular clinical groups, as well as downgrading of a psychiatrist's integrity.

Conclusions: Psychiatrists should submit to the principle of fidelity in working with patients. Since flawed systems undermine fidelity, threatening the patient's interests, psychiatrists are morally responsible for working to improve such systems.

(Am J Psychiatry 2001; 158:1378–1383)

Psychiatrists are under ethical pressure when working in systems of health care that do not adequately meet their patients' needs. We do not refer here to ideal conditions but those that reasonable, informed psychiatrists would deem "good enough." We define this standard more specifically later but pose illustrative questions at the outset, the answers to which suggest care falling below this benchmark: is it "good enough" to provide a few days of inpatient treatment to an acutely suicidal patient? Is a person with a persistent psychotic illness treated adequately with drug monitoring alone? Is it acceptable to limit psychotherapy to a handful of sessions when treating a self-destructive person with a borderline personality disorder? Is it legitimate to proscribe the use of an atypical antipsychotic for a patient who previously experienced extrapyramidal side effects with the typical medications? Unfortunately, these are not hypothetical questions in current systems of health care.

As a result of these types of efficiency-driven issues, the clinician is faced with two moral compromises. First, the ethic of agency is threatened. As Daniels (1) argued, "Considerable autonomy in clinical decision making is necessary if [physicians] are to be effective as agents pursuing their patients' interests." This ensures competent decision making and respect for patients' autonomy and their other rights (e.g., confidentiality) (1). This ethic of agency also applies to systems of mental health care. Second, constraints on the psychiatrist's role may compromise ethical principles and, in turn, harm patients. For example, by participating in a system that withholds information (e.g., through "gag rules"), psychiatrists may undermine informed consent (2). This reflects Menzel's assertion that a health care system "not able...to accord with [patients'] values and considered judgments...morally assaults [their] autonomy and personhood" (3, p. 59).

Policies adversely affecting clinical care have gained ascendancy in many countries since the 1980s. Governmental funding has been cut to hazardous levels, and many private insurers, by their nature, have precluded provision of adequate services. We discuss these trends from macro- and microperspectives. We use managed care to illustrate the former, although we hasten to stress that we are not here concerned with managed care per se, and a case study, in which a preventable death led to a crisis of conscience for the treating psychiatrist, to exemplify the latter. Both circumstances highlight the painful ethical dilemma confronting clinicians: whether to participate in a system known to have deleterious effects.

In exploring this dilemma our aim is to formulate an ethical response that both represents patients' interests and is apt professionally (defining a profession as a group of people who share expertise not readily available to others and assist a vulnerable and dependent clientele) (4). Put another way, we consider how psychiatrists may work "in morally and medically credible ways"(5, p. 114) when clinical circumstances are not good enough. We opt for a professional form of response since this is more likely to preserve the integrity of the protagonists involved. We also address the key question of whether psychiatrists bear any responsibility for the ill effects of flawed systems to which they contribute.

STEPHEN A. GREEN AND SIDNEY BLOCH

The Nature of the Dilemma

Threat to the Principle of Fidelity

First we need to recall a core feature of the relationship between psychiatrist and patient, the framework of trust. This enables people to consign their well-being to professionals who, in turn, serve pivotally in the provision of health care, including working "for the benefit of the sick" (6, p. 6). This principle of fidelity is reflected in diverse ethical theories, including promoting patients' interests in order to maximize the common good, respecting patients' autonomy as a paramount principle, and encouraging professionals to strive toward virtuous actions (7, pp. 62–69).

The current "corporatization" of health seriously undermines the principle of fidelity (8). Policies intrinsically promoting the interests of clinical populations potentially prevent clinicians from serving individual patients and thereby escalate the risk for moral harm. Efforts to control costs result in systems sensitive to economic priorities but "uninformed" about clinical judgment (5, p. 24). For example, curtailed inpatient treatment may allow resources to be distributed among the many but also greatly diminish the well-being of a minority of people suffering from severe forms of mental illness.

Another interference with the principle of fidelity is juxtaposing psychiatrists' financial interests alongside patients' needs. In certain health care systems, for example, income varies according to treatment provided, raising the hazard that decisions will be motivated by economic rather than clinical factors. Psychiatrists may thus withhold certain treatments, information about those treatments, or financial facts that affect proper clinical judgment (5, p. 21). Moreover, recognition by patients of their psychiatrists' conflicts over costs may erode the trust intrinsic to an effective relationship. This situation already prevails in that the public is aware of health care systems' inducement of clinicians to limit treatment (e.g., offering incentives to order fewer special tests) (9, 10). At the same time, clinicians have argued that this intrusion prevents them from working for a particular patient when pressed into weighing relative interests of patients and from obtaining fully informed consent because of "gag rules."

Problems With the Drive for Efficiency

Efficiency, ostensibly the justification for policies of contemporary health care systems, is grounded in the theory that the right action, judged impersonally, gives equal weight to every person's interests (see reference 11). In its most familiar version, the argument runs that the best state of affairs entails the greatest amount of human satisfaction and, therefore, efficient care should receive priority over inefficient care. Efficiency proponents contend that decision making governed by cost-effectiveness not only reaps economic benefit but also avoids arbitrary practices (such as discriminating against the aged), thereby promoting the confluence of efficiency and fairness. (Eddy illustrated the clinical application of this approach across a population of patients [12–14].)

On the other hand, critics of the efficiency argument note that it can impose harm on particular groups by denying them a rightful claim to resources. Harris (15, 16), for example, posited that policy driven by efficiency suffers from a bias favoring treatments and illnesses that require the fewest resources ("economism"). Criticism of managed mental health care reflecting this view highlights the use of cheaper treatments (e.g., medication when psychotherapy is indicated), less intensive care (17), insufficiently trained "gatekeepers" (18, 19) who apply guidelines based on spurious data (20), choice of treatment quality based solely on duration and cost (21), arbitrary limits on the period of treatment (22, 23), and efficiencies that may curb treatment efficacy (24). These practices suggest that while efficiency-dominated policy may profess impartiality, in fact it imposes discrimination against patients with certain conditions or requiring particular treatments (15, 16).

How Maximizing the Common Good Fails the Individual and the Concept of Negative Responsibility

Maximizing the common good encompasses a central limitation—the indifference to the uniqueness of the person. First, in promoting the common good, certain actions that do not advance that end are devalued, even if those actions have intrinsic merit. Second, as Williams (25) discussed, this position is consistent only if it supports the concept of negative responsibility by holding that we are responsible for consequences we fail to prevent (even when not of our own doing) as well as those caused by our actions. In certain instances this is intuitively obvious. Consider the example of a person who encounters a drowning child. It is difficult to condone the morality of walking away because the person has no relationship to the child; rather, a powerful obligation exists to save the child. One argument is the person's negative responsibility to promote the general good. However, negative responsibility can be invoked to justify acts that many would deem excessive—for example, to compel highly altruistic acts of charity (26) or to require actions that compromise the agent's integrity. The latter issue is highly relevant to our discussion concerning the moral responsibility of clinicians in flawed health care systems. By compelling certain actions, negative responsibility challenges the notion of autonomy by undermining the belief that an individual is "specially responsible for what *he* does, rather than for what other people do" (25, p. 35). As Williams argued, the result is that personal integrity "is rendered as a value more or less unintelligible" (25, p. 35), as illustrated by his vivid hypothetical example of Jim, a botanist. Surveying a remote jungle, he unexpectedly witnesses a planned execution of 20 innocent peasants caught up in the cruelty of a revolution. Their deaths are to serve as a deterrent to others who oppose the oppres-

FLAWED MENTAL HEALTH CARE SYSTEM

sive regime. An officer decides to free 19 hostages if Jim will act as executioner of one of their number. Williams discussed the conflicting moral responsibilities—to commit one murder in order to save 19 human beings, or to refuse and bear indirect responsibility for many more deaths. A utilitarian resolution is obvious—killing one to save the many—but this act violates personal integrity given Jim's opposition to taking human life, particularly an innocent life.

This case, albeit extreme, shows how imposing one set of values on a person can so conflict with his or her own values as to undermine integrity. That ethical decision making should depend on such procedure is counterintuitive. To expect a person to "step aside from his own…decision" is "to alienate him…from…the source of his action in his own convictions…attitudes within which he is most closely identified. It is thus…an attack on his integrity" (25, pp. 49–50).

We introduce now a poignant case to illustrate how such integrity may be crushed by policies of a flawed system of health care—in this case by bureaucratic intransigence governed by interests other than those of the patient. A newly graduated psychiatrist (let us call him Dr. Smith) chose to work in a small, rural general hospital in Australia. Among his first patients was Ms. Wing, a 78-year-old woman with severe depression. Notwithstanding prompt treatment with antidepressant medication and supportive care, Ms. Wing's condition deteriorated rapidly, culminating in a state typified by paranoid delusions and refusal to eat or drink. The situation soon became perilous, and the need for ECT was obvious.

At this point Dr. Smith encountered intractable resistance on the part of the administration. ECT could not be arranged because of "practical factors," and Ms. Wing would need to be transferred to a psychiatric hospital 120 km away. By this time her physical state was dire. Dr. Smith's protestations that transfer of such an ill person was tantamount to negligence were to no avail; the administration stood firm. His clinical team supported him inasmuch as all members agreed that Ms. Wing's physical condition precluded a long journey. Moreover, the move would mean losing the support of family members who were not able to travel with her. A contest of wills followed, and the outcome was a stalemate. In the midst of the battle Ms. Wing's health declined, and she died 2 days later.

Dr. Smith felt resentful and anguished, convinced that ECT applied promptly not only would have saved his patient's life but also would have led to alleviation of her psychotic depression, as she had responded well to ECT in the past. His efforts to bring the tragedy to the attention of the regional health authority were frustrated by buck passing and stonewalling. Enraged and embittered, Dr. Smith tendered his resignation, his former eagerness to serve in a remote area entirely squelched.

Personal Integrity and Health Care

The foregoing discussion suggests that a mental health system must adhere to fundamental principles, such as fidelity, in seeking a balance between fairness and efficiency so that its policies not only advance the common good, by expending resources efficiently, but also respect individual claims to care. By definition, such a system necessarily limits clinicians' decision making; however, it must not do so in a way that undermines integrity. Sabin and Daniels (27) usefully reviewed features of an ethical health care system. They espoused a "normal opportunity" model, which embraces a balance between fairness and efficiency (although some patients will not get what they want or all they need) in that it is grounded in a sense of justice, derived from Rawls's concept of fair equality of opportunity (28). (One of Rawls's fundamental goals in this classic work was to articulate a theory of social justice superior to that of utilitarianism.)

Sabin (29) discussed further how clinicians must adopt principles to supplement established codes of ethics in order to create a balance between efficiency and fairness. For example, they should serve as stewards of resources and work for justice in their organizations as they strive to protect patients' interests. Morreim (5) echoed this when noting the tension between efficiency and fidelity. A "morally sound" norm of fidelity for her encompassed

> ordinary and reasonable care, with the proviso that in times of scarcity, what is reasonable will depend in part on what is available. Beyond this, physicians owe patients their own best efforts, skills, thoughtfulness, and competence. They also owe each patient reasonable efforts to secure needed health resources.… And they owe assistance in combating those rules where they distribute resources unjustly or fail to consider the needs of patients as individuals. (5, p. 24)

This is more easily proclaimed than applied. More and more systems of health care are flawed because they fail to guarantee fundamental ethical principles or favor provision of care to certain groups of patients and sacrifice the interests of *individual* patients. Clinicians resorting to dubious strategies to minimize these effects highlight another ominous feature of a flawed system, namely, the manner in which they imperil their own integrity. Handicapped by limited resources, they adopt practices that tax their ability to maintain ethical standards. "Poaching," for instance, is a way of gaining available resources for patients for whom they are not intended. A common practice is cost shifting, whereby affluent patients are charged higher rates in order to support the needy. "Hoarding" refers to securing resources (which might not otherwise be available) by bending rules required by health systems (e.g., providing unnecessary treatment, such as intravenous hydration in an emergency department, to justify brief hospitalization for patients covered by insurance for inpatient care but who cannot afford the copayment for emergency treatment).

Morreim cautioned that such "gaming" of the system may lead to "fudging, even outright fraud, and in turn compromise integrity" (5, p. 24). Evidence accumulates that clinicians increasingly resort to these practices. Most doctors in one survey (30) were inclined to misrepresent a screening test (e.g., a mammogram) as a diagnostic procedure despite any evidence of disease (e.g., a breast lump) in order to obtain third-party funding. They justified their action in terms of consequences by claiming that patients' welfare was of greater value than truth telling. In another study (31), one-quarter of the doctors polled reported nonexistent clinical features to gain reimbursement. Most of them had also manipulated reported diagnoses and exaggerated symptom severity to prevent premature discharge from the hospital.

Ethical Implications for the Psychiatrist

At this point, we need to state more specifically than hitherto what we view as a flawed system of health care. We admit that this is a subjective standard, particularly in the allocation of resources to a population with diverse needs, requiring a combination of preventive, short-term, and long-term treatment. However, criteria for what is "good enough" have been widely acknowledged as valid (e.g., an acceptable quality of treatment, fair access to care, guarantee of key ethical principles) (32). The specifics of a "decent minimum of care" (7, pp. 348–377; 33) may still be the subject of debate, but it is our position that this is precisely the process needed to establish "good enough" criteria. As Mackie pointed out (34, pp. 20–27), so-called objective truths depend on evaluation relative to standards established through an interpretive process:

> Skating and diving championships, and even the marking of examination papers, are carried out in relation to standards of quality or merit which are peculiar to each particular subject-matter or type of contest, which may be explicitly laid down but which, even if they are nowhere explicitly stated, are fairly well understood and agreed to by those who are recognized as judges or experts in each particular field. (34, p. 26)

In other words, reasoned debate by informed people exercising considered judgments "defines" standards. The process may also be applied to determine what constitutes a good enough health care system. The pioneering effort in Oregon, which integrated treatment of physical and mental illness into a unified system, is one means to establish what is good enough (35, 36). Judgment can similarly be made about flawed systems.

Another indication as to the adequacy of a health care system is whether the clinician's integrity is compromised beyond acceptable levels. We agree with Daniels that if a system is to promote communal, as well as an individual's, needs, there must be a limit on clinicians' autonomy. Without that they would be unfettered in their decision making concerning resource allocation, which could lead to waste and/or unnecessary treatment and contribute to morbid-

ity and mortality. On the other hand, autonomy can be so circumscribed that communal concerns are promoted at the expense of the basic interests of individual patients, as well as diminution of their legitimate rights, such as confidentiality and informed consent. The clinician's integrity is then so assaulted that the system is flawed.

We argue that psychiatrists are ethically bound to act in the face of such circumstances. If they shrink from the effort, they become responsible, in part, for adverse effects the system imposes. Their advocacy should accord with Morreim's guidelines: to provide reasonable care and, when patients are unjustly denied this, to assist them in securing the necessary resources. There are explicit precedents for psychiatrists' advocacy, especially when fidelity to the patient conflicts with other interests (e.g., opposing a Jehovah's Witness family's wish that its child not receive a transfusion) (7, pp. 130–131). Similar reasoning should apply when the third party is a managed care organization or governmental bureaucracy. At least three options are available to psychiatrists.

The first is for psychiatrists to serve as stewards for resources by working for justice in their organizations and in the health system as a whole—just as in their clinical role they must promote the welfare of patients (29). For example, psychiatrists should work toward revising criteria of "medical necessity" that they note exert adverse effects on patients, an activity grounded in professional expertise rather than bureaucratic algorithms that neglect clinical reality.

The second is to take political action, either individually or collectively. In this context, Fleck's thesis (37) that health resource allocation is not an "economic, managerial, organizational, or technological problem," but instead "a moral and political problem," is apposite. This echoes Aristotle's notion that ethics and political activity are inextricably linked and points to a role for psychiatrists in translating moral values into political realities. The task can be accomplished in manifold ways, including education (of individual patients, their families, or the public at large), lobbying, or seeking public office in order to promote health policy.

Third, psychiatrists can respond as a professional group by shaping an appropriate ethical position to guide action. Codes of ethics are ideal vehicles. Hitherto, professional bodies have only gingerly initiated the task of identifying ethical principles in the area we are addressing. In some cases, reference is by allusion only. For instance, the American Psychiatric Association's *Principles of Medical Ethics With Annotations Especially Applicable to Psychiatry* (38) consigns the matter to the final principle: "A physician shall recognize a responsibility to participate in activities contributing to an improved community." The annotations that follow provide sensible but slender guidelines. The World Psychiatric Association's Declaration of Madrid (39) is equally minimalist in referring to an advocacy role for psychiatrists as societal members—pushing for fair and equal treatment for all. Other medical bodies have similarly been spare in their statements. The Australian Medi-

FLAWED MENTAL HEALTH CARE SYSTEM

cal Association's Code of Ethics (40) calls on its members to "strive to improve the standards and quality of medical services in the community and more specifically to use special knowledge and skills to consider issues of resource allocation," but that is as far as it goes. One initiative unusual in its detail and explicitness is that of the Royal Australian and New Zealand College of Psychiatrists (41). It shows how psychiatrists as a professional group can weave their societal obligations into a code of ethics and involve themselves in issues involving both service provision and resource allocation. Noteworthy is the progression from the general to the specific (Appendix 1). Australasian psychiatrists have also promulgated a position statement on mental health services (42)—a more comprehensive account of these issues. (Copies are available from us on request.)

Predictably, psychiatrists' attempts to promote good enough services can be thwarted. For example, some managed care organizations threaten to exclude health professionals, an act that can radically hamper their ability to practice, if efficiency standards (e.g., number of patients seen and/or levels of resources expended) are not met. Psychiatrists may obviously opt to extricate themselves from such work conditions, but they do so at the risk of economic vulnerability. This is not a decision most would take lightly even if they had options to practice elsewhere (43).

If, as Morreim argued, clinicians are not obliged to act in excessively altruistic fashion (e.g., sacrificing income to protect patients against the deleterious effects of a health care system) (5, p. 21), or if they cannot alter their patients' situation without incurring personal hardship, the thorny question arises of whether they bear moral responsibility for helping to sustain practices they know are potentially or actually harmful. Does the principle of negative responsibility apply in these circumstances? Or is it too stringent a standard, given that psychiatrists may, by dint of their dependent positions, not have a meaningful voice? Ultimately, the matter revolves around the link between negative responsibility and professional integrity. If they do not act, the result may be what Charlesworth termed "Eichmann-like"—an atmosphere is perpetuated in which clinicians "don't raise questions...and don't worry about so-called ethical issues" but instead do as they are told even if that compromises patients' well-being (44, p. 109).

The question thus remains: Where psychiatrists are unable to reform a flawed system or resign because of the detrimental effects this would impose on themselves or their patients, are they ethically responsible for the impact of unjust policies? We suggest a threshold exists beyond which they cannot be regarded as free moral agents. A system may be so deficient that it is ethically unacceptable. Psychiatrists are then in a position analogous to that of the botanist Jim, in contrast to the adult's encounter with an unknown drowning child. When integrity is so violated, it is much harder to embrace the principle of negative responsibility, and it is debatable whether psychiatrists can be held accountable for the shortcomings of the system in which they function. Direct responsibility is mitigated but not if they evade pursuing actions, professional and/or political, to correct wrongs. Indeed, it is through such actions that good enough health care can be accomplished.

Conclusions

Given the complex questions psychiatrists face when operating in a system patently not good enough, only some of which we have examined, it would come as no surprise if they retreated from the ethical fray out of the sheer need to survive. There is nothing more sapping than grappling with seemingly entrenched defects that affect the professional's central pursuits. Premature retirement and poor recruitment to psychiatry in recent years (45) are probably influenced, in part, by the quandaries we have highlighted.

Our observations point to the following conclusions: 1) psychiatrists are obliged to submit always to the principle of fidelity in working with their patients; 2) since flawed systems of health care jeopardize fidelity, psychiatrists have an ethical responsibility to work for their improvement; 3) ideally, they should respond as health professionals through their associations, but they may also participate as individuals; 4) integrity is compromised by degree in health care systems, depending on how much clinicians are prevented from adhering to ethical principles, and psychiatrists need to be aware of the extent to which the system constrains those principles, because it ultimately defines a threshold of their responsibility to patients; 5) most psychiatrists would consider it unethical if the obligation of fidelity was so curtailed that patients were denied access to needed treatment, and they therefore bear moral responsibility for untoward effects unless they act to improve the system (irrespective of whether they also choose to extricate themselves from it).

APPENDIX 1. Principle 10, and Its First Four Annotations, of the Code of Ethics of the Royal Australian and New Zealand College of Psychiatrists (41)

The Principle
Psychiatrists shall strive to improve the quality of, and access to, mental health services, promote the just allocation of health resources and contribute to community awareness of mental health and mental illness.

The Annotations
10.1 Psychiatrists shall promote the improvement of mental health services recognising that psychiatric patients may be disenfranchised and unable to assert themselves.
10.2 Psychiatrists shall be prepared by virtue of their knowledge and experience to advise and work with those responsible for the provision of psychiatric and other health services.
10.3 Psychiatrists shall be prepared to act as advocates and join with others in ensuring that psychiatric patients have available to them the best possible health services.
10.4 Psychiatrists shall take appropriate action if services, by reason of fiscal restriction or otherwise, fall below minimal standards. Exceptionally, psychiatrists may have to dissociate themselves from such services provided this does not put their patients at serious risk.

STEPHEN A. GREEN AND SIDNEY BLOCH

Received March 20, 2000; revision received Dec. 27, 2000; accepted Jan. 24, 2001. From the Department of Psychiatry, Georgetown University School of Medicine; and the Department of Psychiatry, University of Melbourne, Melbourne, Australia. Address reprint requests to Dr. Green, Department of Psychiatry, Georgetown University School of Medicine, 3850 Reservoir Rd., N.W., Washington, DC 20007; greenm1@gusun.georgetown.edu (e-mail).

References

1. Daniels N: Why saying no to patients in the United States is so hard. N Engl J Med 1986; 314:1380–1383

2. Green SA: The ethics of managed mental health care, in Psychiatric Ethics, 3rd ed. Edited by Bloch S, Chodoff P, Green SA. Oxford, UK, Oxford University Press, 1999, pp 408–410

3. Menzel PT: Some ethical costs of rationing. Law Med Health Care 1992; 20(1–2):57–66

4. Fullwinder R: Professional codes and moral understanding, in Codes of Ethics and the Professions. Edited by Coady M, Bloch S. Melbourne, Melbourne University Press, 1996, pp 72–87

5. Morreim E: Cost containment: challenging fidelity and justice. Hastings Cent Rep 1988; 18:20–25

6. Ancient Medicine: Selected Papers of Ludwig Edelstein. Edited by Temkin O, Temkin C. Baltimore, Johns Hopkins University Press, 1967

7. Beauchamp T, Childress J: Principles of Biomedical Ethics, 4th ed. New York, Oxford University Press, 1994

8. American Medical Association Council on Ethical and Judicial Affairs: Ethical issues in managed care. JAMA 1995; 273:330–335

9. Hillman AL, Pauly MV, Kerstein JJ: How do financial incentives affect physicians' clinical decisions and the financial performance of health maintenance organizations? N Engl J Med 1989; 321:86–92

10. Insufficient patient care. Wall Street Journal, Oct 3, 1994, p A1

11. Schleiffer S: Introduction, in Consequentialism and Its Critics. Edited by Schleiffer S. Oxford, UK, Oxford University Press, 1988, pp 1–13

12. Eddy D: Principles for making difficult decisions in difficult times. JAMA 1994; 271:1792–1797

13. Eddy D: Cost-effectiveness analysis: will it be accepted? JAMA 1992; 268:132–136

14. Eddy D: Cost-effectiveness analysis: a conversation with my father. JAMA 1992; 267:1669–1675

15. Harris J: QALYfying the value of life. J Med Ethics 1987; 13:117–123

16. Harris J: More and better justice, in Philosophy and Medical Welfare. Edited by Bell J, Mendus S. Cambridge, UK, Cambridge University Press, 1988, pp 75–96

17. Boyle PJ, Callahan D: Managed care in mental health: the ethical issues. Health Aff (Millwood) 1995; 14(3):7–22

18. Wells K, Hays R, Burnam M, Rogers W, Greenfield S, Ware JE Jr: Detection of depressive disorder for patients receiving prepaid or fee-for-service care: results from the Medical Outcomes Study. JAMA 1989; 262:3298–3302

19. Eisenberg L: Treating depression and anxiety in the primary care setting. Health Aff (Millwood) 1992; 11:149–156

20. McCarthy P, Gelber S, Dugger D: Outcome measurement to outcome management: the critical step. Adm Policy Ment Health 1993; 21:59–68

21. Sharfstein S, Dunn L, Kent J: The clinical consequences of payment limitations: the experience of a private psychiatric hospital. Psychiatr Hosp 1988; 19:63–66

22. Jellinek M, Nurcombe B: Two wrongs don't make a right: managed care, mental health, and the marketplace. JAMA 1993; 14:1737–1739

23. Van Gelder D: Surviving in an era of managed care: lessons from Colorado. Hosp Community Psychiatry 1992; 43:1145–1147

24. Thompson J, Burns B, Goldman H, Smith J: Initial level of care and clinical status in a managed mental health care program. Hosp Community Psychiatry 1992; 43:599–607

25. Williams B: Consequentialism and integrity, in Consequentialism and Its Critics. Edited by Schleiffler S. Oxford, UK, Oxford University Press, 1998, pp 29–50

26. Singer P: Famine, affluence, and morality. Philosophy and Public Affairs 1972; 1:229–243

27. Sabin J, Daniels N: Determining "medical necessity" in mental health practice. Hastings Cent Rep 1994; 24:5–13

28. Rawls J: A Theory of Justice. Cambridge, Mass, Harvard University Press, 1971

29. Sabin J: General hospital psychiatry and the ethics of managed care. Gen Hosp Psychiatry 1995; 17:293–298

30. Novack DH, Detering BJ, Arnold R, Forrow L, Ladinsky M, Pezzullo JC: Physicians' attitudes toward using deception to resolve difficult ethical problems. JAMA 1989; 261:2980–2985

31. Healing vs honesty: for doctors, managed care's cost controls pose moral dilemma. Washington Post, March 15, 1998, p H1

32. President's Commission for the Study of Ethical Problems in Medicine and Biomedical and Behavioral Research: Securing Access to Health Care: The Ethical Implications of Differences in the Availability of Health Services, vol I: Report. Washington, DC, US Government Printing Office, 1983

33. Buchanan A: The right to a decent minimum of health care. Philosophy and Public Affairs 1984; 13(1):55–78

34. Mackie J: Ethics: Inventing Right and Wrong. London, Penguin Books, 1977

35. Pollack DA, McFarland BH, George RA, Angell RH: Prioritization of mental health services in Oregon. Milbank Q 1994; 72:515–550

36. Boyle PJ, Callahan D: Minds and hearts: priorities in mental health services. Hastings Cent Rep 1993; 23(Sept–Oct suppl): S1–S23

37. Fleck L: Just health care rationing: a democratic decisionmaking approach. University of Pennsylvania Law Rev 1992; 140: 1597–1636

38. American Psychiatric Association: The Principles of Medical Ethics With Annotations Especially Applicable to Psychiatry, revised. Washington, DC, APA, 1995

39. The World Psychiatric Association's 1996 Declaration of Madrid, in Psychiatric Ethics, 3rd ed. Edited by Bloch S, Chodoff P, Green SA. Oxford, UK, Oxford University Press, 1999, pp 517–519

40. Australian Medical Association: Code of Ethics. Canberra, Australian Medical Association, 1995

41. Royal Australian and New Zealand College of Psychiatrists: Code of Ethics. Melbourne, RANZCP, 1998

42. Royal Australian and New Zealand College of Psychiatrists: Position Statement 37: Policy on Mental Health Services. Melbourne, RANZCP, 1997

43. Schreter R: Essential skills for managed behavioral health care. Psychiatr Serv 1997; 48:653–658

44. Charlesworth M: The new ideology of health care: ethical issues, in She Won't Be Right, Mate! The Impact of Managed Care of Australian Psychiatry and the Australian Community. Edited by the Psychiatrists' Working Group. Melbourne, Psychiatrists' Working Group, 1997, pp 104–110

45. Kendell R, Pearce A: Consultant psychiatrists who retired prematurely in 1995 and 1996. Psychiatr Bull 1997; 21:741–745

The Ethical Psychiatrist

[51]

The New Medical Ethics and Mental Health Administration

by ROBERT D. REECE, PhD

Accompanying the transformation in the social and economic environment of contemporary American medicine are major conceptual changes in "medical ethics" that have profoundly affected both therapists and administrators whose responsibility it is to "man" and "manage" mental health facilities. Three significant and interrelated developments deserve special attention:

- the rise of public interest in medical ethics,
- a new emphasis on patient autonomy by the medical profession itself, and
- an increasing demand coming from outside the medical profession that medicine assume greater

Dr Reece is Professor and Chair, Department of Medicine in Society. School of Medicine, Wright State University, Dayton, Ohio.

Address reprint requests to Robert D. Reece, PhD, Department of Medicine in Society, School of Medicine, Wright State University, PO Box 927, Dayton, OH 45401.

> *Until the late 1960s, medical ethics was largely the province of the medical profession.*

responsibility for the common good, possibly even at some sacrifice of the good of individual patients.

These developments in the arena of medical ethics have ramifications that create new challenges in mental health administration.

THE NEW ERA IN MEDICAL ETHICS

Until the late 1960s, medical ethics was largely the province of the medical profession. Some Roman Catholic moralists and a few rabbis had dealt extensively with issues in medical ethics; interest by Protestant the-

ologians and philosophers was not entirely absent. To a considerable extent, however, "medical ethics" meant ethics as defined by physicians. The publication of a book on medical ethics by a well-known American Protestant theologian in 1970 was a milestone signaling that the trend of "lay" participation in medical ethics was here to stay.[1] Soon books on medical ethics were pouring out of scholarly presses, and articles written by an ever increasing number of theologians, philosophers, and physicians were appearing in professional and scholarly journals. Medical ethics became part of the public domain—the first of several incursions into medical territory that have diminished professional autonomy.

Popular interest in medical ethics increased dramatically with the advent of new legal concepts. The famed Karen Quinlan case was followed by court cases and legislation dealing with living wills and brain death. Informed consent became a major issue in legal circles, and a new body of law related to psychiatry emerged. Medical ethics has captured public attention and has become a hot topic on talk shows and television dramas, as well as in popular magazines and books. New organizations have emerged—some to study problems, others to champion particular causes or to advocate specific solutions. One result is the imposition of new constraints on the medical profession and related health facilities. The public is no longer willing to leave medical ethics solely to the professionals.

Moreover, within the medical community a significant shift of perspective and values has occurred, partly because of the influence of nonphysician medical ethicists. Promoting the well-being of the patient has been the overriding norm of the medical profession ever since this commitment was enunciated by the Hippocratic school. This "principle of beneficence" has two dimensions. The negative duty is not to cause harm, a principle immortalized in its Latin formulation *primum non nocere*, "first do no harm." Most positive obligations derived from the principle consist of attempts to reduce or to remove harmful conditions caused by illness or trauma. Undoubtedly at times this has led to subtle or unabashed paternalism, as patient wishes were ignored in the effort to promote what physicians perceived as the patient's best interest.

This concern for patient welfare continues to be the motivating force that energizes physicians, but the past 20 years has seen the flowering of a second principle—the principle of autonomy. This principle,

> A second area where the public is demanding that physicians demonstrate greater social responsibility is in reporting incompetent colleagues.

although not entirely foreign to Western medicine, is rooted primarily in the political theory of the Enlightenment and the history of Anglo-American law. It provides the ethical basis for patient self-determination.[2,3] Although generated largely by external pressures, the recognition of the role of the patient in medical decision-making has not only been endorsed but also internalized by many individual physicians and incorporated into various statements of medical ethics by physician organizations.[4,5] Applying the norms of beneficence and autonomy usually leads to the same result because both the patient and the physician are concerned with the patient's best interest. However, sometimes their perception of what is "best" differs, and with a competent patient the principle of autonomy now takes precedence. The increase in respect for the dignity of patients is laudable, but it will become a travesty if the principle of autonomy so crowds out beneficence that physicians become mere technicians, "providers," who sell whatever services health care "consumers" desire.

The third prominent change in the ethics of medical practice results from growing social pressures on physicians as individual practitioners and as a profession to be concerned with the general welfare of society, not just with the well-being

of individual patients. This broader conception has been a minor theme in the history of medicine, but several forces at work are making it a more important issue today. Laws requiring physicians to report infectious diseases and injuries resulting from violence are examples, as is the "duty to warn" others of certain threats of violence, exemplified in the Tarasoff case. A second area where the public is demanding that physicians demonstrate greater social responsibility is in reporting incompetent colleagues. The challenge to the profession is to fulfill the social obligation without undermining either the very special therapeutic nature of the doctor/patient relationship or the appropriate degree of professional autonomy that promotes responsible professional judgment instead of "cookbook" medicine.

Implications for Mental Health Administration

The changing ethos of medicine is evident in mental health institutions. Mental health administrators may be surprised to hear their decisions being described in the language of ethics, much like Moliere's character who expressed amazement when he discovered that for over 40 years he had been speaking prose without knowing it. The practice of the healing arts is by its very nature an ethical enterprise, concerned with the well-being of people. Now therapists and administrators are becoming more explicit in labeling the ethical dimension and more deliberate in using tools of ethical analysis. Health care institutions now are recognizing that they have a direct obligation to patients, independent of the physician's, as well as a broader social responsibility to the community.

Moreover, many institutions are becoming more self-conscious in articulating their understanding of their ethical responsibility. The drafting of formal statements of institutional philosophies and missions provides an opportunity to make explicit the moral commitments that have existed but have not always been stated. In addition, the adoption of codes of ethics by professional groups, such as the Association of Healthcare Executives, has served to focus attention on the ethical responsibility of professional groups, such as administrators.[6]

Some dismiss such statements of ethics as platitudinous and innocuous, serving as mere decoration or, even worse, as a smoke screen to obscure unethical practice. This objection assumes that any ethic that can be ignored or misused is necessarily defective. But no system of ethical thought is immune to subversion by the unscrupulous. Knowing that the devil can cite scripture for his purpose, the authors of the Code of Ethics of the American College of Healthcare Executives specifically state the duty of its members not to "invoke any part of this Code of Ethics for selfish reasons."[7] Codes of ethics can be useful in identifying and reaffirming ethical ideals for those who aspire to be ethical; they are more limited as instruments for disciplining the unethical.

A second objection, that philosophy statements or codes of ethics are too idealistic to be practical, may sound persuasive. Not infrequently one hears someone complain that circumstances have required unethical behavior because implementing ethical ideals in the situation was impossible. Such statements imply that ethics must be what Max Weber calls an "ethic of ultimate ends," an absolute standard that permits no compromise regardless of circumstances. Such a pure ethic can be fulfilled only by withdrawing from social responsibility into an enclave, Weber argues, and its advocates are really irresponsible. Weber's "ethic of responsibility" assumes that compromise is frequently an ethical imperative. Ethics, like politics, is the art of the possible. Not just any compromise will do, of course. Ideals remain a guiding star that set the direction and the limits for necessary compromises. The person following the ethic of responsibility sometimes reaches a point where compromise is

> **Mental health administrators may be surprised to hear their decisions being described in the language of ethics.**

immoral, and Weber says that then he or she must say with Luther, "Here I stand; I can do no other."[8] Whether or not expressed in a code of ethics, such ideals are essential, lest practitioners set their sights too low.

THE CHALLENGES OF ADMINISTRATION

The ethic of responsibility is the very currency of the administrator. The mental health administrator must respond to several immediate constituencies and perhaps to others more remote. The well-being of the patient and the needs of staff, directors, third-party payers, and the community all place moral demands upon the administrator. Sometimes, the ethical task of the administrator is to make decisions, seeking the most appropriate balance among conflicting duties and values. More often, the task is establishing the framework within which ethical issues will be decided. Adopting and enforcing policies, procedures, rules, and guidelines may promote ethical practice, but ethical formulae will never replace the need for discernment and judgment.

Although administrators may feel powerless in the face of various constraints, they do occupy positions of some power and influence. Part of their responsibility, then, is to exercise that power appropriately to promote their agency's work. This may entail an obligation to appeal vig-

orously for adequate funding, especially as the shortage of funds for public mental health programs becomes more acute. It may mean resisting efforts, especially in proprietary facilities, to let funding drive patient care. However, when financial resources are limited, administrators must lead their institutions in facing several questions. Is it best to do a little for a number of people or a lot for a few? Is it best to provide the most services to those who are most in need, ie, the sickest, or those who may be most likely to benefit, ie, the least sick? When does care become so inferior because of insufficient funding that it becomes unethical to continue to work for the agency?

Administrators also must lead in addressing other conflicts between professional ethics and institutional needs that may result from economic pressures. Ben Bursten raises a serious question, for example, about the requirement that psychiatrists in a supervisory role with other mental health professionals must spend adequate time to provide such supervision; they must not be figureheads who simply sign the charts. The requirement, stated in the American Psychiatric Association's "Annotations on the American Medical Association's Principles of Medical Ethics," is simply impossible to fulfill in many institutional settings, Bursten argues.[9]

Another continuing source of tension for administrators is the potential conflict between teaching, research, and service. In some settings, patient care may be sacrificed in the interest of education. In others, education suffers because residents have excessive responsibilities for patient care, which may be detrimental both to them and their future patients. Likewise, it is possible to err by excessive preoccupation with research, with patients becoming merely means to an end; the opposite mistake is failing to support research that ultimately will lead to improved care.

Perhaps one of the greatest challenges for the entire health care field is helping patients and the public understand what can be reasonably expected from modern medicine. Many people have unrealistic expectations and demand a greater degree of certainty than is possible. Mental health administrators need to foster an environment that encourages open and empathetic sharing of this uncertainty with the patient.

For example, informed consent, viewed as an externally imposed legal requirement that is satisfied by a mechanical recitation of risks and benefits and the signing of a form, may be perceived as threatening by the patient and may result in alienation. Therapists can use the informed consent process as an occasion when they share the patient's distress about uncertainty, and this may promote better understanding and a positive therapeutic alliance.[10]

Sometimes patients' anger following medical "failure" results from physicians' inability to admit the limitations of their craft, or they may not recognize the lasting consequences of the careless use of their power. For example, a mistaken psychiatric diagnosis may well become a permanent feature in a person's life because its existence in the patient's record becomes self-perpetuating.

Psychiatrically trained administrators can be especially helpful in promoting continual self-examination by the therapeutic staff. In addition to providing a check on abuses of power, a good administrator also

will seek to prevent the abdication of power and responsibility by individuals and the profession when it needs to be exercised for the welfare of patients or society.

PROMOTING A NEW ETHICAL FRAMEWORK

In the current ethical climate, administrators are buffeted by competing claims of numerous individuals and groups. "Rights" language seems to be in the ascendancy. Although the concept of rights needs to continue to play an important role in discussions of ethics, it has its liabilities. Excessive individualism, legalism, and an adversarial atmosphere tend to accompany ethical approaches too focused on rights. What may be lost is the appreciation for shared values and goals of individuals in a relationship and a concern for the common good. Conceiving ethical issues solely in terms of rights ignores the commitment of mental health professionals to a therapeutic alliance with their patients.

Moreover, excessive emphasis on patients' rights may lead mental health professionals to pay too little attention to the legitimate public concern for protection from those who are "a danger to others." Even the discussion about health care financing may be skewed if it is conducted only in terms of whether there is a right to health care. Asking what kind of health care should be available in a "good society" may, in

the long run, prove more productive by focusing attention on the common goals that all citizens share. Health care administrators will make an enormous contribution if they can bring their skill in negotiating a harmony of interests into discussions of ethics, which are frequently dominated by debates about competing rights.

REFERENCES

1. Ramsey P. *The Patient as Person.* New Haven, Conn: Yale University Press; 1970.
2. Beauchamp TL, McCullough LB. *Medical Ethics: The Moral Responsibilities of Physicians.* Englewood Cliffs, NJ: Prentice-Hall Inc; 1984.
3. Beauchamp TL, Childress JF. *Principles of Biomedical Ethics.* 2nd ed. New York: Oxford University Press; 1983.
4. Ad Hoc Committee on Medical Ethics, American College of Physicians. American College of Physicians Ethics Manual. *Ann Intern Med.* 1985;101:129-137, 263-267.
5. American Medical Association, Judicial Council. *Opinions and Reports.* Chicago: American Medical Association; 1986.
6. Darr K. *Ethics in Health Services Management.* New York: Praeger; 1987: 33-64.
7. American College of Health Care Executives. Code of ethics. In: Darr K. *Ethics in Health Services Management.* New York: Praeger; 1987:233-241.
8. Weber M. Politics as a vocation. In: Gerth HH, Mills CW, trans. *Max Weber: Essays in Sociology.* New York: Oxford University Press; 1958:115-128.
9. Bursten B. "Medical responsibility" in institutional settings. *Am J Psychiatry.* 1980;137:1017-1074.
10. Gutheil TG, Bursztajn H, Brodsky A. Malpractice through the sharing of uncertainty. *N Engl J Med.* 1984;311:49-51.

[52]

Ethics in Psychiatric Practice: Essential Ethics Skills, Informed Consent, the Therapeutic Relationship, and Confidentiality

LAURA WEISS ROBERTS, MD
CYNTHIA M. A. GEPPERT, MD, PhD
ROBERT BAILEY, MD

Psychiatrists routinely encounter ethical complexities in caring for patients with mental illness, and they are held to the highest levels of accountability in their ethical practices. In this article, the authors first outline skills that are essential to ethical psychiatric practice. They then articulate three domains of clinical and ethical practice that represent the foundation of clinical care for people with mental illness: informed consent, the therapeutic relationship, and confidentiality. Key concepts concerning these domains are presented and relevant empirical evidence concerning each domain is reviewed. An understanding of these clinical and ethical practices will help psychiatrists serve patients with mental illness in their everyday clinical activities in a manner that is respectful, engenders trust, and ultimately fosters optimal clinical care. (*Journal of Psychiatric Practice* 2002;8:290–305)

KEY WORDS: ethics, psychiatric practice, ethical skills, informed consent, therapeutic relationship, confidentiality

Psychiatric care is ethically complex work. This is partly due to the nature of mental illnesses which, by definition, affect one's most fundamental human capacities and relations, and partly due to the roles and skills psychiatrists use in seeking to restore mental health. Psychiatrists are responsible for responding therapeutically to the suffering of a young person undergoing his first psychotic episode, to the devastation of a child who has lost her mother to breast cancer, to the progressive deficits of an elderly widower diagnosed with dementia, to the impulsive and self-destructive behavior of a traumatized person, to the intermittent but severe symptoms of an unemployed adult with bipolar disorder, to the family coping with addiction, to the patient with schizophrenia who starves himself because of fear that his food has been poisoned, to the newly emerging delirium of a hospitalized surgical patient. Mental illnesses in these contexts influence the feelings, experiences, personalities, relationships, self-understanding, and choices of patients. In providing mental health care, psychiatrists thus learn and observe much about the intimate lives of their patients who are often vulnerable because of their illnesses or life situation. For these reasons, psychiatrists routinely encounter extraordinary ethical complexities in caring for patients with mental illnesses, while, at the same time, psychiatrists are held to the highest levels of ethical accountability in their clinical practices.

To help prepare psychiatrists for these important aspects of their work, this article begins with an overview of ethical skills in clinical work. This is followed by descriptions of three practice domains that represent the ethical foundation of clinical care for people with mental illnesses. We present key concepts and review relevant empirical evidence in each of these domains.

ESSENTIAL ETHICS SKILLS

Psychiatrists are often well-equipped to deal with ethical considerations in caring for people with mental illness. Psychiatrists pay attention to motivations that underlie choices and behaviors, and they have a sense of the importance of insight, values, psychological development, and personal history in the lives of their patients, both as individuals and as moral persons in society. Psychiatrists also understand that self-observation and self-scrutiny are essential "habits" in assuring clinical excellence. All of these characteristics help foster optimal ethical reflection and rigorous decision-making in

ROBERTS, GEPPERT and BAILEY: University of New Mexico School of Medicine.

Please send correspondence and reprint requests to: Laura Roberts, MD, Department of Psychiatry, University of New Mexico School of Medicine, 2400 Tucker NE, Albuquerque, NM 87131.

Dr. Roberts gratefully acknowledges support from the National Institute of Mental Health in the form of a Career Development Award (K02MH01918-03).

ETHICS IN PSYCHIATRIC PRACTICE

patient care, and these are qualities that often lead us to choose the field of psychiatry.

Beyond these attributes, there are several essential ethics skills or capacities that should be in the repertoire of all clinical professionals working with people with mental illness (Table 1). The first skill is the ability to recognize the ethical considerations and dilemmas that naturally arise in psychiatric care. This requires sensitivity. It also requires a working understanding of ethical concepts such as beneficence, veracity, respect for persons, justice, nonmaleficence, autonomy, and privacy as they apply to clinical situations. For the psychiatrist who provides care for people with addictive disorders, for example, it will be crucial to be aware of diverse issues ranging from the role of confidentiality protections in minimizing the risk of stigma and discrimination to the importance of helping the person with substance dependence make autonomous choices that are not driven by the addiction.

The second skill is the capacity to honestly examine one's own values, strengths, and biases as they relate to patient care. For instance, in caring for a woman with schizophrenia who is doing well in treatment with atypical antipsychotic medication and now wishes to become pregnant, a psychiatrist may confront her biases about the capacity of people with schizophrenia to be good parents, about the contribution of "nature and nurture" in the upbringing of healthy children, about the rights of people with mental illness, and about the role of the psychiatrist in patients' lives. Being attuned to one's own sense of disquiet or uncertainty (i.e., the feeling of being "in deep waters") is one component of this essential ethics skill. This is important, for instance, when a patient begins asking for special treatment arrangements ("Can you make my prescription dose twice as high, so that I only have to pay the 'co-pay' half as often?" or "Can you see me 'off the record' so that I don't lose my job?"), so that you can be prepared to address these issues constructively within the therapeutic relationship. Moreover, it is important to be able to discern one's own motivations and to examine the possibility that one may be placing one's own needs, convenience, or personal wishes above the needs of the patient. This may arise in the care of a celebrity or "VIP" patient or, alternatively, in the care of patients who are intriguing or exotic by virtue of their background, appearance, illness, or past behavior.

The third skill involves the ability to identify one's areas of clinical competence and, as a corollary, to identify the limits of one's competence. This skill is important because of the linked bioethics principles of

Table 1. Essential ethics skills in psychiatric practice

1. The ability to recognize ethical considerations in psychiatric practice, including a working knowledge of ethical concepts as they apply to the care of mental illness

2. The ability to be aware of one's own values, strengths, and biases as they apply to work with patients, including the ability to sense one's own discomfort as an indicator of potential ethical problems

3. The ability to identify the limits of one's clinical skills and competence

4. The ability to anticipate specific ethical dilemmas in treatment

5. The ability to access clinical ethics resources, to obtain ethics consultation, and to access ongoing supervision of difficult cases

6. The ability to introduce additional safeguards into the clinical care of the patient and to monitor their effectiveness

beneficence, i.e., the duty to do good, and of non-maleficence, i.e., the duty to "do no harm," which are fundamental to the public's trust that clinical professionals will do all they can to serve the well-being and best interests of the patients for whom they accept responsibility. In essence, one should not provide care that is beyond one's ability or expertise, except in the most extraordinary circumstances. In situations where one is likely to be stretched beyond one's competence routinely—for example, in remote areas where there are few healthcare facilities and clinical specialists—it is imperative to make every effort to enhance one's abilities and expertise and to arrange for expert "back up." Even in more resource-rich settings, however, it is important to be aware of the limits of one's clinical competence so that patients receive an appropriate standard of care. This is referred to as an ethical "scope of practice" issue. This requires a very high level of self-honesty, but it also requires an understanding of the clinical competence expectations and clinical care standards that exist within the field of psychiatry.

The fourth skill involves the ability to identify specific situations that are likely to give rise to problems that are ethical in nature and to actively anticipate and prevent their emergence. Examples include outlining the

ETHICS IN PSYCHIATRIC PRACTICE

nontherapeutic role of the psychiatrist who performs a disability and compensation evaluation for a veteran, laying out clear therapeutic boundary expectations when beginning work with a patient who has an extensive trauma history, describing the obligations of physicians to report child abuse and neglect when working with a troubled and violent family, or explaining the limits of confidentiality when evaluating an employee for a security clearance.

While the fourth ethics skill involves identifying the presence of an ethical conflict or an at-risk situation, the fifth ethics skill involves seeking appropriate guidance to help clarify and resolve the conflict. This may simply involve gathering additional information about the patient, finding relevant practice guidelines, or reviewing texts that focus on ethical decision-making in clinical practice. Depending on the complexity of the situation, however, seeking guidance may entail careful consultation with a professional who has ethical or legal expertise and/or obtaining supervision from a wise colleague who will be clear-sighted, knowledgeable, and candid. Other valuable resources include a hospital patient care ethics committee, psychiatrists with a specialized knowledge of ethics in professional organizations such as the American Psychiatric Association, or a clinical ethicist at an academic medical center. Even after the initial dilemma is resolved, it may be necessary to obtain ongoing supervision for a case with difficult ethical and clinical aspects.

Finally, a sixth essential ethics skill is the ability to introduce appropriate additional ethical safeguards into the process of caring for the patient. On one hand, this may only involve remaining cognizant of the ethical problems inherent in a situation as the therapeutic process unfolds and perhaps seeking occasional supervision from a fellow faculty member, a practice partner, or a wise and trusted colleague in another field. On the other hand, more vigorous safeguards may be undertaken in higher risk situations. For example, in the situation in which a patient seeks treatment in an office where a relative works as a staff member, such safeguards might involve keeping patient information separate and locked, i.e., maintaining an appropriate "shadow chart" in parallel with the usual medical record. Other kinds of safeguards might involve having other health care professionals assist in the management of a patient's care, or in some cases carefully transferring the patient to another clinician. In all cases, the psychiatrist should carefully reflect on and document the ethical safeguards implemented in the care of the patient and his or her assessment of their

adequacy in protecting the patient's well-being and interests.

INFORMED CONSENT

Informed consent is a clinical ethics practice that honors the independent decision-making of patients. It is based on the premise that individuals should truly understand and freely make decisions regarding their personal health care. Consent always occurs in the context of a relationship (e.g., between psychiatrist and patient) and in the context of a specific decision (e.g., to have a diagnostic test performed, to be hospitalized, to try a new medication, or to withdraw from a medication). Clinical consent is oriented towards patient benefit, whereas research consent is oriented primarily towards fulfillment of a scientific aim and, depending on the type of study, not necessarily towards patient benefit. In this paper, we focus specifically on informed consent in clinical psychiatric practice.

Elements of Informed Consent

Informed consent involves three elements, as shown in Figure 1. The first component is the sharing of *information* in a manner that enables the patient to freely accept or decline some element of clinical care. Ideally, the psychiatrist gives a patient necessary information regarding the nature of his or her illness, the reason for considering the intervention, the likely risks and benefits of a proposed clinical intervention (e.g., diagnostic test, medication), the procedures involved in the clinical intervention, the alternatives to the clinical intervention (including no intervention), and the expected outcomes. If the acceptance or refusal of a clinical intervention opens or closes future treatment options, it is important to discuss this issue early in the decision-making process.

The level of detail provided should be based on what a reasonable person would want to know. For example, with a new medication, the patient would want to know about target symptoms, major side effects, very serious (even if very rare) adverse events, and follow-up requirements, such as monitoring of serum levels or blood pressure. Under optimal circumstances, the patient will have sufficient opportunity to ask questions and review the information carefully with the psychiatrist.

The second element of informed consent is *decisional capacity*. This is the ability of the patient to evaluate the information and understand its relevance and

ETHICS IN PSYCHIATRIC PRACTICE

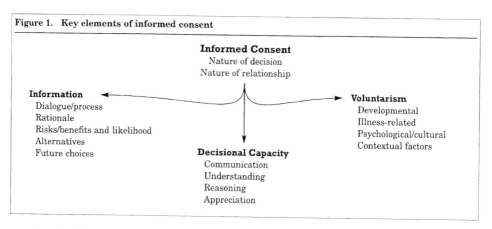

Figure 1.   Key elements of informed consent

meaning within the context of his or her life. Decisional capacity, in turn, has four constituent components. The first is the individual's ability to express a preference (i.e., capacity for expression or communication). The second is the individual's ability to understand pertinent information, such as the nature of his or her illness, its prognosis with and without treatment, and risks, benefits, and alternatives related to the proposed intervention (i.e., capacity for comprehension). In teaching settings, one of us (LWR) refers to this informally as the "Sergeant Joe Friday" criterion ("Just the facts, ma'am, just the facts"), in that it relates to the understanding of factual information.

The third component of decisional capacity is the ability to reason. This refers to the ability to work with information logically and objectively, without the explicit integration of emotions or personal values. (Again, in teaching, we refer to this as the "Mr. Spock" criterion.) For instance, a "rational" individual will consistently choose a medication that poses fewer risks and promises fewer adverse side effects than another medication but that is expected to have treatment benefit. Fourth, and often most importantly, is the person's ability to take the information and what he or she understands about it and use it to make meaning of the decision and its consequences within the context of his or her personal history, values, emotions, and life situation (i.e., the capacity for appreciation). This is the most sophisticated and subtle component of decisional capacity.

In evaluating capacity for consent, listening to and observing the patient and performing a careful mental status examination will help inform an assessment of the patient's decisional capacity. Additional techniques

for evaluating decisional capacity include asking patients to restate the information they have heard in their own words. It is helpful to encourage patients to think through several scenarios and explicitly describe the implications of various choices. Patients should be invited to think about earlier life decisions and their outcomes and explore their relevance for the current decision. A technique that is especially helpful in determining whether the patient appreciates the nature and implications of the decision is to ask the patient to envision the expected consequences of declining a recommended intervention, even if he or she is willing to accept the choice being presented. Eliciting private hopes and fears associated with the decision is subtle work but may be especially important in "high stakes" decisions.

The final element in informed consent is the capacity for *voluntarism*. Voluntarism refers to individuals' ability to act in accord with their authentic sense of what is good, right, and best in light of their situation, values, and history.[1] Voluntarism further entails the capacity to make this choice freely and in the absence of coercion. Deliberateness, purposefulness of intent, clarity, genuineness, and coherence with prior life decisions are implicitly emphasized in this construction.

As with decisional capacity, the capacity for voluntarism in an informed consent decision should be systematically assessed along four dimensions: 1) developmental factors; 2) illness-related considerations; 3) psychological issues and cultural and religious values; and 4) external pressures. Developmental factors include youth or developmental disabilities that may interfere with the generation of personal values and the

ETHICS IN PSYCHIATRIC PRACTICE

capacity for autonomous choice. Illness-related considerations include symptoms such as the negative cognitive distortions and hopelessness associated with depression or the amotivation associated with addiction or psychotic disorders. Psychological issues include the expectations and perceptions of the individual (for example, someone who has served in the military might view recommendations from clinicians as orders from the "commanding officer"). Similarly, cultural and religious values may affect an individual's sense of personal agency vis-a-vis the greater authority that may exist within his or her family or spiritual community. Finally, external pressures such as institutionalization or poverty may diminish the individual's sense of self-efficacy and voluntarism.

What Informed Consent Is, and What It Is Not

It is clear that the ideal informed consent process will be an ongoing dialogue that allows the patient to be informed and to have the time necessary to clarify complex issues, rectify misconceptions, and consult other resources such as family members, friends, another physician, or printed or electronic reference material. It will provide opportunity to clarify personal values and to envision their consequences in health decisions. Strategies for enhancing the consent process in the context of psychiatric care are presented in Table 2.

While this ideal may at times be difficult to attain, it is also worth noting what informed consent is not. First, it is not reducible to a signature on a legal form. Rather the form signifies a richer, more substantive dialogue of importance to the patient. The informed consent process does not end when the form is signed, but rather should provide for opportunities for reconsidering consent as new concerns emerge. For these reasons, the form should be taken seriously as a key medico-legal document—but a signed form is not by itself sufficient to demonstrate a sound consent process.

Second, the ability to give informed consent is not an absolute, and decisional capacity is not reducible to a diagnosis. It is important to keep in mind that decisional capacity is a richer, more complex idea. In relation to a particular decision at a certain point in their lives, individuals with schizophrenia may be decisionally capable whereas individuals with depression or anxiety disorders may not be. Indeed, the presence of a serious symptom (e.g., delusions, memory loss, suicidal ideation, diminished cognitive functioning) or of a serious diagnosis (e.g., schizophrenia, dementia, major depression, developmental disability) or being an elderly person or

---

Table 2. Strategies for enhancing the effectiveness of informed consent interactions

1. Information sharing

- Pay attention to the patient's interpersonal cues and communication style.

- Avoid technical jargon and provide information at the right level to foster understanding.

- Involve translators if necessary.

- Offer verbal, written, and/or audiovisual material whenever possible.

- Be aware of timing and context of information-sharing so that patients do not experience an "information overload" devoid of personal meaning.

- Encourage the patient to seek advice from loved ones.

- Create opportunities for questions and dialogue.

2. Decisional capacity

- Assess the patient for deficits in decisional capacity.

- Provide emotional support and reassurance.

- For patients with deficits in decisional capacity, approach things in a step-wise fashion—seek consent for beginning treatment and, as the patient's symptoms and functioning improve, approach the patient concerning larger decisions.

- If the patient is not capable of providing consent at all, use an appropriate family member as a designated alternative decision-maker.

3. Voluntarism

- Establish a trusting relationship.

- Seek to understand the values and choices of the patient now and in the past.

- Address symptoms and illness phenomena (e.g., negative cognitive distortions, compromised insight) to whatever extent possible.

- Avoid pressuring the patient for a quick decision unless absolutely necessary; reduce pressures in the environment when possible.

ETHICS IN PSYCHIATRIC PRACTICE

a young adolescent does not, *a priori*, imply that one does not possess decisional capacity. A cognitively intact individual in extreme physical pain after a car accident may have tremendous difficulty making an informed, free choice about the decision to undergo amputation of a damaged limb, whereas a chronically ill person with schizophrenia may have demonstrable cognitive deficits but clear decision-making ability about remaining on his depot neuroleptic medication. Decisional capacity, furthermore, differs from "competence" in that decisional capacity is assessed by a clinician according to the four components outlined above, whereas competence is a formal legal determination that relies upon, but is not synonymous with, an evaluation of clinical decisional capacity.[2, 3] Hence, the ability to give informed consent is not an "all or nothing" phenomenon. A person suffering from bipolar affective disorder may be decisionally capable today, but the ability to provide an informed decision while escalating into mania may be predictably problematic. Consequently, the ability to provide informed consent should be conceptualized as a continuum that varies with each patient and may indeed be different for the same patient in different circumstances and at different phases of illness.

Third, the standard for informed consent is not absolute. It is driven by context and consequences for the individual, as shown in Figure 2. The seriousness and complexity of the specific health-related decision together generate a differential standard ("a sliding scale") that determines the rigor of the consent criteria. For instance, the standard for obtaining informed refusal is set higher when a very ill patient refuses a medication that could bring great benefits and has minimal risks. Alternatively, the standard for obtaining informed consent for a routine procedure that is a common and accepted practice (e.g., checking serum cholesterol and lipid profiles, giving a tetanus shot or an influenza immunization) is often more implicit than explicit and requires a less rigorous standard. Critics may complain of a "double standard" in which patients who refuse recommended care are held to a higher standard than patients who accept the recommendation. This is not (or, at least, should not be) the case. The rigor of the standard ethically will rest on the consequences of the decision. If declining a recommended intervention causes few and minimal risks, then ordinarily it is not especially scrutinized, just as acceptance of a recommended intervention with few and minimal risks or which offers the best chance for benefit will not be especially scrutinized. If, on the other hand, the choice to refuse or accept an intervention has very serious conse-

Figure 2.   **Consent standards, risk, and the "sliding scale" model**

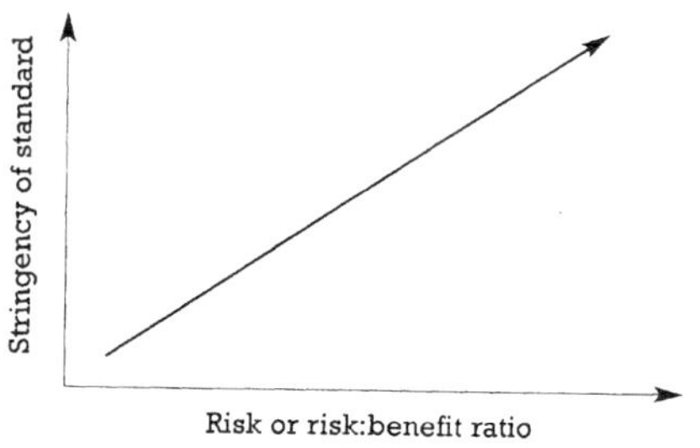

The stringency of the standard for consenting to or declining a recommended treatment increases as the likelihood and severity of the risks associated with that decision increase.

quences, and is not thought to be the patient's "best chance" for benefit, then the standard for the decision should indeed be higher.

Adaptations for Decisional Incapacity

In caring for people with decisional incapacity, whether transient or enduring, it is critically important to safeguard their well-being, best interests, and rights. From the perspective of the bioethics principles of *respect for persons* and *autonomy*, it is also important to honor patients' wishes to whatever extent possible, unless their expressed preferences will lead to significant harm. Efforts to provide understandable, accurate, and balanced information, to provide support, and to obtain assent for treatment may be undertaken (and should be documented) in such situations.

Two formal and specific safeguards have been developed, *advance directives* and *surrogate decision-making*, to help protect the rights and well-being of individuals with significant and/or progressively worsening decisional compromise.

When the psychiatrist anticipates that an individual's decisional capacity may be compromised at some point in the future (e.g., in the case of someone with bipolar or schizoaffective disorder or Alzheimer's disease), advance directives may be valuable tools for clarifying the preferences of mentally ill patients in relation to future choices. Advance directives are usually written documents that notify clinicians, family, and friends of the patient's wishes for treatment if the patient becomes decisionally incapable. Advance directives do not ever replace the wishes expressed by a patient who is currently decisionally capable, and patients should understand that they always retain the power to adapt, or even to reverse, earlier decisions as their preferences and circumstances evolve.

Surrogate decision-making is a second strategy for fulfilling the ideal of informed consent in clinical practice when individuals are decisionally compromised due to developmental or illness factors. Parents are *de facto* decision-makers for very young children, for instance, and substitute decision-makers are often appointed to make healthcare choices for elderly patients who have dementia or other significant cognitive impairments. A surrogate may be a spouse, sibling, adult child, friend, or a court-appointed advocate. The surrogate decision-maker has the responsibility of serving the best interests and well-being of the patient while seeking to make decisions that are faithful to the personal values and prior wishes of the patient. As children mature, it is important to respect their growing autonomy and sense of self and allow them to assent or dissent to their parents' choices for their care. Many adolescents are capable of authentic informed consent and, with support and guidance, can exercise decision-making responsibilities. The decisional capacity of elderly patients must also be accurately assessed, closely monitored, and intensively addressed so that remaining abilities may be optimized and the dignity and choices of patients honored whenever possible.

Research Findings Concerning Informed Consent

Roughly 400 studies have been performed over the past three decades on informed consent.[4] Empirical research on consent in clinical care suggests that this philosophical and legal ideal is difficult to achieve in practice, especially for individuals with mental illness. A full review of this literature is beyond the scope of this article, but is elegantly summarized in an annotated bibliography that was published by the Hastings Center in 1999.[4] While the issues faced in obtaining consent in individuals with mental illness are not dramatically different from those encountered in dealing with patients with physical illness, there are heightened challenges with regard to the more strictly cognitive aspects of consent (i.e., information retention, comprehension, and rationality) for people with psychotic or affective disorders and dementia.[5-7] Studies of advance directives and surrogate decision-making have been carried out prima-

rily with medical patients and patients with dementia and have disclosed that advance directives are underutilized and patient preferences are rarely identified prospectively.[8,9] Early data indicate that persons chosen as surrogates may not be those preferred by the patient; moreover, proxy decision-makers may not accurately assess patients' wishes or may use criteria other than the "best interests" or the values of the patient to make decisions.[10] Fortunately, clear evidence is also emerging that the barriers to consent may be amenable to treatment or to educational interventions, offering significant hope. The observation that educational efforts, symptomatic treatment, and attitudinal obstacles can be addressed suggests a number of constructive approaches to consent in the context of clinical care for the mentally ill.[11-14]

THE THERAPEUTIC RELATIONSHIP

Patients approach the therapeutic relationship with the expectation that the psychiatrist will be able to offer clarity about the causes of suffering and provide treatments that will be effective in addressing symptoms or curing disease. Psychiatrists approach the therapeutic relationship with specialized expertise in diagnosing and treating mental disorders. Psychiatrists have both positive and negative duties in this relationship. Their positive duties include demonstrating respect and regard for the patient, faithfully and competently serving the patient's needs and interests, and being truthful.[15,16] Their negative duties are not to harm or exploit the vulnerability of the patient.[15,17]

Psychiatrists, like other physicians, are entrusted with the power to fulfill certain responsibilities that derive from these positive and negative duties in the therapeutic relationship. For instance, psychiatrists are obliged to preserve the safety of mentally ill individuals who are suicidal or are endangered because of their inability to care for themselves.[2,18] Psychiatrists are also obliged, to whatever extent possible, to intervene to prevent patients with mental illness from harming others through homicidal behavior or impulsivity and compromised judgment.[2,19] These interventions may entail involuntary hospitalization or, in areas with limited services, some other form of supervised, safe detention during the period of crisis. At times, a treatment guardian may be sought. These steps may be, and often must be, taken despite the objections of the patient, and such immediate action is considered to be an ethical use of power due to the seriousness of the safety issues involved.[2,20] Ordinarily in situations such as these in

ETHICS IN PSYCHIATRIC PRACTICE

which an individual's liberties are limited, a legal process is set in motion to assess whether further hospitalization or other constraints on the ill individual should be continued due to therapeutic necessity.

Therapeutic Boundaries

Psychiatrists refer to the patterns of interactions within the therapeutic relationship that serve the well-being of the patient as "therapeutic boundaries." In everyday practice, ethical problems may arise when a usual boundary is crossed or seriously violated in the service of an interest other than the patient's need.[21-23] Examples of boundary crossings include a psychiatrist repeatedly arriving late for a scheduled appointment with a patient, or a psychiatrist who, because of his or her own needs, inappropriately and thoughtlessly discloses personal information to a patient. More serious nonsexual boundary violations that can undermine the therapeutic relationship include accepting substantial gifts from patients, forming friendships with established patients, or having patients run personal errands. Becoming sexually involved with a patient is widely recognized as incompatible with therapeutic work dedicated to the well-being of the patient, may be extraordinarily destructive to traumatized patients, and represents a severe boundary violation according to ethical standards within the profession of psychiatry.[16, 22-24]

Therapeutic boundaries may be influenced by the treatment modality, by the context of care, and by the developmental stage of the patient. For instance, a psychiatrist who handles the medications of a bipolar patient cared for by a multidisciplinary team will attach different meaning to a gift of home-baked holiday cookies than will a psychoanalyst who has worked with a patient for several years. In one case, a graceful "thank you" may be the ethically appropriate response, whereas, in another case, declining the gift and introducing the interaction into the therapeutic work would be the clinical and ethical imperative. When a psychiatrist and patient have overlapping relationships (e.g., the caregiving psychiatrist is a family member, friend, neighbor, or colleague), as is common in small communities, there is a greater risk of real or perceived boundary transgressions because multiple expectations and needs exist in such a situation.[25, 26] Special efforts to define professional and personal roles in such situations are essential to sound clinical practice. Similarly, military and forensic psychiatrists have their own distinctive formulations of the therapeutic relationship that must accommodate the realities of their multiple roles. The developmental stage of the patient is also salient. For instance, giving a child a hug or accepting a child's picture made as a "gift" for the psychiatrist may be appropriate behaviors within the therapeutic boundaries of the relationship. The cardinal principle in clarifying the ethical valence of these actions is whether they seek to alleviate suffering and restore mental health, and whether they serve the needs and interests of the patient or those of the psychiatrist.[21-23]

Research Concerning the Therapeutic Relationship and Boundary Issues

Relatively little empirical study has been done concerning the therapeutic relationship and related boundary issues. Key elements of the therapeutic relationship include iterative trust-building, competence, communication ability, interpersonal regard, and compassion.[26] Positive therapeutic relationships appear to be correlated with improved treatment adherence and better outcomes for diverse illnesses and conditions ranging from schizophrenia and depression to domestic violence and addiction.[27-31] Preliminary work on the therapeutic relationship in very small communities suggests that the overlapping relationships can at times offer benefits to patients (e.g., tracking patient well-being and symptoms in the context of a small, close-knit community) and that perceptions of ethically acceptable therapeutic boundaries differ from those in urban contexts.[32] Survey studies of boundary transgressions (see Table 3) suggest that a small but disturbing minority of mental health professionals engage in both sexual and non-sexual violations, with negative outcomes for sexually exploited patients noted in both survey studies and case reports.[23, 25, 33-38]

The Therapeutic Relationship With the "Difficult Patient"

In both medical and psychiatric settings, the real test of the therapeutic relationship is the "difficult patient."[39, 40] Difficult patients come in all forms. Some are unlikable, irritable, threatening, demanding, and oppositional; others are ingratiating, seductive, and overly familiar; and still others are extremely ill, treatment-resistant, nonadherent, and self-defeating. Difficult patients are those who require or request an investment in time, resources, energy, or emotion that a physician considers inordinate, excessive, or inappropriate.[39, 41] There are at least as many reasons for patients to be considered difficult as there are physician-patient relationships. Research has

ETHICS IN PSYCHIATRIC PRACTICE

Table 3. Examples of ethics studies pertaining to therapeutic boundaries, dual relationships, and sexual boundary violations

Authors	Method	Participants	Key Findings
Hines et al. 1998[36]	Self-report of the number of boundary crossings, including dual relationships and associated countertherapeutic outcomes, with adult patients during the year preceding report	90 military and 191 demographically matched civilian psychiatrists	Military and HMO psychiatrists experienced greater external pressure to engage in dual relationships than non-HMO civilian psychiatrists, but all 3 groups were similar in reported number of such activities.
Perkins et al. 1998[37]	Vignette-based survey assessing ethical dilemmas involving professional role boundaries or client confidentiality	95 psychiatrists and staff members from five community mental health centers	Years of experience and previous ethics training correlated positively with experience of similar situations. Neither variable was related to decisions made or ethical justifications provided. When the analysis controlled for the two variables of experience and training, staff made fewer conservative decisions in boundary dilemmas than in confidentiality dilemmas. Rural providers had experienced more boundary dilemmas and made fewer conservative decisions than nonrural providers.
Epstein et al. 1992[23]	32-question, self-administered questionnaire consisting of the Exploitation Index	532 U.S. psychiatrists and medical psychoanalysts	43% of psychiatrists reported that at least one item on the index made them aware of behavior that could be counterproductive to treatment. 29% were motivated to make specific changes in their practice in response to the survey. Women reported fewer boundary violations than men.
Borys and Pope 1989[35]	Survey of the attitudes and practices regarding dual professional roles, social involvements, financial involvements, and incidental involvements	4,800 U.S. psychologists, psychiatrists, and social workers surveyed (return rate = 49%)	A majority of therapists believed dual role behaviors were unethical in most circumstances and most reported that they had rarely or never engaged in such behaviors. More male than female had been involved in sexual and nonsexual dual relationships. The various mental health professionals showed no difference in a) sexual intimacies with clients before and after termination, b) nonsexual dual professional roles, c) social involvements with patients, or d) financial involvements with patients.
Herman et al. 1987[34]	Written, mailed anonymous survey regarding psychiatrists' attitudes toward sexual contact with patients.	1,423 U.S. psychiatrists	98% responded that therapist-patient sexual contact is always inappropriate and usually harmful to the patient; 29.6% felt that sexual contact after termination of therapy might sometimes be acceptable. 84 psychiatrists who acknowledged sexual contact with one or more patients differed markedly from those who had not engaged in such conduct. 74% of the psychiatrists who had had sexual contact rationalized their behavior as being appropriate after termination.
Gartrell et al. 1986[33]	Nationwide anonymous written survey regarding sexual contact with patients	1,057 U.S. psychiatrists	7.1% male and 3.1% of the female respondents acknowledged sexual contact with their own patients. 88% of the sexual contacts were between male psychiatrists and female patients. All who reported more than one offense were male; 41% sought consultation for the problem.

ETHICS IN PSYCHIATRIC PRACTICE

identified patients with unexplained physical symptoms, psychiatric disorders, substance abuse, psychosocial problems, and those who are nonadherent to treatment or treatment resistant as difficult.[42, 43] Almost any encounter in which a physician feels overwhelmed, incompetent, afraid, guilty, angry, or frustrated will be labeled difficult. Patients who are too similar to the physician in terms of background, culture, socioeconomic status or lifestyle may be experienced as difficult because of an unrealistic positive transference that obscures objectivity.[39, 44] Conversely, patients who differ greatly from the treating physician in these same variables may also be difficult encounters because of problems establishing a therapeutic alliance. From an ethical perspective, difficult patients are those who challenge our capacity to act beneficently, thoughtfully, and wisely.

Moreover, difficult patients are common, as evidenced in a 1996 study of 627 primary care patients, in which Hahn found that on average internists considered 15% to be difficult.[45] Patients considered difficult were more likely to have a mental disorder, most commonly dysthymia, depression, panic, somatoform disorder, generalized anxiety, or alcohol and drug abuse. Difficult patients were also more likely to have functional impairment and higher health care utilization.[45] Jackson and Kroenke looked at difficult patient encounters in the ambulatory setting involving 500 patients and 38 physicians.[46] Patient factors contributing to difficult encounters were having a mental disorder, having more than five somatic symptoms, and more severe symptoms. Physician factors were high scores on poor attitudes toward psychosocial variables. Encounters considered difficult resulted in patients having poorer functional status, more unmet expectations, less satisfaction with care, and higher health care utilization.[46] A 1996 study looked at 34 family physicians' perceptions of difficult patients. Over 80% of these physicians found patients who expected to be cured, who brought up new symptoms at the last moment, or who appeared to be malingering or not taking responsibility for their health to be difficult.[47] A similar more recent study of family physicians identified difficult patients as those who are violent, demanding, aggressive, rude, and who seek secondary gain.[48] Robbins et al. looked at therapists' perceptions of difficult patients, comparing 54 psychiatric outpatients who were considered difficult with 54 control psychiatric outpatients not considered difficult.[49] Difficult patients rated higher on the demanding, help rejecting, and poor-fit scales.

Encounters with difficult patients do not necessarily have to end in mutual frustration and poor care. A number of tactics may help physicians manage difficult patients with compassion and competence.[39, 43, 50] The most important step is to develop an awareness of one's biases, fears, and counter-transferences and to examine how these may play themselves out in interactions with particular "types" of patients. Patients with multiple somatic complaints, or antisocial behavior, or physical disfigurement, or paranoia, or pseudoseizures, or patterns of self-mutilation may be harder for one physician, easier for another. Insight about what makes one uncomfortable may help in efforts to avoid the psychological traps inherent in difficult patient interactions. Difficult patients, by definition, trigger the wish to save, punish, reject, or give in, and clinician self-understanding is important in responding therapeutically, rather than acting on these impulses. It is also valuable to interpret the behavior of difficult patients as a clinical sign, a potent form of communication in the therapeutic relationship, and to try to discern the motivations of difficult patients in a given situation. Similarly, evaluating the multiple factors that contribute to the "difficult" presentation of the patient, using a "biopsychosocial" approach, may allow for a broadened repertoire of interventions that may help improve the patient's overall status and may cause some of the difficult behaviors to diminish.

The clinician who is effective with difficult patients will concentrate on finding some common ground upon which to construct a therapeutic alliance; often patient and clinician can agree that the patient is in pain and needs help, even if other issues in the interaction are very challenging. Seeking consultation, outside expertise, and collegial support when dealing with difficult patients can be extremely helpful and, indeed, is clinically indicated when the interaction between clinician and patient feels more like a struggle than a therapeutic endeavor. Forging a consensus among all caregivers regarding the treatment approach to difficult patients prevents damaging staff splitting. It is also useful to encourage the patient to take advantage of community support or that of family and friends. Each of these approaches can relieve the sense of burden and isolation that clinicians treating difficult patients often experience. Finally, every patient is "difficult" for clinicians who are exhausted. Self-care is important in serving the needs of multiproblem patients therapeutically, effectively, and ethically. Approaching the management of difficult patients as an essential clinical skill to be mastered can turn even the most disturbing patient interaction into a rewarding professional experience (Table 4).

ETHICS IN PSYCHIATRIC PRACTICE

Table 4. **Tactics in managing difficult patients therapeutically**

1. Understand yourself

o Be aware of your own biases and countertransference.

o Understand why certain types of patients upset you.

o Realize you're not a "bad" doctor if you have negative feelings about patients.

o Recognize everyone has trouble managing some patients.

2. Understand your patient

o Every difficult behavior is a form of communication.

o Every difficult patient is trying to express real fears and needs.

o Evaluate your patient from the perspective of a biopsychosocial model.

3. Reflect and think... Don't react

o Remember your duty to help (i.e., not harm, not rescue, not gratify).

o Focus on medical and psychiatric issues you can treat.

o Strive to be empathic, consistent, and stable.

4. Form an alliance

o Find something you can agree upon.

o Educate patients about your limits and responsibilities.

o Reinforce positive behavior, don't reward negative.

5. Treat whatever is treatable

o Screen for medical conditions.

o Screen for Axis I and Axis II disorders.

o Intervene constructively, doing at least a "piece of therapeutic work."

6. Get "back-up"

o Seek advice, obtain consultation.

o Foster team consensus.

7. Take care of yourself

o Find constructive ways of venting frustration.

o Prepare yourself for seeing difficult patients.

o See managing difficult patients as a clinical skill to master.

CONFIDENTIALITY

Confidentiality is defined as an implicit promise that is "present when one person discloses information to another, whether through words or an examination, and the person to whom the information is disclosed pledges not to divulge that information to a third party without the confider's permission" (p. 305).[15] Confidentiality is closely linked to the legal concepts of privacy and privilege. Privacy is the legal right of the individual to be free from unwanted intrusions into his or her physical body and his or her mental or psychological domains. Privilege pertains to the type of information admissible as evidence in court during litigation, with the ultimate goal being to protect the confidentiality of the patient. Privacy and privilege can be conceived of as "rights" belonging to the individual patient, while confidentiality is a duty of the clinician to the patient within the context of the therapeutic relationship. Beyond these legal concepts, confidentiality is also grounded in the ethical principles of respect for persons, beneficence, and autonomy. Respecting the integrity and dignity of an individual who seeks treatment requires that the psychiatrist protect and honor the intimate, often stigmatizing, knowledge and observations that emerge in the therapeutic process dedicated to helping the patient (i.e., beneficence). Part of what enables patients to trust a professional with their confidences is the belief that they retain some choice and control over the information they divulge. This is the connection between confidentiality and autonomy in that confidential information cannot be released without the explicit consent of the patient.

Exceptions to Confidentiality

Confidentiality is not an absolute ethical imperative in contemporary psychiatric practice, however.[2] Competing ethical principles and legal obligations may, in certain circumstances, take precedence. Resolving these tensions and conflicts is often a challenge for psychiatrists. Indeed, many of the ethical conflicts reported to the Ethics Committee of the American Psychiatric Association and many of the ethical problems reported by psychiatrists in survey studies involve ethical and legal exceptions to the physician's duty of confidentiality. Three primary exceptions to confidentiality have generally been recognized as part of psychiatric ethics and are also sanctioned in law: 1) danger to self; 2) danger to others; and 3) abuse of children, elders, or other persons who are dependent or have compromised decisional

ETHICS IN PSYCHIATRIC PRACTICE

capacity. A fourth exception—informing partners of an individual's HIV positive status if he or she refuses to do so and is engaging in unprotected sexual activity—varies according to jurisdiction, but is considered a legal obligation in some states.

It is important to note that the mandates pertaining to a patient's suicidal intentions and plans do not necessarily require the psychiatrist to divulge confidential information. In psychiatric practice, voluntary admission, medication adjustments, more intensive therapy, or, if necessary, involuntary admission and legal commitment are available strategies that may provide for a suicidal patient's safety while protecting his or her confidentiality. If these therapeutic interventions are not sufficient to address the acute crisis, then a physician may need to inform third parties such as friends or family members without the patient's consent in order to prevent the patient from harming him- or herself. Clinician responses to threats of homicide have changed substantively since the Tarasoff rulings regarding the obligations of clinicians to protect society from violent patients were issued in the 1970s in California. The first Tarasoff ruling mandated a "duty to warn" a named individual who is threatened by a mentally ill individual.[51] The second Tarasoff ruling expanded the obligation to a "duty to protect" the named potential victim.[52, 53] Similar legislation has been passed in at least 14 states.[19]

Evolving Confidentiality Regulations

Beyond these established approaches to confidentiality, a host of new regulatory requirements are now under consideration. These requirements, embedded in the Health Insurance Portability and Accountability Act of 1996 (HIPAA), focus on access to and appropriate use of personal health information. HIPAA is the first national, comprehensive privacy act and its rules determine the circumstances in which individually identifiable health information can be released and used. HIPAA guarantees patients four fundamental rights regarding the release of information: 1) to be educated about HIPAA privacy protections; 2) to have access to their medical records; 3) to request correction or amendment of information contained therein to which they object; and 4) most importantly, it requires the patient's permission for disclosure of personal information. Patients may also have access to a documented history of all non-routine disclosures, for instance, for insurance or research purposes. The scope of HIPAA is extensive and applies to almost any institution or individual involved

in health-related electronic transactions, including physicians, group practices, clinics, hospitals, departments of health, billing services that use electronic communications, utilization review, and university and private medical centers. Such institutions and individuals are known as covered entities. The act does not directly extend to insurers or employers but holds "covered entities" responsible for assuring the privacy of sensitive health information transmitted to these agencies. The act will have a pervasive application in health care, since it covers personally identifiable information in any form—oral, written, or electronic. HIPAA does not substantially alter standing public health provisions concerning the reporting of sexually transmitted or other communicable diseases or the reporting of child abuse. The act provides for both civil and criminal penalties for infractions of its regulations and requires that all covered entities designate a privacy officer to oversee policy and arrange for staff training in HIPAA rules. The act provides a baseline of confidentiality protections, but does not supersede state legislation in situations in which the state provides for more stringent confidentiality protections.[54]

The implementation of new privacy rules, such as those outlined in the HIPAA legislation, has important implications for psychiatric practice. Mental illness and addictions are more culturally stigmatizing and result in more social and economic discrimination than other types of medical conditions.[55, 56] Consequently, psychiatric patients are especially vulnerable to the negative consequences of breaches of confidentiality and even of legitimate releases of information and, therefore, extra protections of their sensitive information are warranted.[57, 58] HIPAA represents a strengthening of privacy protections in this area so that, before information can be released to an employer or insurer, the patient must be given a clear and relevant description of the type of information to be disclosed, the reason for the disclosure, the way the information will be used, the recipient of the information, and the expiration date of the release. These requirements are also in force when the patient requests that health information be released. In all cases, traditional practices regarding confidentiality insist that disclosure be the "minimum" necessary to accomplish the goal, although the definition of "minimum" and who will be authorized to determine what meets this standard are somewhat unclear and may be difficult to decide in practice.[59]

Because psychiatric disorders may negatively affect one's ability to give consent for disclosure of information, clinicians may need to take additional and innovative

ETHICS IN PSYCHIATRIC PRACTICE

Table 5. Examples of empirical studies on confidentiality in the care of mental illness

Authors	Method	Participants	Key Findings
Marshall and Solomon 2000[64]	Written survey of members of National Alliance for the Mentally Ill (NAMI) regarding their experiences with mental health professionals and confidentiality	219 members of NAMI	72% of families reported that they received specific information, e.g., about diagnosis and medication. Permission to release information to family members had been requested from few patients. There was a positive correlation between release of information and family's satisfaction with providers.
Binder and McNiel 1996[52]	Interview concerning residents' experiences related to issuing Tarasoff warnings	46 psychiatric residents	22 residents had given a Tarasoff warning, usually in inpatient or emergency room setting. Over half of intended victims could not be contacted but law enforcement was notified. In 75% of the cases, the victim was already aware of the threat. Victims' most common reaction was anxiety, gratitude, and intent to change their behavior to improve safety. Residents felt the warning had a minimal or positive effect on the therapeutic relationship.
Rubanowitz 1987[65]	15-statement telephone questionnaire about expectations for confidentiality in the psychotherapeutic relationship	200 adults from rural (North Dakota) and urban (Los Angeles) communities	Majority responded that therapy information should not be disclosed without client's consent. In general, respondents thought that, when a client disclosed murder (planned or confessed), suicide plans, child abuse, major theft, and treason/sabotage against the United States, confidentiality should be breached. Release of information to spouse, insurance companies, and courts were areas of concern, but not disclosure for purposes of consultation.
McGuire et al. 1985[66]	Questionnaire pertaining to four areas of privacy concerns	50 psychotherapy outpatients, 26 psychiatric inpatients, and 50 hospital employees	Inpatients valued privacy more than outpatients or controls and both groups of patients were unable to distinguish between ethical and legal aspects of privacy. Concerns about intrusions into privacy were higher among patients who perceived a past or current violation of confidentiality in therapy.
Schmid et al. 1983[63]	Semi-structured interview on confidentiality	30 psychiatric inpatients	Results showed patients valued confidentiality highly and were concerned about information being disclosed without their consent, but had little knowledge of their legal rights and options if confidentiality was violated.

ETHICS IN PSYCHIATRIC PRACTICE

measures to communicate information about confidentiality concerns, to determine decisional capacity, and to assure that patients can make authentic choices about their medical information. In addition, psychiatric patients are often members of disadvantaged populations who may not have the financial, educational, or legal resources to seek alternative modes of care or to recognize and address breaches of confidentiality when they do occur. A central consideration for confidentiality in psychiatric practice is the lack of clarity surrounding the distinction between information that is directly "used" versus "disclosed" during routine treatment practices. Some scholars interpret this to mean that clinicians could not freely and fully consult with ancillary staff and colleagues about a case, a practice which is critical to the multidisciplinary nature of contemporary psychiatric practice. Finally, confidentiality issues that arise in caring for children and adolescents are likely to become more complex in the future.[60] Currently, many state laws allow minors to seek treatment for stigmatizing illnesses such as sexually transmitted diseases or substance abuse without parental permission.[61, 62] Older children, particularly adolescents, are often intensely private, and honoring their confidentiality concerns about sexuality, pregnancy, and drug abuse when parents request or demand information are among the most difficult issues in psychiatric ethics. Consultation with colleagues and legal experts and clearly explaining the limits of confidentiality to both parents and children at the beginning of therapy may help avoid confrontations later in treatment.

Research Findings Concerning Confidentiality

Empirical studies of confidentiality (Table 5) affirm the importance of this safeguard for patients and the expectation that confidentiality related to mental health issues will be intensively protected.[63] In survey studies, most patients indicated that they would react negatively to an unauthorized release of information.[65] Many patients reported that their confidentiality had been violated in the past.[66] Patients in a wide variety of settings stated a preference to be better informed about the ethical and legal dimensions of confidentiality, particularly regarding the limits of the concept and their recourse when they feel their rights have been violated.[67] Some studies have reported that clinicians acknowledged underreporting suspected child abuse in order to protect patient confidentiality and because they felt it might damage the therapeutic relationship.[68]

CONCLUSION

Psychiatric practice poses distinct ethical challenges due to the special attributes of mental illnesses and their care. In light of these challenges, the profession of psychiatry has adopted very strict ethical practices primarily related to safeguards in informed consent, the therapeutic alliance, and confidentiality. An understanding of these ethically important clinical practice domains will help psychiatrists serve patients with mental illness in their everyday clinical activities in a manner that is respectful, engenders trust, and ultimately allows for optimal clinical care.

References

1. Roberts LW. Informed consent and the capacity for voluntarism. Am J Psychiatry 2002;159:705–12.
2. Simon RI. Clinical psychiatry and the law, 2nd ed. Washington DC: American Psychiatric Press; 1992.
3. Appelbaum P, Gutheil T. Clinical handbook of psychiatry and the law, 2nd ed. Baltimore: Williams & Wilkins; 1992.
4. Sugarman J, McCrory DC, Powell D, et al. Empirical research on informed consent: An annotated bibliography. Hastings Cent Rep 1999;29:S1–S42.
5. Stanley B, Stanley M. Psychiatric patients' comprehension of consent information. Psychopharmacol Bull 1987;23:375–8.
6. Appelbaum P, Grisso T. The MacArthur Competence Study I, II, III. Law and Human Behavior 1995;19:105–74.
7. Roth LH, Appelbaum PS, Sallee R, et al. The dilemma of denial in the assessment of competency to refuse treatment. Am J Psychiatry 1982;139:910–3.
8. Seckler AB, Meier DE, Mulvihill M, et al. Substituted judgment: How accurate are proxy predictions? Ann Intern Med 1991;115:92–8.
9. Bradley EH, Peiris V, Wetle T. Discussions about end-of-life care in nursing homes. J Am Geriatr Soc 1998;46:1235–41.
10. High DM. Standards for surrogate decision making: What the elderly want. J Long Term Care Adm 1989;17:8–13.
11. Roberts LW, Warner TD, Brody JL. Perspectives of patients with schizophrenia and psychiatrists regarding ethically important aspects of research participation. Am J Psychiatry 2000;157:67–74.
12. Roberts L, Roberts B. Psychiatric research ethics: An overview of evolving guidelines and current ethical dilemmas in the study of mental illness. Biol Psychiatry 1999;46:1025–38.
13. Carpenter WT Jr., Gold JM, Lahti AC, et al. Decisional capacity for informed consent in schizophrenia research. Arch Gen Psychiatry 2000;57:533–8.
14. Roberts LW. Psychiatry: Informed consent and care. In: Smelser NJ, Baltes PB, eds. International encyclopedia of the social and behavioral sciences. Amsterdam: Elsevier; 2001.
15. Beauchamp TL, Childress JF. Principles of biomedical ethics, 5th ed. New York: Oxford University Press; 2001.
16. Council on Ethical and Judicial Affairs. Code of medical ethics. Chicago: American Medical Association; 2002.
17. Jonsen AR, Seigler M, Winslade WJ. Clinical ethics. 4th ed. New York: McGraw-Hill; 1998.

ETHICS IN PSYCHIATRIC PRACTICE

18. Cantor C, McDermott PM. Suicide litigation: From legal to clinical wisdom. Aust N Z J Psychiatry 1994;28:431–7.

19. Anfang SA, Appelbaum PS. Twenty years after Tarasoff: Reviewing the duty to protect. Harv Rev Psychiatry 1996;4: 67–76.

20. Melamed Y, Kimchi R, Barak Y. Guardianship for the severely mentally ill. Med Law 2000;19:321–6.

21. Frick DE. Nonsexual boundary violations in psychiatric treatment. In: Oldham JM, Riba MB, eds. Review of psychiatry. Washington, DC: American Psychiatric Press; 1994.

22. Epstein RS, Simon RI. The Exploitation Index: An early warning indicator of boundary violations in psychotherapy. Bull Menninger Clin 1990;54:450–65.

23. Epstein RS, Simon RI, Kay GG. Assessing boundary violations: Survey results with the Exploitation Index. Bull Menninger Clin 1992;56:150–66.

24. American Psychiatric Association. The principles of medical ethics with annotations especially applicable to psychiatry. Washington, DC: American Psychiatric Press; 2001.

25. Pope KS, Vetter VA. Ethical dilemmas encountered by members of the American Psychological Association: A national survey. Am Psychol 1992;47:397–411.

26. Mechanic D, Meyer S. Concepts of trust among patients with serious illness. Soc Sci Med 2000;51:657–68.

27. Brown PD, O'Leary KD. Therapeutic alliance: Predicting continuance and success in group treatment for spouse abuse. J Consult Clin Psychol 2000;68:340–5.

28. Clarkin JF, Hurt SW, Crilly JL. Therapeutic alliance and hospital treatment outcome. Hosp Community Psychiatry 1987;38:871–5.

29. Frank AF, Gunderson JG. The role of the therapeutic alliance in the treatment of schizophrenia: Relationship to course and outcome. Arch Gen Psychiatry 1990;47:228–36.

30. Fenton WS, Blyler CR, Heinssen RK. Determinants of medication compliance in schizophrenia: Empirical and clinical findings. Schizophr Bull 1997;23:637–51.

31. Svensson B, Hansson L. Therapeutic alliance in cognitive therapy for schizophrenic and other long-term mentally ill patients: Development and relationship to outcome in an inpatient treatment programme. Acta Psychiatr Scand 1999;99:281–7.

32. Roberts LW, Monaghan-Geernaert P, Battaglia J, et al. Personal health care attitudes of rural clinicians: Findings of a preliminary study of 136 multidisciplinary caregivers in Alaska and New Mexico (in preparation).

33. Gartrell N, Herman J, Olarte S, et al. Psychiatrist-patient sexual contact: Results of a national survey. I: Prevalence. Am J Psychiatry 1986;143:1126–1131.

34. Herman JL, Gartrell N, Olarte S, et al. Psychiatrist-patient sexual contact: Results of a national survey, II: Psychiatrists' attitudes. Am J Psychiatry 1987;144:164–9.

35. Boyrs DS, Pope KS. Dual relationships between therapist and client. A national study of psychologists, psychiatrists and social workers. Professional Psychology Research & Practice 1989;20:283–93.

36. Hines AH, Ader DN, Chang AS, et al. Dual agency, dual relationships, boundary crossings, and associated boundary violations: A survey of military and civilian psychiatrists. Mil Med 1998;163:826–33.

37. Perkins DV, Hudson BL, Gray DM, et al. Decisions and justifications by community mental health providers about hypo-

thetical ethical dilemmas. Psychiatr Serv 1998;49: 1317–22.

38. Brown LS, Borys DS, Brodsky AM, et al. Psychotherapist-patient sexual contact after termination of treatment. Am J Psychiatry 1992;149:979–80, discussion 987–9.

39. McCarty T, Roberts LW. The difficult patient. In: Rubin RH, Voss C, Derksen DJ, et al., eds. Medicine: A primary care approach. Philadelphia: Saunders; 1996.

40. Smith RJ, Steindler EM. The impact of difficult patients upon treaters: Consequences and remedies. Bull Menninger Clin 1983;47:107–16.

41. Groves JE. Taking care of the hateful patient. N Engl J Med 1978;298:883–7.

42. Goodwin JM, Goodwin JS, Kellner R. Psychiatric symptoms in disliked medical patients. JAMA 1979;241:1117–20.

43. Vaillant GE. The beginning of wisdom is never calling a patient a borderline; or, the clinical management of immature defenses in the treatment of individuals with personality disorders. J Psychother Pract Res 1992;1:117–34.

44. Wright AL, Morgan WJ. On the creation of "problem" patients. Soc Sci Med 1990;30:951–9.

45. Hahn SR, Thompson KS, Wills TA, et al. The difficult doctor-patient relationship: Somatization, personality and psychopathology. J Clin Epidemiol 1994;47: 647–57.

46. Jackson JL, Kroenke K. Difficult patient encounters in the ambulatory clinic: Clinical predictors and outcomes. Arch Intern Med 1999;159:1069–75.

47. Katz RC. "Difficult patients" as family physicians perceive them. Psychol Rep 1996;79:539–44.

48. Steinmetz D, Tabenkin H. The "difficult patient" as perceived by family physicians. Fam Pract 2001;18:495–500.

49. Robbins JM, et al. Therapists' perceptions of difficult psychiatric patients. J Nerv Ment Dis 1988;176:490–7.

50. Drossman DA. The problem patient. Evaluation and care of medical patients with psychosocial disturbances. Ann Intern Med 1978;88:366–72.

51. Wulsin LR, Bursztajn H, Gutheil TG. Unexpected clinical features of the Tarasoff decision: The therapeutic alliance and the "duty to warn." Am J Psychiatry 1983;140:601–3.

52. Binder RL, McNiel DE. Application of the Tarasoff ruling and its effect on the victim and the therapeutic relationship. Psychiatr Serv 1996;47:1212–15.

53. Felthous AR. The clinician's duty to protect third parties. Psychiatr Clin North Am 1999;22:49–60.

54. Gostin LO. National health information privacy: Regulations under the Health Insurance Portability and Accountability Act. JAMA 2001;285:3015–21.

55. Crisp AH, Gelder MG, Rix S, et al. Stigmatisation of people with mental illnesses. Br J Psychiatry 2000;177:4–7.

56. Markowitz FE. The effects of stigma on the psychological well-being and life satisfaction of persons with mental illness. J Health Soc Behav 1998;39:335–47.

57. Domenici PV. Mental health care policy in the 1990s: Discrimination in health care coverage of the seriously mentally ill. J Clin Psychiatry 1993;54 (suppl):5–6.

58. Phelan JC, Bromet EJ, Link BG. Psychiatric illness and family stigma. Schizophr Bull 1998;24:115–26.

59. Vanderpool D. HIPAA's privacy rule: An update for psychiatrists. Psychiatric Practice and Managed Care 2002;6–12.

60. Proimos J. Confidentiality issues in the adolescent population. Curr Opin Pediatr 1997;9:325–8.

61. Weddle M, Kokotailo P. Adolescent substance abuse.

ETHICS IN PSYCHIATRIC PRACTICE

Confidentiality and consent. Pediatr Clin North Am 2002;49:
301–15.

62. Reddy DM, Fleming R, Swain C. Effect of mandatory parental notification on adolescent girls' use of sexual health care services. JAMA 2002;288:710–4.

63. Schmid D, Appelbaum PS, Roth LH, et al. Confidentiality in psychiatry: A study of the patient's view. Hosp Community Psychiatry 1983;34:353–5.

64. Marshall TB, Solomon P. Releasing information to families of persons with severe mental illness: A survey of NAMI members. Psychiatr Serv 2000;51:1006–11.

65. Rubanowitz DE. Public attitudes toward psychotherapist-client confidentiality. Professional Psychology Research & Practice 1987;18:613–8.

66. McGuire JM, Toal P, Blau B, et al. The adult client's conception of confidentiality in the therapeutic relationship: Depth of self-disclosure as a function of assured confidentiality and videotape recording. Professional Psychology—Research & Practice 1985;16:375–84.

67. Lindenthal JJ, Thomas CS. Psychiatrists, the public, and confidentiality. J Nerv Ment Dis 1982;170:319–23.

68. Brosig CL, Kalichman SC. Clinicians' reporting of suspected child abuse: A review of the empirical literature. Clinical Psychology Review 1992;12:155–68.

Protecting altruism: a call for a code of ethics in British psychiatry

SAMEER P. SARKAR and GWEN ADSHEAD

Codes of ethics have existed for medicine since the time of Hippocrates. However, a written code of ethics (like a written constitution) has so far eluded British psychiatry. In this editorial we discuss the arguments for and against a code of ethics as an essential aspect of our identity as medical professionals. Our professional identity as psychiatrists is coming under scrutiny from the General Medical Council, the emergence of the user movement and the proposals in the draft Mental Health Bill. At a time when psychiatry is seen increasingly as a guardian of public safety, there has never been a more pressing need for a code of ethics.

MEDICAL IDENTITIES: TRADE OR PROFESSION?

Professions differ from trades in important conceptual ways. The 'trade' argument suggests that psychiatrists are what users of services want them to be and – more importantly – are willing to pay for. Consumers negotiate with trades people for their services on an equal interpersonal footing. However, this approach is unconvincing in psychiatry, because mental health is not a commodity that can be bartered for, and therapeutic relationships are more complex because patients are additionally dependent and vulnerable. On this argument alone, psychiatry cannot be a trade and psychiatric patients cannot be consumers.

Professionals have a body of knowledge, a set of standards and an established value system. Professionals acquire their identity with their training, which may or may not be integrated with other social and personal identities. For example, if a call goes out on an aircraft flight asking for a doctor, what should the 'good' psychiatrist do? Is this different from what the 'good' doctor should do, or even the 'good' citizen? A psychiatrist who volunteers to help may be acting as much as a

good citizen as a good doctor, since medically, he or she may be able to do very little.

A profession must have at least three basic components to maintain its standards: entry, education and exit (Dyer, 1999). The professional standards of practice for psychiatrists are laid out in published form in *Good Medical Practice* (General Medical Council, 2001) and *Good Psychiatric Practice 2000* (Royal College of Psychiatrists, 2000). Professions such as medicine and law were formerly exempt from American anti-trust laws (Dyer, 1999); however, in 1975 a US Supreme Court decision ruled that 'learned professions' were no longer immune from anti-trust laws, and could thus be seen as 'trades'. This American example is a reminder that the nature of the financial contract between doctor and patient significantly influences both legal and professional relationships in medicine; and where relationships change, ethical duties and values may also change (Appelbaum, 1990).

Professions exist not only for their own benefit but also to promote the well-being of others, and this is the essence of the fiduciary duty unique to professionals. The altruistic element of professional identity runs in tandem with a specialised body of knowledge, and is encoded in the ethical principles of that profession (Sieghart, 1985).

WHY HAVE A CODE OF ETHICS AT ALL?

Fulford & Bloch (2000) set out the arguments for and against having a code of ethics. Codes may protect and promote a profession, and enhance high standards of practice, based on ethical principles. However, codes may also be self-serving and inward-looking. They may also be derived without appeal to general moral norms or the views of the wider public, especially users of medical services (Beauchamp &

Childress, 1994). The existence of a code may also induce a sense of complacency and encourage professionals to apply it in an unthinking way. Codes may actually reinforce bad practice, if this is the current norm. We know that the existence of a code of research ethics had little effect on the practice of medical members of the Nazi party. There appears to be little evidence that having a code of ethics prevents ethically unjustifiable practice.

However, absence of evidence is not evidence of absence. Relying on evidence of benefit as justification pays no attention to the intentions and characters of clinicians, which relates to the issue of professional identity and to altruism. The intention and values inherent in a code may protect as much as any consequentialist gain. As Fulford & Bloch suggest, the existence of a code of ethics can protect the altruistic identity of the psychiatric professional, especially in politically oppressive contexts. A code of ethics may also help protect the interests of psychiatric patients by emphasising the importance of patient empowerment (World Psychiatric Association, 1996). A code of ethics is another way to maintain standards, even if it cannot ensure ethical behaviour.

PSYCHIATRY AS A SPECIAL CASE

Despite the caveats described above, several psychiatric professional bodies internationally have opted to have a separate code of ethics (derived from existing ethical codes in medicine), presumably in answer to the special ethical dilemmas encountered in psychiatry (American Psychiatric Association, 1973, 2001; World Psychiatric Association, 1977, 1996; Canadian Medical Association, 1980; Russian Society of Psychiatrists, 1994; Royal Australian and New Zealand College of Psychiatry, 1999). Why British psychiatry has not pursued this option is unclear; perhaps it is because British psychiatrists believe that it is not possible to police morality, least of all by a written set of rules. This view may have led to a different type of complacency from that described by Fulford & Bloch: that ethical regulation should come from within the individual, and not be imposed from outside.

The most significant difference between medicine and psychiatry lies in the relative incapacity of psychiatric patients to make

decisions for themselves. They are especially vulnerable not only because they lack
capacity, but also because they are dependent on others to restore that capacity.
There is a need for appropriately regulated
paternalism in the case of patients who
need care but are unable to ask for it.
Furthermore, most mental disorders are of
a chronic and relapsing nature. The loss
of autonomy is not a discrete event but
rather a chronic loss or a fluctuating level
of autonomy. This reduced autonomy
means that our patients are often in a
long-term dependent relationship with
carers, and their autonomy is 'interstitial'
in so far as it is located in a network of
relationships (Agich, 1993).

Patients' dependence on others may
mean that their expressed views and wishes
are ignored. Under current English law, unlike medical patients', psychiatric patients'
competent refusals may be overridden
(Sarkar & Adshead, 2002) even if the intervention can cause direct 'harm' in terms
of the patient's experience. This includes
harm by inducing side-effects, forcible administration of medication and prolonged
involuntary detention. Society gives psychiatrists power that no trade could ever
have. Traders might cheat you in the course
of their business, but they are not legally
allowed to assault you.

Another direct source of harm to patients from psychiatric practitioners arises
from boundary violations and the exploitation of vulnerability. This issue is so rarely
discussed in British or European psychiatry
that practitioners might be forgiven for
thinking that this is a purely North
American problem. However, General
Medical Council data, and information
available from voluntary groups and chari-
ties, suggest otherwise. Despite being pro-
scribed in the Hippocratic oath, it is
entirely legal in the UK to have a sexual
relationship with a patient, so long as the
patient is not detained. However, there is
no reason to assume that non-detained
patients, or out-patients, will be any less
vulnerable than detained patients.

Psychiatry risks harming people by
treating them unjustly. Patients who commit offences may be detained on treatment
grounds for longer than they would have
served in prison. Patients may not be released from hospital (and under the draft
Bill, may have to be admitted) if they present a risk to others, so that the primary
purpose of detention is the benefit of third
parties rather than the patient. The policy

SAMEER P. SARKAR, MD, Institute of Psychiatry at the Maudsley Hospital, London; GWEN ADSHEAD,
MRCPsych, Broadmoor Hospital, Crowthorne, UK

Correspondence: Sameer P. Sarkar, Broadmoor Hospital, Crowthorne, Berkshire RG45 7EG, UK

(First received 24 May 2002, final revision 25 November 2002, accepted 27 November 2002)

of the Royal College of Psychiatrists with
regard to risk assessment is that the
clinician has a responsibility to take action
with a view to ensuring that risk is reduced
(Royal College of Psychiatrists, 1996). It is
a matter of justice that people should know
when they are being assessed for possible
detention, and there is a need for transpar-
ency during the risk assessment.

In the absence of moral guidance from
professional bodies, practical guidance has
to come from various codes of practice
and conduct. An example is the non-
statutory Code of Practice accompanying
the Mental Health Act 1983. Although
Gunn (1996) equates a code of ethics with
a code of practice for trade unions, the
trade *v.* profession distinction above tells
us that this may be an oversimplification.

At some point, codes of conduct or
practice are not sufficient for psychiatrists,
and there is a need for a code of ethics that
serves a different, if not wider, moral
domain. A code of ethics might help to
preserve the link with altruism, which is
arguably the defining intention of the profession. This is important because users of
health services want professionals to intend
to do them good, as well as actually to do
them good. Users of mental health services
have to trust psychiatric professionals to
protect their interests when they are not
well enough to do so for themselves.

Finally, there is the question of multiple
and conflicting duties and values in psychiatry – the so-called 'two hats' problem.
Current legislative approaches in the UK
seem to favour the value claims of third
parties over those of people with mental
illnesses, on the grounds of risk. This
approach is in direct contradiction to the
values espoused in both the Declaration of
Madrid (World Psychiatric Association,
1996) and the National Service Framework
(Department of Health, 1999).

PROTECTING ALTRUISM

The new mental health legislation proposals see the professional role of psychiatry

as treating for risk, especially risk to others.
Pitted against risk, the interests of the individual patient may come a poor second and
ordinary moral claims of patients may be
set aside. One can argue that it is 'good'
for people not to be a risk to others,
although this is not an argument that is applied to the general, non-mentally ill population. However, the traditional altruism of
the medical role is addressed to patients,
not to the public at large. Treatment to
make others feel safer risks treating patients
merely as a means to an end, in the Kantian
sense.

If our traditional professional identity is
so threatened, then a code of ethics might
provide a framework for stability and
further development. The establishment of
such a code, sensitively debated and reflective of the values that are important to
us, could be useful in setting standards
and in training future psychiatrists. It might
also assist with exploring the issue of diversity of values. It is not enough to acknowledge that values may clash: it is also
necessary to understand why different
groups of people may have different sets
of values and to respect the difference.
Recently, the Department of Health has
(as part of the National Institute for Mental
Health in England values framework) asked
the College to provide 'a statement of professional values' for psychiatry. Although
it cannot be guaranteed that our set of values will find favour with the Government,
this may be a particularly opportune
moment to develop our own code of ethics,
reflecting the diversity of values in clinical
practice.

How would a code help? It is true that
it might not prevent poor practice. Furthermore, what should happen when the code
is violated? Should violations be dealt
with internally by the profession, or
through a quasi-judicial sanction? Adoption of a code would raise many questions
like these, not all of which can be answered here. It is our contention nevertheless that a voluntary code of ethics and
self-regulation makes a profession strong
and less open to outside interference.

The General Medical Council's published maxim is 'Protecting patients, guiding doctors'. This ideally should also be the maxim of psychiatric practice. Sadly, it seems that as a profession we are being invited to endorse an ethical position that 'guides doctors to protect the public'. What we need is to define our ethical identity as psychiatrists, based on a system of values that are clinically meaningful and respectful of diversity. We may then be able to protect our medical identity while acknowledging that psychiatric practice has ethical dilemmas distinct from ordinary medical ethics.

DECLARATION OF INTEREST

None.

REFERENCES

Agich, G. (1993) *Autonomy and Long-Term Care.* Oxford: Oxford University Press.

American Psychiatric Association (1973) *The Principles of Medical Ethics. With Annotations Especially Applicable to Psychiatry.* Washington, DC: APA.

— (2001) *The Principles of Medical Ethics. With Annotations Especially Applicable to Psychiatry* (13th edn). Washington, DC: APA.

Appelbaum, P. S. (1990) The parable of the forensic psychiatrist: ethics and the problem of doing harm. *International Journal of Law and Psychiatry,* 13, 249–259.

Beauchamp, T. & Childress, J. (1994) *Principles of Biomedical Ethics* (4th edn). Oxford: Oxford University Press.

Canadian Medical Association (1980) Code of Ethics annotated for psychiatry. *Canadian Journal of Psychiatry,* 25, 432–438.

Department of Health (1999) *The National Service Framework for Mental Health. Modern Standards and Service Models.* London: Department of Health.

Dyer, A. (1999) Psychiatry as a profession. In *Psychiatric Ethics* (3rd edn) (eds S. Bloch, P. Chodoff & S.A. Green), pp. 67–79. Oxford: Oxford University Press.

Fulford, K. W. M. & Bloch, S. (2000) Psychiatric ethics: codes, concepts and clinical practice skills. In *New Oxford Textbook of Psychiatry* (eds M. Gelder, N. Andreasen & J. Lopez-Ibor), pp. 27–32. Oxford: Oxford University Press.

General Medical Council (2001) *Good Medical Practice.* London: General Medical Council.

Gunn, J. (1996) Commentary: comparative forensic psychiatry – USA vs. UK. *Criminal Behaviour and Mental Health,* 6, 45–48.

Royal Australian and New Zealand College of Psychiatry (1999) RANZCP Code of Ethics. *Australasian Psychiatry,* 7, 108.

Royal College of Psychiatrists (1996) *Assessment and Clinical Management of Risk of Harm to Other People.* (Council Report CR53). London: Royal College of Psychiatrists.

— (2000) *Good Psychiatric Practice 2000* (Council Report CR83). London: Royal College of Psychiatrists.

Russian Society of Psychiatrists (1994) *The Code of Professional Ethics of the Psychiatrist.* Reprinted (1999) in *Psychiatric Ethics* (eds S. Bloch, P. Chodoff & A. Green) (3rd edn), pp. 526–531. Oxford: Oxford University Press.

Sarkar, S. P. & Adshead, G. (2002) Treatment over objection: minds, bodies and beneficence. *Journal of Mental Health Law,* 7, 105–118.

Sieghart, P. (1985) Professions as the conscience of society. *Journal of Medical Ethics,* 11, 117–122.

World Psychiatric Association (1977) *Declaration of Hawaii.* Elmhurst, NY: WPA.

— (1996) *Declaration of Madrid.* Elmhurst, NY: WPA.

Name Index